OTHER BOOKS BY TOM AINSLIE

The Compleat Horseplayer
Handicapper's Handbook
Ainslie's Complete Guide to Harness Racing
Ainslie on Jockeys
Ainslie's Complete Hoyle

Ainslie's
complete guide to
THOROUGHBRED RACING

REVISED AND UPDATED

by TOM AINSLIE

SIMON AND SCHUSTER   New York

Copyright © 1968, 1979 by Tom Ainslie
All rights reserved
including the right of reproduction
in whole or in part in any form
Published by Simon and Schuster
A Division of Gulf & Western Corporation
Simon & Schuster Building
Rockefeller Center
1230 Avenue of the Americas
New York, New York 10020
SIMON AND SCHUSTER and colophon are trademarks
of Simon & Schuster

Designed by Irving Perkins
Manufactured in the United States of America
Printed by The Book Press, Inc.
Bound by The Book Press, Inc.
   4 5 6 7 8 9 10 11

Library of Congress Cataloging in Publication Data

Ainslie, Tom.
  Ainslie's complete guide to thoroughbred racing.

  Includes index.
  1. Horse race betting—United States. 2. Horse-
racing—United States. I. Title. II. Title: Complete guide to thoroughbred racing. III. Title:
Thoroughbred racing.
SF332.A43 1979   798'.401'0973   79-12539

ISBN 0-671-24632-1

Contents

9. THE CONDITION FACTOR   160

10. THE CLASS FACTOR   185

Foreword to the Revised Edition

The first version of this book was published in 1968. It became the all-time best-seller in its field. I should have updated it before now. Racing has changed. Leading riders, trainers and other prominent members of the 1968 cast of characters are no longer on the scene. Exotic wagering, year-long racing seasons, legal off-track betting parlors, permissive medication of horses and punitive taxation have each affected the ancient game and the way it should be played.

On the other hand, most of the fundamental truths of racing remain fundamentally true. The Thoroughbred continues to feature a mane, a tail, a leg at each corner and a small person on its back. And handicapping ability continues to be the salient difference between loyal race-goers (who enjoy the sport the most) and transient gamblers (who take a terrible trouncing).

An uninformed gambler approaches the track as if it were a casino, and has no alternative. But a handicapper goes to the track to exercise a skill. Now that legalized casino gambling threatens to abduct gamblers from the tracks, the racing industry has begun to experiment with countermeasures. Some tracks now offer lectures at which experts disclose and explain their personal selections in the day's races. This helps, but not sufficiently. It attracts persons who hope to overhear the name of a winner. It does little for those who would love to learn how to pick winners all by themselves.

By default, therefore, the privilege of transforming needful fans into knowing enthusiasts remains a monopoly of this kind of book.

Tom Ainslie
Millwood, New York
January, 1979

Preface: In Which We Name the Game

This book seeks to fill an enormous void in the literature of American Thoroughbred racing.

Other volumes celebrate the romance of the turf, the feats of champions, the distinctiveness of the breed, the exploits of horsemen dead and gone. This one occupies different territory. It is an encyclopedic review of handicapping theory and technique—the first such work in the long history of the game. Its sole concerns are (1) the competition among horsemen for purse winnings and (2) the competition among horsemen and fans for pari-mutuel winnings. Its goal is to place the fan on approximately equal footing with the horseman by revealing the strategy and tactics that lead to the winner's circle and the mutuel cashier's window.

Racing is unique in American sport. Its paying customer is more than a spectator. He is a participant. He goes to the track not only to see something but to do something. Specifically, he goes to bet. In these pages I propose to enhance his pleasure in the game by helping him to become good at it.

I hasten to concede that one need not be a winning bettor to enjoy an occasional outing at the track. Horse races are incomparably exciting. Moreover, these are prosperous times. Millions of men and women can afford the very minor misfortunes with which racing penalizes innocence. Unless the racegoer gambles insanely, his losing excursion to the track costs no more than a night on the town.

Nevertheless, it is more fun to win than to lose. Nobody with normal emotions can possibly be indifferent to the outcome of the races on which he bets. I therefore find it preposterous that no serious effort has been made (until now) to undress, dissect and analyze this multi-billion-dollar pastime for those whose wagers are its main source of revenue.

Rank-and-file players should know the percentages and probabilities of the game. They should know how horsemen decide what to do with their animals, and when, and why. They should know the criteria on which professional handicappers and successful bettors base their judgments. They should, in other words, be made privy to the what's what, who's who and how come of the game they play.

Inasmuch as human beings tend to concentrate on pastimes in which they are skilled and to avoid those in which they take a thumping, one might fairly ask why racing has been so remiss about educating its own clientele. Why the huge omissions from the tons of literature issued by the racing industry and its able publicists? Has Thoroughbred racing's eminence as our largest "spectator" sport blinded it to the fact that most of its customers, however enthusiastic they may be, are transients? And that, aside from a small minority of neurotically compulsive losers, persons who attend racing regularly do so only because they have learned how to avoid serious financial loss? And that the way to increase the popularity of any game, no matter how popular it may be to begin with, is to teach people how to play it?

The reason that racing fails to grasp such opportunities is that it is afraid to. The fear is understandable. It derives from the sport's checkered past.

Not more than three generations ago, it was taken for granted that the only reputable persons at the track were the high-society types who owned the best horses. Their excuse for having all that fun was that they were perpetuating the glorious traditions of their class, improving the breed. They all bet, of course. But any commoner who went to the track to bet was a practitioner of evil. It surprised nobody when he turned out to be the black sheep of someone's family, or an absconding bookkeeper, or a stage-door johnny, or a degenerate gambler, or some kind of nut. The tracks were overrun with pickpockets and bunco steerers. Anyone with half a brain knew that many races were fixed. Victorian moral standards, or the instinct of self-preservation, or both, discouraged ordinary folk from entering such an environment. The sport was too seamy to mess with.

Great changes have occurred. Victorian morality has all but vanished. People no longer equate excitement with sin. Racing, an excitement if ever there was one, has responded by tidying its house. It now draws customers by the millions from the arts, the sciences, the professions and the upper reaches of the country's business and political establishments. The clientele of racing has become a representative cross section of the American public, as respectable as any other. And the act of going to the track to bet has achieved social acceptance. This is not quite as comfortable as social approval, but is a lap ahead of social toleration. In my opinion, the game will cross the threshold of approval as soon as it recognizes that it deserves to. It has become an industry of immense importance.

Every year, tens of millions of Thoroughbred racing enthusiasts deposit more than $6 billion in the pari-mutuel betting pools at United States tracks. The tracks remit over $350 million to state treasuries, which get another $175 million from harness and quarter-horse racing.

To put it mildly, the state governments welcome these tax contributions. They also enjoy the political jobs made possible by establishment and expansion of commissions charged with supervision of the sport. And they seem to appreciate the highly moral flavor of racing's communications with the voting public. The owners and managers of the game are careful to thwart anti-vice elements and other moralizers by playing down the lure of betting. So that neither they nor their political protectors will be mauled for "encouraging gambling," the tracks promote the spectator aspects of their business. They pretend that the pari-mutuel machines are not the main attraction in the store.

Which returns me to the original point. A major book explaining the game of racing to the bettor should have been published long before now. It might have come from the industry itself, as a goodwill effort to educate the customers toward wiser, less costly betting. Yet one searches in vain for printed matter in which racing officials or active horsemen emit so much as a hint about the art of selecting winners.

So sensitive is the industry to the hostility of anti-gambling fanatics that it even discourages the use of words like "horseplayer." The purple-necked gentleman tearing up a fistful of losing mutuel tickets and bawling abuse at the jockey is not to be called "horseplayer." He is a "racing fan." If it is bad taste to call a horseplayer a horseplayer, what shall we call a poker player?

Let us grant that the sport's modest garb, woven of 100 percent pure, virgin fig leaves, shields it from charges that it promotes vice. Let us applaud anything that frustrates the bluenoses who oppose racing. But let us question whether it is necessary any longer to appease the bluenoses. And let us recognize that the timid failure of racing experts to explain the art of handicapping actually encourages gambling. Their secretiveness is a primary reason why millions of floundering fans waste money on unintelligent bets!

The viewpoint of this book is that few racegoers are emotionally crippled gamblers, hell-bent to make themselves miserable by squandering the milk money. Most horseplayers are capable of learning how to function more effectively at the track—if someone would only do them the honor of showing them how.

How Experts Get That Way

From long experience in a variety of games, I feel qualified to make a most unusual but absolutely valid statement about the handicapping of horse races: It demands no less mental prowess than bridge, poker or chess. The skills of the expert handicapper are, in fact, closely comparable to those of the good bridge, poker or chess player. In any such competition, the player who depends on instinct, trial-and-error, inexpert advice, superstition or reckless guesses is at a disadvantage. He cannot hope to hold his own against persons who have acquired an understanding of the game as a whole.

The bedside table or living-room bookcase of every serious bridge player holds encyclopedic volumes by Charles Goren, Alfred Sheinwold and Louis Watson. Chess players make endless use of comprehensive texts by Reuben Fine, Emanuel Lasker, Fred Reinfeld. Mediocre poker players become tough propositions after studying Oswald Jacoby, Herbert O. Yardley and Irwin Steig. But horseplayers get no such aid and comfort.

Armed only with unreliable tips, insubstantial systems and hope, most horseplayers take a cruel battering in a game that really is not all that tough. Not, that is, for the few players lucky enough to know its theory and technique.

In response to the racing enthusiast's need, this book offers him what Goren, Sheinwold and Watson have given the bridge player. It dismantles the barriers that traditionally separate the paying customer from the professional horseman and professional handicapper. It presents the entire story, the full range of possibilities. Truths about Thoroughbreds and the men who race them are revealed here for the first time. These truths are the essence of sound handicapping, sound wagering.

Above all, the book equips its reader with standards whereby he may judge the relevance of the dizzyingly diverse items of coded technical information which are the handicapper's stock in trade. Believe it or not (and, if you have been going to the races for a while, you will believe it), most players consciously avoid that information, because they don't know what to make of it. Which is like trying to navigate without looking at the map.

The Importance of Predictability

Apart from its neglect of handicapping, published information about Thoroughbred racing is abundant, detailed and accurate. A superb daily newspaper, several magazines and a yearly encyclopedia offer to horsemen, officials and fans a range of news, statistics and commentary unsurpassed in any sport.

These easily available materials are more than merely interesting. They are essential to the orderly conduct of the game. They help the horseman make decisions about his horses. They help the expert fan make decisions about his bets. For both individuals the name of the game is prediction. And published information is the raw material from which prediction is made. Moreover, it provides the background against which errors in prediction may be diagnosed and corrected.

Certain patterns have become well established in centuries of Thoroughbred racing. The running condition of horses improves and declines in cycles familiar enough to make sudden reversals of form both noticeable and suspect. The class, or quality, of horses is also patterned, as is their ability to cope with high weights or unfamiliar distances, or with races in which the early stages are run at unusually fast or slow speeds. For these reasons and many others, race results themselves follow what might be termed a pattern of reasonable predictability.

A limitation on predictability is the unalterable fact that the race is a contest among mute animals of impermanent quality and unstable temperament. Nobody can interview a horse. The creature reveals the truth about itself only after the race has begun and the bets have become irrevocable. Moreover, its ability to do its best is affected by the handling it gets from humans of varying competence and integrity —trainers, grooms, stablehands and jockeys. These circumstances explain why any player able to win 40 percent of his bets in the course of a year is probably a genuine expert. And a marvel of self-discipline. He achieves his winning average by picking his spots with great care. Only a rare day finds him making more than three bets. On some days he makes no bets at all.

Another aspect of racing's predictability is more melancholy, and is closely linked to what I have just said. Anyone who tries to pick a winner in every race will be unable to predict the outcome of more than three races in ten if he persists in the practice for year.

A third aspect is that racetrack crowds do better than that. The crowds function on a blend of hunch, horoscope, hot tip, individual handicapping, the motley forecasts of newspapers and tip sheets

Opening day at Aqueduct.   UPI PHOTO

TOP: *Railbirds at Aqueduct.*   UPI PHOTO

BOTTOM: *"Getting down" on the daily double at Santa Anita.*   UPI PHOTO (which somehow name almost every horse in most races), and the dubious predictions of innumerable selection systems. Yet the crowds pick the winner of one race in every three. That statistic, which holds up year after year, is, of course, the percentage of victories by betting favorites. The public's consistency is one of the inexplicable mysteries of the sport.

If these aspects of predictability seem to impose a ceiling on success at the track, they also suggest the possibility of a floor under failure. The racing industry recognizes this. It understands all too clearly that its hold on public confidence would become infirm if race results were to depart from the established patterns of reasonable predictability. The industry expends much money and a good deal of ingenuity to prevent and/or punish hanky-panky.

Here again, published information is vital. In deciding whether a suspect race was honestly contested, officials have access to video-tapes of it and of previous races involving the same horses and riders. They also avail themselves of the published record about those past races. They do so knowing that the expert fan uses the same informa-tion. His ability to interpret the information is a spur to the authorities. The penalty for official laxness is public indignation—a first step to-ward desertion.

Horsemen, Handicappers and Information

For an example of how horsemen use public information, let us con-sider a trainer. He has a pretty nice kind of four-year-old sprinter which he regards as ready to win a race for $10,000 animals at three quarters of a mile. But his arch rival, the wily Trainer Doe, has just imported a large, bright-eyed colt from Illinois. If our horseman had to wait and see Doe's colt in a race or two before learning anything about him, his ability to manage the affairs of his own horse would be seri-ously impaired. Indeed, such a plight would mean that he and Doe and everyone else in racing had been transported, science-fiction style, to the beginning of the century, when published information was sparse and horsemen resolved their problems by collusion, chicanery and simple assault.

Our modern horseman can learn a great deal about Doe's import without budging from his desk. Chart books and past-performance records offer an almost photographic profile of the creature. Its quality, its running style, its favorite distances, its ability to carry high weight, its liking for wet or muddy running surfaces, and even its capacity for retaining top form after a long journey are all there in the records. If the colt was losing to $5,000 horses in Illinois it had better not jump up and beat $10,000 ones in its debut here, or Doe will find himself in trouble. Such reversals of form were common in the bad old days but, as suggested earlier, are too noticeable to be tolerated now that fans and officials are equipped to recognize them.

The practiced fan has a remarkably accurate bead on every horse in most races. With exceptions that we shall discuss in full detail later, he is able to foretell which entrants are likely to be in contention and which have only negligible chances. The minutely specific information contained in result charts and past-performance records is the foundation of his judgment. He supplements that data by consulting periodic public tabulations that summarize the success or failure of jockeys, trainers, owners and breeders. He also keeps abreast of news about breeding transactions, livestock sales, personnel shifts, owners' and trainers' plans, and equine injury and illness.

His regular presence at the track and the large amounts of money he bets (horsemen and expert customers are the biggest bettors) suggest that the published information works for him. He apparently is able to hold his betting losses at an endurable level—low enough to justify his continued attendance.

Or he may even be a winner. Thousands of fans combine intelligence, knowledge and self-control in proportions adequate to win money for themselves year after year, and even season after season or month after month. In all such cases, including that of the enthusiast whose pleasure in the game outweighs the pain of his small losses, it can be seen that Thoroughbred racing is reasonably predictable.

Yet of the 56 million persons who paid their way into American Thoroughbred racetracks and fed $6 billion into the machines during 1978, I doubt that one in 500 qualified as an expert. I doubt, in short, that more than a handful were able to exploit the predictability of racing by putting available information to profitable use.

Confessions of an Author

My own interest in racing arose more than four decades ago. I was fascinated by the commotion of the break from the starting barrier, the skill of the jockeying on the turns, the tension and suspense of the sprint down the homestretch. But I was a serious-minded type, with a thin billfold. I saw no profit in betting on something about which I knew nothing. I decided to buy some books.

No such thing was to be had. I was appalled. Nostalgic volumes about the history of the turf were available for nine cents on the remainder counter of every bookshop, but a book about the art of picking winners was available at no price.

"The reason they don't publish books for horseplayers," explained one merchant, "is that horseplayers can't read."

Certain magazines contained fragmentary articles extolling the undemonstrated advantages of various handicapping angles or outlining equally unsubstantiated selection systems. Advertisements in the same periodicals hawked pamphlets revealing alleged "secrets" of successful "turf speculation." The pamphlets were similar in quality and substance to the magazine pieces. They offered a glimmering of what might have been wisdom, but nothing remotely like a comprehensive view of the overall problem with which they purported to deal. Also, the mail-order promoters who published these tracts invariably turned out to be tipsters and touts who kept one's mailbox cluttered with promises of riches beyond belief—for a $5 bill. I was young and naive, but it never occurred to me to patronize the touts. I wondered uneasily about the age and worldliness of those who did.

The *Daily Racing Form* published, as it still does, full instructions on how to decipher the notations in result charts and past-performance records. This was helpful. But mastery of the cipher left one with the fundamental problem of how to *interpret* the decoded information. What was important? What was not? Which end was up?

I remained interested in racing for years, without betting a nickel on any race. In spare time I tested various systems on paper, much as a would-be stock investor might attempt dry runs with theories of market analysis. A few bookmakers and several professional horsemen supplied some lore, guiding me toward a beginning grasp of the game. In time, by dint of lonesome, laborious study of a sort so dedicated as to raise questions about the mental hygiene of anyone willing to undertake it, I reached a point where I could go to the track without fear of losing my shirt. It had taken me fifteen years of intermittent study to learn what a decent book could have taught me in a few weeks.

When racing entered its boom period of expansion after World War II, volumes of advice to horseplayers began to materialize in the bookshops. Persons who had never gone near a track now began dropping around to try the daily double. The books were an understandable effort to grab this new market. They continue to appear. I have at least sixty of them and am sure that twenty more must have escaped my attention. With few exceptions, the ones I have seen pose no challenge to the theory that "horseplayers can't read."

Most of them are unreadable, whether one be a horseplayer or not. The worst are not only unreadable but fraudulent. The best, including the very few that have been written by authentic experts, outline systematic methods of prediction. They are serviceable in the limited sense that any more-or-less sound method is superior to no method at all. Their chief weakness is that they leave the reader in the dark about the multitudinous possibilities untouched by their systems. Lacking the time, space, knowledge or willingness to do otherwise, their authors seek to imprison the reader in procedures which, while of some use in special situations, neglect the infinite variety of the game. Also, no single system is likely to be compatible with the temperament, mentality and bankroll of the individual player.

Fond of racing and offended by the book-length material offered to my companions in the audience, I finally decided to write books of my own. In 1966, *The Compleat Horseplayer* * explained a handicapping method based on a more than ordinarily comprehensive view of the total problem. Its illustrative examples were the records of, and reasoning behind, wagers made during a successful week at Monmouth Park, New Jersey. In 1967 came *Ainslie's Jockey Book,* † (later reissued as *Ainslie on Jockeys*), another version of the same method, emphasizing certain previously unpublicized truths about the relationship of the rider to the winning or losing of the race.

These books quickly became the best-selling handicapping manuals in the history of the pastime. They met with unprecedented praise from professional horsemen and other racing experts. But, in my opinion and in that of insiders whose views I respect, both books were too fragmentary to fill the void.

What the racing follower needs is not someone else's method of handicapping, but his own. A book containing a procedure highly esteemed by Tom Ainslie is only a partial help. The chances are that its value derives less from its explanation of Ainslie's method than from what Ainslie discloses about the nature of the game itself.

To evaluate a handicapping procedure, whether he finds it in print or dreams it up himself, the player must understand what the other possibilities are. What other procedures exist? What fundamental principles must be taken into account in the development of any sound approach? Having reviewed the entire array, the individual is well situated to determine his preferences, test them at his leisure and amend them as events and his own developing knowledge may dictate.

To make that possible for its readers is the business of this book.

* (Simon and Schuster, New York, 1966)
† (Simon and Schuster, New York, 1967)

Anyone who has ever spent a precious summer Saturday afternoon watching his five "best bets" run out of the money will agree, I think, that it's high time.

Beginners are also welcome. Anything one might need to launch oneself into the fascinating game of racing will be found in these pages.

How We're Going to Operate

The book begins with a description and explanation of the materials necessary, or useful, to development and maintenance of expert skill.

We then take a good look at the physical layout of racetracks. One should know more than the location of one's seat, the finish line, the $2 window, the cashier's window, the frankfurter stand, the bathroom and the parking lot.

Next we analyze the arithmetic of racing. We start with the percentages of the game—figures with which every expert reckons. We proceed to the pari-mutuel system and how its deductions from winnings affect expert methods of play. We then examine the economics of the industry itself, a kind of arithmetic which has much to do with the outcome of races. We conclude the section with some of the most important arithmetic of all—the cost of the hobby, and how this influences the size of the bet.

We come now to the horse itself. We strip breeding of the hocuspocus that has mystified and confused generations of players. We discuss the size, weight and appearance of the Thoroughbred, explaining what he should look like, and why.

The central section of the book explores the arts of handicapping. After a summary review of the accepted schools of thought, we describe and analyze each fundamental of theory and method. Under appropriate headings, the reader will find concrete information about factors such as distance, form, class, age, sex, consistency, weight, speed, pace, post position, the owner, the trainer, the jockey. And ways to recognize playable-beatable races. And the secrets of the paddock and post parade. And a huge array of supplementary "angles" or "plus factors." And the names of, and strategic differences among, leading tracks; an assortment of professional speed charts and speed-weight formulas; methods of calculating daily track-speed variants; pace-rating procedures; the principles of class handicapping, form handicapping, speed handicapping and pace handicapping; the form cycle and how to recognize improvement or deterioration; the usefulness of workouts; the truth about the drugging and "stiffing" of horses;

the names and characteristics of the nation's leading trainers; the names and specialties of leading riders; the names of leading owners and breeders; methods of recognizing soreness, lameness and illness. And much, much more, with explicit instructions on how to use it all.

The next section contains seventy-seven outstanding selection systems. Some have been sold to players for as much as $500 each. We offer them not as substitutes for actual handicapping but as sources of ideas. Presented as they are—with advice as to how they can be altered or combined—they should provide the fan with endless entertainment, plus unlimited opportunity to practice his growing skills as an analyst of the game.

The final sections of the book contain the official rules of action; complete instructions on how to read result charts and past-performance records in *Daily Racing Form,* and, at the very end, a full glossary of racing terminology.

Acknowledgments

I am indebted to Triangle Publications, Inc., for permission to reproduce copyrighted materials from *Daily Racing Form, American Racing Manual* and from booklets explaining result charts and past-performance records.

Mr. Henry Bomze, late publisher of *American Turf Monthly,* was most gracious in allowing me to use photographs and other materials that had appeared in his magazine. Howard A. Rowe, editor-in-chief of the magazine, and one of the most astute journalists in the field, has given me numerous invaluable suggestions. I thank him warmly and hasten to absolve him of responsibility for the content or tone of the book.

Because much of the information in the book has never been made public before, the reader will deduce that I have been interviewing jockeys, trainers and other experts. That is true, in a sense. The book's insights are the fruit of many years of observation, conversation and successful play. I doubt it would be a kindness to name any of the professional horsemen who, during the years, have contributed (usually unwittingly) to the development of those insights.

1

The Tools of the Trade

Most thoroughbred races are at distances of three quarters of a mile or more, around at least one turn, from a standing start. The margin of victory often is narrow enough to be measurable in inches or hundredths of a second. The best horse usually wins, but not always. Bad luck and human error are factors in the running of every race. They can make an abject loser of an animal that should have won easily. Considering the influence of luck and error in a game of inches and split seconds, it is remarkable that the best horse wins as often as it does.

The horse may be of distinctly higher quality than its rivals. It may also be in peak physical condition. But it may lose its race in the paddock, before it ever gets to the starting gate. A clumsy trainer or groom may fasten the saddle too tightly, or not tightly enough, causing sufficient discomfort to throw the animal hopelessly out of sorts. Or the horse may be upset by the nervousness of another horse, or the sudden roar of a low-flying airplane, or the frightening whiteness of a windblown newspaper. If the handlers misunderstand this and react with more harshness or less firmness than the situation demands, the ensuing fracas can deplete the horse of its winning energy.

If the horse is not familiar with its rider, or does not like that person, or if the rider is not attuned to the animal, the race can be lost during the post parade. Some horses resent being busted with a whip during a pre-race warm-up. In trying to run away from the whip, such a horse may get more exercise than is good for him.

If he is a fast-breaking, front-running animal, eager for action, he may lose the race in the starting gate. The start may be delayed by the sulkiness or unruliness of other entrants, or by this horse's own high-strung behavior. When the bell finally sounds, it may catch him standing cross-legged. Or his jockey may have lapsed into a daydream. The effort of recovering the lost ground may empty the horse of the stamina it needs for the homestretch.

Another nervous type, whose disposition has suffered in the paddock, post parade or gate, may express himself by running rankly, frantically, uncontrollably, exhausting himself in the first half-mile.

A horse may break nicely from the gate and be jarred off stride by a careening neighbor. Bumps and brushes can cost precious split seconds of running time at any stage of a race, especially on the turns. Or an animal's new shoes may fit improperly, throwing his gait into imbalance and crippling him as soon as he attempts to lengthen stride.

Saving ground on the rail, a jockey may find himself without running room in the stretch, hemmed in by horses fore, aft and starboard. If daylight appears, the rider's hesitation for only a fraction of a second may prevent the mount from seizing an opportunity to run to the wire. Or the jockey may ride into a blind switch, swinging a few widths to the inside or outside for room on the turn—and racing straight into a pocket. Or the rider may be forced to check the animal's stride to avoid a pile-up with tiring horses that are backing up to him. Or it may be a timid rider, or a fatigued rider, or a rider weakened by dieting and dehydration, and unable to muster the whoop-de-doo necessary to get the horse's head up at the finish. Or the rider may use the whip too soon and too much, or too late and not enough. Or the horse may stumble on a clod of earth or a hoofprint.

The list of mishaps and errors could be prolonged for pages but need not be. The message is clear: The best horse can be beaten in a multitude of ways. Which is one of the reasons why sages declare, "You can't beat the races." Other sages modify this. "You can beat a race," they say, "but you can't beat the races." A more precise description of the situation is that some players beat the races, and most do not. For those who do not, the chief problem is lack of know-how. Yet some persons with know-how are insufficiently motivated to use the knowledge. They'd rather eat hot dogs and drink beer and have fun in the sun and lose a few hundred dollars a year than expend the effort necessary to catch the extra few winners that would put their accounts into the black. It is their sovereign right. They'd rather cream you on the golf course, or beat you at the poker or bridge table. It's all a matter of taste.

Persons who beat the races are, on the very face of it, knowledgeable players, motivated to use the knowledge. They enjoy winning so much that they are willing to work at it. Yet they may be unable to understand why an expert poker player will lie in ambush at the table for two and a half hours before sandbagging his companions. Again, it's a matter of taste.

As far as I know, horseplayers who win more money than they lose are almost invariably persons who have learned to be expert handicappers. To be sure, a medical friend of mine, who does not know which end kicks or which end bites, financed the establishment of his practice with $60,000 he won on hot tips. He was an intern at the time. The tips came from underworld characters who were grateful for a kindness he had rendered one of their relatives. The horses all won. Every month or two would come a tip on a horse at some small track. And every tip paid off—$60,000 worth in two or three years. It can be assumed that the mob continues to rig a few races at various minor-league tracks and that anyone with access to the information can beat such races. The rest of us are obliged to work for our winnings. We are obliged to learn how to handicap.

Some of the most consistent losers at any track are insiders, or friends of insiders, who depend on stable information. It is nice to know for certain that a certain stable plans to "go" with its horse, and is not simply sending the animal out for exercise. Unfortunately, three or four other stables are also likely to be all-out to win the same race, and may have the horseflesh to do it with. Which is why the player who knows how to handicap does not need stable information or, if he gets it, will not be misled by it.

As a class, professional horsemen are much better handicappers than the paying customers are. But an individual customer can be as effective a handicapper as any horseman. The expert customer's judgment is free of the pressures that result from loyalty to a stable owner or enthusiasm about a particular horse. He learns to mistrust and avoid all enthusiasms except his delight in lining up at the cashier's window to collect the rewards of his judgment.

By the same token, the accomplished player resists the emotional squalls that might be induced by ill fortune. He knows that he can't win every bet. He expects to lose more than half of them. Like the competitive golfer, the homicidal poker player and the expert bridge player—all of whom he resembles in many other particulars—he takes his reverses in stride. When, as happens all too often, the best horse in the race not only loses but loses a bet for him, the handicapper presses onward and upward. There will be other races today, or the next time.

They're off at Churchill Downs. UPI PHOTO

Eddie Arcaro boots Bold Ruler (inside) to new track record in 1957 Wood Memorial at Jamaica, nosing out John Choquette on Gallant Man.

Traffic jam on home turn at Aqueduct.　　　　　　　　　　UPI PHOTO

And every now and then, as he knows full well, he will bet on a horse, discover during the running of the race that it is not the best horse after all, and will cash the bet anyhow, racing luck or human fallibility having made a loser into a winner.

Knowledge, motivation to use the knowledge, self-control and composed self-confidence. These, then, are the primary attributes of the good player. Anyone who begins with the motivation, and enjoys maintaining it, can develop the knowledge, the self-control and the confidence. The latter two qualities are products of experience—successful experience based on knowledge.

In acquiring the necessary experience, the reader probably will use this volume as home base, a primary source of essential knowledge. But he will want additional materials with which to check and test his knowledge and make it firmly his own. Still other materials will help him to replenish and expand what he knows, in light of new developments in the game.

Such materials are the tools of the handicapper's trade. Some are indispensable. Others can be omitted, depending on the amount of effort the player is willing to give to his pastime.

Here are the materials most useful to the hobby of handicapping Thoroughbreds:

"Daily Racing Form" [INDISPENSABLE]

It is impossible to handicap a field of horses without this newspaper. Most players rely exclusively on the individual past-performance records which the paper publishes every racing day. Some also keep files of the official result charts which appear in the paper. The charts are far more detailed than past-performance records. They are especially useful in establishing the actual class of competition against which a horse has been competing. As shall be demonstrated later in this book, among three or four horses that have been winning in $5,000 claiming races, one may actually have been defeating animals of decisively superior quality. The result charts show this—and much else that we shall notice in due course.

Because the hobbyist is likely to be an infrequent visitor to the track, he may find the acquisition of official result charts a greater chore and expense than he wants to incur. Rather than buy the *Form* every day to get the charts, he may prefer to rely on the past-performance records available on the day he goes to the track. Many winning players survive this way, although it must be assumed that they would win somewhat more if they had access to a file of charts.

Another sort of file is almost mandatory, however. To test the concepts and procedures and selection systems he finds in this book or elsewhere, or generates from his own expanding awareness, the player must have a file of *Form*s. A month of back issues would be good. Six months would be twenty times as good. An angle might show a profit in a month's trial simply by accident. But if it holds up well over a six months' trial, it may be worth trying in real life with real money. Back issues are obtainable from the papers themselves, or from mail-order firms that advertise in racing magazines.

The "American Racing Manual" [IMPORTANT]

Every year this magnificent, encyclopedic by-product of the *Form* gives last year's record of every horse, rider, owner, trainer and breeder. Plus track diagrams; track and world speed records; charts of the principal races; lengthy articles summarizing and analyzing the chief developments and accomplishments of the year; tabulations showing who did best in every department of the game; other tabulations showing how often the betting favorites won at every track, and how much purse money was paid out at every track. And several hundred other items, all of keen interest to handicappers.

Magazines [USEFUL]

The most useful are these:

American Turf Monthly, 505 Eighth Avenue, New York, 10018. Frankly addressed to horseplayers, with liberal helpings of the pie-in-the-sky that nourishes their hopes, this monthly contains more handicapping advice than other racing periodicals. Its best column, "Increase Your Horsepower," offers timely inside information about the maneuverings of trainers. Monthly articles by the popular handicapping teacher, Ray Taulbot, cover a wide range of angles and techniques. Every issue contains three or four selection systems, some of which are ingenious enough to merit experimental, self-educational study by the budding player.

Blood-Horse, P.O. Box 4038, Lexington, Kentucky 40504. A splendid weekly that views the game through the eyes of the breeder and will fascinate the player.

Thoroughbred Record, P.O. Box 11788, Lexington, Kentucky, 40578. Breeding, training, economics, who's doing what. Another well-edited weekly, worth keeping up with.

Turf and Sport Digest, 511–513 Oakland Avenue, Baltimore, 21212. The most valuable section of this monthly discusses the racing characteristics of each track. In addition, it publishes feature articles about riders and other horsemen, and produces an occasional selection system, usually with adequate documentation of results. Well worth subscribing to.

Monthly Chart Books [USEFUL]

The official result charts of all races on all American tracks, in convenient book form. Available from Triangle Publications, Inc., 731 Plymouth Court, Chicago, 60605. Triangle is the parent corporation of *Daily Racing Form.*

Notebooks [ESSENTIAL]

Written records are the only reliable means of telling whether one's handicapping is good or not. Notebooks provide a continuous record of what you do and how it works. Some players, as we shall see, use notebooks to record daily track variants, or the actual class of every race, or to keep tabs on horses whose imminent improvement has been noticed in the result charts or at the track.

Local Newspapers [USEFUL]

Few papers ever mention handicapping, much less discuss any of its ramifications, but racing columnists often give significant news of horses and horsemen.

Gadgets [DOUBTFUL]

Advertisers peddle a stupefying variety of metal, cardboard and laminated plastic devices, guaranteed to relieve the player of the need to use his own brain. None is a substitute for handicapping. Most are variants of the slide-rule principle, highly simplified to include the two or three or four factors built into the inventor's system. Those that calculate a horse's percentage of winning or in-the-money races may save enough arithmetical effort to seem worthwhile. For fanciers of pace handicapping, Ray Taulbot's Reliable Pace Calculator, sold by Amerpub, Inc., 505 Eighth Avenue, New York 10018, saves a bit of labor.

Binoculars [IMPORTANT]

Most players sit or stand where they can see the track. But few see much of the race except the finish. A good pair of seven- or eight-power binoculars with a wide field enables a well-positioned player to see the entire race. This is fun. It also is informative, because it helps the player to approach the full truth about how his choices run, and how their jockeys ride. To that extent, binoculars improve his handicapping.

Leisure [INDISPENSABLE]

Some experts can learn all they want to know about a day's program of races in less than half an hour with the *Form*. Others use more elaborate methods which require as much as an hour of careful study per playable race. No matter where one may stand between these extremes, it is safe to assert that only a player of enormous skill and long experience can do his handicapping in the hustle and bustle of the track. The place to figure the horses is in private, on the morning of the race, or—if the racing paper is available—on the previous night. Even with basic handicapping completed before the trip to the track, the player finds plenty to do while there. Eleventh-hour jockey changes, last-minute scratches, unforeseen changes in weights, and the player's all-important visits to the paddock will keep him more than sufficiently busy.

Daily Track Program [INDISPENSABLE]

Not more than eight out of ten persons at the track buy the program, which costs about half a dollar. Many of those who save the money can be seen forking over a couple of dollars for tip sheets. Anybody who cares to be his own master at the track will want a program. It gives all but the final scratches and jockey changes, offers the track's official guess as to what the odds may be (a guess which influences the odds considerably), and lists the leading trainers and jockeys at the current meeting. Expert players do a good deal of pencil work on their programs. To be at the track without one is like playing golf without a putter.

And now some items that every horseplayer should try to do without.

Bookies

Where bookmaking is legal, or otherwise secure from the cops, a player unable to get to the track may sometimes feel like taking a flyer on a horse. The likelihood that the horse will win is somewhat smaller than if the player were at the track. For one thing, no bet is as sound as it should be until the player has seen the horse and has satisfied himself that it is ready to run. Animals that look great on paper often look awful in the paddock.

But the main problem with bookies is that they usually are on the lam from the law. The day you hit them for $700 is the day they vanish over the state line to avoid arrest. I use the sum of $700 because it happened to me many years ago. The guy was not running out on his debt to me. He was literally running from arrest. I suppose he could have mailed me the money, but this obviously was too much to expect.

In more recent years I have had other problems with bookies. They

Old-time bookie parlor—Harold's Club, Reno, Nevada. MODERN PHOTO

have refused to take my action after discovering that I was a consistent winner with whom they could not catch up. Others have limited the size of my bets, apparently for the same reason. It is possible that old-time, gentleman bookies still exist, accepting wagers from anyone with good credit and settling accounts once a week. Such operatives used to welcome the trade of a winner. In the first place, they had good and sufficient reason to expect that he might turn out in time to be a loser. Secondly, his success was a nice advertisement for the game. It provided incentive to other players, losers all.

I no longer fool with bookies. The ones I meet nowadays smell of penitentiary. I'd sooner travel seventy-five miles to the nearest track, or stay home and read a book.

Legal Bookies

The legalized off-track betting shops established in New York and later in Connecticut may have spread west by the time the reader comes across these words. Conceivably, but by no means inevitably, the off-track customer will be able to see a video picture of the odds board and paddock before betting, and of the race itself afterward. No more inevitably, the customer who bets on a winner will be paid off at track odds. As these words are written, the New York OTB customer is being promised information about the changing pre-race odds, a big help, but collects much less on winning tickets than would be paid at the track.

Until OTB mimics Australia and provides the visual aids with which a customer can avoid betting on an unseen horse at unfair odds, the track is the place to go, just as it always has been. Incidentally, none of these words should be interpreted as hostile to OTB. I have long favored it. I think that the off-track establishment should be an outpost of the track itself. If the video facilities were adequate and the odds other than punitively low, many tracks would become outdoor television studios and, therefore, much more pleasant and less congested places to go. Track managements that collected a fair percentage of off-track betting proceeds would not mind the new arrangement at all.

Tip Sheets

As far as I am concerned, this category includes selections published in racing papers, scratch sheets, daily papers and the multicolored leaflets peddled at tracks. It also includes the tips obtainable from "turf consultants" and "information services." As we shall see, none of this information is better than any other. Rather than waste time or money or both, the player should handicap his own horses.

Touts

Although pickpockets have been eliminated from most tracks, touts have not. Many trainers, grooms, stable boys, jockeys, jockeys' agents and track employees supplement their incomes by promoting what are known in the trade as "clients"—persons willing to bet substantial sums for them on horses they recommend. All this hustling of hot information (three quarters of which turns cold after the results are posted) heightens the conspiratorial atmosphere at the track.

Most touts are good enough handicappers to know which four or five horses in a race have the best chances. They "give" one horse to each of four or five tourists. After the race they find the winning sucker and demand the proceeds of a $5 or $10 bet.

Although the small-time tout who buttonholes you at the sandwich stand claims to have intimate stable connections, he almost never does. Even if he did, his information would be of small use, because stable information is itself of small use. Furthermore, while many persons with stable connections supplement their incomes through touting, few would dare to tout a stranger. He might turn out to be a private detective in the pay of the Thoroughbred Racing Associations. At major tracks, the penalty for touting is exile.

A kind of "help" as insidious as that of the tout is the advice given by one's companion at the track. If the player has done his homework and is satisfied, on the basis of past experience, that his selections are as good as anyone else's, he should stick with them. If his companion disagrees, the debate should be resolved by a 25-cent side bet on the race. Occasionally, of course, a trusted friend with superior knowledge and experience can point out a flaw in one's handicapping. That's different.

2

Know the Track

A good handicapper knows something about horses. A superior handicapper is intimately familiar with the ways of horses, trainers and riders. And he knows his track. On his first visit to a strange track, he is likely to turn up hours before the start of the first race, to get the lay of the land.

Here are some of the things he wants to learn about:

Paddock and Walking Ring

As one race ends, the entrants in the next race are led to their covered paddock stalls for final grooming and saddling. They then go to the walking ring, or parade ring. In nice weather they usually parade around the ring twice with their grooms. After the riders mount (in response to the order, "Riders up!"), the horses walk the ring once or twice more and then amble to the track for another parade in front of the stands, followed by pre-race warm-ups which take them to the starting gate.

The design and location of paddock and walking ring are important to the expert player. He needs to see the animals in their paddock stalls. He also needs to see how they look in the walking ring. At most establishments, paddock and walking rings are behind the stands, necessitating a hike. The player is used to this. In a day at the races, pilgrimages from his seat to various other facilities and points of interest will take him at least six furlongs, some of it at a trot. It's the nature of the game.

Walking ring at Aqueduct.   UPI PHOTO

If paddock and walking ring are behind the stands, they may be rather widely separated. In any case, it is most unusual to find a single spot that commands an unobstructed view of both. On a first visit, the provident player takes such problems into account. He plans as best he can to see whatever he can of the paddock preliminaries and then get to the walking-ring rail before it becomes hopelessly congested. An expert player may be fat, but he's nimble.

Among other things that may concern the player during the minutes between races is the trend of betting, as reflected in the shifting odds. Some tracks put electric odds boards where they can be seen from the walking ring. Others do not. If a player is sufficiently dubious about the condition of his horse to want to see how it warms up before the race, he may have no opportunity to study the odds until the warm-up is over, two or three minutes before post-time. This is ample time. The study can be made while standing on line at the mutuel window, where odds boards are always visible. I mention the matter only to demonstrate that a player is likely to become quite busy during the period immediately preceding a playable race. If he does not know where things are, he may be unable to use his time profitably.

Seats

The expert cases the joint to find out where the best seats are. He knows that there is no such thing as a good seat at a racetrack, but that some seats are better than others. In general, the best possible seat is high enough to afford a clear view of the entire race, and close enough to the finish line to permit an accurate guess as to which nose arrived first. At most tracks the very best seats are in the private boxes of the upper crust. If the regular occupants don't show up, the player can sometimes gain admittance by slipping the usher a couple of dollars. First, of course, he has to pay his way into the clubhouse, a ticket to which usually costs two or three dollars more than the general admission to the grandstand.

For some reason, the reserved sections of the grandstand are often in better locations than any but the choicest private clubhouse boxes. And unreserved grandstand seats are often closer to the finish line than unreserved clubhouse ones. A player who does not mind the wrong side of the tracks is far better off in most grandstands than in most clubhouses. The main advantage of the clubhouse (except on summer Saturdays and holidays) is extra elbowroom. Another advantage is the presence of professional horsemen and other sophisticated regulars, who tend to be quieter and more civil than ordinary players. Still another advantage is the comfort of clubhouse dining rooms and bars. But the grandstand has no worse food at better prices. And, unless you happen to sit next to a maniac, you usually have more privacy in the grandstand. They don't know you. You don't know them. They leave you alone to study your figures. In the clubhouse, where you probably know somebody, you talk. The more you talk, the more you miss.

Be all that as it may, it is an excellent idea to get to the track early on one's first day. See where the finish line is situated relative to the grandstand and clubhouse. Then make decisions about seats.

In this connection, the beginning handicapper will find it an excellent idea to plan to leave his seat for the start of at least one race. It should be a race that starts in front of the stands—at mile tracks that would be a race of a mile, or a mile and one sixteenth, or a mile and an eighth. Go to the infield rail, as close to the starting gate as possible. Listen to the commotion. Watch the assistant starters handle the horses. Watch the riders. Especially watch them as the bell rings and the gate opens. An experience or two of that kind is not only interesting but enlightening. It is amazing how the good "gate boys"—jockeys noted for ability to break swiftly at the start—usually get out on top. Their reputations are deserved.

Another place to go during at least one race is all the way to the left of the spectators' area, where you can lean on the rail and watch the horses race around the final turn, their riders maneuvering for favorable position in the stretch drive. Again, the skill, courage and alertness that distinguish the best riders will be compellingly evident.

Racing Secretary's Office

Most horseplayers have never been near the place. But the expert locates it as soon as he can and makes regular visits thereafter. Here, without cost, he picks up the condition books in which the racing secretary prescribes the terms of entry for every race on every program. A player with a complete file of condition books published by his track during the current season is not quite as well off as a player with a complete file of result charts. But he can at least tell with certainty the quality of opposition today's horses faced in their previous starts at the track. The condition book also helps him decide whether he should come back next Wednesday, or whenever. The book tells him exactly what kind of races will be held on each day. He need not wait until the entries are published in his newspaper.

Other useful information published in some condition books includes the names and riding weights of all active jockeys on the grounds; the track's rules; the proportions in which purses are divided among winners and runners-up; track records, and the dates of forthcoming major races.

At or near this office most tracks have a bulletin board on which items of interest are posted. On a Monday, the board contains the names of horses that worked out on Sunday, and the distances they ran, and the speeds at which they were clocked. Because Monday's racing papers are published on Sunday, they cannot report these workouts. The presence or absence of a horse's name on the Sunday list can be a matter of great significance to the player, as we shall explain in a later chapter.

Shoe Board

At modern tracks, a panel on the infield totalisator board tells what kind of shoes each horse is wearing. Elsewhere, the board may be found tucked away near the paddock, or the racing secretary's office, or under the stands. The expert needs this information, and makes sure to find it.

Tracks in General

In a later section of this book, we shall list the names and distinguishing characteristics of all major American tracks. Let us now make sure that the reader knows how to orient himself when he takes his seat and views the course.

The diagram on page 36 represents a typical Thoroughbred track, one mile in circumference. From a seat in the grandstand, to the left of the finish wire, the fan sees the tote board. It is the electric sign that shows the amounts bet on each horse for win, place and show, and the approximate odds on each horse to win. The first odds posted, before any money is bet, are those printed in the track program. They comprise "the morning line"—the track handicapper's estimate of what the final odds will be. The estimate is never anything to bank on. The horse named as favorite may or may not become the favorite and may or may not deserve to. But the morning line influences many bettors, some of whom actually believe that the horse listed as favorite is the horse to bet, regardless of where his odds finally roost.

The tote board flashes new betting totals, and revised odds, every 90 seconds until post-time. It also shows the time of day, the number of minutes remaining until post-time, and the condition of the running surface (fast or sloppy or muddy or slow or good or heavy). During the race it shows the times in which early stages of the running are clocked. At the end it gives the final time, the program numbers of the leading horses and, at last, the mutuel prices they paid.

The finish line is not a line. It is an overhead wire. The various poles on the infield rail are named in accordance with the distance between each of them and the finish line. For example, horses run three quarters of a mile (six furlongs) from the three-quarter pole to the finish line. Races are run counterclockwise, of course, which means that they pass the stands from left to right on the homestretch and from right to left on the backstretch.

At a one-mile track, the first pole encountered in a mile race is the fifteen-sixteenths pole—seven and a half furlongs to the wire. Next comes the seven-eighths pole, followed by the six-and-a-half-furlong pole. That pole might as well be called the thirteenth-sixteenths pole, but it isn't. Similarly, the three-quarter pole is never referred to as the six-furlong pole. But the pole situated five eighths of a mile from

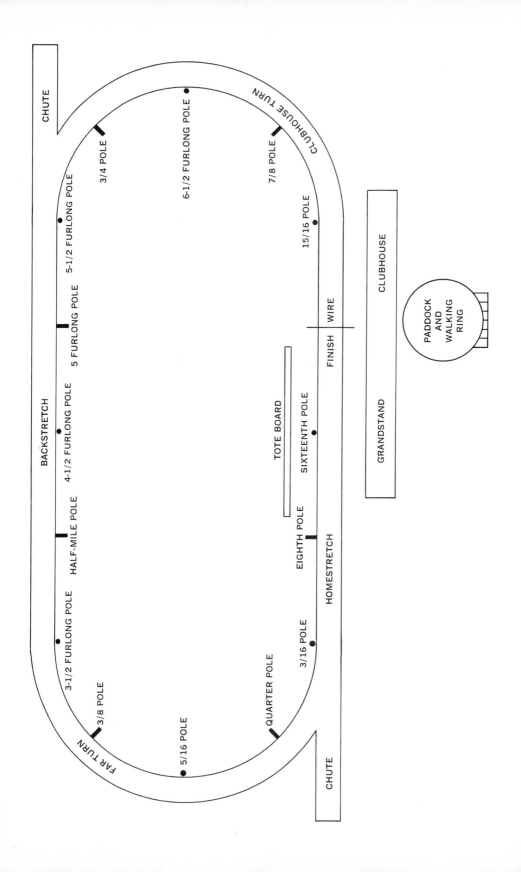

the finish is called, as the diagram shows, the five-furlong pole! And the four-furlong pole is never, but never, alluded to as the four-furlong pole. It's the *half-mile* pole.

The chute in the upper right corner, near the five-and-a-half furlong and three-quarter poles, is where races of six, six and a half and seven furlongs start. The long straightaway is easier for the horses, permitting them to settle into stride before having to negotiate turns. The chute at the head of the homestretch is where races of a mile and a quarter start.

Nowadays, the better tracks are offering more races on grass (turf races) than ever before. The turf course is always situated on the inner perimeter of the main racing strip. This means that the turf course is always shorter, with sharper turns.

If your track is on the following list, it is a mile track and looks very much like the diagram on the opposite page:

Ak-Sar-Ben, Albuquerque, Aqueduct (inner track), Bay Meadows,

The stretch at Aqueduct.　　　PAUL SCHAFER—NEW YORK RACING ASSN.

Start of the Futurity in 1902 at Sheepshead Bay.   JAMES HOLMES

The world's largest window encloses the stands at Laurel.   UPI PHOTO

Beulah Park, Bowie, Calder, Caliente, Centennial, Churchill Downs, Delaware Park, Del Mar, Detroit, El Comandante, Fair Grounds, Fairmount Park, Finger Lakes, Florida Downs, Fort Erie, Fresno, Garden State, Golden Gate, Gulfstream, Hawthorne, Keystone, Latonia, Longacres, Louisiana Downs, Meadowlands, Monmouth Park, Narragansett, Oaklawn, Penn National, Pimlico, Pleasanton, Portland Meadows, River Downs, Rockingham Park, Sacramento, Santa Anita, Santa Fe Downs, Stockton, Suffolk Downs, Sunland Park, Thistledown (main track), Turf Paradise, Woodbine and Yakima Meadows.

The following tracks are a mile and an eighth in length:

Aqueduct, Arlington Park, Atlantic City, James C. Ellis Park, Hialeah, Laurel, Saratoga.

Belmont Park is a majestic mile and a half, Keeneland a mile and a sixteenth.

The Bull Rings

The major tracks in the United States are those that attract the best stables and jockeys by paying the largest purses. All major American tracks are at least a mile in length. Some minor tracks are also a mile or more in length, but most are shorter. The short ones are known to horsemen as "bull rings," because of the sharpness of their turns. Some, like Shenandoah Downs in West Virginia, offer more comfortable seating, more courteous service and better food than one finds at most major tracks. Although the quality of their horseflesh is inferior, the better minor tracks offer races as formful and honest as can be found anywhere. A good handicapper can keep body and soul together at a half-mile oval. An indifferent handicapper is in trouble wherever he goes.

3

The Arithmetic of Racing

The handicapper attempts to unravel a multitude of factors. Some are clear, some obscure. But each relates to all the others in ways that vary from horse to horse, race to race and day to day.

Because the raw materials are numerous, changeable and deceptive, handicapping is a highly personal kind of approximation, closer to an art than to an exact science. Which is why the predictions of experts coincide only part of the time.

Two good handicappers may often play the same horse in the same race. Both may refrain from betting on certain other races. Some races find one of them betting and the other with his wallet buttoned. And, without fail, they frequently bet against each other—picking different horses in the same race. Even if they try to employ identical methods, they reach less than identical conclusions. Differences of this kind are, of course, the fascinating hallmark of any great game.

I enjoyed a demonstration of handicapping's personal aspects after people began reading *The Compleat Horseplayer*. Letters of thanks arrived from racing enthusiasts throughout the United States. Many claimed to have achieved unprecedented success, for which they credited the book. Some of their feats made me drool. Longshots! A Chicagoan gave *The Compleat Horseplayer* full marks for a winner that had paid him more than $90 on a $2 mutuel ticket. I was almost tempted to inquire how he had done it. I had never picked a $90 winner in my life.

Obviously the procedure so painstakingly described in *The Compleat Horseplayer* had been modified by the individual mentality. Some readers had become capable of turning up bonanzas of a magnitude quite beyond my own grasp. No doubt the same readers had also been backing more losers than I could possibly tolerate.

I make these observations about the personal, non-scientific nature of handicapping for several reasons. The first and most urgent is that the reader should harbor no illusions. No matter what theory of handicapping may strike him as most plausible, he will be attempting to predict the future by interpreting past events of uncertain character and inexact significance. Yet his survival at the track will demand predictions of considerable accuracy.

Beating the Percentages

If certainty about the past is so limited, must not certainty about the future be terribly slight? How can anyone wrench a profit from such confusion?

By dealing in probabilities. Or, as they say at the track, working *with* the percentages instead of against them.

It so happens that the old saw "You can beat a race, but you can't beat the races," is quite wrong. It turns reality upside down. The truth is that nobody can be sure of beating an individual race, but lots of people win more money than they lose in a season's activity at the track. There is nothing unusual about this. In any game worth playing, the outcome of any one play (any one race) is rarely a matter of absolute certainty. But someone who plays well finishes ahead in the long run.

Take poker as an example. No matter how expert the player, nothing short of a royal flush provides complete certainty of a winning bet. The expert is lucky if he holds one royal flush in forty years of play. In other words, he can't necessarily beat the race. But he is an expert and he makes out fine, losing a little, winning a little more. He beats the game.

Let us suppose that our poker expert competes with six of his peers in a game of jackpots. After he has been at the table with these sharpers a few times he knows a great deal about their courage, wiles and weaknesses. He undoubtedly knows more about them than any handicapper can know about a field of horses. The usefulness of this knowledge varies from session to session, of course. In poker, last week's tabby is this week's tiger, his mood having modified his style for the time being. A further limitation on the expert's success is that his opponents also are experts and know a good deal about *his* style.

In the end, therefore, the poker expert's main armor against all uncertainties is his knowledge of the game itself—more particularly, his knowledge of the *percentages* that give the game its central character. As long as he is faithful to the laws—the probabilities—embodied in these percentages, he seldom loses. And, when he combines knowledge of the probabilities with accurate guesses about the tactics of his opponents, he becomes a big winner.

Allow me to pursue the matter further. By reminding the reader how the percentages are used in poker, I hope to whet his appetite for discussion of the less familiar, but equally important percentages of racing.

A 52-card poker deck contains slightly less than 2.6 million five-card hands. The exact probability of drawing any specific hand is a matter of established mathematical knowledge. So is the exact probability of improving any hand on the draw. If the expert has a chance to convert his hand into a straight by discarding one card and drawing either a nine or an ace, will he bet the money required for the gamble? It all depends.

He knows that the odds against drawing either an ace or nine are 5 to 1. He may draw the right card and lose the pot to someone who holds a flush or a full house. But he will win in the long run on hands of this kind if he respects the percentages of the game. He will win in the long run if he stays with such a hand *only* when the pot promises to pay him *at least* five times the money he bets. If he draws to this kind of straight on occasions when the pot pays less than a 5 to 1 gamble should, he eventually will lose. Winning one such hand in every six or seven he plays, he will take in less money than he spends on the losing ones.

Identical principles apply to horseplaying. Certain percentages are as cut-and-dried in racing as in cards, and deserve comparable respect. They occur with astonishing uniformity, year after year. They affect the handicapper's choice of horse. They affect the size and frequency of his bets.

What is more, racing is so patterned that a handicapper's own methods are certain to embody percentages of their own. If his methods are consistent (regardless of whether they are profitable or not), they turn up winning horses at a rate that fluctuates hardly at all from one year to the next. Likewise, his annual rate of profit or loss on each invested dollar varies but slightly from year to year. He may encounter long losing streaks and incredible strings of winners, but in the end his handicapping settles at its own percentage level. When he knows this percentage, and the accompanying rate of profit or loss, he is able to judge the efficiency of his methods. He remains uncertain about the outcome of any individual bet, but he knows with considerable certainty that, in due course, he can expect to win a predictable minimum percentage of bets, with a predictable minimum profit or loss per invested dollar.

A life insurance company does the same kind of thing on an incomparably larger scale. It hitches its treasury to the laws of probability. It does not have the vaguest idea when you will die. But it knows, within the practical limits of earthly certainty, the percentage of people your age who will die this year, or next, or twelve years from now. It designs its premium rates accordingly. In the long run its books show a predictable percentage of "winners" and a predictable rate of profit.

Although good handicappers are respectfully attentive to the established percentages of the game, and to the percentages achieved by their own methods, handicapping is not necessarily a mathematical pastime. Some of the best handicappers use pencil and paper only to cross out the names of horses they think will lose. Other good handicappers do simple arithmetic, but not much of it. Still others devise rather elaborate arithmetical formulas in an attempt to introduce reassuring order into the hodgepodge of information with which they deal. Whatever style is most appealing to the individual, he needs no mathematical skill beyond the ability to add, subtract, multiply and divide.

Even the numbers contained in this chapter need not be committed to memory. Far more important than the numbers are the conclusions they permit about the nature of the game.

The Magic Number

Anybody who bets $1,000 on the races and emerges from the experience with less than $800 is doing something dreadfully wrong. A $2 bettor who selected horses with a hatpin, or by using numerology, or by consulting tea leaves, would seldom lose much more than $200 in a series of 500 bets—an investment of $1,000.

It is, of course, more than theoretically possible to go broke at the track. Desperate gamblers do it every day. And victims of inefficient selection methods or wasteful betting systems also manage to run out of cash long before they should.

The shortest route to disaster is to bet too much of one's money at a time. The man with a $1,000 bankroll who plays it all on one horse has a splendid chance of losing it all. The man who bets the $1,000 in five installments of $200 each also risks extinction: In any given series of five bets, no handicapper on earth can be sure of winning so much as one!

How, then, can a less-than-expert player expect to have $800 left after betting $1,000?

The magic number is 20.

Without knowing the slightest thing about horses, and betting entirely at random, the player's long-term losses should not exceed 20 percent of the total amount he bets. To limit his losses to that extent, he need only bet in amounts small enough to assure himself of a large, representative number of bets.

It works like this. Of all money bet on any race, most tracks deduct approximately 18.5 percent for taxes and their own revenue. The remaining 81.5 percent is disbursed to the holders of winning mutuel tickets.

This means that, regardless of how the individual player fares with his bet, the crowd as a whole loses 18.5 percent of its wagered dollar on every race, every day, every week, every year. A random bettor, playing horses at random, should do no worse. A selection system employing daisy petals or playing cards or dice or something else entirely unrelated to handicapping should leave the bettor with close to 80 percent of his wagered money after a series of 500 or more bets.

Any handicapping procedure that results in seasonal losses as high as 20 percent of all money wagered is, therefore, no better than the hatpin method. And anyone who loses more than 18.5 cents of every dollar he bets in a season is—whether he realizes it or not—going out of his way to find trouble.

The high-percentage "take" of racetracks has been compared unfavorably with the smaller levies imposed by gambling houses. A roulette player, for instance, should lose only slightly more than a nickel of each dollar he bets, assuming that the computation is made after a long, representative series of plays. The difference between roulette and racing is, however, a considerable one. The wheel spins every few seconds, all night. The roulette fanatic makes hundreds of bets in one session. No matter how conservatively he bets, the house "take" of 5 percent-plus nibbles away at his capital, and he finally has nothing left.

But the horseplayer encounters only nine races a day, a daily double, some exactas (perfectas) and a trifecta or two. If he confines his wagering to the smallest possible fraction of his betting capital, he might play for months or years before emptying his pocket. For example, a man who allocates $200 to racetrack wagering, and bets $2 on every race, should have about $114 left after going to the track for 28 days. He might have much more or much less, but the track "take" *should* siphon off only $80 or so from the 252 bets he makes. And, if he knows absolutely nothing about the horses and makes no attempt to learn, he very probably will do just about that well.

It follows that anything useful he learns about the horses should enable him to begin reducing the percentage of loss. In this chapter we shall see how to reduce that percentage merely by learning some of the probabilities of the game, and without learning a thing about horses themselves!

Betting on Favorites

An infallible guide to the reliability or intelligence, or both, of a racing expert is his attitude toward persons who bet on favorites. All experts know that, in a representatively large sample of races, one of every three will be won by the betting favorite—the horse on which the most money is bet. The conclusions various writers achieve in light of this statistic are a dead giveaway to their knowledge of probabilities. Anyone ignorant of probabilities is not only unable to evaluate his own chances at the track but is hopelessly unqualified to advise anyone else.

It is fashionable to sneer at "chalk players"—the conservative types who play nothing but favorites. Observing that favorites win only one third of the time, many sages proclaim, with flawless arithmetic, that the crowd is wrong two thirds of the time. They insist that the secret of success at the track is to part company with the crowd, avoid favorites and, presumably, begin winning a lion's share of the two races in three which find the crowd wrong. Such advice is crude nonsense. Whatever truth it contains is strictly coincidental.

Any child will understand the reason for this, after a few facts are set forth. At major tracks, the typical race involves nine horses. This means that about 80 horses go to the post on a representative day. The crowd picks nine of these animals as betting favorites. Three of the nine win. Anyone who thinks it easier to find winners among 71 non-favorites than among nine favorites is thinking backwards.

The fact that non-favorites win two thirds of all races does not mean that non-favorites have twice as good a chance of winning as favorites do. Quite the contrary. Until we handicap the entire field and see which horse is probably the best of the lot (a task few players can perform), we know nothing about the non-favorite except that it is one of eight non-favorites in the race. But we know more than that about the favorite. We know that it wins one race in three. This means that the "natural" odds against it are 2 to 1. But the "natural" odds against a random non-favorite in a nine-horse race are 11 to 1! (This figure is obtained by the statistical process of dividing the number of races that non-favorites win (⅔ by the number of non-favorites (8).)

We now have established that it is foolish to reject a horse simply because it is the favorite, or to stab at another horse simply because it is a non-favorite. We therefore are in better position to appreciate some interesting statistics. We begin with a blazer:

To cut the magic number of 20 just about in half and bring one's losses within striking distance of the break-even point, one need only confine one's bets to horses that are the favorites in their races!

Many years ago, the resourceful Robert V. Rowe studied a series of 7,301 races. He reported in *American Turf Monthly* that a bet on each of the favorites would have produced a loss of 8.4 percent for each dollar wagered. More recently, Burton P. Fabricand studied 10,035 races and came up with a closely similar figure. In a highly original book—*Horse Sense,** proposing a mathematical approach to the game —Fabricand writes that a flat bet on each favorite would have lost the player nine cents per dollar.

Many selection systems, including Fabricand's and several that I describe later in this book, attempt to convert the 9 percent loss into a profit by applying handicapping principles to the past-performance records of favorites. Because the starting point of such systems finds the player only a hop and a skip from profit's promised land, they are among the best possible procedures for persons unacquainted with the game.

Fabricand found that bets on favorites paying extremely short prices (1 to 2 or less) resulted in a small profit. On such wagers, it would seem that the magic number is reduced to zero or thereabouts before a bit of actual handicapping has been undertaken.

In Praise of the Crowd

I have just said some harsh things about experts who base their theories on disdain for the judgment of the crowd. I have showed that the

* (David McKay Company, New York, 1965.)

crowd as a whole does a better job of conserving its money than is likely to be done by someone who refuses in any circumstances to agree with the crowd. The object of this book is, nevertheless, to equip the player to surpass the crowd by means of expert handicapping.

The next step in that direction is to analyze a second accomplishment of the crowd. Insiders have long known that, even though the crowd loses 18.5 cents on the dollar, it does a rather remarkable job of handicapping. If it bets in such proportions as to make a horse a 3 to 1 shot, that horse is more likely to win than the animal that goes off at 4 to 1. Putting it another way, any long series of 5 to 2 shots will win a higher percentage of races for the bettor than a comparable series of horses that run at higher odds.

Fabricand's study of more than 10,000 races included 93,011 horses. Classifying the animals according to the mutuel prices at which they ran, he found the following percentages of winners:

Mutuel Price Range	Percentage of Starts Won	Mutuel Price Range	Percentage of Starts Won
Up to 3.10	71.3	10.00–10.90	16.1
3.20–3.50	55.3	11.00–11.90	15.5
3.60–3.90	51.3	12.00–13.90	12.3
4.00–4.30	47.0	14.00–15.90	11.0
4.40–4.70	40.3	16.00–17.90	9.9
4.80–5.10	37.9	18.00–19.90	8.2
5.20–5.50	35.5	20.00–21.90	8.2
5.60–5.90	30.9	22.00–31.90	6.0
6.00–6.90	28.9	32.00–41.90	4.0
7.00–7.90	23.0	42.00 up	1.4
8.00–8.90	20.9		
9.00–9.90	18.6		

The lower the odds, the greater the likelihood that the horse will win.

Fabricand also demonstrates that it is impossible to turn a profit by playing *all* horses in a given odds range. The very shortest-priced horses on his list earned an insignificant profit when played in that way. But all other odds ranges showed a loss.

However, some important lessons are to be learned from the percentages of loss in each odds range:

1. The largest single group of horses on the list were the 25,044 animals that went off at odds of 20 to 1 or more (mutuel prices of $42 and up). A bet on each of those longshots would have meant a loss of

54 cents on every wagered dollar, even though 340 winning tickets would have been cashed!

2. The odds ranges below 5 to 2 (mutuel prices below $7) yielded losses that clustered around 6 percent of the wagered dollar.

3. Only on horses at 5 to 1 and higher did the percentage losses exceed the normal track take.

4. These results, mind you, were based on uncritical wagering without recourse to handicapping. The sole basis for the paper bet was the odds at which the horse left the starting gate.

It now is possible to modify an earlier statement about the quality of a handicapping procedure that loses as much as 20 percent. A player not only would do far better to play all favorites indiscriminately, but would do still better if he picked himself an odds range below 2 to 1 and played all horses that fell into that range! He would find himself betting on about half of all races, and would lose only 8 or 9 percent of his money in the long run.

If he took the trouble to learn handicapping, he could then move in one of two directions. He could become more sensibly selective about the horses in his pet odds range. Or he could become more selective about horses in general, betting on apparently promising horses regardless of their odds. The test of his method would now be whether or not his bets yielded a loss smaller than 8 percent. His glee at cashing an occasional longshot ticket would remain provisional until he had balanced his books for the season. To hit the dreamed-of longshot or two and end with a loss of 21 cents on the dollar, as many players do, is to carry enjoyment past the point of diminishing returns. For anyone but a person with unlimited means and an uncontrollable yen to gamble, a procedure of that kind is downright foolish.

What Kind of Favorites?

Numerous players believe that certain kinds of races are more formful than others. That is, they believe that the favorites win a substantially higher percentage of one kind of race than of another, producing smaller dollar losses. Statistical surveys that appear to demonstrate the truth of such theories are all based on inadequate studies. More extensive samplings, such as Fabricand's and Robert Rowe's, show that the percentage of winning favorites remains essentially the same in all types of races, and that the profit or loss in each odds range does not vary significantly according to the quality of the race itself.

To show how inflexible the percentages of the game really are, I surveyed the results of all races that paid purses of $30,000 or more during 1965. Of the 215 races of that high quality, the favorites won 39 percent. A $2 bet on each favorite would have netted the player a loss of about 8 percent on his wagered dollars. Which is where we came in.

Extra Ways to Lower the Magic Number

Here are some other well-established statistics that enable a player unacquainted with handicapping to keep long-term losses below 18 percent:

1. Favorites at even money or less produce losses of about 5 percent when bet to win.

2. Odds-on favorites cost about 1 percent when bet to show.

3. All favorites to place cost about 5 percent.

4. Odds-on favorites in major handicaps, stakes races and featured allowance races at major tracks throw off a *profit* of almost 5 percent when bet to place. This exception to all other rules occurs too infrequently to mean very much in the way of riches, but is worth knowing about. It happens because the horses involved are animals of the highest grade, and seldom run worse than second.

And here is something borne in mind by expert players. It may induce non-experts to brush up on their handicapping: If a handicapper's methods customarily yield about one winner in every three attempts, the "natural" odds against any single one of his selections are about 2 to 1. Therefore, when his handicapping points out a horse running at odds of 4 to 1, he is in an enviable situation. The percentages of the game are with him. His position is comparable to that of the poker player who draws to a bobtail straight when he knows that the pot will pay more than the necessary 5 to 1 odds.

The word "overlay" is heard constantly at the tracks. It describes an animal that runs at higher odds than its winning chances would seem to call for. The very best kind of overlay is the horse we have just discussed—picked by the methods of a competent handicapper, and running at odds more than sufficient to repay the handicapper for the losing bets he makes. Those of us who win at the track do so by concentrating on overlays.

Attainable Results

A successful handicapper with a prejudice against betting on favorites is forced to refrain from betting until he finds a race in which the favorite seems undeserving. He then must be able to find a non-favorite that seems clearly superior to the other entrants.

Another successful handicapper, with no prejudice against favorites, must avoid betting on too many favorites that lose, and must bet on a certain number of winning non-favorites, or he will show no profit.

Regardless of the individual's handicapping style, the percentages of the game govern his results. Generally speaking, the more often he bets on longshots, the less often he wins. And the more often he bets on low-priced horses, the more often he wins. But his rate of profit—the only meaningful index to his success—depends on whether he wins enough bets at prices high enough to compensate for his losses.

It has long been taken for granted in racing that a first-class handicapper can win about four bets in ten if he is extremely conservative, bets on relatively few races, and favors horses whose odds average about 2 to 1. Such a level of play brings a profit of about 20 cents for every dollar in bets, increasing capital at a tremendous rate. For example, if his capital is $2,000 and he makes an average of two $100 bets a day for 200 racing days (spread over a period of years, perhaps), his operations return a profit of $8,000, enlarging his capital to $10,000.

A great deal of garbage is published about the 100 percent profits allegedly yielded by one or another winning system. In every instance, the high profits were earned (if indeed they were earned at all), over periods of time too short for significance. During the week of success at Monmouth Park that I recorded in *The Compleat Horseplayer,* my rate of profit was 92 cents on the invested dollar. Profits of that magnitude are entirely beyond reach over the long haul. If I had stayed at Monmouth for the following week I might well have suffered a shellacking.

My usual rate of profit over a period of years has been closer to 30 percent. I employ the word "usual" in a loose sense. Since most of my excursions to the track are for recreation and do not involve grimly serious handicapping, the records on which I base the 30 percent statistic are the records of days such as those at Monmouth Park, when the sole object was to win dough. When I go to the track to laugh and play and get a sunburned nose, I consider myself extremely lucky to break even.

Be that as it may, the percentages of the game and the limits of human capability seem to limit long-range profits to something like 40 cents on the dollar. A more easily attainable rate would be about 20.

Some handicappers hint that through careful selection of their spots they manage to win half of all their bets. I suppose this is possible, but whether it is possible to turn a good profit by doing it is another matter. A far more realistic objective for the handicapper is a bet-winning average in the range of 30 to 40 percent, with mutuel prices high enough for profit.

The reader will be rewarded by a few moments with the following figures.

To earn a rate of profit of 20 cents on the wagered dollar, a handicapper must:

1. Win half of all his bets, at average odds not lower than 7 to 5, or
2. Win 40 percent of his bets, at average odds of 2 to 1, or
3. Win a third of his bets, at average odds of 13 to 5, or
4. Win 30 percent of his bets, at average odds of 3 to 1.

Anyone who hopes to do twice that well, earning profits at the rate of 40 cents on the wagered dollar, must:

1. Win half of all his bets, at average odds of 9 to 5, or
2. Win 40 percent of all his bets, at average odds of 5 to 2, or
3. Win a third of his bets, at average odds of more than 3 to 1, or
4. Win 30 percent of his bets, at average odds exceeding 7 to 2.

Any of the formulas in those two lists is at least theoretically attainable. But the practicalities of the game, and of human self-control, suggest that the beginning handicapper deserves a medal if he can achieve results in the neighborhood of items 2 and 3 on the first of the lists. If he does that well, he will be able to buy his own medal.

Public Selectors

Among the personalities at the track, few are more colorful than the human foghorns who peddle tip sheets to the crowd. Posted in booths directly inside the entrance gates, they use every form of persuasion but gun, knife and fist. The walls of the booths are plastered with yesterday's editions of their sheets. The names of the winning horses are encircled, their mutuel prices scrawled in heavy ink.

It so happens that some (not many) of the men who publish the tip sheets are topnotch handicappers. It also happens that none of the sheets is worth a damn to the player.

The better sheets can claim with accuracy that they "name" the winners of about half of the races. But "naming" winners is different from picking winners. The sheets *name* as many as four horses per race. Let any of the named horses win and the sheet claims a success for itself.

A player interested in knowing which three or four horses are regarded by one or another expert as the livest in each race can get information of comparable quality from the selection pages of *Daily Racing Form,* and from the handicaps published in newspapers of general circulation.

The weakness of all such advice is that no handicapper can show a profit if he attempts to pick the winner of every race on the card. The best proof of this is that no public selector ever shows a long-term profit. Furthermore, even when the public selector attempts to pick a "Best Bet"—the likeliest horse on the entire program—he also fails to show a profit. He may be a fine handicapper, but two obstacles defeat him. The first is that he picks his "best bet" before the horses have entered the paddock, and he therefore misses the essential opportunity to check their pre-race condition. An equally important reason is that his "best bets" become popular choices and pay woefully low mutuel prices. The prices they pay when they win are insufficient to counterbalance the losses.

The January, 1967, issue of *Turf and Sport Digest* showed that anyone who had bet on every favorite at all tracks from March 15 to November 15, 1966, would have cashed 33 percent of his bets and lost 9 percent of every dollar he bet. These figures, as we already know, are par for the course. The most successful public selector on the *Digest* list during that lengthy period was "Trackman," who is not an individual but an assemblage of *Form* experts, each of whom is posted at a track. Trackman's selections were correct 25 percent of the time. His longest losing streak was 30. Repeat, 30 losers in a row for the most successful group of selections on the list.

The loss suffered by anyone who bet on each of Trackman's choices was 11.5 percent. To have played the choices of others among the surveyed public selectors would have meant losses ranging as high as 19 cents on the wagered dollar, after suffering as many as 33 losers in succession.

I observed earlier that anyone who loses more than 20 cents on the dollar is going out of his way to find trouble. The losses recorded season after season by the nation's most able public selectors seldom exceed the magic percentage of 20, but come close enough. They prove the absolute impossibility of profiting from an attempt to pick a winner in every race.

The disadvantages of trying to pick a "best bet" on the day before its race are equally clear. Trackman, the 1966 champion at handicapping entire programs, was correct on only 35 percent of his "best bets." To have played each of them would have meant a loss of 16.5

cents per dollar. By far the top picker of "best bets" during that period was the handicapper known as Reigh Count. Only 27 percent of his spot selections won, but they paid enough to produce a net loss of but 3.5 cents for every dollar bet on them.

Numerous selection systems, including some to be reviewed in this book, apply handicapping angles to the choices of public selectors. The percentages discussed in this chapter suggest rather strongly that the player would do better with similar systems that concentrate on favorites, inasmuch as favorites lose less money to begin with than newspaper and tip-sheet selections do.

Beware the Law of Averages

Statisticians and others acquainted with the laws of probability try, wherever possible, to measure situations in precise terms. They know that averages are misleading. The classic example is of the man who needs to cross a river. Having learned that the average depth is only five feet, and being six feet tall, he tries to wade across. In midstream he sinks like a stone and drowns. A river can be 12 feet deep at mid-stream and still have an average depth of only five.

Or take the following series of numbers: 1, 2, 3, 4, 5, 6, 7, 8, 9, 75. The average of those numbers is 12. But, if the numbers represent the results of something or other—like the odds paid by a series of racing selections—the average distorts reality. Nine of the ten horses ran at odds of 9 or less, yet the striker of averages stumbles around under the delusion that he can expect an "average" return of about 12 on his next series of ten winners. Unless the horse that returned 75—and threw the average out of whack—was a normal, predictable, usual selection, a statistician would prefer to say that the *median* of the series was between 5 and 6. In other words, he would look for the point that falls midway in the series. Five of the numbers in this series were 6 or more. The other five were 5 or less. The median is, therefore, around 5.5. Which ain't 12.

In the handicapping of Thoroughbred horses it is essential to remember the illusory nature of averages. To give an extreme example, the player sometimes encounters a horse that has won over $100,000 in twenty starts—an average of about $5,000 per race. No other animal in the race may show winnings close to that average. To decide that the $100,000 horse is the classiest in the race might be a mistake. It might have won most of its $100,000 in one race last year and have won not a dime since. Indeed, it might have won only two races in its entire career. Another horse in today's race, with average earnings of only $3,000, might have an enormous edge in current class and condition.

Knowing that averages can never be more than rough yardsticks, the good handicapper makes them work for him. He looks beyond them.

Above all, he pays no heed whatsoever to the racetrack superstition known as "the law of averages."

Example: If favorites win one of every three races, and nine races in succession have been won by non-favorites, it is incorrect to suppose that the favorite in the tenth race has a better than ordinary chance to win. The favorite is *not* "due." Aside from what the handicapper may think of the animal's quality, which is quite another matter, its status as a favorite tells only one thing about its winning chances. That one thing is a generality: In the long run, favorites win one race out of three.

But the long run is often a *long* one. Persons who base their play on the inevitability of victory by favorites sometimes increase the amount of their bets after every loss. They lose more than they should. In fact, if they go the route of doubling their bets after each loss, they end in ruin.

It is not unusual for favorites to lose ten races in succession. At Aqueduct during 1966, there was a losing series of 13. At other tracks the losing streaks ran as high as 20. The man who bets $2 on a favorite, loses it, bets $4 on the next, and $8 on the next and continues to double up in hope that the favorite is "due" will have parted with $1,022 after nine successive losses. He will be required to bet another $1,024 on the next race, if he has it. His bet might drive the odds down from the usual 3 to 2 to something like even money. If the horse wins, which is by no means inevitable, the bettor emerges with a profit of $2 on an investment of $2,046.

The law of averages is equally meaningless in connection with the performances of jockeys. Willie Shoemaker and Steve Cauthen may win more than 20 percent of their starts every year, but they also lose as many as 50 races in succession while doing it.

Similarly, the handicapper's carefully recorded knowledge that his selections win almost twice in every five attempts is poor grounds for an assumption that seven losers in a row will be followed by an immediate winner. Or that seven winners in a row make the next selection a sure loser.

Another even more harmful product of this kind of misunderstanding occurs at every track every day. A longshot wins a race. A disappointed bettor consults his *Form* and discovers that the longshot had been timed at 36 seconds in a breezing three-furlong workout a couple of days ago. No other horse in the race had worked so rapidly so recently. Powie! A new system is born! The player now loses eight bets in a row on horses whose records contain that particular workout angle.

Or a player reads a system that seems plausible, tries it on paper for a week and discovers to his delight that it picks eight winners in sixteen attempts for a profit of $1.45 on every hypothetical dollar bet. So he takes it to the track and it hits one winner in the next sixteen races, for a monumental loss. He now discards it. But it might actually be a good system. His first mistake was to assume that it was good without sufficient evidence. His second mistake was to risk money on it. His third was to discard it without sufficient evidence.

To summarize, it is not possible to determine probabilities without a large, representative series of cases. One robin doesn't make a spring. And, even after the probabilities are determined, they remain nothing but long-range probabilities. In no way do they guarantee the outcome of a single, isolated event. Nor do they guarantee the outcome of any short series of events. The feeblest handicapper enjoys winning days and winning weeks. The only inevitability in his situation is that he will end as a heavy loser if he persists in his usual methods. And the best handicapper suffers losing days and weeks, but recovers the ground if his methods remain sensible and he plays in his usual style.

As I have insisted before, and as may seem more agreeable by this time, you can't necessarily beat a race, but you may be able to beat the races. To do so you will have to overcome the unfavorable percentages of the game. You will have to confine your play to situations in which (1) your handicapping knowledge tells you that an animal has an especially good chance to win and (2) the gross returns on your winning bets are more than sufficient to repair your losses.

The House Percentage

Our poker player holds four diamonds and a spade. The odds against exchanging the spade for another diamond are 4 to 1. If it has cost $1 to stay in the game until now, and will cost another $1 to discard the spade and draw a new card, he will do so, provided that the total pot contains at least $10. If he succeeds in getting his flush, it probably will win the pot. And the pot—at least $4 of their money to every $1 of his —will more than compensate for the risk.

Suppose, however, that every time the player won a pot, the owner

OPPOSITE: *Hedley Woodhouse boots one home at Gulfstream.* UPI PHOTO

Dr. Fager and Manuel Ycaza easily win the $100,000 Jersey Derby at Garden State in 1967, only to be disqualified. Second horse, In Reality, was declared the victor.

UPI PHOTO

Kelso, under Milo Valenzuela, beats Gun Bow in the 1964 Washington D.C. International at Laurel. UPI PHOTO of the card table extracted a cut of about 20 percent of the money? The odds against drawing the flush would remain 4 to 1. But the player no longer would be able to break even on such gambles unless the pots offered at least 5 to 1.

Chances are the player would look elsewhere for a poker game. Or, if this were the only game in town, he would revise his methods. He would play much more conservatively. He would incur fewer risks. Where winning probabilities decrease, losses become more costly, more difficult to overcome.

This is exactly what has happened in Thoroughbred racing. Notwithstanding the unfragrance of old-time racing, when pari-mutuel machines were unheard of, a good handicapper enjoyed idyllic advantages. For instance, he often could get 5 to 2 from a track bookmaker on a horse that finally went off at 9 to 5. Nowadays, he would get no more than 3 to 2 on the same horse, because the house keeps a lot of the money for itself. The arithmetic is worth noting; certain bets on which the player used to make $5 in profit now yield him only $3. His profit on a bet of that kind has been reduced by 40 percent. Or, looking at it another way, that profit used to be 67 percent higher than it is now. He therefore plays much more conservatively now. He has to. The house cuts every pot with a cleaver.

The principle of pari-mutuel betting is eminently fair. The odds paid by the winning horse are—in principle—the ratio between the amount of money bet on it and the amount bet on all the losers.

Theoretically, if members of the crowd bet $30,000 on Horse "A" and other players bet a total of $60,000 on all other horses in the race, "A" is a 2 to 1 shot (60 to 30). The mutuel price should be $6, representing the bettor's original $2 plus a $4 profit. In actuality, "A" pays nothing like $6. At most tracks in the year 1978 it pays only $4.80, having been cut from 2 to 1 by the house and the state.

The house deductions are called take and breakage. They finance track operations and provide tax revenues to the state and other governments. Tracks need funds with which to pay purses, hire employees and keep themselves spruce. Governments are undoubtedly entitled to a slice, too. During the 1960's and '70's, unfortunately, state legislatures carried this principle beyond the borders of reason, increasing government's share of racetrack betting pools so remorselessly that tens of thousands of devoted horseplayers no longer could afford to go to the races as frequently as in the past. Many of these worthies took up other pastimes and stopped going to the races at all. And for newcomers unable to handicap horses, the track admission gates became revolving doors. Sensible persons who found themselves losing too

The Tote Board and the Price

This table shows the mutuel prices represented by the figures posted on racetrack odds boards. Horses posted at 4 to 5 or higher may pay more than the minimum mutuel price, but they never pay less. The computations are revised at frequent intervals until post-time.

Odds	Price	Odds	Price	Odds	Price
1-9	$2.20	2-1	$6.00	18-1	$38.00
1-8	2.20	5-2	7.00	19-1	40.00
1-7	2.20	3-1	8.00	20-1	42.00
1-6	2.20	7-2	9.00	21-1	44.00
1-5	2.40	4-1	10.00	22-1	46.00
1-4	2.40	9-2	11.00	23-1	48.00
1-3	2.60	5-1	12.00	24-1	50.00
2-5	2.80	6-1	14.00	25-1	52.00
1-2	3.00	7-1	16.00	30-1	62.00
3-5	3.20	8-1	18.00	35-1	72.00
3-4	3.40	9-1	20.00	40-1	82.00
4-5	3.60	10-1	22.00	45-1	92.00
1-1	4.00	11-1	24.00	50-1	102.00
6-5	4.40	12-1	26.00	60-1	122.00
7-5	4.80	13-1	28.00	75-1	152.00
3-2	5.00	14-1	30.00	99-1	200.00
8-5	5.20	15-1	32.00		
9-5	5.60	16-1	34.00		
		17-1	36.00		

much money simply gave up the game before becoming seriously involved in it.

What had formerly been a combined track-state deduction of 10 percent from the betting pools rose to a standard 17, with some states increasing the bite to as much as 25 percent on trifecta pools. As already observed, these increases meant lower profits for winning bettors, making the game more difficult than ever. The following chart shows how drastically the proceeds of winning bets are affected by apparently small increases in takeout.

Natural Odds	Natural Mutuel Payoff	Payoff With 10% Take	Payoff With 14% Take	Payoff With 17% Take
6-1	$14.00	$12.60	$12.00	$11.60
5-1	12.00	10.00	10.20	9.80
4-1	10.00	9.00	8.60	8.20
3-1	8.00	7.20	6.80	6.60
2-1	6.00	5.40	5.00	4.80
1-1	4.00	3.60	3.40	3.20
4-5	3.60	3.20	3.00	2.60

By "natural odds" of 4 to 1, please remember, the chart refers to a situation in which the bets on the horse amount to one fifth of the betting pool. That is, with $1,000 bet on the horse and $4,000 on its opponents, we have a natural 4 to 1 shot. However, before the payoff to winning bettors, the legislated take is subtracted from the pool, severely reducing the profits awarded to winning bettors. The final column of the chart is the gasser. It shows that someone who bet on a natural 2 to 1 horse at the typical track during the early and mid-1970's collected only $4.80 when the horse won. The natural profit of $4 had been cut to $2.80, a reduction of 30 percent. And the player who collected $2.60 on a natural 4 to 5 shot had been deprived of 62.5 percent, which was outright confiscation.

In mid-1978, under pressure from the New York Racing Association, which operates Aqueduct, Belmont Park and Saratoga, the state legislature rolled back the take from 17 percent to 14. In view of the keenly competitive racing situation in that part of the country, which was cluttered with tracks, it seemed possible that legislatures in New Jersey and Pennsylvania might find it desirable to follow the New York example, give the bettor a break and prevent local racing from disappearing down the tubes.

The Truth about Dime Breakage

Let us now return to Horse "A," on which $30,000 has been bet. The other horses in the race have attracted a total of $60,000. The mutuel pool is $90,000.

The first thing that happens is that the track lifts $15,300 from the pool—representing the 17 percent take provided by law in most states at this writing.

After the take, $74,700 remains in the pool, including the $30,000 bet on the winning horse. The remainder of $44,700 is supposed to be the profit for the winning bettors, but is not. Here is what happens:

$$30,000 \,\big|\, \underline{44,700.00} \atop 1.49$$

The $30,000 has been divided into the $44,700 to see how much money in profit is due per dollar bet on "A." Another way of saying it is that the division gives the dollar odds on "A."

Inasmuch as nobody can bet $1 at a track, mutuel prices are always stated in terms of a $2 bet. Therefore, the next step should be to multiply 1.49 by 2. The product, 2.98, would be the profit on a $2 bet —the odds in terms of $2. To compute the actual mutuel payoff, one then would add the bettor's original $2 to the $2.98, giving a mutuel price of $4.98 on "A."

But it is not done that way.

Instead, the dollar odds of 1.49 are reduced to 1.40. If the odds had been 1.41 or anything else up to and including 1.49, they also would have been cut to 1.40. This is known as "dime breakage." Unless dollar odds turn out all by themselves to end in a string of zeros, they are always cut to the next lower dime. Track and state pocket the leftover pennies—millions of dollars a year.

Back again now to Horse "A" and the poor soul who bet on him to win. Now that the dollar odds are only 1.40, the odds on the $2 bet are $2.80 to 2.00 and the mutuel price becomes $4.80.

There is no logic in the procedure, except as a pretext for raising taxes without seeming to. This legalized pilferage began years ago, when mutuel prices were computed by a slightly different method. Instead of dividing the amount bet on the *winner* into the amount bet on all the *losers,* and coming up with the basic dollar odds, the tracks worked in terms of $2 units. They divided the amount of the entire betting pool by a figure representing *the number of $2 tickets* sold on the winner. The answer was the winner's mutuel price. This is worth exploring further, since it shows how breakage has developed into the larceny that it now is. Let us therefore take another look at Horse "A," this time using the old-fashioned method of calculating his mutuel price.

The $30,000 bet on him represents 15,000 mutuel tickets. The pool, after take, is $74,700. The arithmetic:

$$15,000 \mid \frac{74,700.00}{4.98}$$

Under this old method, the track would have paid $4.90 to any holder of a winning $2 ticket on "A." In those days, furthermore, the track take was no higher than 10 percent, so the mutuel would have been $5.40. But that's another story.

Breakage arose because few mutuel prices came out in neat, round figures. The correct payoff on "A" might have been $5.12. Rather than bother their mutuel clerks with the chore of making chicken-feed change, the tracks adopted dime breakage, reducing the $5.12 to $5.10. As I have now shown, dime breakage under the old method was less costly to the player than dime breakage as currently practiced. Under the old method, the winning player collected a higher mutuel on "A" than he does now.

At some point, a procedure called nickel breakage came into vogue. Odds were computed at the dollar level. If a ticket on "A" was worth 1.45 to 1.00, the mutuel remained $4.90. If the ticket was worth 1.49 to 1.00, the odds were cut to 1.45 and the mutuel stayed at $4.90. Dollar odds were always reduced to the next lower nickel.

Which paved the way for dime breakage calculated in terms of the dollar odds. A whopping increase over old-style dime breakage. Take a horse whose dollar odds are 2.19 to 1.00. Under nickel breakage the odds became 2.15 to 1.00 and the mutuel price was $6.30. But the new, unreasonable dime breakage reduces dollar odds of 2.19 to 2.10. The horse pays only $6.20. Breakage that used to be 8 cents has become 18 cents.

Consider what this means to the holder of a ticket on a short-priced horse. If the dollar odds turn out to be .99, they are reduced to .90 and the animal pays 18 cents less on the dollar than it should have. For a horse in the even-money range this means *a profit diminution of about 18 percent on every winning ticket!*

In New York, breakage of that kind adds slightly more than one full percentage point to the total take. At Aqueduct, Belmont Park and Saratoga during 1975, breakage approached $7 million, of which the state got almost 70 percent. The basic take at the three tracks gave the state another $68 million. Which brings us to the percentages that affect place and show betting.

Place and Show Lunacy

As most players—but not all—understand, the holder of a show ticket collects a profit if the horse wins or runs second or third. A place ticket wins if the horse finishes first or second. A win ticket *loses* unless the horse wins the race.

Obviously, the best horse in the race has a better chance of running second or third than of winning. Some excellent handicappers try to capitalize on this theory. They bet only for place or show. The profits on a successful place or show bet are low, but the players hope to compensate by winning many more bets than they lose.

The profits are low in place betting because the money lost on un-successful bets must be divided between two groups of winners—those who hold place tickets on the animal that won the race, and those who backed the horse that ran second. The profits are even lower in show betting because the profits must be divided three ways.

The arithmetical facts are sobering:

1. To win money on horses that pay $2.20, it is necessary to cash 91 of every 100 bets.
2. To win money on horses that pay $2.40, it is necessary to cash more than 83 of every 100 bets.
3. To win money on horses that pay $2.60, it is necessary to cash more than 77 of every 100 bets.
4. To win money on horses that pay $3.00, it is necessary to cash more than 66 of every 100 bets.

Those are large orders.

The following statements about place and show betting can be accepted as absolute maxims. They derive not from my own prejudices but from the facts of racetrack life, the patterns and percentages of the game:

1. It is harder to make money by betting horses for place and show than by betting on them to win.
2. The number of correct predictions necessary to produce a profit in any representative series of place or show bets is unattainable by any but a supremely expert, supremely patient handicapper.
3. The relatively low natural profits on place and show winnings are drastically reduced by take and breakage, making the task of the place or show bettor even more difficult.
4. The guaranteed profits from place bets on odds-on favorites in high-class races are too low and the betting opportunities too infrequent to alter the overall situation.
5. Anyone able to show a profit from a long series of place or show bets has the ability to make important money on straight betting— betting to win.

Calculating Place and Show Odds

The place pool consists of all the money bet on all the horses for place. Like the win pool, it is subject to take and breakage. Unlike the win pool, it is divided (after take and breakage) between two groups of bettors. Those who bet on the winning horse for place share the profits with those who bet on the runner-up for place. Here is an example which takes the liberty of assuming that the take is only 15 percent, which it well may become in many places where the 17 percent toll has been driving customers away.

Total amount in place pool:	$48,000
Remainder after 15 percent take:	$40,800
Total bet on "A" to place:	$20,000
Total bet on "B" to place:	$12,000

The total profit to be returned to the successful place bettors on this race is $8,800. That figure is obtained by subtracting from the net pool of $40,800 the $32,000 that was bet on "A" and "B." The remainder is what the losing bettors have lost to the winning bettors.

The $8,800 is now divided in half, leaving $4,400 in profits for distribution to the backers of "A" and $4,400 for those who bet on "B."

We'll take "A" first:

$$20,000 \ \big| \ \frac{4,400.00}{.22}$$

The correct dollar odds in "A" to place are .22 to 1.00. Breakage transforms this to 20 cents on the dollar, making "A" a 1 to 5 shot for place. The mutuel is $2.40.

If there were no such things as take and breakage, the mutuel would be $2.80. Take and breakage reduce the natural profits on "A" by a full 50 percent!

Now let us see what happens with "B":

$$12,000 \ \big| \ \frac{4,400.00 \text{ plus}}{.36 \text{ plus}}$$

Breakage reduces the dollar odds to .30 to 1.00 and makes "B's" mutuel price $2.60 for place. But the natural mutuel, without take and breakage, would be $3.33. The profits have been cut by 55 percent.

The difficulties of place and show betting are even more pronounced than these examples indicate. Most notably, the purchaser of a place or show ticket buys a pig in a poke. He may have reason for confidence in the horse's ability to finish second or third, but he cannot begin to know what the place or show ticket will be worth until after the race is over. If he must share the profits with holders of place tickets on an odds-on favorite, his own ticket will be worth little. If his horse wins the race and a longshot finishes second—or vice versa—the place ticket will be worth more. Thus, his position is comparable to that of a poker player with a bobtail straight who agrees to buy a card without knowing how much money is in the pot. He might as well play a slot machine.

To make this clear, let us now see what happens to the place price on the well-backed "A" if Longshot "C" wins the race or finishes second. The pool remains $40,800, after deduction of the take. The crowd has bet $5,000 on "C" to place. That amount, plus the $20,000 bet on "A," is now deducted from the pool, leaving $15,800 for distribution. Holders of tickets on "A" will get $7,900. So will the supporters of "C." Compute the odds on "A":

$$\frac{20,000 \quad | \quad 7,900.00}{.39}$$

The correct dollar odds on "A" are slashed to .30 to 1.00 by breakage, making the mutuel price $2.60. This is more than "A" paid when the pool was shared with backers of the fairly well-supported "B." But now that "B" has failed to finish first or second, the $12,000 bet on him for place has been lost, and the losses have increased the profits available for distribution to owners of cashable place tickets.

I doubt that it is necessary to work out the computations on a show pool. After the take, the amounts bet on all three horses are subtracted from the pool. The remainder is divided into three equal parts, and the show price on each horse is then calculated in the usual way.

Since the place or show price on a horse depends only partly on how much has been bet on it for place or show, but depends also on how well other in-the-money horses were supported, a sensible rule can be suggested:

A time to consider betting on a horse for place is when it is an odds-on favorite and all, repeat all, other likely contenders are longshots. In such circumstances, the horse might pay only $2.40 to win but could pay almost that much—and sometimes more— to place or show. When Roman Brother won the Jockey Club Gold Cup in 1965, he paid $2.40 to win and $2.40 to place. In the Spinaway Stakes that year, Moccasin paid $2.60 to win and $2.60 to place.

Hedging

In this connection, it might be a good idea to analyze the thought processes of players who try to minimize losses by hedging their bets. They bet a horse across the board, or for win and show. Or they bet two horses in the same race, one to win and the other for place or show.

Their results depend, as usual, on handicapping ability and are limited by the effects of take and breakage. And these effects, as we have seen, are most grievous when the odds are short. If a player backs a horse for win and show and the beast finishes third, there is no doubt that the player reduces part of his loss by collecting on the show ticket. Indeed, if he bets about six times as much for show as for win, he may sometimes turn a profit on such a deal.

However, when the horse substantiates the player's handicapping ability by winning the race, the return on combined win and show betting is far less than it would be if the player put all his money on a larger ticket to win.

The inherent problem of all such maneuvering at the mutuel windows is the near-impossibility of making money on place or show bets. Unless the player is able to make such a profit, his attempts to hedge merely prevent him from making as much on his straight bets as he otherwise might. Or, if he also is incapable of making money on straight bets, the hedges will tend to reduce his overall rate of loss to some extent, while increasing his total investment. Finally, if he is good enough to break even or make a small profit on place or show bets, he almost certainly wastes time and money in the effort: He is good enough to make considerably more money than that by betting to win only!

One of the shrewdest handicappers I know often plays two horses in a race. He usually plays one to win and the other to place or show. Occasionally he plays one to win and place, the other to place or show. One of the animals is always a comparative longshot. The other is most often among the top favorites in the race.

My friend wins money, or stays extremely close to neck-and-neck with the game. I happen to think he would do even better if he bought nothing but straight tickets, but his own method of play is more comfortable for him. He is a good enough handicapper to get away with it. And his approach to hedging is the exact opposite of the one most often practiced at the tracks.

Most hedgers play the favorite or near-favorite to win, and the longshot for place or show. Supposedly, the longshot returns enough for place or show to compensate for the possible loss by the favorite. If the favorite wins and the longshot gets no part of the money, a profit remains possible, especially if the player bets at least twice as much on the favorite as on the longshot. If both tickets cash, great.

My friend, who understands what happens in place and show pools, disdains the customary hedging procedure. His handicapping tells him that the longshot has a better than fair chance to finish in the money. *He therefore bets it to win.* He bets the favorite for place or show. When the longshot wins, as it sometimes does, he makes a small fortune, regardless of how the favorite fares. If the longshot finishes second or third, which happens more often, the place and show prices on the favorite are better than usual, because of the longshot's presence in those pools!

Between 1970 and 1978 I was so busy writing about handicapping that I often had no time to handicap. When I wrenched myself away from the treadmill and fled to a track, I found that my handicapping was a bit rusty from disuse. To limit the ego-deflating effects of losing on the rare days when I could bet at all, I took up hedging of a quite effective kind. If my horse was going at 7 to 2 or better and if a little arithmetic a couple of minutes before post-time indicated that the horse's place price would exceed $4.00 even if it shared the place pool with the favorite, I bet for win and place. I well remember a week at Del Mar in 1974 when I managed to pick scarcely any winners but cashed so many fat place tickets that I ended well in the black.

Betting More than One Horse to Win

Jule Fink and his celebrated "Speed Boys" attracted national attention years ago with their practice of betting two and three horses to win the same race. As far as I know, Fink and other successful players still make money that way. It is a perfectly reasonable approach for any good handicapper with plenty of capital. If he can narrow the contention in a race to two or three or four animals, and the odds on each are high enough to assure a net profit, such betting makes sense.

Booking Percentages

Before the advent of mutuel machines, a hustler could shop among the trackside bookmakers for the best odds. Good handicappers made money that way by betting on every horse in a race except rank outsiders, overrated favorites and other animals that figured to lose.

The practice was known as "dutching," supposedly in honor of its originator, a player known as Dutch. Its basis was the bookmaker's scale of percentages, which showed how odds varied according to the fraction of the betting pool represented by the total money bet on each horse. For an easy example, if the player felt that an even-money choice could not win, he would operate as if half the betting pool—the proportion represented by the bets on that horse—were up for grabs. Simply by betting on every other horse in the race in amounts equal or proportionate to their booking percentages, he would win a substantial amount.

I understand that some players try to do the same thing at the mutuel machines. Knowing that the mutuel pool adds up to about 118 percent (the extra 18 being take and breakage), they try to eliminate horses whose odds represent 30 or 40 percent of the pool. Then, by betting the remaining horses in proportions indicated by the table of booking percentages, they beat the race.

It is easier in theory than in real life. Bets must be made at the last possible moment, in amounts that require lightning calculation. Enormous capital and outstanding ability as a handicapper are needed. The player cannot employ the method single-handed, because bets have to be made at more than one mutuel window. How could a solo operative get down bets of $33, $19, $11 and $7 in the same race—and all in the final seconds before post-time? To bet any earlier would risk having the entire deal thrown awry by last-minute changes in the odds.

I do not say that mutuel dutching is impossible. But it requires betting partners of such reliability, capital of such magnitude, and handicapping talent so well developed that the rare person able to carry it off would probably do better by playing alone, betting on two or three good horses a day.

The Percentages

Odds	Percentage	Odds	Percentage	Odds	Percentage
1–9	90.00	8–5	38.46	13–1	7.14
1–8	88.89	9–5	35.71	14–1	6.66
1–7	87.50	2–1	33.33	15–1	6.25
1–6	85.68	5–2	28.57	16–1	5.88
1–5	83.33	3–1	25.00	17–1	5.55
1–4	80.00	7–2	22.23	18–1	5.26
1–3	75.00	4–1	20.00	19–1	5.00
2–5	71.42	9–2	18.19	20–1	4.76
1–2	66.67	5–1	16.67	25–1	3.85
3–5	62.50	6–1	14.29	30–1	3.23
3–4	57.14	7–1	12.50	40–1	2.44
4–5	55.55	8–1	11.11	50–1	1.96
1–1	50.00	9–1	10.00	60–1	1.64
6–5	45.45	10–1	9.09	75–1	1.32
7–5	41.67	11–1	8.33	99–1	.99
3–2	40.00	12–1	7.69		

Simplifying the Booking Percentages

Persons able to narrow the contention in a race to three or four horses can use the following table to guarantee a profit. By betting on each of the contending horses in the precise proportions called for by the odds, the player wins, no matter which of the horses wins. Naturally, if some other horse wins, the entire amount is lost. The only limit on this adaptation of the old-fashioned booking-percentage table is that the total amount wagered may not exceed $42. Of course, if the player wants to double or triple or quadruple the prescribed amounts, his possible outlay increases to the chosen multiple of $42. Note also that the method is not usable with extremely short-priced horses.

Odds at Post-Time	Bet	Odds at Post-Time	Bet	Odds at Post-Time	Bet
8–5	$19	7–2	$11	7–1	$6
9–5	18	4–1	10	8–1	6
2–1	16	9–2	9	9–1	5
5–2	14	5–1	8	10–1	5
3–1	12	6–1	7	11–1 and up	4

Progressive and System Betting

Most betting systems are poison. They require the player to increase his bet after every losing attempt. Their theory is that the player is "due" to win at some point, and that the increased bet will return enough to make up for prior losses. We have already noted the disaster that awaits anyone who, relying on a "law" of averages, doubles his bet after every loss on a favorite, or on a top jockey. One need not double the bets, of course. Modifications of the double-up method are frequently used. But they only modify the player's losses. They cannot produce profits except briefly and accidentally. Also, they require investment outlays out of all proportion to the returns.

A pet method of some players is known as "due-column betting." The racegoer decides that the track owes him a daily stipend—say, $100. He therefore bets as much on each of his selections as will produce the desired return. Let us say that he likes a horse in the first race. Shortly before post-time, the odds board holds the animal at 4 to 1. The player bets $25. If the horse wins, the player has his $100 and goes home. If the horse loses, the player now must win $125 to make his $100 net profit.

The most evident flaw in that procedure is the underlying supposition that anyone can make a profit at any track on any given day. Or in any given week. Due-column betting thus multiplies the player's losses during a losing streak, requiring him to increase the size of his losing bets. Few players can afford it.

A far more sensible arrangement is to abandon "due-columns" and allocate a fixed percentage of betting capital for each transaction. As the capital increases, so does the size of each bet. As the capital decreases, so does each bet, enabling the player to withstand a long succession of losses, if he has to.

The notion that a player should invest more when he is winning and less when he is losing is accepted as wisdom in every game. Players who bet according to that principle make more money—or lose less—than players who defy the principle. Indeed, if two handicappers are capable of turning a 20 percent profit, and each of them starts with a bankroll of $100, the player who bets 5 percent of capital on each of his selections will end the year with far more money than the player who goes in for due-column betting or progressive betting or other upside-down methods that violate the percentages of the game, the principles of sound investment and, last but not least, the tenets of common sense.

The player who bets 5 percent of his capital can stay in business at the track for months, without winning a dime. If he goes there with $100 and loses from the beginning, he will have $45 left even if he encounters twenty successive losses before hitting a single winner. Assuming that he is the kind who can actually make the 20 percent profit we have mentioned so often, he probably will go for years without a series of losers as grievous as that.

The due-column or progressive bettor would put himself out of business in such circumstances, even though he might be just as good a handicapper as the other guy. By the same token, neither the due-column bettor nor the slave of progressive betting systems makes as much money in a series of winning bets as the man who bets a fixed fraction of capital.

By way of demonstrating this, let us analyze the occasional but inevitable blessing of five winners in succession. For the sake of argument, we can assume that each horse pays 5 to 2. The due-column bettor has a bankroll of $400 and wants to make $50 per race. He bets $20 on each of these winners, netting $250 in profits and raising his bankroll to $650. He is happy as a clam.

The adherent of progressive betting also has a $400 bankroll. He bets $20 on the first horse, planning to apply his magic formula in such a way as to require a larger bet on the second horse, if the first one loses. But the first one wins, and so do the next four. He ends by making $250 on the series of bets. His bankroll is also $650, and he is perfectly satisfied.

The man who bets 5 percent of capital also has a $400 bankroll. His first bet nets $50, making the capital $450.

His second bet is $22, netting $55. Bankroll is now $505.

His third bet is $25, netting $62.50. Bankroll: $567.50.

His fourth bet is $28, netting $70. Bankroll: $637.50.

His fifth bet is $32, netting $80. Bankroll: $717.50.

He has done better than the others. Even when his next two horses lose, he will remain in better shape.

He will bet $36 on the first loser, reducing his capital to $681.50.

He will bet $34 on the second loser, reducing his capital to $647.50.

The due-column bettor will lose $20 on the first losing bet and, assuming we are still dealing with 5 to 2 shots, will be trying to win $70 on the second bet. He therefore will wager, and lose, $28. His bankroll is now down to $602.

The progressive bettor, no matter how conservative his system, will lose at least $50 on the two bets, reducing his bankroll to $600 or less.

Daily Doubles and Other Lotteries

The daily double, exacta, perfecta, quinella, trifecta, and similar pari-mutuel attractions at modern tracks are conclusive evidence that the pooh-bahs of racing have no prejudice against outright gambling, as long as they can cut each pot. For that is what these trick bets are—gambling, impure and simple. Moreover, they are forms of gambling without the slightest incentive for a competent player of horses. They are strictly sucker bait. The only knowing bettors who bother with them are tricky horsemen, including some whose trickiness crosses the border of fraud.

Before discussing the tricks, let us agree that it is hard enough to pick one winner at a time without trying to pick two in succession, as in the double, or the winner and runner-up, as in the exacta. Consider what the player of doubles does. If he is any part of a handicapper, he may actually have reason to like one of the horses entered in the first or second race. So he buys a flock of doubles tickets which pair the horse with as many as twelve animals in the other race. So his horse wins, and pays $7. And he wins the daily double, which pays $26. He has spent $24 on doubles tickets. His profit is $2. But if he had put the $24 on the $7 horse, he would have won $60. It happens all the time.

In recent years, major tracks have undertaken to display the changing daily double and exacta payoff probabilities on closed-circuit television monitors during wagering periods. At tracks that render such service, those bets are no longer the ridiculous pig-in-poke propositions that they once were. A doubles fancier who does not wish to be caught with a $26 payoff and a $2 profit on his 12 tickets can take warning from the televised display and either avoid the double or buy an extra couple of tickets on the short-priced combination. Where the probable payoffs are not displayed, doubles and exactas remain beyond the pale for intelligent bettors. And since no track displays probable trifecta payoffs, bets on that attempt to pick the first three finishers in exact order should be avoided entirely.

A valid complaint against the multiple bets is that they encourage and reward dishonesty. Scandalous revelations about the activities of twin-double betting syndicates at harness-racing tracks made that particular wrinkle unfashionable in major Thoroughbred racing. The trifecta is not much better. In 1977, a researcher helped me to establish that the percentage of winning favorites in trifecta races was substantially lower than in other kinds of races. Worse, the favorites ran entirely out of the money far more often than normal. The peculiarly low payoffs in occasional trifecta races won by longshot combinations demonstrate that fixers and other participants in betting coups send heavy money to the trifecta windows.

The well-accepted daily double opens the way to skulduggery of its own. A horseman can stiff his animal with high profit and relative impunity in a daily-double race. If the horse is a short-priced favorite, the horseman is able to enrich himself simply by preventing it from winning, after purchasing daily-double tickets on the other contenders. For a modest outlay, and without confiding in another living soul, he can make more money that way than by collecting the short odds and the wretchedly small winner's share of the purse at the cheap tracks he frequents.

The Economics of Racing

Among the most joyful recollections of any veteran horseman is the time he caught everyone napping and saddled a 70 to 1 shot that romped by four lengths at New Orleans, laughing all the way. Sometimes it was 20 to 1 or 50 to 1 or Empire City or Havre de Grace or Latonia or Havana. It happened over and over again.

"That colt had the tenderest mouth I ever saw," says the old-timer. "Couldn't stand the bit. When I bought him for $200 he hadn't won any part of a purse in more than a year. Soon as he'd feel the bit he'd sulk. Wouldn't run an inch. So I got him down to Hover de Graw and entered him in a $1,500 race and told the boy, 'Keep a stout hold on him all the way. Don't let him run off with you. He needs a lot of rating. Save his run for the stretch.' They break and the boy takes a tight wrap and the horse feels the bit and props and damned near throws the boy and they get beat by sixty lengths. So the next week I put the horse in a $2,500 race and tell the boy, 'Now boy, all I want you to do is sit there and let them reins hang loose. Let the horse do all the work.' Horse win all by hisself. I got almost a hundred bucks down on the race, all I had in the world. One book give me ninety to one and another give eighty-five and another eighty. I sell the horse for two grand and go to Europe for a year on my winnings.''

Times have changed, but not completely. Now, as in the old days, the dream of every journeyman trainer is to find the hole card, the magic formula that converts a losing horse into a winner. The horseman needs to win a purse. He also needs to win some bets. The ideal situation is when the magic formula presents itself after the horse has run out of the money repeatedly, without showing any signs of improvement. The horse wins. The mutuel price looks like the registration number on a freight car. The stewards call in the trainer, to inquire about the miraculous reversal of form.

"The horse was off his feed for months," says the trainer truthfully. "But the other day a kitten wandered into his stall and the bugger

Goats and dogs are standard items in Thoroughbred barns. Race horses love the company.   ARLINGTON PARK PHOTO perked up. I guess he was lonesome, or something. Him and that kitten are thick as thieves. Horse is real frisky all of a sudden.''

Hoof, tail and muzzle, the economics of horse racing are tied to the pari-mutuel machines. The purse money comes from the mutuel betting pools. The funds with which struggling horsemen eke out their purses are earned at the betting windows. The horseman's prime object is to win races with his livestock, but he will go to any permissible length to conceal a horse's true form in hope of getting 5 to 1 on a natural 2 to 1 shot. He has to. He needs the dough.

Let it be agreed that certain leading trainers do not rely on bets for any part of their livelihood. Neither do certain glamorous owners. Many jockeys do not bet. But almost everyone else does, from the candy butchers and tip-sheet hawkers and ushers and sweepers and mutuel clerks to the occupants of the nice boxes in the upper tier.

The player may own a desk full of super-scientific speed charts. He may be able to recite Buckpasser's pedigree all the way back to Tregonwell's Natural Barb. He may know at a glance that yonder filly has bad knees. But his handicapping will be a game of blindman's buff unless he appreciates the significance of the winning bet in the life of the average horseman. The following facts are basic:

1. It costs at least $15,000 a year to feed, house, groom, shoe, doctor and train a Thoroughbred in the big leagues of racing. In lesser environments the cost may fall below $6,000, but not by much.

2. Transportation, jockey fees, entry fees, workmen's compensation insurance, equine mortality insurance and accident insurance may increase the costs by thousands of dollars a year.

3. During 1977, a total of 61,960 Thoroughbreds went to the post at tracks in the United States, Canada and Mexico. They earned purses of almost $336 million.

4. The 35 leading money winners of the year, led by Seattle Slew, earned $9,965,332 (an average of almost $285,000), leaving about $326 million for distribution to other horses. Among these other horses, 1,108 winners of stakes races earned an average of higher than $50,000. And 60,817 less accomplished animals brought home an average of $4,519, meaning that nobody made a dime on their purse earnings.

5. Of 7,500 licensed trainers, thirty won more than $35 million in purses. The remaining 99.6 percent of the brotherhood scrambled after the remaining prizes. Some won none of them. The *American Racing Manual* listed 2,872 trainers whose horses had won $20,000 or more—

The Growth of Racing

Year	Total Races	Total Horses	Total Purses	State Revenues
1915	5,454	3,700	$ 2,853,037	—
1920	6,897	4,032	7,773,407	—
1925	11,579	6,438	12,577,270	—
1930	11,477	8,791	13,674,160	—
1935	15,830	10,544	12,794,418	$ 8,386,255
1940	16,401	13,257	15,911,167	16,145,182
1945	19,587	14,307	32,300,060	65,265,405
1950	26,932	22,554	50,102,099	98,366,167
1955	31,757	26,056	76,643,696	186,989,588
1960	37,661	29,773	93,741,552	257,510,069
1965	47,335	38,502	126,463,984	369,892,036
1970	54,925	47,769	182,313,787	315,863,724
1975	68,203	58,818	291,194,571	361,047,905
1976	69,481	61,083	318,680,094	364,931,707
1977	68,826	61,960	335,720,312	343,075,567
1978	69,498	62,951	367,632,913	Not yet available

meaning that the trainer's 10 percent share had brought him or her at least $2,000.

6. A handful of jockeys enjoyed a monopoly as impressive as that of the top trainers and top horses. Most jockeys made less than $5,000 in winning bonuses during the year.

7. With the field dominated by a few dozen eminently successful personalities, an estimated 98 percent of racing stables lose money every year. Their deficits are compounded not only of high costs and low purses, but of certain other expenses on which no return is ever possible—the cost of purchasing (or breeding) and feeding and training and doctoring animals that suffer injury or illness and never run in a race.

8. Some owners do not mind. An indeterminate number—far fewer than the losing 98 percent—are hobbyist sportsmen, successful in finance, industry or commerce. They deduct their racing losses from personal or corporate taxes.

9. Sportsmen or not, most owners bet. All welcome an extra point or two in the odds.

10. And horsemen who rely on racing for a living not only welcome higher odds, but usually manipulate their horses in ways that encourage higher odds.

A handicapper will be helpless at the betting windows if he does not keep the foregoing facts in mind. He will be unable to interpret past-performance records accurately.

The maneuvering that results in higher odds—the maneuvering that enables many horsemen to remain in the game—is so widespread that it affects the outcome of an overwhelming majority of races.

Do I imply that racing is dishonest, fixed, rigged? Do I suggest that the best horse in the race is pulled or drugged to build the odds for his next outing?

Not really. In big-time racing, when a horse is in shape to win and is entered against animals it can beat, the stable goes all-out for the purse and the bet, regardless of odds. Few horses retain winning form long enough for the kind of odds-building shenanigans that require a ready animal to lose. Next time, when the odds are "right," it may no longer be able to win.

But something else is done. Every day, horses are entered in races that they cannot win except by sheer accident. They are outclassed, or at the wrong distance, or off their feed, or sore-legged, or short of wind. Two interrelated reasons account for their presence on the track:

1. Tracks have to fill nine or ten races a day. Fields of fewer than eight horses are unpopular, but there are not enough fit and ready horses to go around. The tracks therefore expect (to put it mildly) every horseman to keep his stock active. A trainer who refuses to run his animals as frequently as possible finds that the track would rather give his stall-space to a more cooperative stable. Under these pressures, only the stables owned by the big names of racing are permitted to train horses in the proper way—racing them when ready to run at their best, and not before.

2. Most trainers have adapted to these economic and political realities. They now race their stock into shape. They no longer rely on the workouts, the patient nurture and careful doctoring that are the bases of sound training methods. They ruin numerous horses this way, but they have become used to it. They can't fight city hall. As a matter of fact, they have learned to turn the racing of unready horses to their own advantage. Chiefly, they use it to darken an animal's form. They deliberately seek out races in which the horse will look bad, even though its condition actually may be improving. When it finally is ready to win, the crowd may not recognize this in sufficient numbers to make the horse a favorite. It therefore pays gratifying odds, bailing the horseman out of his financial difficulties for the time being.

Fortunately, competent handicappers can usually tell when a horse's condition is improving. The result charts and past-performance records

Man O'War sets world record for mile in 1920 Withers.   UPI PHOTO

contain all the necessary information. Thus, the modern betting coup, in which the stable and its friends bet thousands of dollars, most often finds the horse romping in at modest odds. Members of the paying audience who happen to be good handicappers frequently get in on the coup, and help bring the odds down, by recognizing omens in the past-performance records.

The Cost of the Hobby

There is such a thing as a professional horseplayer. Unless he lives across the street from the track and has a tax-free pass to the place, he must include transportation and admission among his costs of doing business. The hobbyist is well advised to do the same thing. Few players can buy their racing paper, get to the track, pay their way in, eat some lunch, and get home on less than $15.

If he goes to the track twenty times a year, the player's expenses, without betting, are at least $300. I do not regard this as exorbitant. Twenty decent dinners and movies cost more. Twenty baseball games can also cost as much, depending on the location of the ballpark.

One of the pleasures of handicapping is the opportunity to recover the cost of the pastime. There is no need to be grim about it. In fact, being too grim spoils the fun. Yet there she sits, a $300 outlay for twenty afternoons at the track. How do we get it back?

We do *not* get it back with $2 bets. If the player has reached the stage of earning about 20 cents on every dollar he bets, he is likely to make not more than sixty bets in the twenty days. At $2 a bet, the sixty bets are an investment of $120. The profit will be about $24, not enough to pay expenses.

Bets of $20 are far more sensible.

Yet not everyone can afford to bet $20 on a horse.

There would seem to be a contradiction here.

The contradiction is resolved by betting *not one penny* on horses until the results of numerous paper bets demonstrate reasonable handicapping ability. It is as unintelligent to waste money in $2 bets as in $20 bets. Readers of this book will do themselves a great favor by risking no money on its teachings until a series of dry runs has shown that the lessons work.

After achieving that plateau, the player should make the transition to actual betting. But he should bet no money that will be missed after it is lost. Perhaps he will make bets of $2 or $5. If he is a talented handicapper with exceptional self-control, he may discover that he does as well with real money in the hurly-burly of the track as he did on paper at home. If he is less exceptional, it may take a while before he becomes accustomed to the difference between dry run and actual battle.

When his results finally warrant confidence, the player should begin betting in units of not less than $20, which would require investment capital of at least $400. If he does not have the $400, he should wait until he has saved it.

If it costs him $20 a day to go to the track, he may have to make bets of $30 or $40 to retrieve his "overhead."

It's fun to do it. And, depending on the individual personality, well worth the effort.

4

The Mystery of Breeding

Thoroughbreds are a separate, registered breed of horse, as distinctive in purpose and appearance as Percherons, Clydesdales or Appaloosas.

The breed originated in England, where racing has been an aristocratic pastime for more than 2,000 years. Late in the seventeenth century, during the reign of Charles II, numerous Middle Eastern stallions were imported to invigorate the tired blood of native British stock. Efforts to obtain prize specimens continued into the next century. Some of the imports were outstanding. Three of the stallions were so good that their descendants now monopolize the backstretch stalls and breeding barns of the world.

Although it is barely two centuries since the genetic superiority of the three imported stallions became evident in British racing, every single one of today's hundreds of thousands of Thoroughbreds descends in tail male (from sire to paternal grandsire and so on through the male line) from one of the three.

Their names were the Darley Arabian, the Byerly Turk and the Godolphin Barb. The Arabian, foaled in Syria, was held to be one of the foremost specimens of his breed ever seen in England. The Turk had been a military charger. The Godolphin was reputed to have been found in Paris, pulling a water cart. His ancestry was unknown, but he looked like the Moroccan (Barbary Coast) type known as a Barb.

The Darley Arabian's great-great-grandson, Eclipse, foaled in 1764, was probably the greatest runner of his century. All other Darley Arabian lines but his have vanished. But from Eclipse come almost 90 percent of the horses that win major races in the United States.

Among those whose lineage traces to Eclipse in tail male have been Citation, Kelso, Buckpasser, Whirlaway, Alsab, Equipoise, Sysonby, Hoist the Flag, Tom Rolfe, Key to the Mint, Arts and Letters, Round Table, Stage Door Johnny, Johnny D., Prince John, Bold Ruler, Seattle Slew, Secretariat, Foolish Pleasure, Northern Dancer, Hail to Reason, Sir Gaylord, Raise A Native, Affirmed, Alydar, Dr. Fager, Assault, Princequillo, Tom Fool, Roman Brother, Hyperion, Blenheim II, Menow, Nasrullah, Nantallah, Blue Larkspur, Sweep, Count Fleet, Sun Beau, Alibhai, Ben Or, Heliopolis, Sickle, Polynesian, Bull Lea, Teddy, Sir Gallahad III, St. Simon, Black Toney, Roman, Native Dancer, and on and on and on. The American line originated with a horse named Domino, and has been refreshed by frequent imports from Europe, among them Ribot, Princequillo, Ambiorix, Blenheim II, Nasrullah, Alibhai, Mahmoud and Sir Gallahad III.

Descendants of the Godolphin Barb, via his 1748 grandson, Matchem, have not won nearly as many American races, but it is hard to imagine the pastime without them: Man O' War, Seabiscuit, Discovery, War Admiral, Busher, and all their popular kith and kin.

From the Byerly Turk, by way of his great-great-grandson, Herod, foaled in 1758, we have had First Fiddle, Porter's Cap, Whiskery, Royal Minstrel, The Tetrarch, Epinard. The line accounts for the male ancestry of barely 3 percent of American stakes winners, but portions of its blood are found in many more than that. Cross breeding is unavoidable. Kelso, for example, descends in tail male from Eclipse, but his maternal granddam, Maidoduntreath, was a Man O' War mare, from Matchem.

As one might imagine, efforts to breed horses to go farther and faster began on a trial-and-error basis. To a large extent, the work is still largely a matter of by-guess-and-by-gosh. Scientific eugenics are standard in the breeding of cattle, hogs and poultry, but not in the breeding of Thoroughbreds. One reason is that Thoroughbreds are not cattle. They are not something to eat. Their value is not measurable in poundage, but in speed, courage and endurance. Accordingly, a breeder's mistakes and triumphs may not come into clear focus for years—when the foals have grown and raced and ended their careers and begun to produce tested runners or proven washouts of their own.

None of this necessarily rules out scientific study and experimentation, but the keenly competitive, high-pressure economics of racing and breeding are serious obstacles. If given an opportunity, a scientist might be able to argue that a mating of Stud "A" and Mare "B" could produce a promising foal. But the breeder knows that Stud "C" is more fashionable. The progeny of "C" is worth far more on the market. He therefore goes to "C." If the mating turns out poorly and the foal shows little promise, it can always be unloaded at yearling sales, and often for a fancy price, thanks to its glamorous pedigree. So many races are run every day at so many tracks that it is possible to make good money selling horses that would not have been allowed on a track thirty years ago. Moreover, such horses finally win a race or two, after they are entered against animals of their own feeble ability.

Sire vs. Dam

Thoroughbred breeding is so remote from science that completely contradictory theories are practiced without arousing more than mild controversy. Colonel E. R. Bradley used to declaim that 65 percent of a Thoroughbred's quality came from the dam. John E. Madden, breeder of five Derby winners, thought that the *sire* contributed 75 percent of the quality.

The chances are that both were wrong. Does a human being inherit

Colonel E. R. Bradley
ASSOCIATED PRESS PHOTO

his intelligence from his father or mother? Obviously, from both. Horses, like all other living creatures, abide by Mendel's Law.

One of the few qualified persons ever to study Thoroughbred breeding was Dr. Dewey G. Steele, Professor of Genetics at the University of Kentucky. He wrote:

"Pedigrees must be judged primarily on the basis of ancestors in the first and second generation, and individuals beyond the third generation may for all practical purposes be ignored.

"There is no evidence that the tail-female line or any other line exercises a hereditary influence greater than would be expected on a purely chance basis."

Old Colonel Bradley, believing that the "class is in the dam," sought classy dams and got a percentage of classy horses. John Madden, looking at things the other way, used classy sires and got a percentage of classy horses. Why not?

The Unscience of Breeding

Breeders no longer are quite so innocent of genetic rules as they used to be. They formerly tended to evaluate horses in Mayflower terms, poring over pedigrees to see how many champions appeared on remote

Mares and new foals at a California stock farm.   UPI PHOTO branches of the family tree. Bitter experience finally taught them that the best index to an animal's possible class was the class of its parents and grandparents, as demonstrated on the track and in the breeding stall. It made no sense to cherish a man solely because one of his ancestors had been an archduke. The same was true of a horse.

To add a touch of stamina to a line that seemed short of that quality, breeders used to look for "doses" of staying power several generations back, and breed their stock accordingly. Sometimes it worked, more often it did not. Some of them persist in a variation of this, looking for "nicks"—previously successful combinations of bloodlines that might be repeated with equal success.

The simple arithmetic of genetics frustrates most maneuvers of that kind. Any single ancestor five generations removed was, after all, but one of thirty-two great-great-great-grandparents. The hereditary influence of such an ancestor is modified, for good or ill, by the contributions of the sixty-one other recent ancestors whose blood combines in the new foal.

Nowadays, the best breeders try to mate the classiest possible stallion with the classiest possible mare. Extensive research by the late Joseph A. Estes, distinguished editor of *The Blood-Horse,* and his successor, Kent Hollingsworth, has demonstrated that the stallions and mares most likely to produce topnotch runners are animals who themselves were winners of major stakes races.

In general, today's expensive, fashionably bred yearling is the offspring of champions or near-champions or, of course, sires and dams that have already proved themselves capable of yielding good racers. By the same token, the cheap, unfashionably bred yearling is from parents and grandparents that were below the first flight as runners and have done nothing to redeem themselves in the boudoir. But Nature runs a lottery. Every now and then, an expensive yearling proves to be a throwback to the worst of its ancestors. And, every season, several runners of unpromising pedigree turn out to be reincarnations of great-great-grandpa, the champ.

One of the most extreme examples of this kind of thing became noticeable on October 3, 1960, when a highly unfashionable two-year-old colt named Carry Back caught Globemaster in the stretch of the seven-furlong Cowdin Stakes at Belmont Park and won by a length and a half, going away. He paid $14.60.

The opinion makers of racing were unimpressed. Carry Back's sire was Saggy, who had beaten Citation at six furlongs in the mud on a day in 1948 when the great horse was out of condition. Saggy had done nothing else to distinguish himself as a racer and had begotten no outstanding foals in several years of trying. Carry Back's dam was a $150 mare, Joppy. The breeder, Jack A. Price, served also as trainer. Nobody had nominated him for any known Hall of Fame.

A few days after the Cowdin, Carry Back was left at the post and lost the Champagne Stakes. The very notion of Price getting anything much with this beast was so unacceptable that Carry Back paid $18.40 when he sauntered to an easy victory in the Garden State Stakes on October 29. For romping the mile and a sixteenth over a sloppy track, he earned $172,782. All of a sudden the game had a Cinderella horse.

In 1961, Carry Back won seven races, including the Kentucky Derby and Preakness. He earned more purse money that year—$556,874— than any other Thoroughbred and was everyone's choice as champion three-year-old.

Experts who studied Carry Back's pedigree were unable to find any excuse for his championship stamina, speed and soundness. The sire's dam, Chantress, was by the celebrated Hyperion but had such dreadful-looking feet that her owners, the Greentree Stud (Whitney), had unloaded her. The paternal grandsire, Swing and Sway, another Greentree cull, had won some purses without reminding anyone of his daddy, Equipoise. And Equipoise, while a good runner, had suffered from hoof trouble and had been transmitting it to his get. Another blemish in Carry Back's pedigree was the maternal grandsire, Star Blen, which had shown a touch of speed but not a trace of stamina.

By any standards, Carry Back was a freak. He inherited none of the shortcomings to which his immediate ancestry should have condemned him. He was the accidental reincarnation of distinguished forebears. But all Thoroughbreds, even the worst, have distinguished forebears. Nature is fickle. "Breed the best to the best and hope for the best," shrug horsemen.

It would be silly to suggest that any scientist could have foreseen a Derby winner by Saggy out of Joppy. Science ain't all that wise. But, under present, non-scientific auspices, surprises are bred with almost comic frequency. One must assume that the horsemen are running several laps behind Nature. They hope for the best, but are not necessarily able to recognize it when it arrives.

Thousands of examples come to mind. Here are a few notable ones. The capable Sunny Jim Fitzsimmons sold mighty Seabiscuit for $7,500 to C. S. Howard, for whom the colt earned over $400,000 and became 1938 horse of the year. Alsab, two-year-old champion in 1941 and three-year-old champion in 1942, was a $700 purchase. Stymie, eventually to become handicap champion of 1945, was so hard to handle that Max Hirsch, a great trainer, entered him in a $1,500 claiming race. Hirsch Jacobs claimed the rogue and made $918,485 with him.

Ballydam had run in $1,500 claimers. Celestial Blue was a cheap mare. Their coupling yielded a foal that went for $5,000 in the yearling sales. It was Bally Ache, Preakness winner which shared 1960 horse-of-the-year honors with Kelso, earned $758,522, and was sold to a syndicate for $1.25 million.

During the 1970's, the auction prices of well-bred yearlings rose to phenomenal heights. As of 1968, the all-time high price was the $405,000 paid in that year for Reine Enchanteur, a filly by the celebrated French stallion, Sea-Bird. In 1978, no fewer than 9 yearlings each sold for $400,000 or more at the Keeneland, Kentucky, summer sales; 48 went for $200,000 or more, and the sales topper was $1.3 million, with which a British combine purchased a colt by the leading sire in both North America and England, Northern Dancer. Even this was not an all-time high. In 1977, Canadians paid $1.5 million for a Secretariat colt which they named Canadian Bound.

These fantastic price increases attested partly to the severe economic inflation in the United States and the declining international value of the dollar. As well, the prices demonstrated the growing prosperity of world racing, the importance of American bloodstock and the widespread belief that money expended on a prize yearling could be regained manyfold, either on the race track or at the breeding farm. Although this was not always the outcome, it happened often enough to justify the investments. For example, Majestic Prince, who fetched a record $250,000 in 1967, proved to be a great racehorse. He won the Kentucky Derby and Preakness, earned more than $400,000 in purses, was sold to a breeding syndicate for $1.8 million and became a successful sire, begetting Majestic Light among others. In 1970, the $500,000 paid for Crowned Prince (by Raise a Native, sire of Majestic Prince and many other fine runners), was a new record. The colt became a champion two-year-old in England and was syndicated for $1.2 million. In 1973, a new record of $600,000 was well spent on Wajima (by Bold Ruler), who became a great racehorse and was syndicated for $7.2 million.

While all this was going on, bargain purchases continued to produce jackpots. Canonero II, bought in 1969 for $1,200, won the Kentucky Derby and Preakness. Bold Forbes, three-year-old champion of 1976, was bought for only $15,200. Seattle Slew, in 1977 the first undefeated runner to win the U.S. Triple Crown, had been knocked down for a mere $17,500 as a 1975 yearling. That was the year in which disappointments like Elegant Prince cost a record $715,000, Brahms went for $500,000, Four Ten for $410,000, Transworld for $375,000 and I shall not continue with this. The point is made. Big-ticket breeding is a tremendous gamble in itself, and the purchase of expensive yearlings is a bigger one.

Training Beats Breeding

Anybody who pays big money for a yearling Thoroughbred does so on expert advice. The horse's breeding seems to warrant the investment. Similarly, not much is thought of the potentialities of a horse sold for small change or entered in a cheap claiming race. And then the surprises begin. Jack Price, operator of Carry Back, used to argue that the reason cheap horses run cheap is that they are treated cheap. He said that there was no surprise about Carry Back. The dam and foal had been treated properly.

Price was not suggesting that good handling can make a silk purse of a sow's you-know. He was just trying to remind everyone that he was a good handler. In so doing he raised a point often overlooked by the pedigree-conscious: Breeding determines the horse's potential, but training and the luck of the game determine whether the horse will have a chance to achieve its potential.

Thoroughbred auction at Hollywood Park.   UPI PHOTO

Stymie (second from left) *pours it on in home turn of 1947 International Gold Cup at Belmont Park. Assault* (far left) *finished third. Natchez* (on rail) *was second.*   UPI PHOTO

With luck, a good trainer can get more from a mediocre horse than a lesser trainer can from a potential champion. Buckpasser, by Tom Fool out of Busanda, by War Admiral, was a potential champion on paper. Bill Winfrey, who developed him, and Eddie Neloy, who guided him to greatness, provided the nurture without which nature goes awry. Hundreds of trainers could have ruined Buckpasser, and probably would have. The list of potential Triple Crown contenders sabotaged by stupid, greedy mismanagement in their two- or three-year-old seasons would fill this chapter.

Whether making his own mistakes, or doing what his employer demands, the trainer is vital to the career of the horse. So vital that breeding eventually becomes secondary. All Thoroughbreds descend from champions, as we have seen. The humble parents of a Carry Back or Bally Ache may not have been so humble, after all. Their inability to do much as racers may have been a matter of ill fortune or misdirection.

As a two-year-old, Stymie was frantic. He would resist going to the post. He would break tardily from the gate, losing all chance at the very beginning of his races. When Hirsch Jacobs, one of the greatest connoisseurs of Thoroughbred quality in the history of racing, bought Stymie for $1,500, he treated him like a million-dollar horse. He correctly assumed that the poor thing was afraid of people. He spent hours with Stymie, calming him down. He worked the horse by leading him on a rope instead of saddling him with exercise boys. In due course, Stymie acquired the composure that was his birthright and went on to greatness.

H. Allen Jerkens, one of the younger generation of trainers, won lucrative races with Misty Day, after Sunny Jim Fitzsimmons had given up on the animal. Jerkens claimed War Command for $8,000 and six months later won the $25,000 Display Handicap with him. He claimed Admiral Vee for $7,500 and the colt went on to win seven major handicaps and upward of $300,000.

To be fair about it, similar tales could be told about all other leading trainers. All have been able to find the magic formula with horses that have defied the best efforts of other trainers. And all have had failures to match such successes. The purpose at this time is not to compare trainers with each other. We shall do that in the chapter reserved for that pastime. For now, it is important to agree that the horse that runs nowhere for Trainer "A" is the same horse that breaks track records for Trainer "B." His pedigree has not changed.

Moreover, if he is a fractious horse, the kind that exhausts itself in the paddock before getting onto the track, little purpose is served by saying, "He got that from the male line. All Nasrullahs have the tendency." It is impossible to deny that temperamental differences are discernible among the various strains of Thoroughbred, just as size and weight differences and hoof differences and color differences are. But a more essential truth is that any Thoroughbred, regardless of pedigree, can develop a ruinous disposition unless handled intelligently. And a companion truth is that 99.9 percent of every thousand horses with good pedigrees are susceptible to intelligent handling. Some rogues are born, but most rogues are made. Horses that loaf or sulk or hate the starting gate or refuse to run on the rail or stop as soon as they reach the lead or quit when whipped were born with the potential to develop evil traits of that sort. But their handlers deserve full blame for the intensification and perpetuation of the traits.

Where does that leave the racing fan? How can he use a knowledge of breeding in his efforts to pick winning horses? Here are some useful facts to bear in mind:

1. The wise player is aware of the by-guess-and-by-gosh character of Thoroughbred breeding, the haphazard results achieved by breeders, and the variable influences of trainers on their horses. He therefore

Carry Back, the lowborn aristocrat, struts onto the running surface at Aqueduct, with Johnny Sellers up.

Carry Back (far left) *outgames Crozier* (second from left) *to win 1961 Florida Derby. Johnny Sellers rode the "Cinderella Horse." Bill Hartack was on Crozier.*

refers to pedigrees only in special situations where past-performance records are too brief to tell a persuasive story.

2. These special situations are (a) maiden-special-weights and allowance races for lightly raced two-year-olds and (b) the same kinds of races for lightly raced three-year-olds.

3. Pedigrees are absolutely useless in handicapping claiming races. In such races the physically deficient or badly mismanaged offspring of champions are regularly defeated by better conditioned animals of equal or lesser lineage. A claiming race must be handicapped *exclusively* in terms of past performances.

4. Pedigrees also are untrustworthy guides to the route-running ability of Thoroughbreds. Although a Tom Fool colt might logically be expected to defeat an Olympia colt the first time they race at 1¼ mile, too many other factors are at work to permit a reliable selection on the sole grounds of breeding. The 1965 champion handicap mare, Old Hat, had a sprinter's pedigree, and none too classy a one, but won at distances up to 1⅛ mile.

When the most promising new two-year-olds race each other at five and five and a half furlongs in the spring and summer, it often is possible to pick winners by handicapping their parents. After the youngsters have been to the post a time or two or three, their past-performance records usually tell more than can be guessed from their breeding. But, with first-time starters in maiden-special-weights and allowance races, or with other entrants in such races that have been out too sparingly to offer a clear picture, the player looks for the following:

1. A sire listed among the nation's leaders.
2. A maternal grandsire listed among the nation's leaders.
3. A leading breeder.
4. A leading trainer.

Leading Sires

As of the end of 1978, the following stallions were outstanding among sires of North American runners. Their offspring included unusually consistent winners in competition of the highest class. Handicappers who check pedigrees against this list and those that follow will have useful information about the potential class of lightly raced animals entered in maiden or allowance races at major tracks.

EXCLUSIVE NATIVE NORTHERN DANCER
HOIST THE FLAG VAGUELY NOBLE

NODOUBLE
BOLD BIDDER
DEWAN
IN REALITY
GRAUSTARK
CYANE
NIJINSKY II
GUMMO
STAGE DOOR JOHNNY
MAJESTIC PRINCE

RAISE A NATIVE
OLDEN TIMES
MINNESOTA MAC
BOLD REASONING
BEST TURN
AL HATTAB
T.V. COMMERCIAL
VERBATIM
WHAT A PLEASURE
NASKRA

Leading Juvenile Sires

During 1978, two-year-olds sired by the horses on this list won the biggest juvenile stakes races and also entered the winner's circle with relatively high consistency. Good handicappers will enjoy spotting a new two-year-old sired by one of these stallions, preferably out of a mare whose sire appears on the list of leading broodmare sires.

SECRETARIAT
HOIST THE FLAG
ICECAPADE
NORTHERN JOVE
AMASPORT
MONGO
GROTON
RAJA BABA

BOLD BIDDER
MR. PROSPECTOR
FULL POCKET
GREY DAWN II
NO ROBBERY
SHECKY GREENE
LOTHARIO
ACK ACK

Leading Broodmare Sires

A lightly raced horse whose dam was sired by one of the following stallions (or by a stallion on either of the previous lists), has at least a potential advantage over a competitor of lesser pedigree.

CRAFTY ADMIRAL
NATIVE DANCER
DOUBLE JAY
SIR GAYLORD
TIM TAM
FLEET NASRULLAH

PRINCE JOHN
SWAPS
BOLD RULER
TRAFFIC JUDGE
ON-AND-ON
INTENTIONALLY

HASTY ROAD	SUMMER TAN
TOM FOOL	NEARCTIC
ROUND TABLE	BALD EAGLE
BLUE PRINCE	NASHUA
FIRST LANDING	SWOON'S SON
PRINCEQUILLO	TURN-TO

Leading Breeders

The following breeders produce the best stock. They were selected for this list because they breed horses that not only win a lot of money but win with reasonable consistency.

E. P. TAYLOR	HARBOR VIEW
ELMENDORF	SPENDTHRIFT
TARTAN	HOBEAU
CLAIBORNE	NELSON B. HUNT
CALUMET	FARNSWORTH
G. A. POPE	W. S. KARUTZ
F. W. HOOPER	HICKORY TREE
KING RANCH	OLD ENGLISH RANCHO
MEADOWBROOK	MEREWORTH
W. L. JONES	CRIMSON KING
FONTAINEBLEAU	OGDEN PHIPPS
W. R. HAWN	DAN LASATER
GARDINER FARMS	BWAMAZON
J. W. GALBREATH	GREENTREE
JACK STAFFORD	ROBERT SANGSTER

Breeding Procedures

The breeding season runs from mid-February to the end of May. Breeders try to get the job done as early as possible, so that the foals will arrive at the beginning of the following year. Under the rules of racing, every foal becomes a yearling on the New Year's Day after its birth, and has a birthday every New Year's thereafter. A horse foaled in late spring or summer is at a disadvantage as a two-, three- and four-year-old, having to run against more mature animals. Northern Dancer, the fine little Canadian horse, overcame that disadvantage. Foaled on May 27, 1961, he was not yet three years old when he won the 1964 Kentucky Derby.

A broodmare is ready for breeding about a week and a half after dropping a foal. The mare's tail is bound up and she goes to the stall of an unfortunate stallion known in the trade as a "teaser." His job is to make sure that the mare is ready for breeding. If she is not in season yet, the valuable stud with whom she is to mate is spared the frustration of an unsuccessful attempt.

If she proves to be ready, she is hauled away from the eager teaser and led to the big shot's stall. There she is held in position with leg straps. After the stallion is finished, the mare returns to her foal. Three weeks later she is brought back to the teaser. If she is now in foal, she will be indifferent to his advances. If she displays interest it means that the previous "cover" or "service" did not work, and she returns to the court of her mate for another attempt.

Breeding for Mud and Grass

Years ago, when muddy tracks were more common than they now are, handicappers and horsemen could often tell by an animal's pedigree whether it would run well in the heavy gumbo. Reigh Count, a great performer on off-tracks, transmitted the talent to Count Fleet and his other progeny, some of whom relayed it to their own. Man O' War, Petee-Wrack, Challedon and Sailor were other good mudders which begat good mudders. Yet every muddy racing day found horses winning in spite of pedigrees that offered no indication of such ability.

Modern tracks are well drained and contain a great deal of sand. Most of them rarely stay muddy for long. The sandiest and best-drained ones, like Aqueduct, are at their slowest when drying out and labeled "good." When covered with water and called "sloppy" they often are faster than when the tote board says "Track Fast."

Some tracks do get muddy, of course. Those that don't become really gooey nevertheless acquire what horsemen call a "holding" quality while drying out after a rain. When the track is "muddy" or "slow" or "good" or otherwise sticky enough to hold back the horses, the player can be fairly certain that animals that have run badly over similar surfaces in the past will run badly again.

A sore-legged creature that has been having trouble on hard, fast tracks sometimes runs in (wins surprisingly) on a softer footing. Horses with small hooves also seem to move ahead by several lengths on a holding track. Questions of this kind are best settled by looking at the past-performance records and examining the animals in the walking ring. The pedigree is an unreliable guide.

Leon Rasmussen, whose penetrating articles about breeding are a regular feature of *Daily Racing Form,* writes, "Several years ago I indulged in some research on the winners of off-track races throughout the United States. Hundreds of races were studied and the breeding of the winners duly recorded. When I was all through with my analysis, no definite pattern had exposed itself. That is, no particular male line manifested itself, and neither did any particular stallion."

Some horses run well on grass but not on dirt. Some run well on dirt but not on grass. In 1975, Dr. William L. Quirin, of the mathematics faculty at Adelphi University, Garden City, New York, produced a large statistical study which demonstrated beyond possibility of doubt that animals of certain bloodlines are more likely than others to perform successfully on turf courses. Indeed, the study showed that anyone who bet on such animals in their first and second starts on grass would reap substantial profits, ignoring the horses' previously rotten performances on dirt tracks. The leading sire line was that of the European stud, Prince Rose, via Princequillo, Prince Bio and Prince Chevalier. Among grass sires of that and other lines most prominent at this writing were Prince John, Round Table, Stage Door Johnny, Knightly Manner, Exclusive Native, Chieftain, Tentam, Bolero, Sir Ivor, Le Fabuleux, Herbager, Vent du Nord, Grey Dawn II, Hawaii, Mongo, Vaguely Noble, Assagai, T. V. Lark, Chieftain. The list is updated in Quirin's book, *Winning at the Races: Computer Discoveries in Thoroughbred Handicapping,* published in 1979 by William Morrow and Company, New York.

Run-of-the-Mill Breeders

With dozens of tracks demanding seventy or eighty ambulatory Thoroughbreds with which to fill nine races a day, the quality of the breed has declined seriously. There are not that many good horses to go around, nor are purses high enough to pay for them. Accordingly, the woods are full of industrialized breeding establishments, the produce of which have nondescript pedigrees, misshapen limbs, and no more class than is needed to stagger three quarters of a mile. In bygone days, animals as disadvantaged as all this never got to the track. They could not compete with real racehorses. But they now are found in profusion —even at major tracks, where the horse shortage is as severe as anywhere else.

Unable to infuse any real class into this stock, the breeders concentrate on speed. Sometimes a mare from a family that has been showing more staying power than speed is mated with a stud from a line of front runners. All too often, in the words of Charles Hatton, the *Form* expert, the result is a horse that "has the speed of the stayer and the stamina of the sprinter." Errors of that kind also crop up in fancier breeding establishments.

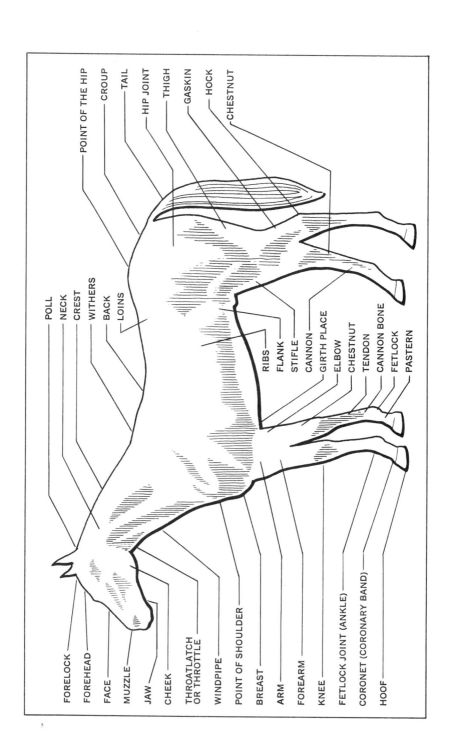

5
Thoroughbred Conformation

When buying a yearling or trying to decide whether to get rid of one, horsemen attach major importance to the animal's physical appearance. The pedigree may be splendid, but if the conformation departs from normal in any major respect, horsemen turn thumbs down.

Yet the test of the Thoroughbred is performance on the racetrack. Every year, horses with dubious pedigrees or unfortunate conformation, or both, finish first in important races. The saying goes that any horse looks good in the winner's circle. Another saying is that there is no such thing as a perfect-looking horse. By the time a horse is two or three and has been to the post a dozen times, earlier judgments of his looks are subject to drastic revision.

Kelso, horse of the year five times in succession, and biggest earner in the history of the sport (almost $2 million), was castrated as a yearling because he was a runt. The theory was that undersized geldings grow more satisfactorily than undersized colts. Sometimes they do. Kelso became a full-sized horse. But Roman Brother, another gelded runt, remained small, ran off with almost $1 million in purses and succeeded Kelso as horse of the year in 1965. Nobody will ever know whether Kelso would have been a great racer if he had not been gelded. All that can be known is that he would now be available for breeding purposes.

No horse in history ever looked better in the winner's circle than Kelso, and he had the bankroll to prove it. But his hocks stuck out farther than is proper. He seemed susceptible to sore stifles. Also, his hooves were delicate. With less discerning care than that of Carl Hanford, his trainer, he might never have won a dollar. His hooves might have cracked if he had been shod less carefully.

Roman Brother had a crooked knee, his pasterns were somewhat too long, and he had hoof troubles. In fact these difficulties finally made it impossible for him to withstand training and he had to be retired. With $1 million.

Buckpasser's knees aroused criticism. Cracked hooves kept him out of races worth hundreds of thousands of dollars. Bold Lad's near (left) foreknee never looked too good to the experts. Gun Bow's hooves were a constant headache for his handlers. The great two-year-old, Hail to Reason, had a curby (suspiciously swollen) hock, which did not prevent him from running like one of the best of all time. His racing career ended accidentally, when he broke a sesamoid (a small bone above the fetlock). Tom Rolfe was faulted for prominent hocks and cannon bones longer than the ideal. Truly, the perfect horse is never seen.

Conformation is important to the racing fan for several reasons:

1. It is fun to appraise the physique of unraced two-year-olds when they come to the paddock and walking ring.

2. It occasionally is possible to pick the winner of a maiden-special-weights race on grounds of conformation—especially when the best-looking horse in the walking ring has a fine pedigree and hails from a leading barn.

3. If you don't know the difference between a hock and a pastern you won't know what horsemen are talking about. You therefore will get less than your money's worth from your racing papers and your days at the track.

Feet and Ankles

Horsemen begin their inspection of a Thoroughbred at the ground and work their way up. They are quite choosy about hooves, and it makes sense. The Thoroughbred weighs in the neighborhood of half a ton. When traveling at full speed—about forty miles an hour—the entire weight lands on one hoof at a time. If the hoof is too narrow, the foot

| NORMAL PASTERN | STRAIGHT PASTERN | LOW PASTERN | SHORT PASTERN | LONG PASTERN |

has to absorb too many pounds of impact per square inch of surface. On today's hard, fast tracks, this is more than the bony structure can bear. Narrow-footed horses go lame more rapidly than horses with wider hooves. They are more susceptible to tendon troubles in the knee region, more susceptible to broken ankle bones and cracked hooves.

Hoofprints are important. If a horse is slightly pigeon-toed he may be a perfectly good runner. But if he toes in considerably, or toes out more than a bit, horsemen downgrade him. The best legs are those with hooves that point straight ahead, leaving hoofprints almost exactly parallel to each other.

As much attention is paid to pasterns as to feet. The pastern should slope at an angle of 45 degrees from fetlock to hoof. If it is more upright than that, it is less springy than it should be. It transmits concussion to the fetlock and knee, which eventually go bad. On the other hand, a pastern with too low a slope flexes more than it should. Such a horse "runs down"—scrapes its fetlocks on the ground while running, and strains tendons and ligaments as well. Furthermore, short pasterns are preferred to long ones. Horses with long pasterns on the forelegs tend to cut their own elbows with their hooves while running. Also, the long pasterns exert undesirable strain on tendons.

On the hind pasterns, a lower slope is accepted. The hind legs provide the horse's forward propulsion and are subjected to less concussion than the forelegs, the vaulting poles of the horse's stride. Therefore, the tendon troubles attributable to faulty pasterns are found often in front and rarely in the rear.

Cannon, Knee and Hock

Horsemen like to see short, sturdy cannon bones, for a longer upper leg and longer stride. Some animals have incredibly fragile-looking cannons. Their legs immediately below the knee are so slender that

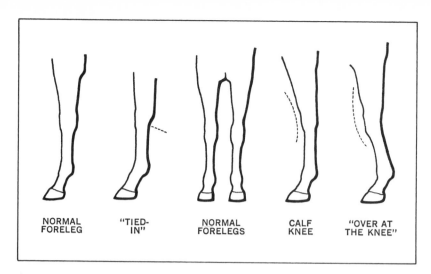

NORMAL FORELEG   "TIED-IN"   NORMAL FORELEGS   CALF KNEE   "OVER AT THE KNEE"

they look, in the language of the trade, "tied-in." Horses with forelegs of that kind are highly susceptible to permanently disabling tendon troubles. The tendons that run down the bone from behind the knee are displaced to begin with and cannot stand the strain of racing.

The knees of the Thoroughbred are located in his forelegs only. The corresponding joint in the hind leg is called the hock. The knee contains seven or eight bones (the number varies from horse to horse and seems to make no difference). These bones help to disperse the concussion of running. Accordingly, Nature intends the normal knee to be situated plumb below the horse's elbow. In other words, straight up and down.

Horses whose forelegs bend somewhat backward at the knee are called calf-kneed or "back at the knee." They are not good candidates for long careers. Their tendons suffer, just as if they had straight pasterns. Horses whose knees protrude forward are called "over at the knee." Many topnotch runners suffer from this blemish. In fact, not many horsemen regard it as a flaw at all, unless it occurs in extreme form.

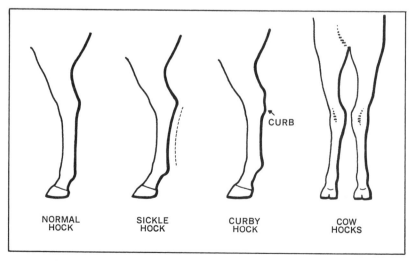

NORMAL HOCK   SICKLE HOCK   CURBY HOCK   COW HOCKS

Horsemen prefer Thoroughbreds whose hind legs drop almost straight down from the hocks. If the hoof is noticeably forward of the hock, the animal is charged with a sickle hock. Pronounced cases lead to curby hocks, swellings of the tendon that often end in serious lameness. Also, it is agreed by one and all that an animal with normal hocks can stride forward more easily, covering extra ground in each jump. However, so many other factors affect the performance of a Thoroughbred (including human factors) that a mild case of sickle hocks is not necessarily calamitous. Kelso did all right on imperfect rear legs, and so have hundreds of other stakes winners.

Cow hocks are another matter. The horse looks knock-kneed from the rear. When he runs, his hooves fly in odd directions, which is no way to get to the finish line in a hurry. Horses with this structural defect can be counted on to develop tendon trouble. Also, they "interfere"—banging their legs together in midair or hitting and cutting one leg with the hoof of the other.

Bandy-legged horses are almost as unpopular. Their hocks bow outward, and the rear hooves are pigeon-toed. The leverage for strong forward propulsion is lacking, the gait is unrhythmical and, as if that were not enough, the animals are odds-on to cut themselves with their own hooves while trying to run.

Shoulders, Hips and Barrel

Long, sloping shoulders are attributes of the horse that runs fast and far. They are associated with short cannons, long forearms and a consequently long, easy, powerful stride. Horses with short, straight shoulders often have short, straight pasterns—the "stilty" look that means a cramped stride.

NORMAL SHOULDER   STRAIGHT SHOULDER

The chest should be deep, the ribs well-sprung rather than straight and flat. Conformation of that kind suggests plenty of lung capacity and stamina. The withers should be fairly prominent, indicating the long spinal muscles of the good strider. The muscles of the loin should also be evident. They tie the horse's rear to his front, creating the "close-coupled" appearance of well-coordinated runners. If "light over the kidney" or "wasp-waisted"—slender-loined and slack in the coupling—a horse has trouble transmitting power from rear to front.

Broad, muscular, rounded (but not fat) hindquarters and close coupling are signs of speed. Narrower rumps and rangy, loose coupling suggest weakness.

Head and Neck

Short-necked horses usually lack balance and stamina. Their strides are too short, and they seldom can be counted on for anything more than a burst of early speed.

Horsemen want the neck to be relatively long and limber, with a slight convexity from withers to poll. The horse with a concave neck, which curves down from the withers and then up to the poll, is called a ewe-neck. He is not pretty but he runs as well as any other horse.

Much attention is paid to the head, ears and facial expression of the young Thoroughbred. A broad, open forehead and large, clear, dark hazel eyes are taken as signs of kindly, manageable intelligence. Ears that seldom move are a warning of sluggishness. But ears constantly twitching bespeak a nervous disposition.

Size and Weight

It is said that a good big horse can always beat a good little horse. On the other hand, little horses are forever beating big horses. Round Table, a leading money winner, was small. So were Roman Brother and Northern Dancer. Tom Rolfe was no giant. Gallant Fox was good and big at 1,100 pounds. Northern Dancer was good and little at 900.

The height of the horse is measured from the withers in "hands"—units of four inches each. A big horse is 16 or 17 hands high, a little horse about 15. If the measurement is 15 hands, 2 inches, it is given as 15.2, or "fifteen-two."

Horsemen work themselves into lathers about the relative merits of big and little horses. Handicappers keep calm. They are guided by past performances and what they see in the paddock just before the race begins.

In trying to differentiate one new two-year-old from another, it seldom pays to prefer the big horse to the smaller. A compact, well-knit juvenile usually learns how to run in a straight line more easily than a bigger, more awkward specimen. The big ones tend to need extra racing and extra training before they settle into winning form. On the other hand, if someone like Frank Whiteley sends out a big youngster for its first start in mid-summer, the player can be sure that most of the green ungainliness has already been ironed out and the horse is ready.

Possibly because they are a bit more nimble, small horses sometimes seem to have an extra edge in races on grass or in mud. They are especially good at picking their way through the traffic jams on the turn for home, finding holes that larger, floundering animals cannot always take advantage of.

None of this constitutes a recommendation to bet on horses because of their stature. The intent is simply to reinforce the observation that the little horse is the best bet in the race if its record is best.

The only other things worth knowing about the size and shape of Thoroughbreds is that blocky animals with bunchy muscles are usually the better sprinters, while horses with staying power seem to be somewhat more lithe, with longer muscles.

Measuring a Thoroughbred for identification purposes at Hialeah Park.

UPI PHOTO

Color and Markings

The official colors:

1. Bay. About half of all Thoroughbreds have the brownish body and the black "points" (black mane, tail and lower legs) that classify them as bay. The body color may be anything from a yellowish tan to a deep, reddish mahogany or a dark brown.

2. Dark Bay or Brown. If the hairs on muzzle or flank are tan or brown, the horse is in this category.

3. Chestnut. The bodies vary from a dark liver to reddish gold, copper and light yellows. Mane and tail are brown or flaxen, never black—although a few black hairs may be present.

4. Black. Sometimes these are unmistakably black. Occasionally they look dark brown, but are distinguishable by the fine black hairs on the muzzle.

5. Gray. A mixture of white and black hairs.

6. Roan. A mixture of black, white and yellow hairs, or black, white and red.

Because the patches known as "markings" are always white, they never are referred to by color.

A *snip* is a small patch of bare skin or white hairs on lip or nose.

A *star* is a small patch of white on the forehead.

A *stripe* is a narrow mark running down the face to the nose or lower.

A *blaze* is a larger patch. When it covers the entire face, the horse is called white-faced or bald-faced.

Markings also are found on the heels, the coronet of the hoof, the pasterns, ankles (half-ankle or full ankle), and above, where they are known as socks, half-stockings or stockings. Many horsemen distrust the bone structure of horses with white legs, ankles or pasterns.

6

Handicapping Theories

Several years ago an animal named Embarrassed won the opening race on an Aqueduct program and paid more than $20. A jubilant lady in the queue outside the mutuel cashier's window explained to all within earshot that she had been dreadfully embarrassed that morning. Something to do with a shoulder strap breaking and her slip landing in a heap at her feet. As soon as she got the paper and saw that Embarrassed was running she knew she had a winner.

A man ahead of me on the line shook his head wryly. "She's some handicapper," he grinned. On impulse, I asked how he had come to play the horse.

"Easy," he said. "It was the only one in the race that ever did three quarters of a mile in less than one-ten."

Months earlier, Embarrassed had covered the first three quarters of a one-mile race in something like 1.09⅗. At lot of water had gone under the bridge since then, of course. The man evidently was a speed handicapper of some kind. He had not noticed, or had not cared, that Embarrassed's previous good clocking at three quarters of a mile had been achieved on the long straightaway which speeds up the early stages of all mile races at Aqueduct. He had seen the raw time figures and become content. Questions of pace, class, weight, condition, and the like had troubled him not. And Embarrassed, the 10 or 11 to 1 shot, had rewarded his hasty judgment. If he could make one successful guess like that in every ten attempts, he could end any season with a profit. And if my aunt were constructed differently, she'd be my uncle.

An orator on the adjoining payoff line was jubilant about the jockey. "Give me Errico every time on a horse like this!" he yelled. Scamp Errico, an able rider of front-running horses, had mounted few winners in recent years. He had suffered several injuries and was out of fashion among the trainers. Anybody who bet on him "every time" would deserve an award for marathon optimism.

"Gee!" exulted a youngster to his companion on the line. "This is some system!" He was waving a booklet. "Bang-bang-bang!" he cried. "Half a minute and you've got a longshot!"

Bang-bang-bang. The miracle system. Half a minute and you've got a longshot. Half a season and you've got an eviction notice.

I returned to the cashier's window a couple of more times that afternoon. The hunch-playing lady, the speed theorist, Errico's loyal fan and the proprietor of the thirty-second longshot system were nowhere to be seen. But some familiar faces were. Faces become familiar at the track. Especially when you see them almost every time you cash a ticket. They are the faces of expert handicappers: Speed handicappers, pace handicappers, class-consistency handicappers, and handicappers whose methods fit no particular label.

On the rare occasions when these people discuss handicapping theory with each other, they discover large areas of disagreement. And yet they have a great deal in common.

First and most prominent is their repeated presence in the payoff line. Ability to win bets is, after all, what identifies them as expert. No other credential counts.

Secondly, they are all "spot players." None attempts to bet on every race. Some go for days on end without betting at all. Many come to the track only when the racing paper's past-performance pages promise a few betting opportunities. Few bet on more than three or four races a day. It goes without saying that they bet only on races that strike them as especially favorable opportunities.

They arrive at these decisions by divergent routes. Some analyze every horse in every race, looking for animals that stand out from the crowd. Others don't bother with all that toil. They regard certain kinds of races and certain kinds of horses as less predictable than others. So they refuse to bet on two-year-olds. Or on females. Or on stakes or handicaps or allowance races. Or they shun maiden races. Or races on the turf course.

Some attach deep importance to handicapping angles, distinct from handicapping fundamentals. For example, some never play a horse that won or finished in the money in its last race. Others go to the

The English Derby at Epsom Downs.   UPI PHOTO

opposite extreme, playing no horse *unless* it won its last race. Some bet only on consistent geldings that won—or did not win—their last races.

Some try to get on the side of the percentages by confining their speculation to favorites whose records can withstand severe scrutiny. Others turn a profit by looking for races in which the favorite is over-rated by the crowd and a longer-priced horse has an outstandingly good chance.

Some play no horses that seem to be moving up in class. Others avoid horses moving down in class. Some give little time to a study of class as such, believing that the true quality of a horse is revealed in its ability to set or overcome a fast early pace and get to the finish wire in good time.

Some play no horse running today's distance for the first time. Others disdain such conservatism, making their selections on the basis of numbers contained in speed charts.

Some mistrust any horse running with substantially more weight than it has been able to carry to victory in the past. Others adjust their speed ratings to reflect pounds added or deducted from the horse's most recent imposts. Some pay no attention whatever to weight, unless it is especially high and the race especially long.

Some give extra credit to horses from favored barns or with leading jockeys. Others insist that the horse is the thing. They ignore trainer and jockey alike.

You Can't Win 'Em All

How contradictory can they get? How can methods so diverse produce long-term winnings in a game as difficult as this?

Answer: Nine races a day make a varied menu. During the height of the season on any major racing circuit, there is seldom a day in which an expert handicapper is unable to find one or more betting opportunities.

Moreover, the differences among successful handicapping methods are more apparent than real. In his own way, each expert takes heed of the fundamentals of the game. The winning player who emphasizes class and consistency may never look at a speed or pace chart, but he is careful to estimate how today's race will be run and whether its pace will suit the style of his horse. And the successful pace handicapper attends to class with numerical formulas which embody the relationship of class to early and late speed. At the same time, he hesitates to give a horse full credit for a fast race run in suspiciously cheap company.

The man who bets only on a horse that won its last race can win money by applying any handicapping method that encompasses the fundamentals of distance, form, class, age, sex, consistency, weight, speed, pace, jockey. So can the man who *refuses* to bet on horses that won their last races. Obviously, neither player encounters as many betting opportunities as he would if his method were less specialized. But both may own the unimpeachable certificate of the expert—the notebook-ledger that shows a long-range profit. The one who favors last-out winners to repeat probably wins a higher percentage of his bets. But his opposite number very likely gets higher mutuel prices.

The player who specializes in bets on claiming races for older horses misses wagering opportunities available to someone with a more varied approach. Yet he may end each season with a higher rate of profit, depending on how well he knows his specialty and how intelligently he manages his money. He might increase his enjoyment and enlarge his profits if he were to learn how to handicap allowance races, and races for two-year-olds, and certain maiden races. But he may not feel like it. He may be getting all the action he wants.

Prescription for Success

We have now reconfirmed a previously emphasized truth: Handicapping is a highly personal pastime. For the 99.9 percent of readers who have not yet found a suitably comfortable and successful method, or

Silky Sullivan, one of the most popular come-from-behind horses in history, trails the field in the 1958 Kentucky Derby. His fans expected him to overtake everybody in the stretch, but he never got under way.   UPI PHOTO

want to improve the performance of a method that is not quite in the black, some general statements will be useful:

1. The fewest bets, the highest percentage of winners, and the highest rate of profit await the player who has the time and patience to apply a method that embraces all handicapping fundamentals in full detail.

2. To the degree that standards relax and one or another fundamental is slighted, the number of bets increases and the percentage of winners decreases. But the median or average mutuel price tends to rise and the rate of profit may decline only slightly, if at all. This explains why some players are forever trying to simplify their own procedures. Some manage to do it quite successfully. In fact, readers who do not care for full-dress handicapping may be able to use this book's teachings to develop their own collections of spot-play systems. A player equipped with an arsenal of five or six such selection methods can "handicap" an entire program in a few minutes, find himself two or three plays a day, and do about as well as the average burner of midnight oil.

3. Rate of profit is important, but it is not everything. In fifteen days at the track, a conservative player might make thirty bets and a less conservative one might make sixty. If the conservative player bets $20 on each horse and realizes profit at the rate of 25 cents per dollar, he makes $150. If the less conservative player also makes $20 bets and his profits are 15 cents on the dollar, he nets $180.

I have prepared the following twelve chapters with such possibilities in mind. Each of the chapters deals with one or more of the fundamentals of handicapping, fully explaining the relations of each to all others. Conservative methods of using each factor are made plain. Less conservative methods—and their possible consequences—also are explained.

7

Finding the Beatable Race

Most races are truly run. The best horse usually gets there first. Next week one of the losers might be in better form and beat him. But not today. Whether he won by a nose or a city block, his victory established certain truths:

1. He was in good enough condition to demonstrate his superiority over today's field.

2. The distance of the race suited him.

3. The weights suited him. (He did not carry high enough weight nor did any other entrant carry low enough weight to alter the outcome.)

4. The pace of the race was comfortable for him. (If he is a front-running type, nothing else was able to keep up with him in the early stages and he had plenty of energy left for the homestretch. If he prefers to run behind the early pace, he either outclassed the field decisively or was helped by the presence of two or more front-runners, which ran each other into the ground, clearing his path to the wire.)

5. His jockey was equal to the demands of the situation.

6. He was not outclassed. (If there were classier animals in the race they lacked the condition to prove it, or were unsuited to the distance or the weights or the pace, or were ridden by jockeys unable to get the best from them.)

It is easy to handicap a winner after the race is over. I have done it myself hundreds of times, wondering how I could have failed to notice *before* the race what suddenly became so obvious afterward. The process of retracing one's steps in hope of diagnosing error is good exercise for the beginner. It encourages careful habits.

The grandstands at any racetrack are cluttered with people who know a great deal about the game but manage to defeat themselves with sloppy handicapping. Experts are careful. They have to be. The percentages provide no margin for careless error. Just as in poker or bridge, a single thoughtless move can convert profit to loss. Knowing this, the expert makes sure that he has a complete profile on every contending horse in any race on which he bets. He knows precisely why he thinks his own choice has an unusually good chance to win. He knows exactly which animals promise to challenge his choice at each stage of the running. When his horse loses—as it does more than half the time—he may re-handicap the field to see if he has made a boo-boo, but he seldom finds one. You never hear an expert say: "I shoulda had the winner but I didn't notice that fast workout he ran the other day." If an expert's choice loses, the reason is usually one or more of the following:

1. **Its condition was not as good as expected.**
2. **Some other horse was in surprisingly good condition.**
3. **The surprisingly good or bad condition of another horse affected the pace of the race, depriving the expert's choice of its predicted advantage.**
4. **The rider failed to exploit his opportunities, or lost unnecessary ground on the turns, or ran the animal into switches, or was victimized by bad racing luck.**

The Expert's Main Problem

That list is worth analyzing. It indicates that the expert's main difficulty is his effort to assess the current condition of horses. Matters like class, weight and distance were not listed because the real expert rarely makes the kind of error that misleads him into selecting an outclassed or overweighted horse, or a horse unsuited to the distance of the race. As we shall see, there is no excuse for *anyone,* expert or beginner, to be misled in that way.

Observation of one simple rule will place the reader in position to save himself from outclassed, overweighted or outdistanced horses.

And it will give him the best possible chance to determine the current condition and the pace preferences of other horses. The rule:

Avoid playing any race in which the relative abilities of the horses are not clearly evident.

Among all reasons why the great majority of players lose, none is more basic than their violation of that rule. They insist on finding a bet in every race. They treat racing as if it were a roulette wheel. One of eight or ten horses has to win, so they take a flyer. They want action. They waste their money on races in which the past-performance records offer inadequate information about the entrants' class or condition or their distance and weight and pace preferences.

Experts call such races unplayable. A more precise term would be "unbeatable."

I have heard losers dispute this. "The favorite wins one out of three, whether it's a claiming race or a turf race or a race for first-time starters," they argue. "This means that one race is like another. No matter what kind of race it is and no matter how hot a handicapper you are, you wind up making a guess. If you don't have a clear picture of class or form or pace, you can find angles to handicap from. Everybody else is in the same boat. Every race is a chance to win. And a chance to lose."

Right. But some races offer a better chance to win, which is why experts concentrate on them.

It is impossible to deny that favorites win unplayable-unbeatable races as frequently as they win any other kind. It also is impossible to deny that an undiscriminating player of favorites winds up 8 or 9 percent behind the game. But the object of the game is to reduce losses to the vanishing point and make inroads into the black. This can only be done by avoiding unbeatable races and looking for beatable ones.

Here are the guideposts.

Seasons and Cycles

When the first edition of this book was written, Thoroughbred racing was a seasonal treat. The major Northern circuits of New York, New Jersey, Kentucky and Illinois opened in April or May and closed during the fall. The major Southern circuits of Florida and California operated during the winter. Maryland offered good racing in the warm months and marginal racing in the cold, modeling the year-around grind that has since become standard in most places.

New York, New Jersey, Illinois, Florida and Maryland now function on a twelve-month basis. Southern California seems headed in the same direction. But the quality of racing continues to change with the seasons. The horses that compete on Aqueduct's winterized inner track or at the rival Meadowlands in New Jersey are inferior to those that run in warm weather—either in Florida or Southern California during the winter, or at Belmont Park, Saratoga and Aqueduct's main track and turf course during more clement periods of the Northeastern year. Now as in the past, the best stables rest their most important runners on Southern farms during the winter and race them only when the hazards of weather are at a minimum.

Horses that cannot get out of their own way at Belmont Park suddenly become tigers when the snow clouds gather over Aqueduct's inner track and superior animals head South. Horses that win everything in sight during the Calder summer meeting and the transitional Tropical Park-at-Calder session of December and January cannot be found at the finishes of Hialeah or Gulfstream races. August killers at Del Mar are January losers at Santa Anita.

Careful handicappers have learned to proceed with great caution when winning stables vacate their barns in the North or South and head for the more suitable weather and fatter purses that await them in the South or North. Each such migration ushers in a new season, a new cast of horses and riders, a whole new ball game. Handicapping becomes more difficult than usual. Every race includes horses whose present abilities are obscure. Some have not run in months. Will they benefit from the rest and win at first asking? Or will they need some actual competition before rounding into form? Some have traveled thousands of miles in vans or planes. Will they need a race or two before becoming acclimated? Or will their journeys agree with them?

Most of the jockeys are familiar enough to the fans, but some are newcomers. Weeks must pass before anyone can know whether the new rider is as good as a New England or Ohio or Illinois record implies—able to perform well with all kinds of horses or less versatile than that.

Watchful waiting and extremely conservative betting are essential during these periods of transition. Wait a couple of weeks until the newly arrived horses have had races over the track. To do this is to liberate oneself from the impossible task of trying to compare apples and pears. It is always easier to rate horses on the basis of what they have done in recent competition with each other at the present track or a nearby sister track.

When It Rains

Many successful players refuse to go to the track unless the weather is pleasant and they know that the running surface is dry. But patient, adaptable handicappers can find lucrative opportunities on off-tracks, just as they do on fast ones.

Several times in every season, the Weather Bureau touts everyone onto a loser. "Fair and warmer," the forecast says. But the morning sun gives way to clouds and the rain begins to fall at noon. By post-time for the first race the running surface is a mess. What to do? Some players go home. Others hunt for spots.

Official information about the condition of the track is posted on the tote board. Not infrequently, the board will pronounce the track "fast" even though everyone can see puddles gathering on it. The tote board is not exactly fibbing. It is doing the best it can. The distinction be-tween a fast track and its immediate inferior, a "good" track, is a matter of judgment. Smart players are wary. They know that horses sometimes run seconds slower than expected and suffer serious losses of stamina on an officially "fast" but damp track.

The sandy, scientifically drained running surfaces at most modern racing plants turn from "fast" to "good" to "sloppy" in a heavy rain. Unless the rain is exceptionally heavy, the track does not even get muddy. Sun and drainage soon combine to upgrade it from "sloppy" to "slow" to "good" to "fast" in a single afternoon. Even if the surface gets actually muddy, the drying process seldom lingers at the stage known as "heavy," when the surface is as gooey as wet cement and horses' hooves sound like suction cups. Aqueduct dries from muddy to fast in a few hours of sunshine. The sequence is usually "muddy," "slow," "good," "fast."

Here is what the various terms mean, and what the handicapper does about them.

Fast: Dry. So dry that the maintenance crew waters it between races, to hold the dust down. The great majority of races are run on fast tracks. Hence, most horses are at their best on such tracks and have little experience on others. Time figures recorded on a fast track stand up quite reliably whenever the same horses run again under the same conditions on the same ground.

Information about the running styles, preferred distances, weight-bearing abilities and class limitations of most horses is based on fast-track performances. The information stands up, as long as today's race is also on a fast track. Therefore, the most conservative, most reliable handicapping is that which refuses to speculate about races held on any but a fast track. In fact, if the tote-board sign says "Track Fast" and the puddles are beginning to form, the ultra-conservative handicapper makes no bets. At any minute the sign may change from "Fast" to "Good" or "Sloppy." Regardless of what the sign says, the weather has already dampened the track sufficiently to alter the complexion of the race. The horses with early speed may not last in the homestretch, or may win with ridiculous ease. You cannot tell until you have seen for yourself how the footing affects them.

Sloppy: The track is covered with large puddles. The rain is still coming down or has ended recently. The drying process has scarcely begun. When modern, sandy tracks are sloppy, the horses run every bit as rapidly as when the surface is dry. Many players proceed with their handicapping as if the track were fast. This is a mistake. It is a mistake because front-running horses have an even better chance on a sloppy track (of the sandy sort) than on a fast track. They seem to hold their speed longer. Their come-from-behind rivals have more difficulty catching them.

It is agreed that the texture of a sloppy track favors the front-runner mainly because his position at the head of the stampede spares him the discomfort of having mud and slop kicked in his face. The horses behind him are obliged to run through a barrage of guck. Few of them appreciate it. It affects their spirit and saps their stamina. Many of them sulk or quit outright.

Therefore, when the handicapper's study shows that the best horse in the race is a front-runner, and that no other front-runner in the race has the speed to stay with him, the horse usually becomes a better bet on a sloppy track. If the horse's most formidable competitor is one that likes to come from off the pace but has done nothing in previous efforts on sloppy tracks, the front-runner becomes an even better bet.

The exception would be a front-runner that simply dislikes slop. A few of them do, and their records often show it.

A more difficult case arises when the best horse in the race is a come-from-out-of-it type. If it has already won in the slop by coming on in the stretch and overtaking the leaders, it may be a rugged sort. The player with access to old result charts would look up the animal's good race in the slop and see if the chart explains how it won. Perhaps it won because two front-runners perished in the stretch and it was the only other living thing in the vicinity of the finish wire. But if the horse ran with authentic gameness, or if today's front-runners seem likely to wear each other out—which can happen in the slop as easily as on a fast track—the player has found a good bet.

Lacking such evidence in results charts, the wise player remains skeptical about the winning chances of the come-from-behinder, even though it may have won in slop before. Unless the animal has a pronounced edge in all departments, and has never showed the slightest inclination to quit in the stretch, it may be wiser to pass the race. On the other hand, if it has won *more than one race* in the slop, it can be certified as a slop runner deserving of support.

As the reader can see, decisions of this kind depend on numerous variables. When in doubt, the expert abstains. It hurts to pass up a winner, but it costs no money. To pass up a loser saves money, and is gratifying in that respect.

Good: While getting drenched, the track passes from "fast" to "sloppy" via "good." While drying out it progresses from "slow" to "fast" with a stopover at "good." A peculiarity of sandy tracks is that "good" refers to conditions not nearly as good as the innocent bystander might think. At Aqueduct, a so-called good track contains less moisture than a "slow" one and more than a "fast" one, but it often works havoc on the figures of an unsuspecting player. In the old days, a "good" track was only a bit slower than "fast," and had no marked effect on the running styles of most horses. But when the sandy track is on the slow side of "good" it holds horses back. Front-runners run out of gas sooner. Races are won by animals that come from off the pace to score victories that would not be likely on a fast track.

The safest approach to the modern track in a situation of this kind is to determine (if possible) how the early speedsters are being affected. If the situation is unclear, bet no horse unless it figured to win on a fast track and either has a clear edge in class or is the determined type that can be rated a few lengths behind the leaders before opening up in the stretch. If it has won in the past on "good," "slow" or "muddy" tracks, it becomes a better risk.

To repeat for emphasis, a pace-setting animal is a dubious choice on a holding track unless it is figured to romp on a fast track, has a decided class edge, and has won on off-tracks in the past.

Slow: Very much the same standards apply to this moister surface. It is slow because it holds. It retards the animals. Front-runners have more difficulty.

Rogelio Olguin rides sadly back to the judges' stand after losing in the mud at Caliente.
JOHN GREENSMITH

Muddy: This kind of footing is wetter than anything but a sloppy track. And it is gummy. The clods that fly from the front-runner's heels adhere to the rearward horses and jockeys like beauty-parlor facials. Hooves slip and slide. Horses become frightened of their unsure purchase on the ground. They sometimes quit running and look for the barn.

The only horse to bet in a race of this kind is one that not only should win if the track were fast but has already proved that it can win in mud. If it does not shape up as the best horse in the race, its previous victory in mud is no evidence that it will win today. Yet, if the mudder is the second- or third-best horse in the race, and the better two have already demonstrated a reluctance to run in mud, you may have something.

As often as not, the winner of a mud race turns out to be a sore-kneed varmint that never raced in mud before but appreciates the cool comfort of the stuff so much that it runs in at huge odds. I repeat, the nearest thing to a safe bet in mud, as on any off-track, is the horse with the double edge—the potential superiority on normal footing *plus* proven ability to cope with today's goo.

Heavy: A surface of this kind is rare at modern tracks. It occurs after a long siege of rain, when enough moisture has evaporated to leave the soil with a consistency comparable to the soft, damp clay used in nursery schools. A heavy track is slower than any other kind. The best hope of the player who tries to handicap races on such a surface is to take the best horse (provided it is not a front-runner), but *only* if it has won on heavy tracks in the past. If he cashes one bet in four he will be extremely lucky. The other three races will be won by a variety of animals, including some that never have done well on off-tracks and others that have never taken the lead in their lives but suddenly move up and set all the pace today.

Bitter experience helps form the attitudes of most players toward rainfall and its consequences. If the past few pages seem to offer hope of success on days when the track is off, and the reader is emboldened to brave the elements instead of staying home, I urge caution. Like anything else in handicapping, wet-track predictions should be tested on paper before actual money travels from the wallet to the mutuel clerk.

The remainder of this chapter deals with the various types of Thoroughbred races, differentiating the less playable from the more so. Here again, a veteran racegoer may find nuggets that seem to promise success with kinds of races that previously have defied his best efforts. I urge once more that he proceed with care. If, for example, he has always avoided races for two-year-olds, having succumbed to the widespread superstition that young horses are unreliable, he should hesitate before deciding that the information in this chapter equips him to bet on a two-year-old. While hesitating, he should see what other chapters of this book can add to his understanding of two-year-olds. And he then should confine his activity to mental bets or paper bets until he has satisfied himself that he can beat such races.

We begin our review with claiming races. They not only are the most numerous races at most tracks, but offer the highest proportion of betting opportunities.

Claiming Races for Older Horses

Without claiming races there would be no racing at all. Owners would avoid the hazards of fair competition. Instead, they would enter their better animals in races against the sixth- and twelfth-raters that occupy most stalls at most tracks. The third-class horse might be unable to win a major race from one end of the year to the other, but would go undefeated in races against his inferiors. This would leave little or no purse money for the owners of cheap horses. The game would perish.

The claiming race changes all that. When he enters his animal in a race for $5,000 claiming horses, the owner literally puts it up for sale at that price. Any other owner can file a claim before the race and lead the beast away after the running. The original owner collects the horse's share of the purse, if it earned any, but he loses the horse at a fair price.

That is, he loses the horse at a fair price if it is a $5,000 horse. If it were a $10,000 horse, in a race for cheaper ones, the owner would get the purse and collect a large bet at odds of 1 to 10, but the horse would be bought by another barn at less than its true value.

Owners sell nothing at cut rates. Not on purpose. Which is why a $5,000 claiming race always matches horses whose value—a reflection of present class and soundness and estimated future earning capacity —is not much higher than $5,000. Their value may, in fact, be a good deal lower. At major tracks, claiming prices usually range from $3,500 to $40,000. Claiming races for $60,000 stock are seen occasionally.

The sophisticated racegoer likes to open his racing paper and find a $5,000 claiming race at six furlongs for three-year-olds, or for three-year-olds and up. He knows that the race may provide his best bet of the day. That is not all he knows. He knows that the reason these horses are running at a claiming price is that they are unfit to run in better company. Some of them showed championship promise as year-lings or two-year-olds, but suffered injury from which they recovered only traces of their ability. Others may be jaded or partly crippled from too much training and racing, and may be on their way down the scale. Next year they'll be running at minor tracks, with $2,000 price tags. Others may be reliable enough animals in their present price bracket. Still others may be reliable animals in a lower price bracket, but over their heads today.

There may be ten horses in the race, and members of the crowd may bet many thousands of dollars on each, but the handicapper usually finds that not more than three or four have a reasonably good chance to win. The rest are short of condition, short of class, running at the wrong distance, or facing animals that figure to cut out the wrong kind of pace for them. Or maybe their jockeys are outclassed.

The trainers of mature claiming horses manipulate the animals like puppets, darkening their form by entering them in races they can't win and then springing them for the money in races that suit them. Expert handicappers know all this, and how to recognize what's afoot. Strangely enough, although these claiming races lack real quality, the winner often turns out to be a horse with a slight edge in class—pro-vided, of course, that its physical condition allows it to demonstrate that inherent superiority. Where no significant class difference exists, the animal in best condition can be counted on to win, assuming that the distance and weights and pace and jockey suit him.

In the urgent effort to subsidize as many stables as possible by giving even the poorest three- and four-year-old and older horses a chance to win, the tracks are unable to rely solely on the class distinctions implied by claiming prices. Identical price tags notwithstanding, a group of $3,000 or $8,000 or $12,000 Thoroughbreds includes widely diversified talents. The tracks compensate for some of these differences by scheduling races at varying distances. But even this is not enough. The track must plan races for the least capable members of any claiming-price group and other races for the better.

In ascending order of quality, the more familiar of these claiming races are:

1. For maiden fillies. A race for four-year-olds of this description is inferior to one that includes three-year-olds or is exclusively for those younger animals.

2. For maiden colts and geldings, or for both sexes. Again, the presence of three-year-olds suggests a better race.

3. For female non-winners of two races at any time. Once more, three-year-olds are generally the best animals in the category.

4. For male non-winners of two, or for both sexes. Three-year-olds are usually of higher quality than their elders.

5. For three-year-old non-winners of one or two or more races since a specified date. The larger the number of permissible previous victories and the more recent the date, the better the competition. Also, a race for males or both sexes is superior to one restricted to females.

6. For three-year-olds and up or four-year-olds and up, with other conditions as in the paragraph above. Among horses of proven winning ability, such as these, four- and five-year-olds usually enjoy clear superiority over three-year-olds of identical claiming price. This is especially true during the first half of the year and in longer races.

7. Open to all in the claiming bracket, aged three, or three and up, or four and up. The best $7,500 animals on the grounds might be ineligible for certain of the races described in Paragraph 6, having won too often and too recently, but can get into this kind of gallop.

The racing secretaries, who plan track programs, resort to many ingenious variations on the foregoing themes. By the end of any representative season, winning opportunities will have been programmed for all but the very sorriest stock. Any trainer who doesn't find a spot for every animal in his barn has only himself—or them—to blame.

Although this is not the place for a discussion of the weight factor, it should be pointed out that the conditions of claiming races grant weight concessions to horses that have won fewer than a specified number of races within a specified time. Additional weight advantages sometimes are given to animals entered to be claimed at less than the maximum price. For instance, a race might be programmed for horses entered to be claimed for $4,500, $5,000 and $5,500. The ones entered at the lower prices would be allowed to carry three or five or seven pounds less than those entered at $5,500.

Older Claiming Maidens and Non-Winners of Two

Maiden claiming races for horses aged three or more are the saddest exhibitions on any card. Most of the entrants have had several opportunities as two-year-olds and have failed. They have done no better at age three. And some have reached four without a single win. The expert almost invariably writes off the four-year-old as hopeless in a maiden claimer. If it has lived this long without winning, there can be little expectation that it will win today.

Among three-year-old maidens entered to be claimed, the majority are equally hopeless. They have shown neither speed, stamina nor spirit. One that has been getting into the money frequently may attract the business of the crowd but is not necessarily a good bet. He very likely is a sucker horse, a chronic loser. His previous experiences have conditioned him to run as fast as is necessary to stay among the lead-

Snow racing at Sportsman's Park   UPI PHOTO

Native Diver (nearest rail) *equals world record for seven furlongs, beating Viking Spirit in 1965 Los Angeles Handicap at Hollywood Park.* UPI PHOTO

ers, but he hates—and that's the word—to get out front, where he can't see any other horses. So he loses and loses and loses, although he often finishes second or third.

I have never known an expert who approached the maiden claiming race for older horses with any expectation of finding a good bet. Some do not bother to handicap such races at all. Others may bet on a three-year-old in a high-priced maiden claimer (about $25,000), if the animal has not yet proved itself a dud. For example, if it has had only a race or two or three in its previous career, has run at least one of them recently without disgrace, has been working out frequently and at respectable speed, and, above all, is from a leading barn, it may be superior to its rivals today. Perhaps the animal's previous race was a maiden-special-weights event, for the most valued non-winners in the place. If it did fairly well in that race and meets other standards, the maiden claiming race may be its dish of tea.

Or perhaps its last was a spirited race against $15,000 maidens and its surprised owner has decided to boost the ante. If the horse is the only thing in the field that looks like a horse, it may be a bet.

Claiming events for non-winners of two races are designed for animals only one step removed from the maiden category. These creatures often are no better than maidens. They prove it by never winning another race at a major track. The best of them is the lightly raced, well-trained three-year-old that wins a maiden race decisively. It has demonstrated an authentic edge in class over non-winners in this price range. The chances are excellent that it retains the advantage when facing non-winners-of-two in the same price bracket.

Another good bet is the occasional animal whose lone victory occurred not in a maiden claimer but in a straight claimer (a race for previous winners). A look at the result chart usually reveals that the race was for non-winners-of-two, but the horse deserves extra credit, especially if it showed any real speed.

Still another possibility is the horse that won a maiden-special-weights race, or has been finishing close to the winners in straight claimers of a value higher than today's. Example: a three-year-old that has been beating half or more of its field when racing against four- and five-year-old winners in a similar price range.

In trying to evaluate races for *female* maidens or non-winners of two races, the criteria remain the same. Certainly, any female that has shown the slightest spark of ability in a recent race against *males* can be assumed to have an extra something going for her when pitted against unpromising females.

Bread and Butter

Straight claiming races for $3,000 to $20,000 horses with multiple victories are the bread and butter of the expert player. The fluctuations of the form cycle, the maneuvering of trainers, and the relative unsoundness of much of the stock make it possible for the player to toss out most of the entrants as probable losers. The real contenders are quite easy to find. But things become stickier when claiming prices exceed $20,000. These higher-priced animals earn their substantial valuations by winning with fair consistency, or at least by indicating that they could do so if entered in suitable races. They are sounder animals and hold their winning form somewhat longer. Thus, a field of $25,000 Thoroughbreds often perplexes the handicapper with four or five animals that have done well enough in fairly fast company—and have done it recently enough—to qualify as contenders. The player's problem may be additionally complicated by the presence of horses dropping down to the claiming ranks after facing superior competition in allowance races.

A race of this kind, in which the handicapper is unable to separate the leading contenders, is every bit as unplayable-unbeatable as a race in which the present capabilities of the horses are unknown or in which no horse has demonstrated enough reliability to deserve a bet.

It is a grievous pain in the neck to spend time handicapping a race and end with two or three or four horses so evenly matched that decision seems impractical. Yet fortune sometimes smiles. One of the horses may be scratched. In the paddock and walking ring, two of the remaining contenders may seem grossly out of sorts. All of a sudden the fourth horse is an outstanding bet. More often than not he pays excellent odds, the crowd having pushed a good deal of its money onto the other prominent contenders.

Claiming races are the staple fare of the expert handicapper. I know none who avoids playing them. I know some who seldom play any other kind.

Races for Good Two-Year-Olds

Let it be asserted at the outset that the better two-year-olds at major tracks are among the most reliable Thoroughbreds anywhere. The prejudice of many players against two-year-olds is unwarranted. Anyone who knows what to look for in juvenile races can profit without nearly the expenditure of time and sweat that other kinds of handicapping demand.

The well-bred two-year-old that reacts well to training is handled like a potential champion. Its first run for money is against other highly regarded juvenile maidens at five or five and a half furlongs under uniform weights prescribed by the racing secretary of the track. Early in the season, most of the entrants in one of these maiden-special-weights affairs are likely to be first-time starters. One or more may be by Secretariat or Northern Dancer or Exclusive Native and trained by Frank Whiteley, Laz Barrera, Jimmy Croll, or other first-rate conditioners who specialize in winning with two-year-olds in the first attempt. What can the player do when confronted by so many attractive unknown quantities? Sit on his hands and wait.

As the season progresses, maiden-special-weights races crop up in which all but one or two of the horses have been to the post a time or three. A high-bred swifty from a good barn is entered. His past performances show that he has been trying, has been missing narrowly but improving, and has been doing it all in excellent time. Frequently, he is the only animal of his description in the race. He is as good a bet as one ever finds.

Official photo that established Tom Fool as winner of the 1953 Suburban Handicap. Royal Vale was second.   UPI PHOTO

The two-year-old may even be a good bet in its very first race. If all other entrants have had a few racing opportunities without demonstrating ability, the well-bred, well-trained youngster making its first start may well go to the post as a solid favorite.

Many players lose money on these sprints for potentially superior two-year-old maidens by overlooking an ancient tradition of the game. This tradition regards the form of a maiden as "the property of its owner." The horse can be sent out *not* to win but to acquire experience in actual competition. Inasmuch as the trainers do not notify the public of their intentions in that regard, a lot of money is wasted at the windows.

Before anyone calls the cops to report corruption, I should point out that no decent barn wants to lose any race. Yet no decent barn will permit a jockey to punish a green but expensive two-year-old in an effort to win. If it cannot win on its own raw talent and courage, it is allowed to lose. Treatment of that sort may be unkind to players, but is good for horses.

To avoid being entrapped into betting on a two-year-old maiden whose connections are not ready to shoot the works, the smart player simply reserves his support for animals that (1) have already tried to win and look like winners today or (2) regardless of prior performance or lack of it, seem to have a clear edge in quality over the zeros in today's field. The handicapping is done mainly in terms of speed, by means to be described in a later chapter. Other basic considerations are breeding, the identity of trainer and jockey, and the swiftness of recent workouts. Class, weight and pace usually are irrelevant in these five-furlong sprints.

Winners of the maiden-special dashes proceed to allowance races, stepping-stones to the lucrative juvenile stakes. If the allowance race is at five or five and a half furlongs, and all entrants have already competed at the distance, the race can be analyzed entirely in terms of speed, with the usual edge to the best barns. If the distance is new to some of the horses, the race is harder to beat. It may even be unplayable, as we shall see in the next chapter.

At distances of six furlongs and up, under allowance or stakes conditions, the player often finds himself with too many sound, evenly matched two-year-olds to choose among. Stickouts like Native Dancer turn up too infrequently to make the player's life simple. But when one does, the juvenile stakes are a joy. A Native Dancer, Citation, Secretariat, Graustark, Moccasin, Ruffian, Hail to Reason or Buckpasser pays miserly odds. But who cares? Animals of that kind figure to win big. Any race is playable in which a horse not only figures much the best but, in the manner of two-year-old champions, can be counted on to give it all he's got. The young champ loses now and then, but not often enough to throw the player's accounts out of joint.

Cheap Two-Year-Olds

Races for inferior two-year-olds are an entirely different matter. When a maiden juvenile is entered to be claimed, his proprietors announce, in effect, that he is a washout. They are so sure of his unsoundness or lack of innate talent that they do not even bother to protect him from sale. The races in which he runs are invariably the slowest at any track, and are not cheering to the eye.

Some players put their money on the supposed class of a glamorously bred two-year-old when it runs in company of this kind. But if the poor thing's breeding meant anything, it would be winning allowance races, not seeking its first win in the company of culls. Once in a great while, the player finds an entrant that has run faster in maiden-special-weights company than any of its competitors have run in their maiden claiming races. Unless the horse displayed that speed recently and has been working out at short, regular intervals, it can be assumed that it has deteriorated and will not equal the previous clocking today. The player who speculates on more than one of every five or six maiden claimers for two-year-olds is guilty of waste—especially at lower claiming-price levels.

Straight claimers for two-year-olds are as playable as other claiming events, but not early in the season. In late summer and fall, after the young horses have run often enough to sort themselves out a bit, the player approaches their claiming races with confidence. In spring, all he really knows about a field of two-year-old claimers is that the entrants have been good enough to win in the past but that something serious accounts for their inability to win in better company. A physical or temperamental flaw of that kind may not prevent the animal from going on to a long, honorable career. Indeed, it may move right out of the claiming ranks and become a stakes winner, like hundreds of underrated Thoroughbreds in the past. But the youngster's failings may be more serious. They may prevent him from ever repeating the swift previous victory that explains why the crowd has made him the favorite in today's race. In short, two-year-old claimers are among the least consistent of horses during the early months of the year, and deserve mistrust for that reason.

Although the horse with the fastest previous race at the distance is the likeliest contender in any two-year-old claiming sprint, the player is well advised to pass the race unless the horse has been active recently and has shown that it can *consistently* cover the ground in substantially faster time than any of its competitors. Even so, it may lose out to a beast that has been performing indifferently in allowance company but runs faster today than it has ever run before. These are tough races. I doubt that anyone beats them.

Allowance Races for Older Horses

The conditions of the allowance race resemble those of the claiming race, except that the horses are not for sale. Eligibility and weight allowances are prescribed in conditions written by the racing secretary. As in claiming races, the conditions usually tend to bar horses that are too good for the field, having won too many purses above a minimum value, or having won too often or too recently. On the other hand, the conditions permit a trainer to enter a horse that has not a prayer of winning, but needs the work.

Most players know that allowance races are designed to provide earnings for horses too good to be lost *via* the claiming route, but not good enough to beat stakes and handicap stars. But most players do not know that allowance races come in almost as many varieties as claiming races. To regard one allowance race as equal in quality to another is to invite losses. To search out those qualitative differences is to open the way to remarkable betting opportunities.

Let us suppose that two three-year-olds seem to be outstanding contenders in an allowance race. Each finished a fast-closing second in its previous start, after running close to the pace all the way. The past-performance records show that both horses have been entered in nothing but allowance races all year, and have been running successfully enough to inspire confidence.

Are they too closely matched? Not a bit of it. The player motivated to dig through the result charts discovers that the last race of Horse "A" was for three-year-olds that had not earned a purse as high as $3,000 on as many as three occasions in the previous six months. "A" was eligible for the race because his earnings had exceeded $3,000 in only two of his five victories. The horse that defeated him in the race was a three-year-old with similar credentials.

The result charts show that "B" has been facing animals of a different order. His last race was for three-year-olds and up. The purse was fatter than the purse in "A's" race. And the conditions of eligibility had permitted entry by several previous winners of handicap and stakes races. In running second, "B" outfooted several high-class animals, older than he. A couple of his earlier victories had been against horses so good that they would not have been allowed into "A's" last race, and would not be allowed into today's race, either.

"B's" trainer has found a soft spot. For a change the horse is running against animals of his own age. They have never demonstrated that they can keep up with the kind of stock "B" has been beating. The player who consults the result charts has found a bonanza. Indeed, if "A" happens to have run his last couple of races in faster time than "B" and if the rider of "A" is the "hot" jockey on the grounds and if, as may be expected, a significant number of newspaper selectors and tip sheets pick "A," the player will collect a robust mutuel after "B" waltzes home in front.

In our chapter on class, means of differentiating one allowance race from another will be presented. Meanwhile, it suffices to say that the occasional racegoer, and others who rely on past-performance records, probably will find many allowance races unplayable. But the player who uses result charts will find them a delightful source of extra revenue.

I do not mean to discourage the casual fan from trying to handicap allowance races. At many tracks, certain allowance fields are composed entirely of animals that have been running in claiming races. The past-performance records give accurate clues to their relative class. In other instances, the past performances of one entrant mark him as the choice. His consistency, his prior earnings, his pace figures, his form cycle, and the identity of his trainer all suggest him as a likely winner. He may not pay much, but you don't have to collect result charts to get the money.

Maiden-Specials for Older Horses

Many a well-bred horse goes through its entire two-year-old season without a single victory. Even after it has lost six or eight times, its owners refuse to enter it in claiming races. Perhaps they think that it may finally come to hand. Or they hope to use it for breeding purposes some day and don't want to lose it. Or the owner's wife loves its limpid hazel eyes and refuses to part with it in any circumstances.

All of a sudden January 1 arrives and the horse is a three-year-old maiden. Indeed, some otherwise successful barns harbor four-year-old maidens, still running in maiden-specials. The tracks are careful to arrange racing opportunities for the creatures. Needless to say, the majority are incurable losers. Some would have serious difficulty winning a $3,000 claimer at a minor track.

But the player misses some excellent bets if he skips past these maiden-specials without a glance at the past-performance records. Most of the four-year-olds are hopeless and can be ignored. But some of the threes *do* come to hand. They put together a couple of brisk races and some bright workouts and proceed to win like winners.

As a general rule of thumb, the likelihood that such an animal will wake up and win becomes smaller as his number of races increases. The fewer races in his record, the better his chances. The best plays of all are horses that did not start at age two, probably because they were late foals and their handlers decided not to overtax them. If they come from leading barns, this is likely to be the explanation. Occasionally, one of these three-year-old first-starters not only wins his race, but deserves betting support by the smart player. If his breeding is promising, his trainer outstanding, his workouts good, his rivals nondescript, and if he looks fit in the paddock, he's worth a chance.

More often, these good three-year-old maidens need a race or two before cracking down. They usually signal readiness by running more competently in their second outing than in their first.

③ MONMOUTH

1 MILE — MONMOUTH PARK

▲Start ▲Finish

1 MILE. (TURF). (1.35) CLAIMING. Purse $7,000. 3-year-olds. Weight, 121 lbs. Non-winners of two races since May 15, 3 lbs. A race, 6 lbs. Claiming price $16,000; for each; $500 to $14,000, 1 lb. (Races entered for $11,000 or less not considered.)

Coupled—Burgee and Hidden Manna; Elyse's Pride and Fairfield Joe.

Hasty Brog

B. c. 3, by Hasty Road—Helen's Crasher, by Crasher
$15,000
Own.—Ja Jo Stable
Br.—Bell S J (Va)
Tr.—Ryerson James

Date	St	1st	2nd	3rd	Amt.
1978	11	0	3	1	$7,510
1977	11	5	2	1	$21,190

113

LATEST WORKOUTS Jun 2 Mth 4f fst :49 b

Burgee

Dk. b. or br. g. 3, by Hoist the Flag—Cream Pie, by Boston Doge
$16,000
Own.—Lopez & Shapiro
Br.—Farish III & Sharp (Md)
Tr.—Lopez Daniel J

	St	1st	2nd	3rd	Amt.
1978	9	2	1	1	$11,755
1977	5	M	1	2	$2,965

115

LATEST WORKOUTS Jly 8 Mth 3f fst :38 b

24Dec77—Awarded Third Purse Money.

Fatalist

B. c. 3, by Distinctive—Jennie's Gem, by Bold Lark
$16,000
Own.—Diamond Jubilee Stable
Br.—Somday Farm Inc—(Fla)
Tr.—Vincitore Michael

	St	1st	2nd	3rd	Amt.
1978	13	4	0	0	$7,400
1977	13	3	3	2	$23,570

115

LATEST WORKOUTS Jun 28 Mth 3f fst :36 b

Promised Road

Own.—Schumer & Berman

B. c. 3, by Santiago Road—Mighty Topsy, by Toby B
Br.—Caple H R (Fla)
Tr.—Gibson Ron

$16,000

										St. 1st 2nd 3rd	Amt.
									1978	2 1 5 2	$3,510
									1977	10 M 5 2	$5,405

3Jly78- 3Mth sly	:48	1:13	1:40%	Clm 16000	2 10	88½ 913 714	513 Lee J N7	109	13.20	58-23 Fortunate Prince 116nk Captain Peter 1161½ Seagay 1094½ Outrun 10
30Jun78- 3GP	fst 1	:47% 1:13	1:46%	Clm c-12000	5 7	613 53 31	1nk Bailey J D	114	10.40	69-19 Promised Road 114nk Chilly Charlie 1162¼ Mr. Olson 116¹ Driving 8
27Dec77- 2Crc	fst	:23½ :47½ 1:20½		Md c-12500	7 4	52½ 53 42	31½ Smith A Jr	120	1.40	85-11 Pirate Kid 116nk Hav'A Happy Day116¹PromisedRoad120¹ Rallied 12
20Dec77- 3Crc	fst	:23½ :46½ 1:13		Md 11500	6 3	44 21	2½ 2nd Smith A Jr	118	2.80	87-14 My Man Nick 120nd Promised Road118¹¼BeeJoyous120²¼ Gaining 12
28Nov77-10Crc	fst	:50 1:15½ 1:41%		Md 10000	5 10	109¼ 89¼ 67½	34 Depass R	120	*2.30	76-14 Mob Scene 116⁴ Master Derek 118nd Promised Road 120² Rallied 11
23Nov77- 4Crc	fst	:22½ :46½ 1:13%		Clm c-7500	2 11	129¼109¾ 78½	21½ Cardone E	116	7.40	81-16 My Dad Dave 114¼ Promised Road 116¹ Coroso 114¼ Rallied 12
10Nov77- 2Crc	fst	:23½ :47½ 1:19		Md 9000	1 8	62½ 34	46 210 Cardone E	118	3.80	64-14 Sum Cash113¹⁰PromisedRoad118¼RamblinDude120³ Gained place 12
10Nov77- 3Crc	fst	:23½ :47% 1:13%		Md 9000	2 10	85½ 45	45 44½ Cardone E	b 118	*1.40	80-12 Michelley 1152 Castro's Velocity 118½ Gunners Step1202 Rallied 11
120ct77- 3Crc	fst	:23½ :47% 1:13%		Md 8000	4 3	2nd 23	22 23 Cardone E	116	*1.40	81-15 Whale OfATale1153PromisedRoad116²MasterDerek120nd 2nd best 9
30Sep77- 1Crc	fst	:23½ :47% 1:27%		Md 10000	10 2	1hd 2nd	66⅔ Cardone E	118	*1.50	72-15 Full Armor 118¹ Double Al 118⁴ Favorite Minstrel 118¹ Tired 10

LATEST WORKOUTS   Jun 30 Mth 5f fst 1:02⅔ b   Jun 8 Mth 3f fst 1:48 b   Jun 3 Mth 3f fst :38 b

Sharpie

Own.—Frank Mrs M & C

B. c. 3, by Hand To Hand—Regal Hint, by Pointer
Br.—Karutz W S (Ky)
Tr.—Weisbord Barry L

$16,000

										St. 1st 2nd 3rd	Amt.
									1978	15 0 2 2	$7,205
									1977	9 2 0 2	$11,940

1Jly78- 4Mth	fst	:22½ :46% 1:12%		Clm c-12500	6 3	31½ 52½ 33	44¾ Brumfield D	116	3.60	74-20 Goodnight Special 119² Attainable 116¹ Kash KsWork107½ Tired 9
15Jun78- 6Mth	fst	:22½ :46% 1:11%		Clm 12500	4 4	42 21½ 21½	22½ Brumfield D	115	*3.10	79-22 Hidden Manna 114² Sharpie 115⁶ Lot of Care 115¾ Gamely 9
8Jun78- 6Mth	sly	:22½ :46% 1:13%		Clm 13000	9 1	65¾ 75¼ 47½	35½ Brumfield D	116	4.90e	65-31 Waltz Note 1104 Kash Ks Work 1132½ Sharpie 116¾ Brushed 9
31May78- 6Mth	fst	:22½ :45% 1:12%		Clm 4000	1 5	41½ 65¾	68⅛ 65 Brumfield D	114	11.10	73-22 Vertee Jr. 120nk No Hassle 1182¼ Captain's Galley 111¾ Tired 7
14Apr78- 4Aqu	fst	:48 1:28%		Clm 10000	1 1	1½ 1½	2hd 2½ Graell A	b 117	4.20	56-34 Clark The Lark 1174¼ Sharpie 117²¾ Dimestore Romeo117¾½ Tired 7
7Apr78- 3Aqu	fst	:46 1:12%		Clm 10000	5 5	22 22½	22¼ 3nk Graell A	117	7.30	82-16 Platforum 1172 Music Man Metz 113nk Sharpie 117nk Gamely 7
29Mar78- 2Aqu	fst	:23 :47% 1:14%		Clm 12500	6 3	36 46½	65½ 74 Tanner R	117	7.50	72-20 Bolyston 119⅝ Ask Joe 117nk Barter Binn 1151½ Tired 8
21Mar78- 5Aqu	fst	:23 :47% 1:14%		Clm 10000	1 3	1hd 2nd	1½ 31½ Graell A	117	*1.90	71-22 American Destiny 1101 Platforum 113½ Sharpie 117¾ Weakened 8
13Mar78- 2Aqu	fst	:23 1:13%		Clm 12500	9 8	3½ 32	32¾ 74 Prosper G	117	6.70	74-20 Clean Edge 112½ Cavalink 110¾ Gun Quill 117½ Lost whip 9
4Mar78- 7Aqu	fst	:23¾ 1:13%		Allowance	2 6	73½ 99¼	69½ 610 Knapp E T5	b 110	17.40	70-23 No Excuses 122¾ ChampagneChappy122¾YouGoFirst115¾ Outrun 7

L. Ryan's Ghost

Own.—Ryan M & F & St Leon

Ro. g. 3, by Native Charger—Adorable Shield, by Cover Up
Br.—International Thoroughbred Assoc (Fla)
Tr.—St Leon Norman E

$15,000

										Turf Record	
										St. 1st 2nd 3rd	Amt.
									1978	15 1 3 1	$5,068
									1977	2 M 0 0	$162

Entered 7Jly78- 6 ATL, finished 6

26Jun78- 5Atl	fm *1⅛ ⑦-:49% 1:14½ 1:47%		Md 4000	2 1	15 11	11½ 11½ Delguidice R Jr	b 113	6.90	79-14 L. Ryan's Ghost 113¹½ FriendlySpirit113½NavelStone120⁴ Driving 6
16Jun78- 3Atl	fst	1:13% 1:47%		Md 7500	6 1	13 15	3nk 2½ Delguidice R Jr	b 113	10.20	68-25 FrankThurman113⁴L.Ryn'sGhost113½Jmie'sDouble115² Held well 8
1Jun78- 4Atl	fst	:22% 1:12%		Md 6500	5 10	811 89½ 37	45½ Delguidice R Jr	b 116	7.70	74-22 Tony's Hideaway 1223 Bold Shan114²FrankCooney122⅛ No threat 12
4May78-10GP	fm *1⅛ ⑦	1:47%		Md 15000	7 5	35½ 32½ 57½	69¾ St Leon G	b 120	25.20	62-18 FifteenthColony114ndBeeJoyous114¼Viennl.d114³½ Wide 1st turn 11
25Apr78-10GP	fst	:47% 1:12½ 1:45½		Md 7500	4 10	911 97½ 813	615 Breen N	b 120	10.00	60-14 I'm Gabbie 110⅛ Honey Bun 115²½ Triple Hold 1151 Slow start 11
11Apr78- 1GP	fst	:21% 1:12%		Md 12500	9 11	12191223	913 76⅔ St Leon G	b 114	30.40	66-20 PeachFlambeau118⅝SeventysixthFloor114nkRoyalRin115² Outrun 12
1Apr78- 3FD	fst	:23½ :46% 1:12%		Md 10000	4 7	54½ 44½ 44	64 McKeever R Jr	b 115	16.50	79-17 Shimmy Back 112⅝ King Oasis 1221 Think Again 110nk Tired 7
25Mar78- 1FD	fst	:22½ :45% 1:12%		Md 10000	9 8	99½ 89¾ 87⅓	67 Vedlago W	b 115	*2.40	74-19 Black Bluffer 1222 Think Again 1102 Shimmy Back 112½ Outrun 10
16Mar78- 7FD	fst	:22½ :46% 1:14%		Md Sp Wt	3 4	56 57	44⅜ 3nk Delaura K A5	b 115	14.90	71-21 Now's My Turn 120nk Salty Peter120noL.Ryan'sGhost1151 Rallied 10
8Mar78- 7FD	fst	:22½ 1:15		Md 7500	1 7	66½ 67½ 67⅓	52⅔ Delaura K A5	b 110	19.90	67-30 Pinnochio 115² Sound Tiger 108no Now's My, Turn 115no Rallied 9

LATEST WORKOUTS   Jun 24 Atl 3f fst :36 b

1087

115

116

Raise the Blade

Own.—Quiet Winter Farm

Ro. g. 3, by Executioner—Down Beat, by Native Dancer
Br.—October House Farm (Fla)
Tr.—Thompson J Willard
$14,000

			Turf Record		St. 1st 2nd 3rd	Amt.
			St. 1st 2nd 3rd	1978 12 3 3 0	$21,265
114			2 0 1 0	1977 3 M 1 0	$1,925

75-15 Cptin'sGlley1106⅓RisetheBlde115₃DFFirfildJo1151⅓ Second best 8

26Jun78- 2Mth fst 1 :46⅗ 1:11⅜ 1:38½						
26Jun78-Dead heat						
14Jun78- 7Mth fm 1⅛ ①:50⅗ 1:14⅗ 1:47	Clm 15000	2 4 52 78⅓ 814 825 Arellano J	b 117	2.50	41-25 Jolly Brent 1176⅓ Noble Sheik 1141 Captain's Galley 111⅓	Tired 9
2Jun78- 6Mth yl 1 ①:49⅗ 1:14⅖ 1:39⅜	Clm 16000	2 6 55⅓ 33⅓ 23 25 MacBeth D	b 122	*2.10	72-32 Jolly Brent 1125 Raise the Blade 1222⅓ NobleSheik1125⅓ 2nd best 10
23May78- 5Mth fst 170 :46⅗ 1:12⅘ 1:44⅗	Clm 15000	1 3 31 2nd 1⅓ 15 Brumfield D	b 117	2.10	77-17 RaisetheBlde1175PositiveBisn1162FortunePrince116³ Drew clear 5
12May78- 5Mth fst 170 :46⅓ 1:11⅖ 1:42⅗	Clm 15000	7 6 58⅓ 34 32⅓ 46⅜ Brumfield D	b 117	*1.50	80-14 JollyBrent1113HolidayCrossing1082⅓FlowingFree1089⅓ No mishap 7
1May78- 6Key fst 6f :23⅗ :47 1:11½	Clm 15000	8 7 87 96 77 66⅓ Thomas D B	122	*2.90	77-16 Kingbird 116³⅓ Warrior's Mark 116ⁿᵒ Savoury 115ʰᵈ No factor 11
22Apr78- 6Key fst 6f :23½ :47 1:11⅓	Clm 22000	7 2 63 42 1ʰᵈ 42 Thomas D B	122	3.40	73-22 Double Threes 116ⁿᵒ Roman Tribute 116¹⅓ Thirst 109⅓ Weakened 7
7Apr78- 7Key gd 7f :23⅗ :47⅓ 1:26⅗	Clm 22000	4 5 33 37 4⅓ 1⅓ Thomas D B	120	7.60	67-34 Raise the Blade 120⅓ Last WhiteHope120ⁿᵏRufflame109ⁿᵏ Driving 7
28Mar78- 8Key gd 120 :47 1:12⅓ 1:45½	Clm 22000	7 6 53⅓ 31 31 55 Thomas D B	120	3.20	69-27 Alcinto 1211 Ne De Gagner 1081⅓ Daring Diplomat 121² Brushed 7
19Mar78- 7Key fst 170 :47⅗ 1:15⅗ 1:49	3↑Allowance	7 7 612 54 31 43⅓ Thomas D B	120	6.50	51-33 Frank Talk 112⅓ Kadahf 112¹⅓ California Prince 115¹⅓ Wide 7

LATEST WORKOUTS   Jly 6 Mth 4f fst :49 b

Elyse's Pride

Own.—Killgman & Pierce Mmes

B. g. 3, by Dominar—Miss Fall River, by Vimy Ridge
Br.—Lasater Farm (Fla)
Tr.—Pierce Joseph H Jr
$16,000

			Turf Record		St. 1st 2nd 3rd	Amt.
			St. 1st 2nd 3rd	1978 12 0 0 0	$2,465
115			8 1 0 0	1977 17 4 2 3	$18,653

31May78- 6Mth fst 6f :21⅗ :45⅗ 1:12⅗	Clm 16000	7 2 63⅜ 42⅓ 33 43⅜ Perret C	116	6.70	74-22 Vertee Jr. 120ⁿᵏ No Hassle 1182⅓ Captain's Galley 111⅓	Rallied 7
20May78- 4Mth fst 6f :22⅗ :45⅖ 1:11⅘	Clm 20000	5 3 43 54⅓ 35 44⅓ Perret C	114	10.60	7-19 Arrariat 116ⁿᵏ Take the Point 116⅓ Burgee 114⅓	Evenly 7
8May78- 8GP fm 1 ①:46⅘1:11½ 1:37	Clm 20500	6 2 2⅓ 23 811 815 Fires E	114	27.80	70-19 North Haven 116ⁿᵒ Full Armor 116² Classic Diamond 114¹⅓ Tired 8
1May78- 5GP fm 1⅛ ⑩ 1:39⅗	Clm 20000	10 3 33 108⅓1012 1015 Crews W	112	27.70	62-21 Sabruff 114ⁿᵒ Solarrian 116¹ North Haven 116¹ Early speed 10
21Apr78- 7GP fm ①*1 1:39⅗	Clm 20000	8 7 96⅓ 97⅓ 77⅓ 77⅓ Fell J	114	8.10	74-22 Frick or Frack 116³ Solarrian 116¹⅓ Lucky 'NRight1121 Tired 10
14Apr78-10GP fm *1⅛ ① 1:45⅗	Clm 20000	9 1 1⅓ 11 32 45⅓ MacBeth D	116	4.30	72-16 Solarrian 116²⅓ Whale Of A Tale 112⅓ MobScene1142⅓ Weakened 10
3Apr78- 5GP fm *1⅛ ① 1:44⅗	Clm 25000	9 1 1⅓ 1⅓ 1ʰᵈ 64⅓ MacBeth D	116	7.40	80-08 I've Got ItAll1132BeforeTheBench116ᵖᵒTatteredEnsign108⅓ Tired 10
23Mar78-10GP fm *1⅛ ① 1:44⅗	Clm 27500	6 2 21 2ʰᵈ 2⅓ 44⅓ MacBeth D	116	14.10	80-13 Frick or Frack 113¹ Orkney Isle 1141 Combatant1142⅓ Weakened 10
21Feb78-10Hia sly 1⅓	Clm 35000	2 3 31 86⅓ 913 916 Perret C	114	26.20	69-19 Double Al 114⅓ Before The Bench 114² Tallow Man 1143 Tired 10
13Feb78-10Hia fm *1⅓ ① :46⅗ 1:12⅓ 1:43⅓	Clm c-25000	2 1 3ⁿᵏ 1⅓ 1ʰᵈ107⅓ Aviles O B	112	8.70	69-19 Tallow Man 1141 Orkney Isle 114⅓ Too Close ToCall118⅓ Stopped 10

LATEST WORKOUTS   Jun 29 Mth 5f fst 1:01 h

Lucky 'N Right

Own.—Kutner J

Dk. b. or br. c. 3, by Subpet—Courting Times, by Court Affair
Br.—LeClaire T (Fla)
Tr.—Heisey Kenneth J
$16,000

			Turf Record		St. 1st 2nd 3rd	Amt.
			St. 1st 2nd 3rd	1978 14 0 1 2	$4,373
115			7 0 1 1	1977 17 2 1 4	$9,947

14Jun78- 7Mth fm 1⅛ ①:50⅘1:14⅗ 1:47	Clm 16000	4 2⅓ 66 711 619 Brumfield D	b 116	7.40	47-25 Jolly Brent 1176⅓ Noble Sheik 1141 Captain's Galley 111⅓	Tired 9
7Jun78- 2Mth fst 1 :47⅖ 1:12⅖ 1:40⅖	Clm 20000	7 4 44 44 46 49⅓ Brumfield D	b 114	18.20	61-22 Cincelari 1121⅓ Combatant 111⅓ Johnny And Joey 1107	Wide 8
31May78- 7Mth yl 1 ①:48⅗ 1:14⅗ 1:49	Clm 20000	1 4 48 64⅓ 712 811 Kiidzia S⁵	b 108	15.80	45-44 Lunar Larvin 118ⁿᵒ Winter Whiz 109¹⅓ Solemn 112⅓	Wide 8
20May78- 5Mth fst 1 :46⅗ 1:12 1:39½	Clm 22500	3 48⅓ 58 611 512 Solomon M	b 114	14.50	65-19 Bumbe 116ⁿᵒ Solarrian 1141⅓ Final Pretext 116⅓	Tired 9
1May78- 5GP fm 1⅛ ①:48⅗ 1:29½ 1:44⅗	Clm 22500	5 2⅓ 21⅓ 42⅓ 62⅓ Thornburg B	b 114	11.20	74-21 Sabruff 114ⁿᵒ Solarrian 116¹ North Haven 116¹	Weakened 10
21Apr78- 7GP fm *1⅓ ①:48⅗ 1:39⅗	Clm 20000	3 6 75⅓ 64⅓ 55 34⅓ Thornburg B	b 116	16.20	77-22 Frick or Frack 116³ Solarrian 116¹⅓ Lucky 'N Right1121	Mild bid 9
11Apr78-10GP gd *1⅓ ① 1:38⅜	Clm 16000	4 2 23 23 24 Solomone M	b 116	3.60	83-19 Sabruff 116⁴ Lucky 'N Right 116¹⅓ Lunar Mike 114ⁿᵏ	Gamely 10
29Mar78-10GP sly 1⅓	Clm 18000	9 2 2⅓ 31 67 69 Brumfield D	b 116	3.10	67-17 Lewis Everett 122² Strike Force 114ⁿᵒ Solarrian 116⅓	Tired 9
16Mar78- 7GP fst 1⅓	Clm 18000	6 2 2⅓ 11⅓ 11⅓ 3ⁿᵏ Brumfield D	b 116	10.90	71-25 Lewis Everett 118ⁿᵏ Nans Bluff 114ⁿᵒLucky'NRight116¹ Good try 10
6Mar78-10GP fm *1⅓ ①:47⅗ 1:13½ 1:46⅗	Clm 20000	2 6 64⅓ 9131017 1024 Arroyo H	b 116	6.90	45-21 What's The Score 116⅓ Dr. Sprunt 116¹⅓ Solarrian 116ⁿᵒ Outrun 12

LATEST WORKOUTS   Jun 30 Mth 5f fst 1:04⅖ b   Jun 23 Mth 5f fst 1:05   bg   May 27 Mth 5f gd 1:02⅘ b   May 19 Mth 3f gd :36⅗ b (d)

Combatant

Own.—Long A F

Dk. b. or br. c. 3, by Bold Reasoning—Dizzy Dame, by Alibhai
Br.—Asbury C A & T H (Ky)
Tr.—Rieser Stanley M
$16,000

							Turf Record						
							St. 1st 2nd 3rd						
							3 0 0 2						

								St. 1st 2nd 3rd		
							1978	10 1 1 2		
							1977	2 M 0 1		

1087

Amt.
$8,020
$1,200

26Jun78- 2Mth fst 1 | :46⅗ 1:11¾ 1:38⅜ | Clm 16000 | 1 | 1 | 11½ 21 | 46½ 513 | Mize W E⁵ | b 110 | *2.10 | 68-15 Cptin'sGlley110⁶ᵈⁿᵏRisetheBide115⁴ᵈⁿᵏFrfieldJoe115½ | Weakened 8
7Jun78- 2Mth fst 1 | :47⅕ 1:12¾ 1:40¾ | Clm 21000 | 3 | 1 | 12½ 13½ | 11 21¾ | Klidzia S⁵ | b 111 | *3.00 | 63-22 Cincelari 112¾ Combatant 111¾ Johnny And Joey 110⁷ | Gamely 8
31May78- 7Mth sf 1 ⅛ ⓣ:48⅕ 1:14¾ 1:49 | Clm 25000 | 8 | 1 | 14 | 12½ 1½ | 52½ Solomone M | b 114 | 4.10 | 53-44 Lunar Lanvin 118ⁿᵈ Winter Whiz 109½ Solemn 112½ | Tired 9
20May78- 5Mth fst 1 | :46⅖ 1:12 1:39½ | Clm 22500 | 4 | 1 | 15 | 12½ 2½ | 42 Barrera C | b 114 | *2.40 | 75-19 Bumbe 116ⁿᵒ Solarrian 114¾ Final Pretext 116¾ | Weakened 9
19Apr78- 6Aqu sly 1 | :46⅗ 1:11¾ 1:38 | 3 ↑ Allowance | 3 | 3 | 41½ 56 | 816 821 | Venezia M | b 108 | 6.30 | 55-24 Stab 121½ Psychosis 109⁶½ Sir Ivorson 121¾ | Fell back 8
23Mar78-10GP fm 1⅛ ⓣ 1:38 | 3 ↑ Allowance | 3 | 3 | 32½ 31 | 31½ 32 | Maple E | b 114 | *2.70 | 83-13 Frick or Frack 113¹⁰rkneyIsle114¹Combatant114²¾ | Finished well 10
2Mar78- 8Hia fm 1⅛ ⓣ 1:51 | | 4 | 2 | 2ʰᵈ 1½ | 1½ 32½ | Maple E | b 114 | 11.00 | 76-26 Svelto 112½ Tattered Ensign 114² Combatant 114½ | Weakened 12
25Feb78- 3Hia gd 1⅛ | :46½ 1:12 1:45¾ | | 3 | 1 | 12 13 | 11½ 1½ | Maple E | b 116 | 3.60 | 76-18 Combatant 116½ No Molesie120ᵐᵏMr.Eldag120²½ | Bumped, driving 8
13Feb78- 3Hia fst 6f | :22⅗ :45⅖ 1:11 | | 10 | 4 | 61¾ 46½ | 811 912 | Maple E | b 116 | 20.60 | 76-12 FmosRlton120⁷ColoniTms120ⁿᵏBconndEggs119ⁿᵏ | Stumbling start 12
23Jan78- 5Hia fst 6f | :22⅖ :46 1:10¾ | Md 60000 | 12 | 8 | 96½ 68½ | 67½ 713 | Maple E | | 122 | 3.90 | 76-14 David El Paso 118⁷ Surf Boarder 122 Sladeless 119ⁿᵒ | Outrun 12

LATEST WORKOUTS   Jly 8 Mth 4f fst :48⅜ h ● Jun 22 Mth 5f fst 1:02⅖ b   May 28 Mth 3f gd :37 b

---

Efrain

Own.—Hobeau Farm

Ro. c. 3, by Peace Corps—A Rose For Charles, by Beau Gar
Br.—Hobeau Farm Inc (Fla)
Tr.—Garcia Efrain T
$16,000

								St. 1st 2nd 3rd		
							1978	3 1 0 0		
							1977	0 M 0 0		

1087

Amt.
$3,165

26Jun78- 1Mth fst 6f | :22⅕ :45⅕ 1:11 | 3 ↑ Md 10000 | 5 | 3 | 2ʰᵈ 13 | 15 15 | Lee J N⁷ | 109 | 10.60 | 85-15 Efrain 109⁵ Whachamacalit 115¹½ Sprung 109ⁿᵏ | Driving 10
19Jun78- 1Mth fst 6f | :22 :45⅗ 1:11½ | 3 ↑ Md 15000 | 5 | 6 | 3½ 51¾ | 87 813 | MacBeth D | b 115 | 10.30 | 68-18 GoodnightSpecial115ⁿᵒStonewllJck123¾HighAstheSky115ⁿᵒ | Tired 9
10Jun78- 1Mth fst 6f | :22⅖ :47 1:12¾ | 3 ↑ Md 15000 | 4 | 2½ | 2ⁿᵈ 43½ | 59½ Tanner R | b 115 | 17.50 | 67-23 On Sail Red 115³GoodnightSpecial115⁴Special Ed115²½ | Weakened 10

LATEST WORKOUTS   Jun 30 Mth ⓣ 3f fm :36¾ b (d)   Jun 24 Mth 3f fst :37   Jun 17 Mth 4f fst :49 bg

---

Noble Sheik

Own.—Bakewell Mrs & P III

B. c. 3, by Noble Descent—Mamounia, by Chanteur II
Br.—Evans T M (Va)
Tr.—Kassen David
$16,000

							Turf Record		
							St. 1st 2nd 3rd		
							4 0 1 1		

								St. 1st 2nd 3rd		
							1978	7 2 0 0		
							1977	7 0 2 1		

115

Amt.
$2,170
$5,590

24Jun78- 5Mth fm 1 ⓣ:48⅗ 1:13 1:38⅛ | Clm 27000 | 7 | 10 | 10¹¹10¹² | 9¹⁴ 9¹¹ | Perret C | b 115 | 31.70 | 73-18 Jolly Brent 115⁵ Rufflame 116¹ T. V. Decree 112ⁿᵒ | Outrun 10
14Jun78- 7Mth fm 1⅛ ⓣ:50⅖ 1:14¾ 1:47 | Clm 15000 | 6 | 9 | 74½ 45½ | 33 26½ | Perret C | 114 | 10.60 | 59-25 Jolly Brent117⁶½NobleSheik114¹Captain'sGalley111¾ | Second best 9
2Jun78- 6Mth yl 1 | :49⅕ 1:14¾ 1:39¾ | Clm 15000 | 1 | 8 | 89½ 6⅖ | 57½ 37¾ | Brumfield D | 115 | 14.50 | 69-32 Jolly Brent 112⁵ Raise the Blade122¾NobleSheik115⁴ | Mild rally 10
20May78- 5Mth fst 1 | :46⅗ 1:12 1:39½ | Clm 25000 | 6 | 8 | 811 812 | 711 713 | Brumfield D | b 116 | 25.30 | 64-19 Bumbe 116ⁿᵒ Solarrian 114¾ Final Pretext 116¾ | Outrun 9
4May78- 5Pim sly 1⅛ | :47⅕ 1:12¾ 1:46½ | Allowance | 5 | 6 | 67½ 612 | 614 621 | Moyers L | b 112 | 10.90 | 53-24 T. V. Crooner 122 D. Flawless 107ⁿᵒ Piscean 114¾ | Trailed 6
24Apr78- 7Pim yl 1 | :47⅗ 1:12½ 1:46½ | Allowance | 4 | 9 | 97¾ 921 | 812 816 | Edwards J W | b 114 | 2.50e | 66-22 George's Duc 107¹ Tomten 112¹¾ Bravo Johnny 112¾ | Outrun 10
14Apr78- 6Pim fst 6f | :24 :47¾ 1:12¾ | | 6 | 5 | 510 68 | 611 614 | Moyers L | b 115 | 21.50 | 70-24 Absurdly Graceful 112²¾ Cocktail Ange112²½NightAsk115¾ | Outrun 6
31Dec77- 9Lrl fst 7f | :23⅖ :47½ 1:27⅛ | Hcp—s | 1 | 8 | 86½ 64½ | 66½ 57 | Moyers L | b 114 | 4.70 | 68-23 StrngeProposl116⁵PrincAlfonso106ⁿᵒHiddnRythm115¹ | No mishap 8
15Dec77- 7Lrl my 7f | :23⅖ :47¾ 1:28⅜ | Allowance | 7 | 9 | 910 74½ | 31½ 1ʰᵈ | Moyers L | b 113 | 6.70 | 70-31 Noble Sheik 113ʰᵈ Boston Warrant 113½ D.Flawless122ⁿᵏ | Driving 9
23Nov77- 4Lrl gd 6f | :23⅕ :47⅗ 1:12⅖ | Md 25000 | 3 | 4 | 1½ 11½ | 12 1½ | Moyers L | b 118 | 7.30 | 82-18 Noble Sheik 118⁴ Before The Bench 122¹½ Its Magic 122⁵ | Driving 8

LATEST WORKOUTS   Jun 21 Mth 4f fst :50 b   Jun 11 Mth 4f fst :50   May 17 Mth 5f sly 1:05 b (d)   May 12 Mth 6f fst 1:17

It makes no sense to bypass maiden-specials for older horses. A highly satisfactory percentage of winners can be found in them by anyone who knows what to look for.

Turf Races

A grass race is likely to be playable if all the horses have already raced on that surface and one or more have demonstrated an affinity for it. *Daily Racing Form* past-performance records now differentiate turf from main-track races by including a "T" on the line that summarizes the particular past performance. Moreover, the Eastern editions of the *Form* summarize each entrant's lifetime grass-racing record, displaying the total number of starts, wins, seconds and thirds. All this helps.

Lucrative opportunities reward handicappers who take the trouble to learn the names of the sire bloodlines known for success on the turf, and supplement that fundamental knowledge with reference works such as the annual *Statistical Review and Sire Book* published by *Thoroughbred Record,* and/or the annual *Stakes Winners* and *Stallion Register* volumes published by *The Blood-Horse,* and, for deeper digging, *Sires and Dams of Stakes Winners,* which lists all such Thoroughbreds from the year 1925 onward and is published by *The Blood-Horse.*

For example, I direct attention to the third race at Monmouth Park on July 10, 1978 (see page 132). A humble claimer for $16,000 three-year-olds at one mile on the grass. On that particular infield course, one-mile races usually favor runners with early speed.

Of the starters that had previously raced on grass, L. Ryan's Ghost had displayed early foot in beating a cheap field of maidens at Atlantic City two weeks before. On the evening of July 7 (considerably less than 72 hours before this July 10 race), the gelding had been roundly trounced on the Atlantic City main track. It was difficult to expect him to recover from that effort and from the subsequent van ride and to expect him furthermore to muster the extra class that might be needed in today's circumstances. Nevertheless, he had won on grass and had to be regarded as a contender.

Raise the Blade, from the track's leading barn, had shown some promise on the turf, but seemed to lack the desired early speed. Elyse's Pride had been out of action for almost six weeks and, in any case, had shown little inclination to hold his speed all the way. Combatant had managed to finish third in two of three grass starts but seemed to suffer from the same shortness of breath as Elyse's Pride. Perhaps they would pickle each other and set things up for a late finish by Raise the

THIRD RACE	1 MILE.(turf). (1.35) CLAIMING. Purse $7,000. 3-year-olds. Weight, 121 lbs. Non-winners of two races since May 15, 3 lbs. A race, 6 lbs. Claiming price $16,000; for each; $500 to $14,000, 1 lb. (Races entered for $11,000 or less not considered.)

Monmouth
JULY 10, 1978

Value of race $7,000, value to winner $4,200, second $1,400, third $770, fourth $420, fifth $210. Mutuel pool $72,319. Trifecta Pool $84,724.

Last Raced	Horse	Eqt.A.Wt	PP	St	¼	½	¾	Str	Fin	Jockey	Cl'g Pr	Odds $1
26Jun78 1Mth1	Efrain	3 108	11	7	11	11½	13	12	12	Lee J N7	16000	10.00
3Jly78 5Mth6	Fatalist	b 3 115	3	3	10½	9hd	73	5hd	2½	Edwards J W	16000	11.90
26Jun78 2Mth2	Raise the Blade	b 3 114	7	10	62	51	2hd	25	32	MacBeth D	14000	2.60
7Jly78 6Atl6	L. Ryan's Ghost	b 3 116	6	11	7hd	7½	61	3hd	44½	Delguidice R Jr	15000	17.10
3Jly78 3Mth5	Promised Road	3 115	4	1	81½	82	51½	62½	5hd	McCauley WHt	16000	32.60
26Jun78 2Mth5	Combatant	b 3 108	10	9	41½	42	41	72	62	Mize W E7	16000	3.40
24Jun78 5Mth9	Noble Sheik	3 115	12	12	9½	6hd	8½	81	7nk	Brumfield D	16000	7.60
1Jly78 4Mth5	Hasty Brog	b 3 113	1	2	112	11hd	94	95	8¾	Wilson R	15000	52.20
31May78 6Mth4	Elyse's Pride	3 115	8	5	21	2hd	31½	4hd	96	Perret C	16000	7.80
14Jun78 7Mth6	Lucky 'N Right	b 3 115	9	8	3½	3½	103	106	105	Solomone M	16000	20.50
19Jun78 6Mth7	Burgee	b 3 115	2	4	12	12	12	12	11no	Thomas D B	16000	6.20
1Jly78 4Mth4	Sharpie	3 115	5	6	5hd	10½	114	11hd	12	Prosper G	16000	46.20

OFF AT 2:32, EDT. Start good, Won handily. Time, :24⅖, :48, 1:12¾, 1:39 Course firm.

$2 Mutuel Prices:	11–EFRAIN	22.00	13.00	6.80
	3–FATALIST		11.60	6.40
	7–RAISE THE BLADE			3.60

$2 TRIFECTA 11–3–7 PAID $1,155.20.

Ro. c, by Peace Corps—A Rose For Charles, by Beau Gar. Trainer Garcia Efrain T. Bred by Hobeau Farm Inc (Fla).

EFRAIN sprinted to the lead on the first turn, increased his margin when roused at the far turn and was not menaced in the final furlong. FATALIST, devoid of early speed, found room to rally on the hedge through the final quarter-mile and was going well at the end. RAISE THE BLADE, forwardly placed early, rallied when called on but flattened out in the final seventy yards. L. RYAN'S GHOST rallied between horses in the final furlong but was too late. COMBATANT tired in the strech. BURGEE was dull.

Blade or L. Ryan's Ghost or one of the horses that had never raced on grass before.

Among these newcomers, the one with the most conspicuously promising bloodlines was Burgee, by Hoist the Flag. The fact that he had shown absolutely nothing in his latest races on dirt would be meaningless if grass turned out to be his element. Turf-bred horses with miserable dirt-track records are forever winning at large mutuels in their first outings on grass. So Burgee had to be accepted as a contender.

The other debutant worth noticing was Efrain, racing in the colors of his breeder, the celebrated Hobeau Farm, the New York division of whose string is superintended by Allen Jerkens. Efrain's sire had been a good grass runner but had not been at stud long enough to show whether he could transmit that talent to his get. On the other hand, the maternal grandsire, Beau Gar, had already begotten several good grass horses. Since breaking his maiden with a display of sprinter's speed on

June 26, Efrain had worked out in excellent time on the Monmouth grass. This horse was definitely a contender.

In the paddock, Efrain behaved like a colt who had come to hand and was ready to demonstrate his quality. He was alert, lively and unfussed. Moreover, his feet were the broad, low-heeled, flat ones so often associated with grass talent. None of the other contenders looked nearly so prosperous. A couple were sweating heavily, as if apprehensive. Burgee had a hangdog look. Efrain was 10 to 1. He won like 1 to 10.

Stakes and Handicaps

Purists will be offended because I lump all handicap races and all the great stakes under one heading. I do so because I think that these aristocratic races offer relatively few betting opportunities. They are delightful to watch, of course. They bring together the best horses in the country, or the best horses at the particular track—animals so well matched that prediction is extra hazardous. In the year of a Secretariat, a Forego, a Kelso, a Count Fleet or a Citation, it is possible to make out nicely on some of the more important events. But most of the other name races simply are too close to bother with.

Overnight handicaps are not much better for the player. In these, top allowance-grade horses compete under handicap conditions—with the weights assigned by the racing secretary according to his evaluation of the entrants' recent performances. As might be expected, the problem is whether the class horse is in good enough condition to win at the particular weights and under the stress of the pace at which the procession is likely to go. Sometimes there is no way of telling whether one of the horses actually *does* have a class advantage. These are tough nuts to crack, and playing the favorite is no way out: it wins a third of the time but the player ends on the losing side of the ledger. Unless, of course, he plays odds-on favorites to place—risking dollars to win nickels.

Starter Handicaps

These are fascinating races. Eligibility is limited to horses that have started at a specified claiming price at some time during their careers, or during a fixed period of time. Weights are assigned by the racing secretary according to his estimate of the horses' abilities. Or the race might be called a "starter allowance," with weights prescribed according to number or value of recent victories.

In no other form of Thoroughbred racing do the maneuverings of trainers become more noticeable than in these regattas. The race may be limited to animals that have run in $3,500 claiming company, yet the field is sure to include several that usually bear price tags as high as $7,500, their $3,500 days long behind them. In fact, trainers have been known to enter $7,500 horses in $3,500 claiming races for no other reason than to make them eligible for subsequent starter handicaps and starter allowance races. (At some tracks, horses cannot be claimed on the first day of the season, enabling a barn to drop an expensive horse into a cheap race and qualify it for later starter handicaps without fear of losing it.)

Certain horses seem unable to win anything but these starter races. They lose when they run in straight claimers for lower purses, but they perk up when the bigger money is on the line. At Aqueduct, many insiders with a nose for large mutuel prices take it as a rule of thumb that the best bet in a starter handicap is the horse that has won such a race in the past, regardless of how poorly he may have been doing in his most recent outings. It is a fact that such horses jump up and win these races—often winning two or three a season without accomplishing much in any other kind of race. Their success can be taken as evidence that their trainers know how to get them ready for a spot without advertising the readiness in the past-performance records.

Optional Claimers

In these races an animal may be entered to be claimed or not, depending on the preference of its management. If it wins when *not* entered to be claimed it is penalized by being declared ineligible for another optional race of the same grade at the same meeting, except if entered to be claimed. Also, the horse's eligibility for future allowance races is affected: The track usually credits its victory as having taken place in an allowance race! But if it *is* entered to be claimed in the optional affair that it wins, it is charged only with a victory in a claiming race.

By and large, these optional races are more difficult to handicap than straight claimers, but are not always as obscure as allowance races. To a player who uses result charts, they pose no special difficulty beyond that of riffling through the charts to see what the past-performance record actually represents. Sometimes the past-performance records suffice, the class of the animals being apparent in the claiming prices and results of their recent efforts.

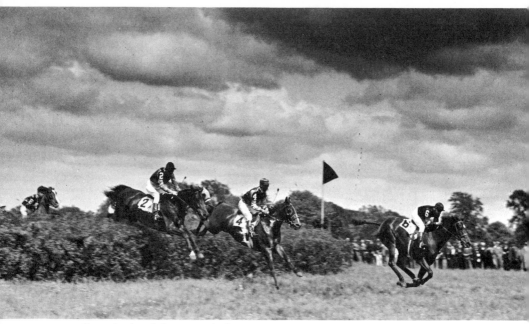

Over the brush in a steeplechase race.   UPI PHOTO

Jump Races

Hurdle races are run over low obstacles. Steeplechase races involve higher fences and water hazards. Both types are extremely dangerous for the horses and their riders and far too unpredictable for betting purposes. They are great fun to watch (except when some poor rider gets thrown onto his skull), but are absolute booby traps for the players. The reason should be obvious—the best horse in the race might meet with interference from a fallen horse, or might fall itself. Flat racing is tough enough. Jumps present the handicapper with an extra unknown factor. Only an incurable gambler risks important amounts of money in such circumstances.

Roll Up Your Sleeves

So much for playable-beatable races. Now for a detailed review of the methods whereby experts play them and beat them. In the next eleven chapters we shall explore matters such as distance, current condition, class, age, sex, consistency, weight, speed, pace, the trainer, the rider, special handicapping angles, the paddock and post parade.

The chapters deal with these factors not in order of importance but in a sequence likely to be most convenient for the reader. Indeed, it is impossible to say which handicapping factor is most important of all. Importance varies according to the particular race and the particular horse. But no factor stands alone. Each affects the others, and must be considered with the others in mind.

8
The Distance Factor

The late Robert Saunders Dowst achieved prominence in the late thir-
ties when his articles in *Esquire* and other magazines of mass circulation explained some of the rudiments of handicapping to the natives.
Dowst enjoyed his fame but found that it had its price. Within a couple
of years after he revealed to the general public that any dodo could
make big money by betting on highly consistent horses, the system
stopped winning.

It stopped winning mainly because the horses were yielding lower
mutuel prices than ever. Dowst's grateful followers had not only been
betting the boodle but spreading the word. Another reason why the
system stopped winning was that a slightly lower percentage of the
consistent horses was finishing first. As if their trainers were rebelling
against the low odds and waiting for more lucrative opportunities.

Dowst himself denied, and rightly so, that any important number of
trainers were deliberately stiffing the best, most consistent horses in
racing rather than win at low odds. He mused that maybe the game
was changing a little. It certainly was. His system had become public
property when the sport was in transition to its present assembly-line
state. The practice of racing Thoroughbreds into shape, long resisted
by conscientious horsemen, was becoming more commonplace.
Hence, an animal's record of consistency (an unusually high percentage of winning or in-the-money starts) could no longer be taken as
absolute evidence that the creature was in condition to vie for the
marbles every time it went to the post. The kind of horse that might

have won a third of its starts in 1935 was unlikely to win more than a quarter of them in 1941, its handlers having discovered the boons and benefits of letting it get some of its training exercise in actual competition. While losing, that is.

From time to time during the years that have elapsed since Dowst's mild embarrassment, I have heard racetrackers cite his system as evidence that it doesn't pay to share the goodies of the game with members of the public. All that happens is that the odds go down, they say. And then, when the odds go down, the horsemen change their methods and the handicapping system or angle or theory becomes obsolete.

Could be. But I doubt it. I especially doubt it as far as the substance of the present chapter is concerned. What is revealed herein about the problem of a Thoroughbred's suitability to the distance of its race is unknown to most players of the game and neglected by many of the few who know it. If hundreds of thousands of players suddenly become aware of it, and begin betting accordingly, and boasting of the results, certain winning horses unquestionably will pay lower odds than before. But the game will not change as a result. The suitability of a Thoroughbred to the distance of its race is a product of heredity and training and cannot be turned on or off like a spigot.

The Law of the Yardstick

Most published material on the art of picking winners urges the reader to avoid betting on sprinters in route races and routers in sprints. The sprint is defined as a race of seven furlongs or less. All other distances are regarded as routes.

To classify an animal as a sprinter or a router, the player usually examines its record to see the kind of races in which it competes most often. More sophisticated analysts look for the kind of races in which it has won or finished close. Few players carry the investigation further. Which is a primary reason for the dismal regularity with which they lose.

Distance is a crucial factor in the training and racing of horses. Confronted with the problem of finding races that his livestock can win, the professional horseman takes pains to learn the *exact* distances best suited to their individual physiques, running styles and temperaments. The wise handicapper is no less painstaking about the distance preferences of the horses on which he bets.

The winning range of most horses is severely limited. If its trainer points at a four-year-old and declares that it can win at any distance in any company, you should remove your hat: You are in the presence of an all-time great Thoroughbred. The $7,000 gelding that beats its own kind every now and then at six furlongs may never be better than second best against the same company at seven furlongs. The slightly sturdier horse able to win at a mile and a sixteenth may lack the zip to beat a similar field at a mile, even though the half-furlong difference between the two races is only a matter of 110 yards. The run-of-the-mill Thoroughbred that steps out of its own distance category and wins is either the beneficiary of freakish good luck or enjoys a pronounced class advantage over the animals it beats at the new distance.

Many years ago, one of the world's foremost authorities on Thoroughbred racing and breeding, Peter Burrell, director of Britain's National Stud, summarized the facts:

"Races are run at all distances from five furlongs to two and a half miles, requiring different types of horse, the sprinter being as different from the stayer as a dairy cow from a beef cow.

"So high is the standard required today at each distance that the individual horse has become specialized for that particular distance, and we must regard the horse which is top class at all distances as something of a freak . . .

"It is not difficult to breed sprinters, but it is an undisputed fact that the more speed one breeds into a horse the less distance he stays, and with the stayers—also a type that breeds true—one can breed them to stay further, but they then begin to lack the turn of speed so essential to the final dash to the winning post.

"Our task would be much simpler if all two-year-old races were run at five to six furlongs and all races for older horses at a mile. After two hundred and fifty years we might and should have produced a definite type. Instead of which, we struggle to produce a sprinter with more stamina, a stayer with more speed, and in between find our classic horse—bred for more and more speed—failing to go the distance."

Because all that has been true for generations, its meaning has been incorporated into a maxim well known on the backstretch of any Thoroughbred track: "Every horse's best distance can be measured with a yardstick."

The player who accepts that truth and puts it to work for him has launched himself toward success at the races. *He stops betting on horses entered at unsuitable distances.* And he clears the air for himself in numerous other ways. Knowledge of the distance factor is essential to any workable understanding of other vital matters such as pace, current condition and the maneuverings of trainers.

How Trainers Use Distance

If you open any copy of *Daily Racing Form* it will take you only a few seconds to find a six-furlong horse. Chances are that its only victories have been at that exact distance. Several weeks ago, let us say, it won when entered to be claimed for $5,000. Seven days later, it ran against $6,000 claimers at the same distance and lost, tiring in the stretch. It probably was slightly outclassed, and may also have lost its keen edge in the exertion of winning its previous race. Ten days later it was back in another $5,000 claimer at its favorite distance and finished a well-beaten fifth. Clearly, it had gone off form.

The trainer rested it for almost a month and brought it back against $6,000 stock at the usual distance. It led to the half-mile call, pooped out and staggered home seventh. Today it again is entered for $6,000, but in a mile race. What goes on?

The animal has run the mile before and has never had a thing left in the stretch. It has never even finished in the money at seven furlongs. Why is the trainer bothering to enter it at a mile today?

Two reasons. First and foremost, the brief layoff seems to have refreshed the horse. It showed a nice lick of early speed in its last race. It may soon be able to win, especially if it runs against its own kind— $5,000 horses—at its own distance. The trainer evidently believes that it needs another tune-up, a "tightener." To make that tightener a mile race may help the horse's condition by requiring it to gallop farther than it likes. Which brings us to the second reason for entering it at the unsuitable distance.

The trainer does not expect to win today's race and has no intention of taxing the horse with an all-out try. Obviously, he would be pleased if the horse took an early lead and managed to hold it all the way to the finish wire. Pleased? Astonished! But he would strangle the jockey with his bare hands if the boy whipped the horse into a state of exhaustion just to finish third or fourth. The trainer's principal interest is to prepare for a race scheduled to take place five or six days from now— a $5,000 claimer at three quarters of a mile. If the beast finishes seventh today, as expected, and loses the predictable six or eight lengths in the final stages, many members of the crowd will refuse to bet on it next week. The odds will be better. The trainer and his employer, the owner, will like that.

The trainer could have entered the horse in a six-furlong scamper on today's program. The race could have been an effective tightener. But the horse might have come close to winning. Its improving form would have been too apparent. When it went for the marbles next week, the odds would be anemic. The trainer and owner would not like that.

What I am getting at here is that the player who bets on a horse entered at an unsuitable distance must assume not only that the horse will violate its own nature and win, but that the trainer will violate *his* nature and go for broke. That is too much to assume.

In virtually every race, most of the entrants have negligible chances to win. Of these all-but-certain losers, some are entered at an uncomfortable distance. Their trainers are darkening their form while doing what they can to improve it. Stayers are encouraged to develop early speed by chasing fleet sprinters out of the starting gate. Sprinters develop needed stamina by chugging behind stayers in the final stages of route races.

How, then, do experts tell if a horse is entered at a suitable distance? Let's see.

The Right Distance

The conservative handicapper is more likely to win than his reckless companion. But it is possible to become too conservative. For example, it is possible to exaggerate the importance of the distance factor beyond all reasonable limits, refusing to bet on any horse that has not already *won* at today's exact distance. Certainly, if a horse has won several times at the distance, its qualifications in this department can be taken for granted. But to eliminate a horse only because it has never won at the distance may be costly.

To illustrate, let us compare the recent races of two animals entered in a $15,000 claimer at seven furlongs.

Horse "A"

6f	23⅕	46¾	1.11⅗	Clm 15,000	4	8	7^5	6^5	5^4	3^4
6f	22⅗	46⅕	1.11¾	Clm 15,000	2	9	8^7	8^6	5^4	3^3
7f	23⅗	46⅘	1.25	Clm 15,000	3	6	5^7	4^4	2^2	$1^{1/2}$

Horse "B"

6f	22⅘	45⅘	1.10⅗	Allowance	3	4	4^2	5^3	6^4	7^5
6f	22⅘	46	1.11⅘	Clm 16,500	1	1	1^2	1^4	1^3	1^{11}
7f	23	46⅕	1.24⅕	Clm 17,000	3	1	1^3	$1^{1/2}$	1no	4^3

Horse "B" is plainly the faster, classier animal. To discard it from consideration because it failed to carry its speed all the way in its only seven-furlong attempt would be a grave mistake. It set the pace in that race but was hooked at the quarter pole by another $17,000 horse (the result chart may show that the other horse was actually a $20,000 one), and continued gamely into the stretch before fading. In a six-furlong race, "B" would be odds-on against "A" on grounds of class, speed, pace, whatever. Its loss to allowance horses can undoubtedly be forgiven.

As to "A," it plainly qualifies for today's distance. Six furlongs apparently is too little ground for it, but it seems able to lumber into contention during the stretch run of a seven-furlong event. At least, it can do that when opposing $15,000 horses incapable of "B's" speed. If "B" is in shape today it should win in a walk over "A."

Problems of this kind are most perplexing early in the year, especially in races for three-year-olds. Many of them have not raced often enough to be ruled out on grounds of inability to win at the distance. The handicapper needs to develop criteria other than previous victories at the distance—unless he wants sorrow.

Later in the year, or in races for four-year-olds and older, the problem subsides. Unless the race is for what my friend Howard Rowe calls "giraffes," several entrants will already have won at the distance. And among the others that have run the distance without winning, several will have covered the ground swiftly enough, and against sufficiently good opposition, to qualify as contenders.

Make Your Own Guidelines

If a horse has already won a race of today's distance, its eligibility as a contender can be accepted. Other questions about its chances can be deferred until the player is ready to consider matters such as form, class, age, sex, consistency, weight, speed, pace.

Many handicappers work that way, one step at a time, systematizing their methods to avoid confusion. Others prefer to take larger bites. If the horse has won or run close-up in a race of today's distance, these players ask additional questions:

1. **Against what kind of animals did the horse do it?**
2. **When did he do it?**
3. **How authoritatively did he do it?**

In attending to such questions, the player recognizes the interrelationships between distance and class, form and pace. He disposes immediately of chores that otherwise would have to be performed later. He gets the job done more quickly.

Mrs. Richard C. DuPont goes to the winners' circle with her wonderful Kelso and a happy Arcaro after the 1960 Jockey Club Gold Cup. WIDE WORLD PHOTOS

Bold Ruler, a good middle-distance runner, beats General Duke in the 1957 Flamingo Stakes at Hialeah. Eddie Arcaro looks over his shoulder while handriding the colt that later became one of the great sires of modern times. UPI PHOTO

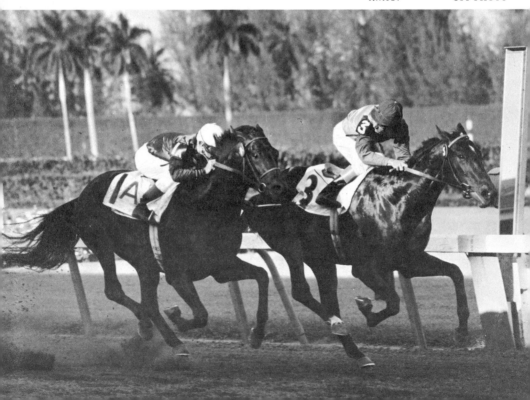

The reader's own approach will depend mainly on his personal tastes and partly on how much experience he has had with past-performance records. As long as he understands and applies the principles set forth in these pages, his eventual method will be as good as any other.

Before deciding *how* to analyze the distance factor, the reader might want to consider whether to dispose of it at the very beginning of his handicapping procedure.

Should Distance Come First?

The Compleat Horseplayer and *Ainslie on Jockeys* recommend a selection method in which the distance factor is handled before the other fundamentals. Excellent results may also be attained by starting with current condition, class, consistency, speed or pace. Since the fundamentals of handicapping are intertwined, the player who deals with one of them must at least touch on some of the others at the same time. Furthermore, no matter where the handicapping process starts, it ends by covering the same ground.

I prefer to take up distance before all other factors because I have found that it saves time. Using fairly simple standards to determine horses' suitability to the distance of today's race, the player often is able to eliminate as many as half of the entrants. This sharply reduces the remaining work. To be sure, similar savings of time are achieved by starting with the factor of current condition. Many experts manage to attend to condition and distance with one sweep of the eye, having been in the game long enough to develop that kind of ease.

For readers who are not already set in their handicapping ways, I should like to propose that they plan to dispose of distance first. However, I shall describe the various methods in such a way that the reader may choose the ones he prefers, and fit them into any sequence he likes.

The Conservative Approach

Some experts refuse to bet on a slow or inconsistent horse, even when it seems to have a clear edge over the other nonentities in its race. These conservatives reason that it is bootless to try to pick the least unreliable animal in an unreliable field. In this same spirit, they bypass a race unless some entrant has already run the exact distance in respectable fashion.

What's more, they never bet that any horse, however good it may be, will be able to do something today that it has not tried to do in the past. They refuse, in other words, to risk their money on a horse running at an unfamiliar distance.

They have a point. They avoid many a loser that way. They also steer themselves off many a winner. More relaxed players do quite nicely with carefully selected bets on cheap races, horses that have never raced before, and horses running at new distances.

Which approach is best? A quick answer would be fraudulent. It all depends on the psyche and talent of the individual player. Those unwilling or unable to dig deeply and imaginatively into the records are best advised to work the conservative side of the street. This might also be the best plan for beginners. As experience accumulates, greater flexibility becomes possible and profitable.

Whether the expert be conservative or not, his study of the distance factor is the very keystone of the work he does on races for two-year-olds. The following review of the best approaches to that problem shows how some players win by playing relatively few such races, and how others win while playing many more.

Two-Year-Olds and Distance

The most cautious approach to the distance factor in juvenile races is this:

1. Consider no two-year-old for play unless (a) it and each of its rivals has already raced at today's distance and (b) the horse has managed to run within two seconds of the track record for the distance.

That rule restricts play to certain high-class allowance and stakes races and a very occasional maiden-special-weights affair. It bypasses the hazards of guessing how youngsters will perform at five and a half furlongs if they have never tried to race farther than five. It protects the player from the first-time starters that sometimes upset the dope and win at long prices. It forbids bets on other, more highly touted debutantes that go to the post as favorites and lose.

The rule requiring a previous speed rating of 90 or better (no worse than two seconds slower than the track record for the distance) guarantees that the player will risk money only on the best two-year-olds around.

A reader attracted to that method will bet on few two-year-olds and seldom will collect a large mutuel payoff. If the remainder of his handicapping procedure is in keeping with his approach to the distance factor, he will hit a high percentage of winners. But he will pass race after race in which other smart, slightly less cautious players find excellent wagers.

To increase his betting opportunities without exposing himself to accusations of recklessness, he might amend his procedure slightly:

2. After making sure that all horses in the race for two-year-olds have already run at today's exact distance, consider only those that have earned a speed rating of 85 or better at the distance.

He now will be able to play additional maiden and allowance sprints. But he will continue to detour races in which some of the horses are strangers to the distance.

A somewhat less conservative outlook permits many experts to cash a satisfactory percentage of bets on juvenile races in which some of the horses have not yet tried the distance:

3. Consider no two-year-old for play unless it has earned a speed rating of at least 87 at today's exact distance.

Observe that nothing is said about whether other horses in the race have run the distance. Yet the method is quite safe. At most tracks, any two-year-old that has traveled today's distance rapidly enough to earn a speed rating of 87 (2⅗ seconds short of the track record) is talented enough to be conceded an excellent chance against first-time starters or other animals which have never tackled the distance before. The horse not only is swift but has undoubtedly profited from the experience of testing its speed in an earlier race at the distance.

If the horse with the previous figure of 87 or better is being asked to face a well-publicized first-time starter from a leading barn and sired by a Bold Ruler, the cautious player may choose to pass the race, depending on his assessment of other factors.

A player who wants to cash in on some of the plausible betting opportunities presented by first-starters and other animals that have never tried today's distance must be prepared for more than occasional losses. If he is essentially a careful type, he may find the following approach comfortable:

4. A well-bred first-time starter from a leading barn qualifies for consideration if (a) it has been working out frequently and rapidly, (b) it is to be ridden by a leading jockey, and (c) none of its rivals has been able to earn a speed rating of 80 or better at today's distance.

In this case the player establishes that none of the horses that has tried the distance is any great shakes at it. The trainer of the high-priced newcomer seems to have found an ideal spot for its debut. Circumstances of this kind arise quite frequently in maiden-special-weights races. The first-starter usually goes to the post as favorite when facing animals that have shown no real speed. The favoritism is deserved.

5. A juvenile that has raced before but has not raced at today's distance qualifies for consideration if (a) no other animal in the race has demonstrated high-class speed at the distance and (b) the horse's races at a distance not more than half a furlong shorter than today's have indicated real ability.

This is not as elaborate as it may sound. If a two-year-old has never traveled six furlongs in competition, one would hesitate to back it against a competitor that has already shown authentic talent at the distance by earning a speed rating of 88 or thereabouts. But if no such speedster is in the race, the horse may be worth a closer look. If it ran at least as fast at five and a half furlongs as any other horse in today's race, it becomes quite interesting. And it qualifies for the most serious consideration if its record shows that it was able to stay fairly close to the pace of the shorter races before *gaining ground in the homestretch.* Whether it won or lost the races, it looks very much like an animal that will be comfortable at the extra sixteenth of a mile. If its own speed ratings at the shorter distance were genuinely high, it may be a splendid risk today.

Why Use Speed Ratings?

The use of speed ratings to determine a Thoroughbred's aptitude for the distance of its race is standard practice, even among many experts who deride speed handicapping and rely mainly on analyses of class and form. The alternative to handling the distance factor in terms of speed ratings is to require the horse's record to show that, regardless of time or speed, the candidate has managed to finish reasonably close to the winner in a race contested over today's distance by a field whose class was not seriously inferior to today's.

In handicapping races for two-year-olds, it is immensely difficult to solve the distance problem *except* by means of speed ratings or actual clockings. Anyone who tries to figure out the class of a maiden-special race for two-year-olds has nothing to go on except the time in which it was run. The same is true of a juvenile allowance race. All that is known about the horses is that they are previous winners of maiden-specials or allowance affairs. The fastest are best. By the end of the season, the slower ones will be running in claimers.

And what about the distance factor in juvenile claiming races? Suppose the player is the less conservative kind who bets on some of the slower two-year-olds and wins at it? How does he do it?

6. In any two-year-old race, if none of the entrants has run the distance rapidly enough to earn a speed rating of 80 or higher, consider betting on any animal that has earned a rating at least 2 points higher than that of any of its rivals.

Every day during the spring and summer, maiden-specials, maiden claimers and straight claimers for two-year-olds are won by horses whose best previous speed ratings have been in the 70's. It is possible to get a satisfactory percentage of winners in these slower races by confining one's action to entrants that have shown slightly more speed than their opponents. Naturally, the player has to be a shrewd analyst of current condition, trainers, jockeys, and—as the season progresses —class. But the distance factor can be attended to by means of speed ratings. Later on, I shall discuss the computation of track variants, which modify running times or speed ratings to compensate for the effects of changes in the inherent speed of racing strips.

The reader who surveys the foregoing information will find in it all he needs for his study of the distance factor in juvenile races. He can tighten or loosen any of the requirements, according to his own preferences and the results he achieves. During the early part of the year, before the youngsters are stretched out to six furlongs and beyond, he will find that his solution of the distance problem is almost all he needs to do about handicapping the race. In these short sprints for two-year-olds, time—speed—is all-important. And time, of course, is what the player uses to decide whether any two-year-old is qualified to run the distance of its race.

Races for older horses are something else entirely. Class distinctions, current condition, weight and pace now become more important. Many experts refuse to look at speed ratings on older horses, even in connection with the distance factor. Others find the ratings convenient indicators of whether a horse can get today's distance in reasonably good time, quite apart from the effects of class, condition, pace and weight. Still others, as we shall see later, do *all* their handicapping in terms of speed.

Older Horses and Distance

In trying to decide whether an animal aged three or more is suited to the distance of his race, the most cautious players of the game often operate on the following line:

1. A horse qualifies if (a) it has won a race of this exact distance, or has finished close to the winner in respectable time and (b) the race took place this season.

Many practitioners of this theory add the further condition that the horse's good race should have been against animals not greatly inferior to those it faces today. In that way they manage to lop off obviously outclassed horses. I mention this merely to suggest that it can be done, but I ask the reader to go through the chapter on class before deciding whether he wants to keep his distance and class studies separated or not.

The phrase "close to the winner," as used in the above rule, usually means a finish not more than three lengths behind. Some experts prefer a finish within two lengths. Others, anxious to qualify more horses on the distance factor, ask only that the animal has run fourth or better. Still others want the horse to have come very close to winning in a cheaper race, but are lenient about its finishing position in a race of higher quality.

As to the term, "respectable time," the following speed ratings can be accepted as adequate, subject to slight variations which arise from unique conditions at the individual track:

90—Sprints for animals of handicap and stakes quality. (In weighing the distance factor in terms of speed, a sprint should be defined as any race run around no more than one turn. At some major tracks, this will include distances up to and including a mile. At others, where there is no mile chute at the head of the backstretch, the longest race run around one turn may be at six and a half or seven furlongs.)

88—High-grade allowance sprints.

85—Handicaps and stakes run around two turns. (If a race is at a mile and an eighth or longer, many experts disregard speed ratings entirely. They evaluate the horse's suitability in terms of the class and stamina it displayed in previous efforts at such distances.)

80—High-grade allowance routes, lesser allowance sprints and sprints for claimers valued above $7,500.

78—Cheap claiming sprints.
73—Route races for better claimers.
69—Route races for claimers valued at $4,000 or less.

A player who tosses out all horses that fail to meet those requirements is well on his way to sharing the success enjoyed by arch-conservative handicappers. He passes race after race. He frequently tosses out the eventual winner of an apparently playable race, but is so strict about other fundamentals of handicapping that he often saves his neck by eliminating the losers at later stages of the work, and passing the race altogether. If some losers qualify on the distance factor, they fail to meet his rigid requirements as to class, condition, consistency, weights, running styles, trainers or jockeys. He may get less action than he might, and far less than most players want, but a handicapper of this kind gets his kicks from winning. Action means nothing to him.

The main flaw in his handling of the distance problem is its requirement that the horse's qualifying race be a recent one. To be sure, a good race last year is no guarantee that a horse will repeat the performance this year. Injuries, illness and overwork make many of last year's $10,000 horses into $3,500 ones by May of this year. But problems of that kind can be surmounted by a player who wants to catch some of the winners that the more cautious player misses. For example:

2. A horse qualifies at today's distance if (a) it has ever finished as close as fourth, or within two lengths of a winner, in a race of today's exact distance at a major track, and (b) it has earned a respectable speed rating at the distance at some time within the past year at a major track, and (c) its record indicates that it may still be able to run well at the distance.

When handicapping horses aged four or more, the requirement of a mere close-up finish at the distance is terribly lenient. Any fully mature horse that cannot meet that requirement is undoubtedly entered at the wrong distance. For that matter, many mature horses that satisfy the rule are also at the wrong distance: a router sometimes produces sufficient steam in the stretch to finish close to the winner of a six-furlong race. But he is still a router, and hardly an ideal choice in a sprint. However, the two additional parts of the rule tend to weed out such duds. So, for that matter, does the common sense of the player. If he sees that most of the races and all of the victories listed in the past-performance record of a mature horse were at distances more than a furlong longer or shorter than today's race, he can be reasonably sure that the horse is out of its element today.

The loose requirement of a close-up finish is most helpful in handicapping lightly raced three-year-olds. Every season, scores of races are won at handsome odds by improving three-year-olds that have never won at the distance before. Their victories occur not only in claiming races but in allowance events for some of the snazzier young horses in the business. Part of the trick of catching these up-and-comers is to give them credit for even a mediocre previous race at the distance.

The notion that a horse can qualify for further attention if it logged good time at the distance within the past year could be dangerous, but need not be. For example, if the horse has declined very much in class since that ancient race, or if it has been running badly or infrequently since the race, the player has good reason to suspect that it has gone sour. He therefore would disqualify it on grounds of form or class, either at this stage of the handicapping or later.

But the idea pays off at the mutuel windows in the late spring and early summer. At that time of year, a rigidly cautious player often discards an animal for failure to show a good recent race at the distance —even though it is perfectly ready to win today. It may be a nice little miler that has been campaigning at tracks where mile events are not programmed. Or it may have been resting for the winter. Its races this year may all have been at distances other than the mile. But if the horse's form has been improving (regardless of whether it has been winning or not), the trainer may be ready to crack down today.

If the approach embodied in this three-part rule is followed alertly, it can be counted on to qualify the ultimate winners of most playable races, and to disqualify a high proportion of the losers. It therefore clears the decks for concentrated study of the genuine contenders.

Older Horses at New Distances

At the beginning of each season and, to a lesser extent, throughout the remainder of the racing year, one encounters races in which three-year-olds attempt to run an altogether new distance. The safest approach is to bypass the race. Alternatively, one can handle the distance factor by methods similar to those employed in evaluating two-year-old races. Preference would go to horses with the best previous records and/or the most successful trainers and/or recent performances suggesting that the new distance might be comfortable for them.

Distance and Speed Charts

As readers of my earlier books are aware, I advocate pace handicapping, in the sense that I recommend inclusion of pace analysis in the player's methods. Some dyed-in-the-wool enthusiasts of pace and speed charts pay no attention to the distance factor, relying on the charted numbers to compensate for all unknowns. But others, whether they favor pace analyses or speed-weight formulas, may be interested in trying to profit from the distance factor. That is, they may want to experiment with the kind of pace handicapping or speed handicapping that applies pace or speed figures only to horses judged suitable to the distance of today's race.

To work in that fashion with pace or speed charts, it is highly advisable to use races that the horse has run at today's exact distance either on today's track or at a sister track on the same circuit. While some players profess to be able to make profits by pace-rating races run at different tracks, I have yet to see any evidence to support the claim.

Accordingly, the reader who contemplates trying a realistic form of pace handicapping (or some down-to-earth version of speed handicapping), should know now that he will be unable to work effectively with horses that have not run reasonably good races at today's exact distance on today's circuit. In my opinion, the races bypassed for lack of such information are more than compensated for by a higher percentage of winning selections.

Naturally, more on speed and pace handicapping will appear in the appropriate chapters.

Sprinters in Route Races

Once in a while, a horse that has never run farther than six furlongs leads from wire to wire in a race at a mile and an eighth. A carefully observant player can sometimes foresee the possibility. It arises most often in route races among animals with no inclination to go to the front in the early stages. If the sprinter is the kind that has been taking the lead in its own shorter races and tiring in the stretch, if not earlier, it probably lacks the stamina to maintain the long, early lead it will enjoy today. But if it is the type that usually is fourth or fifth or sixth at the half-mile call in sprints and seldom quits in the stretch, it may be an excellent bet against today's plodders. Accustomed as it is to a much faster early pace than is characteristic in route races, it will undoubtedly take the lead immediately. If the jockey is good at racing

Count Turf and Conn McCreary fool them all, winning the 1951 Kentucky Derby.   **UPI PHOTO**

Lee Town, a sprinter, leads the 1962 Kentucky Derby at the first turn. The distance was too much for him and he finished far back.   **UPI PHOTO**

horses to conserve their strength, and if the horse does not drop dead of surprise at being out in front so soon, it may last to the wire. The player should not discard it on grounds that it fails to satisfy his distance requirements. Not, that is, unless he is sure that something else in the field has enough foot to catch the sprinter in the late stages.

Routers in Sprint Races

Every spring, last year's stakes and handicap champions begin tuning up for the season's big money races. For many of them, the process includes entry in an allowance race at six furlongs. They usually lose. They lose because they are out for exercise and because they are unsuited to such short distances. Unless the confirmed distance runner entered in a sprint has shown pronounced early speed in its own good races, and unless its opponents in the tune-up are dismally inferior sprinters, the race is not worth a risk.

Among Thoroughbreds of less than championship quality, very much the same facts apply. An animal that wins at a mile and an eighth is odds-on to be out only for conditioning purposes any time it goes to the post in a sprint.

9

The Condition Factor

Of all handicapping problems, none is more challenging than the riddle of condition—the form or fitness or sharpness or readiness of Thoroughbreds. In a representative field of nine horses, three or four may be in such dull form that even a novice can see the signs in their records. But the other entrants are likely to be a puzzlement.

Is the class horse in good enough shape to stand off its sharper, cheaper rivals? Can last week's victor do it again, or did the winning effort blunt its edge? Should one expect improvement from the animal that has been running closer and closer to the pace, or is it past the peak of its form cycle? Can Trainer Doe's gelding return from its six-week layoff and get the job done on workouts alone? Will the speed horse from Santa Anita show its California form in this, its first Maryland race?

The process of attempting to answer such questions is indispensable to success at the track. Knowledge of form prevents the astute player from betting on certain false favorites whose recent good races fool the rest of the crowd. The same knowledge enables him to back animals that win at long prices after apparently poor recent races. Yet, no matter how astute he may be, the subtle complications of the condition factor continue to challenge his best efforts. For every bet he loses through racing luck or a misjudged ride or an error in evaluating the class of a horse, he can expect to lose two because of surprises in the form department.

Most of these surprises derive from the very nature of the Thoroughbred. Contrary to the wishes of every loser, horses are not machines.

They are highly sensitive beings, very much alive. Each is an individual, responsive in its own special way to changes in the weather, delays in feeding or watering, the moods of its handlers, the tensions of other horses, the commotion of the racetrack audience, the discomfort of an aching joint or muscle, the sight, sound or impact of the whip.

A horse's record may proclaim him the class of his field and sharp as a knife. He may breeze through his last pre-race workout in smashing time, without drawing a deep breath. He may eat everything in sight. His coat may shine with the deep gloss of health. But he may take it into his head not to race. His reluctance may be so evident in the paddock and walking ring that sophisticated players immediately cancel any plans they may have had to bet on him. Or his mood may sour when he steps on a sandwich wrapper while trotting to the post, or when one of the assistant starters grabs him too unceremoniously, or when an adjoining horse brushes or bumps him.

Or he may go to the post as spry as can be, and run his race, and be beaten to the wire by a crippled old hide whose chronic disabilities vanish for a minute or two in the warmth of the afternoon and the heat of competition.

Hidden Form

Other reversals of form are more apparent than real. They have less to do with the nature of the Thoroughbred than with the nature of man. From time immemorial, most trainers have regarded it as their sacred duty to conceal or obscure the improving form of a horse. In the old days, when the sport was unsupervised, the object was exclusively to fool everybody and collect big odds. Nowadays, when racing is relatively well policed and detailed past-performance records are published for all to see, trainers have more trouble fooling the experts, but most of them continue to try. Moreover, the game has developed in such a way as to perpetuate the ancient practice of darkening a horse's form.

The demand for horseflesh with which to fill nine races a day is so urgent that only the most aristocratic and/or affluent stables are allowed to condition their animals carefully. All the others are expected to race the livestock as often as possible. This means entering unready horses. Or, as the saying goes, "racing a horse into shape."

The trainer does not live who has not been called into the racing secretary's office for a favor. "I need to fill the fourth race day after tomorrow," goes the request. "How about helping me and putting your filly in there?"

Stable space is hard to get. The uncooperative barn may find itself without house room at next year's meeting. So the typical response from the trainer is, "Sure! Glad to oblige! Any time!"

A less typical answer: "She isn't ready for a race. Needs a few more workouts. But if you say so, I'll enter her and let her work out in public!"

A veteran trainer comments, "Of course we darken a horse's form. How can we help it? How can a horse fail to look bad when it's not in condition to look good? Two or three bad races and it begins to improve, which is when you have to start worrying. You've paid eight or ten grand for the horse and nursed the soreness out of it and you're just beginning to run it into good condition and—bam!—some guy claims it away from you before it's paid for all the time and effort and fees and food you've invested. You've got to try to protect yourself against that, while waiting for it to get in shape to steal a purse.

"If the horse has a pretty fair reputation around the track, you have no choice but to run it over its head—at the wrong distances and at higher claiming prices than anyone in his right mind would pay. And you put stumblebum riders up, who can't handle the horse. And it loses so bad that a lot of people begin to believe you when you cry that something is wrong with it.

"Like as not, the horse is your main meal ticket," he continues. "When it wins, you want it to win at a price. The best way to build the price is to enter it against cheap ones of its own class *before* it is ready to win. Every time you do that, you take an awful chance on having it claimed. But let's say you have the guts to try. You tell the boy not to punish the horse because you've got a better spot picked out for later on. So he lets it pretty much alone and it finishes like sixth. Sure as God made little green mushmelons, half the wise guys in the park notice that the horse picked up five lengths in the backstretch before running into a blind switch on the turn. When next week comes, the horse goes off at 5 to 1 instead of the 20 you've been looking for. Don't let anyone tell you that this is an easy business."

Efforts to inflate the mutuel odds by hiding a horse's improving condition are attributed mainly to smaller stables. But, as I have indicated before, all but the most exclusive barns race their animals into shape. This practice, and the maneuvering whereby trainers seek to protect their cheaper stock from claims, are chiefly responsible for the ostensibly poor form of actually fit and ready horses.

A bad ride by a jockey carrying out the deliberately misleading orders of the trainer sometimes contributes to the build-up, making the horse look worse than it is. But aside from occasional manipulations in daily-doubles, exactas and the like, no trainer in possession of his sanity knowingly defeats one of his horses when he thinks it ready to win. If it can't win, he may prefer it to lose badly. But if it can win, he strikes while the iron is hot, placing the horse in exactly the right company, at exactly the proper distance, with the best rider available. In other words, stables go all-out to win with any horse that has a chance. They go all-out because they know how briefly most horses retain top form. To enter a ready horse in the wrong kind of race is to risk never winning at all.

All this being so, the crucial task of the player is to penetrate the darkness and locate the signs of improvement tucked away in the past-performance records. At the same time, he seeks out equally significant signs of deteriorating condition among horses thought by others to be in the best of shape.

Schools of Thought

The condition factor is so strategic that many successful players devote most of their attention to it, giving only a lick and a promise to matters such as distance, class, weight, pace and jockey. It is possible to win this way, if the player really understands form and is not downright careless about horses that, good condition or not, are severely outclassed or outdistanced or overweighted, or are likely to suffer from an unfavorable pace or an inadequate ride.

A player who begins his examination of a field of Thoroughbreds by applying the same distance and condition factors often finds himself with only two or three qualified contenders when the time comes to proceed to the next phase of his work. This makes life easier.

Other players, especially those who cherish class and consistency, pay no great attention to the condition factor, beyond making sure that the horses they like are not positively out of shape. They often are able to attend to this with a swift glance at the record. If they know what to encompass in the glance, they may be able to survive.

But nobody can ignore the condition factor and come close to winning this game. The more you know about Thoroughbred form and the more attention you give it, the more reliable your selections become.

The Form Cycle

Some horses hold their form for a relatively long time. Others seldom run two really good races in succession. In general, the animals capable of contending for four or five purses in a row are the better ones on the grounds, the ones able to withstand repeated hard efforts. Accordingly, they tend to be males rather than females, and younger rather than older.

Here are typical running lines to demonstrate the form cycle of a cheap, seven-year-old claimer. I have omitted the post position, which is irrelevant to the present discussion. The first column represents the horse's running position at the start of each race:

8	9^4	9^5	9^8	9^8
3	4^3	4^2	4^3	6^4
4	3^3	$2\frac{1}{2}$	$1\frac{1}{2}$	1^2
4	4^5	4^4	3^2	$2\frac{1}{2}$
5	4^2	5^2	6^3	7^5
8	9^3	9^4	9^7	9^{10}

The horse won its third race back and the effort knocked it off form. The improvement that foreshadowed that victory came rather suddenly in the fifth race back, when the horse picked up its feet well enough to stay fairly close to the early pace. In its next race it improved again and gained ground in the stretch. An alert player would have noticed that improvement and would have been careful to consider the animal in its subsequent race, unless it was obviously outclassed or entered at the wrong distance, whereupon the player would have considered it in the race after that. Unless horses of this quality are absolute washouts without a victory in them, they make their winning effort within a race or two of showing improved form. And, unless dropped sharply in class, they seldom run well after winning or finishing close up.

Good horses are always in the money or close to it. If properly managed they hold the winning sharpness for weeks:

4	3^2	4^2	4^3	4^4
3	3^3	2^2	2^2	2^3
2	2^1	$2\frac{1}{2}$	$2\frac{1}{2}$	1no
2	$2\frac{1}{2}$	1^2	1^3	1^4
2	$1\frac{1}{2}$	1^1	1^1	1^2
4	3^2	2^2	2^1	$2\frac{1}{2}$
5	4^5	4^4	4^4	3^3

In its sixth race back, this horse showed that it had approached its best shape. It won three races in succession and now seems to have gone off its feed. It probably will be rested for a month or six weeks and, assuming no injury, will return to the head end of the parade after a preparatory race or two.

Standards of Form

In studying the past-performance records for clues to current condition, the player concerns himself with the following information:

1. The dates and whereabouts of the animal's most recent races and workouts.
2. The probable effects of this activity on the animal's form.
3. Individual variations in the normal form cycle.

Effective form analysis requires a series of decisions, some negative and others positive. In the negative vein, the player discards animals whose records fail to meet his minimum standards. For example, a horse that has been inactive recently might be discarded for that reason alone, regardless of how promising its last race might have seemed at the time. Another horse, recently active, might be discarded because its last race was inexcusably bad, or because the race was too good and unlikely to be repeated!

The records of animals that measure up to the negative standards are then scrutinized for positive indications of winning form. In that phase of the work, the player pits his knowledge against the wiles of the trainer, who may have been trying to conceal or obscure improvement.

Having completed his paper work, the expert reserves decision until he has seen the horses in the paddock and walking ring. Here he often finds that the animal that looked best on paper is wretched in the flesh. The player's detective work at the paddock will occupy a later chapter. For the present, we deal with his studies of past performances.

Recent Action

Every now and then someone breaks into print with the revelation that two thirds of all races are won by horses whose most recent starts occurred within two weeks of the winning effort. Or that a third of all races are won by horses that have had a race within the preceding seven days.

Innumerable systems are based on such statistics. But the facts are that the figures are not nearly so pregnant with meaning as they may seem. For instance, there is no reason why two thirds of all races should not be won by horses that have raced within two weeks: *At least two thirds of all horses that go to the post had had a race within two weeks!* And, while horses that return to the races within a week of their latest start win a third of all races, *at least a third of all starters have had a race within the previous seven days!*

Because of the large number of two-week and one-week horses that race every day, the probability of cashing a bet on either type of horse (without considering any other factor) is something like one in nine. Mathematically, the natural odds against victory by any random one-week or two-week horse are in the neighborhood of 8 to 1. Which are the exact natural odds against any random horse in any typical field of nine horses! In other words, the player has to know more about a horse than that it has been to the post within a week or two.

I make that assertion not to stage a display of statistical wizardry, but to emphasize a truth that recurs frequently in these pages and is, indeed, the most important truth in handicapping: No handicapping factor stands alone. The date of the last race is often important. But only when related to other vital matters.

At a recent New Jersey meeting, the largest single category of winners was the group of 25 horses which won after layoffs of a month or more. Horses in the next largest group—22—had raced exactly five days before their winning efforts! At a recent California meeting, 11 percent of the races went to horses that had not run in thirty days or more. Another 11 percent were won by horses that had run exactly seven days earlier.

The player must concern himself with the dates of the horse's most recent races. But he must bear in mind that a horse that has not run in a month may often be in good enough trim to defeat something else that ran six days ago.

Recent Action in Claimers

In *The Compleat Horseplayer,* I urged rejection of any horse entered in a claiming race unless its record showed a race or workout within twelve days and, moreover, two races or two workouts, or one of each, within seventeen. Players who continue to follow that rigorous advice report success with it, but I think that the approach is outmoded. Research and personal experience demonstrate that an awful lot of horses win claiming races after being out of competition for a full month. It therefore is wasteful to eliminate an animal solely because it has not raced in four weeks.

To repeat myself, the game has changed. The present era is one of severely overworked Thoroughbreds. The trainer sensible enough to refresh a horse with a few weeks of walking and jogging is often likely to have a much improved runner when the animal resumes competitive activity.

As to published dates and distances and times of workouts, it is always reassuring to see that a claiming racer is fit enough to endure such training between starts. On the other hand, the regulations that govern publication of workout reports vary widely from place to place and time to time. The fact that a horse's record includes no recent workouts does not necessarily mean that it has been spending all its time in the barn. In Kentucky, for one current (but not necessarily permanent) example, the horse may have been training strenuously on a farm, or even on the track itself, without news of the exercise reaching the public.

In analyzing claiming races, the safest approach to the problem of recent action hews fairly close to the following guidelines:

1. A horse entered in a race at seven furlongs or less can be accepted if it has raced within the last calendar month, preferably at the present track, a sister track on the same circuit, or a nearby track of equal or superior quality.

2. A horse entered in a race longer than seven furlongs should show a race within the last calendar month plus at least two workouts in the meantime. If it has raced within the last two weeks and shows a workout since, it is acceptable. And if it has raced within the past week, it need show no workouts.

3. A horse entered in a race at seven furlongs or less can be regarded as a potential contender even if it has been unraced for 45 days, provided that it has been working at intervals of four or five days and has previously won after absences of such length.

4. To accept a horse as a possible contender even though it has not raced in the past couple of weeks is a far piece from assuming that it will win its race. Close consideration of other factors may lead to the animal's elimination. Among those factors are, of course, distance, class, pace, weights, post position, trainer, jockey, and how the horse shapes up in the paddock.

The more rigid you become about demanding recent action by claiming horses, the less you need perspire over the remainder of the handicapping, and the less sure you need be of your diagnostic powers at the paddock and walking ring. For an extreme example, it is entirely possible to stay even with the game by playing no claimer that has not had a race within a week—provided one is prepared to apply other simple handicapping rules with equal inflexibility and is willing to pass up a considerable number of races.

With the development of experience and the facile ability to relate form to class, the player becomes more relaxed about recent action (in appropriate cases, that is) and catches some fat mutuel prices that might formerly have been beyond reach.

Recent Action and Better Horses

Allowance, handicap and stakes horses need not race so often to maintain their sharpness. But they seldom are acceptable choices unless they have worked out frequently, recently and with respectable clockings (see page 172). What's more, if the field in an allowance race is composed entirely of authentic allowance horses, the one that has raced well within the last week or two is usually a far better risk than one that has not been to the post for three or four weeks. The most conspicuous exception would be a sparsely raced three-year-old trained by a Frank Whiteley, Allen Jerkens, or similar top-drawer horseman whose animals invariably have a touch of class and usually go to the well only when ready to fill the bucket.

Another prominent exception is a handicap star returning from vacation for a tune-up in allowance company. If the horse's workouts suggest an effort to win today's race, the player must treat the animal with respect, even if it has not raced in months.

The Workout Secret

Like physicians, art critics and losing horseplayers, professional horsemen manage to disagree on a monstrous variety of subjects. In moments of candor, however, the more experienced and competent among them tend to agree that a horse should be at its very best after a freshening layoff from actual competition, followed by a program of workouts.

Once in a great while, the truth of this theory is demonstrated in a claiming race. An honest old animal benefits so much from a lengthy rest that it wins at first asking and pays a mint. It rarely is possible to tell when one of these miracles is going to happen. The assumption must be that the horse will need two or three or more races before recovering its old form. An equally valid assumption is that it has gone bad and will never recover its old form. Once in a while, however, the player notices unusual signs in the workout line of a claiming sprinter about to return from a rest of six weeks or more:

1. **Frequent workouts, including at least one of real speed.**
2. **Long workouts.**

The claimer returning from a layoff is usually sent to the post after only two or three slow works. If it is a sprinter, two of the workouts are likely to be at four furlongs. The third may be at three. But if it has worked four times in the past two or three weeks and has run one or two of the exercise gallops in close to racing speed, it merits attention. And if one of its works was at the distance of today's race, or longer, the player has a problem: He must decide whether to bet on this impressively fresh animal or pass the race altogether.

Sometimes a horse of this kind runs a grand race but lacks the stamina to carry its speed all the way, because it is still short of top condition. But no less often, the workouts mean what they say. The horse is in remarkable shape for its kind. It wins. The safest procedure for the conservative player is to abstain from betting on the race. A more adventurous type might go for the freshened animal, but only if everything else in the race looked awful.

The reader no doubt noticed that I called frequent, fast, long workouts "unusual signs." In the record of a claiming horse, that is. Cheapsters rarely are asked for speed in their workouts: They do not have the speed to spare. They need it for their races. In fact,.whenever a claimer of medium or lower grade ($10,000 or less) shows a swift workout since its last race, the player is entitled to believe that it may be in extraordinarily fine fettle. But, regardless of clockings, the simple presence of a claiming horse on the training track every four or five days between races is ample evidence of physical fitness.

The phrase, "workouts every four or five days" recurs throughout this book and so does the synonymous expression, "frequent workouts." To avoid misunderstanding, I should emphasize that a lapse of six or seven days between an animal's race and its next race or workout is entirely normal. But, when workouts begin, they should almost always recur at regular, short intervals terminated, of course, by the creature's next race. In light of this, the player should wonder about the readiness of a horse that has not raced in three weeks and whose record shows only two workouts during that period. If the latest of the workouts was more than four days ago, doubts should enlarge. Mind you, I say "doubts." Some horses win decisively after going for nine or ten days without a race or workout. Moreover, their victories are predictable on grounds of class, consistency, trainer, jockey, pace and —as far as current condition is concerned—the kind of running the horse did nine or ten days ago.

If I seem to be complicating the reader's existence with these somewhat contradictory interruptions of his train of thought, I apologize. The point, I suppose, is that this is a game in which flexible thinking based on general principles gets more mileage than rigid formulas do. The reader who absorbs the principles of this chapter, and the general guidelines that delineate those principles, will discover sooner rather than later that he is able to modify the guidelines to suit the unique problems presented by the individual race, the individual horse and, of course, the individual track which may be the kind discussed earlier, where workout information is so scanty that the handicapper simply functions without it. While he will accept recent races and workouts as a good sign in the record of any apparently improving horse entered in a claimer, he will be disinclined to eliminate a relatively classy, consistent horse from consideration in the same race merely because it has

Carry Back cools out under the shed at Belmont Park.   UPI PHOTO

Back to the barn at Belmont after a late winter workout on the training track.

been idle for a few days. He will, in sum, relate the factor of condition to that of class, and in due course to those of weights and pace. If he is rigid to that extent—remembering and using the interrelationships among the fundamental factors of handicapping—he will find it necessary to be rigid about little else.

I am sure that all this will become satisfactorily apparent as the reader proceeds through the book.

Workouts by Better Horses

Higher-grade animals that have not raced in recent weeks can be credited with acceptable condition only if they have been working out frequently and show one or two genuinely impressive morning trials. If an allowance or handicap runner produced good speed in a workout seven or eight or nine mornings ago, did not disgrace itself in another gallop four or five days ago, and romped through a final blowout yesterday, it deserves respect. Its last race may have been three or four weeks ago, but the player can be quite sure that the horse is sharp.

Here are standards useful in evaluating the workouts of better-grade horses, including two-year-olds. Obviously, whenever a claiming racer's works approach these standards, he bears watching:

1. At most tracks, a workout is more than satisfactory if the horse breezes (b) (runs entirely without urging) at a rate of approximately 12 seconds for each eighth of a mile. A workout of .36 b for three furlongs or .48 b for four or 1.00 b for five is a definite sign of life. So is 1.13 b for six furlongs, 1.27 b for seven and 1.42 b for the mile. To determine whether your own track is slower or faster than this, check through a few of the workout columns in your racing paper, and alter your par figures accordingly.

2. If a breezing work of .48 is acceptable, so is .47 h—the symbol for "handily." In such an effort, the exercise boy gives what the trade calls a "hand ride," rolling his knuckles along the horse's neck in the familiar pumping motion, which encourages speed. Thus, if two horses do five furlongs in 1.00, but one of them does it breezing and the other handily, the breezer gets the applause. Persons who enjoy arithmetic usually allow a one-second difference between breezes and hand rides in workouts of five furlongs or less. A second and a couple of fifths is more like it at six or seven furlongs. And three seconds is not too much at a mile or more.

3. Another second of credit is given for a workout that begins in the starting gate (g) rather than from the customary running start. Hence .47 hg is as good as .47 b.

4. If the horses work out on a training track (tr.t.) as well as on the main track (m.t.), the workout lines show it. Training tracks are usually deeper and slower, to help the animals develop stamina. Which is why tr.t. .48 h is as good as m.t. .48 b.

5. A longer workout is always more significant than a shorter. It is especially significant if the horse has been away from the races for a while. After a layoff of more than a month, works of three or four furlongs are not too promising for a horse scheduled to race against animals of its own class. But if the race is at six furlongs and the horse spun off six or seven furlongs in good time within the last week or ten days, and has breezed another three or four furlongs in the past 48 hours, one can be reasonably sure that it is ready to try today. Similarly, if today's race is over a distance of ground, the laid-off animal should show a workout or two of at least a mile, and in respectable time.

6. A highly useful way to evaluate workouts is to watch the daily summaries published by the racing papers. An animal whose exercises are impressive enough to earn comment in the bold-face type at the bottom of those columns is usually worth keeping in mind. So is any cheaper horse whose workout was within a few fifths of a second of the better animal's time on the same morning. An advantage of this method is that it compares horses with each other, rather than with par timings. Daily variations in the speed of the track can alter workout figures considerably—especially on damp mornings.

7. In the record of any horse, especially one that has been racing and working out frequently, a nice breezing effort on the day before the race is a highly reassuring sign of fitness.

8. *Daily Racing Form* has recently begun to include the abbreviation "(d)" in workout reports, signifying that "dogs"—rubber traffic cones—were positioned on the racing strip to keep working horses away from the inside rail and allow that strategic sector of the racing strip to recover from the effects of rain. A workout around the dogs is longer than one along the rail and can be credited as one second faster.

Misleading Workouts

A seldom-mentioned aspect of workouts is that they, too, may help a trainer in his hallowed effort to darken his animal's form. Among the techniques:

1. Using a heavy exercise boy, or boosting the horse's burden with lead weights in the saddle pad. If the animal totes thirty pounds or more above the weight it will carry in the race, slow time is a certainty. But the weights carried in workouts are never reported.

2. Wrapping heavy bandages on the horse's legs. Tinfoil beneath a few layers of flannel and gauze used to be a favorite. The weight slows the horse's stride, worsens its time, builds its mutuel price and develops its physique even more effectively than a heavy exercise boy can.

3. Exercising the horse late in the morning. By that time the track has been chewed up thoroughly by hooves, slowing it considerably.

4. Ordering the boy to keep the animal in the middle of the track until it has completed the turn into the homestretch. This deliberate loss of ground adds seconds to the workout time. It does not fool the official clockers, but the past-performance records have no room to explain why the workout was so slow.

5. Ordering the boy to keep as tight a hold as possible, converting a breezing work into a strangling one, a second or two slower.

6. Exercising the horse at night when the official clockers are not around. This seldom is permitted at major racing centers, but remains a favorite tactic on certain smaller circuits.

7. Working the horse not at the track itself but on a nearby private oval, away from prying eyes. If a trainer begins winning with horses whose records show neither recent races nor workouts, you may discover that, yes, he happens to have a workout strip behind his restaurant.

8. Disguising a horse so that the clockers will not recognize it. This is done by dressing the animal in blinkers and saddlecloth of a color never associated with its stable, or putting a strange exercise boy aboard, or wrapping its legs in bandages (which it has never worn and does not need). Some trainers go so far as to give a wrong name to the clockers when they inquire. Again, practices of this kind are rare in major racing, but far from unknown.

The Form of Two-Year-Olds

During the first months of every year, Frank Whiteley wins maiden-special-weights races with well-schooled juveniles that have never raced before. The same trick is routine—spring, summer and fall—for Jimmy Croll, LeRoy Jolley, Buddy Raines, Del Carroll, John Veitch, and, for sure, someone with horses at the reader's local track. The very presence on the entry list of a two-year-old from one of these barns is enough to give pause to any knowledgeable player.

If the player approaches the distance factor in juvenile races along the lines described in the previous chapter, he can assume that any of the logical contenders is in condition, provided it has had a recent race and has been working out briskly at four- or five-day intervals. If it has not raced recently, or has never raced at all, the workouts not only should be frequent but one or more of them should be nice and fast—and the longer the better. A two-year-old in good condition runs as fast as it can at every opportunity. Which is why the speed of recent races or—when real speed is missing in the field—the speed of recent workouts is just about all the player needs to make his selection.

Horses for Courses

I hope it is agreed by now that the winning player prefers a horse that has been running and working out with regularity. And that he appreciates it if a horse of that description shows a fast, long workout. And that he hesitates to discard a horse that has been away from the races for a month or so if it is a higher-grade animal and has been working in something close to actual racing speed, preferably at distances longer than the customary three or four furlongs.

In process of noticing how frequently and how recently a horse has been racing and working out, the smart player takes care to see where all this activity has taken place. An allowance animal that ran nicely last week at Hawthorne might be credited with excellent condition if entered today at the same track. It would be a dubious bet if shipped to Bowie.

Many horses withstand long trips remarkably well. But an enormous majority require a race or two before becoming fully acclimated to a new track. Horses that recover quickly from the stress of travel and the tension caused by new surroundings are known as "good shippers." They sometimes manage to win their first race at the new oval without so much as a workout there. But only sometimes. Not often.

A rule honored with unswerving devotion by most experts is this:

1. Unless a horse outclasses its field and has worked out impressively at today's track, its last race must have taken place here or at a sister track on the same circuit.

A Buckpasser can amble into Chicago, work out a couple of times and break the world's record. And every year some European or South American horse wins the Washington, D.C., International at Laurel, outclassing America's best turf runners in spite of its long journey and its lack of local action. Similarly, Grover Delp manages to win with his claimers in their first attempts at Bowie or Laurel or Arlington Park or Delaware. And Frank Whiteley can train a Damascus in Maryland, yet win with it in New York. Again, the reason is an edge in class.

"Horses for courses," say veterans of the backstretch, nodding their heads sagely. Undoubtedly some horses run better at some tracks than at others. A speed horse does better on the pasteboard surfaces of California than on the sandy, holding tracks of the East. A come-from-behind animal does all right at Bay Meadows and is lucky to reach third money at Golden Gate Fields. But the real meaning of "horses for courses" is that all horses, regardless of running style, are creatures of habit. Until they have become accustomed to a new track, they run below their best form.

Players who care to pursue this line of reasoning will profit from some additional ideas:

2. Unless it is entered at a substantially lower claiming price than usual, discard any claiming horse whose last race was at a track of lower class than today's. The only exception would be a local horse returning from a one- or two-race excursion out of town.

3. Throw out any front-running horse in its first start over a track that favors come-from-behinders. The hotshot from Del Mar is a virtual cinch to perish in its first start at Belmont Park.

4. Throw out any come-from-behind horse in its first start over a track that favors front-runners. The only unvarying exception would be a champion like Forego, an exception to everything, anyhow.

5. In choosing between two animals that have run their most recent races at today's track or on today's circuit, give preference to the one that has been working out at today's track. Horses stabled at Hialeah win races there from rivals stabled at Gulfstream. When the action moves to Gulfstream, the horses that regard the Hallandale plant as home begin beating steeds that have to be vanned from Hialeah. At Aqueduct, the most successful stables are invariably ones with stalls on the premises, rather than at nearby Belmont. Horses that work out at Aqueduct sleep there and win there.

Danger Signals

Some of the most popular selection systems are based on the concept of "last-out-in-the money." The player eliminates any horse that did not finish first, second or third in its last race. If two or more qualify, he bets on the one with the most recent race.

To the extent that such systems take cognizance of class, pace and distance, they are not too bad. Their inescapable weakness is the uncritical assumption that a good race last week foreshadows a good race today. Life is not that simple.

A probable reason that favorites win no more than one race in three is that the crowds tend to make their bets on the basis of "last-out-in-the-money." Failing to appreciate that an animal's good recent effort may have overtaxed its powers, they make it the favorite. But it no longer is in condition to win. The player who recognizes certain signals in the past-performance lines is able to avoid a good many of these false favorites and false second choices. If he finds another bettable horse in the race, he has a good chance to collect a robust mutuel.

Here come some ideas which should enable any player to avoid sucker horses:

1. Throw out any horse that bled, ran sore, or finished lame in its last race. The past-performance records in Eastern editions of *Daily Racing Form* give that information. Western readers must dig up the result charts. Sore-legged animals win every day, but rarely after a race in which the disability was noticeable enough to draw comment. The term "bled" refers to the rupture of blood vessels in the nose or throat under the strain of racing. The flow of blood hampers the animal's breathing. A horse that bled in its last race may not bleed again today, but is unlikely to have recovered from the experience sufficiently to win today.

2. Throw out any horse that lugged in or bore out in its last race. A horse unable to run in a straight line is either badly schooled or ouchy. If it has borne in or lugged out before, it can be discarded without a second thought—unless it seems to enjoy enormous class or speed advantages over the rest of its field, at which point the smart operator resolves to pass the race rather than play roulette.

3. Throw out any horse that is stepping up in class after a race it won while losing ground in a driving stretch run. A horse that has trouble beating its own kind is a poor risk if it tries to tackle superior stock in its next effort. Among cheaper claiming racers, in fact, the exertion of lasting to the finish wire against a gaining rival is usually enough to guarantee that the horse will lose its next start even if it does not go up in class. On the other hand, a horse that merely lopes to the wire, winning easily or handily, can be forgiven if something else gained on it during the stretch. *Racing Form* readers without result charts can safely assume that the horse was engaged in a driving finish if its winning margin was two lengths or less.

4. Throw out any cheap four-year-old or older horse that engaged in driving finishes in each of its last two races. Win or lose, a hard drive knocks the average horse off form. Two drives in succession are murder. Notable exceptions to this rule are handicap and stakes racers from leading barns, better-grade two-year-olds, lightly raced three-year-old fillies of high quality, and three-year-old colts and geldings of almost any grade. Three-year-old males often come to life in the summer, putting together a series of three or more good races against increasingly tough competition.

If the player likes a six-year-old in a claiming race and wonders whether it can do well today after two successive taxing efforts, its past-performance record may show whether it has ever been able to run well in such circumstances before. In the absence of result charts or Eastern *Form* comment lines, the player can assume that the horse was involved in a driving finish if it won by two lengths or less, or finished within a length or less of the winner. If it was similarly situated at the pre-stretch call or stretch call, the drive was that much more prolonged and intense.

It takes a good deal of character to eliminate an animal whose recent record is by far the most impressive in its field, and whose low odds prove that other handicappers think highly of its chances. But the bold step is worth taking—even if nothing else in the race seems worth a play. To fortify determination, and to base the decision on a properly comprehensive analysis of the horse, the handicapper should look for other flaws in its credentials. Like as not, its tired body is now being moved up in class to face a calibre of opposition against which it has never been too successful. Or, if not moving up, it probably is being saddled with more weight than before, or an unfavorable post position or, for some strange reason, a non-winning rider.

The very essence of effective handicapping is, after all, the effort to avoid horses on days when their chances are not as good as others may think, and to play horses whose chances are better than the odds indicate. To shun the apparently overworked horse is basic.

5. Throw out any horse aged five or older whose best effort at today's distance occurred in its last race, unless the horse is a male that demonstrated reserve speed in that race. This is a variation of the overwork discussed above. The simplest way to uncover the flaw is to see whether the horse ran the distance more rapidly in its last race than in any previous try. If so, the presumption must be that the horse ran as fast as possible and will not be able to duplicate the effort today. If the previous rapid effort took place on another track, check pages 273–74 in this book to see whether the track is slower or faster than today's. For instance, if the times are approximately equal, but the earlier race was on a slower track, the more recent effort probably was the less taxing of the two and the horse may be all right.

As to the concept of "reserve energy," if the horse won easily or handily, or, as may happen once in a great while, covered the ground without any great exertion in the kind of race known by the chartmakers as an "even effort," it can be accepted as a possibility today. Also, it can be credited with plenty of reserve juice if it won after staying close to the pace, arriving at the stretch call first or second or within a length of the leader, and gained thereafter. Like one of the following, which are the best kind of races. I call them big wins:

$$3 \quad 3 \quad 3^4 \quad 2^1 \quad 1^1 \quad 1^2$$
$$1 \quad 2 \quad 1^1 \quad 2\tfrac{1}{2} \quad 2\tfrac{1}{2} \quad 1\tfrac{1}{2}$$

6. Throw out any claimer whose last race was a big win more than two weeks ago. A horse able to win that powerfully is at the top of its form. The trainer naturally tries to get it another opportunity, before it loses its edge. If more than two weeks elapse, the player should suspect that something has gone awry with the horse. Exceptions can be made for animals that have been working steadily while awaiting today's race. But if the horse has had little or no public exercise, the player had better plan to look for signs of distress in the paddock and walking ring.

Before proceeding to our next array of negative signs, it might be a good idea to review the circumstances in which smart players overlook or excuse a poor last race, no matter how bad it may have seemed.

The Airtight Alibi

Because the conditioning process finds horses entered in races they cannot win, it is important not to be misled by their dismal performances in such races. Like the trainer who shoots the works after darkening his horse's form, the expert player dearly loves a situation in which his choice's last race looked so bad that today's odds increase. The handicapper who knows when to disregard a horse's latest race is destined for repeated happiness.

A bad race in the wrong company is, indeed, not a bad race at all. If anything, it suggests to the player that things are working out exactly as he and the maneuvering trainer might wish.

Here is a list of the circumstances in which a poor effort is forgivable. Overlook a horse's last race if:

1. It was on an off-track of a kind that the horse has never negotiated successfully in the past.

2. The horse was entered at the wrong distance.

3. The horse ran against animals of a higher class than it has been able to challenge successfully in its most recent seven or eight efforts.

4. The horse carried substantially more weight than is good for it. (Some Thoroughbreds cannot win under more than 115 pounds and look dreadful with 119 or more. Others, able to win with 117 or 118, die with 121 or 122. If a claimer ran poorly with 119 or more, check its record to see if the high weight constitutes an alibi.)

5. The race was the horse's first in more than a month.

6. The race was the horse's first since arriving on this circuit from another part of the country.

7. The horse showed high early speed before tiring or even stopping or quitting. This often is more than just an alibi for a poor finish. It may be a positive sign of approaching form, and of a trainer's imminent readiness to lower the boom. The past-performance line shows that the animal led or ran within a length or so of the early pace (usually to the pre-stretch call) before conking out. Unless the animal is a chronic quitter that does this sort of thing in almost every outing, the player should be delighted to forgive the eighth-place finish. Dollars to doughnuts, if the horse is well placed today it will show early speed again, and carry it farther.

All those solid alibis derive from peculiarities of the modern conditioning process. Other good excuses are more usually attributable to racing misfortune. The expert tosses out the last race if:

8. The jockey had never finished first or second with the horse, is not a national or local leader, and, for today's race, has been replaced by a more successful boy.

9. The jockey lost his whip, or a stirrup broke, or a bandage came undone, or some other mishap fouled the tack.

10. The jockey rode weakly or unintelligently enough to attract comment in the result chart.

11. Other horses prevented the animal from running its race. The chart or Eastern *Form* trouble line might say "Blocked," "Impeded," "Roughed," "Rough trip," "Forced to check," "Shuffled back," "In close," "Close quarters," or "Forced wide." Or it might say "Wide"

Veterinarian William Reed checks Proud Clarion's underpinnings at Belmont Park.
UPI PHOTO

or "Ran wide," indicating a bad ride or interference rather than the affliction of bearing out.

12. The horse got off to a poor start, but seldom has that kind of trouble.

Inexcusable Performances

Assuming that the horse ran in its own class range and at its best distance and had no excuse for its last performance, it can be eliminated on grounds of poor condition if:

1. It failed to beat about half its field—finishing fifth or worse in a field of seven, sixth or worse in a field of eight or nine, seventh or worse in a field of ten or more—and earned a speed rating at least 5 points below the ones recorded in its better local races.

2. It failed to gain on the leader at any call in the race and finished out of the money more than six lengths behind. (Some players use this kind of standard in preference to the first. Others use both in sequence.)

3. It lost more than two and a half lengths between the stretch call and the finish.

4. It got off to a poor start, and poor starts have been one of its problems.

5. It earned an uncomplimentary chart comment such as "Dull," "No speed," or "Showed nothing."

Signs of Improvement

"Accentuate the positive, eliminate the negative," wrote Johnny Mercer in a song that was popular during the Stone Age. Numerous horseplayers take the advice literally. They look for horses whose most recent races gave notice of better things to come. They ignore other horses.

In my opinion, a little more work than that pays dividends. A player who follows a sequence similar to the one in this chapter achieves a considerable edge by discarding horses that figure to be out of contention today. He then decides what to do about the remaining horses. If he is really hipped on the condition factor, he can toss out any of the surviving contenders that fail to check out on the positive angles described below. But if he cares to consider some advice from an old hand, he may refrain from crossing off such horses until he has evalu-

Kelso and the farrier.   UPI PHOTO ated them in terms of class, pace and other fundamentals. My reasons for suggesting this are readily understandable: A horse that has been sufficiently active and has earned no black marks in its recent performances may well be in good enough shape to win today, even if its last race or two were unspectacular. For one thing, the horse might have run an alibi race last time out and this in itself might be a sign that the trainer's gears are meshing. Even without the evidence of an alibi its trainer might be a master at concealing improvement from the public, whereupon the player would live to regret eliminating the animal.

Players not already committed to a different way of doing things really should see if their winning percentage does not increase when they accept as contenders any animals that qualify on the distance factor and show none of the signs of unreadiness reviewed earlier. A player who does not care to excuse a bad last race on grounds of one of the alibis discussed earlier should then look for negative signs in the horse's next-to-last race. If the race took place in the past three weeks and was a good one, the player had better not eliminate the horse.

In setting forth the following methods of spotting improvement or other signs of current readiness in the past-performance records, I recommend that the player regard them as plus factors. A horse may show none of these angles in his record, but may be the class of the race and win in a walk. Where these factors are especially useful is in separating contenders that (1) qualify on distance, class, pace, etc., (2) have checked out successfully against the negative standards of condition, and (3) need to be differentiated from each other. In such circumstances, a horse that showed one or more of the signs of improvement would ordinarily be the better bet (see Chapter 16). Another use of the signs of improvement is as a homing device for lovers of long-shots. As everyone knows, many players hate to handicap, but enjoy a longshot more than anything. If they check out a field of horses against the following series of improvement angles and bet on the longest-priced horse whose record contains one or more of the angles, they can count on an entertaining run for their money.

A horse that has not been eliminated for any of the reasons reviewed earlier can be expected to run a good race today if it:

1. Won its last race easily or handily.
2. Won its last race in big-win style (see page 179).
3. Lost its last race but gained at least two lengths in the stretch, earning favorable comment such as "Rallied," "Gaining," "Game try," "Sharp try," or "Good effort."
4. Lost ground in the middle stages but gained in the stretch. A

horse may lose ground to the leader while hunting for racing room, but if it is in a running mood, it often demonstrates that fitness by recovering the lost ground and more:

$$6 \quad 6 \quad 4^2 \quad 4^4 \quad 4^3 \quad 3^1$$

5. Showed high early speed (see page 180).

6. Ran within the past week.

7. Ran in the money in its first effort after a long layoff or a long trip.

8. Steps down in class today after a race in which it ran well enough to earn a comment like "Evenly" or better.

9. Steps down in class today to a level at which it has never been beaten by more than half a length.

10. Ran the final quarter of its last race in 24 seconds or less. (The famous Colonel E. R. Bradley invented this one. He found that any horse able to cover the last two furlongs that rapidly was an especially good bet next time out. To calculate a horse's final-quarter speed in a six-furlong race, subtract the race's official half-mile clocking from its official final time. For every length the animal gained on the leader from the half to the finish, deduct one fifth of a second. If the horse lost ground, add a fifth for every length it lost. The only other kind of race in which this calculation is possible for most fans is the mile, wherein the three-quarter-mile and final clockings are used.)

11. Ran closer to the early pace than in its previous race or two.

12. Was closer at the stretch call than in its previous race or two.

13. Finished closer to the winner and earned a higher speed rating than in its previous race or two.

14. Gained three or more lengths between the first and second call, or between any other two calls in the race.

15. Is a front-running type that carried its speed farther than in its previous race or two, even though it tired toward the end.

16. Ran an even race, in second or third position all the way, earning a substantially higher speed rating than in its previous race or two.

17. Has earned increasingly high speed ratings in its past three races, even though out of the money in its latest.

As the reader has noticed, many of these positive signs are infinitesimal. Most players overlook all but the more obvious of them. The handicapper sophisticated enough to understand that even slight improvement is often a prelude to major improvement can expect to make extra money by exploiting the above list, along with similar subtleties that will appear in later chapters.

10

The Class Factor

They claim that the late Saul Silberman, ebullient president of Tropical Park, decided one day to make a splendid and unusual gesture of goodwill toward his paying customers. He would go to the grandstand with sheaves of currency and give it all away. For free.

It turned out to be quite an experience. When Silberman offered greenbacks to strangers, many not only refused the gift but behaved as if he were trying in some way to take advantage of them.

I can understand that. Racing is a weird game. A proportion of its clients become so accustomed to calamity that they cannot recognize good fortune when they see it face to face. This self-defeating turn of mind reflects itself in their betting. Let me illustrate.

Class Bonanzas

The nearest thing to a cinch at any track is a sharply conditioned horse of substantial class, when entered at a suitable distance against inferior animals. Did I say racing was weird? Racing is astonishing. One of its most astonishing features is the frequency with which betting opportunities of this kind occur. At the height of the season on major circuits, the discerning player finds at least two such bonanzas every week.

What makes them bonanzas is that the best horse usually wins and almost invariably pays longer odds than it should. Even at Aqueduct, where a relentlessly shrewd crowd sometimes makes odds-on choices

4 ATLANTIC CITY

6 FURLONGS. (1.08¾) ALLOWANCE. Purse $5,500. Fillies & Mares, 3-year-olds and upward. Which have never won two races. Weights, 3-year-olds, 117 lbs.; Older, 122 lbs.; Non-winners of $4,200, allowed, 2 lbs.; Maidens, 4 lbs.; (Winners preferred.)

Smooth M. Out

Dk. b. or br. f. 3, by Aforethought—Cavan Clay, by Clay Ground
Br.—Baker Development Co Inc (Tex)
Tr.—Menarde Frank J

Own.—Loyle & Menarde

1105

				St	1st	2nd	3rd	Amt.
				1978	9	0	2	0	$5,575
				1977	10	1	0	3	$7,665

10May78- 9 Key gd 6f	:22⅗ :47⅗ 1:13⅗ 3 + ⑤Allowance	8 1 42½ 88 812 816 Kotenko R	112	11.90	60-24 Sadance 115½ Minna E. 112² That's Luck 114½ Done early 10
30Apr78- 7 Key fst 6f	:23 :46⅗ 1:12⅖	1 4 1hd 2nd 22½ 21½ Kotenko G	116	15.60	78-16 Luffer 115¹½ Smooth M. Out 116ᵐᵏ Flower Legend 116ⁿᵒ Gamely 8
22Apr78- 9 Key fst 6f	:22⅖ :47½ 1:13 3 + ⑤Allowance	3 4 31½ 65½ 811 714 Kotenko G	109	27.50	63-22 Hey Nancy 114³ Coiled 107½ Minna E. 110ⁿᵏ Tired 11
3Apr78- 7 Key fst 6f	:22½ :45⅗ 1:12½ 3 + ⑤Allowance	7 1 76 56½ 58½ 57½ Kotenko G	110	17.20	73-25 Yearn For Peace 112ʰᵈ Coiled 108¹½ Loyal Ana 123⁴ Outrun 8
3Mar78- 6 Key fst 6f	:23⅗ :48 1:15	7 1 52½ 55 45½ 44½ Kotenko G	115	19.10	63-33 Michael's Sweetie 115½ Bibianna K.1173ᵐMyChang115½ No mishap 7
24Feb78- 7 Key fst 6f	:22⅗ :46½ 1:12⅗	2 3 87½ 817 824 821 Osani J R Jr.10	106	19.90	58-28 Bimbo Sue 115⁵ Beaver River 115⁵ Sew Proudly 115¹½ Outrun 8
20Feb78- 7 Key fst 6f	:23½ :47 1:13½	1 1 31½ 36½ 28 28 Kotenko G	116	8.80	65-23 CynthisWhistle120⁸SmoothM.Out116⅜MissBinny0.1163½ No match 8
10Feb78- 7 Key fst 6f	:23⅗ :48½ 1:13⅗	7 1 1hd 21 33 46 Kotenko G	116	15.80	67-24 Luffer 109¼ A Rough Win 111¹½ Miss Benny 0. 107⁴ Weakened 9
2Jan78- 9 Key fst 6f	:22⅗ :48⅗ 1:15	6 1 31½ 34½ 46½ 48½ Kotenko G	116	4.00	58-31 Acts Like A Queen 120² A Rough Win 113¹½ Obvious 1115 Tired 9
10Dec77- 6 Key fst 6f	:23⅗ :46⅗ 1:12⅖	1 1 11 21 33½ 49½ Kotenko G	115	13.10	75-18 Sheldy'sDrem107ʰᵈSpringInVirgini114⁸Judy'sHop112¹½ Weakened 6

Final Glow

Ch. f. 3, by Restless Wind—Island Spot, by Windsor Ruler
Br.—Glen Hill Farm (Fla)
Tr.—Clark Max

Own.—Clark & Steinberg

115

				St	1st	2nd	3rd	Amt.
				1978	1	1	0	0	$2,520
				1977	1	M	0	0	

| 27Jly78- 3 Atl fst 6f | :22⅗ :45⅗ 1:10⅗ 3 + ④Md 14000 | 7 1 1½ 12 13 13 Nied J Jr | 116 | 5.20 | 89-14 Final Glow 116³ Congenial Diplomat 1154 Scuffle 111½ In hand 7 |
| 30Sep77- 4 8M fst 6f | :23 :46⅗ 1:11⅗ ⑤Md Sp Wt | 2 7 1hd 23 24 614 Diaz A | 117 | *2.60 | 68-20 Bag of Spooks 112⁸ Delta Debbie 112ⁿᵏ Lambay 117¹ Tired 8 |

LATEST WORKOUTS   Jly 22 Atl   6f fst 1:16⅗ b   Jly 13 Atl   4f fst :49   bg   Jly 8 Atl   4f fst :49⅘ b

Double Rhythm

B. f. 3, by Spring Double—Mile Dianne, by Call Over
Br.—Polk H H (Md)
Tr.—Boniface J William

Own.—F J V Stable Inc

117

				St	1st	2nd	3rd	Amt.
				1978	8	0	0	0	$350
				1977	4	1	2	1	$8,600

10Jly78- 5 Pim fst 6f	:23 :46⅗ 1:12⅗	3 5 58 712 713 712 Passmore W J	b 114	7.30	71-13 Diane's Porsche 114⅓½ Tawny 107³½ Solo Darlin 114ⁿᵏ No menace 7
23Jun78- 7 Pim fst 6f	:23½ :46½ 1:12½	8 4 51½ 911 1016 1018 Lillis R J	b 112	76.40	66-20 A Symphony 107³½ Mike's Dream 112¹½ Civil Defense 112½ Tired 10
31May78- 7 Pim fst 6f	:23 :46⅗ 1:13⅗	6 1 54 68 69½ 615 Lillis R J	b 112	13.80	73-19 Bold Melody 115³½ Hagleys World 108⁶ Tupamara 114¹ Outrun 7
9May78- 4 Pim gd 5f	:22⅗ :46⅗ :59½	4 2 42½ 47 49½ Ardoin R	b 114	4.00	79-24 Flowing Troy 117⁴½ Diane's Porsche 114ⁿᵒ Tripleen 114⁵ Tired 4
29Apr78- 5 Pim fst 6f	:23⅖ :46⅗ 1:12½	3 2 54 64 65½ 57½ Turcotte R L	b 114	13.80	78-18 CopprConjurr112²⅓SunshinButy112¹StpGirlfrind115²½ No mishap 6
20Apr78- 8 Pim my 1	:47⅗ 1:13½ 1:48½	6 2 21 32 68½ 615 McCarron G	b 112	9.60	49-24 Tina'sMusic1142DoubleIndemnity112¾DancersReveltion1142 Tired 7
6Apr78- 8 Pim fst 6f	:22⅗ :46½ 1:12⅗	2 2 22½ 35 45 77¾ Turcotte R L	b 114	11.00	76-20 Worthy of Flowers1202BetterTurn115ⁿᵏSubRosa117¹ Speed, tired 7
29Mar78- 5 Pim fst 6f	:23⅗ :47⅗ 1:13	2 4 34½ 65½ 65½ 69½ Turcotte R L	115	11.10	71-21 Banderole 115¹ LaDiscotheque120²Janet'sJustin107¹½ Done early 7
21Jun77- 3 Bow fst 5½f	:22⅗ :45⅘ 1:06	2 2 2nd 22 22½ 11 Hinojosa H	119	*.90	89-23 Double Rhythm 119¹ Comaneci 119² Fight For Gold119¹½ Driving 7
8Jun77- 4 Bow fst 5f	:46 :58⅘	8 4 21½ 22 24 26 Hinojosa H	119	3.50	90-18 DangerBearing119⁶DoubleRhythm119¹FightForGold119⁶ 2nd best 10

LATEST WORKOUTS   Jly 8 Pim   4f fst :48   h   Jun 29 Pim   6f gd 1:16⅗ b   Jun 19 Pim   4f fst :48   h

Kate Coventry

Ch. f. 4, by Viceregal—Sphinxlike, by Princequillo

Own.—Edwards J F Br.—Taylor E P (Md) Tr.—Harraway Thomas P

		St	1st	2nd	3rd	Amt.
	1978	5	0	0	0	$990
	1977	8	1	0	1	$7,480

Date										
26Jly78- 3Mth fst 6f	:21⅗	:44⅖ 1.10	3↑ⓕAllowance	4	8	916 813 811 79¾	Broussard R	b 118	21.60	81-13 Fascinadora 114¹¼ Jancinto Girl 107² Misty Native 110² Outrun 9
11Jly78- 8Mth fst 6f	:22½	:45⅗ 1.11⅜	3↑ⓕAllowance	7	2	78 59 411 412	Broussard R	b 118	50.80	70-21 Tabler 114ᵐᵒ Misty Native 1139 Fascinadora 108³ Rallied 8
17Jun78- 4Mth fst 6f	:22	:45 1.11⅗	3↑ⓕAllowance	4	9	99½ 916 813 815	Miceli M	b 119	15.40	67-19 PorcelainFlower117⅜Fascinadora114ᵐᵒSilverCrown107³ No factor 9
10Jun78- 7Mth fst 6f	:22	:45½ 1.10⅗	3↑ⓕAllowance	6	2	42 42 49 411	Miceli M	b 119	28.00	75-23 Forbidden Isle 111⁴ Tegawitha 117⁴ Ericka Downs 108²½ Tired 8
24May78- 8Mth sly 6f	:22	:45⅗ 1.11⅗	3↑ⓕAllowance	2	4	32½ 44 57½ 79	Solomone M	b 120	21.70	72-24 Merrimac Valley 111² Fascinadora 113¾ Ericka Downs108²½ Tired 8
18Nov77- 6Med fst 6f	:23⅗	:46⅗ 1.12⅘	3↑ⓕAllowance	2	4	67 68 613 521	Arellano J	b 114	31.40	63-24 HevenlySunshine116⅜HevenlyWind114ᵐᵈLdyMcJy116¹⁰ No factor 6
2Nov77- 8Key fst 170	:48½	1.14½ 1.45⅘	3↑ⓕAllowance	8	6	64 46 46½ 515	Black A S	b 118	7.20	56-25 Marge Wells 121¾ Wysox 107¹ Sailor Girl 114⁸ Outrun 8
15Oct77- 5Med gd 6f	:22⅗	:46⅖ 1.13⅗	3↑ⓕAllowance	1	1	12 1½ 31½ 55¼	Miceli M	b 119	7.90	74-15 Ernest Ruler 113ᵐᵈ Lady McJay 116²⅓Peggy'sPleasure119¹½ Tired 6
7Oct77- 5Med fst 6f	:22⅗	:46 1.12⅘	3↑ⓕAllowance	2	7	76½ 811 814 816	Miceli M	b 119	15.20	65-18 Our Paige 113¹½ Whistling Menace 109¼LeanAndMean114² Outrun 8
30Sep77- 4Med fst 6f	:23⅗	:46⅗ 1.13⅘	3↑ⓕMd Sp Wt	1	5	31 2½ 13½ 14½	Miceli M	117	14.50	— — Kate Coventry 117⁴½ Lt. Lady 117ʰᵈ Grand Tumbler112²¾ Handily 8

Some Clip

Ch. f. 4, by Tony's Chance—Citation Clip, by Sky Clipper

Own.—O'Connell E F Br.—O'Connell E F (N J) Tr.—O'Connell Eugene F

		St	1st	2nd	3rd	Amt.
	1978	5	0	1	0	$3,701
	1977	4	M	1	0	$700

Date										
3Aug78- 2Atl fst 6f	:21⅘	:45 1.11⅛	3↑ⓕⓢAllowance	5	4	52½ 55 68 46½	Pagano S R	b 115⁴	34.10	79-22 Tony's Hideaway 120² Victorious Val 108³Romanean1131½ Evenly 9
	3Aug78-Dead heat									
22Jly78- 3Atl fst 6f	:22	:45⅗1.10⅘	3↑ⓕⓢAllowance	6	2	55 53½ 54 46	Lanci H L	b 120	7.70	85-21 Make Mine Mink 120¹ Victorious Val 113² Lorelei J.114³ No rally 6
15Jly78- 4Atl fst 6f	:22⅘	:46⅗ 1.13⅘	3↑ⓕⓢMd 8000	9	1	31½ 2nd 1½ 12½	Lanci H L	b 122	3.70	75-21 Some Clip 122²½ Kristi Dutchess 120¾ Dust of Snow 114³ Driving 9
30Jun78- 2Atl fst 6f	:22⅘	:46 1.13⅗	3↑ⓕMd 5000s	4	2	31½ 32½ 35½ 47¼	Castaneda J A	b 109	33.40	77-21 Little Indian 114² Walter Kaplan1165¼Jake'sLate118ᵐᵏ Early speed 8
12Jly77- 3Atl fst 6f	:22⅘	:47½ 1.13	3↑ⓕⓈMd 5000	11	2	41½ 44½ 49 49	D'Agusto J G⁵	b 117	38.40	65-24 Milucky Marge 122¹⁰ Bold Mist 122² Some Clip 117² Held evenly 12
12Jly77- 2Atl sly 6f	:22⅘	:45⅗ 1.13⅘	3↑ⓢMd Sp Wt	8	1	811 816 819 721	Boulmetis S A Jr	b 110	35.60	63-23 Blue Onion 110³ Belltree 115ᵐᵏ Harold's Sons 115¹⁰ Outrun 10
10Jun77- 2Key gd 6f	:23	:48½ 1.14⅘	3↑ⓕMd 5000	4	4	3½ 56½ 27 27½	Saumell F R 11⁷	109	5.90	60-28 Come OutSmokin116¾⅓SomeClip109½Fool'sTune116¾ Lugged in 10
1Key fst 6f	:23⅘	:49½ 1.17⅘	3↑ⓕMd 5000	5	5	1hd 2nd 42½ 85¾	Ramos R	116	14.60	51-30 Retrospective 116¹ Hemi Demi 116ᵐᵏ Sifsari 124¹½ Used up 12
31Mar77- 3GS fst 6f	:22⅗	:47⅘ 1.15	3↑ⓕMd Sp Wt	1	12	1218121812201221	Lovato F	112	63.20	47-31 Forli Clover 112¹¼ ColonelShula113³SocietyDance113² Poor start 12

Linda Faye

Dk. b. or br. f. 3, by Proud Clarion—Rositer, by Native Dancer

Own.—Jones John P Jr Br.—O'Quinn C (Fla) Tr.—Jones John P Jr

	Turf Record				St	1st	2nd	3rd	Amt.
	St 1st 2nd 3rd			1978	12	1	0	0	$4,140
	1 0 0 0			1977	0	M	0	0	

Date										
28Jly78- 7Atl fst 6f	:22	:45⅘ 1.10⅗	3↑ Allowance	1	9	912 912 912 69¾	Black A S	b 113	9.30	80-16 HolidyCrossing116¹¼Mr.tie'sAngr114⁴¾Tom'sLuck114ʰᵈ No factor 9
12Jly78- 1Atl fst 6f	:22	:45⅘ 1.11⅘	3↑ⓔMd Sp Wt	10	1	13 12½ 13 16	Boulmetis SAJrb	116	18.80	83-22 Linda Faye 116⁶ Rivers Edge 116⁴ Jolie J. G. 122ᵐᵏ Driving 10
22Jun78- 3Atl fst 6f	:21⅘	:44⅘ 1.10⅗	3↑ⓔMd Sp Wt	4	6	42½ 37 511 615	Broussard R	b 119	8.70	76-15 Mighty Lura 116ᵐᵒOneForMyBaby109²MissBrownwood116½ Tired 9
15Jun78- 5Mth fst 170	:46	1.12⅘ 1.44	3↑ⓔMd Sp Wt	5	1	11½ 31 618 733	Broussard R	b 118	13.30	45-22 Merci Sha 110½ Estaciones 108¾ Pouliche D'Espace 115⁷ Stopped 7
1Jun78- 6Atl fm *1	(T):49⅕	1.15⅗ 1.42⅗	3↑ⓔMd Sp Wt	7	6	77½ 712 715 724	Calderon F	112	75.20	50-30 Love Star 118⁶ Stage Door Dolly 115³½ Rozzie Green 105¹ Outrun 8
8May78- 1Key fst 170	:48½	1.13⅘ 1.44⅘	3↑ⓔMd Sp Wt	9	4	42 2nd 42½ 511	Castaneda K	b 114	8.50	65-19 Hgley'sKitten113ᵐᵒDeluxeBinding118¹¼OurJointVentur114⁶ Tired 10
22Apr78- 9Key fst 6f	:22⅘	:47½ 1.13	3↑ⓔAllowance	9	10	841109110171020	Castaneda K	b 114	17.50	57-22 Hey Nancy 114³ Coiled 107¹¼ Minna E. 110ᵐᵏ Outrun 11
31Mar78- 2OP fst 6f	:22	:45⅘ 1.11⅗	3↑ Md Sp Wt	8	5	53½ 56 45½ 47½	Maple S	b 113	12.40	80-13 Screamer 123¹ MasterRichard113⁴⅜BreezingWind113¹½ No mishap 12
15May78- 8OP fst 6f	:22	:45⅘ 1.11⅘	3↑ⓔMagnolia	3	9	77½ 811 811 910	Vasquez G	b 113	59.50	73-20 Miss Baja 118¹½ Powder Room 113¹½ Bionic Babe 115²¾ Outrun 10
6Mar78- 5OP fst 170	:46⅘	1.13⅗ 1.44²½	3↑ⓔMd Sp Wt	4	2	2nd 33 78¾ 712	Snyder L	b 112	6.00	62-17 Bubble Act 111³¼ Indyson 113¾ Bold Jane 121² Tired 10

LATEST WORKOUTS ●Aug 9 Atl 3f fst :36 bg

Romanean

Dk. b. or br. f. 3, by Hyberborean—Jems Roman, by Trajan

Own.—Kollmansberger Doris
Br.—Kollmansberger Doris & R (NJ)
Tr.—Kollmansberger R

115

	1978	St.	1st	2nd	3rd	Amt.
	1978	5	1	1	0	$5,948
	1977	0	M	0	0	

3Aug78-	3Atl	fst	6f	:21⅗	:45	1:11⅘	3↑⑥⑤Allowance	9 1	3¹ 3² 2³ 3⁵	Thornburg B	113	7.50
20Jly78-	3Atl	fst	6f	:22⅗	:45⅗	1:11⅗	3↑⑥⑤Md Sp Wt	1 4	11½ 11½ 13	Thornburg B	116	.90
8Jly78-	1Atl	fst	6f	:22⅗	:45⅘	1:12⅗	3↑⑤Md Sp Wt	6 3	3² 3¹ 3¹ 2½	Thornburg B	116	20.10
3Jly78-	4Atl	sly	6f	:22⅗	:46⅘	1:12⅘	3↑⑤Md Sp Wt	11 7	5⁴½ 6⁴½ 9⅓ 9²¹	Lee R F	b 111	24.40
9Jun78-	9Atl	gd	6f	:22⅗	1:13	3↑⑤Md Sp Wt	4 7	6³½ 45 69½ 6¹⁴	Thornburg R	b 116	13.50

LATEST WORKOUTS   Jly 18 Atl   4f fst :49   b

Muffies Jet

Gr. m. 5, by Determined Man—Petite Astre, by Helfast

Own.—Taylor J R
Br.—Hengen E C (Va)
Tr.—Taylor John S

120

Turf Record	St.	1st	2nd	3rd					Amt.
1 0 0 0					1978	5	0	0	2	$2,357
					1977	10	0	0	3	$2,703

24Aug78-	7Atl	fst	6f	:47⅘	1:12½	1:45⅘	3↑⑥Clm 12000	3 2	22 43 49½ 416	Lukas M	b 116	14.80
24Jly78-	8Atl	fst	6f	:46⅘	1:12½	1:46	3↑⑥Clm 11500	6 4	58½ 57½ 67½ 610	Lukas M	b 116	3.00
8Jly78-	7Atl	fst	7f	:21⅘	:44⅗	1:24⅘	3↑⑥Allowance	7 2	37½ 57 3ⁿᵏ 2ʰᵈ	Lukas M	b 120	11.20
28Jun78-	6Atl	fst	6f	:21⅘	:45⅗	1:12½	3↑⑥Allowance	2 10	8¹¹ 918 47½ 56¼	Henderson R⁷	b 113	25.20
3Jun78-	8Atl	sly	6f	:22⅘	:46⅗	1:11⅘	3↑⑥Clm 13000	3 1	2¹½ 3²½ 36	Henderson R⁷	b 109	10.90
16Nov77-	7Key	fst	6f	:22⅗	:45⅘	1:12	3↑⑥Allowance	3 8	8¹² 8¹⁴ 8¹⁷ 8¹⁸	Moseley J W	b 113	29.00
2Nov77-	8Key	fst	170	:48⅘	1:14½	1:45⅘	3↑⑥Allowance	2 3	43 8¹³ 715 727	Maita A	b 115	12.10
1Sep77-	5Key	fst	6f	:22⅘	:46½	1:12	3↑⑥Allowance	6 7	6⁴½ 65 68	Meszaros G5	b 109	6.10
23Aug77-	6Atl	fst	6f	:21⅘	:45	1:10½	3↑⑥Allowance	4 7	712 79½ 56⅓ 33	Henderson R⁵	b 109	30.90
13Aug77-	6Atl	fst	6f	:22	:45	1:10½	3↑⑥Allowance	1 9	87½ 810 67⅓ 58	Meszaros G5	b 109	11.20

LATEST WORKOUTS   Jly 1 Atl   3f fst :36   b

I'm For Triggs'z

B. f. 3, by I'm For More—Triggs'z, by Successor

Own.—Kaplan M O
Br.—Triggs D (Fla)
Tr.—Taylor Robert J

115

Turf Record	St.	1st	2nd	3rd					Amt.
2 0 0 0					1978	9	1	1	2	$5,850
					1977	0	M	0	0	

25Jly78-	9Del	fst	170	:47	1:13½	1:44½	3↑⑥Allowance	2 1	13 12 2½ 35	Franklin R J5	b 107	25.70
14Jly78-	6Atl	fst	1⅟₁₆	:46⅘	1:12½	1:47⅘	3↑⑥Clm 16000	1 4	2¹½ 22 46¼ 418	Pronesti B	b 116	*2.60
8Jly78-	7Atl	fst	7f	:21⅘	:44⅗	1:24⅘	3↑⑥Allowance	8 1	5⁸½ 36 2ʰᵈ 32	St Leon G	114	3.50
28Jun78-	5Atl	fst	6f	:22⅘	:45⅘	1:11⅘	⑥Clm 15500	6 2	62½ 56½ 34 2½	Haldar A	116	27.60
10Jun78-	6Atl	fst	sf	:51	1:18½	1:55⅘	Clm 15500	1 4	4⅓ 54 810 819	Calderon F	111	50.70
1Jun78-	7Prim	fm	1	⊕:48	1:13⅗	1:39⅗	⑥Clm 23500	6 6	9¹² 9¹⁰ 717 720	McCarron G	114	17.70
5May78-	7GP	fst	6f	:21⅘	:45	1:10⅗	⑥Clm c-17000	1 2	21 33 69½ 8²⁸	Hussey C	114	6.60
27Apr78-	1GP	fst	6f	:23½	:47⅘	1:12⅘	⑥Md c-7500	2 2	12 13 16 110	Thornburg B	119	*1.70
11Apr78-	4GP	fst	6f	:22½	:46	1:13½	⑥Md 15000	6 7	79½ 813 79⅘ 68⅓	Zippi D M7	112	86.80

LATEST WORKOUTS   Aug 11 Atl   3f gd :40   b   Aug 3 Atl   5f sly 1:02⅘ b   Jly 22 Atl   4f fst :48   b   Jly 7 Atl   3f fst :39   b

Silver Crown

... Own.—Whitney C V

Ch. f. 3, by Bold Bidder—Spit and Polish, by Herbager
Br.—Whitney C V (Ky)
Tr.—Rieser Stanley M

117

	Turf Record					St.	1st	2nd	3rd	Amt.
	St.	1st	2nd	3rd						
	1	0	0	0	1978	8	0	1	0	$3,855
					1977	7	1	0	0	$4,225

Date											Jockey		Odds	Company	Finish
2Aug78- 5Mth sly 6f :22 :45¾ 1:12⅗ 3↑⑤Allowance	7	2	2½	3½	4½	6¹¹	Mize W E⁵	107	5.90	66-22 Zip Qui 112²¼ Misty Native 114³¼ Jancinto Girl 108² Tired 7
21Jly78- 4Atl fm *5¼f ①:22 :46¾ 1:05¾ 3↑⑥Allowance	9	4	4½	3½	3¹¼	5⁵¾	Whitley K	114	5.70	79-11 Diplomatic Lady 116²¼ Sweetly 112² Kathy Who 109no Tired 10
26Jun78- 7Mth fst 6f :21⅗ :44¾ 1:10⅘ 3↑⑥Allowance	10	1	2nd	52¾	88¾	Asmussen C B K⁷	107	9.20	80-15 Tegawitha 117³ Heavenly Wind 117¹¼ Misty Native 114¾ Tired 10
17Jun78- 4Mth fst 6f :22 :45 1:11¾ 3↑⑥Allowance	1	6	3nk	1½	1hd	3¾	Asmussen C B K⁷	107	29.30	81-19 PorcelainFlower117²Fascinadora114hdSilverCrown107³ Weakened 9
10Jun78- 7Mth fst 6f :22 :45⅗ 1:10⅘ 3↑⑥Allowance	2	6	11½	3¹	6¹¹	8¹⁷	DiNicola B	111	11.60	69-23 Forbidden Isle 111⁴ Tegawitha 117⁴ Ericka Downs 108²½ Tired 9
2Jun78- 7Mth fst 6f :21⅗ :45¾ 1:11¾ 3↑⑥Allowance	2	1	1hd	1½	4¹½	48¼	Nemeti W	112	4.60	74-21 Sugarbush Baby 117²¼ Minaretta 108¾Fascinadora114⁵ Weakened 8
5May78- 7CD gd 6f :22 :45⅗ 1:11⅗ ⑥Allowance	6	1	11	1hd	23	37¾	Hirdes R J Jr⁷	108	2.80	82-15 White Song 121⁷ Love To Tell 121nkSilverCrown108⁵¼ Weakened 9
14Apr78- 6Kee fst *7f :22⅗ :46 1:29 ⑥Allowance	5	2	12½	12	22	Brumfield D	117	2.70	76-19 Native Look 117² Silver Crown 117²¼ Danshua 112⁸ Second best 8
4Nov77- 7Aqu fst 6f :23⅗ :46¾ 1:11⅘ ⑥Allowance	8	4	44¾	5⁴	8¹²	8¹³	Turcotte R	114	25.00	73-20 Four Angles 114² Dr. FeelGreat116¾SallysFlight114no Tired badly 8
10ct77- 1Bel fst 6f :22⅗ :46⅘ 1:12⅗ ⑥Allowance	3	2	21	5³¾	81⁴	82¹	Venezia M	b 114	25.30	60-14 Lucinda Lea 119¹¾ Sallys Flight 114no No No-Nos 114¾ Tired 8

LATEST WORKOUTS Aug 10 Mth 4f fst :48 h ● Jly 31 Mth 4f fst :47 h ● Jly 17 Mth 4f my :47⅘ h (d) Jly 10 Mth 4f fst :48 h of animals that might pay 4 to 1 elsewhere, the kind of near-cinch I have in mind often pays 3 to 2, when it ought to be 4 to 5.

And sometimes the odds are even more robust—especially when the classy animal's superiority is less than conspicuously evident, escaping the attention of most players. An interesting yet familiar example occurred in the fourth race at Atlantic City on Saturday evening, August 12, 1978. I do not pretend that the winner of the race was a mortal cinch but I am sublimely certain that its record and the records of its weak opponents formed a pattern which the reader should bear in mind for future use. At the odds the winner paid, the handicapper can prosper even if the pattern yields a winner only 25 percent of the time.

The conditions of the race and the past performances of the starters are reproduced here as originally published in *Daily Racing Form*. The reader will note that the race was at six furlongs, for fillies and mares that had never won two races of any kind. A quick glance at the past-performance records showed that most of the starters had been running in claiming and maiden-claiming races, some of them woefully cheap. If a horse could be found without so humble and discouraging a background and with some kind of racing ability in better company, it could be credited with probably superior class and an excellent chance to win. Let us now run down the list.

Smooth M. Out had shown early speed in moderate claiming company but had not raced since May. ELIMINATE.

Final Glow, the favorite at an incredible 7 to 5, had broken her maiden in a $14,000 claiming race for non-winners 16 days ago. Winners of $14,000 maiden claiming races do not ordinarily jump up and beat legitimate allowance runners in their next starts. If an allowance horse is in this field, the favorite has little chance. ELIMINATE.

Double Rhythm has not raced since July 10 and has been showing little in her allowance and claiming attempts. ELIMINATE.

Kate Coventry has never run with a claiming tag but beat half her opponents in each of two recent attempts against decent allowance horses at Monmouth Park, where the opposition is far better than at Atlantic City. POSSIBLE CONTENDER.

Some Clip beat $8,000 maidens here and has been performing indifferently in allowance races for state-bred stock. ELIMINATE.

Linda Faye's record is one of non-accomplishment, although she has been entered repeatedly against far superior fields, including males. Her only victory came against maidens, when she got a huge early lead and was not caught. If today's field is really soft, she might have a chance, provided she leaves the gate on time, which is not inevitable. POSSIBLE CONTENDER.

Romanean has been racing against state breds and has done nothing to suggest ability to beat a class animal. ELIMINATE.

Muffie's Jet has been unable to get the early lead in longer races against inexpensive fields and does not figure to sprint well against better. ELIMINATE.

I'm For Triggs'z would rather sprint than go long, but has shown none of the quality we look for in an allowance race like today's. ELIMINATE.

Silver Crown, from no less a stable than that of the celebrated Cornelius Vanderbilt Whitney, liked neither the slop nor the grass in her latest two starts, but showed authentic early speed against substantial opponents in previous main-track sprints at Monmouth Park. She has been working extremely well and is accompanied by Monmouth's leading rider, Don MacBeth. She should have no difficulty capturing the early lead against this weak field, and is not very likely to be caught. At 5 to 1, she is an excellent risk.

At any track, analysis no more elaborate than the kind just demonstrated can be depended on to produce dozens of winners each year. Horses that display even a little foot while being outgunned in stakes

---

FOURTH RACE
Atlantic City
AUGUST 12, 1978

6 FURLONGS. (1.08⅗) ALLOWANCE. Purse $6,500. Fillies & Mares, 3–year–olds and upward. Which have never won two races. Weights, 3–year–olds, 117 lbs.; Older, 122 lbs.; Non–winners of $4,200, allowed, 2 lbs.; Maidens, 4 lbs.; (Winners preferred.)

Value of race $6,500, value to winner $3,900, second $1,300, third $715, fourth $390, fifth $195. Mutuel pool $63,783.

Last Raced	Horse	Eqt.A.Wt PP St	¼	½	Str	Fin	Jockey	Odds $1
2Aug78 5Mth6	Silver Crown	3 117 10 3	1 4	1 5	1 6	1 4	MacBeth D	5.00
26Jly78 3Mth7	Kate Coventry	b 4 122 4 6	7½	6hd	5½	2 1½	Sierra J A	23.30
10Jly78 5Pim7	Double Rhythm	b 3 117 3 4	2½	2 1½	2 1½	3nk	Landicini C Jr	27.10
3Aug78 2Atl4	Some Clip	b 4 120 5 7	8½	7 1½	6 3	4 3	Black A S	24.70
27Jly78 3Atl1	Final Glow	3 115 2 10	7½	5 1	3 1½	5 1½	Nied J Jr	1.40
10May78 9Key8	Smooth M. Out	3 110 1 2	6 1	10	7hd	6nk	D'Agusto J G5	30.20
2Aug78 7Atl4	Muffies Jet	b 5 120 8 8	9 2	9 1½	8½	7no	Lukas M	22.10
29Jly78 7Atl6	Linda Faye	b 3 115 6 9	10	8½	9 1½	8 2	Weipert D	11.80
25Jly78 9Del3	I'm For Triggs'z	b 3 115 9 5	4hd	3 1	4hd	9 4	Barrera C	3.90
3Aug78 2Atl3	Romanean	3 115 7 1	3 1½	4hd	10	10	Thornburg B	4.90

OFF AT 9:06, EDT. Start good, Won easily. Time, :22⅕, :45⅖, 1:11⅗ Track good.

$2 Mutuel Prices:

12-SILVER CROWN	12.00	6.60	5.20
4-KATE COVENTRY		18.40	13.00
3-DOUBLE RHYTHM			10.40

$3 TRIFECTA 12–4–3 PAID $6,321.

Ch. f, by Bold Bidder—Spit and Polish, by Herbager. Trainer Rieser Stanley M. Bred by Whitney C V (Ky).

SILVER CROWN broke alertly and quickly established a comfortable lead, wasn't menaced and won under wraps. KATE COVENTRY unable to keep up early, made a mild late bid. DOUBLE RHYTHM raced in closest pursuit of winner for much of the journey and lacked a stretch rally. SOME CLIP passed tiring rivals. FINAL GLOW broke slowly, made a mild bid in backstretch then tired I'M FOR TRIGGS'Z tired. ROMANEAN was through early. ESTHONIA failed to arrive in the paddock and was ordered scratched by the stewards. All monies wagered on her were refunded.

races are always threats when entered at the proper distance in allowance fields. Horses lowered in claiming price, or dropping from allowance to claiming company, are always threats if the distance is suitable and recent activity contains signs (however slight) of improving condition. Finally, the handicapper should remain alert to situations in which claiming runners hold class advantages over weak opponents in allowance races. A hard-knocking campaigner with several victories at the track's highest claiming level may romp when entered in an allowance affair for animals that have never won a race or two other than maiden or claiming. Indeed, at Aqueduct's winter meeting each year, former claiming runners invariably win a few stakes without arousing extraordinary surprise. To take advantage of opportunities provided by claiming horses entered in weak allowance or stakes fields, it is helpful to keep track of local purse and claiming-price schedules, noting at which point on the scale certain claiming races command purses roughly equivalent to those offered in certain allowance races. Knowledge of the running times normal for races in these closely related class categories also helps, often revealing that the claiming animal consistently runs faster than the supposedly superior field it faces in its allowance debut.

Leading Money Winners of All Time

As of March 1979, the following horses were the biggest earners in the history of the sport.

Kelso	$1,977,896	Secretariat	1,316,808
Forego	1,938,957	Nashua	1,288,565
Round Table	1,749,869	Ancient Title	1,252,791
Affirmed	1,609,318	Susan's Girl	1,251,668
Exceller	1,599,003	Carry Back	1,241,165
Dahlia	1,535,443	Foolish Pleasure	1,216,705
Buckpasser	1,462,014	Seattle Slew	1,208,726
Allez France	1,380,565		

What Class Is

Thoroughbred class, or quality, is easy to recognize and hard to define. From Eclipse to Seattle Slew and Affirmed, the horses of highest class —the champions—have been the ones whose physical soundness, speed, stamina and competitive willingness enabled them to beat everything in sight. They won under serious weight disadvantages. They won on off-tracks. They won by narrow margins after overcoming serious lack of running room in the stretch. And sometimes they won by exhausting their opponents in the first three quarters of a mile and romping home all alone, a city block in front.

Many of the horses they whipped were every bit as sound. Some were speedier. Some had no less stamina and as much courage. But the champions combined those traits in maximum quantity. And, lest we forget, they were trained well enough to remain sound and consistent in race after race. Not many trainers can make a champion of a potential champion. Indeed, nine out of every ten trainers can be relied on to ruin any potential champion they handle. Competence is as rare a quality in this field as in any other.

Class and Speed

One of the hallmarks of superior class is speed. But it is speed of a special kind. Most good horses (professional horsemen seldom say "great") set speed records only when pressed by an able, ambitious rival or an overly eager jockey. Otherwise, they run just hard enough to win. Their failure to break watches during the early stages of their three-year-old seasons—when they are big and strong enough to do so —is terribly misleading to racetrack crowds. Large numbers of customers, impressed by the speedy past performances of relatively undistinguished three-year-olds, make the mistake of backing them against classier animals whose own clockings have been slower.

An illustration is in order. The sixth at Aqueduct on November 3, 1966, was a seven-furlong allowance race for three-year-olds and up that had never won two races other than maiden or claiming. Nothing in the race looked like an imminent national champion, but class distinctions are as important among second- or third- or tenth-rate stock as among the champs. The co-favorite at slightly less than 5 to 2 in this particular sprint was a nicely bred three-year-old, Second Venture, which had been in the money in each of its four starts, winning two of them. In its only effort at seven furlongs, it had run within half a length of an excellent early pace of .45⅕ to the half-mile, tiring in the stretch and finishing third, four and a half lengths behind a winner clocked in 1.23⅗. In its most recent start, exactly a week before, it had set a pace of .46⅖ to the half in a six-furlong allowance race and had lost by a nose in 1.11⅖, after swerving under its apprentice rider. The superb John L. Rotz would be up today.

The Best of the Best—Thoroughbred Champions Since 1948

	Two-year-old Male	Two-year-old Filly	Three-year-old Male	Three-year-old Filly	Handicap Horse	Handicap Mare	Turf Horse	Steeplechase Horse	Horse of the Year
1948	Blue Peter	Myrtle Charm	Citation	Miss Request	Citation	Conniver	—	American Way	CITATION
1949	Hill Prince	Bed o' Roses	Capot	Two Lea Wistful	Coaltown	Bewitch	—	Trough Hill	CAPOT
1950	Battlefield	Aunt Jinny	Hill Prince	Next Move	Noor	Two Lea	—	Oedipus	HILL PRINCE
1951	Tom Fool	Rose Jet	Counterpoint	Kiss Me Kate	Hill Prince	Bed o' Roses	—	Oedipus	COUNTERPOINT
1952	Native Dancer	Sweet Patootie	One Count	Real Delight	Crafty Admiral	Real Delight	—	Jam	ONE COUNT
1953	Porterhouse	Evening Out	Native Dancer	Grecian Queen	Tom Fool	Sickle's Image	Iceberg II.	The Mast	TOM FOOL
1954	Nashua	High Voltage	High Gun	Parlo	Native Dancer	Parlo	Stan	King Commander	NATIVE DANCER
1955	Needles	Double-dogdare	Nashua	Misty Morn	High Gun	Misty Morn	St. Vincent	Neji	NASHUA
1956	Barbizon	Leallah	Needles	Double-dogdare	Swaps	Blue Sparkler	Career Boy	Shipboard	SWAPS
1957	Nadir	Idun	Bold Ruler	Bayou	Dedicate	Pucker Up	Round Table	Neji	BOLD RULER
1958	First Landing	Quill	Tim Tam	Idun	Round Table	Bornastar	Round Table	Neji	ROUND TABLE
1959	Warfare	My Dear Girl	Sword Dancer	Royal Native	Sword Dancer	Tempted	Round Table	Ancestor	SWORD DANCER
1960	Hail to Reason	Bowl of Flowers	Kelso	Berlo	Bald Eagle	Royal Native	—	Benguala	KELSO
1961	Crimson Satan	Cicada	Carry Back	Bowl of Flowers	Kelso	Airmans Guide	T.V. Lark	Peal	KELSO
1962	Never Bend	Smart Deb	Jaipur	Cicada	Kelso	Primonetta	—	Barnabys Bluff	KELSO

Year									
1963	Hurry to Market	Tosmah	Chateaugay	Lamb Chop	Kelso	Cicada	Mongo	Amber Diver	KELSO
1964	Bold Lad	Queen Empress	Northern Dancer	Tosmah	Kelso	Tosmah	—	Bon Nouvel	KELSO
1965	Buckpasser	Moccasin	Tom Rolfe	What a Treat	Roman Brother	Old Hat	Parka	Bon Nouvel	ROMAN BROTHER
1966	Successor	Regal Gleam	Buckpasser	Lady Pitt	Buckpasser	Open Fire	Assagai	Mako	BUCK-PASSER
1967	Vitriolic	Queen of the Stage	Damascus	Furl Sail	Damascus	Straight Deal	Fort Marcy	Quick Pitch	DAMASCUS
1968	Top Knight	Gallant Bloom	Stage Door Johnny	Dark Mirage	Dr. Fager	Gamely	Dr. Fager	Bon Nouvel	DR. FAGER
1969	Silent Screen	Fast Attack	Arts and Letters	Gallant Bloom	Arts and Letters	Gallant Bloom	Hawaii	L'Escargot	ARTS AND LETTERS
1970	Hoist the Flag	Forward Gal	Personality	Office Queen	Fort Marcy	Shuvee	Fort Marcy	Top Bid	FORT MARCY
1971	Riva Ridge	Numbered Account	Canonero II.	Turkish Trousers	Ack Ack	Shuvee	Run the Gantlet	Shadow Brook	ACK ACK
1972	Secretariat	La Prevoyante	Key to the Mint	Susan's Girl	Autobiography	Typecast	Cougar II.	Soothsayer	SECRETARIAT
1973	Protagonist	Talking Picture	Secretariat	Desert Vixen	Riva Ridge	Susan's Girl	Secretariat	Athenian Idol	SECRETARIAT
1974	Foolish Pleasure	Ruffian	Little Current	Chris Evert	Forego	Desert Vixen	Dahlia	Gran Kan	FOREGO
1975	Honest Pleasure	Dearly Precious	Wajima	Ruffian	Forego	Susan's Girl	Snow Knight	Life's Illusion	FOREGO
1976	Seattle Slew	Sensational	Bold Forbes	Revidere	Forego	Proud Delta	Youth	Straight and True	FOREGO
1977	Affirmed	Lakeville Miss	Seattle Slew	Our Miss	Forego	Cascapedia	Johnny D.	Café Prince	SEATTLE SLEW
1978	Spectacular Bid	It's in the Air Candy Eclair	Affirmed	Tempest Queen	Seattle Slew	Late Bloomer	MacDiarmida	Café Prince	AFFIRMED

6th Race Aqueduct

7 FURLONGS — AQUEDUCT

7 FURLONGS. (Chute). (Rose Net). (Rose Net, Sept. 17, 1962, 1.21⅖, 6, 114.) Allowances. Purse $6,000. 3-year-olds and upward which have never won two races other than maiden or claiming. Weights 3-year-olds 122 lbs., older 124 lbs. Non-winners of a race other than maiden or claiming since October 1 allowed 3 lbs., of such a race since August 27, 5 lbs., of such a race since July 30, 7 lbs.

Fence Rider
Ch. g (1963-Ky), by Middleground—Friponne, by Shut Out
King Ranch — Max Hirsch — (King Ranch) — 115 — 1966 14 2 1 1 $8,035 — 1965 1 M 0 0

Date						Race							Jockey	Wt	Odds		Finish	
27Oct66-7Aqu	fst 1⅛	.48	1.13½	1.51	Allowance	1	5	5 5½	44	23	42¾	JRuane	b 112	2.80e	78-20	Bol 'n Jac 115 2½ Without Warning 112no Naturalist 116nk	Tired 7
2Oct65-6Aqu	sl 7f	.23½	.46½	1.25	Allowance	5	9	109 1015	89	65	55½	D'Amigo	b 112	31.0	7o-3	Glenrose 116 2½ Prince Graff 115nk Lord Byron 118¹	Began slowly 10
29Sep56-4Aqu	fst 7f	.22⅘	.45⅘	1.23⅘	Allowance	5	9	66 66½	64	55¾	JLRotz		b 115	23.80	83-18	End Man 113 1½ Mountainside 120nk Golden Buttons 113 3¾	No factor 6
16Jly66-6Aqu	fst 7f	.22⅘	.45⅘	1.23⅘	Allowance	6	9	88½	77½	78	79¼	WBoland	b 117	10.30	79-18	Woodford 112½ Vail Pass 1124 Second Venture 117¹	Never close 9
30Jun66-6Mth	fst 1	.46	1.12¾	1.45	Allowance	3	3	31½	77½	76	78	SBoulmetis	b 117	3.20	76-18	Fence Rider 117nk Ready All 117 1¾ Ridgid 1154	Narrowly best 8
20Jun66-6Aqu	hd 1¼⊕			1.52¾⊕		3	3	31½	11½	11nk	564	JLRotz	b 114	7.50	67-27	Prince Rico 115¹ Tartan Dance 113½ Gourmand 111¹	No factor 8
31May66-5Aqu	fst 1⅛	.48½	1.13½	1.52½	Md Sp Wt	7	6	77½	76	41½	1½	JLRotz	b 113	5.30	74-22	Fence Rider 113½ Intangible 114h Poker Table 113nk	Driving 8
25May66-3GS	fst 170	.47½	1.11½	1.42½	Md Sp Wt	6	5½	54	24	24	23¼	SBoulmetis	b 115	2.90	79-16	Gallant Flash 115 3¾ Fence Rider 1158 Black River 115¹¾	Gamely 8
12May66-3Aqu	fst 1⅛	.48½	1.13½	1.53½	Md Sp Wt	4	3	23	21½	3½	44	JLRotz	b 113	4.40	63-20	Densaland 113no Intangible 113½ Poker Table 113 3¾	Broke whip 7
LATEST WORKOUTS	Oct 31 Bel m.t. 6f fst 1.16 h			Oct 24 Bel m.t. 6f fst 1.14½ h						Oct 17 Bel t.c. 6f fm 1.16 h				Oct 15 Bel m.t. 7f fst 1.30 h				

Absolute Power X
B. c (1963-Ky), by Bold Ruler—Who Dini, by Hypnotist II
High Tide Stable — L. S. Barrera — (E. G. Burke) — 115 — 1966 7 1 1 0 $5,350 — 1965 1 1 0 0 $2,750

Date						Race							Jockey	Wt	Odds		Finish	
27Oct66-5Aqu	fst 6f	.23	.45¾	1.11⅘	Allowance	4	4	4½	54½	57½	EBelmonte		112	27.90	78-20	Lord Byron 118no Second Venture 1113½ Tom Poker 110 1¼	Swerved 7
1Mar66-7SA	fst 1¼	.45⅘	1.10⅘	1.43⅘	Allowance	2	1	34½	45	710	715	EBelmonte		118	6.40	71-17	Vague Image 116h Triple Tux 116 3½ Keen Kutter 116 2½	Early foot 7
19Feb66-3SA	fst 1⅛	.47⅘	1.11⅘	1.41⅘	Allowance	5	1	1½	2½	26	210	EBelmonte		120	16.20	84-7	Boldnesian 11810 Absolute Power 1206 Mejor 118 1½	2nd best 10
15Feb66-7SA	fst 1⅛	.46⅘	1.10⅘	1.42⅘	Allowance	2	4	3½	66½	77½	MYanez		113	2.00e	82-12	Boldnesian 1138 Fleet Shoe 1158 Wingover 117²	Lost ground 7
5Feb66-3SA	fst 1⅛	.46	1.11	1.45	Allowance	5	2	21½	11½	11	EBelmonte		115	5.50	78-12	Absolute Power 115¹ Plimenek 115¹ Go It Alone 115nk	Driving 12
13Jan66-4SA	fst 6f	.22⅘	.45⅘	1.10⅘	Allowance	7	7	54½	64¾	64½	EBelmonte		116	7.70	84-13	Vague Image 118nk Royal Step 1185 Perfect Prince 116 3¾	Tired 11
5Jan66-6SA	fst 6f	.22¾	.45¾	1.17	LosFeliz	7	3	21½	68	79¾	EBelmonte		122	8.50	81-12	Brand Royal 122² Twins Orbit 122½ Golden Buttons 122½	Tired 10
29Dec65 4SA	sly 6f	.22¾	.46	1.11½	1nk EBelmonte	1	7	3¹					118	16.30	85-19	Absolute Power 118nk Fact Seeker 1185½ Dominar 118 1¼	Driving 12
LATEST WORKOUTS	Oct 21 Bel m.t. 5f fst 1.00⅘ hg			Oct 13 Bel tr.t. 5f fst 1.02½ b						Oct 8 Bel tr.t. 5f fst 1.05 b				Oct 4 Bel tr.t. 4f fst .48⅘ h				

The Los Feliz Stakes run in two divisions, 6th and 8th races.

Second Venture
Ch. c (1963-Ky), by Porterhouse—Blue Rcbe, by Shut Out
H. S. Nichols — E. Jackson — (Mr. R. W. P. Johnston) — 115 — 1966 4 2 1 0 $8,205 — 1965 0 M 0 0

Date						Race							Jockey	Wt	Odds		Finish	
27Oct66-5Aqu	fst 6f	.23	.45¾	1.11⅘	Allowance	6	2	31	1h	2no	JJMartin7		111	6.90	86-20	Lord Byron 118no Second Venture 1113½ Tom Poker 110 1¼	Swerved 7
16Jly 66-6Aqu	fst 7f	.22⅘	.45¾	1.23⅘	Allowance	4	5	2h	2½	34½	WBlum		117	*0.90	83-18	Woodford 112½ Vail Pass 1124 Second Venture 117¹	No excuse 9
7Jly 66-6Aqu	fst 7f	.22⅘	.45⅘	1.23⅘	Allowance	3	7	2½	1h	WBlum			117	*1.10	86-15	Second Venture 117h Rogo 110½ Happy Noble 112½	Lost whip, up 7
29Jun66-1Aqu	fst 7f	.22⅘	.46⅘	1.13⅘	Md Sp Wt	2	1	1h	1½	14	WBlum		115	3.00	86-17	SecondVenture 1154 Age of Reason 115h NightCloud 115h	Handily 8
LATEST WORKOUTS	Nov 2 Bel tr.t. 3f fst .35½ h			Oct 22 Bel m.t. 5f gd 1.01 h						Oct 15 Bel tr.t. 5f fst 1.02 b				Sep 9 Bel tr.t. 5f fst 1.07 b				

Sermon
Ch. c (1963-Ky), by Nadir—Edified, by Jacopo
W. H. Perry — J. W. Maloney — (Claiborne Farm) — 122 — 1966 4 2 2 0 $7,405 — 1965 1 M 0 0 $210

Date						Race							Jockey	Wt	Odds		Finish	
26Oct66-8Aqu	fst 6f	.22⅘	.46⅘	1.10⅘	Allowance	7	4	42½	32½	1h	1h	EBelmonte		121	4.40	89-19	Sermon 12¹h Counsellor 113½ It's Blitz 1074	Strong urging 10
17Oct66-6Aqu	fst 7f	.23	.46⅘	1.24⅘	Allowance	4	3	3nk	1h	2½	2½	EBelmonte		121	*1.60	82-19	Hurry Akal 115½ Sermon 12¹h As You Like 121 2½	Held on gamely 7
60ct66-5Aqu	fst 6f	.22¾	.47⅘	1.12¾	Md Sp Wt	1	1	15	18	111	EBelmonte		121	*1.60	81-24	Sermon 12111 Vocalist 121¼ Birdsofafeather 1214	Won easily 10
29Sep66-1Aqu	fst 6f	.23½	.47	1.12⅘	Md Sp Wt	7	7	74½	89½	68½	54	BBaeza		120	*1.30	77-18	Emerald Talent 115h Soldier'sStory120½ Birdsofafeather120¾	No exc. 10
14Aug65-1Sar	fst 5½f	.22⅘	.46½	1.05¾	Md Sp Wt	12	8	44½	53½	42½	LAdams		b 122	*1.70	87-6	Total Talent 12¹ Gig 122¹ Royal Step 122nk	Going well at end 12
LATEST WORKOUTS	Oct 31 Bel tr.t. 5f fst 1.01¾ h			Oct 25 Bel tr.t. 3f fst .37¾ b						Oct 22 Bel tr.t. 4f fst .50 b				Oct 14 Bel tr.t. 4f fst .50½ b				

Red Beach X

B. c (1962), by First Landing—Recite, by Citation
Saddle Rock Farm   J. P. Conway   (H. B. Phipps)   **117**

		1966	6	1	3	0	$1,000
		1965	12	1	1	0	$7,100

Date											
2Oct66-6Aqu	sl 7f	.23⅖	.46⅗1.25	Allowance	9	5	5⁴	3³	66¼	89¼	HWoodhouse	b 115	21.80	72-23	Glenrose 116²¼ Prince Graff 115ⁿᵏ Lord Byron 118¹	Early factor 10
11Oct66-8Aqu	fst 6f	.22⅖	.46½1.11⅗	Allowance	8	3	3¹	86	81⅖	815	HWoodhouse	b 115	7.70	70-21	Yucatan 118ⁿᵏ Tom Poker 110² Stands to Reason 112ʰ	Stopped 8
18Feb66-6Hia	fst 7f	.23	.45³⁄₅1.23⅗	Allowance	3	3	1¹	1½	12	21	EGuerin	b 115	4.50	90-19	Full of Fun 108¹ Red Beach 115³½ Yucatan 108¹	Drifted out 8
8Feb66-9Hia	fst 7f	.23	.45³⁄₅1.23⅗	Allowance	4	3	2ʰ	22	34	69	EGuerin	b 116	17.90	84-13	Sky Wonder 116¹ Tronado 113⁷ Dogeola 113ʰ	Hard used early 8
26Jan66-7Hia	sly 7f	.23⅗	.46⅗1.25	Allowance	5	6	44	61²	91³	88¼	EGuerin	b 116	15.30	75-17	d-GrandMarais 109³ Comprehensive 114ⁿᵏ HurricaneTim 114¼	Tired 11
12Jan65-8TrP	fst 6f	.22½	.45⅖1.09½	Allowance	2	8	76¼	89⁴	816	81³	DBrumfield	b 119	2.40	83-14	Judge Morris 119ⁿᵒ Admiral Clove 109²¼ Hill Chance 109ʰ	Bore out 8
30Dc65-9TrP	fst 6f	.22	.44³⁄₅1.09²⁄₅	Allowance	6	4	2¼	23	36¼	78¼	DBrumfield	b 115	5.40	86-17	I'm Rusty 110⁴¼ Red Redeemer 113¼ Hill Chance 108¼	Tired 11
21Aug65-5Sar	fst 7f	.22½	.45³⁄₅1.23⅗	Allowance	8	3	5³½	22	32½	32¼	SHernandez	119	3.40	88- 9	d-Timurid 117¼ Tudor Manor 112² Red Beach 119⁵	Taken up sharply 9

21Aug65—Placed second through disqualification.

| 13Aug65-5Sar | fst 1¼ | .47³⁄₅1.12½1.50⅖ | Allowance | 2 | 2 | 3²¼ | 21 | 12 | 18 | SHernandez | 112 | 4.30 | 91- 9 | Red Beach 112⁸ Alackaday 112ⁿᵒ Known Quantity 115ʰ | Easily 8 |

LATEST WORKOUTS   Nov 2 Bel m.t. 3f fst .37⅖ b   Oct 27 Bel tr.t. 4f fst .52 b   Oct 8 Bel m.t. 5f fst 1.00⅗ h   Oct 4 Bel m.t. 1m fst 1.41⅗ b

Tom Poker

B. h (1961), by Tom Fool—Miss Stripes, by Big Game
Hob-au Farm   H. A. Jerkens   (Shawnee Farm)   **112⁵**

		1966	3	0	1	1	$1,850
		1955	11	2	2	3	$8,680

2/Oct66-5Aqu	fst 6f	.23	.45³⁄₅1.11⅖	Allowance	2	2	2ʰ	32	33½	ECardone5	b 110	*0.60	82-20	Lord Byron 118ⁿᵒ Second Venture 111³¼ Tom Poker 101¼	No exc. 7
2Oct66-6Aqu	fst 6f	.22⅗	.46³⁄₅1.25	Allowance	4	4	2¼	54¼	Bolteo	WBoland	b 115	*1.10	—	Glenrose 116²¼ Prince Graff 115ⁿᵏ Lord Byron 118¹	Rein broke 10
11Oct66-8Aqu	fst 6f	.22⅖	.46½1.11⅗	Allowance	1	2	21	1ʰ	2ⁿᵏ	ECardone5	b 110	6.70	85-21	Yucatan 118ⁿᵏ Tom Poker 110² Stands to Reason 112ʰ	Gamely 8
11Dec65-9Aqu	fst 7f	.23½	.46½1.25½	Allowance	5	4	64¼	53¼	42½	32¼	WBoland	b 124	3.50	80-26	Twin Teddy 124⁴ Yucatan 112² Tom Poker 124²¼	Wide, mild bid 9
6Dc65-8Aqu	fst 7f	.23½	.47	1.25⅗	Allowance	3	4	43	3½	13	13	WBoland	b 118	2.10	77-22	Tom Poker 118³ R. Anniversary 113¹ Thirty Pieces 113⁷	Easily 6
25Nov65-8Aqu	gd 7f	.23	.46½1.25³⁄₅	Allowance	2	3	3½	38	410	56½	WBoland	117	5.70	71-26	Round Table Pet 115¼ El Premiere 110⁴ GreatDepths122²	Weakened 8
25Oct65-4Aqu	fst 6f	.22⅖	.45³⁄₅1.11	Allowance	2	4	51¼	31¼	31¼	SHernandez	119	5.50	77-18	Brooklyn Bridge 121⁸ Mount Noble 113²¼ Tom Poker 119²¼	No mis'p 8
19O't65-8Aqu	fst 6f	.22½	.45½1.12	Allowance	2	1	87¼	86	5¼	42	JLRotz	121	5.10	81-18	Twin Teddy 117ⁿᵒ Great Depths 115ⁿᵒ Vail Pass 115²	In close 9

LATEST WORKOUTS   Nov 1 Bel m.t. 3f fst .39⅖ b   Oct 25 Bel tr.t. 4f fst .51 b   Oct 19 Bel tr.t. 4f sly .53 b   Oct 10 Bel tr.t. 4f fst .50⅖ b

The other co-favorite, Sermon, was not only well bred but a product of the spectacularly successful Claiborne Farm. Its owner was the renowned William Haggin Perry. The trainer was Jim Maloney, one of the nation's leaders. These credentials spell class. The colt had made its only two-year-old start at Saratoga in August, 1965, coming on strong at the end of a losing race at five and a half furlongs. Its potential class had made it the betting favorite in that maiden affair. It returned to the wars in September, 1966, at Aqueduct, again in a maiden-special, again as the favorite. Again it lost while gaining in the stretch, this time at six furlongs.

It broke its maiden in October, again as favorite, winning by eleven lengths at six furlongs, after Eddie Belmonte hustled it into an early lead. Its next was a seven-furlong allowance affair. It lost in a game effort, after leading at the half-mile in .46⅗—more than a second slower than Second Venture's early speed in a similar race. And the final clocking of the race was 1.24⅗, a full second slower than the Second Venture race. On October 26, Sermon ran in a six-furlong allowance and won by a head in the excellent time of 1.10⅗.

Plainly, the horse had more than a smidgeon of class and was beginning to get its sea legs. Why would anyone pick a Second Venture over an animal of this kind? True, Second Venture had run more swiftly at seven furlongs. But Sermon had run more determinedly, and under 121

Results of 6th Race Aqueduct—November 3, 1966

SIXTH RACE
Aqu - 29224
November 3, 1966

7 FURLONGS. (Chute). (Rose Net, Sept. 17, 1962, 1.21⅕, 6, 114.)
Allowances. Purse $6,000. 3-year-olds and upward which have never won two races other than maiden or claiming. Weights 3-year-olds 122 lbs., older 124 lbs. Non-winners of a race other than maiden or claiming since October 1 allowed 3 lbs., of such a race since August 27, 5 lbs., of such a race since July 30, 7 lbs.
Value to winner $3,900, second $1,200, third $600, fourth $300. Mutuel pool $271,281.

Index	Horse	Eqt A Wt PP St	¼	½	Str	Fin	Jockey	Owner	Odds $1
29097Aqu¹	Sermon	b 3 122 4 2	1½	2³	1³	1½	E Belmonte	W H Perry	2.40
29103Aqu³	Tom Poker	5 112 6 1	3½	3h	3½	2³	E Cardone⁵	Hobeau Farm	2.80
29050Aqu⁸	Red Beach	b 4 117 5 3	2¹	1h	2½	3no	H Woodh'use	Saddle Rock Farm	14.80
29105Aqu⁴	Fence Rider	b 3 115 1 6	6	5h	5³	41½	W Blum	King Ranch	10.20
29103Aqu²	Second Venture	3 115 3 4	4½	42	4³	52½	J L Rotz	H S Nichols	2.40
29103Aqu⁵	Absolute Power	3 115 2 5	5²	6	6	6	B Baeza	High Tide Stable	4.20

Time .23, .45⅗, 1.10⅗, 1.23⅘ (with wind in backstretch). Track sloppy.

$2 Mutuel Prices:

4-SERMON	6.80	3.20	2.60
6-TOM POKER		3.60	3.20
5-RED BEACH			5.60

Ch. c, by Nadir—Edified, by Jacopo. Trainer J. W. Maloney. Bred by Claiborne Farm (Ky.).

IN GATE AT 2.59. OFF AT 2.59½ EASTERN STANDARD TIME. Start good. Won driving.

SERMON sent along inside to make the pace under good rating, shook off RED BEACH to draw clear in upper stretch and was fully extended to hold TOM POKER safe. The latter, never far back, raced wide throughout and was slowly getting to winner. RED BEACH weakened after duelling for lead to upper stretch. FENCE RIDER was forced to steady when caught in close quarters leaving backstretch. SECOND VENTURE failed to seriously threaten. ABSOLUTE POWER was outrun.

pounds. And had followed that effort by traveling six furlongs in faster time than Second Venture ever had.

Knowing how horseplayers think, I believe that many of them preferred Second Venture because (1) he looked like a speed horse, a grabber of the early lead, (2) he had run the half-mile in considerably faster time than Sermon, (3) he might have been short of condition in his last race, having been away for three months, and (4) he might benefit enough from a ride by Rotz to show all his speed today.

Those who recognized the signs of class in Sermon's record collected a $6.80 mutuel. Second Venture was no factor in this race against able older horses. But young Sermon took an early lead and held it. Pressed by the four-year-old Red Beach and the five-year-old Tom Poker, he ran the half in .45⅗, the three quarters in 1.10⅗ and the full distance in 1.23⅗—better time than Second Venture had ever traveled.

The example shows how a young horse of superior class exceeds its best previous clockings when the occasion demands. It demonstrates that the identity of owner, trainer and breeder are excellent tip-offs to superior class in a lightly raced young Thoroughbred, as is the determined manner in which it has contested its few races. Determination and class go together. The classy horse may tire in the stretch, but it does not quit.

Cheap Horses Know It

The ability of better horses to turn on the speed when they need to is noticeable at every level of Thoroughbred class. In the pell-mell two-year-old sprints at five and five and a half furlongs, the better juveniles log excellent speed ratings, because the races are run lickety-split, little pace strategy is employed, and the distances are short enough to permit a speedy animal of little class to reach the wire without dropping dead. Therefore, the better horse must run swiftly, too.

After the races are stretched to six furlongs, and especially after the animals have turned three, the horse with the fastest previous time at the distance is no longer a copper-riveted certainty to be the one with the fastest potential at the distance. When it faces a genuinely superior Thoroughbred, it invariably loses in slower time than it has recorded in the past.

Horsemen are so accustomed to this phenomenon that they seldom even discuss it. A $5,000 horse able to get the half-mile in .45 and the six furlongs in 1.10 when racing with utmost courage against its own kind, has not a prayer of equaling those figures against an allowance runner which may never have done better than .45⅗ and 1.10⅘.

Invariably and inevitably, the class horse prevails. Whether on the backstretch, on the turn, or in the homestretch, the better horse makes a run, easily overtakes the speedster, keeps pace with it for several strides and pulls ahead with little effort. During those few moments, the cheaper horse gets the message. It acknowledges its own inferiority and gives up. The better horse wins, perhaps in 1.10⅘. It will not run the three quarters in the 1.09⅕ of which it is capable until challenged by an animal more nearly its match.

It is unnecessary to become mystical about the ease with which a class horse trounces its inferiors, the authority with which it bullies them into running more slowly than usual, the "knowledge" they seem to display in promptly accepting defeat by a superior. Students of animal intelligence and animal psychology would not be surprised by this, and would find nothing mystical in it. Every known species of bird, fish and mammal has its own social order in which physical superiority wins privileges.

Thoroughbred horses, whose function in life is to run, evidently establish their own social order in the process of running. How? Horsemen agree that animals of higher class possess greater reservoirs of racing energy. They can turn on the speed at will, or whenever the rider asks for it. And they can maintain the speed for as long as may be necessary to demonstrate the prowess that discourages a lesser rival. In most cases, it does not take long. The inferior horse hoists the white flag. Whereupon the good horse relaxes into a less taxing stride and ambles home as he pleases.

This curious physical and psychological dominance of higher-quality Thoroughbreds over lower is misinterpreted by many players and more than a few horsemen. Having noticed that the good horse beats the cheap one in slower time than the cheapie has run in the past, they conclude that time is irrelevant to the handicapping of races. They overlook the fact that the speed potential of most horses is thoroughly tested long before the end of the three-year-old season. Except for out-and-out champions, virtually all horses aged four or more have shown repeatedly what they can do in the speed department when subjected to the *extremely accurate test of races against their own kind*. In such races they are obliged to run as fast as they can.

The Triple Crown

Only eleven three-year-olds have managed to win the celebrated Triple Crown of American Racing—the Kentucky Derby, the Preakness Stakes and the Belmont Stakes:

1919—Sir Barton	1941—Whirlaway	1973—Secretariat
1930—Gallant Fox	1943—Count Fleet	1977—Seattle Slew
1935—Omaha	1946—Assault	1978—Affirmed
1937—War Admiral	1948—Citation	

The following horses won two of the three great races: Man O' War (1920), Pillory (1922), Zev (1923), Twenty Grand (1931), Burgoo King (1932), Johnstown (1939), Bimelech (1940), Shut Out (1942), Pensive (1944), Capot (1949), Middleground (1950), Native Dancer (1953), Nashua (1955), Needles (1956), Tim Tam (1958), Carry Back (1961), Chateaugay (1963), Northern Dancer (1964), Kauai King (1966), Damascus (1967), Majestic Prince (1969), Canonero II (1971), Riva Ridge (1972), Little Current (1974), Bold Forbes (1976).

Because that is so, and because races among seasoned animals of roughly equal quality are a majority of all races run in this country, one of the most reliable ways of determining subtle differences in class is by means of time figures and pace analyses. (See Chapter 13.)

Class and Form

We agree, then, that a horse of higher class is physically and temperamentally superior to one of lesser class. If he is a handicap star, he has proved it by starring in handicaps. If he is a $10,000 animal, he can walk away from $7,500 ones. It does not matter how sharp their condition may be, if his own is good. But, no matter how keen his edge, he cannot beat well-conditioned $15,000 stock.

Class and physical condition are closely related. A horse may drop down the scale to $4,000 before it wins a race. It it is still young, it may suddenly iron out its own kinks, get its legs under it and turn hot. Or a new, perceptive trainer may repair the aches and pains or correct the bad habits, as Hirsch Jacobs did in promoting Stymie from a $,1500 claiming race to a national championship.

Rarely does a horse spend an entire career at one class level. Rather, it moves up and down the scale. For most, the peak of class is attained during the three-year-old season. And then injury, overwork and unintelligent handling begin to take effect. Anyone who qualifies as an experienced racing fan has seen more than one former Kentucky Derby contestant struggling to win part of a purse in $3,500 claimers. At every bull ring in the land, animals of former high class pit their arthritic limbs and stout hearts against beasts that would not have been allowed in the same yard with them a few years earlier.

Quite apart from the pathos of such cases, they demonstrate that the effective class of a horse is related to its current condition. It does no good to ask what kind of fields the horse has beaten. One needs to know what kind it has beaten lately.

Schools of Thought

The dedicated class handicapper looks for the top-quality animal in the race, employing any of several standards and techniques which we shall examine shortly. If he thinks the horse is in shape, he plays it. Otherwise, he goes to the one that rates second or third or fourth on his scale of class values.

His opposite number, the fervent speed handicapper, regards speed ratings as expressions of class, and rarely looks further.

Some class handicappers are as keen on arithmetic as any speed-chart fancier. They assign each contending horse a class rating, usually $\frac{1}{10}$ or $\frac{1}{100}$ of its supposedly true claiming price or class value. They modify the figure by adding or subtracting other homemade numbers in which they try to embody the probable significance of average earnings, consistency, weights, recent form, the winning averages of rider and trainer, and whatever other angles appeal to them.

Players less inclined toward paper work may also concentrate on the class horses in the race, eliminating all but the final choice on the basis of current condition, distance, weight, pace, jockey or whatever.

In my own play, I attend to distance and form eliminations first. I then check the survivors to see if any is clearly outclassed and can be discarded for that reason. By the same token, if one of them is obviously the class of the field, and nothing about the jockey or weight assignments or probable pace seems likely to undermine its class superiority, I regard the handicapping process as completed, pending the routine visit to the walking ring. There is, of course, good reason to do a more thorough handicapping job than that on the other contenders, outclassed though they may be. They are, after all, in shape and suited to the distance. If the class horse is scratched, it's nice to know which of the others might become a good bet.

Certain astute speed handicappers depart from their rigid speed-weight formulas sufficiently to credit a horse for a good recent performance in superior company. Some of them do very well at the mutuel windows, having broadened their methods to that extent.

I doubt that anyone who does *not* pay due deference to the class factor can win money at the races. On the other hand, abundant rewards await the player willing to probe beneath the surface of the past-performance records to obtain a really accurate notion of each contender's current class. To adopt any of the procedures that involve such digging is to gain an unbeatable advantage over the rest of the crowd.

Basic Principles

Thousands of racegoers make the costly assumption that a horse has an advantage if it has run against higher-class animals than it meets today. Such reasoning is never valid unless:

1. The horse beat at least half its field or showed high early speed in the higher class.

2. Nothing has happened in the meantime to indicate that the horse has gone bad.

3. The horse is in good enough condition today to demonstrate whatever class advantage it might have.

The first point is basic. Few horses begin their careers in $5,000 claiming races. They descend to that level because they are unable to earn their keep in better company. Until each has found a class in which it can win, or give promise of winning, the experienced horseman assumes, quite properly, that its true class is probably lower.

The horse that never wins but sometimes gets into the money at a given level is usually conceded a good chance of improving when entered against cheaper stock. This is especially true if it has shown pace-setting tendencies or willingness in the stretch. A fairly widespread and entirely valid concept holds that any animal able to finish within three lengths of a winner may be expected to come out on top in the same company at a later date, and should have a class advantage if entered with cheaper animals while still in condition.

In any list of entries at any track, the player finds horses whose records show that they have defeated better fields than challenge them today. A horse is entered at $5,000 today, but has won here at $8,000. Should the player credit it with an edge in class? Not too quickly. In assessing the class of claiming animals that have been racing steadily, without long layoffs, it usually is hazardous to consider any performance that occurred more than three months ago. In fact, the safest procedure is to find the *latest* victory or in-the-money effort and base the class evaluation on it. If the horse won with great authority, or ran close in excellent time, the player should be fairly confident of its ability to hold its own against another field of the same or even slightly higher class. Provided, of course, that it is in shape.

If a claiming horse's record shows an absence from racing of six weeks or more at any time since its good performance in the higher class, the player has stronger reason than ever to suspect that it no longer is able to cut the mustard with better animals. Unless its most recent performances have been powerful enough to indicate that it is as good as it used to be, it should be credited with class no higher than that of the horses it lately has been beating or running close to.

Among bettors who try to do their own handicapping, the customary approach to the class factor is quite simple: The player accepts at face value the class notations in past-performance records. But, as we have already seen on several occasions in this chapter, significant qualitative differences often exist among horses entered at the same price, or in allowance races.

The Purse Is the Thing

By and large, the better the field of horses, the higher the purse. At your track, allowance races may offer purses as low as $5,000 and as high as $20,000, with numerous gradations between. The best claiming races probably involve purses and horses superior to those of lower-grade allowance races. Lesser handicaps sometimes pay no more than better allowance races and attract the same horses.

For the professional horseman, the purse is the thing. Whether a big bettor or not, his primary business is the winning of purses, as large and numerous as possible. He watches the racing secretary's condition book like a vulture. Far beyond the ken of an innocent public, that book often provides soft spots which permit a trainer to drop a horse in class without seeming to. The horse that chases allowance animals without success in races for $7,500 purses can be run into shape and given a soft touch in an allowance that offers only $6,500. The public does not realize that the animal is moving down in class to steal some money. The horse often wins at good odds.

A thorough handicapper cashes in on escapades of that kind and deserves to, having worked hard. The key to such success is a file of *Daily Racing Form* result charts, which contain information for which there is no room in past-performance records. The past-performance lines show only that the horse has been running in allowance races. But the result charts show that the horse has been running against non-winners of three allowance races while still eligible for races restricted to non-winners of one or two. And, of course, the charts also show that the purses (like the horses) are better in the races of higher quality.

As usual, there are complications. Purse schedules often are revised upward or downward during the course of a single race meeting. Last month's $11,000 purse has now become $10,000 or $12,000. Moreover, the horse that wins a race for a $20,000 pot at Hollypark or Belmont is no cinch when competing for a $15,000 one at Del Mar or Monmouth. It is quite a job to keep abreast of the class relationships embodied in purse schedules at one's local track and at the nearby tracks at which local horses also race.

In recent years, state legislatures have supplied an additional complication. Laws ostensibly designed to foster agriculture and animal husbandry provide enormous bonuses for the breeders and owners of winning Thoroughbreds foaled in the governing states. In some states not previously noted for the quality of their runners, purses awarded to state-bred races (restricted to horses bred in the particular state) are as much as 25 percent higher than those paid to superior fields in open competition. These breeding programs offer large incentives which have already stimulated marked improvement in the quality of horse-flesh foaled in New York, New Jersey and the State of Washington, to name a few. But the inflated purses paid in state-bred races confuse and defeat a purse-conscious handicapper who does not take pains to differentiate them from the better races that get lower purses. And a handicapper who still regards an individual horse's gross or average purse earnings as a true index to its class is absolutely doomed wherever state-bred races are programmed.

The Golden Notebook

The player who saves the *Form* result charts of all races run on his local circuit not only has the purse values at hand, but the special conditions of each race, plus revealing comments about the performance of each horse. His deliberations about class and form are sure to become far more rewarding than in the past.

A somewhat more efficient procedure is to transcribe the purse value and main eligibility conditions of each race into a notebook. This takes a few minutes, but saves time later.

The main reason to go to any part of this trouble is that it leads the way to extra windfalls. The conditions of entry in claiming and allowance races are often quite complicated. Just as identical claiming prices may hide fields of widely diverse quality (from maidens to non-winners this year to non-winners of three in the last two months to any horse entered at the required price), so may identical purses. Beyond the state-bred races with which we have already dealt, numerous occasions arise in which a racing secretary finds it expedient to offer identical purses to fields of significantly divergent class.

For example, an allowance race might offer a $7,500 purse to three-year-olds that have not won two races of $2,925 in four months. (Translation: Two races in which the winner's share was $2,925. At some tracks, the winner gets 65 percent of the total purse, the runner-up earns 20 percent, the show horse 10 and the fourth horse 5. In allowance conditions, "races of $2,925" are races run for purses of $4,500.)

In offering a purse of $7,500 to animals that have not won twice when competing for far less money in recent races, the racing secretary invites trainers to move some of their three-year-olds ahead in class. He also opens the door to better stock, such as one of last year's juvenile stakes winners in its first or second conditioning start of the season. Or a lightly raced animal whose only victories in a brief career may have occurred in a maiden race and in an allowance of today's value or better!

Another allowance race might offer an identical purse, but confine eligibility to horses that have won a somewhat larger number of recent races, or races of higher purse value. And it might admit older horses along with the three-year-olds.

The player who wants to unearth the opportunities buried in such conditions must know the kinds of races in which the contenders have been competing. He can make the check by referring to his file of result charts, or he can consult his notebook. It might look like this:

1. 4200-MSW3up
2. 3700-f3500-4up-NW2 mile 8/1
3. 5500-10.5-12.5-3up
4. 5000-fAlw-2s-NW2
5. 7500-Alw-3up-NW3 of 2925 12/7

Any similar shorthand will do. The above notations say that the purse in the first race on this particular day was $4,200, under maiden-special-weights conditions, for horses aged three and up.

The second was a claimer for $3,500 females, aged four and up, which had not won two races of a mile since August 1. The purse was $3,700.

The third was a $5,500 purse for three and older, entered to be claimed at $10,500 to $12,500.

The fourth offered $5,000 under allowance conditions to two-year-old fillies that had never won two races of any kind.

The fifth was a $7,500 allowance purse for threes and older that had not won $2,925 three times since December 7.

It is not necessary to include distances in such notes, since that information appears in the past-performance records which the notes are designed to supplement.

Absolutely the most de luxe notebooks are the kind maintained by players so enamored of the game that they handicap every race every day. Rather than depend entirely on purse sizes and eligibility conditions for their evaluation of the quality of a horse's past performances, they jot down the age, sex and class of the horses that finish first, second or third in each race. In the right hands, notes of this kind are like a telescope into the future.

Let us pretend that we are trying to get a line on Horse "A," a five-year-old. The past-performance record shows that its last outing was a strong victory when entered at $6,000. The conditions of the race accommodated four-year-olds and up, at claiming prices of $6,000 to $7,000. So far so good. It was not simply a $6,000 race, as one might conclude from the past-performance record. But it was not simply a $7,000 race, as one might conclude from the conditions.

The player who keeps handicap figures on every race finds in his notebook that "A" beat a four-year-old rated at $5,500, and that the show horse had been a five-year-old rated at $5,000. "A's" own rating prior to that race had been $6,000. If there were any legitimate $7,000 animals in the race they were not in condition to demonstrate that superior class. "A's" rating remains $6,000. If one of its opponents in today's field ran third in a good effort last week, behind horses rated at $8,000 and $8,500, the opponent might be a good bet at splendid odds today.

Decisions about class ratings are often tricky. Some note-keepers work entirely in terms of purse value, rather than claiming price. For example, if yesterday's purse was $5,000 and the winner went into the race with a rating of $4,400, based on previous accomplishments, the player would not increase the rating to $5,000 unless the animal whipped horses that (1) had such ratings and (2) ran well enough to justify them. Thus, the relationship between class and condition is kept in view.

By the same reasoning, if each of the first three finishers went into the race with $5,000 ratings, the winner would retain that rating. The second and third horses would be reevaluated on the basis of their performances. If it was a close finish, and the two horses ran extremely well, they might remain at $5,000. If they were beaten decisively, or ran in such a way as to suggest a decline in condition, their ratings would be decreased. One man I know operates on the basis of 50 points a length, assuming a truly run race: If "A" and "B" both rated at 5,000 and "A" beats "B" by a length, gaining in the stretch, "A" might emerge from the race with a rating of 5,050, and "B" with 5,000. If "A" won by the length only because "B" tired, "A" might retain 5,000 and "B" get 4,950.

Working on the basis of claiming prices rather than purse figures, I have had good results by giving full value to a victory or a finish within one length, deducting $500 for a second-place finish or a finish within two lengths, and $1,000 for show. Hence, if the first three finishers went into the race with ratings of 3,700, 3,300 and 3,600, respectively, the winner would retain its original rating (unless it were a young, improving horse that had won most decisively and powerfully). The second finisher might be promoted to 3,700 for running only a jump behind, and the third finisher would end with anything between 2,700 and 3,700, depending on how well it ran, and where the race fit into its own form cycle.

Although this kind of method allows the player to operate at the very nub of the class-condition problem, it requires more attention and is more complicated than the casual hobbyist may like to be bothered with. I include it only because some of the more enthusiastic players in the audience might enjoy a fling at it someday. It works with special efficiency in handicapping allowance races, especially the kinds that find high-priced claimers all mixed up with handicap animals.

Needless to say, if any horse suffers interference serious enough to affect the outcome of a race, the player must make due allowances in assigning his post-race class ratings.

Track Class

Two months ago, the horse won a couple of allowance races at Shenandoah Downs and here it is in a $3,500 claimer at Aqueduct, facing the cheapest stock on the New York circuit. Does the West Virginia horse have an advantage in class? Almost certainly not. Its victories occurred in allowance races for purses of less than half the amounts for which $3,500 New York horses compete.

Experienced players usually discount the chances of any animal entered in a race at a major-league track until it runs well in a race at such a track. The Shenandoah Downs horse travels but a few miles to Laurel or Bowie, but the Maryland ovals are worlds removed from West Virginia, as far as class is concerned. Similarly, a Laurel animal would

Class in action. Damascus wins the 1967 Preakness from In Reality and Proud Clarion. **UPI PHOTO**

Kelso romps home in the 1963 Woodward Stakes at Aqueduct. Never Bend, three lengths back, got there before Crimson Satan. **UPI PHOTO**

deserve little support in its first effort at Saratoga, unless it had been beating the best available stock at the Maryland plant, came from a leading barn and was fracturing the clockers' watches in its workouts.

The class differences among major tracks and minor ones, and the difference between one major track and another, are essentially matters of purse money. The best stables take the best horses where the most money is to be won. A stable that cannot earn its way at one track migrates to another, where the competition is more suitable and, to be sure, the purses are lower. The player need not wonder whether the New England horse has been defeating animals as good as those it faces today in Delaware. *Daily Racing Form* result charts show that, in competing for lower purses, the New England horse has been running against less formidable opposition.

On occasion, the shipper from a lesser track turns out a winner, whether it has been running against weaker fields or not. As mentioned earlier, the handicapper should respect any shipper from a leading barn. Why should the topnotch Maryland trainer, Dick Dutrow, send a veteran like Double Edge Sword to New York, and why should Angel Cordero ride the animal? The hard-knocking runner showed why by winning stakes—and many a smart New York handicapper lined up at the cashier's window, having realized that the Maryland horse had quality and that the Maryland stable did not ship horses to New York just for fun.

That is always an important clue. When George Handy raced his horses in New England, he always managed to ship to New York for two or three wins a year. Now that he operates in New Jersey, he continues that happy custom. New Yorkers have learned as well to respect the chances of shippers from other Jersey stables such as those of Warren (Jimmy) Croll, Willard Thompson, Jim Crupi, Larry Jennings, Joe Pierce and Jimmy Iselin.

Years ago at, I think, Aqueduct, I noticed that the leading Maryland horseman, King Leatherbury, had an unraced animal named Boone the Great in a maiden claimer. Why on earth would Leatherbury ship such a specimen to New York unless to win a check and perhaps cash a bet? The horse won, some friends and I cashed tickets and the horse was claimed by John Campo, who proceeded to develop Boone into a stakes runner.

If the horse from a top barn at a lesser track is a threat when entered at a better track, what of the horse that ships from a major to a minor track? A second question answers the first. Why would anybody stabled at Hollywood Park (where $7,000 horses run for $7,000 purses), ship a $7,000 horse to Sante Fe Downs or Turf Paradise to compete for much less money? Answer: The horse has gone bad and the barn hopes it will be claimed. As a generality subject to few exceptions, no good reason exists to send a horse from a better to a lesser track unless the better track is between seasons or the horse is a stakes or allowance animal for whom no suitable opportunities appear in the big track's current condition book.

Track Class: What They Paid in Purses, 1977

The official "daily average purse distribution" statistics of race tracks are inflated by inclusion of the large purses offered in stakes races. The tracks need rich stakes races to attract the big-name stables and riders that generate publicity and increase attendance. However, the larger the proportion of available purse money spent on glamorous stakes events, the smaller the proportion that remains for the bread-and-butter claiming and allowance races which dominate the daily programs. Needless to say, the best index to the actual class of a track is the class of its claiming and allowance runners. The following tabulation closely approximates the average amount of purse money various tracks paid for a non-stakes race during 1977.

Santa Anita	$11,600	Laurel	6,000
Belmont Park	11,500	Churchill Downs	5,800
Hollywood Park	11,300	Golden Gate	5,800
Aqueduct	11,300	Bay Meadows	5,700
Saratoga	11,200	Fair Grounds	5,700
The Meadowlands	10,500	Bowie	5,600
Oaklawn	9,300	Delaware Park	5,600
Del Mar	7,800	Keeneland	5,500
Arlington Park	7,300	Hialeah	5,400
Ak-Sar-Ben	7,300	Keystone	5,300
Monmouth Park	7,000	Rockingham Park	4,900
Hawthorne	7,000	Atlantic City	4,800
Gulfstream	6,500	Longacres	3,700
Sportsman's Park	6,300	Suffolk Downs	3,500
Pimlico	6,200	Calder	3,900

Note: During 1977 Gulfstream had the prized "middle dates" at the height of the Florida tourist season, and Hialeah the less lucrative "late dates." Their purse schedules reflected this.

Consistency

An honest, relatively sound campaigner is likely to be a factor in the running of every race that finds it entered at the right distance against animals of its own quality. Modern conditioning methods are such that a consistent animal's only severe losses occur when it is entered at the wrong distance, or on wet footing, or over its head, or after a long trip or a long layoff. This applies whether the horse be a handicap champion or a $5,000 meal ticket.

In every price bracket, some horses are sounder and more reliable than others. Many are so unreliable that they never win and rarely run in the money. Having failed to establish class of any kind, they warrant betting support by nobody. But what of the creature that has won only once in its last fourteen attempts yet seems properly placed today?

It may be a winner. It may beat off a horse that has won 20 percent of its own races, and has run somewhere in the money half the time. Inconsistent horses beat consistent ones every day.

Some of the worst sucker bets at all tracks are "consistent" horses that run second, third or fourth in race after race, yet almost never win. Another sucker bet is the truly consistent animal that finally runs one race too many and comes out of it incapable of another good race for weeks.

The key to a workable knowledge of consistency is that it means little unless the animal is in good condition and properly placed as to class and distance. And notwithstanding a record of inconsistency, a horse is a threat if entered today at a class and distance that have found it a winner on every similar occasion listed in its record. As far as the record shows, that horse is admirably consistent when in today's company.

Many old-time players refuse to consider an animal that has been unable to win at least one of every five of its starts—the traditional yardstick of Thoroughbred consistency. Some also demand that the horse have finished in the money at least half the time. They count its wins, places and shows, and compare them with its total starts this year, or this year and last.

An even more conservative approach makes additional requirements. Even if its overall record is one of consistency, the horse must show at least one victory in its last two or three races, and two or three victories and/or three to five in-the-money finishes in the published past-performance lines that represent its ten or twelve most recent races. Some players go still further, demanding four in-the-money finishes in the last five races, or not less than four victories in the list of itemized past-performance lines.

Anyone who adheres to such principles of consistency and applies other simple rules involving distance, recent action, basic class and pace can expect to catch a high percentage of winners. Most of the horses turned up by a method of that kind run at short prices, but the player loses very little money betting on them, and may even be a winner in the long run.

Between two horses whose most recent good races were against authentic $7,500 stock, the smart player would naturally tend to favor the one that had been in the money with substantially greater consistency than its rival. And if the more consistent horse had been displaying that enviable quality in its latest races, the proposition would become even more inviting.

But what do you do when confronted by two horses, each entered for $7,500, if one has run at a price that high only once in its career and the other has run at a price that *low* only once in its career? And what if both races at that level were good performances within the last ten days? And what if the horse that stepped up to $7,500 and ran well was a truly consistent animal at lower claiming prices, whereas the other had been quite inconsistent when entered at $8,500 and $10,000, winning only two races of its last fifteen?

Some players automatically go to the consistent horse. Others automatically go to the "class" horse—the one with victories at a higher claiming price. On any given day, either or both players may be entirely wrong. Assuming both animals are in condition to run their best, the pace of the race may be such as to prevent either from winning. Because pace is so often a determining factor in situations of this kind, I advise the reader to be chary about eliminating relatively inconsistent horses or, at the other extreme, backing them simply because they have won at higher prices in the past.

To my way of thinking, downright inconsistent horses should be eliminated on grounds of class. Horses of middling consistency should be retained—unless obviously outclassed by a truly superior animal.

For anyone who cares to undertake a comprehensive brand of handicapping, moving from distance to form to class to weight to pace to trainer to jockey to special angles and finally the paddock, I recommend the following standards of consistency:

1. Accept as a potential contender any horse with at least one victory in seven to thirteen starts or two victories in fourteen or more starts this year. If it has had fewer than seven races this year, make the computation on the basis of its races this year and last.

2. Accept any horse, regardless of consistency, if it finished in the money or within a length of the winner in its last race, or had an excuse.

3. Accept any horse, regardless of consistency, that steps down in claiming price at least $1,000 to a level at which it has been able to win or run within a length of a winner at today's distance.

These rules are, of course, useless in handicapping maiden races. They also do not apply to two-year-olds. In handicapping older, more experienced claiming horses, they have the great virtue of allowing the player to prepare himself for the upsets that are standard at all tracks —the "surprise" victories by horses that have seldom won but, regardless of prior inconsistency, happen to be well suited to today's race. Handled this way, consistency is not overlooked. On the contrary, the player may find that the only advantages of one horse over its main rival is a more consistent record, plus its superior jockey, plus its superior barn. In a contest of that sort, consistency becomes a plus factor of great significance.

Average Earnings

Because races of higher class usually pay larger purses, a quick means of separating two horses in point of class is to consult their earnings records. If both have made ten starts and have run in the money five times, the one that has earned $6,500 has obviously done so in more demanding races than the one whose earnings total only $4,400—provided, of course, that the earnings of the more successful animal have not been inflated by the premiums paid to state-bred races.

Some players are so confident of the earnings tabulations published with the past-performance records that they incorporate the figures into their methods. Thus if the above two horses are rated at 50— meaning that each has won or run close when entered for $5,000—the player might add 7 to the rating of the horse that has won $6,500, and add 4 to the rating of the horse that has won $4,400.

Other players go to the bother of adding the total earnings of the entire field for this year and last. They then divide the total by the number of entrants. All horses whose earnings are below the average are discarded. Horses with earnings above the average are looked upon as the class. I have no idea whether this works or not. I can think of numerous circumstances in which it would not, especially in better claiming races and allowance races at major tracks. Yet, if the player who went in for these calculations were a good judge of form and carried his class studies beyond the arithmetical stage, he might have a fighting chance.

The late Les Conklin once published a book-length system, *Payday at the Races,** which defined consistency among claiming animals as the ability to earn money at the rate of $500 a start. Twenty-five years have passed, but the principle continues to stand up. Confining his bets to geldings in medium-priced claiming races and betting only on those that have run recently and have either averaged $1,000 a start or won their last races while gaining in the stretch, an acquaintance of mine is several thousands of dollars ahead of his bookmaker, and extends the lead by a few hundred dollars a year.

The earnings table is perhaps most useful when the casual racegoer tries to make head or tail of allowance races and handicaps. Not knowing one horse from another, he can be confident of the class superiority of any entrant that *not only has won and finished in the money consistently* but has managed to amass higher earnings than its other consistent rivals. The higher earnings mean that the horse has been running for larger purses, and doing it effectively.

Age

A properly handled Thoroughbred achieves the pinnacle of its speed and endurance in the late summer of its four-year-old season and does not necessarily lose these fundamental attributes of racing class until age six or seven. Unfortunately, most Thoroughbreds are not properly handled. Many are so badly abused that they begin to deteriorate at three.

Because of this, one finds three-year-olds winning races of a mile and longer in the spring and summer of the year against older animals that should leave them many lengths behind. If the feat is performed by a Buckpasser or Tom Fool, it should surprise nobody. But when it happens in ordinary races, experts have every right to gnash their teeth.

Four- and five-year-olds are supposed to outclass the threes, especially at distances in excess of seven furlongs. They usually do. Which is one of the chief reasons why the expert player keeps an eye on purse values or on the eligibility conditions of races. The three-year-old that has been losing by narrow margins to older horses does considerably better against animals of its own age. The five-year-old that has been victimizing threes may be unequal to more mature competitors.

On the other hand, many claiming racers are so badly off by the age of four or five that a relatively sound three-year-old handles them with no difficulty—especially toward the end of the year.

* (Citadel Press, New York, 1953.)

Here are some tested rules that help experienced players to cope with the age problem:

1. No horse aged four or older is likely to win a handicap or stakes race unless it usually runs in such company and either has won or finished in the money when so entered.

2. No three-year-old is a good candidate in a handicap or stakes race against older horses unless it has already beaten such a field, or has been running with exceptional power against its own kind, suggesting a clear edge in intrinsic class and condition.

3. No three-year-old is a good bet against older horses in allowance or claiming races during the first eight months of the year unless it has a noticeable advantage in class. In the fall it remains a dubious bet if any older horse is not only in condition but seems superior as to class.

4. In maiden races and races for non-winners of two races, three-year olds are almost invariably better prospects than the older, chronic losers they meet in such fields.

Sex

Except at the lowest claiming prices or in the richest European and American grass races, female Thoroughbreds have less strength and stamina than males. They retain winning condition for briefer periods, and seldom are able to win the second of two successive driving finishes. They need jockeying of intelligence and sensitivity, because they react badly to punishment. Also, their sexual cycle affects their form.

For these reasons, no filly (a female aged four or less) or mare (a female aged five or more) is a good bet against males unless it enjoys a pronounced edge in class.

In *The Compleat Horseplayer* I disclosed a gimmick that I had found helpful in comparing the class of female and male horses: Deduct 20 percent from the claiming price at which a female beats other females, to determine the kind of geldings, colts (whole males, aged four or less) and entire horses (aged five or more) against which she might have a chance. In short, victory in an f-6,000 is rated at $4,800—not quite good enough to beat a $5,000 colt or gelding.

Among males, geldings usually are regarded as the most reliable claiming racers. Having been castrated, they have nothing in mind but racing. Indeed, they often are easier to train and ride than colts.

Some useful ideas embodying the class distinctions between male and female Thoroughbreds:

1. No female is a likely contender against males unless it has already beaten males of today's value at today's distance or longer, or has run close to males of higher value, or has beaten females when entered at a price substantially (25 percent) higher than today's top claiming price.

2. No female is a likely contender against males if the top claiming price listed in today's conditions is $500 or more above the price for which the female was entered in her last race. If that last race was an f-claimer, reduce its value by 20 percent before making the comparison. An occasional exception to this rule is the filly that scored a powerful win over males in its last race, finishing first by a comfortable margin after gaining in the stretch.

3. No female can be expected to win today against males or females if it is stepping up in class after a race in which it engaged in a driving finish and failed to gain ground during the stretch run.

Rises in Class

Vigorous three-year-olds often improve tremendously. The horse that beat $4,000 claimers at 15 to 1 in June may continue to win, despite boosts in class, and may be a 7 to 5 favorite when it goes to the post against $10,000 animals in August.

Older horses also climb the class ladder, but less often and less spectacularly. Unless a horse ran an exceedingly promising race in its last try, it probably has no business stepping up in claiming price today. The most frequent reason for running it in superior company is that the trainer is trying to work it into condition and wants to protect it from a claim while doing so. If the horse not only is out of its class but is entered at an unsuitable distance, the trainer's motives become that much more apparent.

But the player needs to wrinkle his brow over a rise in class by a horse that won, ran close or showed signs of important improvement in its latest effort. Ability to perceive those signs of improvement (see Chapter 9), when combined with a solid understanding of the class factor, enables a good player to catch winners at nice prices. Racetrack crowds sometimes bet on a horse that moves up in class, but are unlikely to do so unless its most recent race was an obviously strong performance. As the reader now knows, some signs of improvement are by no means obvious.

As in other aspects of handicapping, it is possible to become too mechanical about rises in class, and miss wonderful betting opportunities. The animal that ran well in its last race, entered for $7,500, may not be stepping up in class at all today, even though its price has been raised to $9,000. A notebook-keeper or a collector of result charts would see at a glance that the horse defeated animals every bit as good as those it meets this afternoon. In other circumstances, a horse that remained at $7,500 today might be facing better stock, and might even be tossed out on grounds of inability to handle the assignment.

Step-ups in class are a serious handicapping problem only to the player who depends entirely on past-performance records and must guess the actual quality of the races described in the record. Such players will find some helpful ideas in the remainder of this section.

Class Ratings Without Charts

A horse that was entered for $3,500 in its last start, and runs today in a race for animals priced at $3,500 to $4,000, may be stepping up slightly in class, or may be running under precisely the same eligibility conditions as last time. The best way to solve the problem is to assign the horse the most accurate possible class rating, based on its best recent race or races, and see how it compares in that department with other leading contenders. Later, an accurate pace rating will help to settle the question.

By and large, if today's top claiming price is *within the range of the entered prices at which the horse has run well in the past,* the apparent step-up need arouse no anxiety. (I take it for granted that the player is careful to judge the horse's basic class in terms of recent races or, in exceptional cases, good recent performances that strongly suggest an ability to match the high quality of races run last season.)

A concept of claiming-price ranges is extremely important to the player who depends on the class notations in past-performance records. For example, a confirmed $2,000 horse seldom wins in $2,500 company, except after moving to a lesser track. Other difficult step-ups in entered claiming prices:

$2,500 to $3,000	$5,500 to $6,750	$12,500 to $15,000
$3,000 to $3,500	$6,000 to $7,250	$15,000 to $20,000
$3,500 to $4,250	$6,500 to $7,750	$20,000 to $25,000
$4,000 to $4,750	$7,500 to $8,750	$25,000 to $35,000
$4,500 to $5,250	$8,500 to $10,250	
$5,000 to $6,250	$10,000 to $12,500	

A horse that runs the overpowering kind of race described on page 179 and earns the accolade of a big win can, however, be conceded a good chance to step up as much as 50 percent in price, when his entered price in that good race is compared with the top claiming price stated in the conditions of today's.

Indeed, when dealing with a three-year-old coming off a big win, it makes a good deal of sense to credit it with class no lower than the bottom price in today's eligibility conditions. Horses of that kind should never be underrated, and should be allowed to make huge jumps in class. They can do it. They often are the best bet of the day, week and month.

Here, for persons who depend exclusively on past-performance records, are additional ideas about step-ups in class, supplementing other notions set forth on pages 213–217.

1. To be acceptable as a contender in an allowance race, a horse whose last start was in a claimer should (a) have won an allowance race on this circuit or one of equal class, or (b) should be facing other non-winners of such allowance races, and (c) should not be asked to beat another contender that has run in the money in a handicap race within the last three months.

2. No female may step from a claiming race to an allowance race, or from an allowance to a handicap, unless today's race is for females and no other entrant has ever been able to finish in the money when entered in a race of today's class. An obvious exception is the female stakes winner that tuned up for today's effort by running in an allowance race.

3. A female running against other females may seem to be stepping up in class after a race in which it was entered against males at a lower price. But it may actually be an excellent prospect whose trainer has maneuvered it into a concealed soft spot. For example, if it ran well against males last week, when entered to be claimed for $7,000, it is actually dropping in class if entered against $8,000 fillies and mares today (see page 215).

Drops in Class

A horse rarely drops very much in class unless something is wrong, and the barn has lost hope of winning any money with it at its customary price level. Yet races are won every day by animals entered at lower prices than those listed in their most recent past performances. These are not usually authentic class drops. They merely are proper placements of well-conditioned horses, restoring them to the proper class after running them into shape against better stock.

A player who considers the factors of distance and form before concerning himself with class can save a lot of effort. A horse out of shape is a horse out of shape: it may be dropping in class by $2,500 today, but if it is not in condition to run its current best, nobody should hazard a bet on it.

Assuming that the player restricts his attention to animals entered at suitable distances, and in sufficiently good form to qualify as contenders, the following ideas about class drops will prove useful:

1. The horse should improve today if the highest claiming price allowed in the race is lower than the price at which it was entered in its last race.

2. The horse may improve if it stepped down in price for its last race and is entered today at the same price, especially if it ran at the wrong distance in its last race, or will have a better rider today.

3. The horse should improve if it went up in claiming price for its last race and is entered today at a price lower than in its next-to-last. For example, if it is entered at $4,000 today, it might have been entered for $5,000 in its last race, and $4,500 in the race before.

4. A female should improve if it ran against males in its last race and is entered at a lower claiming price today in a race for females. This is a significant reduction in class.

5. A horse should improve today if it is running at a price lower than any listed in its past performances. An allowance horse is invariably a threat when entered in a claiming race for the first time.

6. A horse should be conceded a chance in a claiming race if it has won an allowance race on a major circuit within the last three months.

7. A horse should improve today if it is entered at a price lower than the price at which it was claimed, especially if it was claimed within the past two months and has had not more than three races in that time —all of them losses at a higher claiming price.

The Class of Two-Year-Olds

Until the juveniles are asked to run three quarters of a mile and beyond, nobody has more than a hazy idea of their real class. In the shorter dashes, the two-year-old that has demonstrated its ability to cover the ground in the shortest time is the best bet. He may beat a youngster that goes on to stakes victories at more representative distances. And he may end as a $3,000 claimer himself. Forget it. He remains the best bet today, because speed is all that counts today.

For the same reason, an apparent drop in class from a maiden-special-weights to a maiden claimer, or from one claimer to another of less value is unimportant among two-year-olds entered at distances of less than six furlongs.

Later in the year, when most two-year-olds are running at six and seven furlongs, things change. The player welcomes the presence in a high-priced claimer of a youngster that has run middling well in an allowance race of today's distance. If all other things are equal, the former allowance runner may have a decisive edge in class.

Likewise, the speediest two-year-old in the field is a good bet in any juvenile allowance or stakes race at less than six furlongs, even if its only victory was in a maiden race. But when the distances are stretched out a bit, and the ready stamina of superior class becomes operational, no juvenile should be considered in a stakes unless it has proved its mettle in allowance company.

Class in Handicaps and Stakes

The fields in handicap and stakes events for horses aged three or older are normally so closely matched that victory goes to the animal in best condition—a superiority which may be impossible to foresee in the past-performance lines. On other occasions, especially at secondary tracks, the player may note the presence of a horse that has been doing most of its running in the very best company on the very best circuits and has the earnings to prove it. If its rider is one of the nation's best and its barn is also one of the leaders, the horse probably has a class advantage. The player then checks the weights, the condition factor, and the probable pace, and often as not finds himself with a nice bet.

Class in Starter Races

One of the neatest ways to separate the sheep from the goats in the tricky starter handicap and starter allowance races that complicate the programs at some tracks is to keep records of purse sizes. These races often are run at longer distances, which demand superior endurance and determination. An animal that has displayed those qualities while running for higher purses is very likely a good bet in starter races at a mile or beyond.

11

The Weight Factor

To differentiate themselves from mere horseplayers, racing fans who analyze the past performances of Thoroughbreds like to call themselves handicappers. It is an impressive term, well deserved. Technically and traditionally, however, a handicapper is a racing official, not a customer. His job is to heighten the sporting aspects of the game—and make life more difficult for its players—by attempting to equalize the winning chances of horses. He does this by saddling better horses with relatively heavy weights, allowing inferior horses to carry relatively light weights.

The procedure is at least four centuries old. It originated in common sense: A horse with less weight on its back retains more energy for the stretch run. Whenever a longshot carrying 110 pounds noses out a favorite carrying 123, there is little room for doubt that the favorite could have reversed the order of finish under a lighter burden.

In contests among well-conditioned Thoroughbreds of approximately equal quality, with first-rate riders aboard, the only measurable, tangible, fully predictable advantage is lighter weight. During the actual race, this advantage may be insufficient, of course. Horses carrying heavier loads may prove to be in sharper condition, or better suited to the pace, or unapproachably superior in class, or better ridden. Professional horsemen know all this very well. It is their duty to avoid or minimize whatever disadvantages they can. So they look for spots in which their horses will be required to carry the lightest possible weights. In some circumstances, they try to augment that advantage by employing apprentice jockeys, reducing weight by the additional three, five, seven or ten pounds allowed as bonuses to trainers who risk the services of inexperienced riders.

When the late Ben Jones trained for the mighty Calumet Farms, he kept his horses out of countless rich races in which they would have been freighted with a few more pounds than he liked. His son and successor, H. A. "Jimmy" Jones, allowed the great Citation to carry as much as 130 pounds only four times. The horse lost all four of the races and never won with more than 128 throughout its career. As far as the Joneses were concerned, track handicappers had but one goal in life—to beat Calumet with high weights.

At the bottom of racing's totem pole, Trainer Joe Blow maneuvers for months with an arthritic nag until he finds a cheap race in which the poor thing must carry only 109 pounds. He fires the gun. The horse wins in a walk. Joe Blow feels like a genius. His horse might have whipped the identical field under 119 pounds, but don't try to argue that with Blow. He wants the largest possible bulge in the weights. In a game of perilous uncertainty, weight is something of which he can be sure. Only a fool, says Blow, would think that 109 pounds ain't ten pounds less weight than 119.

The commonsensical belief that a horse is best off with least weight on its back has become a kind of springboard. From it, horsemen, track officials and vast numbers of paying customers dive headlong into error and confusion. "Weight," they say, "brings 'em all together." By this they mean that a competent racing secretary-handicapper can assign weights of such exquisite accuracy that all entrants in a given race will have almost exactly equal chances to win. Nonsense.

Condition, class, distance, pace and jockey are factors of such fundamental importance that weight differentials seldom obscure them. Of the 54 races run every week at a major track, the outcome of one or two may be attributable to the effects of weight. In the other 52, weight is one factor among many, and not decisive.

The Scale of Weights

The tabulation on page 224 is the most honored of all the weight formulas. It derives from rulings propounded in the middle of the last century by Admiral John Francis Rous, who was unchallenged czar of British racing. The old salt knew something about Thoroughbreds and a great deal about human beings. His scale put the damper on certain

Jockey Club Scale of Weights

(a) The following weights are carried when the weights are not stated in the conditions of the race.

Distance	Age	Jan.	Feb.	Mar.	April	May	June	July	Aug.	Sept.	Oct.	Nov.	Dec.
Half Mile	Two years	x	x	x	x	x	x	x	105	108	111	114	114
	Three years	117	117	119	119	121	123	125	126	127	128	129	129
	Four years	130	130	130	130	130	130	130	130	130	130	130	130
	Five years & up	130	130	130	130	130	130	130	130	130	130	130	130
Six Furlongs	Two years	x	x	x	x	x	x	x	102	105	108	111	111
	Three years	114	114	117	117	119	121	123	125	126	127	128	128
	Four years	129	129	130	130	130	130	130	130	130	130	130	130
	Five years & up	130	130	130	130	130	130	130	130	130	130	130	130
One Mile	Two years	x	x	x	x	x	x	x	x	96	99	102	102
	Three years	107	107	111	111	113	115	117	119	121	122	123	123
	Four years	127	127	128	128	127	126	126	126	126	126	126	126
	Five years & up	128	128	128	128	127	126	126	126	126	126	126	126
One and a Quarter Miles	Two years	x	x	x	x	x	x	x	x	x	x	x	x
	Three years	101	101	107	107	111	113	116	118	120	121	122	122
	Four years	125	125	127	127	127	126	126	126	126	126	126	126
	Five years & up	127	127	127	127	127	126	126	126	126	126	126	126

		x	x	x	x	x	x	x	x	x	x	x	x
	Two years..........	98	98	104	104	108	111	114	117	119	121	122	122
One and a	Three years	124	124	126	126	126	126	126	126	126	126	126	126
Half Miles	Four years	126	126	126	126	126	126	126	126	126	126	126	126
	Five years & up	126	126	126	126	126	126	126	126	126	126	126	126
	Three years	96	96	102	102	106	109	112	114	117	119	120	120
Two Miles	Four years	124	124	126	126	126	126	126	125	125	124	124	124
	Five years & up	126	126	126	126	126	126	126	125	125	124	124	124

(b) In races of intermediate lengths, the weights for the shorter distance are carried.

(c) In races exclusively for three-year-olds or four-year-olds, the weight is 126 lbs., and in races exclusively for two-year-olds, it is 122 lbs.

(d) In all races except handicaps and races where the conditions expressly state to the contrary, the scale of weights is less, by the following: for fillies two years old, 3 lbs.; for mares three years old and upward, 5 lbs. before September 1, and 3 lbs. thereafter.

(e) Welterweights are 28 lbs. added to the weight for age.

(f) In all overnight races except handicaps, not more than six pounds may be deducted from the scale of weights for age, except for allowances, but in no case shall the total allowances of any type reduce the lowest weight below 101 lbs., except that this minimum weight need not apply to two-year-olds or three-year-olds when racing with older horses.

(g) In all handicaps which close more than 72 hours prior to the race the top weight shall not be less than 126 lbs., except that in handicaps for fillies and mares, the top weight shall not be less than 126 lbs. less the sex allowance at the time the race is run; and scale weight for fillies and mares or three-year-olds may be used for open handicaps as minimum top weight in place of 126 lbs.

(h) In all overnight handicaps and in all claiming handicaps, the top weight shall not be less than 122 lbs.

(i) In all overnight races for two-year-olds, for three-year-olds, or for four-year-olds and upward the minimum weight shall be 112 pounds, subject to sex and apprentice allowances. This rule shall not apply to handicaps, nor to races for three-year-olds and upward.

larcenies by using weights to neutralize the natural advantages of older horses over younger, and males over females, at various distances and at various times of year.

It is quite a good scale. It is so good that it virtually eliminates weight as a prime factor in weight-for-age stakes races. When both horses are weighted according to the scale, victory in a contest between a three-year-old and a four-year-old invariably goes to the animal that rates best on the distance, condition, class, pace and jockey factors. To observe that this probably would remain true if the scale's weight differentials were lowered or increased by a pound or two does not belittle the admiral's accomplishment.

When assigning weights for handicaps, or in writing conditions for allowance and claiming races, track officials employ the scale's guidelines, but seldom its exact poundages. For example, the conditions of a typical allowance race at six furlongs in April stipulate basic weights of 113 pounds for three-year-olds and 126 for older horses. Non-winners of a certain number of races, or of races of a specified value, get lighter imposts than these. But the deductions are made from the basic weights, according to the age of each horse. The purpose of using 113 and 126 instead of the official scale's 117 and 130 is to make the proposition more attractive to trainers. It allows mediocre older horses to run under weights they are able to carry.

There can be no doubt that the differentials suggested by the official scale of weights are highly useful in the management of the sport. They bestow rules and standards on an area where chaos and chicanery might otherwise prevail. But there is no magic in them. They are far from precise in their effects on Thoroughbred performance. They do not begin to nullify class and condition—nor are they intended to.

Some horsemen complain that the scale is considerably off base in its treatment of four-year-olds during the early months of the year. They argue, with considerable justice, that it is unfair to require these young horses to run at equal weights with older, stronger animals in March, April, May and June.

The complaint would be worth acting on if significant numbers of races found horses running under weights at all close to the basic age differentials prescribed by the official scale. But factors like class, consistency and form are *also* embodied in the eligibility conditions of races. By the time weight concessions have been granted for failures to win, or for entry at slightly lower claiming prices, or for lower earnings, the extra poundage which a trainer might regard as unfair to his four-year-old has been compensated.

Handicappers' Weight Formulas

Because weights are precisely measurable, are an integral part of the eligibility conditions of every race, and are much on the mind of every horseman, efforts have been made to develop formulas expressing the effects of poundage on running time. One set of formulas is widely accepted among racing secretaries, newspaper selectors, trainers and players, many of whom concede it the authority of Holy Writ:

1. Four extra pounds of weight slows a horse by one fifth of a second, or one full length, in a sprint.

2. Three extra pounds have the same effect at a mile.

3. Two extra pounds have the same effect at a mile and an eighth.

4. One extra pound has the same effect at a mile and a quarter.

It may be so. But nobody can prove it. Horses are living beings whose fitness and mood improve or deteriorate from day to day according to the fluctuations of the individual form cycle. Condition, class, pace and jockey invariably are so decisive in the running of a race that the effects of small differences in weight become less exact than the formulas pretend.

Horse "A" loses by a neck under 115 pounds this week. Next week, under 110, the creature runs the same distance in the same time, losing by five lengths. Or runs slower and wins. Horse "B" does three quarters in 1.11⅗ under 112 pounds this week, losing to a classier animal. Next week, with 119, he beats his own kind in 1.11 flat. Someone who pays close attention to the weight formula at the expense of other factors condemns himself to grief.

Where the weight formula is more useful is in the work of racing secretaries. Like the official scale of weights, the formula has the virtue of being orderly. It is as good an aid as any in the process of deciding how many pounds to assign to each horse entered in a handicap race. Traditionally, and justly, the horse that has been winning the biggest races is burdened with higher and higher weight in each succeeding effort. The horses that have been chasing him get less and less. When one of them finally beats him, weight may be to blame—especially if he has been required to carry genuinely high weight. More often, however, his handlers refuse to run him under really heavy imposts. He loses simply because he has reached the downcurve of his form cycle, and something else not only has rounded into shape but is able to demonstrate it under a low impost.

Weight in Handicap Races

The handicap race is the supreme test of the theory that "weight brings 'em all together." Here the racing secretary has comparatively free rein. The only limitation on his experiments is the reluctance of certain barns to accept high weights. He sometimes solves the problem by assigning their champion horses the minimum top weight allowable under the rules of racing, and lightens the weights on all other entrants as much as necessary to provide a reasonable handicap.

If his calculations result in a close finish, he not only is good at his work, but lucky. Weight does not bring 'em all together. Not even in handicaps.

I have just reviewed the charts of the 62 richest handicap races run in the United States during 1977. They dispel for all time the theory that weight differentials come close to equalizing the chances of horses whose class, condition, jockeys and pace and distance preferences are unequal. If the theory were valid, horses carrying the highest weights in each handicap field would win no more races than horses carrying the lowest weight. But here is what actually happened in 62 races:

1. Horses carrying the lowest weight in their fields won only one of the races and finished in the money in only 15.

2. Horses carrying the highest weight in their fields won 14 of the races and finished in the money in 36.

3. Horses carrying the highest weight finished last in only four of the races.

4. Horses carrying the lowest weight finished last in 20 of the races.

These statistics indicate most strongly that the weight concessions given to inferior horses and the weight penalties imposed on better horses do not cancel the more fundamental factors of class, condition, pace and jockey.

The number of high-weighted winners was strikingly below normal. High weights usually win about 33 of every hundred handicaps. That an indeterminate number of the high-weighted losers might have done better with lower weights is undeniable. Yet, of three starters carrying 129 pounds, two won and the other ran in the money. And the immortal Forego won twice when carrying 133, second when burdened with 137 and second again under 138.

A perhaps more convincing indicator of the failure of weight to "bring 'em all together" is the margin of victory that separates the typical handicap winner from the horses that pursue him. Of the 100 leading handicaps during 1965, only 36 were won by a margin of half a length or less. And in only 26 of the races was the last horse to cross the finish line as close as 15 lengths to the winner! The usual gap was about 30 lengths, weights notwithstanding!

When Weight Counts

As the results of handicap races demonstrate, large weight concessions rarely make winners of outclassed or unfit horses. The principle stands up in all kinds of races, including the cheapest claimers.

For this reason, the expert turns his attention to weight only after deciding which horses are in decent form, are not outclassed, are suited to the distance and, therefore, qualify as contenders. At this point, the following ideas become helpful:

1. Weight usually is no factor in two-year-old races at less than six furlongs. If the fastest animal gets in with as many as five pounds less than its leading rivals and is being handled by a good rider, the bet becomes more inviting. But weight spreads large enough to neutralize superior speed are unheard of in these short dashes.

Handsome Boy, 116 pounds, defeats the mighty Buckpasser, who carried 136, in the 1967 Brooklyn Handicap at Aqueduct.   UPI PHOTO

2. Three-year-old and older horses, and two-year-olds entered at distances of six furlongs and beyond, vary in their weight-carrying ability. If well-placed as to class, distance, condition and pace, and if assigned a weight no higher than it has carried in previous strong performances, a horse can be backed confidently, regardless of any weight concessions to other entrants. But if the horse has never run well at today's distance when carrying as much weight as it is assigned today, it probably is a bad bet. This is especially true of front-running horses with a tendency to tire in the stretch. It is almost equally true of one-run horses that win only by coming from far off the pace.

3. If today's weight is higher than the horse has ever carried in the past, but if the assigned weight is below 120 pounds, the player checks to see how the horse has fared with three or four pounds less. Is it the kind of cheapie that seems comfortable only with 114 and below? Does it die in the final stages whenever it has 116 or more? If it seems a fairly courageous runner, and qualifies on other counts, it usually can be conceded ability to carry four or five pounds more than it has ever won with in the past—provided today's race is a sprint. At longer distances, three pounds is an equally safe assumption.

4. For most horses, 120 pounds is the beginning of difficulty at any distance. Except for young, sharp animals of allowance quality or better, no horse should be granted ability to carry 120 or more unless (a) it has already done so with aplomb in a race of today's distance or longer, or (b) it has run a powerful, reasonably recent race at the distance or longer, under 118 or more.

5. In races at a mile or longer, weights in excess of 120 pounds become most burdensome. A horse entered in a race of that kind under such an impost can be backed with confidence only if (a) it has demonstrated its ability to tote the load, (b) it is in superb form and does not come to the race off a recent tough effort under similar high poundage, and (c) no other fit animal of equal class has a weight advantage of five pounds or more.

6. In races at a mile or more, it pays to keep an eye peeled for weight shifts. Assuming that Horse "A" had a five-pound advantage when it beat "B" by a nose last week, "B" deserves consideration if the advantage is canceled or reversed today.

7. At any distance, weight in excess of 120 pounds becomes additionally unfortunate if the track is muddy or slow or heavy, and other contenders have lighter burdens.

8. A horse running with less weight than it carried in its last race should be viewed with extra respect when it qualifies on the distance,

Quick Pitch shows that weight is not everything by carrying 172 pounds to victory over the jumps at Aqueduct in 1967. **UPI PHOTO**

The mighty Citation, shown winning the 1948 Kentucky Derby, never won a race when carrying more than 128 pounds. **UPI PHOTO**

form and class factors. Trainers being poundage-conscious, today's weight shift, however slight, may represent opportunity to the barn.

9. If the track announcer reports that a horse will carry four pounds or more in excess of the weight prescribed in the conditions of the race, the horse is probably out for exercise. Being weight-watchers, horsemen want every pound of advantage they can scrounge, and do not ordinarily accept the services of an overweight jockey on a day when the horse has a good chance to win.

10. If the track announcer says that the horse will carry one pound of overweight in an important race, the player has reason to suspect the physical fitness of the rider. Presumably the horse has a good chance—or the player would be paying no attention to it. Presumably the rider has tried to make the low weight to which the horse is entitled. If he has failed by a pound, he may be woozy-headed from dehydration. Has he been winning many races lately? If he has been in a slump, his weight problem may be the answer. The horse should be viewed with extreme caution.

11. If a trainer waives an apprentice weight allowance in order to put a leading rider on his horse, the bettor should perk up and take notice. On the other hand, if the trainer has switched from a hot apprentice to a run-of-the-mill boy who never has won with the horse, the player should beware.

12. Except in dealing with races over a distance of ground among extremely well-matched horses of superior class, it is a waste of time to worry about weight shifts or weight advantages of less than three pounds. A pound or two does not make that much difference, but other factors do.

13. When in doubt as to the weight-bearing ability of your leading contender, pass the race.

12

The Speed Factor

Horsemen agree that most Thoroughbreds are unable to maintain full speed for more than three-eighths of a mile. When three-furlong baby races were a standard feature of January and February programs, the player who put his money on the previously demonstrated speed could expect to be right seven or eight times out of ten.

As distances lengthen, the ability of horses to run full tilt does not. Courage, endurance, nimbleness and responsiveness to the rider come into play. Day in and day out, relatively slow horses defeat faster ones by running more efficiently and with greater determination.

In racing parlance, a "speed horse" is the kind that leaves the starting barrier swiftly and contends for the lead at once. It performs best when allowed to set the early pace without serious challenge, running well within its limits and consuming its fuel gradually enough to have some left at the end. Its past-performance record is full of one's and two's—at least at the early calls of its races.

Players who understand the peculiarities of Thoroughbred speed, and the role played by speed horses, pay a great deal of attention to early pace. They are known as pace handicappers. We shall get to them in the next chapter. In preparation, we now discuss the outlook and methods of their country cousins—the large, loyal, somewhat mystical cult of speed handicappers.

The Theory of Speed

Theories of speed handicapping derive from an undeniable fact: The winning horse is the one that gets to the finish wire in the shortest time.

The faster he gets there, the better he is, the speed handicappers say. The ultimate demonstration of class and condition, they assert, is the time it takes the horse to run the race. Accordingly, they concentrate on final time—the minutes, seconds and fractions of seconds that measure the interval between start and finish. Everything else is secondary.

I sometimes think that speed handicappers have more fun than anybody. For them, the game is an arithmetical pastime. Its subtleties, contradictions and intangibles are digested in speed charts, supplemented by formulas for calculating the significance of weight, beaten lengths and variable track conditions. The charts and formulas award each horse a number. The one with the best number becomes the choice.

This approach is most popular, and understandably so, wherever the racing favors pace-setting speed horses. For example, speed handicappers flourish at bull-ring tracks, which feature short sprints around sharp turns. The horse with the fastest final time at these minor ovals is usually a comparatively sound front-runner. Given reasonable readiness, an even break in the weights, and an inside post position today, he can be expected to break on top, save ground by monopolizing the rail on the turns, and lead from wire to wire. The speed handicapper will cash tickets, having been tipped off by his charts.

For another example, many of the top public selectors and high-rolling punters in Southern California are expert speed handicappers. The running surfaces at Del Mar, Hollywood Park and Santa Anita are exceptionally fast. At distances up to seven furlongs, sharply conditioned front-runners tire much less noticeably than on the deeper, holding tracks of the conservative East. Early pace has comparatively slight effect on the outcome of such California races. The horses require less sophisticated jockeying. The animal with the fastest previous final time, or the fastest recent final time, may still be in form, a good bet.

At tracks like Aqueduct, Saratoga and Belmont Park, which have long homestretches and deeper footing, early pace is a primary factor. Come-from-out-of-it horses have a good chance to win, if the pace is favorable to them. Previous final times are, therefore, an uncertain guide. The player needs more information than that. Mechanical speed-handicapping formulas are disdained. Howard Rowe, a New Yorker, once quipped in *American Turf Monthly,* "Very few speed handicappers are lolling in loot . . . In fact, one of them we know is rarely permitted out of the attic, and steadfastly maintains that he is Martin Van Buren."

This chapter and the next will supply ample basis for decision as to whether speed handicapping should be embraced, ignored, or perhaps adapted in part to the reader's own methods. For now, it might be a good idea to list situations in which the use of final time is uncontroversial. A handicapper of any persuasion should find final time useful for the following purposes:

1. As an indicator of a horse's suitability to a particular distance (see pages 152–155).

2. As an indicator of improving or deteriorating form (see pages 181 and 184).

3. As the most reliable means of handicapping short sprints for two-year-olds (see pages 150–152).

4. As an occasional indicator of class (see pages 193 and 198).

How Speed Handicappers Work

Speed handicappers deal in numbers. Beginning with the final time of a previous race, they use their charts and formulas to produce a numerical rating which embodies that time figure and modifies it to compensate for beaten lengths, today's assigned weight, the relative slowness or speed of the track on which the race was run, and, perhaps, the manner in which the horse ran.

Some speed handicappers attend to the form factor by refusing to consider any animal that has not been to the post in ten days or two weeks, or whatever other standard of late action inspires them with confidence. They then consider only the horse's latest race. Or, if the race was unimpressive for some excusable reason, they use the next previous one. Other speed handicappers, after invoking a standard of late action, look for the fastest race in the animal's entire record, and base their figures on its final time.

Many speed handicappers pay no attention whatever to the distance factor. Their charts purport to show how quickly a horse should cover any distance, given its final time at any other. More realistic types believe that a horse should be rated only on the basis of a race not more than a furlong shorter or longer than today's. Relatively few use the distance factor as rigorously as this book recommends in Chapter 8. In truth, California tracks are so kindly to a pace-setting horse that it is not at all unreasonable to expect a winner at six furlongs to hold his speed for seven. This happens in the East less often, and should rarely be expected there unless the horse is the type that gains authoritatively in the stretch of the shorter race.

Most speed handicappers trouble themselves not at all with class. Final time, they say, is a reflection of class, just as it is of everything else that goes into the making of a winner. Rather than split hairs about class and condition, worrying whether the one will outfoot the other, they throw the whole thing into their arithmetical meat-grinder and accept the figures that emerge from the other end.

Lest anyone think I am being unfair, let me hasten to acknowledge that good speed handicappers hold their own with any other kind. What makes the good ones successful, of course, is that they regard their charts and formulas as conveniences, rather than as gospel. By whatever route they follow to their final speed ratings, they are careful to attend to the fundamentals of handicapping. Their results are sometimes downright astonishing, as when the guy in the seat next to you at Del Mar shows you that his handicap figures predicted the exact order of finish in an eight-horse race.

As to the ability of less thoughtful speed handicappers to survive at the track, all I can say is that their comparative success demonstrates that any orderly procedure—even a somewhat irrational one—gives the player of this game a fair chance to overcome a large part of the 18 percent loss that befalls random guessers and stabbers.

Speed and Class

In Chapter 10 I observed that horses usually generate maximum speed and fastest final times when challenged by animals of equal class. But a $7,500 horse may defeat a $5,000 one in time that would not tax the abilities of a $3,500 one.

Although class differences explain the outcome of a substantial fraction of races, and occasionally cause untypically slow final times, an orderly pattern exists. All responsible studies of the final times of races show that races of higher purse value tend to be run more quickly than races of lower value.

I once riffled through an entire season of Aqueduct result charts and found that the average $5,000 claiming race on a fast track at six furlongs was run in about 1.11⅗. The average $10,000 claimer was about two fifths of a second faster. The average allowance race was almost a second faster than the $10,000 claimer. Averages being unreliable, I took due note of the *range* of final times in each category. As might have been expected, some $5,000 claimers were faster than some $10,000 ones. But the majority clustered around 1.11⅗, whereas the majority of the better claimers were about two ticks swifter.

If a large preponderance of $10,000 races were exactly two or three fifths more rapid than an equal preponderance of $5,000 races, it might be reasonable to credit any horse with superior class on the simple evidence that it has run two or three fifths faster than its rival. This, of course, is not always reasonable, but it is what speed handicappers do, whether they spell it out in such terms or not. Moreover, their weight computations sometimes involve numbers large enough to cancel whatever genuine class differences may have been reflected in their original speed ratings. On my desk is an assortment of speed charts and speed-weight formulas that allow the unwary player to rate a $3,500 horse above a $7,000 one, simply ignoring the class factor, and trusting the clock and the weights.

Am I saying that some speed handicappers bet their money on out-classed horses? I most certainly am. At half-mile tracks, of course, speed and current sharpness are the main determinants of victory, and

American Speed Records

Distance	Time	Horse, Age, Weight	Track	Date
3f	:33½	Atoka (6) 105	Butte, Mont.	9/7/06
3½f	:38.4	Tango King (6) 116	NP*	4/22/78
4f	:44.3	Norgor (9) 118	Rui	8/14/76
4½f	:50.2	Kathryn's Doll (2) 111	TuP	4/9/67
		Dear Ethel (2) 114	MP	6/4/67
		Bold Liz (2) 118	Sun	3/19/72
		Scott's Poppy (2) 118	TuP	2/22/75
		Foxen Canyon (2) 119	TuP	4/13/77
5f	:55.2	Zip Pocket (3) 122	TuP	4/22/67
		Big Volume (4) 120	Fno	10/15/77
5½f	1:01.3	Zip Pocket (3) 129	TuP	11/19/67
6f	1:07.1	Grey Papa (6) 116	Lga	9/4/72
6½f	1:13.4	Best Hitter (4) 114	Lga	8/24/73
7f	1:19.4	Triple Bend (4) 123	Hol	5/6/72
1m	1:32.1	Dr. Fager (4) 134	AP	8/24/68
1m70y	1:38.4	Drill Site (5) 115	GS	10/12/64
1¹⁄₁₆	1:39	Swaps (4) 130	Hol	6/23/56
1⅛	1:45.2	Secretariat (3) 124	Bel	9/15/73
1³⁄₁₆	1:52.2	Riva Ridge (4) 127	Aqu	7/4/73
1¼	1:58.1	Noor (5) 127	GG	6/24/50
		Quack (3) 115	Hol	7/15/72
1⅜	2:14.1	Man O' War (3) 126	Bel	6/12/20
1½	2:24	Secretariat (3) 126	Bel	6/9/73
1⅝	2:38.1	Swaps (4) 130	Hol	7/25/56
2m	3:19.1	Kelso (7) 124	Aqu	10/31/64

*Abbreviations of track names explained on page 438.

American Turf-Course Records

Distance	Time	Horse, Age, Weight	Track	Date
5f	:56	Reb's Policy (4) 114	Hol*	4/22/71
		Black Tornado (5) 119	GG	5/10/75
		L'Natural (4) 114	GG	5/28/77
		Neat Claim (5) 113	GG	5/30/77
5½f	1:02.1	Faneuil Hall (5) 108	Hia	2/25/71
6f	1:08.4	Canal (8) 118	WO	7/9/69
7f	1:20.4	Beau Bugle (4) 112	Bel	6/6/74
7½f	1:28.1	Uniformity (4) 115	Dmr	9/4/76
1m	1:34	Portsmouth (3) 116	Lrl	10/30/65
		Fiddle Isle (5) 126	Hol	5/30/70
		Step Forward (4) 114	GP	3/13/76
		Clout (4) 114	Bel	6/26/76
1m70y	1:37.1	Aborigine (6) 119	Pen	8/20/78
1¹⁄₁₆	1:39.1	Fleet Victress (5) 115	Bel	6/25/77
1⅛	1:45.2	Tentam (4) 118	Sar	8/10/73
		Crystal Water (4) 116	SA	2/20/77
		Waya (4) 115	Sar	8/21/78
1³⁄₁₆	1:51.2	Toonerville (5) 120	Hia	2/7/76
1¼	1:57.2	Double Discount (4) 116	SA	10/6/77
1⅜	2:11	Cougar II (6) 125	Hol	4/29/72
1½	2:23	Fiddle Isle (5) 124	SA	3/21/70
1⅝	2:37	Tom Swift (5) 110	Sar	8/23/78
2m	3:18	Petrone (5) 124	Hol	7/23/69

*Abbreviations of track names explained on page 438.

class is often nonexistent, or close to it. In California, class is most definitely a factor, but is perhaps not so formidable at sprint distances as it is in the East.

At distances of a mile and beyond, by the way, the best speed handicappers suspend their arithmetical operations sufficiently to take heed of class, stamina and pace, which are fundamental factors in the outcome of longer races. In this respect, their methods vary in no essential particular from the methods of more conventional handicappers.

How Many Lengths Per Second

Races are timed in fifths of seconds. Traditionally, a Thoroughbred is thought to cover its own length in a fifth of a second. Most speed handicappers use that equation in calculating a losing horse's final time. If the beast finished four lengths behind a winner clocked in 1.12, its own time is recorded as 1.12⅘.

Like so many other widely accepted traditions of this unbelievable game, the one-fifth-per-second theory is utterly wrong. Its only virtue is convenience. It allows the player to think in terms of fifths. Five lengths per second. The horse beaten six lengths is one and one-fifth second behind the winner. And so forth. Very convenient.

But horses happen to drive across the finish line more rapidly than that. At the finish of a sprint, good horses travel at a rate close to seven lengths per second. In longer races, or among cheaper horses, or for any horse—winner or loser—that may be tiring and shortening its stride at the finish, the rate is about six lengths per second. The animal that moves as slowly as five lengths per second—one fifth per length —is the horse that is only loping, having dropped out of contention.

In case anyone cares to check this out, let him understand that a length is between eight and nine feet. Horsemen prefer nine, but eight is closer to the fact. To travel at the rate of five lengths per second, a nine-foot horse must slow down to 14.6 seconds per furlong (660 feet). Milk wagons move faster than that. No matter how long the distance, or how cheap the competition, the contending animals cross the finish line much more rapidly. And the finish line is, of course, where the final time is recorded and the speed handicapper does his work.

On the assumption that anyone who wants to tinker with speed handicapping should have better charts and formulas than are generally available, I have composed some especially for this book. They permit the player to crank out speed ratings which respect actuality. They are based on the notion that a horse travels across the finish line at a rate of about six lengths per second. This is not accurate in all cases, of course, but is 20 percent closer to reality than the conventional one-length-per-fifth theory.

Speed Charts

All speed charts embody the principle of parallel time. By grace of a logic that collapses under the slightest scrutiny, they show that a horse that travels six furlongs in a final time of such-and-so should go a mile and a quarter in so-and-so. Charts differ from each other by as much as two seconds in their separate versions of this phenomenon. I shouldn't wonder. No power on earth can predict how fast any horse will run in competition at a new distance.

I urge the reader not to use this book's speed charts in that way. Today's horses should be rated off races at today's distance on today's track. To stretch a point, they can be rated off races not more than a furlong longer or shorter than today's.

The experienced speed handicapper will note with some surprise that the charts award 12 points for each fifth of a second of running time. Most charts are laid out in intervals of 5, 10, 50 or 100 points, depending on preference. The reason for designing the present charts in units of twelve is mathematical. With 60 points allowed for each full second of running time, it becomes easy to work out a formula for beaten lengths. If a full second of running time is equal to 60 points, and a horse covers six lengths in a second, it can be seen that one length—equal to a sixth of a second—is worth 10 points. No complicated arithmetic is required. The formula is clearly presented with the charts.

To those who hope to use the charts for best effect, I make the following suggestions:

1. Eliminate all outdistanced, outclassed, and out-of-form horses by applying standards set forth earlier in this book.

2. Rate each surviving contender off the winner's final time in its most recent good race, but do not be afraid to use a race run last season at this track, as explained on page 155.

3. If tempted to rate the horse off a race at another track, adjust its rating by using one of the track-speed compensation methods described below.

4. Use the beaten-lengths and weight-shift formulas to arrive at a final rating.

5. Test the method on paper for weeks before risking a dime on it. In fact, if your natural habitat is the East Coast, read the next chapter, on pace, before deciding whether to bother with speed handicapping at all.

Track-Speed Adjustments

To make accurate comparisons of running times logged at different tracks, it is necessary to know the normal running times of the given class of horse at the particular distance at each of the tracks. If these times differ, as is usually the case, adjustments must be made accordingly. But this is only the beginning. So-called normal or "par" times are averages. On any day at all—indeed, on most days—running times may diverge from the norm because of the effects of weather and track maintenance on the speed of the racing strip. Conscientious speed handicappers who live in the busy Northeast find themselves compiling daily speed records for as many as seven tracks at a time, an amount of labor beyond the capability or preference of the casual hobbyist.

When the first edition of this book was written, *Turf & Sport Digest* featured a monthly tabulation of the best recent times at each distance at each track. The recency of the information permitted a fair guess about inherent differences between tracks. Handicappers unable to compile daily speed variants could nevertheless make useful time comparisons by finding three or four races in the desired class-distance category at each track, compensating for the best-recent-time differences, and seeing whether any significant time difference remained.

The magazine abandoned that expensive feature years ago. But in 1977 a researcher came to the rescue. William L. Quirin, Ph.D., Associate Professor of Mathematics (Computer Sciences) at Adelphi University, Garden City, New York, wrote a booklet called *Par Times,* which presented the normal running times for each age-sex-class-distance at each major track in North America, along with clever means of approximating daily variations in track speed. The material appears in Quirin's book, *Winning at the Races: Computer Discoveries in Thoroughbred Handicapping,* published by William Morrow and Company, New York.

In my own various pronouncements on the subject since the first edition of this book appeared, I have suggested, among other things, that speeds at different tracks can be compared fairly satisfactorily by determining (through research) the normal times at six furlongs and the most popular local longer distance for a single middle- or high-grade class of claiming runners. For most major one-mile tracks this would mean the average fast-track running times of $10,000 or $20,000 four-year-old males at six furlongs and a mile and one sixteenth. If the handicapper then confined time comparisons to races at those prevalent distances, results would be better than those achieved by no comparisons at all.

Daily Speed Variants

The sun shines bright. The track is fast. A detachment of $8,000 animals races a mile in 1.39⅗, breaking no records. A week later, sun still shining, track still fast, the same field runs the same distance in 1.37⅗. Why?

Any number of reasons. Fluctuations in the form cycle, for instance. Horses that pressed the pace last week may drop out of contention sooner this week, giving the winner an easier time. Or a rider's strategy may misfire. Attempting to reserve his stretch-running mount until the last possible moment, he finds himself without racing room at the quarter pole. By the time he navigates to an opening, the horse has thrown in the towel. It declines to run another yard, and allows the early leader to stagger home alone.

Speed handicappers pay little heed to such nuances in the actual running of a race, but are alert as hawks to variations in final time. While overlooking the effects of running style and racing strategy on their figures, they make careful adjustments for the effects of weather and the changing texture of the racing surface. The effort of calculating these daily track-speed variants is vital to their success. It protects them from crediting an undeserved edge in speed to some nag whose apparently swift final time was a result of lightning-fast footing rather than any great swift of its own. It protects them from assuming that a horse with slow final time is off its feed—if the track was slower than usual on the day the horse ran. And, most important, by making allowances for these external influences, the process helps the speed fanciers to recognize the horse whose recent speed at the distance has actually been fastest. This, of course, is the goal of speed handicapping.

It is forgivable to complain, as I do, that pace or class may annul an advantage in speed. But it would be idiotic to pretend that an expert speed handicapper who knows how to calculate track variants cannot stay ahead of the game. The horse with the best previous final time at the distance (after adjustments for weights and variants) wins often enough.

Variations in track speed result from combinations of the following circumstances:

1. Moisture on or near the surface of the racing strip. Even when labeled "fast," a track may be considerably slower than usual. On other days, it may be faster than usual.

2. When the maintenance crew harrows the surface, it becomes deeper than usual, producing slower final times.

3. After the track is rolled, the hard-packed surface permits greater speed.

4. As the season advances, hooves exert an effect similar to that of motor-driven rollers, compressing the surface. Faster clockings result.

5. High winds slow or accelerate horses, just as they affect anything else that moves.

Speed Chart for Races with OneTurn

Half *Mile	Basic Rating	5f	5½f	6f	6½f	7f	1m
.43	500	—	—	1.08	1.14—2	1.20—2	1.33
—1	488	.56	1.02	—1	—3	—3	—1
—2	476	—1	—1	—2	—4	—4	—2
—3	464	—2	—2	—3	1.15	1.21	—3
—4	452	—3	—3	—4	—1	—1	—4
.44	440	—4	—4	1.09	—2	—2	1.34
—1	428	.57	1.03	—1	—3	—3	—1
—2	416	—1	—1	—2	—4	—4	—2
—3	404	—2	—2	—3	1.16	1.22	—3
—4	392	—3	—3	—4	—1	—1	—4
.45	380	—4	—4	1.10	—2	—2	1.35
—1	368	.58	1.04	—1	—3	—3	—1
—2	356	—1	—1	—2	—4	—4	—2
—3	344	—2	—2	—3	1.17	1.23	—3
—4	332	—3	—3	—4	—1	—1	—4
.46	320	—4	—4	1.11	—2	—2	1.36
—1	308	.59	1.05	—1	—3	—3	—1
—2	296	—1	—1	—2	—4	—4	—2
—3	284	—2	—2	—3	1.18	1.24	—3
—4	272	—3	—3	—4	—1	—1	—4
.47	260	—4	—4	1.12	—2	—2	1.37
—1	248	1.00	1.06	—1	—3	—3	—1
—2	236	—1	—1	—2	—4	—4	—2
—3	224	—2	—2	—3	1.19	1.25	—3
—4	212	—3	—3	—4	—1	—1	—4
.48	200	—4	—4	1.13	—2	—2	1.38
—1	188	1.01	1.07	—1	—3	—3	—1
—2	176	—1	—1	—2	—4	—4	—2
—3	164	—2	—2	—3	1.20	1.26	—3
—4	152	—3	—3	—4	—1	—1	—4
.49	140	—4	—4	1.14	—2	—2	1.39
—1	128	1.02	1.08	—1	—3	—3	—1
—2	116	—1	—1	—2	—4	—4	—2
—3	104	—2	—2	—3	1.21	1.27	—3
—4	92	—3	—3	—4	—1	—1	—4
.50	80	—4	—4	1.15	—2	—2	1.40
—1	68	1.03	1.09	—1	—3	—3	—1
—2	56	—1	—1	—2	—4	—4	—2
—3	44	—2	—2	—3	1.22	1.28	—3
—4	32	—3	—3	—4	—1	—1	—4
.51	20	—4	—4	1.16	—2	—2	1.41

Adjustments

If the horse **lost,** reduce the basic rating of its race by 10 points for every beaten length; 5 points per half-length; 3 points per quarter-length or neck.

*For use in pace handicapping. See page 265.

Speed Chart for Races with Two Turns

Basic Rating	1m	1-70	1 1/16	1 1/8	1 3/16	1 1/4
572	1.33—1	—	1.39—4	1.46—3	1.53—1	1.59—2
560	—2	—	1.40	—4	—2	—3
548	—3	—	—1	1.47	—3	—4
536	—4	1.39	—2	—1	—4	2.00
524	1.34	—1	—3	—2	1.54	—1
512	—1	—2	—4	—3	—1	—2
500	—2	—3	1.41	—4	—2	—3
488	—3	—4	—1	1.48	—3	—4
476	—4	1.40	—2	—1	—4	2.01
464	1.35	—1	—3	—2	1.55	—1
452	—1	—2	—4	—3	—1	—2
440	—2	—3	1.42	—4	—2	—3
428	—3	—4	—1	1.49	—3	—4
416	—4	1.41	—2	—1	—4	2.02
404	1.36	—1	—3	—2	1.56	—1
392	—1	—2	—4	—3	—1	—2
380	—2	—3	1.43	—4	—2	—3
368	—3	—4	—1	1.50	—3	—4
356	—4	1.42	—2	—1	—4	2.03
344	1.37	—1	—3	—2	1.57	—1
332	—1	—2	—4	—3	—1	—2
320	—2	—3	1.44	—4	—2	—3
308	—3	—4	—1	1.51	—3	—4
296	—4	1.43	—2	—1	—4	2.04
284	1.38	—1	—3	—2	1.58	—1
272	—1	—2	—4	—3	—1	—2
260	—2	—3	1.45	—4	—2	—3
248	—3	—4	—1	1.52	—3	—4
236	—4	1.44	—2	—1	—4	2.05
224	1.39	—1	—3	—2	1.59	—1
212	—1	—2	—4	—3	—1	—2
200	—2	—3	1.46	—4	—2	—3
188	—3	—4	—1	1.53	—3	—4
176	—4	1.45	—2	—1	—4	2.06
164	1.40	—1	—3	—2	2.00	—1
152	—1	—2	—4	—3	—1	—2
140	—2	—3	1.47	—4	—2	—3
128	—3	—4	—1	1.54	—3	—4
116	—4	1.46	—2	—1	—4	2.07
104	1.41	—1	—3	—2	2.01	—1
92	—1	—2	—4	—3	—1	—2
80	—2	—3	1.48	—4	—2	—3
68	—3	—4	—1	1.55	—3	—4
56	—4	1.47	—2	—1	—4	2.08
44	1.42	—1	—3	—2	2.02	—1
32	—1	—2	—4	—3	—1	—2
20	—2	—3	1.49	—4	—2	—3

Adjustments

If the horse **lost**, reduce the basic rating of its race by 10 points for every beaten length; 5 points per half-length; 3 points per quarter-length or neck.

6. The intense humidity of midsummer depletes the stamina and jangles the nerves of Thoroughbreds, affecting their running time.

Calculating the Variant

The most familiar method of computing daily track variants is to compare the final time of each race with the track record for the distance. Simple arithmetic then discloses the *average* number of fifths by which a day's races fell short of the records. Thus, if the *Daily Racing Form* past-performance line contains the figure 82-14, the player knows that the horse ran $1\frac{4}{5}$ slower than the track record (82 + 18 = 100) on a day when the average winner ran $2\frac{4}{5}$ seconds behind the record ($1\frac{4}{5} = 2\frac{4}{5}$). Many players add the 82 and the 14, crediting the horse with a 96. Naturally, they prefer horses that rate at 101 or better, believing that a sign of sharpness is the ability to come closer to the track record than a day's average winner did.

The difficulty of the published variants is that they rise and fall not only with changes in the holding properties of the racing strip but with variations in the quality of the day's racing. All other things being reasonably equal, the official track variant is higher on a Tuesday than on a Saturday. The Saturday average is affected by races among top-grade animals able to run closer to record times than Tuesday horses do. Accordingly, a player might tend to underrate the performance of a $3,500 horse that earns a perfectly nice 80 on a Saturday, when the track variant is only 12. By the same token, he tends to overrate the performance of a good allowance horse that logs an unremarkable 88 on a Tuesday, when the track variant is 22.

To avoid the inevitable penalties of using track variants that fail to differentiate the effects of moisture or harrowing on final time from the effects of low-grade racing, conscientious speed handicappers calculate their own track variants. They make adjustments for the distance of each race and the quality of its field. In no area of handicapping are players more resourceful, or their formulas more complicated.

There is no easy way to do it well. The simplest of the genuinely useful methods begins with a session in the library. Go through last season's charts of the results at your track. Ignore all occasions on which the track was labeled anything but fast. Write down the *distance, purse or class, and final time* of every race except grass and jump races. Record two-year-old and maiden races separately.

If you use purse sizes to separate your class categories at a big-league track, it is a good idea to peg them at $500 intervals up to about

Buckpasser sets a new world record for the mile—1.32⅘—in winning the 1966 Arlington Classic. Creme de la Creme was second.   UPI PHOTO

$7,000. From that amount to $12,000, the categories can be $1,000 apart. Above $12,000, a $6,000 spread is all right, ending with a top class of $35,000 or over.

In using claiming-price brackets, a typical breakdown at a middle-class track would be $3,500 or below; $4,000–$4,500; $5,000–$6,000; $6,500–$7,500; $8,000–$9,500; $10,000–$12,000; $12,500–$15,000; over $15,000 plus allowance races with a purse value of $8,000 or less; better allowance races; handicaps; stakes. The top claiming price stated in the conditions of each race would determine the class of the race.

The next step is to determine the most typical running time in each class-distance category. To do this, you should begin with the categories in which you have jotted down at least five examples each. In some you may have ten or more. Start with those. For example, if you have a dozen figures for $5,000 claiming races at six furlongs, and most of the figures are between 1.11⅘ and 1.12⅖, you know immediately that the usual time for such a race at your track is 1.12 or 1.12⅕. The occasional 1.13⅖ or 1.11 is untypical and should not affect your reckoning.

After you scan the most crowded class-distance categories and assign typical final times to each, a pattern should become clear. At each distance, the times should improve as class increases. Do not accept any sample that makes the usual final time in one class grouping faster than the time in the next higher grouping. Chances are 100 to 1 that the sample is too small. Do not be afraid to raise or lower the figures in any category by a fifth to make them logical. Example: You might find that the time for $4,500 animals is 1.11, and is no higher for $6,000 ones, but that the $7,500 class rates at 1.10⅖. Simply make the $6,000 figure 1.10⅖.

Very well. You emerge from the library with a splitting headache and a page of invaluable figures—typical times for each distance and each class of horse at your home track. After making one simple adjustment, you will be ready to approximate the inherent speed of the racing strip on every day of the next meeting. The adjustment consists of increasing the typical final-time figure in each class-distance category by four full seconds, converting them from typical times to par times. The sole reason for doing this is to guarantee that the final times of most races will be faster than par. If par were closer to reality, some races would be slower and some faster, requiring complicated arithmetic later on.

Here is how to use the par figures to work up your daily track variant:

1. At the end of each racing day, note the number of fifths of a second by which the final time of each race failed to equal par in its class-distance category (almost always, the time will be faster than par).

2. After the nine figures are written down, divide them into two lists —one for races around one turn, the other for races around two turns.

3. Add the numbers on each list. Then divide each sum by the number of items on its list. The resultant averages are the day's track variant for distance races and the day's variant for sprints.

4. Adjust the official final time of each sprint race by adding the daily sprint variant. Add the daily route variant to the final time of each route race. Enter the adjusted times in a notebook.

5. When computing speed ratings, use the adjusted times instead of the official times.

The only problem likely to arise with this method—aside from that of remembering to keep the records up to date—occurs on days when the track has only one route race on its program. If the difference between the final time of that race and par for its class-distance category is within two or three fifths of the day's sprint variant, you are probably home free. If in doubt, check back to see what the route variant has been on other days when the sprint variant was the same as today's, and be guided accordingly.

An excellent, time-saving substitute for all the labor of computing par times and daily variants is supplied by an ingenious slide rule called Amer-Var. It is printed on the back of another gadget, Ray Taulbot's Pace Calculator, with which it sells for $20 at *American Turf Monthly*. Although its class-distance figures are compromises which may be out of kilter to some extent at certain distances on some tracks, Amer-Var comes close enough to get the job done more than adequately.

More Sophisticated Approaches

Effective though the daily variant is by comparison with no variant at all, it compromises with reality. Gusty, shifting winds, rainfall or a drying-out strip can produce several wide variations in track speed during a single racing program. To strike a daily average in such circumstances is to settle for second best. The same is true, surprisingly, in cloudless Southern California and Arizona where the Hollywood Park and Turf Paradise strips are often slower at the beginning of a program than at its end.

During the 1930's, an anonymous author wrote a treatise (now long out of print and virtually unobtainable) called *How To Select Winning Horses,* published by the defunct Montee Publishing Company of Baltimore. The book revealed a method of rating races on the basis of the speed expected of individual horses when in form and entered at the proper distance. If a 1.12 horse won in 1.13 in a truly contested race, showing signs neither of improvement nor of deterioration, it remained a 1.12 horse and the speed ratings of its pursuers were calculated accordingly. Instead of rating the speed of racing strips, the procedure concentrated on the actual performances of the horses.

Start of a six-furlong race at Aqueduct, where early speed often lasts to the finish wire.   NEW YORK RACING ASSN.

A similar approach was set forth by Andrew Beyer in his *Picking Winners* (Houghton Mifflin, Boston) and *My $50,000 Year at the Races* (Harcourt Brace Jovanovich, New York). Speed figures calculated in that way have long been a feature of *Today's Racing Digest,* available at Southern California tracks, and of the Ainslie-Kuck Ratings, sold to mail subscribers by Woodside Associates, New York. Not many handicappers have the time or experience to compile such ratings for themselves. The few who can perform the labor enjoy the results.

13

The Pace Factor

Ask any competent trainer of Thoroughbreds what strategy he would employ with a ready miler on a day when it meets its own kind at its favorite distance. He replies with a shrug: "How do the other horses run? How does my horse run?"

Racing strategy is entirely a matter of pace, which is determined mainly by the running styles of the contestants and partly by class, condition, distance, weights and the texture of the racing strip. After a horse wins a truly run race, the trainer knows that his strategy was correct. The player with the negotiable mutuel ticket knows that his own handicapping was correct. And they both know that—in particular circumstances of the particular race—the class, condition, distance preferences, weights and running styles of the other horses were advantageous to the winner. In other words, he was a ready Thoroughbred, well placed.

Because pace is the very crux of the trainer's pre-race calculations, it should occupy no lesser position in the mind of the player. Whatever school of handicapping thought may claim his loyalty, his results improve as soon as he budgets a few minutes of intelligent attention for a study of pace.

This applies with special emphasis to speed handicappers, whose arithmetic takes place on the outskirts of pace handicapping. The mutuel machines are invariably kinder to the speed fancier who makes no bet unless reasonably sure that the pace of the race will help his choice to run back to its best previous clockings.

Pace wins the race. Sprint races are won or lost in the first half-mile —more often in the first quarter. Longer races are won or lost in the first three-quarters. This remains true whether the ultimate winner be a front-runner which leads all the way, or a stretch-runner which steams out of the pack to win in the last jump. The pace analyst looks for the horse able to set or overcome the fastest probable early pace without tiring too badly in the homestretch. It is as starkly simple as that.

How Pace Works

In the last chapter I observed that Thoroughbreds are able to produce top speed for about three furlongs. The rider's problem is to consume this energy efficiently. His ability to do so is limited by the physique and temperament of his mount, which govern its racing style.

The cheap front-runner has only one way of going—lickety-split from the gate and decelerating from exhaustion in the last quarter-mile.

Better front-runners can be rated on the lead, restrained just enough to avoid premature fatigue while staying in front.

The familiar "one-run" horse allows itself to be rated behind the pace and then expends its strength in a single burst—losing if the jockey lets it run too soon, or if he waits too long, or cannot find racing room, or if the leader simply ran too fast and too far.

A really useful horse of rare versatility may be able to lead from wire to wire in some races, or run slightly behind the early pace in others, allowing the rider to adapt to the demands of the situation.

The rider is limited not only by his mount's style but by the effect of the racing surface on that style and, of course, the effect on the horse of its opponents' styles. A front runner is fortunate if (1) it races on a day when the track is kindly to early speed and (2) its opponents include no other front-runner of equal class and condition. In such circumstances, the jockey wins by rating the animal, allowing it to run just quickly enough to stay in front, but slowly enough to have plenty left in the stretch. Even a rank quitter can win once in a while when the situation is so favorable that it develops an early lead too large for the plodders to overcome.

Any front-runner encounters trouble when opposed by another early speedster or two of equal or superior class. In such competition, the outclassed horse gives way a few seconds after it is challenged. On days favorable to early speed, one of the other two may go on to win the race, if its class and condition permit. When the track is deeper and more tiring, the two surviving front-runners are more likely to defeat each other, giving way in the stretch to a horse that has run slightly behind the early pace, awaiting its turn. Or, if the track is exceptionally deep and holding, the winner may be a horse that was many lengths behind the early pace but comes along in the final yards.

In any truly run race, as we have observed before, a decided class advantage tells the tale. The really superior horse wins if in shape to do so, regardless of running style. If a front-runner, it pickles others of that persuasion and proceeds to win. If it prefers to run behind the early pace, it turns on the engine in the stretch and leaves the others behind, like a Buckpasser or Kelso.

Without a pronounced edge in class, a stretch-gainer wins its race pretty much by default. It wins by staying sufficiently close to the early leaders and waiting for them to beat each other. Quite often, they have no choice. Should one of them slow down in the early running, in an attempt to conserve strength, its front-running rival almost invariably does the same. When both slow down too noticeably, the shrewd rider of an off-pace horse smells the rat, speeds up, takes the lead ahead of schedule and holds it to the wire. Eddie Arcaro used to do that sort of thing at every opportunity.

The Right Track

Most Thoroughbreds being prisoners of their own inherited or acquired running styles, owners and trainers select their stock with that in mind. Horses with early speed are found in greatest profusion at tracks most favorable to that style. Horses more laggard out of the starting gate are in demand at places where the finishing kick has a better chance to win.

One of the most important handicapping discoveries of the past decade was made separately by Frederick S. Davis in Pennsylvania and Dr. William L. Quirin in New York. Each found that North American tracks are considerably more hospitable to early speed than to the late gain in the homestretch. Slightly more than 55 percent of all races are won by horses with enough early speed to run first, second or third at the half-mile pole. Davis reported that horses of that kind won 62 percent of all races on dry footing at the main track at Aqueduct. When the strip was wet, the percentage rose to 75. At Belmont Park, long thought to favor come-from-behinders, dry tracks enabled quick-starting animals to win 52 percent of the time, a record that improved to 70 percent in slop and mud. At Monmouth Park, the figures were 62 percent when dry, 60 when wet. And at Fair Grounds, although early speedsters won only 45 percent of the races on a dry strip, they won 65 percent when the New Orleans track was in its familiar, soggy state.

Among major tracks that generally confer extra advantage on runners with early speed are Aqueduct (main and inner dirt tracks), Arlington Park, Del Mar, Golden Gate, Gulfstream Park, Laurel, Keystone, The Meadowlands, Monmouth Park and Woodbine. And slower starting animals seem to have a closer-to-even chance when the footing is dry at places like Bay Meadows, Churchill Downs, Ellis Park, Fair Grounds, Fort Erie and Sportsman's Park.

On the other hand, Sportsman's Park becomes a front-runner's paradise when wet and, to be sure, most tracks are more favorable to the quick starters during and immediately after rainfall. What all this means is that any mechanical pace-handicapping formula is doomed unless by some wild and totally unexpected chance it makes adjustments for daily variations in the resilience of the individual racing strip.

Many years ago, in *The Compleat Horseplayer*, I presented a pace-rating formula which handled track variations by avoiding them. Play was confined to fast tracks and such sloppy ones as benefited early speed. The fact was overlooked that fast tracks also vary from day to day and even from race to race. The procedure remained in the black only because it permitted play on few races and only on horses that were conspicuous standouts. Because of that book and the success many players had with its advice, I became identified as an all-out pace handicapper, dependent on arithmetical calculations. I am not. In these pages I hope to persuade uncommitted readers that pace *analysis* is far preferable to numerical pace ratings, and that the essence of pace analysis is knowledge of how early speed is doing on the particular track that particular afternoon or evening.

The Illusion of Stretch Speed

Because of the dominance of early speed on most days at most tracks, and because the rider who falls too far behind the early pace invites other horses to run away and leave him hopelessly behind, the fast start has become a fundamental of the sport. Precious speed is spent in the rush from the gate and the duel for favorable position at the head of the line, and/or on the rail, and/or on the dry center of the strip, or wherever the riders want to be.

The finish being a product of what took place earlier, practically all races are run more rapidly in the beginning than at the end. Most players are unaware of this. But it is crucial to an understanding of pace and of jockeying.

The front-runners in a typical six-furlong sprint at Aqueduct cover the first quarter-mile in less than 23 seconds. They require at least 25 seconds to run the final quarter. Whenever a horse runs the last quarter in .24 it rates headlines.

The sensational sight of a Thoroughbred coming on strong to pass four or five others in the stretch is mostly optical illusion. It obviously is running faster than the others. But it may actually be slowing down: It passes its rivals because they are "backing up"—decelerating more rapidly. Whether slowing down or not, the stretch-gainer in no circumstances runs as rapidly as it did in earlier stages of the race. If it manages to win, its victory is attributable not only to its class, condition and rider, but to the inability of earlier leaders to keep going.

The optical illusion deserves further comment. A come-from-behind type that wins in 1.11⅗ very possibly ran the first quarter in .23⅗, the second in .23⅗ and the last in .24⅖. This is what the racing brotherhood knows as an "even race." The horse holds its stride comfortably all the way to the stretch and loses relatively little motor power when it gets there. To the crowd in the stand the horse may seem to be flying, but it is not. Good riders run such races on good horses. Riders like Bill Shoemaker, Angel Cordero, Steve Cauthen, Jorge Velasquez, Darrel McHargue, Laffit Pincay, Sandy Hawley, Jeffrey Fell and other masters of pace do it frequently. A speed-minded, whip-conscious public chews its fingernails and unburdens itself of oaths when such a horse loses by a nose, wondering why the boy did not let it run sooner. But pace is tyrannical. Energy expended earlier is unavailable later. When Shoemaker wins or loses by a nose, it is an odds-on bet that a whoop-de-doo rider would have lost by lengths, having wasted the horse prematurely.

Varieties of Pace Handicapping

The public confuses pace with speed. Some persons who call themselves pace handicappers are no such thing. They are speed handicappers. Rather than study the records for a clue as to the possible pace of the race, they use ordinary speed-rating charts and deal entirely with final time. Some of the charts are known as "average pace" charts, on the assumption that the horse with the best final time has covered each yard of ground at the swiftest average pace. This is beyond refute: As final time improves the horse can be said to run the distance at a faster rate, or pace. But this is word-mongering. "Average pace" is merely a different way of expressing final time. It has nothing to do with the running style of any Thoroughbred, and is no help whatever to a player who cares to figure out how today's race may be run.

Confusion about the meanings of speed (or final time) and pace may explain why Damon Runyon pinned the label, "Speed Boys," on the brilliant pace handicapper Jule Fink and his colleagues. Fink specialized, and still does, in cashing large bets on speed horses. But he bets them only after analyzing track conditions and pace and satisfying himself that the speed horse has a better chance of remaining in one piece all the way.

Many practitioners of pace handicapping concentrate their attention on the two, three or four horses in the race that seem to deserve the highest pace ratings. By whatever methods they assign such ratings, they single out the best of the lot and ignore everything else. For some reason, they usually rate the horses indiscriminately, on the basis of races run anywhere, in any year, at any distance. Their choice, more often than not, is the highest-rated animal whose recent record suggests that the trainer may be trying. They hit enormous mutuel prices. But their indifference to distance, current class and the fine points of form produces a lamentably high percentage of losers.

A somewhat more rational group tosses out entrants that have not raced in the last week or two, accepts the rest as contenders, and pace rates them. Again, little attention is given to class or distance. Speed or pace charts (which are one and the same thing) are used to compare a race at Fair Grounds with one at Suffolk Downs, or a race at Hawthorne with one at Calder. These players also get high prices, but enough losers to condemn them to the scrambler category. The high prices they get are by no means accidental, of course. Any horse that has ever run well enough to deserve a superior pace rating is a threat to jump up and win whenever it gets into shape.

In my view, the most profitable pace handicapping consists of analyzing the running styles of all sharply conditioned horses that are suited to the distance and are neither outclassed nor overweighted. The key to handicapping is to waste no time on animals whose records disqualify them as logical contenders. Pace analysis then becomes a prime means of differentiating one contender from the others.

Analyzing Pace

Let us examine the fractional times and running lines of the best recent races of two horses. Let us make the dangerous assumption that track conditions were identical for both races, justifying comparison of their raw times.

"A:" $22\frac{2}{5}$ $45\frac{3}{5}$ $1.10\frac{2}{5}$ 4 2 1^2 $1\frac{1}{2}$ $1\frac{1}{2}$ 1no

"B:" $22\frac{2}{5}$ $45\frac{1}{5}$ $1.10\frac{2}{5}$ 5 4 4^3 3^1 $2\frac{1}{2}$ 1^2

Given no important difference in the weights, a conventional speed handicapper or "average pace" handicapper would regard Horse "A" as better by a fifth of a second, or one full length. It broke swiftly, was well in front after a quarter-mile, led at the half in .45⅗ and held its lead to the finish, although closely pressed all the way. Horse "B" was not too far off the pace in the early stages (a fact that most speed handicappers and other arithmeticians might overlook), but took a full fifth longer to get home. The believers in charts would go to "A" by a large majority, and would be wrong.

A pace analyst would prefer "B" and would be right. His object, as described earlier, would be to find the animal able to set or overcome the fastest early pace and hold its lick to the end. "B" overcame a half-mile pace of .45⅕ and had so much left at the end that it won going away. Its own time to the half-mile was faster than "A's," about .45⅗ (figuring six or seven lengths per second). The power of its subsequent performance suggests that it would have enough juice for a stout stretch run even after chasing a pace-setter that did the half in .45 or .44⅗. An early pace of that kind would wreck "A." Indeed, it is possible that "B" might pickle "A" shortly after they leave the half-mile pole, and might beat the poor thing by ten lengths. The only kind of front-runner with a reasonable chance against a well-conditioned "B" would be one able to finish comfortably in 1.10⅖ or better after reaching the half in .45 or better.

For an example of another kind, try this:

"C:" 23 45 $1.23\frac{3}{5}$ 5 2 2^1 2^1 1^1 1^2

"D:" 23 $45\frac{2}{5}$ $1.23\frac{3}{5}$ 3 5 5^5 4^4 3^2 2^1

This time the speed handicapper picks the off-pace horse because its final time is better. But the on-pace horse happens to be the superior risk, unless today's track is unfriendly to its style. "C" was able to run the half in less than .45⅕, yet retained enough energy to pull ahead and draw out in the stretch. If his only problem today is "D," he can throttle all the way back to .46 or more, which will make him unbeatable in the stretch. Worse, if "D" tries to stay close to "C" in the early stages, so as to be in striking range later, he will have less left at

Ruffian carries Jacinto Vasquez to an easy victory over an Aqueduct allowance field on April 14, 1975. During that brief season, which ended with her tragic death in July, the three-year-old filly established herself as one of the great runners of all time. **NYRA (BOB COGLIANESE)**

Two front-runners exhaust each other in a typical speed duel at the old Jamaica track. **UPI PHOTO**

the end than he did in his best race. The record shows that "D's" ability to win in 1.23⅗ depends on the presence of one or two tiring front-runners. But "C" was able to outclass the leader in his own race, and could probably have done 1.23⅗ if pressed through the last eighth of a mile.

Pace-Class Ratings

Numerical ratings help the player to expose fine differences between sharply conditioned contenders. Where one horse enjoys a slight class superiority over another, or seems to, it also may earn a higher pace rating. The two numbers, one for class and the other for pace, confirm the original impression. Or, if the horse with the higher class rating emerges with an inferior pace rating, the player realizes that the contenders are closely matched and seeks other ways to separate them. I would guess that for every player able to encompass such variables without use of pencil and paper, at least five will find that the time spent in working up formal pace-class ratings saves a good deal of confusion and perplexity.

Two principles should be borne in mind:

1. Even when carefully applied, numerical ratings supplement but do not replace analysis of prevailing track conditions and the running styles, quality and present form of the horses. On a day when front-runners are perishing in the final furlong, the handicapper should discount the chances of all front-running types except the rare ones that enjoy large advantages in class.

2. Without accurate track variants, numerical ratings are likely to be extremely misleading—especially in the kinds of rating procedures that single out the best-looking one of each contender's recent past performances.

Basis of the Class Rating

Means of assigning class ratings were suggested in Chapter 9. For purposes of the present discussion, I shall assume that the player attempts to determine the highest grade of competition in which the individual contender has a winning chance. Most often, the information is found in the past-performance record. Examining the running lines of the animal's best recent race or races, the player should be able to approximate its current class. The most convenient rating method awards the horse a figure of approximately $\frac{1}{100}$ of the claiming price at which it ran its best recent race. For instance, if it won at $7,500, its rating would be 75. If its victory or close-up finish were at $3,250, the rating would be 33.

As usual, possession of result charts permits more precise work. The horse that won when entered at $6,500 would deserve a rating of 75 if the result chart showed that it had defeated $7,500 animals in that race. Arbitrary adjustments are made to give less value to a horse that ran its best in a race restricted to non-winners since a remote date, giving higher value to non-winners of a certain number of races since a more recent date, and full marks to a race of the same claiming price but open to any horse on the grounds.

An alternate method is to use the purse values of the races. This is particularly helpful in attempting to rate allowance and handicap runners—provided that the handicapper is alert to upward or downward mid-season fluctuations in purse schedules, and remembers to discount earnings in races limited to horses bred in the track's own state. It is extremely helpful to use not only the purse values but the varying conditions that governed eligibility for entry in these past races. If one horse raced in a field limited to non-winners since a certain date, or non-winners of a certain number of races, it probably met a better field than competed in a race for non-winners since a more distant date, or non-winners of one race fewer.

With experience, the class rating tends to become less frequently a statement of the class level of the previous successful race, and more often the handicapper's estimate of the class level at which the horse might perform in its impending race.

Basis of the Pace Rating

To obtain a numerical expression of the fastest pace that a contender can set or overcome, the player looks for the race with the fastest fractional and final times in which it won or finished encouragingly close to the winner. At distances up to seven furlongs, the rating is based on the quarter-mile and/or half-mile time of the race, plus the final time of the horse itself (in case it did not win the race). With races of a mile or longer, the half-mile and three-quarter-mile race times and the individual's final time are used. Facts:

1. In choosing the race on which pace ratings are to be based, it is important to find one properly representative of the horse's present condition, and readily comparable to the situation in which it will find

itself in its upcoming try. The rating should be taken from a race of today's distance, on today's track and, most urgently, recent enough to relate to the horse as it now is, rather than as it may have been in better days.

2. Lacking dependable track variants, the practice of deriving pace ratings from one past-performance per contender exposes the handicapper to the real risk of underrating horses that ran on relatively slow tracks and overrating ones that ran when the track was relatively fast. This hazard exists even when the handicapper confines ratings to performances at the local track on days when the strip was labeled "fast."

3. Users of the East Coast editions of *Daily Racing Form* can reduce the ill effects just mentioned by using the *Form*'s daily variant figure, which adjoins each horse's speed ratings on the past-performance lines. As pointed out on page 245, the *Form* variant is only partly a reflection of the speed of the track on a given day. Nevertheless, studies have demonstrated that, when added to *Form* speed ratings, it supplies greater accuracy than can be obtained with the speed ratings alone. For even greater accuracy, it is possible to determine the average *Form* variant at any track by going through a few random days of past-performance pages, jotting down the variants given for that track on days when it was "fast" and, after compiling a list of at least 20 such days, striking an arithmetical average. If, for example, the average for a track is 15, the handicapper assumes thenceforth that the track was normally fast on days when horses earned speed ratings accompanied by *Form* variants of 15. Their speed ratings and/or final and fractional running times would then be taken literally, without modification by a variant. When a speed rating appeared with a variant of 18, the handicapper would assume that the track was three-fifths slower than normal and would modify the horse's times accordingly. Dr. William L. Quirin offers an ingenious way of handling all these numbers for speed-handicapping purposes in his *Winning at the Races*. For pace ratings, it is necessary to divide and distribute the variant among the fractional and final times, as I shall show below.

4. Users of Western editions of the *Form*, which publishes no variant, can cushion the pitfalls of pace-rating procedures by basing them on two or more races per horse—all at the local track, the particular distance, on "fast-track" days and, of course, all representative of the horse's ability when in form. The use of at least three races can be counted on to blunt distortions of running times caused by relatively fast or slow racing strips—mainly by giving a larger sample of the horse's work and, in many cases, permitting fast and slow distortions to cancel each other.

5. The policy of using three past performances per horse, and of limiting their recency, distance and whereabouts, seriously reduces the number of occasions on which the handicapper can resort to pace ratings. This is probably just as well. It produces a situation in which the handicapper passes race after race or begins to resort to pace analysis and other handicapping fundamentals rather than to numerical ratings.

6. As implied but not stated previously, to pace-rate past performances at different distances and/or at different tracks, it is necessary to have accurate variants not only for the different distances at one's own track but for different distances at the other tracks. This alone should propel the recreational handicapper away from pace ratings and toward pace analysis. Any briefly experienced and reasonably attentive player knows enough about the differences among local or regional tracks to make useful pace analyses of past performances logged at most of them.

For example, the alert New Yorker knows why the courageous front-runner with an inside post position has an advantage on a fast or sloppy track in a nine-furlong race at Saratoga. The distance to the first turn there is only 344 feet. The horse gets out fast, captures the rail position and, before any other horse can run with it, the turn has arrived and the horse is saving ground. At Belmont Park, on the other hand, such a race involves only one turn after a start out of the chute and a long run down the backstretch. That Belmont race is like a long sprint in which neither front speed nor an inside post is much help.

Computing Pace Ratings

In the upcoming example, pace ratings are awarded on the basis of one past performance per contending horse. Having pointed out that this is a risky procedure unless the running times are modified to reflect the relative speed of the track when the times were recorded, I now shall show how to modify the times. The reader should bear in mind that we shall be dealing with arithmetical conveniences which only approximate the realities of racing. Nevertheless, the subject deserves detailed attention. Numerical pace ratings are central to the operations of many successful handicappers and, despite their flaws, may suit the individual newcomer.

We have already stated that the most dependable way to base pace ratings on single past performances is to confine those performances to races that were run at today's distance on today's track on days when the track was labeled "fast" and—above all—to modify the running times with an accurate, home-made variant. An acceptable alternative is to modify the running times with a figure based on the track's average *Form* variant, as described above.

Let us assume that Horse "A" ran a good recent race at six furlongs on a day when our home-made or adjusted *Form* variant was SLOW by 3. The official running times of Horse "A's" race were .22⅗ for the quarter-mile, .45⅗ for the half-mile and 1.10⅗ for the full distance. If the track was three-fifths of a second slow for the full distance, the presumption can be made that it was only ⅕ slow for the first quarter-mile, which is one-third of the distance. By that reasoning, the official time of .22⅗ represents .22⅖ on a normally fast track. And the .45⅗ for the half-mile can be reduced to a flat .45, with the 1.10⅗ being promoted to a flat 1.10.

Lacking one's own variant or the average Eastern *Form* variant for the local track, the Eastern handicapper might use the *Form* variant itself, adding it to the *Form* speed rating and substituting the resultant sum for the horse's actual final time when making the subsequent calculations. Failing as it does to modify fractional times in proportion to varying track speeds, this procedure can cause serious mistakes which defeat the purpose of pace ratings. A preferable but more complicated approach is to compare the *Form* variants posted for each contender's best recent past performance. If one speed rating is accompanied by a 16, another by an 18 and a third by a 14, one can arbitrarily decide to base the final pace ratings on a day when the *Form* variant was 14. This means that the running times of the third contender's race will be taken at face value, unmodified. The first horse's running times will be modified as if it had raced on a day when the track was SLOW by 2. And the other contender's running times would be modified as if the track had been SLOW by 4.

Handicappers without their own variants and without access to the Eastern *Form* and its published variants can achieve satisfactory accuracy only by finding two or more recent and representative local past performances for each horse. As already emphasized, these will be useless unless they took place on "fast" tracks and at today's distance. Which makes them hard to come by. Having found two or three for a horse, the handicapper arbitrarily decides the fractional and final times most typical of the horse. To return to Horse "A," its three most recent good performances might resemble these:

.22	.44⅗	1.09⅗
.22⅕	.45	1.10⅕
.22⅖	.45⅕	1.10

The picture would seldom be so symmetrical, but the example will serve us better than a more complex one would. Clearly, the running times of this horse's better races cluster about .22⅖, .45 and 1.10. The fact that the horse's one race with those fractional times ended in 1.10⅕ rather than 1.10 might persuade the handicapper to prefer the 1.10⅕, and the handicapper might be right to err on the conservative side in that way. Unfortunately, the entire procedure involves so much compromise to begin with that little is to be gained by fretting over a vagrant fifth of a second. As often as not, the decision to add or subtract a fifth will cancel some other error. Also, since traditional pace ratings use only *fractional official times* of a past performance but crank in the horse's *own final running time,* the handicapper who tries to function without a variant often saves his or her neck by assigning the horse whatever final running time it seems most likely to achieve in a race with those official fractional and final times.

Although the first quarter-mile of running is usually the fastest and most important segment of the typical six-furlong sprint, and although the use of both the official quarter-mile and half-mile running times lends an air of precision, many handicappers have found that time can be saved and results improved by ignoring the quarter-mile time and concentrating on the half-mile time. If this is more effective, and I believe it often is, the reason may well be that the fatigue factor has often become operational after a half-mile of running. Thus, a horse that finishes in relatively good time after a relatively fast official half-mile time can be thought to have performed well during the most rigorous part of the race, after the cheap speedsters have begun to exhaust themselves and the real contenders have been put to the test.

In pace rating the contenders in the example race, I shall use only the half-mile time of each past race, plus each contender's own final time. The race in question is a six-furlong affair with a top claiming price of $5,500. Nine entrants have been eliminated for failure to measure up in terms of distance, form, class, sex or consistency. Each of the remaining three horses has run good recent races in $5,000 company and poor races when entered at $6,000. Each therefore earns a class rating of 50.

The best recent race of each at today's track and today's distance is broken into its components:

> "A:" .45   1.10—beaten by 2 lengths
> "B:" .44⅘ 1.10⅗—beaten by a nose
> "C:" .45⅘ 1.11⅕—won ridden out

The simplest method of comparing these performances makes the traditional assumption that one length equals a fifth of a second. The final time of each horse works out as follows:

"A:"   1.10⅖
"B:"   1.10⅗
"C:"   1.11⅕

Having calculated these individual final times, the player now uses numbers to rate the fractional times of the three races, and the final times of the three horses. In each instance, he awards 10 points to the fastest time and deducts a point for each fifth of a second by which other times are slower. Here is how it would work in the present example:

"A:"   9 + 10 + 10 = 29
"B:" 10 + 7 + 9 = 26
"C:"   5 + 4 + 6 = 15

"B" earned 10 points in the first column, because its race was run in .44⅗ to the half-mile. It got only 7 points in the second column, because the 1.10⅗ final time of its race was three ticks slower than the "A" race. Similarly, "B" gets a 9 in the last column because its own running time in the race was a fifth of a second slower than the final time of "A," who looks like the best bet, at least for now.

A player who cares to undertake a bit more work will be able to make finer distinctions by using the speed charts on pages 243 and 244.

Again, the fractional and final times of the three races are rated. However, instead of using the approximate final times of the horses, beaten-length adjustments are made, as prescribed on the speed charts themselves. The ratings would look like this:

"A:"   380 + 380 + 360 = 1120
"B:"   392 + 344 + 344 = 1080
"C:"   332 + 308 + 308 = 948

In using the chart to pace rate races of a mile or more, the three-quarter-mile fractions are awarded whatever number of points the chart would give them if they were final times.

Having computed the pace-rating figures, the player must decide how to interpret them. Before getting into that, he might be interested in reading about some elaborate methods of developing pace-rating figures—methods used by certain successful professionals.

The Pace Handicapper's Notebook

Pace handicappers who keep track of daily speed variants, purse sizes and other such information usually compute a pace rating for every race, every day.

To do this, they use speed charts such as the ones on pages 243–244. They may even rate quarter-mile clockings, which is extra work but helps clarify things to the maximum. For work with the charts in this book, a quarter-mile time of 22 would be worth 440.

If the track-variant formula announces that the day's racing at a mile was four ticks slower than par, the handicapper reduces the official fractional and final clockings in proportion. Those clockings, in case anyone has forgotten, give the time of the race (sprint) at the quarter, the half, the three quarters and the finish. If the player believes, as is most likely, that the track was slower than usual because of dampness, he distributes the four fifths of a second evenly. He lowers the official quarter-mile time by a fifth. He takes another fifth at the next quarter-mile—meaning that he lowers the half-mile time by an aggregate of two fifths. He takes three fifths from the three-quarter-mile time, and the full four fifths from the final time.

Speed handicappers, being unconcerned with pace, get this part of their work done by slapping the variant onto the final time alone. But the pace handicapper is plagued by the knowledge that *final time is a result of pace*. If the track was four fifths off par, it did not suddenly slow down at the finish wire. Its slowness probably was operational throughout the race. For that reason, the pace handicapper parcels out his track variant in a plausible way: The entire variant is applied to the final time, and proportionate shares of it are added to or subtracted from fractional times.

If the chart of the race shows that the horses were assisted by a tail wind in the backstretch, or retarded by a head wind, the player may decide to use a larger share of the variant on the early fractions. For that matter, even if the pace handicapper ignores daily variants, he can make profitable allowance for winds by checking result charts and recognizing that the animal that ran the half in .46 against an Aqueduct head wind is at no great disadvantage against one that bettered .45 with a tail wind.

Be that as it may, the pace handicapper's notebook contains a pace rating for every race, compounded of fractional times and variants. Using this book's speed chart, plus columns for the quarter-mile and half-mile calls, the player produces a string of numbers like 254, 268,

280, 268, representing the point value of the fractional and final times. He adds them, getting a total of 1070 for the race. Later, when time comes to give a pace rating to an animal that ran in the race, he awards it the full 1070 if it won, and deducts points at the rate of 10 per length if it lost.

Needless to say, the more simple methods presented earlier can also be extended to include the quarter-mile time in sprints and the quarter and mile times in longer races. I do not think it necessary, however.

At this point I might mention that some players otherwise drawn to pace handicapping but afraid of arithmetic can get the satisfactions of the one without the discomfort of the other. Ray Taulbot's Pace Calculator is a handy device, sold in combination with the Amer-Var track variant gadget by *American Turf Monthly*. Constructed like a slide rule, it does its own arithmetic, turning out pace-rating figures in terms of the five-lengths-per-second concept.

The only trouble with the Pace Calculator is that it uses *Form* speed ratings instead of the final times of the horses. No harm comes of this as long as the player rates only performances that occurred at one distance at his own track. If he attempts to compare races run at different distances or different tracks he is well advised to ignore the official speed ratings. They can throw his figures off by many lengths, being based on records set by horses of varying quality under varying conditions.

Interpretation of the Ratings

I have already emphasized that numerical pace ratings are no substitute for intelligent analysis of the probable running of the upcoming race. No set of numbers, regardless of the sophisticated complexities that produce them, can tell a handicapper whether today's track favors early speed or not. On the other hand, where analysis of that kind takes place, and the handicapper eliminates horses whose running styles are out of place under prevailing track conditions, the pace ratings help to differentiate one likely contender from another—especially if the pace ratings have been developed with a dependable track-variant factor.

Situations frequently arise in which one contender has a materially higher pace rating than that of a horse with apparently superior class. This kind of thing can be maddening to pace enthusiasts, who often argue that their numbers are the best possible indicators of class. To the degree that a good track variant is employed, the situation arises less often, but arise it will. Here are suggestions about it and similar dilemmas:

1. Beware of high pace ratings earned by horses that lead from wire to wire without encountering close challenge at any stage. The cheaper the horse, the less likely that it can match its high pace rating when collared by another animal and forced to contend for the lead.

2. Bear in mind that class and present condition are inseparable. Unless the past-performance records suggest that the horse is ready to display some of last year's class, do not credit it with formerly high quality. The most accurate class rating, and the one least likely to conflict with good pace ratings, would project the handicapper's notion of how the horse is likely to perform in its next start.

3. In allowance races involving lightly raced but previously successful three-year-olds from good barns, it is best to expect continued improvement from any contender that seems suited to today's distance and today's track conditions. Stated differently, it is best to expect improved class and an improved pace rating.

4. In attempting to differentiate among seasoned horses whose present class levels are evident, discard any whose class and pace ratings are each 10 points lower than those of another contender. When using the six-lengths-per-second approach, discard any horse whose rated class is below the average of those awarded to other contenders, and whose pace rating is 120 points lower.

5. Discard all females whose pace and class ratings are not superior to those of all male contenders.

6. Before August, do the same with three-year-olds running against older horses. After August, accept any three-year-old whose pace and class ratings are as high as any in the field.

7. After checking its condition in the paddock and walking ring (see Chapter 17), prepare to bet on any remaining contender that (a) rates among the top three on pace and on pace plus class and (b) has a running style favored by today's racing strip and (c) will run at attractive odds.

8. On days when no particular running style seems to be at a conspicuous advantage, prefer (a) the only front-runner that rates among the top three on pace and class or (b) one of the top three contenders who is the only one that runs slightly off the pace and promises to defeat the other two in a stretch drive.

9. If none of the foregoing situations presents itself, separate the top three contenders by means of the handicapping fine points discussed in Chapter 16.

MONMOUTH 4

1 1-16 MILES. (1.41) ALLOWANCE. Purse $10,500. 3-year-olds and upward which have not won a race other than maiden, claiming or starter Weights, 3-year-olds, 116 lbs. Older, 122 lbs. Non-winners of $6,000 in 1978, allowed 2 lbs. $3,600 since may 10, 4 lbs. $3,600 in 1978, 6 lbs.

Baederwood
B. c. 3, by Tentam—Royal Statue, by Northern Dancer

Own.—Bright View Farm
Br.—Taylor E P (Md)
Tr.—Bardaro Anthony J

114

						St. 1st 2nd 3rd	Amt.
					1978 3 1 1 1	$6,515
					1977 0 M 0 0	

2Aug78- 2Mth sly 1¼	1:11¾ 1:47½ 3↑Md Sp Wt	6 1 2hd 11½ 16 Nied D	117	*1.70	83-22 Baederwood 117⁶ Revivalist 122⁶ Silent Bid 110²	Easily 8
18Jly78- 5Mth fst 6f	:22⅗ :46 3↑Md Sp Wt	7 4 3nk 11½ 1½ 21¼ Nied D	116	3.80e	77-27 Ray A Day 122¹¼ baederwood 116⁵ ColumbusBound116²¼ 2nd best 8
1Jly78- 9Mth fst 6f	:21⅘ :45⅘ 1:11 3↑Md Sp Wt	12 4 57½ 58 48 310 Nied D	116	6.00	75-20 Really And Truly 116⁵ RayADay122⁵Baederwood116nk No mishap 12

LATEST WORKOUTS Aug 10 Mth 5f fst 1:04⅗ b Jly 31 Mth 4f sly :49 b Jly 26 Mth 5f fst 1:03⅗ b Jly 17 Mth 3f my :37⅘ b (d)

Turn For The Best
Dk. b. or br. c. 3, by Best Turn—Detag, by Prince Taj

Own.—Capricorn Stable
Br.—Davidson A H (Ky)
Tr.—Nieminski Richard

114

					Turf Record	St. 1st 2nd 3rd	Amt.
					1 0 0 0	1978 11 1 1 2	$11,310
						1977 0 M 0 0	

28Jly78- 9Bel fst 1¼	:46⅘ 1:11½ 1:42⅗ 3↑Md 35000	7 3 4½ 1hd 2hd Venezia M	116	8.40	89-12 TurnForTheBest116hdSlowtoAngr114²¼mARoughOn114no Driving 8
24Jly78- 4Bel fm 1 ⊕:23⅗ :45⅘ 1:22⅗ 3↑Md Sp Wt	7 7 811 712 613 617 Venezia M	114	34.80	71-15 Ivan Skvinsky 114² Cheating Arthur 114⁸ SunFlame122²¼ Outrun 8
4Jun78- 2Bel fm 1¼ ⊕:49 1:38⅘ 2:04 3↑Md Sp Wt	7 9 910¹⁰ 921 921 Velasquez J	114	10.20	53-16 Hereditary 114nk Robin's Song 114¾ Knapper 115nk No factor 11
19Aug78- 3Aqu fst 1 :46¾ 1:12 1:38⅞ 3↑Md Sp Wt	1 8 814 511 56 33 Cauthen S	113⅜	*2.60	72-19 MightHvBn113²ProudVctory113²[DH]TurnForThBst113 Wide turn 9

19May78-Dead heat

12May78- 4Aqu fst 1	:46¾ 1:11⅘ 1:38 3↑Md Sp Wt	4 4 66 32½ 65 612 Velasquez J	113	*2.30	64-21 Judge Advocate 113¼ Addison 113½ Murtaugh 114²¾ Bid, tired 9
21Apr78- 6Aqu gd 1	:47⅕ 1:12⅘ 1:38⅝ 3↑Md Sp Wt	2 8 84½ 84¾ 75 73½ Maple E	122	3.40	70-18 Buck N Fool 122¹¼ Dead Stick 122no Stick Game 122no Steadied 8
16Apr78- 4Aqu fst 1	:48 1:13⅛ 1:39⅛ 3↑Md Sp Wt	9 6 52 43 21½ 2no Velasquez J	113	*1.90	70-23 DancingWizrd113noTurnForTheBest113²¾MyBestPie115¼ Gaining 10
6Apr78- 6Aqu fst 7f	:23⅘ :46⅗ 1:25 3↑Md Sp Wt	2 6 76 75½ 45 22 McCauley W H	113	9.40	74-23 Montalvo 126² Turn For The Best 113²¼FirstAndTen126½ Blocked 8
18Mar78- 4Aqu gd 1¼ ⊡:49 1:14⅜ 1:47⅜ 3↑Md Sp Wt	9 6 73¾ 64¾ 75 66¾ Prosper G	113	6.00	70-14 Man. Reason 113nk Gymnast 113¼ Third Reich 114¼ Outrun 10

LATEST WORKOUTS Aug 9 Bel 4f fst :50 b Jly 26 Bel 3f fst :36⅘ h Jly 21 Bel 5f fst 1:03 b Jly 8 Bel 5f fst 1:01 h

Mysto Hill
Ch. g. 4, by Amarullah or Miracle Hill—Mysteclin, by Happy Go Lucky

Own.—Walton Jay
Br.—Maybrier H (Ky)
Tr.—Walton Jay

116

					Turf Record	St. 1st 2nd 3rd	Amt.
					2 0 1 0	1978 16 0 8 3	$9,035
						1977 26 4 8 3	$32,227

5Aug78- 7Mth sly 1¼	:48⅘ 1:13⅘ 1:47⅘ 3↑Allowance	4 2 2hd 2½ 23 Thomas D B	b 116	20.60	64-31 Ne De Gagner 108³ Mysto Hill 116⁵ Rufflame 116²¾ Gamely 8
28Jly78- 4Mth sly 6f	:22⅕ :45⅘ 1:12 3↑Clm c-16000	5 5 64½ 67¾ 69¼ 58¼ MacBeth D	b 116	3.60	71-30 Gallant Courier 109² Fiddlefish 116²¼ Rebounding 113² Wide 6
6Jly78- 6Mth fst 6f	:22 :45 1:11⅕ 3↑Clm 14000	3 5 58½ 55 43 2no Edwards J W	b 114	8.50	84-20 Slow Joe 116no Mysto Hill 114hd NoConventions116¾ Just missed 7
29Jun78- 4Mth fst 6f	:22⅗ :45⅘ 1:11¾ 3↑Clm 12500	3 6 77½ 56 56¾ 31¾ MacBeth D	b 114	9.00	80-27 Clip The Coupons 116¼ Blue Streaker113¼MystoHill116nk Rallied 7
8Jun78- 7Mth sly 1¼	:48 1:14½ 1:48½ 3↑Clm 12500	3 5 57 42 77½ 616 Kupfer T5	b 111	9.00	46-31 Liquid Asset 114⁴ Proudest Spartan 119⁴ Dot The T. 119⁴¼ Rallied 7
1Jun78- 5Atl fst 6f	:22 :45½ 1:10⅛ 3↑Clm 15000	5 3 75½ 66½ 57¼ 58½ Kupfer T5	b 111	7.50	82-22 Big Star 116½ Thou Fool 116⁵ Danny Boy 116no No threat 7
18May78- 5Mth gd 6f	:23 :46⅗ 1:12½ 3↑Clm 14000	1 2 2hd 3½ 3nk Kupfer T5	b 109	6.90	79-26 Fiddlefish 116nk Limited Funds 116no Mysto Hill 109² Weakened 6
11May78- 6Mth fst 170	:46½ 1:11¾ 1:43⅜ 3↑Allowance	7 5 56½ 59 615 631 Kupfer T5	b 115	26.20	49-24 Silent Cal 119⁵ Dream Time 120⁵ China Clipper 112⁸ Outrun 7
20Apr78- 5Pim my 6f	:23 :46⅗ 1:12½ 3↑Clm 11500	2 5 56½ 67 55½ 57 Kupfer T5	b 109	5.60	76-24 B. African 114⁴ Sandargent 109¼ Oak Cross 114¼ Outrun 6
11Apr78- 4Pim fst 1¼	:48 1:12¾ 1:45 3↑Clm 14500	1 2 34 36½ 34 411 Kupfer T5	b 109	2.00	69-22 Man In Red 119nk Rough Powder 119⁵ Turn To Fright 114⁶ Tired 6

LATEST WORKOUTS Jly 26 Mth 4f fst :49 b Jly 20 Mth 4f fst :48⅔ h Jly 12 Del 5f fst 1:07 b Jun 27 Mth 5f fst 1:02 b

Rufflame

Own.—Baker Joann

Ch. c. 3, by Ruffled Feathers—Famous Flame, by Bagdad
Br.—Pollinger M (Md)
Tr.—Baker Joann

				Turf Record	St. 1st 2nd 3rd	Amt.
				St. 1st 2nd 3rd	1978 15 1 2 2	$11,787
				3 0 1 0	1977 0 0 0 0	

5Aug78– 7Mth sly 1¹⁄₁₆	⊕:48⅘ 1:13¾ 1:47⅘	3↑Allowance	8 5 47½ 37 36½ 38	Sierra J A	116	26.50	Rallied 8
22July78– 9Mth fst 6f	:22 :44⅘ 1:09¼	3↑Allowance	5 9 99¾ 11¹² 71² 51³	Sierra J A	114	62.20	No threat 11
14July78– 6Mth fm 1¹⁄₁₆	⊕:48 1:12¾ 1:45¼	Clm 30000	7 2 2½ 2½ 33 58¼	Sierra J A	116	6.50	Tired 8
24Jun78– 5Mth fm 1	⊕:48⅘ 1:13 1:38½	Clm 27500	3 3 32 22 25 25	Sierra J A	116	67.80	Tired 8
3Jun78– 9Mth fst 6f	:22 :46½ 1:12¾	3↑Allowance	5 6 811 813 76¼ 78¾	Mize W E	113	85.00	2nd best 10
27May78– 5Mth gd 6f	:22⅘ :46 1:11¾	3↑Allowance	4 1 42½ 32½ 35 46¾	McCauley W H	113	70.60	Swerved 7
22May78– 8Mth fm 1	⊕:48 1:13½ 1:38⅘	3↑Allowance	4 4 44 68 713 823	McCauley W H b	113	76.70	Tired 9
11May78– 6Mth fst 170	:46⅘ 1:11¼ 1:43¾	3↑Allowance	1 2 2hd 1hd 42¼ 413	McCauley W H b	112	10.60	Checked 7
25Apr78– 7Key fst 170	:46⅘ 1:12 1:42	3↑Allowance	4 2 3nk 2nd 55½ 611	D'Agusto J G⁵	b 107	4.90	Tired 8
16Apr78– 7Key fst 170	:47⅛ 1:13¾ 1:44⅘	Allowance	5 2 2½ 21 21¼	D'Agusto J G⁷	b 107	3.90	Good try 6

Banging Bill

Own.—Middletown Stable

Ch. c. 3, by Vent Du Nord—Carol's Choice, by Activate
Br.—Stavola M J (Fla)
Tr.—Raymond William T

				Turf Record	St. 1st 2nd 3rd	Amt.
				St. 1st 2nd 3rd	1978 3 1 0 0	$5,400
				2 1 0 0	1977 5 M 0 1	$605

21July78– 7Mth fm 1	⊕:47⅘ 1:12½ 1:45⅘	Clm 27500	4 4 41½ 55 912 917	Klidzia S	b 117	4.30	Early ft 10
14July78– 6Mth fm 1	⊕:48 1:12¾ 1:45¼	Clm 15000	5 5 33½ 1½ 12½ 13	Klidzia S	b 112	25.50	Handily 8
8July78– 9Mth fst 6f	:22 :45¾ 1:11¾	Md 15000	3 9 99¾ 812 86¼ 68½	Klidzia S	b 116	12.80	Outrun 10
120ct77– 3Key fst 6f	:22½ :46⅘ 1:14	Md Sp Wt	2 10 811 714 714 710	Santage J L	b 120	25.70	Outrun 12
70ct77– 4Med fst 6f	:23 :46⅔ 1:12½	Md Sp Wt	3 9 99¼ 10¹² 711 811	Miceli M	b 119	25.70	Outrun 12
27Sep77– 4Med gd 170	:48 1:13½ 1:44⅘	Md Sp Wt	8 4 42 412 718 727	Perret C	b 119	17.20	Wide 9
15Sep77– 3Key fst 5½f	:22⅘ :47¾ 1:06⅘	Md Sp Wt	8 8 85½ 86½ 45 39½	Barrera C	b 118	47.80	Sluggish 8
27July77– 4Mth fst 6f	:21¾ :45½ 1:11¾	Md Sp Wt	3 6 811 912 911 99¾	Perret C	b 118	16.60	No factor 10

LATEST WORKOUTS Jly 27 Mth 4f fst :47¾ hg · Jly 20 Mth 3f fst :36⅗ b

Johnny And Joey

Own.—Baer S M

Gr. g. 3, by Jim J—Foxiness, by Native Dancer
Br.—Petrie Juanita (Va)
Tr.—Tammaro John III

				Turf Record	St. 1st 2nd 3rd	Amt.
				St. 1st 2nd 3rd	1978 12 1 2 1	$7,325
				2 0 0 0	1977 0 M 0 0	$510

5Aug78– 2Mth sly 1¹⁄₁₆	⊕:48⅘ 1:14½ 1:48⅛	Clm 20000	6 5 56½ 34½ 33 2nk	MacBeth D	b 114	10.40	Sharp 8
29July78– 3Mth yl 1	⊕:48½ 1:14 1:41¾	Clm 20000	3 9 10¹⁴ 96½ 96 74	Prosper G	b 115	17.00	Outrun 10
11July78– 9Mth fst 1	⊕:48½ 1:13¾ 1:38⅘	3↑Allowance	11 12 12¹⁸ 11¹² 98 812	Prosper G	b 112	38.90	Outrun 12
3July78– 5Mth sly 1	:47⅘ 1:13½ 1:40⅘	Clm 21000	1 4 44 49 412 210	Prosper G	b 119	6.90	Outrun 12
7Jun78– 2Mth fst 1	:47⅘ 1:12¾ 1:40⅘	Clm 19000	1 5 54½ 23½ 33 32¼	Kupfer T⁵	b 110	10.50	Gamely 8
27May78– 5Mth gd 6f	:22⅘ :46 1:11¾	3↑Allowance	7 7 74 42¾ 55½ 68	Kupfer T⁵	b 107	11.90	Evenly 8
22May78– 1Mth fst 6f	:21¾ :45¾ 1:11	3↑Md 15000	1 7 48 21 1½ 1nk	Kupfer T⁵	b 110	11.90	Driving 10
10Apr78– 3Aqu fst 6f	:22⅘ :46½ 1:12½	Md 20000	7 3 76 79½ 76¾ 67¾	McCauley W H b	118	30.60	No threat 12
16Mar78– 3Aqu fst 1¹⁄₁₆	⊡:48 1:13¾ 1:47¾	Md 20000	8 3 44½ 58¼ 614 613	McCauley W H	122	22.90	Tired 10
1Mar78– 4Aqu fst 170	⊡:49 1:15 1:45¾ 1:29	3↑Md 20000	5 4 64¼ 67½ 511 69¼	Kupfer T⁵	108	10.10	Tired 9

LATEST WORKOUTS Jly 26 Mth 7f fst 1:29 b · Jun 29 Mth 3f fst :35⅗ b

Pace in Long Races

At races beyond a mile and one sixteenth, the safest procedure is to hunt for the animal that has already demonstrated suitability to the route, is in condition and, if you are lucky, has an edge in class. More often than not, a record of coming on in the stretch is a reassuring sign, especially if the late gains have taken place recently and the animal is otherwise in good trim. Should a couple of fast-breaking front-runners be in the field, the come-from-behinder looks even better. There seldom is any occasion to resort to arithmetical pace ratings in races of this kind.

If the track, like so many, presents route races in which the horses run only about 100 yards before reaching the first turn, it pays to keep an eye peeled for front-runners with inside post positions. Moreover, if the field includes two front-runners of which one is not in particularly sharp condition and will break from an outside post position, possibilities remain bright for the horse with the inside post.

Once in a while an especially sharp player spots a sprinter in one of these longer races. If the horse is the only speed in the field, it may be a lucrative bet. The player must be careful that it is not being entered at the longer distance for purposes of exercise. It should have genuine speed to begin with, and no prospect of competition for the early lead. Even if it has had difficulty holding the lead in shorter races, its chances to carry its speed farther and more comfortably should not be dismissed without careful analysis of the probable pace of the impending race.

A representative example occurred in the fourth at Monmouth Park on Saturday, August 12, 1978 (page 268). In a field of five three-year-old colts and geldings and a four-year-old gelding competing at $1\frac{1}{16}$ miles for a $10,500 purse for which only non-winners of an allowance race were eligible, Baederwood seemed an obvious qualifier. By Tentam out of a Northern Dancer mare, the colt was bred to run all day but had not yet gone beyond three-quarters of a mile. In the most recent two of his three lifetime starts, he had reached the lead before the half-mile pole. No other horse in this field had shown such a running style when sprinting or even when running in longer races. Furthermore, the colt had just broken its maiden on the same kind of footing as today's—slop—after gamely overtaking the early leader and proceeding to draw away by six lengths. Baederwood went off at a measly 3 to 2, yet seemed an overlay at those odds.

I should point out that Baederwood was the only starter that had

FOURTH RACE	1 $\frac{1}{16}$ MILES. (1.41) ALLOWANCE. Purse $10,500. 3-year-olds and upward which have
Monmouth	not won a race other than maiden, claiming or starter Weights, 3-year-olds, 116 lbs. Older, 122 lbs. Non-winners of $6,000 in 1978, allowed 2 lbs. $3,600 since may 10, 4 lbs.
AUGUST 12, 1978	$3,600 in 1978, 6 lbs.

Value of race $10,500, value to winner $6,300, second $2,100, third $1,155, fourth $630, fifth $315. Mutuel pool $134,341.

Exacta Pool $116,048.

Last Raced	Horse	Eqt.A.Wt	PP	St	1/4	1/2	3/4	Str	Fin	Jockey	Odds $1
2Aug78 2Mth¹	Baederwood	3 114	1	3	1½	1hd	1½	1hd	1hd	Thomas D B	1.50
28Jly78 9Bel¹	Ⓓ Turn For The Best	3 114	2	5	6	6	5⁵	2½	2⁴	Adams L	3.30
5Aug78 2Mth²	Johnny And Joey	b 3 112	6	1	3 1½	2hd	2 1½	3³	3⁴	MacBeth D	2.80
5Aug78 7Mth²	Mysto Hill	b 4 116	3	2	4hd	3hd	3hd	4½	4²	Wilson R	4.20
5Aug78 7Mth³	Rufflame	3 116	4	4	2hd	4³	4½	5⁸	5¹⁰	Sierra J A	11.20
21Jly78 7Mth⁹	Banging Bill	b 3 114	5	6	5²	5½	6	6	6	DiNicola B	16.30

Ⓓ—Turn For The Best Disqualified and placed third.

OFF AT 3:01 EDT. Start good, Won driving. Time, :24⅖, :48⅕, 1:13, 1:39⅖, 1:46⅗ Track sloppy.

$2 Mutuel Prices:

3-BAEDERWOOD	5.00	3.20	2.40
8-JOHNNY AND JOEY		3.60	2.40
4-TURN FOR THE BEST			2.60

$2 EXACTA 3-4 PAID $17.00.

B. c, by Tentam—Royal Statue, by Northern Dancer. Trainer Bardaro Anthony J. Bred by Taylor E P (Md).

BAEDERWOOD set or forced the pace between rivals from soon after the start, responded gamely in the final sixteenh and held TURN FOR THE BEST safe. The latter, outrun, early, rallied outside horses when roused on the final turn, drifted in entering the stretch, continued to respond after Adams dropped his whip in the upper stretch but bore inward, badly impeded JOHNNY AND JOEY near the sixteenth ple and could not quite overhaul the winner. Following a steward's inquiry into the stretch run, TURN FOR THE BEST was disqualified and placed third for impeding JOHNNY AND JOEY. JOHNNY AND JOEY, close contention outside horses from the outset, was severly impeded in the stretch. MYSTOHILL flattened out in the stretch.

never run for a claiming price. He was every bit the kind of lightly raced, well-bred, well-managed, improving three-year-old that can be expected to continue winning as long as its record remains conspicuously more impressive than that of any of its opponents. That he won this race by only a narrow margin after a lengthy stretch drive (and without ever enjoying a long lead) was evidence of his quality.

Pace and Post Position

We have discussed the advantage of an inside post position to a fast-breaking front-runner when the first turn is only a few hops from the starting gate. Logically enough, an outside post position is a serious disadvantage to such a horse in a race of that kind, unless it is the class of its field.

Needing to get out front in a hurry so that it can run with maximum ease at the slowest possible pace over the shortest possible distance, the front-runner needs extra class and stamina to overcome the handicap of the outside post. Lacking those qualities, but imprisoned by its running style, it may defeat itself in the effort to get to the rail, in front, before reaching the first turn. Or, if the rider does not try to get to the rail that soon, the mount must cover extra ground on the turn and may lose that way.

In circumstances of that sort, a stretch-running type with a more favorable post position is often a better bet. When ridden by a good postboy able to get it out in a hurry and find a good position in the pack, it is able to lay slightly off the pace and, with ordinary luck, find the room it needs to pass the fatigued front-runner in the stretch.

Races with a long, straight run to the first turn are quite different for the jockey and the player. The front-runner is at no serious disadvantage in any post position. Even if it breaks from the extreme outside, its rider has plenty of time. He may ease over to the rail at any point before the first turn occurs, losing little ground and expending practically no extra energy in the process.

The slow-breaking horse with an inside post position is in grave trouble, however. Unable to get out of the gate as fast as many of the others, it often is pinched back as they fight their way toward the rail. To its difficulty in gathering stride and momentum is added the exertion of staying out of trouble and, finally, the problem of trailing everyone around the turn and, as the stretch arrives, finding—as often as not—that the only way home is on the outside of the pack, covering extra ground.

An added complication, for front-runner and off-pace horse alike, is the condition of the running surface. On muddy days, the deepest, most difficult running is often along the rail. The speed horse, which usually needs to save as much ground as possible, can now do so only at the risk of tiring itself in the deep gumbo. The competition now becomes a struggle for room in mid-track. The stretch-runner with a touch of stamina and class sometimes manages to come on along the rail at the end, deep footing or not.

Handicappers can make extra money by keeping tallies of the winning post positions at each distance and in each kind of track condition. To note that the inside post is a detriment at six furlongs on days when the track is labeled "fast" is to become aware of a situation not at all uncommon in many places, yet often overlooked by the crowd. And to discover that one or more of the middle posts is a great advantage when the track is drying out after rain is to place oneself in the way of jackpots.

How Leading Tracks Differ

When your track is dry (fast, good or slow), do horses with early speed enjoy an advantage? How great is that advantage on most days of that kind? Does the situation change when the footing is wet (sloppy, muddy or heavy)? To what extent?

In his celebrated research study, *Percentages and Probabilities,* Frederick S. Davis showed that North American racing strips can be divided into four categories, according to the percentage of races won by horses that ran first, second or third at the first call (after a quarter-mile of running in sprints and a half-mile in races at a mile or longer). With thanks to Fred, who is my friend and frequent colleague, his findings are updated and reproduced in the following list of tracks and their characteristics. The early-speed categories are:

1. 44–49% winners
2. 50–59% winners
3. 60–69% winners
4. 70–75% winners

The tabulation also includes the circumference of each track (in parentheses after its name), and the distance from its finish line to the beginning of the first turn. In general, when a race starts fewer than 400 feet from the first turn, horses with inner post positions have the large advantage of being able to save ground on that turn. And horses that combine inner posts with early speed are even more fortunate. The reader will notice that many one-mile tracks seldom program races at that distance. Races at a mile and 70 yards or a mile and one-sixteenth extend by 210 or 330 feet the distance to the first turn, making for more competitive racing.

One final observation before presenting the list: Regardless of how friendly or hostile to early speed a track may seem in light of its long-term statistics, no guarantee exists that it will reproduce typical running conditions on any given day. During or after changes in weather, or on the first day of each new racing week, good handicappers take nothing for granted. They watch a race or two to see whether the track is behaving in its normal fashion.

| Track | Early Speed | | Finish Line |
	Dry	Wet	to First Turn
Ak-Sar-Ben (1)*	3	2	350
Aqueduct Inner (1)	2	3	333
Aqueduct Main (1⅛)	3	4	330
Arlington Park (1⅛)	3	3	375
Atlantic City (1⅛)	3	3	700
Bay Meadows (1)	1	2	330
Belmont Park (1½)	1	3	843
Bowie (1)	3	3	256

| Track | Early Speed | | Finish Line |
	Dry	Wet	to First Turn
Calder (1)	2	3	330
Churchill Downs (1)	1	1	113
Delaware Park (1)	3	2	325
Del Mar (1)	3	3	488
Fair Grounds (1)	1	3	150
Fort Erie (1)	1	3	260
Golden Gate (1)	4	3	383
Gulfstream (1)	4	3	315
Hawthorne (1)	2	2	184
Hialeah (1⅛)	2	3	325
Hollywood Park (1)	2	2	340
Keeneland (1¹⁄₁₆)	2	4	146
Keystone (1)	2	2	313
Laurel (1⅛)	4	4	480
Meadowlands (1)	3	3	330
Monmouth Park (1)	3	2	440
Oaklawn (1)	2	2	330
Pimlico (1)	2	3	162
Rockingham Park (1)	2	4	330
Santa Anita (1)	2	2	330
Saratoga (1⅛)	2	4	341
Sportsman's Park (⅝)	1	4	114
Woodbine (1)	3	4	375

*Numbers in parentheses are in miles.

14

The Stable Factor

During 1978, the owners of approximately 25,000 licensed racing stables competed for net purses of about $330 million at Thoroughbred tracks in the United States, Canada and Mexico.

If the money had been divided equally, which it was not, the average stable owner would have grossed about $13,000—not quite enough to keep one horse training and racing on a major racing circuit.

The economics of stable ownership are even more severe than the statistics suggest. During 1977, fewer than 3,500 stable owners (roughly 14 percent of all), won as much as $20,000 in purse money. Not only did 85 percent of owners fall below that modest earnings level, but it is quite likely that at least 10,000 owners won less than $3,000 each. In a typical year, between 40 and 45 percent of owners win less than 8 percent of the available money. On the other hand, the 100 most successful stables (the ½ percent that we hear about most often), usually take 20 percent of the loot.

Now we know why stable owners are called "sportsmen and sportswomen." The sport is founded on their willingness to spend more than they take in. Most can afford to. If they could not, they would quit. Indeed, many remain owners for only a few years, moving to other pursuits after Internal Revenue no longer permits them to deduct stable losses from their taxes. To be tax-deductible, a racing stable must show occasional profits, thereby qualifying as a business rather than a hobby. Some manage to show profits and qualify for tax deductions by buying and selling horses in claiming races, or by merchandising attractive livestock at the auction sales which punctuate race meetings.

Socialites and Pros

Owners come in all shapes, sizes, sexes and ages, from all walks of life. Those who form the political backbone of the big-time sport and supply it with most of its famous glamor are persons of inherited wealth. The breeding and racing of Thoroughbreds is a traditional avocation of their families. They share dominance of the pastime with a few millionaires of more recent vintage and a scattering of professional horsemen who rose to the top the hard way and now own important stables.

Diverse though owners may be, they fall into two categories. The smaller (by far) is composed of those with sufficient sense and taste to leave horsemanship to horsemen. A more numerous group includes owners whose desire for prominence exceeds their interest in horseflesh. If certain trainers behave like con artists and seem to know as much about soft soap as they do about the care and schooling of Thoroughbreds, it is from years of coping with bubble-headed employers.

Many owners want the trainer to pretend that they know something about horses. They crave to make strategy. They sulk if the trainer fails to adorn each horse with a popular rider. They want to know why the trainer spends so much money on straw. They get sore if the trainer doesn't tip them off to a longshot once in a while. They fume if they don't win stakes races and get on television. They make general nuisances of themselves. But they pay bills.

One of the most celebrated owners of modern times was Elizabeth (Arden) Graham, the cosmetics queen who owned Maine Chance Farms. During her thirty-five years in the sport, she employed at least sixty-five trainers. Some of the most competent horsemen of the era were unable to achieve lasting rapport with the lady. For examples, Eddie Neloy, Clarence Buxton, Eddie Holton, H. Guy Bedwell, George Odom, Frank Christmas, Tom Barry, Mose Shapoff, Ivan and Monte Parke, Ben Stutts, W. O. Hicks, Frank Merrill, Jr., Casey Hayes, Willie Molter, Randy Sechrest, Al Scotti and George Poole.

The player needs to know something about owners. He especially needs to know the names of the most successful ones. Generally, he will pay much more attention to the doings of trainers, who are the most decisive influences in the life of a Thoroughbred. But trainers move from owner to owner, their fortunes rising or falling according to the kind of livestock the owner provides. And year after year the same owners appear on the list of leading money winners. It pays to know who is who.

Leading Owners

To qualify for a player's alert respect, a stable should not only win a lot of money but should win at least 15 percent of the races it enters. The following owners have established their ability to meet these standards, and are likely to merit attention for years. I list them alphabetically.

AISCO STABLES
AUGUSTIN STABLES
S. M. BAER
OSCAR S. BARRERA
MARIBEL G. BLUM
BROOKFIELD FARMS
MRS. J. W. BROWN
BUCKLAND FARM
BWAMAZON FARM
CALUMET FARM
CARDIFF STOCK FARM
E. C. CASHMAN
CHRISTIANA STABLES
CRIMSON KING FARM
J. P. DORIGNAC, JR.
ELMENDORF FARM
EL PECO RANCH
B. R. EVANS
MARTIN L. FALLON
W. S. FARISH, III
BERTRAM R. FIRESTONE
DANIEL M. GALBREATH
GOLDEN CHANCE FARM
GREENTREE STABLE
HARBOR VIEW FARM
D. J. HEARD
HICKORY TREE STABLE
HOBEAU FARM
FRED W. HOOPER
STANLEY M. HOUGH et al.
AARON U. JONES
KEMLING BROS.

KINGHAVEN FARMS
KING RANCH
J. W. LACROIX
DAN LASATER
LAZY F RANCH
J. L. LEVESQUE
O. C. & P. MAXWELL
MAY-DON STABLE
MRS. H. D. PAXSON
WILLIAM HAGGIN PERRY
LEONE J. PETERS
OGDEN M. PHIPPS FAMILY
PROLER & STRAUSS
QUALITY HILL STABLES
BERNARD J. RIDDER
ROKEBY STABLES
SAMVAN STABLES
ROBERT E. SANGSTER
SARON STABLE
L. P. SASSO
J. M. SCHIFF
E. A. SELTZER
SIGMUND SOMMER
STAFFORD FARM
TARTAN STABLE
JACK C. VAN BERG
REGINALD N. WEBSTER
RANDOLPH WEINSIER
C. V. WHITNEY
DANIEL WILDENSTEIN
WINDFIELD FARMS

Man vs. Horse

Horsemen sometimes convey the impression that the sport would be more to their liking if a way could be found to eliminate the horses.

Eddie Arcaro once complained that three out of four horses don't want to win their races. Other riders say that unwillingness is even more prevalent than that. Throughout the industry, a standard conversational theme is the perverse, mulish, erratic contrariness of these animals.

After centuries of selective breeding, racing apparently remains alien to the essential nature of the Thoroughbred. Despite training routines intended to bring any fairly sound horse into some kind of racing trim, the breed continues to balk.

Exactly what is wrong?

Human stupidity and greed, intensified by the economics of a highly precarious business.

Owners of Champions

The first family of modern American racing is named Phipps. At this writing, Ogden Mills (Dinny) Phipps is Chairman of the New York Racing Association, which operates Aqueduct, Belmont Park and Saratoga. His father, Ogden Phipps, preceded him in that eminent position. His grandmother, Mrs. Henry Carnegie Phipps, headed the celebrated Wheatley Stable, in which Dinny Phipps was active as a youth. Ogden Phipps, Dinny Phipps and Mrs. Ogden Phipps each own and race good horses. Among them, the members of this dynasty have owned 18 American champions, and at least that many near-champions. They lead the list of currently active stables that have won championships.

Phipps-Wheatley: Ancestor, Bold Lad, Bold Ruler, Buckpasser, Castle Forbes, High Voltage, Impressive, Mako, Misty Morn, Neji, Numbered Account, Oedipus, Queen Empress, Queen of the Stage, Straight and True, Successor, Top Bid, Vitriolic.

Calumet Farm: A Glitter, Armed, Barbizon, Bewitch, Citation, Coaltown, Forward Pass, Mar-Kell, Our Mims, Real Delight, Tim Tam, Twilight Tear, Two Lea, Whirlaway, Wistful.

A. G. Vanderbilt: Bed o' Roses, Discovery, Native Dancer, Next Move, Now What, Petrify, Social Outcast.

Greentree: Capot, Devil Diver, Jungle King, Malicious, Stage Door Johnny, Tom Fool.

Rokeby: American Way, Amerigo Lady, Arts and Letters, Fort Marcy, Key to the Mint, Run the Gantlet.

C. V. Whitney: Bug Brush, Career Boy, Counterpoint, First Flight, Phalanx, Silver Spoon.

Montpelier: Benguala, Mongo, Proud Delta, Shipboard, Soothsayer.

Responsible racing journals are replete with articles on the techniques of breaking and schooling yearlings, maintaining equine health, and preparing a horse for its race. Regardless of disagreements on technical matters, virtually all the articles play variations on a single theme: A Thoroughbred treated with rough impatience is unlikely to amount to much.

If kindness, patience and intelligence were dominant characteristics of the racing industry, such articles would be unnecessary. But they are necessary. Anyone can prove it to himself by wandering around the barns of a morning, or keeping his eyes and ears open at the paddock in the afternoon.

Many trainers, stablehands, exercise boys and jockeys truly love and understand horses. Many more do not. The heart of the misunderstanding seems to be the unwarranted assumption that modern racing is a natural activity for horses and that the animals, though mentally dim, should adopt a more human attitude toward their work and be grateful for the opportunity to participate. When the bland manageableness that passes for equine gratitude is withheld, and sulkiness or rebelliousness sets in, the tendency of the human being is to react with resentment of his own. In due course, there arises the peculiarly negative, self-defeating, quite widespread feeling that the meal-ticket, the horse, is an infernal nuisance, a necessary evil.

Noms de Course

The player ought to know that he is talking about John Hay Whitney when referring to "Greentree." Here are some of America's most important racing stables, and the names of the persons who own them.

Aisco Stables (Marvin S. Savin)
Aisquith Stable (Raymond E. Aisquith)
Ardboe Stable (James B. Moseley)

Augustin Stables (George Strawbridge, Jr.)
Balmak Stables (Mary S. Streit)
Bohemia Stable (Allaire C. du Pont)

Brandywine Stable (Donald P. Ross, Jr.)

Briardale Farm (Anthony Imbesi)

Buckland Farm (Thomas M. Evans)

Calumet Farm (Lucille P. Markey)

Christiana Stables (Jane du Pont Lunger)

Claiborne Farm (Mrs. A. B. Hancock, Jr.)

Elmendorf Farm (Maxwell H. Gluck)

Greentree Stable (John Hay Whitney)

Harbor View Farms (Louis E. Wolfson)

Hickory Tree Stable (Alice du Pont Mills)

Hobeau Farm (Jack Dreyfus, Jr.)

Kinghaven Farms (Donald G. Willmot)

Lazy F Ranch (Martha Farish Gerry)

Llangollen Farm (M. E. [Liz Whitney] Tippett)

Meadowhill (Morton Rosenthal)

Meadow Stable (Helen C. [Penny] Ringquist)

Montpelier (Marion du Pont Scott)

Pen-Y-Bryn Farm (William W. Bancroft)

Pillar Farms (William du Pont III)

Rokeby Stables (Paul Mellon)

Saron Stable (Corbin J. Robertson)

Stafford Farm (Jack Stafford)

Tartan Stable (James H. Binger)

Windfields Farm (Edward P. Taylor)

Woodside Stud (Sally Bierer)

The truth is that racing is no more natural for horses than the hundred-yard dash is for men. To engage successfully in activities of that kind, a horse (or man) must be carefully schooled and tended. To survive any great number of races or training workouts without breaking down, the muscles, joints, heart and lungs of horse or man must be trained for undue stress. The difference, of course, is that a human footracer can discuss his pain. And he can make choices.

But horses cannot. They are entirely dependent on man. Like other domesticated animals such as the dog, they thrive or wilt according to the treatment they get from humans. A well-nurtured Thoroughbred tolerates the hullabaloo of the track, the repeated exhaustion of training and racing, the sometimes frightening ministrations of handlers, blacksmiths and veterinarians. He is willing to race. He sometimes even seems to like it. When he is retired he may act, like an Exterminator or Kelso, as if he missed the excitement, and may perk up considerably when brought back to a track to parade in front of the stands.

But the unwilling Thoroughbred is a different specimen. He fears noise, or people, or some particular handler, or his knee hurts after repeated concussion of hoof on racing strip, or his lungs are congested, or he was soured on the whole game by unpleasant early experiences. Sometimes he can be whipped into cooperating and running a good race. More often, the punishment frightens him into losing his stride. Or he retaliates in the only ways he knows, which are to sulk or swerve or duck or stop.

As the Hirsch Jacobs experience with Stymie illustrates, and as has been shown in many other cases of the same kind, a trainer with time, skill and motivation may sometimes undo the previous experiences or present afflictions that cause unwillingness in a Thoroughbred. Unfortunately, the tempo and pressures of the business make most such speculative experiments uneconomical. The horse is a commodity on which a quick return is craved. Either it delivers or it goes elsewhere. The need for the quick dollar, earned from minimum investment, affects what happens to most Thoroughbreds from the moment of birth. Financial pressures influence the behavior of trainers, grooms, exercise boys and stablehands—all but a lucky few trainers and their backstretch help.

While most owners fully expect to lose money, each wants to win every purse he can—and some specialize in nagging about it. The goal of the average trainer and his staff is to keep the owner quiet—if not happy—by providing maximum action. Moreover, backstretch incomes are tied to purse revenues. The trainer gets 10 percent. Bonuses go to everyone else, including the humblest swipe.

Under those pressures for quick returns, and with the track's racing secretary screaming for horses with which to fill out his programs, it is perhaps no wonder that comparatively sound animals are grievously overworked. And that they continue to race even after overwork begins to take its toll. And that they finally break down forever. And that the year never passes without half a dozen good three-year-olds going permanently bad before they ever get to Churchill Downs. And that many three-year-old champions poop out at four. And that a topnotch six-year-old is a rarity.

You can argue until you turn blue that a horse might last longer and earn a great deal more money if raced more sparingly, prepared more carefully for each race. The trainer answers with a grimace, "Horses make no money standing in their stalls or browsing in pastures. I'm not Johnny Nerud or Frank Whiteley. I'm not working for Mr. Whitney or Mr. Guest. I've got payrolls to meet and my owners are breathing down my back. Horse either gets up and does it or I go rustle me another horse."

Scores of trainers—possibly hundreds—do the very best that can be done for their animals, on the sound theory that proper care will be repaid at the finish wire some afternoon. Their ability to function this wisely depends not only on their own competence but on the dispositions of their employers—the owners—and on the quality of their stable help. Good stablehands are hard to find nowadays. The others tend to give as little time and care as possible to a horse, thereby helping to worsen whatever quirk or ailment may be preventing it from winning. I have seen the trainers of world-famous stables seethe in helpless rage at the barbarically stupid impatience with which exercise boys and grooms handle frightened animals. "I'll fire that bum as soon as I can find another," is a familiar refrain in the front offices of racing barns.

How Horses Learn

All scientific studies of horses reveal them to be less intelligent, in the human sense, than apes, dolphins, elephants, pigs or dogs. But they are keenly sensitive to their surroundings and to the experiences they undergo at human hands. And they have memories that would do credit to any elephant. It is easier for them to learn than to forget what they have learned. A bad habit implanted by a misused whip, an ill-advised shout or cuff, or an accidental collision, may persist for years.

It is unlikely that any horse actually understands the difference between winning and losing. Yet horses obviously do what they can to avoid or resist discomfort. There seems no doubt that they do best when taught their trade with a minimum of fear and pain, and when convinced by repeated experience that the rewards of good performance are worth the considerable effort.

It all begins with the yearlings. Patient, gentle treatment being costly, because it consumes the time of expensive personnel, an appalling number of Thoroughbreds are ruined at this, the earliest stage of their careers.

The process known as "breaking" is meant to accustom the young horse to the feel of the rider and his tack. It is a hideously frightening experience for the yearling, unless the handlers take their time. All writings on the subject (and trade journals are at it constantly), emphasize that human violence during the breaking period often spoils the disposition of a horse, leaving it dispirited or fractious.

Damage at that stage is compounded for many horses by impatience and carelessness during their first months of drill on the training track. They must learn to run straight, and to respond to the rider's voice,

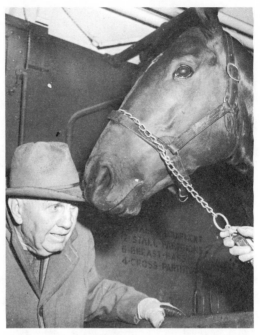

The late Sunny Jim Fitz-simmons, one of the most successful trainers of all time, with his great Na-shua.   UPI PHOTO

hands and reins, and to change leads on the turns, and to break from a standing start at the gate. It is a tricky business in which, once again, the future abilities of the animal may be impaired by unintelligent handling.

Yet the pressures are to school 'em as fast as possible (to save money) and get 'em to the races as early in the two-year-old season as possible (to get the money back). Thousands never make it to actual competition, having broken down from running too fast too early in their lives.

Horses do not grow a complete set of adult teeth until they are five! One of the chief reasons why young horses break down is that their immaturely soft bones give way under the concussion of running full tilt over hard surfaces. Incredibly, some veterinarians assert that the problem is worsened and disaster assured by ill-fitting shoes, which throw the animals off balance when they run.

Among horses that finally get to the races, few are without quirks of temperament or running style. Horsemen ascribe many of these idiosyncracies to equine family traits. But candid ones agree that proper handling from the very start of schooling could minimize the effects of these inherited characteristics and, above all, could prevent development of other bad habits.

Mares and foals at Dickey Stables in the Florida Green Grass country.
UPI PHOTO

When the jockey grumbles that he always has to whip a particular horse to get some run from it in the early stages of a race, he refers in most cases to an animal whose earliest handlers taught it, altogether unintentionally, to behave that way. Horses that panic in the paddock or do not like to run on the rail, or between horses, or behind horses, or in front of horses, or on the turns, or that quit when whipped, or refuse to run unless whipped, are victims of their early conditioning. Horses whose tongues must be tied down with straps are, most often, horses whose first handlers did not know how to break them to the bit.

One of the best-known facts about Thoroughbreds is that their first experiences in competition often have a decisive effect on their later performances. A horse whose trainer is careful to give it an easy first race or two has a much better chance of going on to better things than a horse that almost expires of exhaustion in its first outings. Even better at the beginning is an easy *winning* race. The horse that loses its first races in all-out efforts may take months to recover from the experience. It usually behaves as if it is *supposed* to chase the others, not beat them.

In 1961, *The Thoroughbred Record* provoked considerable debate with a series of articles by the veteran horseman Colonel Phil T. Chinn. Among other statements uncomplimentary to modern racing, Chinn declared that the bucked shins, osselets and other arthritic ailments that afflict today's overworked two- and three-year-old horses were virtually unknown in his era. Horses were not subjected to premature strain when he was a lad. When they turned sore, he said, they were rested. And rest was more beneficial to bones and joints worn and torn by overstrain than the modern practice of cauterizing damaged tissue with a red-hot iron.

During the ensuing uproar, *The Thoroughbred Record* polled horsemen for their opinions. Three out of five agreed that the modern Thoroughbred is less sound than its ancestor of thirty years before. Those who agreed tended to blame today's harder tracks, the demand for more speed, the failure to rest modern horses during the winter, and the strain of breaking from the stationary starting gate.

Some of the comments were enlightening.

Sam Sechrest said, "It's not a question of soundness. If horses were given more time as two-year-olds and at the time of breaking, and not started so soon, I don't believe there would be so many bucked shins and osselets."

Max Hirsch: "Horses not raised with common sense."

Robert L. Dotter: "Asking for too much speed from horses that have not finished growing."

Stephen Di Mauro: "Bad exercise boys—snatching, twisting and turning horses too sharply. Same for hot walkers. All in all, careless help."

John H. C. Forbes: "Thirty years ago there was time to rest a horse."

R. H. McLellan: "Starting juveniles at the start of the year and racing the majority of them too often thereafter."

W. C. Freeman: "Too many sprint races which force a trainer to rush his young horses before they have achieved their growth."

Dale Landers: "Racing and breaking colts too young."

Other articles in authoritative trade periodicals have deplored abuses visited on horses that survive the rigors of premature racing. Writer after writer pleads with horsemen to give ailing or jaded Thoroughbreds the rest they need. But rest takes time. And time is money. From stakes winners to $1,000 derelicts, lack of rest is a prime factor in the development of disability.

Veterinarians agree, and many have written, that a horse with cold symptoms should be rested. In recent years, outbreaks of what horsemen call "cough"—actually influenza—have caused alarm throughout racing. The proper treatment includes rest—an absolute termination of training and racing. But the lung capacities of innumerable Thoroughbreds have been impaired permanently by the strain of racing while infected with flu.

"I know, I know," says a top trainer. "I'm as sad as you are that the sport is not as gracious as it was when lords and their ladies sat under parasols and watched Arabian chargers run around their pastures for side bets. But this thing is bigger than all of us. It's just a reflection of changes that have taken place in every area of life. If you want to get indignant about the industrialization of the Thoroughbred, be my guest. But while you're at it, you might consider the industrialization of everything else. When was the last time you saw a piece of homemade bread, or milk fresh from a cow, or a new-laid egg, or an automobile that looked like the guy who made it cared about his work? You go get indignant about horses. Me, my main worry is whether I can get my horses onto the track for their exercise tomorrow morning before the strip is shut down for rolling. And whether I can talk some snot of an exercise boy into taking my filly around the track twice before he runs off to pick up another few bucks working some other guy's horse. And whether tomorrow's shipment of feed will have mold in it like the last one. And whether the damned accountant will get the stable's books in order for the next damned tax examination."

All of this has a good deal to do with the handicapping of horse races. The player is better off when he realizes that most trainers are not more competent than most haberdashers or auto mechanics and are under no greater compulsion to be. That realization surely clears the air for the player and inspires greater respect for the feats of those very few trainers who manage somehow to surmount all obstacles, winning far more than their share of races every season. These are the trainers the smart player favors. They have better horses and/or induce more racing readiness and willingness in their stock than other trainers do. Between two evenly matched contenders—one trained by a national or local leader and the other by a scrambler—the expert player grants an advantage to the horse from the more successful barn.

Trainers to Watch

A Frank Whiteley, Jr., or Charles Whittingham handles nothing but good horses, or potentially good horses, and races them only when he believes they are ready for a genuine effort. Such horsemen operate that way because they prefer to, and because they are fortunate enough to be employed by owners willing to be patient. Other trainers may be every bit as knowing but have less to work with. Handling the discards of better barns, or struggling with stock spoiled by others, they hang on by their fingernails and wait for luck to smile.

Who are the best trainers in the business? Insiders award the palm to those who manage to make the most of whatever horseflesh they may have. All lists include the aforementioned Whittingham and Whiteley and the remarkable H. Allen Jerkens, who for years has specialized in transforming apparently ordinary animals into authentically good ones—and beating champions with them.

Held in much lower regard are horsemen lucky enough to train the expensively bred stock of wealthy stables yet seldom able to keep the animals in condition long enough to win the big victories to which their bloodlines may have entitled them. And almost nobody has a kind word for trainers who (1) win races but ruin their horses in the process or (2) seldom enter horses at the right distance or in the right company yet consider themselves victims of ill fortune when smarter operatives claim the horses and begin winning with them.

It is fun to nominate trainers as best or nearly best. And it is essential to know, as implied above, that a horse claimed by Barn "A" from Barn "B" is likely to improve dramatically. One's ability to know such things has less to do with the difficult job of comparing horsemen's talents than with the relatively easy one of comparing their performance statistics. Whether Trainer "A" actually is more gifted than "B" is beside the point. What counts is "A's" superior record as revealed in statistical compilations during the present race meeting and those of the recent past.

Here is how to do it:

1. Never bet on the trainer alone. The best seldom win more than one race in every four or five attempts.

2. If the horse seems to be a leading contender in its race and is being handled by a reliable trainer, it deserves extra favor. Indeed, it is rarely a mistake to differentiate closely matched horses on such grounds. Successful trainers get that way by beating the unsuccessful ones.

3. A contending horse deserves special consideration if its trainer meets one of the following standards:

   a. Mention on the published daily list of leading trainers at the current meeting, with a winning average of at least 17 percent.

   b. Mention on the list of consistent trainers that appears on the facing page. The list should be revised and updated by consulting *The American Racing Manual* each year. From the player's point of view, a high percentage of victories is more important than high total earnings.

The suggestion that a winning average of 17 percent be the timberline between reliably consistent trainers and their rivals is based on the knowledge that the most reliable trainers manage in the long run to win a race in every four or five attempts. A trainer capable of such a winning average can be regarded as off his feed or in bad luck if he falls much below 17. But, unless he loses his good horses, he will improve his average before long. This is why the list on the next two pages should be used in conjunction with the current list of local leaders, and should be updated annually.

Super-conscientious handicappers carry the statistics beyond the trainer's winning percentage. They record his performances with horses returning from layoffs, and with previously unraced horses, and with newly claimed horses, and with routers as distinguished from sprinters. Not content with discovering whatever strengths, weaknesses and areas of specialization may seem evident in these records, the handicappers also try to ascertain training patterns that might be associated with the individual's all-out attempts to win. What about drops in class? Rises in class? Switches in distance? Frequency of workouts? Preferences for one or another rider?

Factual compilations of that kind are a great deal of work but reward any handicapper sufficiently attuned to the realities of the sport to understand that a good trainer's methods are dictated not only by personal preferences but by the variable nature of the horses in his barn and, of course, by pressures from owners.

The Consistent Ones

Most of the best and some of the best-connected trainers in the U.S. and Canada are listed here. They win consistently and can be expected to do so whenever they have the horses.

RON ALFANO	BILL BONIFACE
NED ALLARD	JIM BRACKEN
PETE ANDERSON	LOU BRANDT
DALE BAIRD	FRANK BROTHERS
LAZARO S. BARRERA	ELLIOTT BURCH
OSCAR BARRERA	SUNSHINE CALVERT
JOE BOLLERO	GORDON C. CAMPBELL
BERNARD P. BOND	DEL CARROLL
J. BOWES BOND	BEN CIBORON

Charles Whittingham

Frank Y. Whiteley, Jr.

H. Allen Jerkens

HENRY CLARK
DON COMBS
JIM COWDEN
WARREN A. (JIMMY) CROLL
JIM CRUPI
ROBERT DE BONIS
HAROLD DELAHOUSSAYE
GROVER G. (BUD) DELP
A. T. (TOMMY) DOYLE
RICHARD E. DUTROW
GENE EUSTER
MARTY FALLON
JERRY FANNING
FLOREANO FERNANDEZ
MIKE FERRARO
JOHN R. S. FISHER
BERNARD FLINT
LAWRENCE FONTENOT
JACK FORAN
JOHN FORBES
BOBBY FRANKEL
CARLOS GARCIA
JOHN M. GAVER, JR.
FRANK GOMEZ
WALTER GREENMAN
EDWIN GREGSON
MEL GROSS
KARL GRUSMARK
ROBERT GUCIARDO
EVERETT HAMMOND
JERRY HAMMOND

DAN HASBANY
RICHARD HAZELTON
DENNIS HEIMER
RAMON HERNANDEZ
ROBERT HILTON
STAN HOUGH
PETER M. HOWE
DOM IMPRESCIA
BOB IRWIN
JIMMY ISELIN
LARRY JENNINGS
H. ALLEN JERKENS
JUNE JOHNSON
PHILIP G. JOHNSON
LEROY JOLLEY
GARY JONES
DAVE KASSEN
MICHAEL KAY
EDDIE KELLY
TOMMY J. KELLY
ALLEN S. KING, JR.
FRANK KIRBY
FRANK LA BOCCETTA
ROGER LAURIN
KING T. LEATHERBURY
P. O'DONNELL LEE
JOHN J. LENZINI, JR.
BUDD LEPMAN
MILT LONGERBEAM
DANNY LOPEZ
D. WAYNE LUKAS

Dale Baird   *Lazaro S. Barrera*   *Elliott Burch*

JIM MALONEY
RICHARD MANDELLA
ALAN B. MARCUS
FRANK (PANCHO) MARTIN
JOSE MARTIN
RAUL MARTINEZ
PETE MAXWELL
BRIAN MAYBERRY
RON McANALLY
HENRY MERCER
FRANK H. MERRILL
JERRY C. MEYER
MACKENZIE MILLER
ZEKE MINASSIAN
H. STEWARD MITCHELL
MIKE MITCHELL
JOHN C. MOBBERLY
JIM MORGAN
JIM W. MURPHY
JOHN NERUD
V. J. NICKERSON
HOMER PARDUE
ANGEL PENNA
ORAL PICKARD
JOE H. PIERCE, JR.
GORDON POTTER
TOM PRATT
BILL PRICKETT
VIRGIL RAINES
WALTER REESE
SCOTT REGAN
LOREN RETTELE

CLYDE RICE
THOMAS L. (LOU)
  RONDINELLO
LARRY ROSE
GIL ROWNTREE
JOHN RUSSELL
CHARLIE SANBORN
AL SCHWIZER
JONATHAN SHEPPARD
JIM SIMPSON
GERALD SINNE
BURTON K. SIPP
RICHARD W. SMALL
DEWEY SMITH
FRANK SMITH, JR.
JERE R. SMITH
RON SMITH
J. Y. SOILEAU
JOHN STARR
WOODY STEPHENS
JOHN TAMMARO
JOHN TAMMARO, III
J. WILLARD THOMPSON
NOBLE THREEWITT
JIM TONER
JOE TROVATO
EDDIE TRUMAN
BILLY TURNER
JACK VAN BERG
DAVE VANCE
JOHN VEITCH
CHRISTINE VIERA

JAIME VILLAGOMEZ
KATHY WALSH
JAY WALTON
SID WATTERS
JACK WEIPERT
HARRY WELLS

ROBERT L. WHEELER
DAVID WHITELEY
FRANK Y. WHITELEY, JR.
CHARLES WHITTINGHAM
NEAL J. WINICK
DAVE ZAKOOR, JR.

Who's Who

CHARLES WHITTINGHAM—The eminent Californian has conditioned more champions and near-champions than has any American trainer since the glory days of Calumet Farms' father-son combination, Ben and Jimmy Jones. International turf moguls such as Nelson Bunker Hunt and Robert E. Sangster stock his barn with the kinds of European, South American and U.S. animals needed to win the huge purses offered in Southern California's stakes program for older horses. With help from the peerless rider, Willie Shoemaker, the Whittingham string dominates those races every year. When the money calls, he ships individual runners and Shoemaker to special events at Saratoga and Belmont Park, where he more than holds his own. In 1978, for one example of many, he sent Exceller to Belmont and beat Seattle Slew and Affirmed. His other champions have been Ack Ack, Cougar II, Fiddle Isle, Oil Royalty, Porterhouse, Pretense, Tallahto and Turkish Trousers. Smart handicappers have learned to abstain from backing inexperienced Whittingham runners until he has completed their education and is ready to try for important purses, which often does not happen until they are four. He is particularly adept at coddling high-priced imports until they have adjusted to American conditions, whereupon he wins big stakes with them and enhances their commercial attractiveness as potential sires and broodmares. His son, Michael, appeared on the scene during the mid-1970's and quickly established himself as a talented trainer in his own right.

FRANK Y. WHITELEY, JR.—Little appears in print about the Marylander except that he is laconic. It is his right. He lets his horses do the talking, usually winning at least a third of his starts. In 1977, he won 41 percent of the time. His champions have been the incomparable Ruffian, Damascus, Tom Rolfe and, in 1976–77, Forego. Others of his first-class runners were Chieftain, Honorable Miss, Northernette, Bronze Babu, Hedevar, Tyrant and Icecapade. He rarely gives house room to animals that lack stakes potentiality, and he never sends one to the post unless it has an excellent chance to win. The sophisticated New York crowds always bet heavily on his horses, taking his first-time starters on faith, but you can occasionally collect a decent mutuel price when he races in New Jersey, Maryland or Delaware. Son David carries on in the tradition, specializing in better horses from affluent owners and winning around 25 percent of the time.

H. ALLEN JERKENS—I have never heard a professional horseperson speak of this former polo player except in tones of awe-struck admiration. The attitude is appropriate. Jerkens has made a career of demonstrating that intelligent training will overcome glamorous breeding much more often than not. The homebred livestock supplied him by his chief client, Hobeau Farm, is generally related to Beau Gar, a soundly but not spectacularly bred stallion whose achievements at stud would undoubtedly be less notable if Jerkens were not trainer of the offspring. Hobeau homebreds not sired by Beau Gar are from matings of Beau Gar mares with stallions so obscure that their stud services command $2,000 or less. Accordingly, Jerkens seldom turns up with a contender for one of the annual championships. Instead, he cons and coddles middling horses into beating champions. No horseman in history has been his equal in that department. He beat the great Kelso three times with Beau Purple. He beat Buckpasser with Handsome Boy. He beat Secretariat with Onion and Prove Out. He beat Wajima with Group Plan. In 1955, he won the Display Handicap with War Command, whom he had claimed a few months earlier for $8,000. He won seven stakes with Admiral Vee, a $7,500 claim. He won stakes with Shirley Jones, Kilmoray, Choker, Canal, Never Bow, Tunex, Peace Corps, Vertee, King's Bishop, Blessing Angelica and Sensitive Prince. When he enters a sprinter in a race at a mile or longer, the handicapper had better assume that the horse can go the distance.

DALE BAIRD—This owner-trainer has a lien on the winner's circle at Waterford Park, the West Virginia night-racing resort near Pittsburgh. He usually enters around 1,500 races a year, winning around 15 percent of them, which is invariably enough to place him among the nation's top ten trainers. That his horses and their competitors are usually $1,500 claimers is a tribute to the efficiency of the man's assembly-line methods. He always has 18 or 20 fresh and fit runners in his Waterford barns, and 30 or 40 more resting or training at his two farms. When he enters them to race, he is careful to put them where they belong. That is, in races (a) for which they are barely eligible and (b) in which they enjoy something of an edge in form. In 1973, Baird won 305 times in 1,558 starts for a nifty percentage of almost 20. It was the first time any trainer had ever won 300 races in a year.

LAZARO S. BARRERA—In 1978, the Cuban horseman became the first trainer ever to achieve purse winnings of more than $3 million in a single year. That was when his extraordinary three-year-old from Harbor View Farm, Affirmed, won the U.S. Triple Crown, standing as the very model of what a first-class trainer can do with top-grade material. In years previous to that, Barrera had no immortals in his charge but had established his high competence in major-league racing on both coasts and way stations between. In 1976, he astounded the industry by stretching out a dyed-in-the-wool sprinter, Bold Forbes, winning the Kentucky Derby and Belmont Stakes. Always in the running for trainer championships at Santa Anita, Hollywood Park, Belmont Park, Saratoga and Aqueduct, Barrera has the advantage of extremely versatile runners supplied by Harbor View and other important owners such as Aaron U. Jones. He wins with two-year-olds (Affirmed was the 1977 champion), sprinters, routers, grass runners and first-time starters.

OSCAR BARRERA—One of Laz's several brothers in the profession, Oscar for years was a chronic non-winner around New York but came into his own (and then some) with the opening of Aqueduct's winterized inner track. He did so well with his claiming stock (most of which he owned himself), that his name began appearing on *Daily Racing Form* tabulations of the nation's leading money-winning owners. His conditioning techniques leave his competitors goggle-eyed. He thinks nothing of racing a horse five or six times in a single month. In the process, he cashes a lot of checks, although his winning percentage seldom surpasses 15 percent.

J. BOWES BOND—No longer quite as active as when he handled champions Ahoy, Process Shot and Silent Screen, Bond is always a threat with two-year-olds at Monmouth Park. He can be counted on to win 20 percent of his annual starts. His distinguished brother, Bernie, is a high-percentage winner on the New Jersey and Maryland wheels.

ELLIOTT BURCH—As son and grandson of celebrated trainers Preston and William Preston Burch, Elliott Burch astonished nobody by rising to the top of the profession on his own considerable merits. For the Brookmeade Stable of Isabel Dodge Sloane and the Rokeby Stable of Paul Mellon, he trained champions Amerigo Lady, Arts and Letters, Bowl of Flowers, Fort Marcy, Key to the Mint, Run the Gantlet and Sword Dancer. Ill and absent for a while, he returned hale and hearty in 1978 with a few horses for Alfred G. Vanderbilt and Mrs. George M. Humphrey. His starters are always well schooled, impeccably groomed and never in need of lead ponies to escort them to the starting gate. It can be assumed that he will assemble another powerful

Warren A. (Jimmy) Croll   *Grover G. (Bud) Delp*   *A. T. (Tommy) Doyle*

stable by the time this reaches print. If so, the reader had best respect anything he enters in a race.

GORDON C. CAMPBELL—The Canadian horseman specializes in topnotch runners on Southern California tracks. Given a promising animal, he sends it out prepared to win its first start. And he is unlikely to race it on any subsequent occasion unless it has a prime chance. The champion handicap filly of 1977, Cascapedia, was a good example. So was Flying Paster, the sensational two-year-old of 1978.

MARY M. COTTER—By the mid-1970's, female trainers were no longer a novelty in the sport at large. To Mary Cotter went the distinction of being the top female trainer based in New York. Although her winning percentage was not high, she established herself as an exceptionally capable claimer of horses. Time and again, she won at good mutuels with newly claimed animals that had benefited from her methods. Professionals say that her barn is one of the most orderly.

WARREN A. (JIMMY) CROLL—Every spring, the New Jersey trainer turns up with a herd of well-bred two-year-olds, many of which win their first starts and at least one of which survives to compete in major stakes races. It is an unusual year if he does not win more than 20 percent of his attempts.

JIM CRUPI—Another shrewd user of the claiming box, the New Jersey horseman is dynamite with new additions to his string, and is always high in the Meadowlands and Monmouth Park standings.

GROVER G. (BUDDY) DELP—For years, he, Dick Dutrow and King Leatherbury have dominated Maryland and Delaware racing with their industrialized claiming operations. In the process, they have invariably earned placement on the upper rungs of the national standings. In 1978, Delp became the first of the trio to handle a national champion—the mighty two-year-old, Spectacular Bid.

A. T. (TOMMY) DOYLE—The Irishman with a steeplechase background has found a home in Southern California, where he is well entrenched as a developer and conditioner of good horses. Some say he is best with fillies and mares, citing his national champion, Typecast. Others insist that he does best with young sprinters. But these judgments overlook good Doyle runners like Avatar and Mr. Redoy. The truth is that he can handle anything that can run and will usually top a 15 percent winning average.

RICHARD E. DUTROW—In 1975, the Marylander won 352 races, which not only led the nation but was an all-time record subsequently broken by Jack Van Berg. In 1977, Dutrow finished second on the national list, behind his local rival, King Leatherbury. How do they do it? While one draft of horses is racing, another is farmed out for freshening and cranking up. Nothing mysterious about that. Maryland's liberal medication rules help, too. Dutrow is always good for at least one win for every five annual starts. Perhaps surprisingly, he is deadly when he ships a horse to New Jersey, Pennsylvania or New York.

MARTY FALLON—The ex-jockey trained Hillsdale, a national champion, but in recent years has been entirely content to operate a New Jersey–Keystone claiming stable, owning most of the runners himself. Justly regarded as a great patcher of cripples, he bides his time with a horse, not asking it to run until ready. Winning average ranges between 15 and 20 percent. Always a threat with a newly claimed horse, or one moving up in claiming price, or one returning from a long layoff.

BOBBY FRANKEL—The young New York bettor wanted to learn the game from the inside, and took employment in the barns of Buddy Jacobson and Bill Corbellini. Next thing you knew, he was a trainer in his own right, winning stakes races with claimed animals like Baitman and Barometer. When his principal client, Mrs. Marion Frankel (no relation), migrated to Southern California, so did Bobby and the horses. There he quickly asserted himself, leading the trainer standings at major meetings and proving himself to be as canny a claimer of other folks' horses as has ever brandished a halter. Winning percentage often hovers around 25.

JOHN M. GAVER, JR.—His father trained Capot, Devil Diver, Stage Door Johnny and Tom Fool during the heyday of the Greentree Stables. And during 1978, young Jack began cranking out wins at such a rate (better than 32 percent through September), that New Yorkers

Richard E. Dutrow   *Marty Fallon*   *Bobby Frankel*

Richard Hazelton

Philip G. Johnson

foresaw a real resurgence for the Whitney outfit. Advice: Regardless of what the future brings in terms of Greentree champions, never bet against a Greentree favorite. They win.

RICHARD HAZELTON—Usually rules the roost at Turf Paradise, and is there or thereabouts in the Chicago standings. Although mainly a claiming operative, always has a few hard-knocking candidates for better competition. Perhaps the best of his career was Full Pocket, a rugged sprinter which won 27 of 47 races in a four-year career. Annual winning percentage has exceeded 20 several times and rarely drops below 15. Uses his horses to the utmost, striking repeatedly as long as the iron is hot.

STAN HOUGH—The Florida winner has become a one-man owning-training industry, dominating the standings at Calder Race Course's lengthy meetings year after year. Wins more than 20 percent of the time and should never be underestimated by any handicapper with a sense of self-preservation.

LARRY JENNINGS—A thoroughly competent New Jersey trainer who wins his share in extremely tough company. When the *Form* past performances suggest even slight improvement in a Jennings runner, the handicapper should expect additional improvement next time out.

JUNE JOHNSON—In 1977, the Canadian became the first woman to finish in the top ten in the U.S. list of race-winning trainers. Headquartered at Charles Town–Shenandoah Downs in West Virginia, she took over the string from her husband, Wade, who formerly was among the leaders there. Dealing entirely with cheap claimers, she sometimes wins as much as 25 percent of her starts—a prodigious statistic that represents talented claiming and superb orthopedic nursing.

PHILIP G. JOHNSON—Peegee scuffled for years with cheap horses in Chicago and New York but has been a respected member of New York's top flight for more than a decade. Gifted in all departments, he is especially good at maintaining the condition of a horse. His charges repeatedly run well, once they reach peak form. Has not yet developed a national champion, but is the peer of most of those who have done so, and is sure to bob up in that select circle before calling it a career. Meanwhile, any horse he enters in a race deserves close scrutiny, and any horse he ships out of town is a genuine threat.

LEROY JOLLEY—The trainer of champions Foolish Pleasure, Honest Pleasure, Optimistic Gal, Ridan and What a Summer. He gets superbly bred stock from his main client, the Bertram Firestones, and is always in the running for national honors in one or another division. Wins from 15 to 20 percent of the time. His first-time starters are often ready to win.

GARY JONES—The son of the esteemed Farrell Jones is Bobby Frankel's main rival—and absolute peer—among the claiming operators in Southern California. As of September 30, 1978, he had won 23 percent of his races. During 1977, he won 18 percent. Specializes in moving claimed sprinters up the class ladder. Does not do quite that well with dropdowns. Wins with his first-time starters. Regardless of the class or previous experience of the Jones horse, it is likely to be at its best when a leading rider is up.

MICHAEL KAY—This alumnus of Elliott Burch's barn won 18 percent of his starts in 1977, his first year as a full-fledged New York trainer. As if that were insufficient, he won the national grass-racing championship with Johnny D. His operation is distinguished by old-time patience in the Burch tradition.

TOMMY J. KELLY—Running one of New York's quietest and most successful public stables, Tommy Kelly seldom wins fewer than 20 percent of a year's starts and rarely fields a cheap horse. Has trained three champions—Droll Role, Fast Attack and Limit to Reason—and made a pass at a grass championship with the imported Noble Dancer II. With well-heeled enthusiasts like Townsend B. Martin, James B. Moseley and John M. Schiff supplying the livestock and respecting his horsemanship, Kelly enters nothing but ready runners. Excels on grass. So does his brother, Eddie, high-percentage trainer for Brookfield Farm.

FRANK LA BOCCETTA—During the past decade, New York racing has seen an enormous turnover among young trainers, several of whom

Gary Jones

Tommy J. Kelly

King T. Leatherbury   *D. Wayne Lukas*   *Frank (Pancho) Martin*

have logged sensational winning records and then, after stern lectures from the stewards, have virtually disappeared from view. New York, you see, tries to stamp out unauthorized medication and some of the bright young men have depended on secret potions. Not Frank La-Boccetta. Maintaining a win average above the timberline of 15 percent, he has become a fully accepted member of the high-powered New York training colony, and can be expected to remain so as long as he chooses. Makes good claims and rarely enters a horse that does not run to form.

KING T. LEATHERBURY—In 1977, the Maryland talent led all North American trainers with 322 victories in 1,475 outings. His 22 percent was a remarkable accomplishment, considering the tremendous number of races he entered. During 1978, he carried on in the same vein, winning 304 starts and again leading the national standings. To do that well, a trainer needs plenty of horses and commodious private facilities in which to rehabilitate the ones that need a vacation. Leatherbury has it all. Whether he or Bud Delp or Dick Dutrow win the annual three-way battle for Maryland-Delaware supremacy, they all make fortunes, all win national ranking, and all face the next season with sublime optimism. When two or more of them are entered in the same race, and no significant differences appear in the past-performance records, the handicapper who insists on betting might as well play the one that goes at the best odds.

D. WAYNE LUKAS—During the mid-70's, America's top trainer of quarter horses decided to try his hand with Thoroughbreds. His clients had a lot of money and, as one California observer cracked, he seemed to have their credit cards. During 1978, he had the exciting Secretariat two-year-old, Terlingua, who challenged for the filly championship. With his other stock he won at the approved 20 percent rate and showed a great facility for keeping a runner in good form. His first-time starters and horses returning from layoffs were not as remunerative as those that were beginning to show improvement.

ALAN B. MARCUS—The Texan waited a long time for success in New York but when it was within grasp he was ready. Usually most effective at Aqueduct, he is especially dangerous with horses returning from layoffs. Does well with new claims moving up in price. Wins between 15 and 20 percent.

FRANK (PANCHO) MARTIN—After years with a public stable, the Cuban horseman settled down as trainer for the New York real-estate magnate and daily racegoer, Sigmund Sommer. To enter 738 races and win 138 of them (19 percent), as Martin did in 1977, is a tremendous feat for someone who seldom races outside of New York. Martin leads most meetings there, thanks mainly to his gifted work as a claimer and restorer of horseflesh. Loves to switch distances, a practice that produces few repeat wins but helps handicappers who wait for him to enter horses at distances that have suited them in the past. No sentimentalist, he does not hesitate to drop tired horses from high to low claiming prices in one jump. They seldom win. With better stock, he can be more patient. For example, he put up with the winless high-priced purchase, Tom Swift, for seasons until finding the hole card and winning a few on the grass. Otherwise, he does little on that surface.

JOSE MARTIN—Pancho's son started out in the conveyor-belt tradition and proved that he could do it. In recent years, he has been upgrading his outfit with stock provided by Randolph Weinsier, owner of the Martin-trained 1977 champion, Lakeville Miss. Jose started only 355 times in that year, but won 65 for an 18 percent score. He performed at a comparable level in 1978. If one of his charges shows even slight improvement in the running line of its latest or next-to-last race, watch out.

FRANK H. MERRILL—Now that Lou Cavalaris, Jr. has become a part of track management, Frank Merrill's hold on Ontario's annual races-won championship seems more secure. Relying on large numbers of entrants rather than outstanding horses, Merrill seldom wins more than 15 percent of his starts. But if the past-performance record of a Merrill entrant looks promising to the handicapper at Woodbine, Fort Erie or Greenwood, that handicapper probably has found a winner. How else do you suppose the man tops the standings year after year?

MACKENZIE MILLER—The specialist in grass runners took over the Rokeby string from Elliott Burch and continued to perform at his usual 20 percent clip. During his years as trainer of the late Charles Engelhard's mighty Cragwood Stable, Miller loved to give grass horses experience on the main track, where they ran poorly, and then win their first attempts on the turf course. His champions have been Assagai, Hawaii, Leallah and Snow Knight.

John Nerud

Angel Penna

JIM MORGAN—King of the hill in Ohio, where he always wins at least 20 percent and usually has a stakes winner or two. In excursions to New York and elsewhere, he has won authoritatively enough to demonstrate that he is not simply a big fish in a small pond, but a first-class horseman. If he ever ships an animal to your track, think twice before betting against it.

JOHN NERUD—The public knows this veteran as the developer of the great Dr. Fager. His rivals know him as a supremely patient conditioner who gives his charges plenty of rest between starts and to whom the usual handicapping rules about recent races should not be applied. While continuing to handle the Tartan Stable, he has been running more horses under his own colors in recent years. Winning average is not as high as when the Tartan string was going strong, but a Nerud runner that shows some run in good company is a good bet to show even more run next time out—as when his Dr. Patches beat Seattle Slew at the Meadowlands in 1978. In 1979, he relinquished the actual training to son Jan, but remained in charge of the Tartan operation.

ANGEL PENNA—After winning everything available in his native Argentina and Venezuela, he came to the U.S. and became a factor on the New York circuit, where he handled all kinds, from cheap claimers to stakes winners. In 1970 he decamped to France and promptly took command. He saddled San-San to win the 1972 Arc de Triomphe and won that richest of all international races a second time in 1974 with Allez France, one of the great mares of all time. Returning to the U.S. in 1978 with Waya, Flying Water and other good horses belonging to Daniel Wildenstein, Penna made straight for the winner's circle. He then took over the stables of the Phipps family, instantly becoming one of the two or three most powerful trainers in the Western Hemisphere. Look for him on the lists of top money-making barns and among the outfits with high winning percentages. As they say in football, this man knows where the end zone is.

JOE H. PIERCE, JR.—Son of a popular midwestern horseman of days bygone, Pierce winters in Florida, summers in New Jersey, and always has a couple of useful turf runners in his stalls. His better ones perform consistently. When dealing with the others, the handicapper is advised to check a race or two immediately previous to the latest. If the latest was nondescript, but the next-to-last promising, the horse may be ready.

THOMAS L. (LOU) RONDINELLO—As trainer for the Galbreath family of Darby Dan fame, the New Yorker is given young horses regarded as potential candidates for championships. Accordingly, he schools them to go distances of ground, reserving their big runs for the final stages. They seldom show much during the sprint phases of the two-year-old season, but come into their own when the distances stretch out at ages three and four. In 1974, his Little Current (who had set nobody afire as a two-year-old but had shown a nice finishing kick), won the Preakness, the Belmont and the three-year-old championship. In 1977, Cum Laude Laurie was narrowly outvoted for the three-year-old filly title. Indeed, it is a rare year that finds Rondinello without a leading contender for one of the titles.

JOHN RUSSELL—The Britisher galloped horses for Ben Jones at Calumet, started on his own in Canada, developed the great champion Susan's Girl while training the Fred W. Hooper stable, and then took over the Phipps strings. Highly considerate of his horses, in the European style, Russell can be depended on for a 20 percent winning average and multiple stakes victories when training for owners who appreciate his gift of patience. Replaced by the more aggressive Angel Penna in the Phipps operation, Russell departed for California to handle runners for Penny Ringquist (the former Penny Tweedy, whose Meadow Stable owned Secretariat and Riva Ridge).

WOODY STEPHENS—No Eastern horseman has won as many stakes races as Stephens, developer of champions Bald Eagle, Bold Bidder, Never Bend and Sensational. His winning average is generally in the vicinity of 20 percent, as befits a man who trains only expensive stock owned by leaders of the racing industry. On the other hand, the

Thomas L. (Lou) Rondinello

Woody Stephens

John Tammaro

J. Willard Thompson

Jack Van Berg

year never passes in which he fails to win stakes races with longshots. As the knowing Howard Rowe remarked in *American Turf Monthly,* "Stephens is a man who can get a horse ready for the big dough without tipping his mitt to the entire turf world." Furthermore, a Stephens winner is extraordinarily likely to play an encore in its next start.

JOHN TAMMARO—Formerly a leader on the Maryland circuit, and a winner everywhere else in the East, the round man is now in Ontario, where he continues his hallowed practice of claiming somebody's sprinter, tinkering with it and then using it to win some races around two turns, often at a price. Besides that, he is getting some well-bred stock from Kinghaven Farms and, with Lou Cavalaris retired, should soon be running one-two with Gil Rowntree and John Starr in the big Canadian races. His son, John III, is a force at New Jersey tracks.

J. WILLARD THOMPSON—Is always at or near the top of the races-won standings in New Jersey. Does well with claims and is especially dangerous when he takes the trouble to ship something to New York or Pennsylvania.

BILLY TURNER—The developer of triple-crowner Seattle Slew objected when the geniuses who owned the horse insisted on shipping it to California for one race too many after its victorious Belmont Stakes. In due course, Turner was no longer the trainer and resumed his quiet ways as a winner of at least 20 percent on New York tracks. In a style that no longer prevails but is deadly effective, he prepares horses to win on workouts alone, and then keeps them in shape for repeated good performances.

JACK VAN BERG—His late father, Marion H. Van Berg, was one of the phenomenal owner-trainers in history. The father led all North American owners in races won during 1952 and 1955, shared that honor in 1956, and then monopolized it for eleven consecutive years, 1960–70. He also led in purse earnings in 1965 and 1968 through 1970. He did all this with several divisions of claiming and allowance cavalry which he ran simultaneously at various secondary tracks throughout the Middle West. The son bobbed up as the continent's leading trainer of winners in 1968 and has repeated on five subsequent occasions. In 1976 he saddled an incredible 496 winners in an equally incredible 2,362 starts (21 percent) and won $2,976,196, an all-time record surpassed in 1978 by Laz Barrera. Aside from details of ownership, Jack's operation resembled that of his father—lots of horses at lots of tracks, and all in the care of fully competent assistants. In 1977, the Nebraskan decided to cut down a little. During 1978, he had 40 horses under his direct supervision in Southern California, 30 in Detroit, 20 in Kentucky and another 50 resting or training on his Kentucky farm. More to the point, he started getting better runners. In April, his Landscaper won the $111,600 Century Handicapper at Hollywood Park, defeating luminaries like the great Exceller and Properantes. A California expert told me, "If I could have anybody whispering in my ear, it would be Van Berg. A flat bet on his horses would have returned a very substantial profit out here. Anything he claims wins promptly, even if it has run poorly before coming into his hands."

JOHN VEITCH—In 1976, Calumet Farm was in the doldrums with no discernible prospect of recovering its former place as one of the mightiest stables in American racing history. The livestock was not there anymore. Some prominent horsemen had tried to turn things around, but it was an impossible task. Or so the experts said. Then John Veitch took the helm and the belittled Calumet stock underwent a miraculously prompt transformation. In 1977, Veitch fielded the champion Our Mims and the near-champion Alydar. In 1978, Alydar's stupendous duels with Affirmed established him as an authentic great. In 1979, the stable leader was Davona Dale, undoubtedly the best filly since Ruffian and very possibly one of the best of all time. Beyond consummate horsemanship and a high winning percentage, Veitch is notable for a self-deprecating wit that brightens the solemn atmosphere of Eastern racing. He is the son of trainer Sylvester Veitch.

ROBERT L. WHEELER—Long recognized as a trainer of fillies and mares, the California trainer came up with two more good ones in 1978: Taisez Vous and B. Thoughtful. In previous years he had the champions Silver Spoon and Bug Brush and the colt Malicious. When

John Veitch   *Robert L. Wheeler*   *Neal J. Winick*

a Wheeler animal seems ready to run well, it does so. His first-time starters are dependable, especially when they draw at least moderate betting support from Southern California's legion of clockers and snoopers.

NEAL J. WINICK—Arnold Winick used to be a dominant force in Chicago, Florida and New Jersey. Son Neal continues to train successfully for Mrs. Maribel G. Blum, and does especially well in the Florida standings. Now, as in the past, the stable makes exceptionally successful claims, is dynamite with first-time starters, and does not hesitate to drop a horse in class to win a purse. No outfit has a better line on the local horse population than this one.

Photo credits: NYRA (BOB COGLIANESE): *Whiteley, Jerkens, Barrera, Burch, Croll, Johnson, Martin, Nerud, Penna, Rondinello, Stephens, Tammaro, Veitch.* TURFOTOS (JIM RAFTERY): *Thompson, Winick.*

15

The Jockey Factor

Except for a dozen professional golfers and tennis players who amass fortunes in television fees and advertising testimonials, the richest athletes on earth are American jockeys. A really good one takes home not less than $200,000 a year for a decade or two, if he keeps his weight down, his nose clean and his mind on his work.

By tradition, the victorious rider gets 10 percent of the purse. Many owners sweeten this bonus with other gifts, such as the proceeds of a large bet on the horse. As pin money, the big-league jock also earns $50 for winning, $40 for finishing second, $30 if third, and $25 for fourth or worse. The fee for winning is usually regarded as part of the 10 percent bonus, although no rule forbids an owner to pay both.

This sounds like a splendid career for any little person who likes horses. It certainly is, in the same sense that a top executive position with General Motors is a splendid career for anyone who likes cars. The trouble is that a man can be wild about cars and spend his career in the grease pit of a filling station. And a little fellow who likes horses may become a jockey without ever making big pay at it.

Success as a race rider requires more than small size and large desire. Talent is essential. Luck helps. An ingratiating personality does no harm. The top riders have those qualities in abundance. Most do not, which is why there are so few top riders.

Many jockeys are untalented to begin with. Others, fearful of injury, fail to exercise what little talent they may have. It is not at all unusual to see races in which one or more of the riders do nothing but cling to the reins and wave the whip.

According to the Jockeys' Guild, about half of all active riders earn $5,000 a year or less. Recent editions of *The American Racing Manual* spell this out. An amazingly small group of riders dominates the profession. They own the winner's circle, lock, stock and bonus. They are so much more successful than their colleagues that there simply is no comparison.

About 4,000 men and women have riding licenses. In the course of a year, fewer than 3,000 of them ride in actual races. Of those who do, almost half get 100 or fewer mounts, compared with the 1,000 to 1,800 assignments obtained by successful jockeys.

Of the 2,900 who ever ride during a year, about a third win not a single race. More than half the races are won by perhaps 200 riders—the middle and upper classes of the profession. Each of these goes to the post at least 500 times a year, either because the trainers vie for his services or because they regard him as the least of the available evils and give him the try.

And now we reach the heart of the matter. An elite group of less than four dozen riders—hardly more than 1 percent of the profession—wins more than 9,000 races a year. Members of this tiny elite win one race in every seven! Moreover, they win about $85 million in purses for their employers—fully a quarter of the purse money paid at all tracks!

Betting on Jockeys

Awareness of the enormous statistical edge enjoyed by a handful of leading riders leads some players to center their handicapping on the jockey rather than the horse. If the handicapping is fairly competent, taking due account of the horse, the player who refuses to bet on any but a top rider has an excellent chance to get by. Unfortunately, such players usually ignore the horse. They "follow" individual jockeys, often betting according to the formulas supplied by progressive betting systems. As pointed out on page 54, this leads straight to ruination. Any jockey inevitably encounters streaks of from twenty to fifty consecutive losers.

Neither does the player do himself a favor by going to the opposite extreme. "The horse is the thing," some say. "All I do is look for the live horse in the past performances. I let the trainer pick the jockey." Bad logic. The actual "liveness" of a horse often is revealed in the identity of its rider.

Players are right in supposing that most trainers know which riders to put on their horses. But most jockeys and their agents know something, too. They know which horses are the likeliest contenders. Successful riders have their pick of the best mounts. The presence on a horse of an obscure or relatively ungifted rider is frequently a sign that the trainer is marking time, or that the horse is less ready than its record implies.

In any case, the probability of victory by a leading rider is so disproportionately high that it should not be overlooked. The past performances of the jockey should always be evaluated, as part of the evaluation of the horse.

The Importance of the Ride

In 1966, Avelino Gomez led all North American riders with 318 victories in 996 attempts. His winning average of .321 was a record among champions in the races-won department, surpassing the .301 achieved by Bill Shoemaker in 1954. Gomez had long been one of the finest reinsmen in the world, an extraordinarily consistent winner wherever he rode. He preferred to ride in Canada and Mexico. He had his choice of mounts in those places. When he rode in New York, pickings were less easy. Other outstanding jockeys competed with him for the best mounts. He got fewer winners.

The point of this is that no rider can make a winner of a non-contender, except by accident. To be a consistent winner, the jockey must get the mounts. And even the consistent winner loses about eight of every ten races in which he rides. Most of the losses are simply part of the form cycle. It's a nice horse, but it won't win for another two or three weeks, and the leading rider is content to stay with it in the meantime, so that he may cash in later.

Other losses find the topnotcher on some downright rotten animals. Contractual commitments, the politics of the business, or the wish to do a friend a favor often result in Sandy Hawley or Bill Shoemaker going postward on a hopeless hulk. Because the Shoe has the mount, the odds drop. But the chances of victory remain as slim as they would be if Joe Nobody were aboard.

Where good jockeys come into their own is on fit, well-placed horses. As their riding records illustrate, they bring something extra to the assignment. They win the big ones and the close ones. The trainer able to induce one of them to ride his animal knows in his heart that he has done everything possible for victory. The owner loves him for it. And if the horse loses, the owner blames the horse and consoles the trainer. Trainers would rather be consoled than blamed.

Does the second- or third-best horse in the race win because its rider

Willie Shoemaker   *Sandy Hawley*   *Angel Cordero, Jr.*

is the best in the race? It happens somewhere every day. And it happens everywhere several times a week. The frequency with which it happens depends, of course, on the class of the track. In a field of nine horses at the height of the Aqueduct season, one usually finds that each of the three or four logical contenders is being ridden by a first-rate jockey. Yet there are occasions when this is not so, and the player is able to make his choice on grounds that one or two of the contenders are carrying outgunned boys.

Some horsemen maintain that New York riders are so evenly matched that none can move a horse more than a neck farther than any of a couple of dozen others. Races are won, however, by necks and heads and noses. Cordero, Velasquez, Cauthen, Cruguet, Fell, Maple and Vasquez do it often enough in New York to warrant the eagerness with which trainers seek their services. Yet, if the best horse in the race is ridden by José Amy, Ruben Hernandez, Antonio Graell, Jean-Luc Samyn or Mike Venezia, no knowledgeable player would refrain from betting on that account. These five riders had a combined winning average of less than 11 percent during 1977, but are widely respected in the sport and can be regarded as hindrances to no Thoroughbred. They won far fewer races than the local leaders, whose averages ran from Vasquez's 13 percent to Cauthen's 24. Yet they accounted for more than $7 million in purses.

What is the New York player to do? If so many of the riders there are better than their records indicate, how is he to tell one from another?

He should do exactly what he would do at any other track, where the distinctions among riders are often easier to recognize. He should bear in mind that the most successful riders are those most sought after by trainers. They get the best mounts. They get more good mounts—and the statistics prove it—than are assigned to riders who may be equally good but are less successful. Therefore, the player bears the percentages in mind. He scrutinizes the field in terms of distance, condition, class, weights, pace, barns. At some point—whether sooner or later depends entirely on his preference—he eliminates horses to which non-winning riders are assigned. A leading rider should never be dismissed, of course. But a good rider with unimpressive winning statistics can often be ruled out. A bit later I shall present some ways of making these decisions.

Riding Ability Defined

The ideal rider has an instinctive sense of the needs, capacities and peculiarities of his mount. Developed through years of experience in the barns, on the training tracks and in money competition, this sensitivity enables him to get extra effort from any kind of horse, with or without helpful instructions from the trainer.

The ideal rider is an expert judge of pace. He can tell whether the early going is too slow or too fast for his horse, and he adjusts the animal's stride accordingly. Unless the horse is unmanageably rank, he runs it as slowly as possible before the final turn for home, giving it the breather it needs for that last burst of effort.

The ideal rider is a master strategist. He takes the trouble to learn all about changes in the footing, so that he can navigate his horse over the fastest part of the track. If the rail is the place to be, he will be there, even if behind horses. His knowledge of his own mount, and of its rivals, and of the other riders, usually enables him to find daylight and come through at the end, still on the rail.

The ideal rider has extraordinarily quick reflexes and remarkable powers of anticipation. In the split second that he recognizes the development of a potential traffic jam, he steers his horse away from the trouble. In the split second that a hole begins to open in front of him, he takes advantage of it.

The ideal rider is unswervingly courageous. His confidence is unshaken by the dreadful spills that he and all other jockeys suffer from time to time. He takes calculated risks. He goes through holes from which battle-weary jockeys back off. Yet he is not reckless. He knows when to take up or go wide rather than risk harm to himself, his horse and the others in the race.

Jorge Velasquez   *Darrel McHargue*   *Laffit Pincay, Jr.*

Leading Riders of All Time

As of January 1, 1978, the following jockeys had won more races than any others in the history of American racing.

	Victories	Total Purses
WILLIE SHOEMAKER	7,327	$64,789,155
JOHNNY LONGDEN	6,032	24,665,800
EDDIE ARCARO	4,779	30,039,543
STEVE BROOKS	4,451	18,239,817
WALTER BLUM	4,382	26,497,189
BILL HARTACK	4,272	26,466,758
AVELINO GOMEZ	3,945	11,006,284
TED ATKINSON	3,795	17,449,360
RALPH NEVES	3,772	13,786,239
ROBERT LEE BAIRD	3,653	11,617,211
BOBBY USSERY	3,611	22,714,074
LARRY SNYDER	3,602	15,062,742
LAFFIT PINCAY, JR.	3,329	36,726,251
ANGEL CORDERO, JR.	3,299	37,027,480
SANDY HAWLEY	3,278	20,675,551

The ideal rider is alert at the gate. He keeps his horse on its toes in readiness for the start. He gets out of there as quickly as the horse can manage it, to achieve the all-important racing position that enables him to save ground later.

The ideal rider has unlimited competitive spirit. As long as his mount has a chance, he refuses to give up. He continues trying until the race is over. This, combined with his knowledge of pace and strategy, makes him what the trade calls a "strong" rider—a strong finisher. If he wasted his mounts in the early going, they would have nothing left at the end, and his finishes would be less strong.

The ideal rider uses the whip no more than necessary. He gets all he can by exploiting the pace of the race, and by distributing his weight evenly on the withers (which is comfortable for the animal), and by using voice, reins, legs and, above all, hands. He rolls his hands on the horse's neck, in rhythm with its stride, urging it forward. When he whips, the emphasis means something to the horse, and it usually reacts by lengthening stride.

The ideal rider spares his horse in other ways. He is able to win by a neck when less capable jockeys might need the security of a three-length lead. Similarly, if the horse is clearly beaten, he does not bother to whip it in a spurious display of determination. He eases it, saving it for next time.

The ideal rider has no weight problems. Without having to resort to the self-denial, the steam baths and the deliberate heaving after meals which make ashen, wasted, weakened, prematurely old men of other jockeys, he rides at full strength. A well-nourished, clear-headed rider is an asset to a horse. A starved rider is likely to conk out at any time.

The ideal rider brings absolute concentration to the job. Like any other athlete, he does whatever is necessary to remain in decent physical and mental condition. His private life is an orderly one that helps, rather than disrupts, his frame of mind. If he boozes or wenches, the recreation is never excessive enough to harm his performance and generate disfavor among trainers. If he gambles, he does it according to the rules, betting only on his own mounts, through their owners. He does not become so immersed in the gambling aspects of the game that his ''investments'' distract him from his riding.

Among riders now active, many come close to these ideal standards. With all due respect to the good old days (whenever they were), I doubt that any era has luxuriated in as many authentically great race riders as now patrol the major circuits of the East and West coasts. Bill Shoemaker, Sandy Hawley, Darrel McHargue, Steve Cauthen, Angel Cordero, Jorge Velasquez and Laffit Pincay, Jr., are so good that handicappers can safely credit them with adding lengths to the ability of any horse. In the final years of his unparalleled career, Shoemaker displays no weaknesses of any kind, riding every race with supreme skill. He is tops. Hawley, McHargue and Cauthen seem to be cut from the Shoemaker pattern, with an almost supernatural sensitivity to their mounts. Hawley, the most seasoned of the three, rarely commits an error in riding judgment and never loses concentration. Velasquez, the best rider never to have won the Kentucky Derby, Preakness Stakes or Belmont Stakes, occasionally delays his stretch run too long in lesser races, but only occasionally. When he reaches the lead with a horse, he seldom relinquishes it. Pincay sometimes suffers from weight problems. Also, his furious aggressiveness gets him in periodic difficulty with stewards, but at his best he is the equal of any rider I have ever seen. As for Cordero, he rides as the situation demands. His Belmont Stakes victory on the tiring sprinter, Bold Forbes, was a masterpiece of horsemanship, but only a sample of what he does on lesser horses day in and day out.

Riders for Courses

During 1966, Bill Shoemaker accepted 246 mounts in New York. He won on 37 of them, for a batting average of .150. Outside New York

—mainly in California—he won 194 times in 791 attempts, for an average of .245. This made his overall statistic a nifty .213.

It is no disgrace to score with only 15 percent of one's mounts on the New York circuit. But Shoemaker always does better than that elsewhere. He is one of the rare riders able to win at least once in every five races—the brand of consistency most significant to players. But he cannot win that often if he does not get the horses. The reason he has fewer good horses to ride in New York is simple enough: Trainers tend to stay with topnotch boys who they know will remain available for the entire season. If rider Doe is good enough to be among the six or seven leaders at Aqueduct, he is good enough for any horse—even though he may lack the virtuoso qualities of a Shoemaker. Rather than antagonize Doe and Doe's noisy agent by using Shoemaker during the champ's irregular trips East, the trainer stays with the local rider, and Shoemaker has to take the leavings.

Earlie Fires, leading apprentice rider of 1965, when he scored in 19 percent of his starts, invaded New York in 1966 and made a splendid impression. But he won only 8 percent of the time, as contrasted with the 15 percent he was able to log during the same year in less rugged company elsewhere.

Sammy Boulmetis and Jimmy Stout, heroes of New Jersey racing and thorough pros in their own right, could never get much in New York. Nor could Johnny Longden, the wizened godling of the West Coast. On the other hand, Laffit Pincay, Jr., a 1966 sensation in Illinois, was no less sensational in New York, and proceeded to maintain the level when he wintered in California.

Generally speaking, a rider who has distinguished himself sufficiently to earn national ranking is a fair bet to win on any track—provided his horse qualifies for support. However, he *usually is a much better bet on his home circuit or on some lesser circuit.* To take an extreme, hypothetical case, if he breaks records in Arizona, he must prove himself all over again before meriting support in New Jersey. But if he is Hawley, he rates as tops anywhere.

Among the first things the expert does in handicapping a field of horses is check the current jockey standings at the track. He carefully notes the names of the two or three top riders, and any others whose listings show that they have been winning at least 16 or 17 percent of their starts. These are the boys who are getting the live horses. And who are justifying the trainers' confidence.

In conjunction with this, the player refers to national listings. Good ones appear on the opposite page and on pages 314 and 315.

The Very Best

Most of the following riders win high percentages of their starts in the fastest company and can be expected to do more of the same on any major circuit where they decide to sink roots. Although Marco Castaneda, John Lively, Eddie Maple, Don Pierce, Jean-Luc Samyn, Fernando Toro and Jacinto Vasquez do not necessarily win as many as 15 percent, each is fully capable of doing so when more selective about his mounts. In the meantime, each wins when on the best horse and is good enough to win on the second- or third-best horse.

ANTHONY BLACK	DARREL McHARGUE
VINCE BRACCIALE, JR.	CRAIG PERRET
MARCO CASTANEDA	DON PIERCE
STEVE CAUTHEN	LAFFIT PINCAY, JR.
ANGEL CORDERO, JR.	ROBIN PLATTS
JEAN CRUGUET	MIGUEL A. RIVERA
EDDIE DELAHOUSSAYE	JEAN-LUC SAMYN
JEFFREY FELL	WILLIE SHOEMAKER
SANDY HAWLEY	LARRY SNYDER
RUBEN HERNANDEZ	JORGE TEJEIRA
JOHN LIVELY	FERNANDO TORO
EDDIE MAPLE	JACINTO VASQUEZ
SAM MAPLE	JORGE VELASQUEZ
CHRIS McCARRON	

Apprentice Jockeys

The chronic shortage of first-rate riders impels horsemen to beat the bushes for promising new talent. To encourage the search and expedite the development of newcomers to the trade, trainers are allowed weight concessions for any horse on which they seat an apprentice jock.

If the apprentice wins a race or two in fairly authoritative style, he usually gets more work than his skills warrant. He rides and wins, while full-fledged journeymen sit in idleness and grumble about the politics of the game.

Politics has something to do with it. The notorious eagerness of many owners to see fashionable riders aboard their horses combines with the weight allowance to make the "hot" apprentice an attractive proposition to certain trainers.

Of course, apprentices often lose on horses that might win with better jockeying. But this is not always a negative factor from the trainer's point of view. A player who takes ten minutes to study any random issue of *Daily Racing Form* will notice that some horses seem to lose when the apprentice is up, and win only with a leading rider. The function of the apprentice in such cases is to give an unready horse a brisk workout in actual competition under light weight. If the horse accidentally wins, so much the better. Certain stables specialize in manipulations of that kind, and attentive players have ·no trouble recognizing the signs in the records.

A more wholesome, widespread and significant reason for the popularity of apprentices is their eagerness. They ride the cheapest race as if it were the Kentucky Derby. When the eagerness occurs in combination with genuine ability—as sometimes happens—the trainer of a cheap horse often prefers the apprentice to an older hand. The boy may be green, but his spirit is beyond doubt. It frequently enables him to finish ahead of more experienced riders whose own competitiveness has been dulled by prosperity. Apprentices rarely get mounts in important races, and seldom win when they do. But they have an extra something going for them in lesser races.

Underrated Riders

In the riding profession, last year's hero is this year's bum. The jockeys on this list have had their moments as heroes and remain able to become national leaders at any time. None of them harms the chances of a well-placed horse.

JERRY BAILEY	JORGE SALINAS
DAVE BORDEN	ANGEL SANTIAGO
KELLY CASTANEDA	LARRY SAUMELL
PATRICK DAY	GARY STAHLBAUM
BERNIE GONZALES	DOUG THOMAS
ANTONIO GRAELL	ANGELO TROSCLAIR
DON MACBETH	RUDY TURCOTTE
DARYL MONTOYA	RICK WILSON
GONZALO PROSPER	

José Amy

Anthony Black

Dave Borden

In recent years Sandy Hawley, Chris McCarron and Steve Cauthen have each been an authentically hot apprentice. After losing the weight allowance (see Rules of Racing, pages 407–429), each has continued to get good mounts and win numerous races. The transition from bug-boy to journeyman is usually more difficult than that. Most leading apprentices disappear from prominence as soon as the rules require them to ride at equal weights against polished jockeys. Trainers no longer assign them the live horses. The boy who could do nothing wrong suddenly becomes an also-ran.

As might be expected, apprentices do their best work on horses that require the least jockeying. To win a six-furlong sprint on a sharply conditioned pace-setter, the boy need only get out of the gate in a hurry and remain in the saddle for an additional minute and eleven seconds or so. A more experienced rider might use the animal's energies more efficiently, but horsemen often prefer the five- or seven-pound weight concession for a sprinter of that type.

The Comers

Any of the promising riders listed below is capable of leadership on a major circuit.

CASH ASMUSSEN	RON HIRDES
JEFF BLUM	GEORGE HOSANG
KEN BOURQUE	EDDIE KING
TOM CHAPMAN	JEFF LLOYD
RICHARD DE PASS	BILL MIZE
BRYAN FANN	MIKE MORGAN
RAMON FIGUEROA	JIM POWELL
RONNIE FLETCHER	WAYNE RICE
RICHARD HEDGE	DOUG ROLFE

Hawley, McCarron and Cauthen were remarkable for their precocious ability to win at all distances on horses that required rating off the pace. Ordinarily, off-pace horses are poor risks when ridden by apprentices. At sprint distances, the kid has too little time to recover from his mistakes or solve the problems presented by traffic jams. At longer distances, he is worse off: his sense of pace is not yet trustworthy. Also, the extra turn of the track presents additional headaches for which the best cure is experience.

Accordingly, expert players bet on an apprentice jockey only if his mount is a front-running sprinter or, in rare cases, if the boy has shown that he can win at the distance with the particular come-from-behinder.

Match the Rider to the Horse

An approach to the jockey factor becomes sensible as soon as it embraces a key reality: the high percentage of races won by the leading riders. The player who favors leading riders directs himself toward live horses.

Yet the player must reckon with the fact that other riders also win races. And that some of those less prominent riders are uniquely suited to certain horses which refuse to run for more successful jockeys.

Here is a good way to handle the jockey problem:

1. Accept as a contender any ready, well-placed horse ridden by a journeyman jockey who (a) is a national leader or (b) is a leader in the current standings at the track or (c) has won at least 16 percent of his races at the meeting or (d) has won with the horse in the past.

2. Eliminate any horse ridden by an apprentice jockey unless (a) it is a front-running type entered in a race around not more than one turn or (b) the boy has won with the horse in the past or (c) the boy rates among the most successful riders at the current meeting and has been winning at least 16 percent of his starts.

3. Play no apprentice in route races unless he has demonstrated in the past that he can handle assignments of that kind.

Needless to say, these suggestions are valid only as part of a comprehensive approach to handicapping.

The most convenient and productive time to analyze the rider's qualifications is at the end of the handicapping process, after the more fundamental questions of distance, condition, class, weight, and pace have been attended to. It makes no sense to eliminate a horse on the jockey factor until then. The penalty for doing so is exacted on the afternoon of the race, when the trainer switches from the unsuccessful jockey to McHargue. If the player has not checked the horse for distance, class, etc., he has no idea whether the switch is as meaningful as it might seem.

Who's Who

JOSÉ AMY (1953)*—The hard-working Puerto Rican waited in the wings of big-time New York racing for several years, galloping horses in the mornings and riding what little he could get on an occasional afternoon. In 1977 it began to dawn on some of the brighter trainers that the youngster had developed considerable polish. He got better mounts and won over $1 million in purses. In 1978, he really took hold, boosting his percentage to a respectable level. Should be a staple on the circuit for many years. Can ride anything.

JERRY D. BAILEY (1957)—A consistent winner in Chicago and Florida, this comparative newcomer sits a horse nicely, handles it considerately and is powerful in the stretch. A likely star of the future.

GARY BAZE (1955)—From a prominent family of Northwestern trainers and riders, he got scarcely a tumble when he invaded the East a few years ago, but he later caught on in Chicago, displaying the kind of versatility that should keep him a winner on any circuit where he can find mounts.

ANTHONY BLACK (1951)—The conscientious New Jerseyite spends much of his time winning lots of money and a high percentage at Keystone, and is perfectly comfortable anywhere else. The early rough edges are long gone. He gets the most from every horse he rides.

DAVE BORDEN (1956)—The Clevelander would probably have been the apprentice sensation of 1977 if someone named Cauthen had not come along at the same time and on the same Chicago circuit. Borden followed Cauthen to New York and, at this writing, is beginning to get deserved recognition as an exceptionally promising rider who leaves the gate promptly, uses his alert brain in close quarters and finishes strongly.

VINCE BRACCIALE, JR. (1953)—The son of a West Virginia horseman was one of the keenest apprentice jockeys of modern times and suffered no setbacks when he lost the bug. He can win wherever he hangs his tack, as already demonstrated in Maryland, New Jersey, Pennsylvania and New York.

* Year of birth

Vince Bracciale, Jr.   *Donald Brumfield*   *Marco Castaneda*

DONALD BRUMFIELD (1938)—The Kentucky veteran may not be able to go all-out nine times a day anymore, but his performances in his home state, and in Florida and New Jersey continue to be models of professional competence. No matter what the distance of the race or the quality or running style of the horse, this hardboot improves its prospects.

MARCO CASTANEDA (1950)—The Colombian made a good impression on knowing observers after he began riding in New York. He then left for California, where the competition for mounts was not quite so keen. Known primarily as an off-the-pace rider with special gifts on the grass course, he will fool you on a front-running sprinter, if he ever gets the opportunity. Now wins purses at the rate of over $2 million annually, but does not ride enough live mounts to achieve the high percentage of which he is capable.

WAYNE CATALANO (1956)—This whoop-de-doo booter may be one of the most alert gate boys in the country. Won better than 20 percent during 1977 on the year-long Detroit circuit, mainly with front-running horses. All he needs is experience on tracks less favorable to early speed, and on horses that like to lie behind the early leaders.

STEVE CAUTHEN (1960)—No rider in history had won as much as $6 million in purse money in a single year until the apprentice sensation of 1977 exceeded that figure, winning 487 races and almost 24 percent of his starts. His riding style was as spectacular as his statistics. Not since the early Shoemaker had a young rider displayed such affinity for running horses, allowing them to settle into comfortable stride before asking them for full speed. In 1978, he suffered a severe spill and the temporary absence of his celebrated agent, Lenny Goodman. Some felt that his concentration was not as great as it once had been. That was the year in which he rode Affirmed to the triple crown and, while winning less purse money and fewer races, performed at a level of which few other jocks could even dream.

ANGEL CORDERO, JR. (1942)—Perennially among the national leaders in purse money won and always one-two-three in the race for New York honors, the high-spirited Puerto Rican is surely an all-time great. If the horse can run, Cordero will bring it home in front or close thereto. Front-runners, late runners, grass horses and two-year-olds are equally suitable. He does it all and, contrary to frequent supposition, he does it without inflicting unnecessary punishment on the animal.

JEAN CRUGUET (1939)—The outspoken Frenchman has had his ups and downs in the hearts and minds of New York trainers, but in recent years the ups have outnumbered the downs. Of all riders now active, he is probably the most knowledgeable all-around horseman, which means that he often knows more about the horse than the trainer does. In 1977, Billy Turner knew everything necessary about Seattle Slew and Cruguet won the triple crown with the horse. His ride in the Kentucky Derby was one of the most brilliant and courageous escapes from trouble ever seen in that classic. In 1978, having been dismissed by the Slew's owners, Cruguet consoled himself aboard the sensational grass runner, MacDiarmida, and also began riding first string for the powerful stable of Angel Penna. When wintering in Florida or patrolling his beat in New York, Cruguet has always been a threat aboard long shots, and in recent years has been selective enough about mounts to win more than 15 percent of his starts, including many at fat prices.

PATRICK DAY (1953)—After standing the Fair Grounds on its ear in 1976, the little Coloradan went to New York and established himself as a hard-finishing booter with enough horse sense to deserve good mounts in important stakes. For some reason which could have been related to the youngster's belligerence in the jockey room, the stewards' dim view of such altercations, and trainers' reluctance to ride someone at whom other riders are sore, Patrick headed West. As of September 30, 1978, he had won more than 20 percent of his starts on the Chicago circuit. He will be around, and effective, for a long time.

Wayne Catalano   *Steve Cauthen*   *Jean Cruguet*   *Patrick Day*

Eddie Delahoussaye   *Jeffrey Fell*   *Antonio Graell*   *Ruben Hernandez*

EDDIE DELAHOUSSAYE (1951)—This member of a family of out-standing Louisiana horsemen got it all together in 1977, when he won more than $2 million in purses and almost 19 percent of his starts. During 1978, he won 384 races, tops in the sport, and proved that he could compete with the best in California, Illinois, Kentucky, Louisiana, wherever. I remember him from a New Jersey season as an intelligent, energetic jock whose main problem was inadequate horseflesh. That difficulty seems to have been overcome.

JEFFREY FELL (1956)—After an astonishingly successful apprenticeship in Florida and his native Canada, and after leading at least one Florida and a few Canadian meetings as a journeyman, Fell went to New York and quickly took his place among the top riders on that toughest of circuits. He is good out of the gate, resourceful on the turns, and a strong finisher. He still makes occasional mistakes (who doesn't?), but he wins between 15 and 20 percent of his races, has a superbly professional attitude, continues to improve, and must already be included in any accurate list of North America's ten best.

ANTONIO GRAELL (1944)—One of the numerous Panamanians in U.S. winners' circles, Graell was a rather late comer to the big time after winning several hundred races in Ohio, where he ruled the sport and earned a high place on national races-won rankings. If he has any flaw as a race rider, it is not conspicuous. When he has the horse, it wins. The only reason that he no longer appears on national lists is that he is competing for mounts with too many other first-class riders in New York. Warning: When he arrives in your town with a New York shipper, do not rush to bet against him.

SANDY HAWLEY (1949)—In 1973, the brilliant Canadian became the first rider ever to win 500 races in a single year. His 515 broke the record of 485 set by Willie Shoemaker in 1953. And his 27 percent winning average was almost as spectacular as the 29 percent achieved by the Shoe. Hawley has been a big winner in New York, California, Florida and Maryland but in 1978 he spent most of the time in Ontario, for tax reasons. Naturally, he won his usual 27 percent. Although his riding style is busier than those of Shoemaker, Cauthen and Mc-

Hargue, he resembles them in an uncanny ability to suit the tactics to the needs of the horse, rather than vice versa. He is so gifted at conserving a horse's energies that he frequently goes wide on the turns, losing ground, but staying out of trouble—and having more than enough horse at the finish.

RUBEN HERNANDEZ (1950)—After success in his native Panama, this strong, aggressive rider made a big hit in Florida and proceeded straight to New York, where 1978 found him winning more than 15 percent of the time, collecting well over $2 million in purse money, and firmly ensconced as a full-fledged member of that most competitive of riding colonies.

JOHN LIVELY (1943)—Always does well at the big-league Oaklawn meeting and elsewhere in the middle of the continent. In his rare appearances elsewhere, has impressed as a thorough pro who knows all the tricks, including the most important one of all—saving some horse for the finish of the race. Appears every year among the leading money-winning jockeys, although his batting average is not as high as his ability might permit. Won the 1976 Preakness on Elecutionist after wisely allowing Bold Forbes and Honest Pleasure to defeat each other.

DON MACBETH (1949)—The Canadian has become a stalwart at New Jersey tracks, winning his annual 15 percent and $2 million or so in purses. A quiet man with a quiet riding style, he rides for some of the best barns on the circuit. Formerly more at home on fast-closing horses, he has adapted to the prevailing reality of Monmouth Park racing and now is smartly adept at nursing a front-runner on the lead.

EDDIE MAPLE (1948)—One of the solid citizens of New York and Florida racing, the Ohio rider is not an especially colorful performer but enjoys the respect of leading trainers and gets the job done for them about 15 percent of the time, while winning as much as $3 million a year. This makes him a major-league star and means that he would be a cinch to win everything in sight in a less difficult environment.

SAM MAPLE (1953)—Eddie's brother was a Midwest bigwig for several years and continued to win better than 15 percent of the time after arriving at the Meadowlands in New Jersey. Like Eddie, he rides

John Lively   *Don MacBeth*   *Eddie Maple*   *Sam Maple*

Chris McCarron

Craig Perret

every race with great determination and is not likely to be outfoxed when he has the best horse.

CHRIS McCARRON (1955)—In 1974, the Bostonian accepted a record 2,199 mounts (mostly on the Maryland circuit), and won with 546 of them (25 percent). Nobody had ever won that many races in a year. And he was only an apprentice. He is now a fully seasoned professional who spends most of his time on the Southern California circuit, where only Shoemaker, McHargue and Pincay win 20 percent. Nevertheless, young Chris fits in. He is accepted not only as one of the best of the Santa Anita–Hollywood Park jockeys but as one whose greatest achievements lie ahead. He is a rider in the classic mold—patient, intelligent and attuned to the needs of the horse in the particular situation.

DARREL McHARGUE (1954)—As this was being written in late 1978, the smooth Oklahoman was certain to win more purse money than any other rider of the year. Indeed, his main concern was an effort to surpass Steve Cauthen's one-year purse record of slightly more than $6 million. Nobody was surprised when McHargue set a new record —$6,188,353—on Dec. 31. McHargue has been a phenomenally good rider from his days as an apprentice when he rode at Liberty Bell and Oaklawn for the Dave Vance division of Dan Lasater's immensely powerful stable. By now he has performed with invariable success as a free-lance jock in Southern California, Maryland, New York and New Jersey. With a flawless riding style and an apparently unflappable temperament, he is among the two or three leading candidates to succeed Bill Shoemaker as best in the business.

FRANCISCO MENA (1947)—Paco does not often have his pick of the best mounts at Santa Anita and Hollywood Park but is a solid professional who would lead the standings on most other circuits. His annual purse winnings usually are around $1 million, and his winning average exceeds 10 percent. Better trainers prize his ability to relax a front-running horse, parceling out its energies over the entire distance of the race.

CRAIG PERRET (1951)—He came out of New Orleans as a 16-

year-old apprentice who won everything in sight on Chicago's tracks, did nicely in New York and, in due course, settled down as the solid man of the New Jersey–Florida stables. Wins his 15 to 20 percent and his $1.5 million in purses. Drops into New York occasionally, when a big outfit needs a topnotcher to handle an important horse. Can win in front or from behind. Knows all the angles. Makes very few mistakes. Good on two-year-olds.

DON PIERCE (1937)—This shrewd navigator has had a good deal of publicity describing him as an underrated and under-publicized jock. Every year, he wins big stakes in Southern California, using the first-rate brain, quick reflexes and courage that have kept him among the purse-earnings leaders for many years. If he has the best horse in a stakes race, the horse will probably win, regardless of who the other riders may be. On the other hand, smart players have learned to expect less of Pierce in humdrum claiming races, as if his adrenaline did not really begin kicking until $100,000 were on the line.

LAFFIT PINCAY, JR. (1946)—Son of a fine Panama rider, this great jockey burst on the scene in 1966 and promptly seized a place among the top five riders in the country. A leader in New York, California, Florida and wherever else he has chosen to ride, he has been troubled by weight problems which in recent years have kept him in the warmer weather of Southern California. Like other outstanding jocks, he has a magical effect on horses, often getting them to run much faster than their recent form would seem to promise. His style is much less suave than that of a Shoemaker, involving a good deal more whipping, but he is second to none as a judge of pace. Always wins more than 20 percent of his races.

ROBIN PLATTS (1949)—Although obscured in the shadows of Sandy Hawley and Jeff Fell, this English-born Ontarian is a complete rider who manages to win more than 15 percent, holding his own against the other two stars in races of all classes at all distances and on any surface. A trainer would be an idiot not to want Hawley, but would be wrong to assume that his horse is at a serious disadvantage with Platts.

Robin Platts

Don Pierce

Miguel A. Rivera   *Jean-Luc Samyn*   *Angel Santiago*

MIGUEL A. RIVERA (1943)—For reasons of his own, the brilliant Puerto Rican prefers to ride in Florida most of the year, accepting only occasional mounts in important Northern stakes. As he showed in winning the Preakness and Belmont Stakes on Little Current in 1974, he is a masterful comer-from-behind, who yields nothing in finishing strength to other top appraisers of pace.

JEAN-LUC SAMYN (1956)—I like to think that I recognize riding promise when I see it, but I did not recognize this Frenchman's potentialities when I saw him struggling on bad horses as an apprentice at Monmouth Park. By the time he arrived in New York, during 1977, he had gained enough experience and confidence to attract the favor of good trainers. During 1978, thanks mainly to the excellent runners of Phil Johnson, he took his place among the most dependable journeymen in New York and found his way to the upper reaches of the national purse-earnings list. Strong, brave, smart and responsive to instruction, Samyn is unquestionably for real.

ANGEL SANTIAGO (1950)—Injuries and the presence of numerous other first-class riders detoured this Panamanian from what seemed at first to be an inevitable place at the very pinnacle of his profession. He competed successfully with Cordero, Velasquez and the others for leadership at several New York meets, winning a great many important stakes races in that process. In 1978, after a couple of comparatively slow years of subnormal winning percentages and earnings not much above $1 million, his riding seemed to be as sharp as it had ever been. On that basis, it can be forecast that he soon will attract assignments on live mounts and will regain prominence. His talents are fully rounded. He rides anything well.

LARRY SAUMELL (1957)—This son of jockey Frank Saumell has led enough Florida meetings and has done well enough in New Jersey to rank as one of the more promising riders in the country. He wins more than 15 percent of his attempts, rides two-year-old maidens, older stakes runners and ordinary claiming stock with equal ease, and is cool around two turns.

WILLIE SHOEMAKER (1931)—The incredible craftsman entered

1978 with a world-record total of 7,327 victories, world-record purse winnings of $65.8 million and 717 victories in stakes races, another world record. In his 30 years of race riding, he had led the continent in annual wins five times and in earnings ten times. His winning percentage in 30,939 career starts was 23.7. To call him the greatest of his time and among the greatest of all time is obvious but obligatory. Having studied his style through binoculars, I recommend that kind of observation to anyone who wants to understand race riding. It is as if Shoemaker's reins were in direct telephonic communication with the horse's central nervous system. I do not claim that Shoemaker actually talks to horses, but I am positive that they know precisely what is on his mind. They appreciate his gentle handling so greatly that they do everything in their power to please him.

ROBYN C. SMITH (1944)—Thoroughbred racing has not been especially enthusiastic about female liberation or, for that matter, any other kind of liberation. That women grooms and exercise riders upgraded the performance of many a barn during the 1970's was attributable less to social enlightenment than to a desperate shortage of dependable male help. Good riders also were scarce, which provided grudging opportunities for females, mainly at secondary tracks. Denise Boudrot, Patty Barton, Rochelle Lee, Violet (Pinky) Smith, Joan Phipps and many others proved entirely capable of competing on equal terms with male jockeys on various circuits. In the big time, only Robyn Smith made the grade, and not for very long. Let it be stated for the record that the courage, competitiveness, concentration, horse sense and athletic reflexes required of good jockeys are found in little women as well as in little men. The inability of a highly competent rider like Robyn Smith to obtain live mounts is no reflection on her or on other women jockeys.

LARRY SNYDER (1942)—In 1969, this slick veteran led the list with 352 victories—a winning percentage of 21. He has not equaled that number of victories since, but has invariably been found among the national leaders in races won, with his average situated comfortably between 15 and 20 percent. No less an authority than Jack Van Berg

Robyn C. Smith

Larry Snyder

has been quoted as saying that Snyder can do everything on a horse. During 1978, he rode in the murderous competition of Southern California, dropped in for a while at Keystone and then took his annual two-month vacation. I do not know where he will decide to ply his trade in 1979 and thereafter, but I urge handicappers to respect his well-rounded skills.

MICKEY SOLOMONE (1942)—One can never be sure when this personality will come up with one of his better seasons and contend for leadership at whatever meeting he favors with his presence. By the same token, one can never be sure when he will toss in a bummer. Having already dominated Chicago on more than one occasion, he turned hot in Florida and New Jersey during 1977. In the following year, he again was hot in Florida but not quite himself in New Jersey. Nevertheless, the riding standings as of September 30 showed that he had already won 110 races, more than $1.2 million, and that he had finished first in 15 percent of his starts. When he feels right, he has no discernible weakness, is a splendid judge of pace and an exceptionally strong finisher able to win on grass or dirt—often with the second- or third-best horse.

JORGE TEJEIRA (1948)—Riding for the mighty Dan Lasater stable in 1976, this talented Panamanian won 360 races and more than $2.5 million in purses. His winning percentage with 1,414 mounts was a stunning 25.5. In 1977, he barely missed 20 percent while winning 307 races and over $2 million. With Lasater's activities drastically reduced, Jorge found 1978 less rewarding, but his future must be regarded as bright. As rider of the celebrated Nodouble in the pre-Lasater days, as repeated champion at Keystone and frequent winner in the fastest company on both coasts, his credentials are sound. He is extremely difficult to dislodge from a lead, and is a master at getting there on the turn or at the head of the stretch. This means that he takes care to husband his mount's resources.

DOUG THOMAS (1945)—After a bright apprenticeship in New York, the strong-finishing Canadian suffered the customary post-bug problems. In recent years, he has been a fixture at Keystone and the New Jersey circuit, winning around $1 million a year and flirting with the magic 15 percent winning average. During 1978, he finished in the money in a remarkable number of Trifecta races. Indeed, he was so deadly in that company that certain wise operators began wheeling his horse—regardless of how the past-performance record looked. Although all riders make tactical errors from time to time, I cannot recall having seen Thomas commit a serious booboo in the hundreds of his

Jorge Tejeira   *Fernando Toro*   *Angelo Trosclair*

rides that I have watched in the last few years. If he got better mounts, his talents would make him a real star.

FERNANDO TORO (1941)—The Chilean master has a lock on Southern California turf racing, which is to say that he wins around $3 million in purses during a typical year, and that many of his important victories find him leading Shoemaker and Pincay to the finish on the grass. Why does he do so well on that footing? For one thing, they do a lot of such racing in Chile. He was raised on it. He saves ground and cuts the corner on sharp turf turns with remarkable timing, and always has a lot of horse for the final straight run to the wire. He sometimes wins more than 15 percent of his total starts, indicating that he is not exactly helpless on the main course, either.

ANGELO TROSCLAIR (1957)—This kid is usually king of the hill at Fair Grounds in his native New Orleans. On expeditions to Northeastern tracks, he has shown that his riding talents are not merely regional. He gets out of the gate alertly, is courageous and intelligent in close quarters, and—after all that constructive experience through the long homestretch at Fair Grounds—knows the importance of saving ground.

JACINTO VASQUEZ (1944)—A mainstay on the New York circuit for many years, winning many important stakes on horses of the highest quality, this Panamanian fell below his customary $3 million in purses and 15 percent winning frequency during 1978. On the other hand, when he won he still looked like his former self—a consummately skillful rider with the indispensable ability to adapt his tactics to the style of his mount and the demands of the particular situation. If, as is by no means certain, the accomplishments of Fell, Hernandez and Samyn have made Vasquez permanently less fashionable than he was, he can always move across the river and lead the list in New Jersey, Pennsylvania or Maryland.

JORGE VELASQUEZ (1946)—Among the great Panamanian riders, this one shares with the retired Braulio Baeza the classic riding style associated with victory in the richest races of Europe and North America. That is, he waits for a late-running horse to settle into stride and

Jacinto Vasquez   Mike Venezia

then steers it to the wire by the most appropriate and least troublesome route. Like Baeza, this virtuoso is equally effective on a front-runner. In New York it is taken for granted that, if he enters the stretch in front, he is not likely to be overtaken. That he has never won a triple-crown race is one of the weird accidents of modern racing. On the other hand, he always contends for leadership among New York riders, logging $4 million in annual winnings, and a percentage that approaches 20.

MIKE VENEZIA (1945)—The little Brooklynite was one of the sensational apprentices of modern times and, like others, could scarcely get a mount for years afterward. If ever patience and fortitude have been rewarded in racing, Venezia may be Exhibit A. Merely by remaining on the scene, stubbornly available and, above all, by riding in championship style whenever given the opportunity, he rehabilitated himself on his home circuit, and is now a leading member of the cast. His winning percentage seldom exceeds 12, because of the killing competition for live mounts. But when his horse figures to contest the outcome, you can take it for granted that the jockey will be a help.

Photo credits: NYRA (BOB COGLIANESE): *Cordero, Velasquez, Pincay, Amy, Borden, Bracciale, Cauthen, Cruguet, Fell, Graell, Hernandez, E. Maple, Perret, Rivera, Samyn, Santiago, Smith, Toro, Vasquez, Venezia.* MICHAEL BURNS: *Hawley, Platts.* TURFOTOS (JIM RAFTERY): *Delahoussaye, MacBeth.*

16

The Plus Factors

You have eliminated seven of the eight horses, including the favorite in the race. The remaining animal seems admirably situated as to distance, class, weight and pace. It is in good form. Its jockey's name is Velasquez. The crowd is letting it go to the post at 4 to 1. You buy a ticket.

The horse finishes second, a few jumps ahead of the favorite. The winner is a 20 to 1 shot. You turn back to the past-performance records to see if you missed anything. No. The horse had fallen on its face every time it had tried to go farther than a mile. And it had never been in the money against animals of today's caliber.

On the other hand, the horse was ridden by the only jockey who had ever won with it before. And was carrying seven fewer pounds than in its last race. And had worked out only yesterday. As they say in the trade, it had a few angles going for it.

Because racing is a game in which victory rewards the shrewd as often as it does the swift, innumerable players do their handicapping entirely in terms of angles—patterns in the past-performance record which reveal significant maneuvers by a trainer or possible improvement by the horse itself. Distance, form, class, pace and jockey are all surveyed in such figuring, but seldom in any fundamental way. The angle player hits longshots, as does anyone else who takes a cavalier attitude toward the basics of the sport. Naturally, he also suffers long droughts and generally ends by losing more money than he wins.

But angles have their place in handicapping. They are especially useful as a means of separating well-placed, legitimate contenders whose pace and class ratings are too close for easy decision.

Readers of *The Compleat Horseplayer* and *Ainslie's Jockey Book* will recall that each contained a compilation of selection angles helpful in singling out live horses. I called them "plus factors" and urged the reader to use them only *after* more fundamental analyses. I renew the advice in this chapter, with the admission that almost any of the plus factors might constitute the basis of an interesting selection system. Players drawn to the idea of mechanical systems, which require no effort beyond the application of rules, will find that Chapter 18 of the present volume offers the most fetching array of systems ever published in one place. Before attempting to adapt any of the plus factors to system play, it might be a good idea to look through the assortment of mechanical methods in the later chapter.

In the meantime, anyone who prefers to do his own handicapping will find the following wrinkles a useful adjunct to whatever method he favors. If unable to separate two or three horses by ordinary means, see whether any of the following factors applies to one or more of the horses. Generally, a contender is a good bet if it earns four more of these credits than any other contender does.

1. Winning Favorite: A horse that goes to the post as betting favorite in its race deserves extra credit if its barn customarily wins more than a third of the races in which its horses run as favorites.

2. Consistent Stable: Whether the horse is favorite or not, it deserves credit if its trainer is among the leaders at the current meeting or is shown by *The American Racing Manual* or the daily racing program or the tabulations in this book to be exceptionally consistent.

3. Consistent Jockey: If the rider is an unusually consistent winner or a national or local leader, the horse gets credit. If the horse happens to be the betting favorite and the jockey is good on favorites, the horse gets an additional check or star or whatever symbol you prefer.

4. Favorable Jockey Shift: Credit any contender that lost its last race but is to be ridden today by a different jockey, provided the boy is a national or local leader, or has a winning percentage of at least 16 at the meeting, or has won with the horse in the past. Likewise, a shift to the hot apprentice of the meeting also deserves credit. A switch to a winning rider is almost invariably a sign of readiness, especially in a horse that qualifies as a legitimate contender on more fundamental grounds.

5. Won Last Race Easily: Such horses are among the best bets to repeat unless the last race was against cheap stock or the horse led all the way, without being challenged for the early lead.

6. Won Last Race Handily: The difference between "handily" and "easily" is not great. An animal that wins handily usually retains enough of its form to win at the next asking, provided it is properly placed (a question that should be settled at earlier stages of the handicapping).

7. Last Race a Big Win: The most powerful kind of victory is that in which the horse leads at the stretch call, or is close to the pace, and wins going away.

8. Lost Last Race but Gained in Stretch: If the result chart or past-performance line says "rallied," "just missed," or "finished fast" and the horse picked up at least two lengths in the stretch, it may do better today. Unless, of course, the effort dulled its form (which the player should have noticed in analyzing the form factor).

9. Lost Ground in Middle Stages but Gained in Stretch: A horse may be shuffled back by heavy traffic after a good start. If it at least regains the lost ground, it demonstrates the willingness and condition that win races. The past-performance line might look like this:

$$3 \quad 3 \quad 2^3 \quad 5^5 \quad 4^4 \quad 2^2$$

In seeking this angle—known to old-time punters as the "Up and Down System"—little attention need be paid to running position. Lengths behind the leader are more important, although it is nice to note that the horse managed to pass others while closing in on the leader.

10. Gained Three Lengths or More at Any Call: A burst of speed at any stage of a race is often a sign of improvement:

$$3 \quad 4 \quad 5^5 \quad 3^2 \quad 4^3 \quad 5^4$$

The horse turned it on sufficiently to gain three lengths between the quarter-mile and pre-stretch calls. Or, if it was a route race, between the half-mile and three-quarters.

Racegoers prefer to stand, as this Bowie crowd demonstrates.   UPI PHOTO

11. Passed More than Half the Field: If an animal that usually breaks alertly got off to a poor start and, though losing, passed more than half the other horses in the race, it probably will improve today.

12. Ran Closer to the Early Pace than in Its Previous Two Races: An almost invariably reliable sign.

13. Was Closer at the Stretch Call than in Its Previous Two Races: Ditto.

14. Finished Closer to the Winner than in Its Previous Two Races: Ditto.

15. Is a Front-Running Type that Carried Its Speed Farther than in Either of Its Two Previous Races: More of the same.

16. Ran an Even Race, No Worse than Fifth All the Way, Earning a Higher Speed Rating than in Either of Its Previous Two: A particularly telling sign, often overlooked.

17. Has Earned Increasingly High Speed Ratings in Each of Its Last Two Races: Not necessarily as obvious a sign as it might seem, especially if horse has not been finishing in the money.

18. Has Earned Increasingly High Speed Ratings in Each of Its Last Three Races: Dynamite.

19. Displayed Early Speed: A fast start is often a better sign than a fast finish. Unless the horse is an habitual quitter (which should have been eliminated early in the handicapping), it deserves credit for leading or running close to the leader of its last race, whether it carried the speed beyond the first call or two or not.

20. Led or Ran Within Two Lengths of the Winner to the Stretch Call before Losing Ground in the Stretch Run of a Longer Race than Today's: The reference, as usual, is to the animal's last race. The horse might have won if the race had been at today's comfortable distance. The distance switch, combined as it often is with a class drop and jockey shift, is a dead giveaway that the stable is shooting.

21. Has Led from Wire to Wire in a Race at Today's Distance: The type of horse able to get out on top and stay there is an extra-good bet when in shape and properly situated. He encounters none of the problems that befall off-pace animals.

22. Last Race Easy, Previous Race Good: The last race was easy if the horse never challenged for the lead, finished fourth or worse, and earned chart comment like "No excuse," "No mishap," "Ran evenly," "Wide," or "No rally." If everything else in the record suggests a good performance today, and if the animal's next-to-last race was a good one, the chances are that its last outing was a conditioning effort—a tightener.

23. Alibi: A horse that lost because it was misplaced or because it ran into trouble is often a nice bet when properly placed in its next effort. The public often overlooks the reason for its last defeat, seeing only that it lost badly.

24. Last Race within Seven Days of Today: A horse good enough to survive close scrutiny in terms of distance, condition, class, weight, jockey and pace, deserves extra consideration if its trainer is running it within seven days of its last race. There can be little doubt that the animal is ready and that the barn is trying.

25. Last Race within Five Days of Today: Five days is so much more impressive than seven that the player can give the animal an extra star on that account.

Morning workout at Saratoga.   PAUL SCHAFER—NEW YORK RACING ASSN.

26. Second Start after Long Layoff or Long Trip: Horses usually do far better in the second effort at a new track or after a layoff.

27. Ran in Money after Long Layoff or Long Trip: If the horse ran second or third in its first attempt at the new track (or after a vacation), and did so without the all-out effort of a hard stretch drive, it almost certainly will improve today. An especially good sign is early speed that petered out in the later stages of the race. The horse was undoubtedly short of wind, and should improve today.

28. Stabled at Today's Track: Horses stabled at Belmont Park win a lower proportion of races at Aqueduct than horses that sleep at Aqueduct. The workout line in the past-performance record tells where the horse lives—a good plus factor at any track.

29. Worked Yesterday: Many trainers believe in giving the horse a breezing workout on the day before a winning effort.

30. Recent Long Workout: If the horse has been tiring in the stretch, or has been away from the races for a while, a six-furlong workout for today's sprint or a workout of a mile or more for today's route is an indication that the trainer has been building the animal's stamina. The workout should have occurred at least three days ago, to enable the horse to recover from it.

31. Three Workouts in Two Weeks: A racer that works every five days is in adequate physical condition and is being prepared for something.

32. Six Pounds Less Weight than in Best Race: If the trainer has found the spot in which the horse can run with considerably less weight than it carried in its best effort at the distance, he is likely to want to cash in on the opportunity. The fact that the horse qualifies as a contender suggests that the trainer knows what he's up to.

33. Five Pounds Less than in Last Race: Trainers like to get weight off. Even though the last race may have been a much different kind of affair than today's, the lighter burden remains significant.

34. Distance Switch: Today the horse is running at a suitable distance or the player would (I hope) have eliminated it. If it ran at the wrong distance last time, the effort probably was for conditioning purposes, which may pay off today.

35. Down in Class: If the top claiming price at which horses may be entered in today's race is lower than the price at which the horse was entered in its last start, today's company is probably easier pickings.

36. Steps Down after "Even" or Better Race: A horse bears watching when it drops in class after a race in which it neither exerted itself nor earned unfavorable comment. If the comment was "Even," the player can assume that the trainer had today's race in mind and was merely preparing the horse. If the comment was "Good try" or "Rallied" or something equally complimentary, the horse probably will be an odds-on favorite today.

37. Steps Down Today and Stepped Down Last Time: If the horse's recent record qualifies it as a contender, repeated drops in class may not be the woeful signs that they are in the case of a worn-out animal. They may only mean that the barn is desperate for a purse and a bet.

38. Stepped Down Last Time, Runs in Same Class Again: The trainer evidently thinks that the horse has found its best level. Since the horse is plainly one of the leading contenders in the race, the trainer may be right. If the check mark is added to others earned on the bases of distance switches, weight shifts, jockey switches and the like, the player may be in on a betting coup.

39. Up One Notch Last Time, Down Two Today: Good manipulators get nice prices with this one. For example, the horse might be entered for $5,500 today and its last two races might look like this:

Clm 6500
Clm 6000

If the $6,000 race was fairly good and the $6,500 one pretty bad, the trainer may be wound up for a killing. Racetrack crowds seldom penetrate the past-performance records deeply enough to notice maneuvers of this kind. They see that the horse is dropping $1,000 in price after a bad race. They do not notice that it also is dropping $500 in price after a previous, but recent, good race. Naturally, the good race should have taken place within two or three weeks.

40. Drops from Claimer to f-Claimer without Face-Value Drop: A filly or mare entered in a race for $5,000 females is dropping in class and will have a better chance than she did if her last race was for $5,000 animals of both sexes.

41. Drops from Claimer to f-Claimer with Apparent Value Rise: A filly that ran in a Clm 5000 last week is not stepping up in class if today's is an f-6000. At most tracks, she will pay extraordinarily good odds, because the crowd will think she is being pushed up the class ladder. Review the 20 percent formula on page 215.

42. Properly Placed Three-Year-Old: A three-year-old that has been running fair races against older horses is a cinch to move ahead by several lengths when the trainer finally drops it in with its own kind. If the maneuver is combined with an apparent increase in class—a rise in claiming price of not more than $1,000—it is an especially powerful gimmick and should get a second check mark.

43. New Low Class Today: A contender deserves credit if it is meeting the cheapest field of its career.

44. Has Never Lost by More than Half a Length at This Distance against This Class or Lower: A strong indication that the trainer has found the right spot for the horse.

45. Highest Class Rating: A horse should be credited if its class rating is the highest among the leading contenders.

46. Highest Class Rating by 15 Points: A $1,500 edge in class merits an extra check mark. Or, if the player prefers to use purse values, a $500 difference is significant.

47. Has Won Allowance Race at Major Track: This is significant in handicapping claiming races.

48. Has Won Handicap Race at Major Track: This occurs in claiming races sometimes, and should get an extra check. It also is well worth noticing in allowance races.

49. Recently Claimed: The rules of racing require a recently claimed animal to be run in a higher bracket during the first month it is in the new hands. Exceptions occur when one meeting ends and a new one starts, whereupon the animal is let out of jail and can run at any price the trainer chooses. Horses claimed within the last month that have not yet won for the new proprietors are among the best bets a handicapper finds—provided he has already assessed distance, condition, class, weights, jockeys and pace.

50. Drops Below Price at Which It Was Claimed: A busy claiming trainer does this all the time—winning his first attempt with a newly

Official finish-line photo shows Affirmed beating Alydar in the 1978 Belmont Stakes. Steve Cauthen rode Affirmed, Jorge Velasquez was on Alydar.

NEW YORK RACING ASSN.

Distance runners begin the clubhouse turn at Aqueduct.

claimed horse, and insuring the win by entering it for less than he paid. In general, if a horse qualifies as a live contender, was claimed within two or three months, and is running for the first time at a price lower than the owner paid, an all-out effort should be expected.

51. Consistency: This is one of the most powerful of plus factors, provided, of course, that the horse has adequate pace and class ratings, is in shape and likes the distance. A horse qualifies for the credit if it has won 20 percent of six or more races this year or, if less active this year, has won 20 percent of all its races this year and last.

52. Only Consistent Horse: If no other contender meets the consistency standards, the consistent one should get a second check mark.

53. Gelding: A gelding in shape to run its best is the most trustworthy of Thoroughbreds.

54. Entry: A contender coupled in the betting with another horse has something extra on its side. Because the contender is ready to go, the trainer undoubtedly will use the other half of the entry to make the pace easier for the contender. Therefore, if the contender is a stretch-running type, and its stablemate is a front-runner, and the contender's chief rival in the race is another front-runner, it pays to give the contender not one but two checks. The player is safe in assuming that the stablemate will run the rival pace-setter into the ground, clearing the way for the winning half of the entry.

55. Fast Final Quarter: Colonel E. R. Bradley, the professional gambler who had the Kentucky Derby in his hip pocket, used to make money betting on horses that had run the final quarter-mile of their latest races in 24 seconds or better. The angle is especially useful if the horse qualifies on other counts. To tell how fast a horse traveled the final quarter of a six-furlong race, subtract the half-mile time of the race from the final time. If the horse gained ground from the pre-stretch call to the finish, allow one fifth or one sixth of a second for each length it gained and subtract from the previous figure. Or, if the horse lost ground, add. If the horse's last race was at a mile, subtract the three-quarter-mile clocking from the final time, and then adjust the result according to the number of lengths gained or lost by the horse. It is impractical to attempt this calculation except if the race was at six furlongs or a mile. The angle is so good that it deserves not one but two check marks.

17

Paddock and Parade

When off-track betting finally is legalized in a state with any sense, the customer will spend his afternoon in a neighborhood establishment similar to the branch office of a brokerage house. In air-conditioned splendor, safe from wind, rain, sun or chill, he will surrender his spending money to an electronic tax collector, and will watch his horses lose on closed-circuit television.

"This," he will say, "is the life!"

A close approximation of "the life" already exists. Among the more popular facilities at modern tracks are indoor seating areas, completely walled off from any direct view of the race course. Throngs of punters congregate in these sanctuaries beneath the stands, handicapping, betting and watching four-legged shadows move across the screens of TV monitors. Legal off-track betting will be a great convenience for such folk, sparing them the ordeal of travel to and from the track on congested highways or jouncy rails. They will find everything at the state or municipal bookie parlor that they now get at the track itself.

The Thoroughbred racing industry regards off-track betting as a peril to its existence. If this is true, which I doubt, the industry has only itself to blame. As I complained in the preface to this book, the rulers of the sport are so afraid to offend morality that they fail to educate their customers in the theories and techniques of handicapping. They fail, therefore, to publicize the overwhelming advantage that accrues to the player who does his betting at the track: The horse is at the track! The player cannot see the horse in the flesh unless he makes the trip. And if he does not see the horse in the flesh he does not know what he is betting on.

The helpless innocence of Thoroughbred racing's loyal clientele is displayed most nakedly in its unawareness of the need to look closely and critically at a horse before risking good money on its chances. In a typical racing crowd of 20,000, hardly 1,000—many of them tourists —go to the paddock and walking ring to inspect the animals before the race. A much larger faction mills around beneath the stands, hoping to stumble onto a hot tip.

The paddock and walking ring are where the expert makes his final decision about the winning chances of his horse. Before going there to see the animal, and preferably before leaving home for the track, he has done his preliminary handicapping. He probably has from one to three contenders in mind. One may seem clearly superior on paper.

The wonderful Seattle Slew parades to the post with Jean Cruguet at Belmont Park before winning the 1976 Champagne Stakes and that year's two-year-old championship. NEW YORK RACING ASSN.

The other one or two interest him only if the first turns out to be in unready condition.

The player therefore devotes main attention to the likeliest horse. If he approves what he sees, and regards the odds as reasonable, he makes his bet and awaits Destiny. However, if the appearance or behavior of the horse arouses mistrust, he studies the secondary contenders. At times, his observations may last throughout the ceremonies at paddock and walking ring, the parade in front of the stands, and the pre-race gallops.

Recognizing Readiness

When a good barn sends a fit horse to the races, the animal looks the part. Whether a two-year-old maiden or a five-year-old handicap champion, its class and condition are usually recognizable without the aid of a scoreboard. Its healthy coat glows like well-oiled, hand-rubbed wood. Its mane and tail are carefully groomed. Its eyes are bright, head up, ears erect and forward, muscles firm, ribs barely visible. Its stride is long, easy and free. Its nervousness, if any, resembles the wound-up tension of a human athlete eager for action.

The handsomest, soundest-looking, best-behaved, most devotedly groomed horse in the field is an extraordinarily good bet—but only if it seemed a likely winner during the paper-and-pencil phases of the handicapping. Relatively unimposing Thoroughbreds often win championships, and some of the finest-looking horses you ever saw never got beyond the allowance stage.

Kelso was unimpressive in the walking ring. There have been $4,000 horses with snazzier-looking coats. Yet the player who noted from the past-performance records that Kelso was the best horse in the race could not possibly have been put off by the great gelding's looks. Kelso did not look bad. He just looked unremarkable.

And there you have the main point of the jaunt to the saddling enclosure. You go there to see if there is any reason to refrain from betting on your choice. You hunt for negative signs.

The professional horseman and professional bettor enjoy a considerable advantage in this setting. Because they are on the scene every day, they know which few horses are able to run well even after displays of pre-race fretfulness. They know which horses are running in bandages for the first time. They know which horses customarily race with special shoes or special bits, and which are heavier or skinnier or more languid than usual.

The hobbyist or infrequent player is unable to keep abreast of such things. But if he knows what to look for and what, in general, it all means, he guarantees himself more winners, fewer losers and a higher rate of profit than can possibly be achieved by omitting the paddock visits.

Nervousness and Reluctance

Loyd (Boo) Gentry was roundly criticized because Graustark, the best-looking colt in years, broke down before getting to the 1966 Kentucky Derby. I sang in that critical chorus myself and shall never believe that the horse's ruination was unavoidable.

If Gentry offered any excuses, I did not read about them. A man with an ironic, rather cynical view of things, he kept his own counsel. He also kept his job as trainer of the high-class animals which his father, the celebrated Olin Gentry, bred and raised for John W. Galbreath's Darby Dan Farm.

Coming into 1967, word got around that Boo might have a fresh chance at the Derby with a nice colt called Cup Race, a half-brother of Graustark. But Cup Race went the way of so many others. Injuries knocked it out of the entry box. Gentry then decided to see what might be done with a second colt, Proud Clarion.

This particular animal had suffered so severely from the sore shins that plague today's hard-worked two-year-olds that it had raced only three times during 1966 and had failed to win. A slow learner, and set back still further by the shin ailments, it also suffered from extreme nervousness. However, it showed enough promise early in the year to deserve a shot at Louisville.

On two afternoons during the week before the Derby, Gentry took the trouble to come to grips with Proud Clarion's nervousness. He paddocked the horse. That is, he brought it to the paddock amid the uproar of actual racing and saddled it, as if for actual competition.

"He shook so, his teeth rattled," said Gentry.

On each occasion, the horse did not recover its composure until safely back in the barn.

Derby Day came. Gentry again brought Proud Clarion to the paddock—this time not merely to be saddled but to run in the big race. This time the horse was quite calm. It finally had become accustomed to the noise of the track. Proud Clarion won the Kentucky Derby at 30 to 1.

The betting favorite on that day was Damascus, trained by Frank Y.

Whiteley, Jr. Like other Whiteley horses, this handsome son of Sword Dancer had been the beneficiary of patient, careful handling. It had long since overcome its natural fear of human crowds and of the special tension associated with pre-race ritual. It might get keyed up, but was not the skittish type that exhausts itself before the race starts.

Yet Damascus was nervous before the Derby. Unaccountably nervous. So nervous that certain New Yorkers who had seen the horse win the Wood Memorial at Aqueduct now changed their minds about betting on it in the big one. They suspected that something was wrong. So did Frank Whiteley.

Bill Shoemaker brought Damascus from the gate in a rush, found the horse unusually rank, but managed to snug it back slightly off the pace until the turn for home. Coming into the stretch, he located daylight, pointed Damascus at it and asked for speed. The colt started after the leader, Barbs Delight, as if able to eat it up and win by yards. And then the predictable happened. Damascus ran out of gas and was lucky to finish a well-beaten third. It had left its race in the paddock.

I do not know why Damascus was nervous on Derby Day. But I do know that 99 out of 100 noticeably nervous horses use up so much energy before the start of their races that they stop in the stretch.

Among two-year-olds and certain lightly raced threes such as Proud Clarion, the chief cause of serious nervousness is fear of a strange environment. A frequently complicating factor is dread of the discomfort which the animal has learned to associate with the sights, sounds and tugs and hauls to which it is subjected on the day of a race. Many horses seem literally to dread the prospect of the stressful dash from the starting gate or the punishing drive to the wire.

Later, after becoming adjusted—or resigned—to the demands of racing, Thoroughbreds manifest reluctance—or the nervousness it often begets—only when returning to the track from a long vacation, or when running for the first time at a strange place, or when ill or in pain or when jaded from too much work.

Here are signs of reluctance severe enough to warn the player that the horse may be out of kilter:

Fractiousness. Instead of walking cooperatively from the receiving barn to its paddock stall, the animal fights its handler. It tosses its head, swishes its tail restlessly, kicks, tries to wheel. The behavior may become more intense in the stall, or may not erupt until that point (as if the animal suddenly realized that it had not merely been out for a stroll but was actually going to be asked to race). It may try to kick down the walls of the stall. It may resist the saddle. It may try to savage its handlers with its teeth.

Later, in the parade around the ring, the horse may calm down—a good sign, if accompanied by other good signs to be described below. But if the fractiousness or unhappiness persists, the player knows that precious, unrecoverable energies are being squandered.

Note well that a horse that jogs, toe-dances and whinnies before its race should not be charged with undue nervousness unless it presents other signs of the condition. It may simply be keyed up, which is better than being uninterested.

Note also that inexperienced horses display more nervousness than seasoned animals do. Allowances must be made for this, although the really frantic juvenile seldom has anything left for its race. It is most comforting to discover that the two-year-old with the best previous clockings is also a cool cat in the walking ring.

Human Failure. The reaction of the horse's handlers to its fractiousness is frequently a dead giveaway to their estimate of the animal's prospects. When the groom or trainer displays viciousness or impatience of his own, he reveals that he has no more liking for the race than the horse does. If the horse had a substantial chance, the handler would do everything possible to protect his bet and his share of the purse. This, incidentally, is why stakes horses of notoriously erratic temperament, such as certain members of the Nearco-Nasrullah-Nantallah line, win even after giving their handlers fits. The thing is that they *are* stakes horses and the handlers are under orders to accept the trouble or find employment elsewhere. A fractious claiming racer seldom is treated with such deference. Once the battle starts in the paddock, little is done to improve the animal's disposition, or relieve the fears that account for the misbehavior. Not, that is, unless the horse has an excellent chance in the race and the handlers are willing to suffer injury and indignity in an attempt to salvage the situation.

Washiness. A lather of nervous sweat appears early in the paddock proceedings and the dampness spreads along the horse's neck and flanks like a stain.

In very hot weather, all healthy horses are expected to sweat. Indeed, horsemen worry about the condition of an animal that remains dry when most others are wet. But a nervous, washy horse has a particularly distressed air, no matter what the weather may be. His handlers sponge off the foam, yet he generates more. The sweatiness usually occurs in combination with other signs of nervous strain, such as rapidly flicking ears, or ears that lie flat, or a tossing head, or outright fractiousness.

Kidney Sweat. Nervousness betrays itself with an accumulation of white foam between the animal's rear legs. Occasionally, this is the only visible sign of unease. If the nervousness is not severe, the kidney sweat should diminish or disappear before the horses leave the walking ring for the track. If it becomes more profuse, the horse is probably out of sorts. On closer or more expert inspection, other signs of unreadiness may become apparent.

It is useless to speculate about the causes of any individual case of paddock distress. Whether produced by inexperience, physical discomfort or a sudden, perverse reluctance to play the game, it prevents horses from winning. The player need know no more than that. Even if the horse's record proclaims it the best runner in the race, the player who sees signs of serious reluctance or apprehensiveness had better not risk his money, unless the horse snaps out of its difficulties in short order. Or unless it is the kind of freak that always acts like a loser before it wins.

Bandages

Short bandages around fetlock and pastern are beneficial to a horse that tends to scrape its ankles on the surface of the track, a difficulty known in the trade as "running down." If the horse seems otherwise fit, these short bandages can be ignored.

Long bandages on the hind legs often are applied for much the same reason that a handball player wears a wrist strap—to give extra support. In this case, muscles and ligaments held firmly together enable the animal to propel its weight forward with greater comfort. A really sound horse requires no such artificial assistance, but hind bandages are acceptable unless the horse seems reluctant to race. In those circumstances, the bandages can be accepted as an additional sign of trouble and the horse should be tossed out.

Long bandages on the forelegs are strong signs of tendon trouble where the horse can least tolerate it. If an animal wearing these things seems ready to run, and figures to be the best in its field, the wise player passes the race. The horse might indeed win, but nobody should bet on it. Sooner or later, horses with foreleg ailments break down. Naturally, if the leading contender bobs up in front bandages and shows no liking for the day's activity, the player goes to his second choice with considerable confidence.

Soreness and Lameness

Some gallant old campaigners have legs so gnarled and knotted with wear-and-tear that it hurts to look at them. It surely hurts worse to run on them. But the horses get out there and win. Accordingly, the player should hesitate to rule out a contender whose knee is swollen or who has an alarmingly prominent tendon. Far better to assume, as racing officials do, that any horse able to get to the post is probably "racing sound" and may occasionally overcome its ouchiness and finish on top.

The trick is to recognize "racing sound" animals that are hurting too badly to stand the gaff. Most give fair warning by the unwillingness with which they surrender to saddle, rider and post parade. Others, more stoical about it, seem quite content to run, but reveal in their gaits that they are too stiff and sore to do it well. The goings-on in the paddock stall also help the player to spot such trouble.

In Arkansas, New York and New Jersey, which forbid pain-killing drugs for racing purposes, the law-abiding trainer of a lame or sore horse is forced to rely on bandaging, liniments and the analgesic properties of cold water. It is by no means unusual to walk into a receiving barn and find half the entrants in a claiming race standing in tubs of ice. The ice relieves discomfort by dulling the nerves that transmit pain. It also counteracts inflammation, at least briefly. To prolong its effects, trainers often wrap the sore member in a bandage soaked in the ice water. On arrival at the paddock stall, the bandage is removed. So are less significant bandages known as shipping, standing or stall bandages, which protect the legs from accidental kicks and scrapes.

It is not a particularly good idea to cross out the name of a contending horse that comes to the paddock in cold-water bandages. The soothing comfort may be all the animal needs to run in its best possible form.

Before making up his mind, the player should watch what goes on in the stall after the bandage is unwrapped. If trainer and groom fuss over the suspect joint, feeling it for signs of inflammation, one can assume that they are worried. Or if the horse shies away from the attention, the player knows that it hurts at a touch and is unlikely to run well.

After a few weeks of experience, the player can recognize horses that are stiff and sore. Their walking gait is less fluid than it might be.

They favor the ouchy limb or foot, getting off it as quickly as possible in what amounts to a limp.

In the absence of an outright limp, the horse's head or hips may tell the tale. The head rises when a sore foreleg touches the ground, and then it nods to the opposite side. In the case of a painful rear leg, the opposite hip drops noticeably while walking. If the forelegs spread and seem about to straddle, as if the animal were on a skating rink, it has a sore knee or two, and will confirm the diagnosis with a mincing, choppy stride when it tries to run.

Every now and then, a horse's gait is so stilted in the walking ring that the player has no trouble deciding to bet on something else, or pass the race entirely. Perhaps more often, the player waits to see whether the animal eases out of its stiffness en route to the starting gate.

The Final Minutes

The horse that arouses expert suspicion in the walking ring generally confirms it during the post parade or the pre-race gallops. Like a child being dragged to the woodshed for punishment, it sweats, strains, has difficulty keeping its feet under it, and needs to be escorted under a tight hold by an outrider on a lead pony. Head high, eyes wild, chewing on the bit, the horse looks like the embodiment of defeat. Its occasional victory does not make a sucker of the player who refuses to bet on it.

Affirmed and Steve Cauthen are unable to overtake Seattle Slew and Angel Cordero in the 1978 Marlboro Cup at Belmont Park. NYRA (BOB COGLIANESE)

Bobby Ussery enjoys the scent of roses and the taste of triumph on Proud Clarion after the 1967 Kentucky Derby. UPI PHOTO

This kind of animal is not a good bet to begin with, and it proves this over the long haul by losing far more often than not.

Other unready horses do not have to be carried to the post, or held in check to prevent them from bolting to the stable. They simply run sore. The jockey sets them down for a gallop in front of the stands and they do not step out with the characteristically long stride of the Thoroughbred. Short, choppy steps, often with head unusually high or unusually low, reveal soreness. When the rider gets to the backstretch and busts the horse a couple of times with his whip, it may seem to lengthen stride and run more easily, a sign that it is working out of the trouble and may be able to run. No magic formula can be offered to help the player decide whether to bet or not. The only safe prescription is familiar enough: When in doubt, pass.

For my taste, the best bet is the horse that navigates to the starting gate under its own power, without a lead pony and without any special exercises beyond a brief gallop or two. Lead ponies have become so common in modern racing, however, that the bettor would cut his play below the reasonable minimum if he made the lack of a pre-race escort a large factor in his handicapping.

Shoes

Horseshoes come in a multitude of varieties, most of which are of absolutely no interest to the player.

In the old days, when horsemen solved their economic problems by conniving with each other to cash large bets on fixed races, deliberately poor shoeing was a favorite means of stiffing a horse. Nowadays, purses are more numerous, and big-time horsemen have little incentive to hobble a potential winner. The ancient custom of stiffing it today so that it may win at long odds next time is hard to practice in an era of overworked horses which seldom retain winning form from one race to the next. And an era of relatively vigilant policing. And of claiming races which help a trainer to darken improving form until ready to crack down at a price.

It also is an era in which some veterinarians swear that horses would last longer if greater attention were paid to their shoes. I mention this only for background. The player may deplore the incompetent handling of horses, but is powerless to act against it. As far as shoes are concerned, his role begins and ends with a glance at the official shoe-board and a close look at the feet of his horse.

He should bet money on no horse that wears steel shoes, now that aluminum ones are the mode. The aluminum weighs several ounces less than steel and, as the saying goes along shed row, "an ounce on the foot is like a pound on the back."

The player also should bet no money on a horse that wears bar shoes. These differ from the usual open-ended footwear. A bar is built across the opening. The purpose is to prevent a weak hoof from spreading and cracking under the animal's weight. Winners rarely wear these.

On tracks that tend to get gooey when wet, or on any kind of track labeled muddy or heavy, the player should favor a sharp, well-placed horse whose handlers have spent the $20 necessary to equip it with stickers, or mud calks. These cleats provide extra traction.

Blinkers and Bits

The track's printed program advises the player whether a horse that has been running in blinkers will run today without them ("blinkers off") or vice versa ("blinkers on"). The purpose of the hoods is to keep the horse running in a straight line, with his mind on his work. They prevent him from seeing what he might ordinarily shy away from or veer toward—such as other horses, or the inside rail or the grandstand. The heavy reliance of horsemen on trial-and-error is demonstrated by their experimentation with blinkers. A two-year-old that runs a couple of unaccountably erratic races when blinkered is quite likely to be sent postward without them in its next attempt. Sometimes the change works wonders, but don't bet on it. By and large, the change to favor is "blinkers on," when the two-year-old is from a smart barn, has never run hooded, and needs only to improve its previous clockings by a fifth or two to win a maiden race.

Bits come in as many varieties as shoes. The only interesting one is the extension, run-out bit. If the horse has been lugging in, it may go to the post with a bit that is longer on the off (right) side, enabling the rider to develop greater leverage with the reins. Similarly, a bearing-out horse benefits from an extension on the near (left) side. If the player gets to the races frequently enough to notice this change in equipment, and if the horse shapes up well with respect to class, condition, distance and the like, the mutuel ticket may be a better investment than usual.

Drugging and Stiffing

Heroin is known as "horse" because trainers used to dose racehorses with it. The dreaded opium derivative is a powerful stimulant of horses. Its effect is exactly the opposite of the lethargy associated with human addiction. Indeed, a heroin-stimulated horse may become uncontrollably wild, thereby frustrating its handlers, who had hoped only to dull its pain and shock its nervous system into condition for a winning effort.

I mention heroin because it is interesting. What is perhaps most interesting about it is that it has gone out of fashion at the tracks. More reliable, less dangerous, and far less easily detected stimulants and pain-killers are now in use.

The rules of racing forbid the administration of such chemicals. Concern for the betting public, to say nothing of concern for the well-being of the Thoroughbred, explains why official track laboratories test saliva and urine samples taken from the winners of all races. In some jurisdictions, tests are required for any horse that runs in the money. And in several, tests are run on any animal whose form is suddenly and inexplicably better or worse than expected, regardless of whether it finishes in the money or not.

Unfortunately, the intent of all this policing is more impressive than the results it achieves. For one thing, at least three of every four horses need medication of some kind to withstand training and racing. Secondly, in an age of wonder drugs, horsemen constantly stumble upon marvelous new preparations which not only help relieve pain but stimulate a horse's nervous system and, when administered in proper dosage, are exceedingly difficult to detect in saliva or urine samples.

In racetrack chemistry, as in war, the offense is always a jump or two ahead of the defense. By the time the track chemists have discovered how to detect a new drug, unscrupulous horsemen have found an even newer one.

Thus, one of racing's strongest weapons against stimulation of horses is its network of undercover intelligence agents. In plain language, spies. If these shoeflies were not padding around the barns pretending to be other than what they actually are, and if trainers and stablehands were not thoroughly conscious that Big Brother is watching, the game would be much less orderly and predictable than it is.

Every year, about one tenth of 1 percent (.001) of urine and saliva tests turn out positive. Which is to say that racetrack chemists find traces of one or another banned drug. Heads roll. The crime often is blamed on a stable boy, who then vanishes. Once more, calm descends on shed row. Or the trainer, after serving a brief term of suspension, becomes more vigilant than ever. In some cases this means vigilance against hanky-panky. In other cases it means vigilance against getting caught at hanky-panky.

Nobody really knows how many horses go postward under the influence of drugs which relieve discomfort and augment the animals' natural energies. But the high degree of predictability in racing strongly suggests that the problem need alarm no player. Most races are won by horses whose records of increasing readiness are confirmed by good appearance and pleasant deportment in the paddock. If, as seems highly improbable, the victory is often a triumph of medication, the situation is potentially dangerous and deserves even more attention than it already gets behind the scenes of the sport. But, as nearly as I or anyone else can tell at present, drugs have not yet become a factor as important as distance, class, condition, pace or jockey. Nor are they likely to.

Another use of drugs is for purposes of preventing victory by the best horse in the race. It would be naive to pretend that horses never are stiffed, either by their handlers or some other bettor. Barbiturates, which turn up in twenty or thirty horses a year, are a favorite means of inducing languor and defeat. No doubt other chemicals, less easily discovered, are also in use. But stiffing—and of this you can be sure —is an extremely rare occurrence in major racing, and is by no means common in minor racing. Whatever else the boys may do, they want those purses. To stiff one horse does not assure victory to any other horse unless all the jockeys and/or trainers are in collusion. With Big Brother watching, that kind of conspiracy is riskier than it is worth. So the stiffing, when it is done, is done surreptitiously, as a gamble. If the gambles were uniformly profitable, there would be more of them and racing would be in the throes of a dreadful problem.

Tote-Board Tips

Privileged insiders, who supposedly have a better-than-fair idea about what's what before the race starts, are known enviously as the smart money. When the odds on a horse drop sharply before post-time, the crowd convulses. Hundreds stampede to the windows to join the smarties in the good thing, thereby weighing down the odds still more.

It is true that stable owners, trainers, grooms and clockers—and their relatives, friends and clients—bet thousands of dollars on a horse deemed ready to win. If the horse is unready, or is considered so, they don't bet on it. And, if they *do* bet, the odds decline.

Is it possible to tell whether smart money is on a horse? Sometimes. Is smart money smart enough to bother about? Sometimes.

In my opinion, the tote board is an interesting object but should be allowed to play no role whatever in the player's handicapping. His first problem is to find himself a horse. If he finds it, the tote board tells him whether the odds are reasonable. The better his handicapping, the less attention he need pay to the odds, of course. But if he is a neophyte, and not sure whether his horse merits a bet, low odds may well be sufficient reason to abstain.

This, of course, flies in the face of the belief that the player's handicapping is confirmed whenever his horse goes to the post at lower odds than expected. Confirmed by what? By smart money? But what about the two or three other platoons of smart money that have sunk the family jewels on two or three other horses in the same race?

The smart money is not a formally organized league of superlatively knowledgeable bettors. It does not move in a single phalanx to the mutuel windows. Any individual insider or group of insiders is as likely to be wrong about a horse as anyone else. Assuming, of course, that "anyone else" is a good handicapper.

The test of whether smart money is on a horse is whether relatively more is bet on it to win than to place or show. The insiders bet to win, because that's where profit lies. Accordingly, if bets on the horse account for a fifth or sixth of the win pool but only a seventh or eighth of the place or show pool, the player knows that certain presumably smart plungers expect big things and have backed their opinion with cash. Exception: an odds-on horse. The public often bets as heavily on such a horse to place or show as to win.

A last-minute drop in the odds on a horse may or may not reflect inside action by the stable. Occasionally, it means nothing but the infectiousness of a wild rumor. Not so many years ago, I was button-holed by two hustlers in five minutes, each trying to tout me onto the same two-year-old. I thought it had no chance in its race, and was fascinated to see the odds drop. The horse ran out of the money at 7 to 5. A 4 to 1 shot won. That night I heard from a quite reliable source that several thousand dollars had been wagered on the winner by some smart guys who had employed a few hot-walkers to circulate through the crowd touting the other nag. This kind of thing happens quite often at smaller tracks.

At all racetracks in this country, a sharp drop in the tote-board quotation during the final minutes before post-time usually is a result of a rumor that somebody has loaded up on the horse in the win pool. The news spreads and the rush begins. For the record, let it be noted that the smart money, if it be involved at all, usually feeds its bets into the machines gradually, in an effort to elude discovery. Or, in some cases, it bets at the very start of wagering.

Now that I have done my level best to discourage the reader from allowing himself to be swayed by what he sees on the tote board, I should admit that it seldom pays to buck such betting trends in maiden races at major tracks. This is particularly true when a first-time starter goes postward at odds considerably lower than its morning-line quotation. The reason is simple enough. The only reliable dope about first-starters and lightly raced maidens is the opinion of clockers and other horsemen who have seen it in the mornings. Including, of course, its own handlers. When the slightest amount of extra cash shows up for such a horse in the win pool, the word spreads through the crowd with great rapidity and the odds plummet. I have never kept records of the results attainable through bets on such maidens, but I should not be surprised if profits await anyone who bets on them—provided that he does so only when he thinks that nothing else in the race has an obviously superior chance.

Another kind of tote action worth watching is the *lack* of change in the quotation on a medium-odds horse when the odds drop on another. Plainly, when odds drop sharply on one horse, carrying it into the even money range or thereabouts, odds should rise on everything else in the race. If one horse holds steadily in the 3 to 1 to 6 to 1 range, somebody is hurrying the money in on it. If your handicapping has already singled out that animal, it might pay you to increase your bet.

18

Seventy-seven Selected Systems

The typical system player stands in awe of the expert handicapper. He plucks at the cashmere sleeve and begs for secrets. The handicapper replies with the scorn that insiders reserve for outsiders. The only secret, he growls, is comprehensive knowledge of the game.

True. A system is a set of rules, a mechanical procedure, a formula. But handicapping is different. To tell one race from another and one horse from another, the handicapper makes personal evaluations of many interrelated, variable factors. No rules concise enough for practical use could possibly encompass all those variables. The handicapper's secret is his mental store of the general concepts from which rules derive. Examining a field of horses, he uses his knowledge in an orderly way—*systematically,* if you like—but he relies in the end on what he knows and believes and foresees, rather than entrusting his game to canned rules.

Because the theories and techniques of genuine handicapping have been guarded as jealously as the secrets of Voodoo, it is not surprising that racing fans pay hundreds of thousands of dollars a year for selection systems. Some of the formulas cost $100 each and arrive in plain white envelopes. Others are obtainable for pennies in the pages of *American Turf Monthly* and *Turf and Sport Digest.* I have a file drawer full of the things and have seen thousands more. Most are quite worthless, including some that sell at high prices. The best, including many published in the two major fan magazines, are substantially useful, especially in the hands of someone who knows enough about handicapping to evaluate the rules and adapt them to his own purposes.

Having gone to some pains to make a handicapper of my reader, I shall not now invite him to become a system player. Yet I have filled this chapter with some of the most plausible of workable systems ever published. I have done this for several reasons. First, I believe that the analysis and dry-run testing of systems is an interesting way to enlarge one's grasp of handicapping. Secondly, I believe that a player who *knows* handicapping might well prefer to attack the mutuel machines with three or four valid spot-play systems. Knowing what he does, he is able to choose the right method for the right occasion. Sparing himself most of the labors of actual handicapping, he remains able to invoke the principles of handicapping whenever he recognizes the special situations in which system rules must be stretched or ignored.

Systems are not supposed to be played that way, of course. What makes them systems in the first place is the reassuringly inflexible set of rules which the player is required to apply unquestioningly. So be it. The systems in this chapter are composed of rules. Each is supplemented, however, with suggestions which show any fairly well-informed player how he might improve matters by using his own noodle.

How to Evaluate Systems

Systems cover a wide spectrum. Some are ingenious attempts to codify basic principles of handicapping in relatively simple form. Some apply handicapping standards to the business of locating exceptionally worthwhile favorites, or the likeliest selections of newspaper handicappers. Some are angle systems that point out a horse as playable without regard to the potentialities of the other horses in the race. Some stress class, some consistency, others current condition or speed or jockey.

Before describing this book's systems in detail, I think it important to agree on methods of evaluating them. And of evaluating other systems which the reader might encounter elsewhere or dream up himself. First, a system should contain no eccentric rules. It should be attuned to the established realities of the sport. It should make sense from a handicapping standpoint.

I have in mind hundreds of systems I have seen which advise the player to back the least consistent horse in the race, or the only maiden in the race, or the horse with the poorest recent performance, or the horse moving furthest up in class, or the horse carrying the least weight, or the horse with the apprentice rider, or the only female in the field, or the only three-year-old in a race against older. It is quite easy, but thoroughly dishonest, to "substantiate" such a system by citing longshot victories. Any attempt to make money by departing so far from the percentages of Thoroughbred racing is doomed. The player who persists in a disregard of the laws of equine nature and the principles of handicapping must end without a dime.

Given a system that seems compatible with some of the basic probabilities of the game, the player needs to find out whether its mechanical rules cover a sufficient range of circumstances to permit a profit. The only way to find out is to run a test. Test it on paper, preferably over a period long enough to permit at least 100 paper bets. For most systems and most tracks, this would mean checking through the racing papers of an entire meeting.

A less extensive test is likely to be misleading, like the brief published "workouts" that "prove" the validity of bets on the only maiden in the race, or the only horse carrying an apprentice. A profitable system might show a loss in any random series of 50 plays. A losing system might show a profit in a similar test.

Beware of the system that yields a paper profit of less than 10 percent on the hypothetically wagered dollar. This is better than losing, but is hardly sufficient profit to sustain one's enthusiasm, unless the bets are huge.

Beware especially of the system that produces frequent fallow periods of more than seven or eight successive losses. One or two such losing streaks may be endurable in a system that yields clusters of winners. But give it some thought. Do you really want to stretch your nerves with a procedure that bails itself out with a $24 winner after nine successive losses? Adventurous though you may be when betting on paper in the privacy of your den, would you deliberately suffer nine or ten losses in a row when risking your own money?

Beware also of systems that require a large financial outlay without a proportionate return. The system that produces two plays a day and a 20 percent profit is far more suitable to most players than the kind that obliges him to bet on two or three horses in each of four or five races, and ends with a 2 percent profit. The first system lends itself to supplementation. For example, the player can use it in conjunction with another that picks a fair percentage of winners in other kinds of races. He then can make a total of three or four or five bets a day. But the second system jams him up, requires too much capital, and, no matter how nice some of its mutuels may seem, it pays too little in the end.

Shun systems full of "tie-breaking" rules which sound suspiciously as if they were added during, rather than before, the test of the system. Good systems separate qualified contenders by means of fundamental handicapping factors. For example, a system based on speed ratings and class should use distance and current condition to eliminate the less likely contenders. Tear it up if it says something like, "In case two or more horses qualify, play the one that carries the highest weight today; if still tied, play the one that was closest to the leader at the pre-stretch call of its next-to-last race." In breaking ties among horses selected by any of the systems in this chapter, always, but always, use whatever fundamentals are not covered in the system. Apply those fundamentals in this sequence: distance, current condition, sex, age, class, consistency, weight, jockey.

Beware most earnestly of the system that depends for its paper profits on a couple of boxcar mutuels. When you disregard the $76 winner does the system still show a profit? If so, it may merit further testing. If not, the system probably is a waste of time. For most temperaments, any system that throws off fewer than 25 percent winners is no use at all, the $76 bonanza notwithstanding. Far more significant than the big longshot is the price range of *most* winners produced by the system. If it hits one out of four or five, with mutuels large enough to make the difference, and if its long losing streaks are few and far between, perhaps you can tolerate it.

Finally—if I may repeat my warning against the ever-present temptation to adopt or invent eccentric rules—avoid any system that gets its longshots by making unreal requirements. For example, you may notice that the system would have caught a $96 winner if it had accepted horses idle for nineteen days instead of the prescribed fourteen. Before embracing the idea, be sure to recheck. How many losers would it *add* by extending the late-action rule? Is it a longshot system to begin with, or was the $96 thing a freak occurrence? Most urgent of all, was your test extensive enough to be meaningful?

System Principles

Most systems are silent about one or more of the fundamentals of handicapping. The great delight, of course, is to find one that shows a profit anyhow, requiring a minimum of toil. You will see several in this chapter.

Others, which perform erratically, are subject to revision. You can tighten them by supplying additional rules to cover distance or condition or weights or sex or class or consistency or jockey—reliable factors that seem most pertinent. If in doubt about the kind of rule to add, you might riffle through whatever chapter in this book covers the particular factor.

The player unwilling or unable to test a variety of spot-play systems in hope of working up a battery of the things may be equally unready to test his own handicapping with real money. He will find excellent alternatives in some of the more comprehensive systems that appear late in this chapter. After putting one or two through a dry run for several weeks, he is certain to notice certain aspects of handicapping falling into place for him. He may adopt part of the system to his own blossoming method of selection. Or he may revamp the system radically and make it entirely his own. If his changes comply with the fundamentals of the game, he will discover in due course that he has become a pretty good handicapper. Welcome to the club.

Class-Consistency Systems

Some interesting selection systems emphasize Thoroughbred class and/or consistency. Like most canned methods, they are least likely to disappoint when the following restrictions are observed:

1. No maiden races.
2. No races for two-year-olds at less than six furlongs.
3. No jump races.
4. No races on other than a fast track.
5. No females against males.
6. No horses whose best races have been run at tracks inferior to today's.
7. No horses carrying more than 120 pounds in races which find the competition less severely burdened.
8. No horses making their first starts after long trips or lengthy layoffs.

Having issued those warnings, I urge the reader to use his knowledge of handicapping to find occasions on which some of the warnings may be ignored.

SYSTEM 1

Principle: Play a horse entered for a claiming price at least $2,000 below a price tag it has carried in the past, provided it is

the only such horse in the race and is regarded highly enough to go postward at odds of 15 to 1 or less.

Reasoning: Class will tell.

Comment: All minor tracks and some major ones are replete with gimpy, cut-rate horses that used to win allowance races or $15,000 claimers. However, the published past-performance records are brief. They seldom cover more than the most recent six or eight months of an active animal's career. For that reason, this system tends to point out horses that have only recently declined in market value. Such a Thoroughbred unquestionably has gone sour, but it may still have enough class to beat the cheapies it faces this afternoon.

Fantastic results have been recorded in tests of this idea. E. R. DaSilva and Dr. Roy M. Dorcus, faculty members at the University of California at Los Angeles, reported in their interesting book, *Science in Betting* (Harper, New York, 1961), that the method turned up 27 plays at a 55-day meeting at Hollywood Park. Thirteen of the bets won, at a profit of $1.50 on every wagered dollar! Somewhat more action— 37 plays in 55 days—occurred at Santa Anita, with only a slight reduction in profits. At Aqueduct, a 50-day workout produced 11 plays and an 82 percent profit.

I ran through three weeks of a Delaware Park meeting and found that plays arose at the rate of three or four a week. The sample was too small for significance, but I was interested to note that four of ten selections won and that the prices were long enough to return almost exactly 100 percent of every dollar invested. To achieve this, however, certain elaborations were necessary. Like other apparently simple notions about racing, the one embodied in this system produces endless confusion unless shored up with additional rules.

Suggestions: The player should avoid maiden races, because drops in claiming price mean little in such company. Similarly, if he finds that an entrant in a straight $5,000 claimer once ran in a race for $10,000 maidens, he dare not qualify the animal on such grounds, but should confine his interest to horses that qualify on the basis of a race for previous winners. Moreover, danger lurks in the assumption that a filly entered against $6,000 males should be bet because it once ran in an f-8000. The player should take pains to adjust the value of the f-claimer (see page 216) or should pass the race entirely.

Another problem is that of the horse whose only qualification is that it ran in an allowance race or a higher-bracket claimer at a minor track.

Such stock should be ignored. Finally, high-priced claiming races at major tracks frequently involve animals that have run in allowance company. Unless the player is satisfied that the allowance race was substantially classier than today's claimer, he should toss out the horse or pass the race.

The player attracted to this system should run it through a full season at his own track. See what happens when its basic principle is taken literally, without regard to the previous winning status or sex of the horses, or the tracks at which they have run their apparently classier races, or the real value of the allowance races in which they have started. Also see what happens when my suggestions are applied. And see how things work out when rules affecting distance and/or recent action are added. I believe that tightening of this kind would leave the player with two or three bets a week, a high percentage of winners, an excellent rate of profit and, most important, a sound procedure likely to withstand the test of time.

SYSTEM 2

Principle: Play any horse running in a claiming race for the first time, provided it has been racing and working out regularly, was beaten by not more than five lengths in its last start, and either led or was within two lengths of the leader at some stage of the race.

Reasoning: An allowance or maiden-special competitor in good enough physical condition to race and work frequently must be conceded an excellent chance when it drops into claiming company after a race in which it showed signs of life.

Suggestions: If in doubt as to what constitutes sufficient recent action, consult Chapter 9. Or require at least one race in the past eighteen days, with workouts at the rate of one per five days for any horse that has not raced in eight days or longer. A distance rule is probably less necessary with this system than in other methods of selection: The trainer who drops a formerly promising horse into a race from which it may be claimed is likely to put it where it can do its best.

SYSTEM 3

Principle: Play a horse that led or ran within a length of the leader at one or more of the early calls of its last race and drops down today to a class at which it has won in the past.

Reasoning: Trainers do this sort of thing all the time.

Comment: This system should produce profits if supplemented with a late-action rule. A pace-setting type that tires in the late stages after showing some run is usually brought back to the races in a hurry, to exploit its apparently improving form. When dropped in with cheaper company than it has been facing, it usually holds its speed longer. The trainer probably places it at the right distance in a situation of this kind.

Suggestions: In addition to a condition rule, the player should resolve to bypass turf races. The only exception would be a horse that has won on the grass against a field exactly like today's.

SYSTEM 4

Principle: Bet any horse that was claimed in one of its last three races and is entered today at a price lower than the new owner paid for it.

Reasoning: Horsemen sometimes make dreadful claims, but not very often. If the horse has been running and working regularly and the owner now risks losing it for less than he paid, the player knows that the barn wants today's purse. Badly.

Comment: An occasional horse goes to pot during the very race from which it is claimed. Others conk out during their first days in the new barn. But a majority of the remainder give the new owners some run for the money, having been chosen on grounds of impending good form. Certain shrewd haltermen often win with the horse on the first try, even though it runs against better company than it has been meeting in the recent past. Others take a couple of races to prepare the animal for the crackdown, and do not hesitate to enter it for $500 or $1,000 less than the purchase price, to insure the best possible results. This system probably will not make money if played indiscriminately, but should be a powerful instrument for anyone who knows the habits and gimmicks of his local track's leading trainers.

Suggestions: The system is unworkable with maidens. It gains strength if the player checks the horse in the paddock, to make sure it is ready. It also improves with tight distance and condition rules, and when the jockey is among the local leaders. Addition of such rules eliminates the most spectacular longshots turned up by this system, but increases the winning percentage greatly and should bring the player onto the profit side of the ledger, where he belongs.

SYSTEM 5

Principle: Play a horse stepping down in class after a race in which it ran out of the money, provided that (1) it had stepped up in class for that race and (2) it was never worse than third at any call in its next-to-last race.

Reasoning: This combines Plus Factors 22 and 23 (see Chapter 16). They often are accompanied by as many as six or seven others, signifying an authentic "go."

Comment: Formal handicapping procedures often single out this system's horse as a contender, yet it may pay a handsome mutuel because of its apparently bad last race.

Suggestions: Distance and current-condition rules make this system a nice addition to anyone's collection of spot-play methods.

SYSTEM 6

Principle: Play a horse stepping down in class after a race in which the chartmaker's comment indicated that it ran an "even" or better race.

Reasoning: This is Plus Factor 36. A horse that did not disgrace itself in competition with better horses might move ahead a few lengths today.

Comment: Years ago, I used to finish no worse than even, and sometimes with a nice seasonal profit, using this system in races where I could find (1) no truly consistent horse with a clear edge in class and (2) none that ran powerfully enough in its last race to look like a serious threat on grounds of current form. I believe the system is most effective in races for animals aged four and older and, of course, only when more fundamental factors fail to suggest a likely play.

Suggestions: Recent action and a liking for the distance should be a routine part of this one.

SYSTEM 7

Principle: Play a horse that finished second in its last race if (1) it runs in the same company or cheaper today and (2) the winner of its last race has subsequently stepped up in class and won.

Reasoning: The horse lost to something that was much too good for the field. But it beat everything else and should be a good bet today.

Comment: This is what is called a "follow-up" system. A player who already keeps a notebook record of results, the true class of races, and the like, can turn a pretty penny with this angle. It produces not more than one or two plays a week, but the winning percentage ranges between 33 and 50, depending on how careful the player is about avoiding females against males, three-year-olds against older horses on the down slope of the form cycle, and horses that have not had sufficient recent work to deserve support.

Suggestions: If you do not maintain a notebook, the infrequent plays produced by this system may not seem worth the trouble. On the other hand, the results are most gratifying for anyone with the necessary patience. The system is particular dynamite with fillies and mares that finish second to males and seem to be stepping up in class when entered at a slightly higher price against females. As readers of Chapter 10 are aware, such a step up is really a step down. The system gets equally good results with three-year-olds that race against their own kind after running second to older horses. In any case, careful observance of the form cycle is necessary. A horse that runs second may get so tuckered out that it can't beat anything in its next effort. Check Chapter 9 and devise rules to assure bets on ready horses.

SYSTEM 8

Principle: Play a horse that has gone to the post as betting favorite in at least 40 percent of the races described in its past-performance record, provided that it (1) has earned more money this year than anything else in the field and (2) has finished in the money in at least half the races for which detailed past-performance lines are published and (3) has won no less than 25 percent of its total races this year and last.

Reasoning: A horse of established consistency and recognized class (note the frequency with which it runs as favorite) is seldom a hopeless risk.

Comment: Strangely enough, this system puts the player on cheapies as well as stakes runners. It gets surprisingly good prices at times. The crowd often discounts the chances of a vigorous young three-year-old against better stock than it has faced in the past. Odds also rise when a well-backed horse loses two or three times in succession.

Suggestions: The system is at its best when the player takes pains to avoid jaded horses. Sufficient late action and, among older horses, not too many hard recent races, should be minimum requirements. A distance rule should also be used—preferably one that demands a previous victory at today's exact distance. Two-year-olds are not covered by this system, which calls for consistency over a period of two years.

SYSTEM 9

Principle: Play a horse that has won at least 25 percent of no fewer than six races this year, or this year and last combined, provided that (1) it has run within the past ten days at this track and (2) has won at today's distance against animals of today's class.

Reasoning: An authentically consistent horse, properly placed and physically fit, is usually a real contender.

Comment: This one is typical of better systems. It saves the player the labor of handicapping the entire field, yet directs him to a horse whose record suggests ability to hold its own.

Suggestions: The results improve if the condition rule is enlarged to include negative factors like overwork. A simple pace analysis, a walk to the paddock, and avoidance of horses unlikely to do their best under today's weights will reduce the number of losing bets. Also, they will tout the player off an occasional longshot! But the long-run results should be satisfactory.

SYSTEM 10

Principle: Play a horse that has won and/or finished second at least ten times during this year and last, provided that (1) it has finished first or second in at least half its races during that period and (2) has won at least 25 percent of its total starts during that period and (3) has raced within the past eight days and (4) has won or finished second within the past two months.

Reasoning: A genuinely consistent horse that ran eight days ago should be fit enough to live up to its record today.

Comment: Even more potent than System 9, this one seldom gets more than two or three plays a week. Prices range from odds-on to $30 and better, with the majority somewhere between 2 to 1 and 5 to 2. *Turf and Sport Digest* published a full-season New York workout of a closely similar system many years ago. It hit 40 percent winners and the profit exceeded 100 percent.

Suggestions: A player would diminish losses by tightening the condition rule to avoid bets on older horses that have been raced too strenuously in their recent starts. A distance rule would reduce the action still further, but would probably push the winning percentage above the 40 mark.

SYSTEM 11

Principle: Of all entrants that ran within the past ten days and finished out of the money, play the one whose record shows a victory at today's exact distance in a field of today's class.

Reasoning: The recent losing race and the proper placement suggest an effort to win at a price.

Comment: Like so many methods of its kind, this one leads to the poorhouse unless the player fortifies it with sensible condition rules. Otherwise, its losing streaks will be more compelling than the long-shots it finds.

Suggestions: With condition rules, this kind of play becomes an especially promising bet, particularly when the maneuvering trainer assigns the mount to a leading jockey.

SYSTEM 12

Principle: Play a horse that lost its last race but earned a "Form" speed rating of 95 or better.

Reasoning: It takes an exceptionally good horse to earn such a rating, win or lose. An animal of such class should win next time out if given any part of a break.

Comment: Like most systems, this one improves in the hands of a player willing to supplement mechanical rules with knowledge of the game. For example, no cut-and-dried condition formula is much help in evaluating the readiness of the stakes and allowance runners likely to qualify under this method. Yet an analysis of their fitness is most important, and so is analysis of the assigned weights. The player who uses the system in that fashion should find it helpful in big races.

Suggestions: Do not try this on turf races. Watch the opportunities it presents at secondary tracks, when big-league stakes runners are entered. Also watch it in top-grade sprints at major tracks.

SYSTEM 13

Principle: Play the horse that has won or finished closest to the front end most often in its last seven races. Add the finishing positions in those races, counting a victory as 1, a second-place finish as 2, and so on, but giving nothing worse than a 5, even if the horse finished tenth in one of its races. The horse with the lowest total is the play. If any horse has fewer than seven races, but has won any, pass the race.

Reasoning: Recent consistency is the best kind.

Comment: Surprisingly good prices await anyone who plays this mechanically, in nine races a day, breaking ties by means of distance, class and recent action, in that order.

Suggestions: Profits are possible for the player willing to convert this from a mechanical system to a simple handicapping method. The key elements to be added are class and its relationship to form. Grant high-class animals the ability to win in second-rate company after a layoff. Likewise, be lenient about demanding recent races of consistent claiming animals which have shown in the past that they can win in their own class off workouts alone. Be careful about betting females against males.

Form Systems

Thousands of systems purport to zero in on ready horses without requiring the player to ponder the numerous subtleties of the current-condition factor. To the degree that they deal in fundamentals of form and take heed of class, they do quite well.

SYSTEM 14

Principle: Bet a horse that won its last race easily, provided that the race took place not more than a week ago.

Reasoning: An easy winner is at top form. The trainer seeks a repeat victory as soon as possible.

Comment: A sound idea, except when the animal steps up to meet one or two classier animals whose own condition is sharp.

Suggestions: Worth trying if the horse is the only one of its kind in the race. In allowances, handicaps and stakes, and in top-grade claimers at major tracks, the one-week rule might be eased to ten days.

SYSTEM 15

Principle: Play a horse that won its last race by gaining in the stretch after leading or running within two lengths of the leader at the stretch call, provided the race occurred within two weeks.

Reasoning: The big win (see page 179) is the most reliable sign of powerful form. But if the horse is kept out of action for more than two weeks, one must assume that illness or injury has prevented the trainer from cashing in again.

Comment: The player who is careful about age, sex, and jockey can beat the game with this spot-play system.

Suggestions: Play no race in which more than one horse qualifies. Avoid three-year-olds against older, except in allowance sprints, or if you know that the three-year-old beat older in its big win. Also avoid females against males. Otherwise, do not worry about animals moving up in class. This kind does it and wins. Flexibility about the two-week rule also helps: If the horse has been working briskly at four- or five-day intervals, it can be allowed up to three weeks since its last race. Obviously, however, the situation is rosier if not more than a week elapses.

SYSTEM 16

Principle: Bet a horse that gained in the stretch in its last race, provided that it beat at least three horses, has average earnings of at least $1,000 per start, and does not step up in class.

Reasoning: Class, consistency and form.

Comment: An excellent spot-play method for claiming races, but only when not more than three animals qualify and no other apparently sharp entrant has superior consistency. Gets excellent prices.

Suggestions: Try combining this with Systems 13 and 14, using it when they fail to produce a play in a medium-grade claimer. A severe late-action rule is needed for best results. I would not bother with a horse unraced for more than two weeks unless it had worked out at least twice in the last eight or ten days. To break ties, discard an animal that seems less than ideally suited to the distance. If the tie persists, favor the horse stepping down in price. If still a tie, go to the one that raced most recently and/or got the most favorable chart comment.

SYSTEM 17

Principle: Play a horse that ran close to the early pace of its last race, slowing down in the later stages, provided that (1) it had not showed as much early speed in its previous two races and (2) it earned a higher speed rating in the last race than in either of the previous two.

Reasoning: Early speed is a reliable sign of improvement.

Comment: Innumerable systems derive from this idea. Their virtue is in steering the player away from obvious choices, many of which turn out to be past the peak of form.

Suggestions: Try this with horses that have raced in the past seven days or have worked out at short intervals since racing not more than two weeks ago. Concentrate on claiming races, and favor a horse entered at a class and distance which it has handled successfully in the past. In testing the system, notice whether results improve if the jockey factor is introduced. Also notice how the winning percentage increases when the probable pace of the race suits the animal's running style. Finally, see if you can steal a few hours to see what happens when these horses are played three times in succession, stopping the play sooner if the horse wins.

SYSTEM 18

Principle: Play a horse that lost its last race provided that it was first, second or third at the pre-stretch call and that (1) it had been at least two positions farther back at that call in each of its previous two races and (2) it earned a higher speed rating than in either of the two previous races.

Reasoning: Another sign of improvement, representing a sign of life in the semifinal stages of the race.

Comment: Everything said about System 17 applies here.

SYSTEM 19

Principle: Play a horse that was first, second or third at the stretch call and, while losing, earned a higher speed rating than in its previous two races.

Reasoning: Another hint of imminent victory.

Comment: See System 17.

SYSTEM 20

Principle: Play a horse that finished two positions closer to the winner and earned a higher speed rating than in its previous two races.

Reasoning: Still another sign of improvement.

Comment: See System 17.

SYSTEM 21

Principle: Play a horse that ran an even race, in second, third or fourth position (it does not matter which), at each of the four calls (ignoring the "Racing Form" notation of the animal's position at the start). The horse should have earned a higher speed rating than in either of its previous two races.

Reasoning: Such a horse is on the verge.

Comment: See System 17.

SYSTEM 22

Principle: Play a horse that has earned increasingly high speed ratings in each of its last three races without winning, and has been increasingly close to the winner at each of the four calls in each race. Judge closeness to the winner either in terms of running position or number of lengths behind. If the horse led at any call in its third race back or its next-to-last race, it should have led at the same call in the following race.

Reasoning: The occasional animal whose record shows an overall improvement of this kind is on its way to the winner's circle.

Comment: See System 17.

Suggestions: Consider combining all these improvement-angle systems into one. A careful study of results at your own track will disclose the blend of distance, class, consistency, sex, jockey and pace rules that yields the most satisfactory profits.

SYSTEM 23

Principle: Play a horse that raced twice in the past fourteen days but did not win, provided that it has won at today's distance and class at some time in the past three months.

Reasoning: A properly placed animal fit enough to race three times in two weeks is fit enough to win, perhaps at a price.

Comment: This one gets longshots, but misleads the player toward animals that are being raced into shape and have not yet achieved it.

Suggestions: Things improve considerably if the player requires that the horse's record shows a bit of improvement in either of its last two efforts. It also pays to avoid any four-year-old or older animal that lost in close, driving finishes in both of its most recent starts.

SYSTEM 24

Principle: Play a horse that has raced within two weeks, has worked out every four days since, worked out yesterday, and is dropping in claiming price.

Reasoning: Such a recent record portrays a trainer getting ready to shoot the wad with a physically able animal.

Comment: A nice system. Losing streaks are no problem if the player digs into the past-performance record instead of leaving everything to the trainer. Trainers, as we know, are not infallible.

Suggestions: Avoid allowance races and higher-bracket claimers. The system is best in medium-grade claimers and maiden claimers for three-year-olds and up. In testing, note the effects of the distance, sex, weight and jockey factors.

SYSTEM 25

Principle: Among entrants that have raced in the past seven days, finishing out of the money, play the one that has run in the highest-grade race in the last two months. Break ties by finding the qualifier that has earned the highest "Form" speed rating in the past month.

Reasoning: A race within seven days is always a good sign. Many successful players refuse to bet on any other kind of animal.

Comment: This is a longshot special, best used when other selection methods fail to produce a candidate.

Suggestions: If you want to try this as a last resort, after your other systems come up empty on a race, your chances of breaking even with it will be enhanced by giving first preference to horses that have already shown ability at the particular distance and class. The presence of a winning jockey also means a good deal on a horse of this kind.

SYSTEM 26

Principle: Play the horse that finished in the money most recently.

Reasoning: What better clue to top form than a recent good performance?

Comment: The last-out-in-the-money system may be the most popular of them all. It requires absolutely no work and tends to protect the player against serious losing streaks by directing him to animals whose trainers are trying to cash in on good form. It can be used in any kind of race.

Suggestions: The player who understands the form cycle increases the winning percentage of this system by ruling out horses whose in-the-money finishes are forecasts of deterioration rather than improvement. See pages 176–179. Distance, class, sex, consistency, weight and jockey rules each help the system, although they rob it of its extreme simplicity. I can think of no better drill in the principles of handicapping than a long workout with this system, including a study of how its results vary with the addition and modification of fundamental handicapping factors.

SYSTEM 27

Principle: Play a horse that finished in the money in its last two starts, provided that (1) it won not more than one of them, (2) was out of the money in its third race back, (3) steps up not more than $1,000 in claiming price today and (4) is the only qualifier in the race.

Reasoning: The horse demonstrated improvement in its next-to-last and either improved still more in its last or ran well enough to get some of the money. It may still have enough on the ball to win today.

Comment: Frank Bouche served this one to readers of *American Turf Monthly*. It gets good prices, encounters few long losing streaks, and locates a play or two on most racing days. Its ingenious rules cover the kind of animal that lost last time because it was stepped up in class after a victory. Also covered are the animals that won last time but which may be able to win again because they step up only $1,000 or less today. The rule against races with more than one qualifier prevents confusion. It also tends to turn up races in which the one horse, regardless of odds, is a form standout.

Suggestions: A distance rule would help the player to avoid losers that won their next-to-last, tailed off slightly in their last and are being entered today at the wrong distance for exercise. A rule requiring recent races and/or works might cancel an accidental longshot or two, but also would eliminate bets on horses that have not run in months. A rule eliminating older horses that ran to the limits of their ability in their last two races would spare the player bets on animals that should be resting instead of racing.

SYSTEM 28

Principle: By reading the official result charts, including the chartmaker's comments, note the name of any horse that finished fast in the stretch and reached the wire not more than two lengths behind the winner. Note also horses that encountered interference of some kind but showed late speed. And horses that go off at 2 to 1 or less but finish out of the money after a poor start or interference of some kind. Play each horse each time it races again until it wins, but do not play it more than four times. Compile the list from charts of all races except jumps, two-year-old and maiden races.

Eddie Arcaro (at right) *wins the 1958 Wood Memorial on Jewel's Reward. Photo shows how narrowly horses and their riders avoid collision in the effort to get there first.*   UPI PHOTO

Bill Hartack and Gen. Duke nip Eddie Arcaro and Bold Ruler at the wire in the 1957 Everglades at Hialeah.   UPI PHOTO

Reasoning: The stout stretch finish is a splendid clue to impending victory. The alibi (see pages 179–181) is a strong plus factor in cases of this kind.

Comment: The man who introduced me to Thoroughbred racing forty-five years ago used to make a pretty penny with a follow-up system quite similar to this. In 1949, R. H. Matthews explained the present version to readers of *Turf and Sport Digest*. He published a workout covering 1,752 bets at seven tracks in a period of almost a year. The winning percentage was 23 (418 winners), and the profit was a robust 57 cents for every wagered dollar. Some of the mutuel payoffs were extraordinary—one horse paid $94.90, another $87.20, another $86.70. And so on, including dozens at 5 to 1 or better. The system beat every one of the seven meetings.

Suggestions: All this takes is patience, alertness and access to the daily result charts. Winning percentage and, I am quite sure, rate of profit would be increased by using a distance rule to avoid bets when the horse is being sent out to build its speed or stamina. In testing the method at your own track, try expanding it to include horses that show early speed and tire in the stretch. If you happen to patronize book-makers (shame on you), it pays to follow the listed horses even if they ship to out-of-town tracks.

SYSTEM 29

Principle: Play a horse that runs within four days after being scratched from a race, provided that (1) the track was fast on the day the horse was scratched and (2) the horse was assigned a post position for the race from which it was scratched and (3) the horse has been racing and working out regularly.

Reasoning: The trainer scratches the horse because a better oppor-tunity is in prospect a few days later. If he were not hoping to win with the animal, he would let it get its tightener in the earlier race and would not bother to scratch it.

Comment: A sound enough idea, limited by the inescapable fact that the wish to win and the ability to win are two different things. The post-position rule is important. Often, more entries are received than can be accommodated in a race. The extra horses are placed on an "also-eligible" list and are assigned no post positions. If one of the others is scratched, a horse is moved into the race from the also-eligible list. Therefore, a horse whose name appears on the also-eligible list may be scratched for no reason other than that the race was filled.

Suggestions: If the trainer and the horse are both consistent winners, it may be possible to work this nice little angle with no more handicapping than that. Otherwise, it will pay to make sure that the horse is properly placed as to distance, is not outclassed, has demonstrated at least a hint of improvement in its last race or two, and will enjoy the probable pace.

SYSTEM 30

Principle: Consider only horses that ran within ten days and finished out of the money. Determine the number of lengths by which each was beaten in each of its three most recent races (counting a victory as zero). Add the number of beaten lengths. Play the horse with the smallest total.

Reasoning: A horse that has been getting close to the winner, or winning itself, benefits from an easy, out-of-the-money race. If it then returns to the wars within ten days, it is in adequate physical condition. Its poor last race will inflate the mutuel price.

Comment: This is a nice angle for players sensible enough to steer away from animals that are on the downgrade.

Suggestions: Use the form factor and alibis as carefully as you can. Watch distance and class.

SYSTEM 31

Principle: Play a horse that finished fourth in its last race provided that it (1) gained at least two lengths in the stretch or (2) led or ran within a length of the leader at any call or (3) steps down at least $1,000 in claiming price.

Reasoning: The fourth-place finish, being out of the money, discourages a certain amount of public play, augmenting the odds. A horse that ran fourth after giving notice of improvement, or that steps into easier company, should never be overlooked.

Comment: Some of the best longshot systems concentrate on horses that run fourth or fifth or sixth. This one turns up winners at all sorts of prices but cannot be counted on for sustained profits without additional, protective rules.

Suggestions: As usual with systems that supposedly emphasize current condition, it pays to make sure that the horse is improving rather than deteriorating. And that it is entered in the right company at the right distance. And, of course, that the race under scrutiny took place recently enough to mean something.

SYSTEM 32

Principle: Play a horse that returned to racing after a layoff of six weeks or more and, in its first or second outing, led or ran within a half length of the leader at the first three calls, but tired in the stretch and lost.

Reasoning: The "short" horse needed that race to build its stamina and demonstrate the benefits of its freshening layoff.

Comment: A player who exercises the slightest discrimination about the pace factor should be able to make profits with this, especially at tracks that favor horses with front-running styles.

Suggestions: Make sure the horse's promising race took place within the last week or two or three. If more than a week ago, workouts are essential. It also pays to check the distance and class factors. As to pace, the player should make certain that the animal has more than enough early speed to show its heels to other front-runners that may be entered. Or else that it is the only front-runner in the field.

SYSTEM 33

Principle: Play a horse that finished out of the money but within five lengths of the winner.

Reasoning: The apparently poor finish conceals the fact that the horse was actually quite close to the winner. Good mutuels are likely.

Comment: This is a cousin of System 31. It gets enormous prices. The difficulty is that as many as four or five horses in a single field may qualify. Means of separating them are likely to become as complicated as actual handicapping, unless one decides to bet on more than one animal per race, whereupon investment costs soar.

Suggestions: It is best to demand a lot of recent action from an animal whose sole recommendation is that it finished within five lengths of the winner. Try demanding one race within eight days or a race and two workouts within two weeks. In case of a tie, favor the horse that has run within ten days or less. If still tied, try the distance factor. If still tied, go to the horse that has won the highest-class race in the past three months. If, as often happens with the kind of animals spotted by this system, none has won in three months, go to the winning jockey and finally, in desperation, to the horse that goes postward at the highest odds. When playing this system, there seldom is any sense in betting on one of its horses that goes off at less than 4 to 1. The system is meant to discover longshots and is not geared for the kind of handicapping that points out solid, relatively short-priced animals.

SYSTEM 34

Principle: Play a horse that ran out of the money in its last race, if (1) it finished not more than a length behind the second-place horse and (2) the winner of the race crossed the wire at least five lengths in front.

Reasoning: A horse that wins by five lengths or more has demonstrated unusual superiority over its field. In those circumstances, an out-of-the-money finish, a length or less behind the second-place horse, is evidence of form.

Comment: This is another longshot system that gets prices because of the failure of racing crowds to differentiate between a badly outclassed or badly conditioned horse and one that ran quite close to the leaders, even though it failed to get into the money. As usual, efforts to reduce the number of losers also reduce the number of longshots.

Suggestions: Make sure the horse is suited to today's distance, is not carrying substantially more weight than seems good for it, has been racing and working regularly, and is not stepping up in class. These grade-school rules give the system a good chance of paying off at the mutuel window, although the cherished $100 winners—and the series of fourteen consecutive losers—may be eliminated.

SYSTEM 35

Principle: Play any horse that ran as betting favorite within the past six days and finished in the money.

Reasoning: The trainer strikes while the iron is hot.

Comment: This gets a high percentage of winners, which can be increased by closer attention to the form factor.

Suggestions: Do not be afraid of a horse stepping up in class. But be careful not to risk money on overoptimistic trainers who send older horses back to the post too soon after grueling races. If the animal's last couple of races have not been the kind likely to exhaust it, its race today may well be a victory. The distance factor is unlikely to be as important as usual here, since the trainer is all-out for a win and—except in the case of an occasional incompetent—figures to place the animal properly.

SYSTEM 36

Principle: Play a horse that has been in the money in each of its last four races.

Reasoning: The horse is due.

Comment: No horse is ever "due" on these grounds alone. Furthermore, some horses, especially two- and three-year-olds, become habitual runners-up, unwilling to pass the leader. Within these limitations, the system can be used to catch a fair percentage of winners. Moreover, the prices are often not bad, possibly because the crowd tends to lose faith in horses of this type.

Suggestions: Confine play to secondary tracks, or to horses stepping down in class, or horses switched from ordinary jockeys to local or national leaders.

SYSTEM 37

Principle: Play a horse that was the favorite in its last race but lost, provided it gained in the stretch.

Reasoning: The animal wanted to run. Perhaps it was victimized by lack of racing room or a badly judged ride.

Comment: Some racegoers play every beaten favorite they can find. The advantage of this system is its usual avoidance of false favorites, the sucker horses that get the public's money after they have begun to lose their racing sharpness.

Suggestions: If the selection was entered at the wrong distance last time, expect big things today. If the last race was at the right distance, it is safest to require that the horse stay in the same class or step down a bit. Make sure that the last race was recent, or that the animal has been working out regularly. Welcome a change of riding assignments, especially if today's jockey is a leader.

Repeaters

Among the rules most familiar to system fanciers is, "Eliminate any horse that won its last race." The reason is statistical: Many horses are incapable of winning twice in succession. Yet many others win two or three or four in a row. Among the best methods of locating potential repeaters are Systems 13 and 14. Here are some other good ones.

SYSTEM 38

Principle: Play a horse that goes to the post within six days after a race in which it led at every call and won by two lengths or more.

Reasoning: The horse is hot.

Comment: Indeed it is.

Suggestions: Unless the horse gained in the stretch it is unlikely to repeat the victory in a substantially higher claiming bracket. If the top claiming price in the last race was $6,000 or less, today's should be not more than 20 percent higher. If the last race was in a higher range, the animal can step up 25 percent. An exception would be the horse that previously has won in today's class or better.

SYSTEM 39

Principle: Play a horse that won its last race "handily," "easily" or "going away" provided that (1) the race took place within ten days and (2) the horse has won at least 25 percent of its starts, finishing out of the money in fewer than half.

Reasoning: This catches good horses at the peak of their form.

Comment: Incredibly, not all the horses unearthed by this system are short-priced favorites.

Suggestions: If the horse has had ten or more races this year, it is safe to calculate its consistency on this year's record alone. Otherwise, combine this year's total with last year's. Do not attempt to use this method with two-year-olds. Somewhat bigger class rises can be permitted than in System 38. But if the animal moves from a claimer to an allowance race, do not bet on it unless it has already won in such company.

SYSTEM 40

Principle: In starter-handicap races, play the horse that has won such a race earlier in the season. If more than one qualify, pick the horse that has won the highest percentage of its starter-handicap efforts. If still tied, play the one that won a race of this kind most recently.

Reasoning: Each season a different group of trainers dominates the starter races, winning these tough races with animals that run for Sweeney in straight claimers.

Comment: This is not strictly a repeater system. The horse probably has been doing poorly since its last romp in a starter race. The mutuel prices are excellent. This system has shown an annual profit for years.

Suggestions: Ignore everything but the horse's propensity for winning this kind of race.

Favorites

Endless profits await the player able to identify 45 percent of winning favorites *before* their races. System fanciers tinker by the hour with gimmicks designed to eliminate false favorites. Here are a few wrinkles well worth studying.

SYSTEM 41

Principle: In races with a purse value of $10,000 or less for four-year-olds and up, play the favorite if (1) it has won at least 20 percent of its races this year and (2) it has won at least 20 percent of its races this year and last and (3) its list of recent performances includes at least three wins and two places, or four wins and one place, or five wins, and (4) it finished in the money in its last start, which occurred at today's track not more than eighteen days ago and (5) it has won at today's exact distance.

Reasoning: A four-, five- or six-year-old of proved consistency and fitness is the steadiest of all Thoroughbreds. This is especially true in races of less than top quality, where the competition is less severe. The system bars races open to three-year-olds only because animals of that age frequently have not yet found their proper class level: An apparently inconsistent one might actually be the class and speed of its field. A handicapper could discern this, but·the means of doing so are too complicated for inclusion in a system of this kind.

Comment: When Lawrence Lalik published this method in *American Turf Monthly,* the magazine reported that tests at Bowie, Fair Grounds and New York had produced winners in 55 to 63 percent of its selections, with profits ranging between 40 and 60 percent. Plays arise two or three times a week.

Suggestions: Females should not be backed against males. Animals that have had two hard races in succession should be avoided. Lawrence Lalik also eliminated horses that had won their three previous races and "any horses showing races at a foreign track." These two angles are worthwhile to the extent that a winner of three straight races may have overexerted itself and that a horse whose overseas races show in the past-performance list may not have done enough racing here to prove its consistency. Canadian racing is not regarded as foreign, of course.

SYSTEM 42

Principle: Play an odds-on favorite to place in any race with a purse of $10,000 or more.

Reasoning: Year in and year out, bets of this kind show a small profit.

Comment: As far as I know, this is the only kind of place or show betting on which profit is assured without resort to handicapping. The explanation is that the animals are especially good ones, less susceptible than others to sudden lapses of form. They win or finish second about two thirds of the time. The place prices are customarily wretched, but perk up a bit when the place pool is shared with backers of a longshot.

Suggestions: Unless yours is a track of authentically major caliber, you had better test this on the few races of $10,000 value that were run there last season. In my experience, odds-on favorites are most reliable at New York, California, Illinois, Maryland, New Jersey and Delaware.

SYSTEM 43

Principle: When the track is sloppy, play a front-running horse that goes to the post as favorite.

Reasoning: Front-runners have a special advantage in the slop.

Comment: This is a particularly good bet for a player equipped to do a bit of handicapping on matters like distance, class and pace.

Suggestions: If the horse happens to qualify under one of the other systems concerned with favorites, it can be supported with considerable confidence. Otherwise, the player should see whether the animal is the only apparently fit front-runner in the field. In case another seems capable of running with it, and there is doubt about the favorite's staying power in such circumstances, the next factor to examine is class. If the favorite is moving up in class and does not seem completely capable of surviving early competition for the lead, pass the race.

SYSTEM 44

Principle: Play a favorite if (1) it is male, (2) it raced not more than five days ago and (3) it won the race.

Reasoning: It may still be at peak form.

Comment: In 1956, *Turf and Sport Digest* reported a fifteen-month test, covering about 2,800 races at all major tracks. This simple system yielded a profit of 13 cents on every wagered dollar.

Suggestions: A test at your track might produce considerably higher paper profits, but less action, if play were confined to animals that won their last races easily, handily, or going away. It also would be worthwhile to see how four-year-olds and older horses did after hard stretch drives in their two latest races.

SYSTEM 45

Principle: If the favorite did not win its last race, or goes to the post at odds higher than even money, play the second choice in the betting, provided that (1) it is male and (2) it won its last race within the last five days (ten days if today's purse is $10,000 or higher).

Reasoning: The crowd's second choice wins about one race in five. This means that, in almost two races on an "average" afternoon, the crowd overestimates the favorite's winning chances by comparison with those of its second choice. This system directs the player to a kind of race in which the crowd errs rather frequently.

Comment: Jud Onatsirt, who also devised System 44, reported a six-month test of this one. It cranked out a 55 percent profit. Plays occurred at the rate of about two a week at major tracks. In combination with 44, this system is as simple and rewarding as any purely mechanical selection method I have ever seen.

Suggestions: I can think of no reason why Systems 44 and 45 should not work as effectively nowadays as they did in the 1950's. Try them on your own circuit.

Speed

Conventional speed handicapping is as mechanical as any predigested system, demanding nothing of the player but willingness to follow rules. Because those rules require a good deal of time and patience, many speed fanciers prefer to take their chances with systems which quickly single out the fastest horse in the race. Hundreds of methods are in circulation. The following are quite useful, especially in sprints. Avoid wet weather and grass races.

SYSTEM 46

Principle: Among horses whose last races were at today's track, note the three that earned the highest "Form" speed ratings at today's exact distance within the past thirty days. Play the animal that earned the rating in a higher class and/or when carrying more weight than today's. In case of a tie, favor the horse that drops the most weight.

Reasoning: If it is still in decent shape, the horse should be able to run at least as well under today's more favorable conditions.

Comment: The effectiveness of this sort of thing depends greatly on the kind of racing programmed at the individual track. A four-week test of claiming races for three-year-olds and up should show whether the method warrants further study on your own home grounds. One of the strong merits of the system by comparison with most speed-rating methods, is that it concedes the possibility of victory by a higher-class horse over a cheaper one, even though the cheaper may show a higher speed rating.

Suggestions: There is little reason to expect help from this system in allowance or handicap or stakes races. Also, be careful of animals that have not raced or worked out with recent regularity.

SYSTEM 47

Principle: Consider any horse entered in a claiming race that earned a 90 while finishing fourth or better in one of its two most recent starts. Also note any horse that earned an 85 or better while finishing in the money in one of its two most recent starts. If more than two qualify, play the horse that won or finished closest to the winner in its good race. Break any remaining tie by playing the horse whose good race was most recent.

Reasoning: At most tracks, speed ratings of this kind are the marks of able claiming horses.

Comment: This would be best at secondary tracks, where most of the action for claiming prices is at six furlongs and the animals race frequently.

Suggestions: Addition of distance and late-action rules could make a solid winner of this one, especially if play were limited to sprints and no horse were expected to win in company more than $500 more expensive than it had beaten at some time in the past three months.

SYSTEM 48

Principle: In races no longer than six furlongs, find the highest speed rating earned by each horse when running at today's exact distance in the past month. Add or subtract 1 point for each three pounds of difference between today's weight and the weight carried in the rated race. If the horse goes with lighter weight today, add the difference. If the horse carries more weight today, subtract the difference, Play the horse with the highest net figure.

Reasoning: Many speed handicappers do little more than this.

Comment: Dorcus and DaSilva, who gave us System 1, recorded profits of almost 50 cents on the dollar in lengthy workouts with this one at

Hollywood Park and Aqueduct. Prices were not large, but more than 40 percent of the choices won.

Suggestions: In using speed to make selections in dashes for two-year-olds, there is no need to bother about weights.

SYSTEM 49

Principle: Add the running positions of each horse at the pre-stretch and stretch calls of its last two races. Play the horse with the lowest total.

Reasoning: The horse closest to the front during the middle stages of its last two races is certain to be in contention today.

Comment: Best suited to the speedy tracks of California and Illinois and some of the half-milers, which favor front-runners. Gets good mutuels sometimes.

Suggestions: Addition of simple form and distance rules ought to make this a profitable system at certain tracks.

SYSTEM 50

Principle: Among horses that finished in the money within the past week, play the one that has earned the highest speed rating in a race of today's exact distance on the present circuit during the past three months. If a tie, play the one that carried the highest weight when earning the top rating.

Reasoning: A horse that races twice in a week is physically fit and might show its previously superior speed.

Comment: The seven-day rule saves this one. A bit of attention to the class factor would help, too.

Suggestions: The system lends itself to experimentation. More detailed examination of current condition would permit play on horses other than those that have run in seven days.

SYSTEM 51

Principle: To the highest speed rating earned by each horse during the past thirty days, add 1/100 of the claiming price for which

it was entered, and add the weight it carried. Play the horse with the highest total.

Reasoning: Speed, weight and class are the bases of many successful handicapping procedures.

Comment: This one gets winners. Because it disdains distance and form, some of the winners pay high prices, but long strings of losers are a positive certainty.

Suggestions: It would be fun to see what combinations and modifications of distance, form, consistency and jockey rules might shorten the losing streaks without eliminating all the longshots.

SYSTEM 52

Principle: Play the horse that has earned the highest speed rating in the past sixty days, provided the rating was earned in a higher-class race than any in which the other horses earned their highest speed ratings during that period.

Reasoning: The class edge and the superior speed rating make a formidable combination.

Comment: This one should earn profits at most tracks, but not until condition and distance rules are added.

Suggestions: The horse should be suited to the distance and should have offered a hint of form in its last race or two. If the rider is a local or national leader or has won with the animal in the past, the bet might be well worth making.

SYSTEM 53

Principle: Among the three entrants that have earned the highest speed ratings in the past month, play the one that (1) has won at least 20 percent of its races during this year and last, (2) has had two races, or a race and two workouts, or three workouts in the last eleven days, and (3) has won at today's distance when entered at a claiming price not more than $1,000 below the price at which it is entered today.

Reasoning: This is comprehensive enough for relative safety, yet permits good mutuel prices by directing the player to animals that may have been running indifferent races at odd distances and at lower claiming prices in their most recent starts.

Comment: The heavy late action and the horse's established ability at the distance make this a more substantial method than most of its kind.

Suggestions: In case of ties, try to use the jockey factor for separation purposes.

Jockeys

Followers of jockeys learn in time that it is a good idea to pay some attention to the horses which the young men ride. Almost any of the more solid systems in this chapter will suffice. And here are a few others designed expressly for the purpose.

SYSTEM 54

Principle: Play one of the five leading jockeys at the current meeting when he rides a horse that (1) lost its last race, (2) finished in the money in at least one of its latest three attempts, (3) has won 20 percent of its starts this year and last combined, and (4) raced not more than ten days ago.

Reasoning: A fit, consistent horse that lost its last race should go off at better-than-usual odds today.

Comment: The good prices obtainable with some of the choices of this system would not be sacrificed by addition of a distance rule. Moreover, a player familiar with the fluctuations of Thoroughbred form could safely relax the ten-day rule.

Suggestions: Break ties by going to the higher-class animal.

SYSTEM 55

Principle: Play a horse that lost its last race provided that (1) the jockey has won with it at today's exact distance but in better company than today's and (2) the jockey is either a national leader or ranks among the top riders at the current meeting.

Reasoning: This is another fairly reasonable effort to get occasionally higher mutuels than one might expect when a leading jockey is aboard a class horse.

Comment: Recent races and workouts would make this more reassuring and, in fact, would permit elimination of the rule requiring a leading rider.

Suggestions: Note how often horses of this type come to life when switched from an apprentice or a rank-and-file journeyman to a leading reinsman or one who has won with the animal in the past.

SYSTEM 56

Principle: Play the horse listed at lowest odds in the track program's morning line, provided that it is ridden by one of the two leading jockeys of the meeting.

Reasoning: Hot jockey, hot horse.

Comment: The morning-line favorite does not always turn out to be the public's choice, but seldom pays better than 5 to 2. The stinginess of the odds are compensated by a good winning percentage.

Suggestions: The player may not believe that the jockeys listed at the head of the official "leading riders" tabulation are the best on the grounds. And he is probably correct. If he prefers, he can use the two jocks with the highest winning averages, or the two whom he regards most highly. But, since trainers tend to assign their best horses to the riders with the best reputations, the player had better not depart too far from that group.

Tote-Board Systems

The handicapper usually gains confidence in his bet when he notices significant tote-board activity on the horse. Certain system players omit the handicapping and look for omens on the tote board. Here are some of the more sensible systems that depend on betting trends.

SYSTEM 57

Principle: Using any reliable selection method, favor one of the top five horses in the race when the tote board shows that disproportionately high sums are being bet on it to win, by comparison with what is being bet on it to place or show.

Reasoning: Horsemen do not fool around with place and show betting. When they bet, they bet to win.

Comment: If the bets on a horse account for 20 percent of the win pool and only 15 percent of the place pool, it is obvious that someone is loading up on the front end. Indeed, if the place bets account for 17 percent of that pool a similar supposition is warranted. The only time place or show bets should be high in proportion to win bets is when the horse is odds-on. In such circumstances, lots of money, smart and otherwise, goes on place and show tickets.

Suggestions: If you like the horse and notice even slight overactivity in the win pool, it is safe to assume that some big bettors also like the horse. It is more than merely conceivable that these bettors include the owner and trainer and those who follow their tips.

SYSTEM 58

Principle: Bet on a horse whose tote-board odds a minute before post-time are less than 50 percent of the odds given in the track's morning line.

Reasoning: If the track handicapper thought the horse would go off at 8 to 1 and the crowd makes it 4 to 1, some smart money is on the animal.

Comment: The morning line is an effort by the track to forecast the final odds. At many tracks, the job is done by clerks with no particular qualifications. Moreover, late scratches can undermine even the canniest morning line. And so can the predictions of newspaper handicappers and tip sheets and the effects of wild rumor.

Suggestions: If none of the four top morning-line contenders is scratched, and if the track morning line is relatively competent, you can assume that a horse bet down to half of the morning odds is thought to be alive and well. If you plan to risk money on these suppositions, the best chances of profit lie in confining play to animals listed at 8 to 1 or less in the morning line.

SYSTEM 59

Principle: Bet on a horse that lost its last race and steps up in class today but goes to the post at lower odds than in the cheaper, losing race.

Reasoning: The insiders must have a coup cooking.

Comment: Ordinarily such a horse should be running at higher odds today. If the player's handicapping suggests that the animal is in shape, the lower odds may indeed be a sign of inside action.

Suggestions: Don't bother with this unless you have confidence in your handicapping.

SYSTEM 60

Principle: If one horse is heavily bet and its odds fall below 8 to 5, any horse whose odds do not rise is worth backing.

Reasoning: When the odds on the favorite drop, the odds on the other horses should rise. If the 4 to 1 or 5 to 1 shot holds steady when the favorite drops from 5 to 2 to 7 to 5, you know that many people have been buying tickets on the longer-priced animal.

Comment: Again, good handicapping is the key. If the favorite looks to you like a sucker horse, and you like the other, the steadiness of its odds are an indication that other smart players feel the same way.

Suggestions: Nothing but grief awaits the person who plays this system without bothering to examine the records of the horses.

SYSTEM 61

Principle: In the second race of the day, play a horse on which proportionately more money was bet in the daily double than is being bet in the win pool of the race.

Reasoning: Rather than drive down the odds on his entrant in the second race, many a trainer or owner buys daily-double tickets on it. After the first race, the track posts the mutuel price that the double will pay on each horse in the second race. If the daily-double price on a horse is lower than it should be, considering the odds at which the horse is held in the win pool of the race itself, somebody must have plunged on the double.

Comment: Such things happen. If the stable holds a sufficient number of daily-double tickets which couple its horse with the winner of the first race, and if the daily-double price is right, the boys can sweeten the profit with only modest bets on the win end. Modest bets at high odds. This is preferable to betting a wad on the horse, driving the odds down, and collecting peanuts later.

Veterinarian takes saliva sample for chemical testing.

Secretariat, voted Horse of the Year as a two-year-old in 1972, wins the Hopeful Stakes under Ron Turcotte at Saratoga.   NYRA (BOB COGLIANESE)

Suggestions: Two minutes before post-time for the second race, divide the posted daily-double price on each horse by the latest toteboard quotation. Thus, if the daily-double price is $200 and the present odds against the horse are 20 to 1, the answer would be 10. If the daily-double price on another entrant is $24 and the odds against it to win the second race are 2 to 1, the answer in its case is 12. Clearly, the longshot was heavily backed in the daily double. Horses of this kind win once in a while. Not often enough to show a profit, however. The time to bet one is when its record offers some explanation for the vigor with which people bet on it in the double.

Public Selectors

Thousands of systems handicap the newspaper handicappers. Starting with the assumption that a good public selector, or a consensus of several, names horses with legitimate chances to win, the systems deploy simple handicapping procedures in an attempt to avoid the losers. Some of these systems produce lengthy strings of winners at low prices. Like other systems, they perform best when the track is fast.

SYSTEM 62

Principle: Play the "Form" consensus choice in an allowance, handicap or stakes race, provided that the horse (1) has won a third of its races since the beginning of last year and (2) either was in the money in its last race or lost by not more than two lengths and (3) has been in the money in at least five of its last seven races and (4) carries not more than 124 pounds, unless the race is a weight-for-age stakes.

Reasoning: Not only do the experts like it, but it clearly is an outstanding Thoroughbred.

Comment: A system like this hits few losers, and few payoffs above $4. Profits are possible.

Suggestions: Beware of cheaper allowance races at secondary tracks.

SYSTEM 63

Principle: Play the consensus ("Form") choice, provided that it has had a race and one workout within seven days.

Reasoning: A high proportion of winners have had a race and a workout in seven days. When the racing paper's consensus favors a horse with those qualifications, it ought to have a splendid chance.

Comment: This system has been around for years. It finds about one play a day at a typical major track, and is quite reliable.

Suggestions: Test it at your own track.

SYSTEM 64

Principle: Play "Trackman's" best bet of the day whenever the "Form" consensus selection (1) is another horse and (2) is picked by another selector as his best bet.

Reasoning: The racing paper representative known as Trackman is on the scene, where the racing is. Also, he often is a topnotch handicapper. If the consensus picks another horse and, moreover, that horse is highly enough regarded to be the best bet of some selector other than Trackman, better-than-usual payoffs reward Trackman's winning choice.

Comment: The logic is flawless. The system produces profits if the player does a little handicapping of his own.

Suggestions: At the very least, apply some consistency rules. Also, it helps to insist on a winning rider.

SYSTEM 65

Principle: Bet the consensus choice when no other horse in the field has raced more recently or is more consistent or has earned a higher speed rating in its last three races.

Reasoning: Consistency, fitness, overall speed and the high regard of experts should produce winners.

Comment: Do not be surprised if this one produces seven or eight short-priced winners in succession—at the rate of one play every ten days or so.

Suggestions: Try a prolonged dry run at your own track.

SYSTEM 66

Principle: Play any horse named by Trackman, provided that no other "Form" selector picks it to finish in the money.

Reasoning: Trackman has the advantage of being there every day to see the animals with his own eyes. If he thinks that a horse has improved enough to get part of a purse, and if no other selector thinks so, the odds may be magnificent.

Comment: The same idea can be applied to the choices of any other competent public selector. Prices are excellent, profits nil—unless the player does some handicapping.

Suggestions: On a casual outing to the track, this kind of play is easy fun.

SYSTEM 67

Principle: Play any horse picked to win by all selectors listed in the "Form" consensus.

Reasoning: Such unanimity must be deserved.

Comment: This system will lose little in the long haul.

Suggestions: A good way to sharpen your skills is to study the past-performance records of horses that lose after being chosen by this system. Also note the kind of animals that beat them. Do not expect a pattern to emerge quickly, but pay special attention to the effects of high weight in distance races and long layoffs in allowance races.

SYSTEM 68

Principle: Using a graded handicap such as that of "Hermis" or "Sweep," determine whether it predicts odds of 3 to 1 or higher on its first choice in the first and/or second race of the day. If so, cross out such a horse or horses. Now buy nine daily-double tickets which pair the top three remaining choices in the first race with the remaining top three in the second.

Reasoning: A horse held so lightly that the handicapper thinks it may go off at 3 to 1 is a good candidate for defeat. Pairing the other top animals in the double is an excellent way to hit a stout mutuel in circumstances of this kind.

Comment: If you insist on playing the double, this is as good a way as any.

Suggestions: Another comparatively plausible approach is to use any of the other systems in this chapter and, after three horses are found in each race, pair them in every possible combination—an $18 investment.

SYSTEM 69

Principle: Clip the "Horses to Watch" column which appears in the "Form" on Mondays. Play each horse three times or until it wins—whichever occurs sooner.

Reasoning: These are tips from chart-callers, clockers and other experts.

Comment: Profits are conceivable for a player who makes sure the animals are properly placed.

Suggestions: Do a dry run in which no paper bet is made unless the horse has had a race or a workout within a week, is entered at a suitable distance, and is assigned a leading jockey.

SYSTEM 70

Principle: Play any "Form" consensus choice that rates at least 25 points above the consensus second choice in the race, provided that the top choice (1) was favorite in its last race but lost, or (2) won its last race.

Reasoning: Only formidable animals achieve large margins in the consensus. A beaten favorite must be especially well placed to merit such esteem. The same is true of a horse that won its last race.

Comment: Lots of long winning streaks, the profits from which are annulled by only a few losers.

Suggestions: The remarks made in connection with System 67 apply here as well.

Arithmetical Systems

I now offer some methods that require paper work. The more elaborate are comprehensive enough to qualify as legitimate handicapping procedures. The reader may find one a pleasant way station between straight system play and independent handicapping.

SYSTEM 71

In 1964, Robert Rowe offered *American Turf Monthly* followers a selection method in which weighted percentages reflected the relative
importance of each handicapping factor. It was not the first system of
its kind (I have seen a few that employed algebraic equations), but it is
by far the simplest and most sensible. It takes time but is logical and
orderly enough to fall well within the grasp of any player.

Rowe recommended that the system be used only on fields of seven
or fewer horses, where the purse was at least $5,000. The limitation on
the size of the field saves work, and the minimum purse size strength-
ens the possibility that the system's choice will be a good, reliable
animal.

The procedure applies the following table of values:

Current Condition	25%
Class	20
Consistency	15
Sex	10
Weights	6
Jockey	6
Distance	6
Liking for Track Condition	6
Age	6

The player deals with the race as if he were an old-time bookmaker.
He works up booking percentages proportionate to the winning
chances of each horse. He begins with the statistically valid assumption that, until further information arises, each horse must be granted
an equal chance to win. In a five-horse field, therefore, each horse
would have one chance in five. The natural odds against it would be 4
to 1, expressed in a percentage figure of 20. In a six-horse field, the
percentage would be 17 per horse (obtained by dividing the number of
horses into 100). The player's worksheet for a five-horse field would
now look like this:

A	20%
B	20
C	20
D	20
E	20

From here on, the player decides which horses qualify as contenders
in terms of each handicapping factor. If, for example, he feels that
three of the five have shown positive signs of winning condition, he
credits each of the three and penalizes the other two. Condition, as

shown above, is worth 25 percent in this method. If three horses are in condition, each is awarded 8 percentage points—its share of the 25. The two animals that seem to be out of condition are each penalized by 12 points—25 divided by 2.

The list now has changed:

```
A ..................... 28%
B ..................... 28
C ..................... 28
D .....................  8
E .....................  8
```

Note that the sum of the percentages remains 100, or close to it. Therefore, the percentage finally earned by each horse is an approximation of its actual chance in the race. Whether it is a good approximation or not depends entirely on how carefully and knowingly the player appraises the animals in terms of each handicapping factor.

Rowe suggested that the class, consistency and weight factors should be handled as follows:

Class: Add the total earnings of the field, using this year's and last year's records. Divide the sum by the number of horses in the field, producing an average. Horses with earnings above the average are the class of the field. Divide the 20 points among them. Each horse below the average is penalized by whatever number of points represents its share of the 20. Thus, if Horses "A" and "C" were regarded as the class of the race, each would get 10 points, whereas 7 each would be taken from "B," "D," and "E." The list would now look like this:

```
A ..................... 38%
B ..................... 21
C ..................... 38
D .....................  1
E .....................  1
```

Consistency: Add all starts made by the entrants this year. Divide by the total number of times they have run in the money. Use the resultant average as in handling the class factor.

Weight: Add the weights assigned to the horses, and determine the average weight by dividing the number of entrants into the total. Horses carrying less than the average get credit. Those above the average are penalized.

If all entrants are male or female, no adjustment is made on grounds of sex. But if there were a female in a five-horse field, she would be penalized 10 points, and each of the others would get 2. Similar procedures would subtract 6 points from the only three-year-old running against older horses, or 3 points from each of two three-year-olds in such a fix. Another 6 points might be redistributed if one or more of the entrants were ridden by other than leading jockeys, or if one or more were a sprinter entered in a route race or a router in a sprint, or if the track were muddy and some of the horses were uncomfortable on such footing.

Rowe postulates a situation in which the final figures make "A" best with 41 percent, followed by "B" with 22. He suggests that the player calculate each horse's proper odds on the basis of these percentages, but allowing a fat 20 percent for take and breakage. Thus, assuming that the betting pool has been reduced to 80 percent, of which 41 represents "A's" chances, the proper odds against the animal's victory become 39 to 41—or almost exactly even money. The odds against "B" are 58 to 22, or 3 to 1.

The player should not, says Rowe, regard "A" as a good bet if the crowd sends it to the post at less than 3 to 1! Indeed, if "A" goes off at 5 to 2, and "B" at 10 to 1, the horse to bet is "B." Only by waiting until the actual odds are at least 200 percent better than those calculated by the system can the player be sure of having the percentages on his side, argues Rowe.

It's all a matter of individual taste, really. A player is unlikely to worry too much about the odds on any single bet if his handicapping cranks out a satisfactory percentage of winners at prices large enough to produce a comfortable profit. For such a player, some horses are worth backing at 2 to 5, and others are a waste of money at 20 to 1. The real merit of the Rowe system and, in fact, of all the others in this chapter, is not in its rules but in the concepts from which the rules develop. I imagine that the only unchangeable part of this system is the business of assigning each horse an equal percentage chance of winning, and then increasing or diminishing that chance according to values found in the horse's record.

Surely, many readers will prefer to modify every other rule of the system, especially the handicapping procedures used on each factor. In doing so, and testing the results, the experimenter will not only refine his handicapping skills but take a huge step toward developing a winning method that bears his own imprint.

SYSTEM 72

In 1958, Robert Saunders Dowst, the daddy of class-consistency handicapping and the first purveyor of betting advice to reach the general public with books and articles, published an extremely simple rating system in *American Turf Monthly*. It went like this.

Class: If the horse has never raced in a claimer, give it a 1. If it has raced in a mixture of claimers and non-claimers, give it a 2. If it has raced only in claimers, it gets 3.

Consistency: Winning average is calculated on the basis of ten or more races run this year. If the horse has been in fewer than ten this year, use this year's and last year's totals together. An animal that has won 70 percent of its races gets 1. For 40 to 70 percent, 2. For 20 to 40 percent, 3. For less than 20 percent, 4.

Using the same minimum number of starts, the player then computes the percentage of races in which the horse has finished in the money. The same percentages and point awards are used.

Weights: Using the Jockey Club Scale of Weights, add to each horse's assigned weight whatever sex and age allowances it should be getting on the scale. Horses whose adjusted weights fall into the middle range of the field get 2 points. Horses carrying a good deal less get 1. Horses carrying much more—giving as much as eight pounds to members of the middle group—get 3.

Form: Obvious non-contenders that have not been in contention for months get 3. Horses that have run poorly in their recent starts, but have done better in the past get 2. Everything else gets 1. Dowst was never much of a believer in form. He thought that class and consistency told the real story.

Picking the Winner: Add the five figures. Play the horse with the lowest total, provided it is not a female running against males.

The best bets are horses that earn ratings of 9 or less. A player who cares to jigger around with this system—especially in an effort to make it more realistic about the importance of current condition—should be able to hit a satisfactory percentage of winners with it.

SYSTEM 73

A fascinating, highly workable basis for almost any selection system starts with the assumption that a second-place finisher in a twelve-horse field has accomplished more than a second-place finisher in a smaller field. When the class of the race is incorporated into this idea, ratings can be assigned.

The system assumes that a winner deserves a rating of 100, regardless of the size of the field it may have beaten. The following ratings are used for other horses:

Horses in Race	Finish Position												
	2	3	4	5	6	7	8	9	10	11	12	13	14
5	67	43	25	0									
6	71	50	33	20	0								
7	75	56	40	27	17	0							
8	78	60	45	33	23	14	0						
9	80	64	50	38	29	20	13	0					
10	82	67	54	43	33	25	18	11	0				
11	83	70	57	47	38	29	22	16	10	0			
12	85	72	60	50	41	33	26	20	14	9	0		
13	87	74	63	53	44	37	29	24	17	12	8	0	
14	89	76	65	55	46	40	31	27	19	14	11	7	0

After eliminating any horse entered at an unsuitable distance or clearly unready to win, the player assigns each a class rating based on the price at which it was entered when it ran its best race at today's distance during the past month or two. If it was entered at $4,000, the class rating would be 400. If another was entered at $3,750, its class rating would be 375.

The second step is to use the chart of finishing positions and field sizes to modify the class rating. For example, if the animal entered at $4,000 in its good race ran third in a nine-horse field on that day, its rating would be 400 + 64 = 464. If the $3,750 horse ran second in a field of ten, its rating would be 375 + 82 = 457.

A logical sequence of additional steps might be:

1. Calculate winning percentage this year, or this year plus last, and add it to the rating.

2. Calculate percentage of starts in the money and add it to the rating.

3. Calculate average earnings per start and add it.

4. Add the speed rating earned in the good race.

5. Add 5 points for each plus factor (See Chapter 16).

6. Add or subtract the difference between today's weight and the poundage that the horse carried in its good race.

7. Add 2 points for each workout and 4 points for each race in the past two weeks.

Players unwilling to rely on their own evaluations of the distance factor could remain in the ball game by rating only those animals that have run in the money at today's distance, or at a distance within half a furlong of today's. Those who prefer mechanical rules to personal analysis of the form factor could survive by rating the horse's three most recent races, and adding the total, provided that the latest race

had taken place not more than two weeks ago and all three had occurred in the past month.

SYSTEM 74

**Here is a simple, arithmetical method which catches a fair per-
centage of winners in wide-open races among animals of indifferent consistency and obscure current form. It is especially useful during the first weeks of the Florida and New York seasons,
when each field includes horses that have not raced recently at
the local track:**

1. Eliminate all entrants except those whose last races took place at
today's track within the past nine days, at today's distance or shorter.

2. Now eliminate all those that did not finish within five lengths of
the winner of that recent, local race.

3. Assign each remaining contender a class rating equal to $\frac{1}{100}$ of the
price at which it was entered in that latest race. A horse entered at
$7,500 would get a rating of 75. A horse entered at $4,250 would get a
rating of 43. A horse entered at $10,500 rates 105.

4. To the class rating add ten times the number of lengths each horse
gained in the stretch of its race. If a horse gained 3½ lengths, add 35.
If it gained 2¼ lengths, add 23. If it gained 1¾ lengths, add 18.

5. If a horse led at the stretch call and won its race while increasing
its lead, multiply its winning margin by ten and add that to the class
rating. Do not use the stretch-gain figure for a horse of that kind.

6. If a horse led at the stretch call and *lost* ground in the stretch,
multiply its margin at the stretch call by ten and add that to the class
rating.

7. If the horse carries more weight today than in its last race, deduct
the number of extra pounds from the rating. If the horse carries less
weight, add the number of pounds.

8. Play the horse with the highest rating.

Players who wish to take on animals whose last races were at longer
distances than today's can do so by using Item 6 above, especially if
the horse ran at seven furlongs last time and today's race is at six, or if
the horse ran at a mile and an eighth last time and goes at a mile today.
If today's distance is more than a furlong shorter than the distance of
the last race, the player should make sure that the horse is properly
placed. If it has never run a good race at today's distance, it should be
eliminated.

In claiming races which produce no play for this system, System 6 works especially well. Look it up.

SYSTEM 75

Here is one for players who have copies of "The American Racing Manual." Without requiring the player to do any handicapping of his own, it puts him on the consistent horse, trainer and jockey.

Obtain the following figures:

1. The horse's percentage of victories in all its starts this year and last.

2. The horse's in-the-money percentage this year and last (combined).

3. The jockey's current winning average, as shown in the official track tabulation of leading riders at the meeting. If the jockey is not listed, eliminate the horse.

4. The jockey's winning average last year, as shown in *The American Racing Manual*.

5. The trainer's current winning average, as shown in the official track tabulation of leading trainers at the meeting. Eliminate any horse whose trainer is not listed.

6. The trainer's winning average last year, as shown in *The American Racing Manual*.

7. Add all the percentages. Play the animal with the largest total.

The player who confines play to animals with a recent race and with proved ability at today's distance will be rewarded with a high percentage of winners. If he adds 5 points for each plus factor shown in the horse's record (see Chapter 16), results will improve even more.

SYSTEM 76

Now comes one of the oldest of all systems. It commands undying loyalty among thousands of players throughout the country.

1. Look at the horse's finishing position in each of its last three races. Give it 30 points for each victory, 20 points for a second, and 10 for a third. Anything worse than third gets no credit.

2. Add the points.

3. Subtract the total from today's assigned weight.

4. Play the horse with the lowest net figure.

This system improves when the player eliminates horses that have not raced within three weeks (a month for stakes and handicap animals), and is careful to demand a recent workout of any horse that has not raced in twelve days or more. Another great help is a rule confining play to animals that have proved their ability at today's distance. A search for plus factors also boosts profits.

SYSTEM 77

This, the last but not the least useful of our systems, gets upward of 40 percent winners for anyone patient enough to use it. Not more than two plays a week will be found. Most of the choices are favorites, although a surprisingly high mutuel occurs every now and again.

Play is confined to high-class races with purses in excess of $10,000. Races for two-year-olds are not suitable.

Contenders are picked on the following bases:

1. Qualify the three entrants that earned the highest speed ratings in their last outings. If two or more tie and you find yourself with more than three horses, no harm is done.

2. Qualify any other horse if it has won a third of all its races this year and last.

To separate the contenders, award points as follows:

1. Two points for a winning average of 20 percent in all races this year and last.

2. Two points for finishing in the money in half of all races this year and last.

3. Two points to each contender whose average earnings per start are among the top three averages in the field. Compute average earnings on the basis of total races this year and last.

4. Two points to any contender that has finished in the money in each race for which a running line is shown in the past-performance record. Do not count races run over off-tracks.

5. One point to any contender that has been out of the money not more than twice in the races listed in the record.

6. One point to the contender that has run in the most stakes races at major tracks. If a tie, award a point to each horse involved in the tie.

7. One point to any contender that has finished in the money in two of its last three races.

8. One point to the contender or contenders that ran on the most recent date.

9. One point to any contender that worked out yesterday.

10. One point to the contender or contenders that have gone to the post as favorites most often in the past four months.

11. One point to each contender for every race it has won when ridden by today's jockey. Three points to the contender ridden by the leading jockey at the current meeting, or by a recognized national leader.

12. One point to the contender chosen as winner by the "Form" consensus. Two points if named as Consensus Best Bet.

13. One point to each contender for each plus factor, as explained in Chapter 16.

14. Play the horse with the highest total. In case of tie, pass the race, or play the tied horse that goes postward at 5 to 2 or better.

The seventy-seven systems described in this chapter are food for years of recreational thought. Some will win money as is. Others need tinkering to bring them into phase with the individual track and the individual temperament. Thousands of variations are possible. Have fun.

19

The Rules of Racing

The rules of the sport vary slightly, but insignificantly, from state to state. Here are the rules of the Jockey Club of New York.

PART I.
Definitions and Interpretations

1. A recognized meeting is:

(a) A meeting held with the sanction of the Commission upon a race course operated by a duly licensed Association, for the time and at the place where such meeting is licensed to be held.

(b) A meeting held in other portions of the United States, or in any foreign country, with the sanction of any turf authority whose jurisdiction over racing of any nature is recognized by The Jockey Club and which gives effect to sentences imposed by The Jockey Club upon those guilty of improper turf practices.

2. An "Association" is a person, or persons, or a corporate body, conducting a recognized meeting.

3. A "Horse" includes mare, gelding, colt and filly.

4. A horse is "bred" at the place of his birth.

5. The age of a horse is reckoned as beginning on the first of January in the year in which he is foaled.

6. A "Maiden" is a horse which, at the time of starting, has never won a race on the flat in any country.

7. A "Race" includes a stake, a purse, a sweepstakes, a private sweepstakes, a match or an overnight event, but does not include a steeplechase or hurdle race.

8. A "Purse" is a race for money or other prize to which the owners of the horses engaged do not contribute.

9. A "Sweepstakes" is a race in which stakes are to be made by the owners of the horses engaged, and it is still a sweepstakes when money or other prize is added, but, within the meaning of this rule, no overnight race, whatever its conditions, shall be considered to be a sweepstakes.

10. A "Private Sweepstakes" is one to which no money or other prize is added and which, previous to closing, has not been advertised, either by publication, or by circular, or entry blank, or in any other way.

11. A "Match" is a race between two horses the property of two different owners on terms agreed upon by them and to which no money, or other prize, is added; it is void if either party dies.

12. An "Overnight Race" is one for

which the entries close seventy-two hours (exclusive of Sundays), or less, before the time set for the first race of the day on which such race is to be run.

13. A "Handicap" is a race in which the weights to be carried by the horses are adjusted by the handicapper for the purpose of equalizing their chances of winning.

14. A "Free Handicap" is one in which no liability is incurred for entrance money, stake or forfeit, until acceptance of the weight, either directly or through omission to declare out.

15. A "Highweight Handicap" is one in which the top weight shall not be less than 140 pounds.

16. A "Post Race" is one in which the subscribers declare, at the usual time before a race for declaring to start, the horse or horses they are to run, without limitations of choice other than that prescribed by the rules of racing or the conditions of the race.

17. A "Produce" Race is one to be run for by the produce of horses named or described at the time of entry.

18. An untried horse is one whose produce are maidens.

19. (a) A "Claiming Race" is one in which every horse running therein may be claimed in conformity to the rules.

(b) An "Optional Claiming Race" is a race restricted to horses entered to be claimed for a stated claiming price and to those which have started previously for that claiming price or less. In the case of horses entered to be claimed in such a race, the race will be considered, for the purposes of these rules, a claiming race.

20. The "Nominator" is the person in whose name a horse is entered for a race.

21. "Owner" includes part owner or lessee, and singular words include the plural, except where the context otherwise requires.

22. The "Breeder" of a horse is the owner of his dam at the time of foaling.

23. (a) An "Authorized Agent" is a person appointed by a document, accompanied by a fee of $1, signed by the owner and lodged annually at the office of The Jockey Club and approved by it, or if for a single meeting only, with the Clerk of the Course for transmission to The Jockey Club.

(b) An authorized agent may appoint a Sub-Agent only when authorized so to do by the document lodged as above and when the appointment approved by The Jockey Club, of the Sub-Agent is lodged as above, accompanied by a fee of $1.

Rule 24 (a) and (b). (Stricken out.)

25. "Weight for Age" means standard weight according to these Rules. A "weight for age" race is one in which all horses carry weight according to the scale without penalties or allowances.

26. A "Walkover" is when two horses in entirely different interests do not run for a race.

27. The publications of The Jockey Club are the Racing Calendar and the Stud Book, and such other publications as hereafter may be designated by The Jockey Club.

PART II.
Calculation of Time

28. (a) When the last day for doing anything under these Rules falls on a Sunday, it may be done on the following Monday, unless a race to which such act relates is appointed for that day, in which case it must be done on the previous Saturday.

(b) "A month" means a calendar month; "a day" means twenty-four hours.

PART III.
Regulations for Race Meetings

29. After May 31st in each year, only four overnight events for a distance less than a mile for horses three years old and upwards shall be given on any race day, except upon approval by the Stewards.

30. After June 30th in each year, there shall be no race less than five furlongs.

31. The number of starters in overnight races shall be limited by the width of the track at the starting post, the maximum

number to be determined by the Stewards. The number of starters in such overnight races, except handicaps, shall be reduced to the proper number by lot, or by division, also by lot, of the race, at the option of the Association. The division of overnight handicaps shall be made by the Racing Secretary in his entire discretion.

32. By permission of the Stewards of The Jockey Club, races may be run over a race course other than the one over which they have been announced to be run.

33. (a) If a horse runs at any unrecognized meeting, he is disqualified for all races to which these rules apply.

(b) Any person owning, training or riding horses which run at any unrecognized meeting is disqualified, as are also all horses owned by or in charge of any such person.

(c) Any person acting in any official capacity at any unrecognized meeting may be disqualified.

PART IV.
Powers of the Stewards of The Jockey Club

34. (a) The Stewards of The Jockey Club have power, at their discretion, to grant and to withdraw the approval of The Jockey Club to Associations in the conduct of meetings.

(b) The appointment of a general Racing Secretary, the handicapper, clerk of the scales, starter and judge or judges and all minor racing officials shall be made by the Stewards of The Jockey Club subject, when required by the rules of the Racing Commission, or by the laws, of any State, to the approval of said Racing Commission.

35. The Stewards of The Jockey Club

have charge of the forfeit list, the registry office, and the registration of partnerships and other documents required by Rule 86 or other Rules to be registered or filed with The Jockey Club.

36. The Stewards of The Jockey Club have power to make inquiry into and to deal with any matter relating to racing, and to rule off, or otherwise less severely punish, any person concerned in any impromptu turf practice.

37. The Stewards of The Jockey Club shall hear cases on appeal as provided for in these Rules.

PART V.
Stewards

38. Whenever the word "Steward" or "Stewards" is used, it means Steward or Stewards of the Meeting, or their duly appointed deputy or deputies.

39. (a) There shall be three Stewards to supervise each race meeting. One of such Stewards shall be appointed by the State Racing Commission, one shall be appointed by The Jockey Club, and one shall be appointed by The Association conducting such race meeting.

(b) The Jockey Club may designate one of its members to visit each race meeting in an honorary capacity in association with the Stewards.

40. Each Steward may appoint a deputy to act for him at any time. If there be but one Steward present, he shall, in case of necessity, appoint one or more persons to act with him. If none of the Stewards are

present, the officers of the Association shall request two or more persons to act during the absence of such Stewards.

41. In case of emergency, the Stewards may, during a meeting, appoint a substitute to fill any of the offices for that meeting only.

42. Every complaint against an official shall be made to the Stewards in writing signed by the complainant.

43. The Stewards have power, as they think proper, to make and, if necessary, to vary all arrangements for the conduct of the meeting, as well as power to put off any race from day to day until a Sunday intervenes.

44. The Stewards have control over, and they and the Stewards of The Jockey Club and members of the State Racing Commission of the State wherein the rac-

ing is being conducted, or their duly appointed representatives, have free access to all stands, weighing rooms, enclosures and all other places within the grounds of the Associations.

45. (a) The Stewards shall exclude from all places under their control every person who is warned or ruled off.

(b) They may so exclude any person who, by the turf authorities of any country, or by the Stewards of any recognized meeting, has been declared guilty of any improper turf practice.

46. The Stewards have supervision over all entries and declarations.

47. The Stewards have power to regulate and control the conduct of all officials, and of all owners, trainers, jockeys, grooms and other persons attendant on horses.

48. If the Stewards shall find any person has violated these Rules of Racing or has been involved in any improper turf practice, they may impose a punishment no greater than the exclusion of such person from the grounds, or any portion of such grounds, of the association conducting the meeting, for a period not exceeding the remainder of the meeting, or the suspension of such person from acting or riding for a period not exceeding twenty racing days after the meeting, or by fine not exceeding two hundred dollars, or by more than one of such punishments; and if they consider

necessary any further punishment, they shall immediately refer the matter to the Stewards of The Jockey Club. Whenever under these Rules of Racing a matter has been referred to the Stewards of The Jockey Club, they shall take such action as they shall deem proper and appropriate.

49. The Stewards have power to determine all questions arising in reference to racing at the meeting, subject to appeal under Part XIX. Should no decision have been arrived at by the Stewards within seven days of an objection being lodged, the Clerk of the Course shall then report the case to the Stewards of The Jockey Club, who may at their discretion decide the matter, and who, if they consider there has been negligence, may order any additional expense arising therefrom, to be defrayed out of the funds of the meeting at which the case occurred.

50. The Stewards have power to call for proof that a horse is neither itself disqualified in any respect, nor nominated by, nor the property, wholly or in part, of a disqualified person, and in default of such proof being given to their satisfaction, they may declare the horse disqualified.

51. The Stewards have power at any time to order an examination, by such person or persons as they think fit, of any horse entered for a race, or which has run in a race.

PART VI.
Officials of Meetings

52. (a) The Secretary of the Association, or his deputy, shall be Clerk of the Course. He shall discharge all duties, expressed or implied, required by the Rules of Racing, and he shall report to the Stewards all violations of the Rules of Racing or of the regulations of the meeting.

(b) He shall keep a complete record of all races.

(c) He shall receive all stakes, forfeits, entrance moneys, fines, fees, including jockeys' fees.

(d) Within fourteen days, exclusive of Sundays, from the close of the meeting, he shall pay, to the persons entitled to it, all the money collected by him; and at the expiration of the same period he shall notify The Jockey Club of all arrears then

remaining unpaid, and all arrears not then reported shall be regarded as having been assumed by the Association.

(e) Before acceptance, he shall submit to The Jockey Club, all entries and transfers of engagements for all races except those opened and decided during the meeting.

53. The handicapper shall append to the weights for every handicap the day and hour from which winners will be liable to a penalty and no alteration shall be made after publication except in case of omission, through error, of the name or weight of a horse duly entered, in which cases by permission of the Stewards the omission may be rectified by the handicapper.

54. (a) The Clerk of the Scales shall ex-

hibit the number (as allotted on the official card) of each horse for which a jockey has been weighed out, and shall forthwith furnish the starter with a list of such numbers.

(b) Any extra or special weight declared for any horse, or any declaration to win, or any alteration of colors shall be exhibited by the Clerk of the Scales upon the Notice Board.

(c) He shall in all cases weigh in the riders of the horses, and report to the Stewards any jockey not presenting himself to be weighed in.

(d) He shall, at the close of each day's racing, send a return to the office of the Secretary of The Jockey Club, of the weights carried in every race, and the names of the jockeys, specifying overweight, if any.

55. (a) The Judge or Judges must occupy the Judge's box at the time the horses pass the winning post, and their sole duty shall be to place the horses. They must announce their decisions promptly, and such decisions shall be final, unless objection to the winner or any placed horse is made and sustained. Provided, that this rule shall not prevent the Judges from correcting any mistake, such correction being subject to confirmation by the Stewards.

(b) A camera approved by the Stewards of The Jockey Club may be used to make a photograph or photographs of the horses at the finish to assist in determining their positions as exclusively indicated by their noses.

56. The official time of each race shall be determined by the official timer. The time recorded when the first horse crosses the finish line shall be the official time of the race.

57. The Judge or Judges shall, at the close of each day's racing, sign and send a report of the result of each race to the office of The Jockey Club.

58. The Judge or Judges shall determine the order of finishing of as many horses as they may think proper.

PART VII.
Registry Office and Registration of Horses

59. Except as provided in section (b) of this Rule, no horse may start in any race unless duly registered in the Registry Office and duly named.

(b) If for any reason ineligible for registration, or pending inquiry as to eligibility, a horse foaled outside of the United States or its possessions, Canada, Cuba or Mexico, and imported into the United States, may be submitted by the owner for approval solely for racing purposes if the application is accompanied by such information as the Stewards of The Jockey Club shall require; whereupon if said Stewards shall consider that the horse has an outstanding racing record and that the application and accompanying information meet the requirements prescribed by said Stewards, they may direct the Executive Secretary or other person authorized by them to issue a permit granting racing privileges only for such horse. Application for such a permit for such a horse must be made to The Jockey Club within thirty days of the original arrival of the horse in the United States—the application to be accompanied by a fee of $50, which will include the permit if granted. In case of failure to apply for a permit within the thirty-day period, and upon proof that failure to do so was unintentional or accidental, application for such a permit may be made within three months after original arrival. Such application shall be accompanied by a fee of $200, which will include the permit if granted.

60. The Registry Office, which is the office of The Jockey Club, is established for the identification of all race horses, whether foaled in the United States or its possessions or in other countries, and for the certification of their pedigrees.

61. Except as provided in Rule 65, horses foaled in the United States or its possessions, Canada, Cuba or Mexico must be registered with the Registry Office before October 1st of the year in which they are foaled.

62. (a) The registration shall comprise the name, if any; the color and marks, if any; whether a horse, mare or gelding; and the names of its sire and dam. If the mare

was covered by more than one stallion, the names or descriptions in full must be stated.

(b) In any case of doubt regarding the true parentage or identification of an animal, blood tests may be required, and, taking into consideration the results of such tests and/or such other information as may be available, the Stewards may authorize such corrections in the records as may be determined to be necessary or appropriate.

63. The registration fee shall be $30 for each animal, which will include certificate.

64. Only those horses are eligible for registry which authentically trace, in all of their lines, to animals recorded in the American Stud Book or in a Stud Book of another country recognized by The Jockey Club, and which are eligible under the rules and regulations from time to time adopted by the Stewards of The Jockey Club. A horse born in the United States or its possessions, Canada, Cuba or Mexico may not be registered unless both its sire and dam have been previously registered in The American Stud Book. The only exception to this rule is a foal imported in utero whose dam is properly registered in The American Stud Book after importation, and whose sire was not imported but is properly recorded in the Stud Book of a country recognized by The Jockey Club.

65. Upon failure to register a horse before October 1st of the year of his birth, he may be registered prior to January 1st of his three-year-old year by special permission of the Stewards of The Jockey Club, but not thereafter. If the application to register be made prior to the January 1st next following his birth, the payment of a fee of $60 will be required; if made after that date and prior to January 1st of his two-year-old year the required fee will be $150; and if made after that date and prior to January 1st of his three-year-old year, $300.

66. A name for each horse may be claimed gratis through the Registry Office before January 1st of his two-year-old year. On or after that date, a horse may be named upon payment of a fee of $50 and then only if the name is claimed and allowed at least two days before the date of his first start.

67. (a) All names are subject to approval or disapproval by the Stewards of The Jockey Club.

(b) No name that has been used during the previous fifteen years, either in the stud or on the turf, shall be duplicated, and no name may be claimed for any unregistered horse.

68. By special permission of the Stewards of The Jockey Club a name may be changed but only upon the payment of a fee of $100, except that when a horse's name is changed before January 1st of his two-year-old year, permission is not necessary and the fee is only $10. However, no change of name will be permitted after a horse has started.

69. (a) No horse foaled out of the United States or its possessions, Canada, Cuba or Mexico, shall be registered until the owner has filed in the Registry Office a certificate stating age, color, sex, distinguishing marks, if any, and pedigree as recorded in the recognized Stud Book of its native country or of that country from which it is exported; or unless, in respect of the age and identity of the horse, the owner has otherwise satisfied the Stewards of The Jockey Club. In both cases there must be filed after importation a veterinarian's certificate of identification.

(b) All such applications must be accompanied by a certified copy of the horse's complete racing record in all countries; such record to state date, the type race, distance and the amount of money won in each race.

(c) This registration must be made at the Registry Office within sixty days after the horse's original landing in the United States or its possessions, Canada, Cuba or Mexico and the registration fee shall be $30 for each horse, which will include certificate of registration.

(d) If it be proved to the satisfaction of the Stewards of The Jockey Club that the failure to apply for the registration of a horse within the 60-day period provided in paragraph (c) of this rule was the result of an excusable inadvertence, such registration may be permitted thereafter, provided, however, that such application to register is made within two years after original arrival in the United States or its possessions, Canada, Cuba or Mexico and provided further that the Stewards are furnished with such authenticated information, in respect of the age and identity of the horse and other relevant matters, as they may require.

If the application to register be made within six months after the original arrival, the fee will be $100 for each horse; if made within one year after original arrival, the fee will be $400.

PART VIII.
Entries, Subscriptions, Declarations and Acceptances for Races

70. Every person subscribing to a sweepstake or entering a horse in a race to be run under these Rules accepts the decision of the Stewards or the decision of the Stewards of The Jockey Club or the decision of the State Racing Commission, as the case may be, on any question relating to a race or to racing.

71. At the discretion of the Stewards of The Jockey Club or of the Stewards or of the Association, and without notice, the nominations or entries of any person or the transfer of any nomination or entry may be cancelled or refused.

72. A horse is not qualified to run in any race unless he is duly entered for that race.

73. No horse shall be permitted to start unless his certificate of registration or his racing permit is on file at the Identification Office of The Jockey Club, except that the Stewards, in their discretion, for good cause, waive this requirement if the horse is otherwise properly identified.

74. No horse is qualified to be entered or run which is wholly or partly the property of or leased to or from, or in any way under the care or superintendence of, a disqualified person. Disqualification of a husband or wife from racing horses applies equally to both.

75. Any horse which has been the subject of improper practice may be disqualified for such time and for such races as the Stewards shall determine.

76. (a) Entries and declarations shall be made in writing signed by the owner of the horse or of the engagement or by his authorized agent or some person deputed by him; and in order to secure privacy all entries to overnight races must be made at a specially designated booth.

(b) Entries and declarations by telegraph are binding if promptly confirmed in writing.

(c) Entrance money is not returned on the death of a horse nor on his failure to start, whatever be the cause of the failure.

(d) Entries to all races, excepting those which are opened and decided during the meeting, must be posted on the bulletin boards at the track where the meeting is being held.

77. (a) A horse of a partnership cannot be entered or run in the name, whether real or stable name, of an individual partner in accordance with Rule 87, unless that individual's interest or property in the racing qualities of that horse is equal to at least 25 per cent.

(b) All horses owned wholly or in part by the same person or the spouse of any such person or trained by the same trainer, must be coupled and run as an entry.

(c) Not more than one horse owned by the same person or two horses trained by the same person shall be drawn into any overnight race, or on the also eligible list, to the exclusion of another horse.

(d) For purposes of paragraphs (b) and (c) of this Rule 77, a horse shall be deemed "owned wholly or in part" by a particular person or "owned" by a particular person if that person holds the entire property interest in the horse or if, by lease or ownership, he controls the racing qualities of the horse or if he holds a proportionate interest of 25 per cent or more in a partnership which either holds the property interest in the horse or, by lease or ownership, controls the racing qualities of the horse.

(e) No licensed or authorized trainer shall have any interest, either by ownership of the horse or by lease of its racing qualities in a horse of which he is not the trainer and which may be racing at the same track where the trainer is licensed or authorized and currently racing.

78. (a) The list of entries for overnight races shall be closed at the advertised time and no entry shall be admitted after that time, except that, in case of an emergency, the Racing Secretary may, with the consent of a Steward, grant an extension of time.

(b) The list of entries for all other races shall be closed at the advertised time and no entry shall be admitted after that time unless the nominator can prove to the Stewards that the entry was mailed before the advertised time of closing; and starters must be named through the entry box by the usual time of closing on the day preceding the race.

79. (a) Except as provided in paragraph (b) of this Rule, entries shall be in the name of one person or a stable name, and shall state the name, or the stable name, of the owner, the name or description of the horse, if unnamed, and if the race be for horses of different ages, the age of the horse entered.

(b) Entries may be made in the name of a corporation or a partnership, but, in order to remain eligible, such entries must be transferred to one name on or before January 1st of the two-year-old year of the horse or horses entered.

80. (a) In entering a horse for the first time, it shall be identified by stating its name (if it has any), its color and sex and the name or description of its sire and dam as recorded in the Stud Book. If the dam was covered by more than one stallion, the names or description of all must be stated.

(b) Except as provided in Rule 81, this description must be repeated in every entry until a description of the horse with his name has been published in the Racing Calendar or in the program or the list of entries of an Association.

(c) In every entry after such publication, his name and age will be sufficient.

81. If a horse be entered with a name for the first time, in several races for the same meeting, closing at the same place on the same day, the description need not be added in more than one of the entries.

82. Upon any change of name of a horse which has run in any country, his old name as well as his new name must be given in every entry until he has run three times under his new name over the course of an Association.

Produce Races

83. In making an entry for a produce race, the produce is entered by specifying the dam and the sire or sires.

84. If the produce of a mare is dropped before the 1st of January, or if there is no produce, or if the produce is dead when dropped, or if twins are dropped, the entry of such mare is void.

85. In produce races, allowance for the produce of untried horses must be claimed before the time of closing, and are not lost by subsequent winnings.

Partnerships and Stable Names

86. (a) A horse may be owned by an individual or by a partnership of any number of persons, but no horse shall be entered and run by an owning partnership if it contains more than four members or if the proportionate interest of any member is less than 25 per cent.

(b) A horse owned by a partnership in which the number of members or proportionate interest of any member does not meet the requirements of paragraph (a) of this Rule 86 may be entered and run only by a lessee of its racing qualities, which lessee shall be an individual or a partnership in which the number of members and the proportionate interest of every member meets the requirements of paragraph (a) of this Rule 86. In such a case, the lessee may be a member of or may include one or more members of the owning partnership.

(c) All partnerships having any property, ownership or racing interest in a horse, and the name and address of every individual having any such interest in a horse, the relative proportions of such interest, and the terms of any sale with contingencies, of any lease or of any arrangement, must be signed by all the parties or by their authorized agents and be lodged annually at the office of The Jockey Club or with the Clerk of the Course for transmission to that office, and must be approved by The Jockey Club and a fee of $1.00 per horse be paid, before any horse which is a joint property or which is sold with contingencies or is leased can start in any race.

(d) In the case of a partnership which, by ownership or lease, controls the racing qualities of a horse, all of the partners and each of them shall be jointly and severally liable for all stakes and obligations.

(e) No statement of partnership of a partnership which proposes, by ownership or lease, to control the racing qualities of any horse will be accepted unless proportionate interest of each such partner is at least 25 per cent.

(f) The Jockey Club shall not be required to lodge under paragraph (c) of this Rule 86 any lease of the racing qualities of a horse or horses which is contrary to the law or officially declared public policy of any State in which racing is authorized to be conducted. As a condition of the acceptance of a lease, The Jockey Club may require lessors and lessees to supply such information concerning the identity of their members or participants as is reasonably necessary to insure compliance with this paragraph.

(g) The Jockey Club reserves the right to disapprove any partnership, sale with contingencies, lease, or other arrangements required to be lodged with and approved by The Jockey Club pursuant to paragraph (c) of this Rule 86 when, in the opinion of The Jockey Club, the effect of the partnership, sale, lease, or other arrangement would be to deceive or improperly mislead the public as to the identity of the persons holding an interest in a horse.

87. All statements of partnerships, of sales with contingencies, of leases, or of arrangements, shall declare in whose name the horse will run, to whom winnings are payable (which must be the name of the nominator), and with whom rests the power of entry.

88. In cases of emergency, authority to sign declarations of partnership may be given to The Jockey Club by a telegram promptly confirmed in writing.

89. No member of a partnership which owns a horse or leases the racing qualities of a horse shall assign his share or any part of it without the written consent of the other partners lodged and approved by paragraph (c) of Rule 86. No assignment of an interest in a partnership, which, by ownership or lease, control the racing qualities of a horse will be accepted, if the effect of the assignment would be to create a partnership, which would not be accepted under the terms of paragraph (c) of Rule 86.

90. (a) An individual may adopt a stable name under which to race horses by registering it annually with The Jockey Club and by paying annually a fee of $100. Such a registration shall be effective only during the calendar year for which it is made, and all such names shall be subject to the approval or disapproval of The Jockey Club.

(b) An individual cannot have registered more than one stable name at the same time, and, so long as an individual has a stable name registered, he shall not use or permit the use of his real name to identify the ownership interest in the racing qualities of any horse.

(c) A partnership which, by ownership or lease, controls the racing qualities of a horse or horses shall race such horses under the name, either real or stable name, of a member of the partnership whose proportionate interest in the horse meets the requirements of paragraph (a) of Rule 77. All horses the racing qualities of which are controlled by a given partnership shall be raced under the same name.

(d) A stable name may be changed at any time by registering a new stable name and by paying the fee of $100.

(e) An individual cannot register as a stable name one which has been already registered, or one which is the name of a race horse, or one which is the real name of an owner.

91. Any individual who has registered a stable name may at any time abandon it by giving written notice at the office of The Jockey Club; notice of such abandonment shall be published in the next Racing Calendar, after which all entries which have been made in the stable name shall be altered as may be approved by The Jockey Club.

92. No trainer of race horses shall register a stable name, but the partnership of which a trainer is a member may use the stable name of another member, provided the use of such other member's stable name is otherwise authorized by these Rules.

93. (Stricken out.)

94. Provided the identity of the horse is satisfactorily established, incorrect or imperfect description in the entry of a horse

or failure to register a partnership, may be corrected at any time before the horse is announced as a starter and his number exhibited for the race concerned; or in a handicap before the weights are announced; but this rule shall not be construed so as to allow any horse to start in any race for which he is not otherwise completely qualified under these Rules of Racing.

95. Except in overnight races, if the hour for closing of entries or for declarations be not stated, it is understood to be midnight of the day specified.

96. In the absence of notice to the contrary, entries and declarations of forfeit, due on the eve of and during a meeting, are due at the office of the Clerk of the Course where the race is to be run.

97. A person who subscribes to a sweepstakes may, after approval by the Stewards, transfer his subscription.

98. An entry of a horse in a sweepstakes is a subscription to the sweepstakes. Such an entry or subscription may, before the time of closing, be altered or withdrawn.

99. Subscriptions and all entries or rights of entry under them shall not become void on the death of the person in whose name they were made or taken. All rights, privileges and obligations shall attach to the continuing owners including the legal representatives of the decedent.

100. No horse shall be considered as struck out of any of his engagements until the owner or his authorized agent shall have given notice, in writing or by telegram, promptly confirmed in writing, to the Clerk of the Course where the horse is engaged.

101. (a) The striking of a horse out of an engagement is irrevocable.

(b) Omission by the vendor to strike a horse out of an engagement, not sold or transferred with him, does not entitle his owner to start him, or to the stakes if he wins.

102. (Stricken out.)

103. (a) If a horse is sold by private treaty, or at public auction, or claimed out of a claiming race (unless the conditions of the claiming race stated otherwise) the written acknowledgment of both parties is necessary to prove the fact that it was transferred with its engagements.

(b) When a horse is sold with his engagements, or any part of them, the seller cannot strike the horse out of any such engagements.

(c) If only certain engagements be specified, those only are transferred with the horse.

104. A sale to a person ruled off, or to an unqualified or disqualified person, will not entitle such person to be recognized as an owner under these Rules of Racing.

PART IX.
Stakes, Subscriptions, Etc.

105. In the absence of conditions or notice to the contrary, entries for overnight races are to be made at the office of the Clerk of the Course by 2 P.M. on the day before the race.

106. Every horse shall be considered as having started and be liable for whatever is due for so doing, when its jockey has been weighed and its number displayed, unless the Stewards shall otherwise determine.

107. (Stricken out.)

108. No horse shall be allowed to start for any race and no jockey shall be weighed out for any horse until there have been paid or guaranteed to the Clerk of the Course

(a) Any stake or entrance money due by the owner in respect to that race.

(b) The jockey's fee.

PART X.
Rules 109 through 116 were repealed by The Jockey Club years ago.

PART XI.
Qualifications of Starters

117. (a) A horse shall not be qualified to start in any race unless, not less than 30 minutes before the time set for the race, his presence on the grounds of the Association be reported to the paddock judge, he be announced to the Clerk of the Scales as a starter, and the name of his jockey given to the latter official.

(b) Any subsequent change of jockeys must be sanctioned by the Stewards, who, if no satisfactory reason is given for the change, may fine or suspend any person they may think culpable in the matter.

(c) All horses must be saddled in the paddock.

(d) The paddock judge shall be in charge of the paddock and inspect all race horses and their equipment prior to each race, and shall report forthwith to a Steward any violation observed by him.

(e) No one not actually connected with its stable shall touch a horse while in the paddock preparatory to starting a race, except as provided in Rule 117(f).

(f) A representative of the Association conducting a meeting shall inspect the plating and bandaging of each horse as it enters the paddock before the race, and record the plating on a board provided for the purpose in the paddock.

118. The Stewards may permit or direct the withdrawing of a horse after weighing out.

119. The time fixed for the first race shall be printed on the program.

Post time is the time designated by the Stewards at which horses are to arrive at the post for each race, and such time shall be shown on the dial provided for that purpose.

PART XII.
Weights, Penalties and Allowances

120. (a) The following weights are carried when the weights are not stated in the conditions of the race:

Scale of Weights for Age

Distance	Age	Jan.	Feb.	Mar.	April	May	June	July	Aug.	Sept.	Oct.	Nov.	Dec.
Half Mile	Two years	x	x	x	x	x	x	x	105	108	111	114	114
	Three years	117	117	119	119	121	123	125	126	127	128	129	129
	Four years	130	130	130	130	130	130	130	130	130	130	130	130
	Five years & up	130	130	130	130	130	130	130	130	130	130	130	130
Six Furlongs	Two years	x	x	x	x	x	x	x	102	105	108	111	111
	Three years	114	114	117	117	119	121	123	125	126	127	128	128
	Four years	129	129	130	130	130	130	130	130	130	130	130	130
	Five years & up	130	130	130	130	130	130	130	130	130	130	130	130
One Mile	Two years	x	x	x	x	x	x	x	x	96	99	102	102
	Three years	107	107	111	111	113	115	117	119	121	122	123	123
	Four years	127	127	128	128	127	126	126	126	126	126	126	126
	Five years & up	128	128	128	128	127	126	126	126	126	126	126	126
One and a Quarter Miles	Two years	x	x	x	x	x	x	x	x	x	x	x	x
	Three years	101	101	107	107	111	113	116	118	120	121	122	122
	Four years	125	125	127	127	127	126	126	126	126	126	126	126
	Five years & up	127	127	127	127	127	126	126	126	126	126	126	126
One and a Half Miles	Two years	x	x	x	x	x	x	x	x	x	x	x	x
	Three years	98	98	104	104	108	111	114	117	119	121	122	122
	Four years	124	124	126	126	126	126	126	126	126	126	126	126
	Five years & up	126	126	126	126	126	126	126	126	126	126	126	126
Two Miles	Three years	96	96	102	102	106	109	112	114	117	119	120	120
	Four years	124	124	126	126	126	126	126	125	125	124	124	124
	Five years & up	126	126	126	126	126	126	126	125	125	124	124	124

(b) In races of intermediate lengths, the weights for the shorter distance are carried.

(c) In races exclusively for three-year-olds or four-year-olds, the weight is 126 lbs., and in races exclusively for two-year-olds, it is 122 lbs.

(d) In all races except handicaps and races where the conditions expressly state to the contrary, the scale of weights is less, by the following: for fillies two years old, 3 lbs.; for mares three years old and upward, 5 lbs. before September 1, and 3 lbs. thereafter.

(e) Welter weights are 28 lbs. added to the weight for age.

(f) In all overnight races except handicaps, not more than six pounds may be deducted from the scale of weights for age, except for allowances, but in no case shall the total allowances of any type reduce the lowest weight below 101 lbs., except that this minimum weight need not apply to two-year-olds or three-year-olds when racing with older horses.

(g) In all handicaps which close more than 72 hours prior to the race the top weight shall not be less than 126 lbs., except that in handicaps for fillies and mares, the top weight shall not be less than 126 lbs. less the sex allowance at the time the race is run; and scale weight for fillies and mares or three-year-olds may be used for open handicaps as minimum top weight in place of 126 lbs.

(h) In all overnight handicaps and in all claiming handicaps, the top weight shall not be less than 122 lbs.

(i) In all overnight races for two-year-olds, for three-year-olds, or for four-year-olds and upward the minimum weight shall be 112 pounds, subject to sex and apprentice allowances. This rule shall not apply to handicaps, nor to races for three-year-olds and upward.

Estimated Winnings

121. (a) In estimating the value of a race to the winner, there shall be deducted only the amount of money payable to the owners of the other horses and to other persons out of the stakes and out of the added money.

(b) In estimating foreign winnings, the current rate of exchange at the time of such winnings shall be adopted.

(c) The value of prizes not in money will not be estimated in the value of the race to the winner.

(d) In estimating the value of a series of races in which an extra sum of money is won by winning two or more races, the extra sum shall be estimated in the last race by which it was finally won.

122. In all races, should there be any surplus from entries, or subscriptions over the advertised value, it shall be paid the winner, unless stated by the conditions to go to other horses in the race.

123. (a) Winnings during the year shall include all prizes from the 1st of January preceding to the time appointed for the start, and shall apply to all races in any country; and winning shall include dividing or walking over.

(b) Winning of a fixed sum is understood to be winning it in one race, unless specified to the contrary.

124. (a) In a case of a walkover, one-half of the money offered to the winner is given.

(b) When a walkover is the result of arrangement by owners of horses engaged, no portion of the added money nor any other prize need be given.

125. Any money or prize which by the conditions is to go to the horse placed second, or in any lower place in the race, shall, if the winner has walked over or no horse has been so placed, be dealt with as follows:

(a) If part of the stake, it shall go to the winner; or

(b) If a separate donation from the Association or any other source, it shall not be given at all; or

(c) If entrance money for the race, it shall go to the Association.

126. If a race never be run or be void, all moneys paid by an owner in respect to that race shall be returned.

127. A race may be declared void if no qualified horse covers the course according to rule.

Penalties

128. No horse shall carry extra weight, nor be barred from any race for having run second or in any lower place in a race.

129. When the winners of claiming races are exempted from penalties, the exemption does not apply to races in which

any of the horses running are not subject to being claimed.

130. Penalties and allowances are not cumulative, unless so declared by the conditions of the race.

Allowances

131. (a) Any male between the ages of sixteen and twenty-five years who has never previously been licensed as a jockey in any country, and has of his own free will and, if under age, with the written consent of his parents or guardian, bound himself to an owner or trainer for a term of not less than three nor more than five years (subject to written extension if made for less than five years) by written contract approved by and filed with The Jockey Club, and after at least one year service with a racing stable, may claim in all overnight races, except handicaps, the following allowances:

(1) Ten pounds until he has ridden five winners and seven pounds until he has ridden an additional 30 winners; if he has ridden 35 winners prior to the end of one year from the date of riding his fifth winner, he shall have an allowance of five pounds until the end of that year.

(2) After the completion of conditions above, for one year he may claim three pounds when riding horses owned or trained by his original contract employer provided his contract has not been permanently transferred or sold since he rode his first winner.

(3) The holder of the contract at the time the boy rides his first winner shall be considered the original contract employer.

(b) All holders of apprentice contracts shall be subject to investigation as to character, ability, facilities and financial responsibility; and shall, at the time of making the contract, own in good faith a minimum of three horses in training, or, if a trainer, shall operate in good faith a stable of at least three horses.

(c) Contracts for apprentice jockeys shall provide for fair remuneration, adequate medical attention and suitable board and lodging for the apprentice; and approved provision shall be made for savings out of his earnings.

(d) Under exceptional circumstances which would prevent an apprentice jockey from riding during the full periods specified above, such as (a) service in the armed forces of the United States; (b) personal injuries suffered in the course of his occupation or otherwise; (c) a disabling illness; (d) restrictions on racing; (e) or other valid reason, the Stewards may extend said period and the term of his contract to compensate therefor.

(e) No apprentice shall be permitted to acquire his own contract.

(f) All apprentice contracts described in this rule shall be filed with The Jockey Club within thirty days after execution thereof or upon filing application for license with the New York State Racing Commission.

(g) The failure of an owner or trainer to file such contract or to obtain the approval of The Jockey Club thereto, may subject such owner or trainer to the revocation or suspension of his license or to such other disciplinary action by the Commission as in its judgment may seem proper.

132. No horse shall receive allowance of weight, or be relieved from extra weight, for having been beaten in one or more races; provided that this rule shall not prohibit maiden allowances, or allowances to horses that have not won within a specified time, or that have not won races of a specified value.

PART XIII.
Weighing Out

133. (a) Every jockey must be weighed for a specified horse not less than 30 minutes before the time fixed for the race, and the number of the horse shall be exhibited officially as soon as possible.

(b) Only equipment specifically approved by the Stewards shall be worn or carried by a jockey or a horse in a race.

(c) Every jockey, apprentice jockey and other rider, whether in a race or when exercising or ponying a Thoroughbred horse, shall wear a safety helmet of a type approved in writing by the Stewards; and no change shall be made in any such helmet without the approval of the Stewards.

134. If a horse run in muzzle, martingale, breastplate or clothing, it must be put on the scale and included in the jockey's weight.

135. No whip, or substitute for a whip, blinkers or number cloth shall be allowed on the scales, nor shall any bridle or safety helmet approved by the Stewards be weighed.

136. If a jockey intends to carry overweight, he must declare the amount thereof at the time of weighing out, or if in doubt as to his proper weight, he may declare the weight he intends to carry.

137. If a jockey intends to carry overweight exceeding by more than two pounds the weight which his horse is to carry, the owner or trainer consenting, he must declare the amount of overweight to the Clerk of the Scales at least 45 minutes before the time appointed for the race, and the Clerk shall cause the overweight to be stated on the Notice Board immediately. For failure on the part of a jockey to comply with this Rule he may be punished as provided by Rule 48.

138. No horse shall carry more than five pounds overweight except in races confined exclusively to amateurs or to riders who are Officers of the United States Army or Navy or of the National Guard.

139. The owner is responsible for the weight carried by his horse.

PART XIV.
Starting

140. (a) The Starter shall give all orders necessary for securing a fair start.

(b) He shall report to the Stewards by whom or by what cause any delay was occasioned, and any cases of misconduct by jockeys when under his orders.

141. If a horse whose number has been exhibited or whose starting is obligatory does not start and run in the race, the Stewards may fine or suspend any person or persons responsible therefor.

142. After the horses are ordered to the starting post, and until the Stewards direct the gates to be reopened, all persons except the racing officials shall be excluded from the course to be run over.

143. A bell shall be rung to indicate the time to saddle and a bugle sounded to indicate the time to go to the post.

144. (a) All horses shall parade and, under penalty of disqualification, shall carry their weight from the paddock to the starting post, such parade to pass the finish line.

(b) When by permission of the paddock judge and upon payment of $10 a horse is led to the post, he is excused from parading with the other horses, but nevertheless he must, on his way to the post, pass the Steward's stand.

145. (a) The position of horses when starting shall be determined by a lot, i.e., a numbered ball shall be drawn from a bottle by the Clerk of the Scales.

(b) The Starter may place vicious and unruly horses on the outside and behind the line.

(c) A horse in the hands of the Starter shall receive no further care from anyone at the starting post except the assistant starters, provided that if any accident happen to a jockey, his horse or his equipment, the Starter may permit any jockey or jockeys to dismount and the horses to be cared for during the delay; otherwise no jockey shall dismount.

146. (a) Except in cases provided for in paragraph (b) of this Rule, all races shall be started by a starting gate selected by the Association conducting the meeting if approved by the Stewards of The Jockey Club.

(b) By permission of the Stewards, a race may be started without a gate.

(c) When a race is started without a starting gate, the start shall not be official until, and there shall be no recall after, the recall flag has been dropped in answer to that of the Starter.

147. A start in front of the post is void, and the horses must be started again.

148. All horses shall be schooled properly before starting and, upon the report of the Starter, the Stewards may fine or sus-

pend any trainer who, after being notified, shall start any unruly horse.

149. The horses shall be started as far as possible in a line, but may be started at such reasonable distance behind the starting post as the Starter thinks necessary.

150. (a) The Starter may fine or suspend a jockey for disobedience of his orders at the starting gate or for attempting any unfair advantage; and the Starter may impose upon an offender a fine not exceeding $200 and suspension not exceeding ten days, with or without reference to the Stewards for further action, but such suspension shall not take effect until after the last race of the day of his suspension.

(b) All fines and suspensions by the Starter must be reported in writing by him to the Clerk of the Course, and they may be modified or remitted by the Stewards only.

151. The concurrent statements of the Starter and his assistant as to incidents of the start are conclusive.

PART XV.
Rules of the Race

152. An owner running two or more horses in a race may declare to win with one of them, and such declaration must be made at the time of weighing out, and it is to be immediately posted on the Notice Board. A jockey riding a horse with which his owner has not declared to win must on no account stop such horse except in favor of the stable companion on whose behalf declaration to win has been made.

153. (a) When clear, a horse may be taken to any part of the course provided that crossing or weaving in front of contenders may constitute interference or intimidation for which the offender may be disciplined.

(b) A horse crossing another so as actually to impede him is disqualified, unless the impeded horse was partly in fault or the crossing was wholly caused by the fault of some other horse or jockey.

(c) If a horse or jockey jostle another horse, the aggressor may be disqualified, unless the impeded horse or his jockey was partly in fault or the jostle was wholly caused by the fault of some other horse or jockey.

(d) If a jockey wilfully strike another horse or jockey, or ride wilfully or carelessly so as to injure another horse which is in no way in fault or so as to cause other horses to do so, his horse is disqualified.

(e) When a horse is disqualified under this rule, every horse in the same race belonging wholly or partly to the same owner, in the discretion of the Stewards, may be disqualified.

(f) Complaints under this rule can only be received from the owner, trainer or jockey of the horse alleged to be aggrieved, and must be made to the Clerk of the Scales or to the Stewards before or immediately after his jockey has passed the scales. But nothing in this rule shall prevent the Stewards taking cognizance of foul riding.

(g) Any jockey against whom a foul is claimed shall be given the opportunity to appear before the Stewards before any decision is made by them.

(h) A jockey whose horse has been disqualified or who unnecessarily causes his horse to shorten his stride with a view to complaint, or an owner, trainer or jockey who complains frivolously that his horse was crossed or jostled, may be fined or suspended.

(i) The extent of disqualification shall be determined by the Stewards as in these rules provided.

154. If the Stewards at any time are satisfied that the riding of any race was intentionally foul or that any jockey was instructed or induced so as to ride, all persons guilty of complicity shall be suspended and the case shall be reported to the Stewards of The Jockey Club for such additional action as they may consider necessary.

155. If a horse leaves the course, he must turn back and run the course from the point at which he left it.

156. If a race has been run by all the horses at wrong weights or over a wrong course or distance, and an objection be made before official confirmation of the number of the horses placed in the race, or if a Judge is not in the stand when the

horses pass the winning post, the race shall be run again after the last race of the day, but in no case less than 30 minutes after the finish of the wrongly run race.

Walking Over

157. In a sweepstake, if only one horse remains to start, the Stewards may dispense with a walkover.

PART XVI.
Weighing In

158. Every jockey must, immediately after pulling up, ride his horse to the place of weighing, dismount only after obtaining permission from the official in charge, and present himself to be weighed by the Clerk of the Scales; provided that if a jockey be prevented from riding to the place of weighing by reason of accident or illness by which he or his horse is disabled, he may walk or be carried to the scales.

159. Except by special permission of the official in charge, every jockey must, upon pulling up, unsaddle his own horse, and no attendant shall touch the horse, except by his bridle. Upon the returning of a jockey to the winner's circle to dismount after a race has been run, no one may touch the equipment of the jockey until he has been weighed in, except upon the approval of the official in charge.

160. If a jockey does not present himself to weigh in, or if he be more than one pound short of his weight, or if he be guilty of any fraudulent practice with respect to weight or weighing, or, except as provided in Rule 158, if he dismount before reaching the scales, or dismount without permission, or if he touch (except accidentally) before weighing in any person or thing other than his own equipment, his horse may be disqualified and he himself may be fined or suspended, as provided by Rule 48.

161. If a horse carry more than two pounds over his proper or declared weight, his jockey shall be fined, suspended or ruled off, unless the Stewards are satisfied that such excess weight has been caused by rain or mud.

PART XVII.
Dead Heats

162. When a race results in a dead heat, the dead heat shall not be run off, owners shall divide, except where division would conflict with the conditions of the race.

When two horses run a dead heat for first place, all prizes to which first and second horses would have been entitled shall be divided equally between them; and this applies in dividing prizes, whatever the number of horses running a dead heat and whatever places for which the dead heat is run. Each horse shall be deemed a winner and liable to penalty for the amount he shall receive.

When a dead heat is run for second place and an objection is made to the winner of the race, and sustained, the horses which ran the dead heat shall be deemed to have run a dead heat for first place.

163. If the dividing owners cannot agree as to which of them is to have a Cup or other prize which cannot be divided, the question shall be determined by lot by the Stewards.

164. On a dead heat for a match, the match is off.

PART XVIII.
Claiming Races

165. (a) In claiming races any horse may be claimed for its entered price by any owner presently registered in good faith for racing at that meeting who has nominated a starter up to or including the race in which the claim is made, or by his authorized agent, but for the account only of the owner making the claim, or for whom the claim was made by the agent; provided, however, that no person shall claim his own horse or cause his horse to be claimed directly or indirectly for his own account.

(b) The minimum price for which a horse may be entered in a claiming race shall be twelve hundred dollars, but in no case shall it be entered for less than the value of the purse to the winner.

(c) If a horse is claimed, it shall not start in a claiming race for a period of 30 days from date of claim for less than 25 per cent more than the amount for which it was claimed.

(d) If a horse is claimed, it shall not be sold or transferred to anyone wholly or in part, except in a claiming race, for a period of 30 days from date of claim, nor shall it, unless reclaimed, remain in the same stable or under control or management of its former owner or trainer for a like period, nor shall it race elsewhere until after the close of the meeting at which it was claimed.

166. All claims shall be in writing, sealed and deposited in a locked box provided for this purpose by the Clerk of the Course, at least fifteen minutes before post time. No money shall accompany the claim. Each person desiring to make a claim, unless he shall have such amount to his credit with the Association, must first deposit with the Association the whole amount of the claim in cash, for which a receipt will be given. All claims shall be passed upon by the Stewards, and the person determined at the closing time for claiming to have the right of claim shall become the owner of the horse when the start is effected whether it be alive or dead, sound or unsound, or injured before or during the race, or after it. If more than one person should enter a claim for the same horse, the disposition of the horse shall be decided by lot by the Stewards.

An owner shall not be informed that a claim has been made until after the race has been run, and any horse so claimed shall then be taken to the paddock for delivery to the claimant.

167 No person shall claim more than one horse in a race.

168. Each horse shall run for the account of the person in whose name it starts.

169. When a claim has been lodged with the Secretary or Clerk of the Course, it is irrevocable, and is at the risk of the claimant.

170. In case of a dead heat, each of the dividing horses is the winner for the purpose of these rules.

171. (a) Should the Stewards be of the opinion that any person is claiming a horse collusively for the benefit of another interest or in order to evade the provisions of Rule 165, they may require him to make an affidavit that he is not so doing, and if upon proof it is ascertained that he made a false affidavit he shall be referred to the Stewards of The Jockey Club for further action.

(b) Should the Stewards within twenty-four hours after the running of a race be of the opinion that the lease or the entry of a horse was not made in good faith but was made for the purpose of obtaining the privilege of entering a claim, then in each case they may disallow or cancel any such claim and order the return of a horse that may have been delivered and refer the case to the Stewards of The Jockey Club for further action.

172. A horse's liability to be claimed is not affected by his walking over, but he shall receive all the money offered by the conditions of the race to the winner.

173. No horse shall be delivered except on a written order from the Secretary or Clerk of the Course.

174. Any person refusing to deliver a claimed horse shall be suspended and his case may be referred to the Stewards of The Jockey Club. The horse is disqualified until he is delivered to the purchaser.

175. (a) When a stable has been eliminated by claiming, the owner so affected, if he has not replenished his stable before the close of the meeting, may obtain a cer-

tificate from the Stewards of the meeting, and on presention thereof the owner shall be entitled to claim during the next thirty racing days at any recognized meeting operating under the jurisdiction of The Jockey Club, until he has claimed a horse. Stables eliminated by fire or other hazards may also be permitted to claim under this Rule by the discretion of the Stewards.

(b) Any person who shall attempt to prevent another person from claiming any horse in a claiming race, or any owners running in claiming races who may make any agreement for the claiming of each other's horses, may be fined or suspended by the Stewards and referred to the Stewards of The Jockey Club for further action.

PART XIX.
Disputes, Objections, Appeals, Etc.

176. When a race is in dispute, both the horse that finished first and any horse claiming the race shall be liable to all the penalties attaching to the winner of that race until the matter is decided.

177. Every objection shall be decided by the Stewards, but the decisions shall be subject to appeal to the Stewards of The Jockey Club so far as relates to points in-volving the interpretation of these rules, or to any question other than a question of fact, on which there shall be no appeal unless by leave of the Stewards and with the consent of the Stewards of The Jockey Club. Notice of appeal must be given in writing to the Clerk of the Course within forty-eight hours of the decision being known.

Objections, When and Where Made

178. Every objection must be made by the owner, trainer or jockey of some horse engaged in the race, or by the officials of the course, to the Clerk of the Scales or to one of the Stewards, or an objection may be made by any one of the Stewards.

179. All objections except claims of interference during a race must be in writing signed by the objector.

180. An objection cannot be withdrawn without leave of the Stewards.

181. All costs and expenses in relation to determining an objection or conducting an inquiry shall be paid by such person or persons, and in such proportions as the Stewards shall direct.

182. Before considering an objection, the Stewards may require a deposit of $25, which shall be forfeited if the objection is decided to be frivolous or vexatious.

183. If an objection to a horse engaged in a race be made not less than 15 minutes before the time set for the race, the Stewards may require the qualification to be proved before the race, and in default of such proof being given to their satisfaction, they must declare the horse disqualified.

184. An objection to any decision of the Clerk of the Scales must be made at once.

185. An objection to the distance of a course officially designated must be made not less than 15 minutes before the race.

186. An objection to a horse on the ground of his not having run the proper course, or of the race having been run on a wrong course, or of any other matter occurring in the race, must be made before the numbers of the horses placed in the race are confirmed officially.

187. (a) An objection on the ground

(1) Of misstatement, omission or error in the entry under which a horse has run; or

(2) That the horse which ran was not the horse nor of the age which he was represented to be at the time of entry; or

(3) That he was not qualified under the conditions of the race or by reason of default; or

(4) That he has run in contravention of the rules of partnership or registration, may be received up to 48 hours exclusive of Sunday after the last race of the last day of the meeting.

(b) In any other case an objection must be within 48 hours of the race being run, exclusive of Sunday, save in the case of any fraud or willful misstatement, when there shall be no limit to the time of objecting provided the Stewards are satisfied that there has been no unnecessary delay on the part of the objector.

188. The Stewards are vested with the power to determine the extent of disqualification in case of fouls. They may place the offending horse behind such horses as in their judgment it interfered with, or they may place it last, and they may disqualify it from participation in any part of the purse.

189. If by reason of an objection to a horse a race or place is awarded to another horse, the money for such race shall be distributed in accordance with the final placing, and the owner of a horse to which the race or place is finally awarded can recover the money from those who wrongfully received it.

190. Pending the determination of an objection any prize which the horse objected to may have won or may win in the race, or any money held by the association holding the meeting, as the price of a horse claimed (if affected by the determination of the objection) shall be withheld until the objection is determined.

PART XX.
Licenses or Authorizations for Participants in Racing

191. Except as provided in Rule 192, no person shall be allowed to start, ride or train horses, and no person may pursue any other occupation or be employed at race meetings, in any State where it is or shall be required that such person be licensed, or obtain an authorization, in order to pursue his occupation or employment upon the grounds of an Association, unless such person shall have been licensed or shall have obtained such authorization.

192. Unless otherwise provided by the rules of the Racing Commission, or by the laws, of the State concerned:

(a) No jockey license or authorization shall be granted to anyone less than sixteen years of age;

(b) Each owner, to be eligible for a license or authorization, shall be required to submit an affidavit, as to his ownership or lease of all horses in his possession;

(c) Boys never having ridden in a race may be allowed to ride twice, if approved by the Stewards, before applying for a license or authorization; but a license or authorization shall not be granted to boys who have never ridden in a race;

(d) In an emergency, the Stewards may permit owners, trainers, assistant trainers and jockeys and others to start, train or ride or pursue their other occupations or employments pending action on their application; and

(e) Any amateur wishing to ride in races on even terms with jockeys shall obtain leave, good until revoked, from the Stewards of The Jockey Club;

(f) No person shall be eligible for an owner's or trainer's license or authorization, if, during the term of such license or authorization, he would practice as farrier or veterinarian with horses racing under the jurisdiction of The Jockey Club; provided, however, that a duly licensed or authorized owner may personally shoe a horse owned by him upon applying for and receiving a certificate of fitness therefor from the Stewards;

193. Trainer and assistant trainers are responsible for the condition of horses in their care and are presumed to know these Rules.

Jockeys' Betting, Etc.

194. (a) No jockey shall bet on any race except through the owner of and on the horses which he rides, and any jockey who shall be proved to the satisfaction of the Stewards to have any interest in any race horse, or to have been engaged in any betting transaction except as permitted by this Rule, or to have received presents from persons other than the owner, may be punished as provided by Rule 48.

(b) Any person knowingly acting in the capacity of part owner or trainer of any horse in which a jockey possesses any interest, or making any bet with or in behalf of any jockey except as provided in Rule 194(a), or otherwise aiding or abetting in any breach of these Rules of Racing, may be punished as provided by Rule 48.

195. (a) No jockey shall be the owner of any race horse.

(b) A jockey may not ride in any race against a starter of his contract employer unless his mount and his contract employer's starter are both in the hands of the same trainer.

196. (a) A jockey or trainer under sus-

pension in any state or foreign country, shall not be permitted to train or ride in a race for anyone during the period of his suspension. Any person who shall employ a jockey or trainer in contravention of this Rule may be punished as provided by Rule 48.

(b) All fines imposed upon jockeys must be paid by the jockeys themselves. Any other person found paying the same shall be punished as well as the jockey.

197. In the absence of a specific contract, jockey's fees shall be as follows:

Purse	Winner	Second	Third	Loser	Purse	Winner	Second	Third	Loser
$400	$25.00	$15.00	$12.00	$10.00	1,200-1,300	42.00	27.00	23.00	18.00
500	26.00	16.00	13.00	11.00	1,400-1,500	44.00	29.00	24.00	19.00
600	27.00	17.00	14.00	12.00	1,600-1,700	47.00	32.00	25.00	20.00
700	34.00	21.00	19.00	15.00	1,800-1,900	50.00	35.00	27.00	22.00
800-900	37.00	22.00	21.00	17.00	2,000 & up	50.00	40.00	30.00	25.00
1,000-1,100	39.00	24.00	22.00	17.00					

198. (a) The terms of all contracts between jockeys and their employers shall be filed with The Jockey Club, accompanied by a fee of $1, and must be approved by it (in the cases of apprentices, before a license or authorization be granted), and such contracts shall contain a provision that in case a jockey's license or authorization be revoked or suspended, the salary of the jockey shall in the former case cease, and in the latter case cease during the time of his suspension. The terms of all contracts between jockeys and jockey agents shall be filed with The Jockey Club accompanied by a fee of $1 and must be approved by it before being effective.

(b) A jockey shall be compensated and insured by either the owner or trainer of the horse according to which one is the employer as defined by the applicable Workmen's Compensation Law.

199. If a jockey engaged for a race, or for a specified time, refuses to fulfill his engagement, he may be punished as provided by Rule 48.

200. Employers retaining the same jockey have precedence according to the priority of the retainers as specified in the contracts.

201. Conflicting claims for the services of a jockey shall be decided by the Stewards.

Stable Employees

202. No owner or trainer shall engage any person who has not a written discharge from his last employer, but any person prevented by this rule from obtaining or retaining employment shall have the right of appeal to the Stewards against the person withholding his written discharge.

203. Any owner or trainer employing a person in violation of any of Rules 191 to 202, inclusive, may be punished as provided by Rule 48.

PART XXI.
Racing Colors and Numbers

204. (a) Racing colors shall be registered annually on payment of $5, or for five years on payment of $15. Colors so registered shall not be taken by any other

person. All disputes as to the right to particular colors shall be settled by the Stewards of The Jockey Club.

(b) No person shall run a horse in colors other than those registered in his own or a stable name without special permission of the Stewards.

205. Jockeys must wear a number on the saddle cloths corresponding to the numbers of the horses as exhibited after weighing out.

206. Any deviation from the recorded colors of the owner that may be granted by the Stewards is to be immediately posted on the Notice Board.

207. Under special circumstances, a horse may be permitted by the Stewards to run in colors not those of the owner.

PART XXII.
Corrupt Practices and Disqualifications of Persons

208. (a) If any person give, offer or promise, directly or indirectly, any bribe in any form to any person having official duties in relation to any race or race horse, or to any trainer, jockey or agent, or to any other person having charge of, or access to, any race horse; or

(b) If any person having official duties in relation to any race track, race or race horse, or if any trainer, jockey, agent or other person having charge of, or access to, any race horse, solicit, accept, or offer to accept any bribe in any form; or

(c) If any licensed person, or person permitted within the grounds of any Association, shall be approached with an offer or promise of a bribe or with a request or a suggestion for a bribe or for any improper, corrupt or fraudulent act or practice in relation to a race or racing, or that any race shall be conducted otherwise than fairly and in accordance with these Rules of Racing, and if such licensed or other person shall not immediately report the matter to the Stewards; or

(d) If any person wilfully enter, or cause or permit to be entered, or to start, in any race a horse which he knows or has reason to believe to be disqualified; or

(e) If any person shall have in his possession in or about any race track, or shall use, appliances—electrical, mechanical, or otherwise—other than the ordinary equipment, of such nature as could affect the speed or racing condition of a horse; or

(f) If any person be guilty of any improper, corrupt or fraudulent act or practice in relation to racing in this or in any other country, or shall conspire with any other person to commit, or shall assist in the commission of, any such act or practice;

Any person found by the Stewards to have violated Rule 208.(a), (b), (c), (d), (e) or (f) shall have such penalty imposed upon him and the Stewards shall take such other action in the matter as they may deem proper under any Rules of Racing, including reference to the Stewards of The Jockey Club.

(g) If the Stewards shall find that any drug has been administered or attempted to be administered, internally or externally, to a horse before a race, which is of such a character as could affect the racing condition of the horse in such a race, such Stewards shall impose such penalty and take such other action as they may deem proper under any of these Rules of Racing (including reference to the Stewards of The Jockey Club) against every person found by them to have administered, or to have attempted to administer or to have caused to be administered or to have caused an attempt to administer, or to have conspired with another person to administer such drug.

The trainer, groom, and any other person, having charge, custody or care of the horse, are obligated properly to protect the horse and guard it against such administration or attempted administration and, if the Stewards shall find that any such person has failed to show proper protection and guarding of the horse, they shall impose such penalty and take such other action as they may deem proper under any of the Rules of Racing, including reference to the Stewards of The Jockey Club.

The owner or owners of a horse so found to have received such administration shall be denied, or shall promptly return, any portion of the purse or sweepstakes, and any trophy in such race, and the same shall be distributed as in the case of a disqualification. If a horse shall be disqualified in a race because of the infraction of this Rule 208(g), the eligibility of other horses which ran in such race and which have started in a subsequent race before announcement of such disqualification, shall not be in any way affected.

(h) No person within the grounds of a racing Association where race horses are lodged or kept, shall have in or upon the premises which he occupies or has the right to occupy, or in his personal property or effects, any hypodermic syringe, hypodermic needle, or other device which could be used for the injection or other infusion into a horse of a drug without first securing written permission from the Stewards. Every racing Association, upon the grounds of which race horses are lodged or kept, is required to use all reasonable efforts to prevent the violation of this Rule. Every such racing Association, the Commission, and the Stewards, or any of them, shall have the right to permit a person or persons authorized by any of them to enter into or upon the buildings, stables, rooms or other places within the grounds of such an Association and to examine the same and to inspect and examine the personal property and effects of any person, within such places; and every licensed person and person authorized to pursue his occupation or employment within the grounds of any Association, by accepting his license or accepting such authorization, does consent to such search and to the seizure of any such hypodermic syringes, hypodermic needles or other devices, and any drugs apparently intended to be used in connection therewith, so found. If the Stewards shall find that any persons have violated this Rule 208(h), they shall impose such penalty and take such other action as they may deem

proper under any of the Rules of Racing, including reference to the Stewards of The Jockey Club.

(i) Every person ruled off the course of a recognized Association is ruled off wherever these rules have force.

(j) Anyone who has been ruled off or who has been suspended, whether temporarily for investigation or otherwise, and anyone penalized as above by the highest official regulatory racing body having jurisdiction where the offense occurred, shall be denied admission to all race tracks until duly reinstated.

(k) A person whose license or authorization has been revoked or has been suspended, whether temporarily for investigation or otherwise, and so long as his exclusion or suspension continues shall not be qualified, whether acting as agent or otherwise, to subscribe for or to run any horse for any race, either in his own name or in that of any other person.

(l) All horses in the charge of a trainer who has been ruled off or has been suspended, whether temporarily for investigation or otherwise shall be automatically suspended from racing during the period of the trainer's exclusion or suspension. Permission may be given by the Stewards for the transfer of such horses to another trainer during such period, and upon such approval such horses shall again be eligible to race.

(m) In the event that a horse establishes a track or other record in a race and it should be determined by competent authority that the chemical analysis of any sample taken from such horse shows the presence of a drug which is of such character as could affect the racing condition of the horse in such race, then such record shall be null and void.

PART XXIII.
Discretionary Powers

209. If any case occurs which is not or which is alleged not to be provided for by these Rules, it shall be determined by the Stewards or by the Stewards of The Jockey Club, as the case may be, in such manner as they think just and conformable to the usages of the turf.

210. These Rules of Racing or any

rules, not consistent therewith, made by the State Racing Commission of the State concerned, supersede the conditions of a race or regulations of a meeting when they conflict.

211. The Stewards shall not entertain any disputes relating to bets.

212. The Jockey Club may contract

with racing authorities, racing Associations and other bodies for the rendition of such advisory or other services as may be desired.

PART XXIV.
New Rules

213. No new Rules of Racing can be adopted by The Jockey Club nor can any of its Rules be rescinded or altered unless the proposed new rule, rescission or alteration shall have been previously advertised twice in the Racing Calendar nor unless notice shall have been given in such advertisement of the meeting of The Jockey Club at which it is to be acted upon, except that:

(a) In the event of an "Emergency," so declared by the Stewards of The Jockey Club, new rules may be passed and any existing rule rescinded or altered at a meeting of The Jockey Club called upon twenty-four hours' notice, which notice shall contain the reason for the meeting.

(b) The Stewards of The Jockey Club may sanction variations in these Rules to conform with local conditions.

20

How to Read Past Performances

Not one racegoer in a thousand is fully conversant with the symbols and abbreviations employed by *Daily Racing Form* in past-performance records. Spending a few minutes with this chapter is highly recommended. The first section of the chapter reproduces the *Form*'s own instructions for users of the tabloid editions published in the middle and far West and Canada. The second section contains instructions for users of the full-size Eastern editions.

DETAILED EXPLANATION OF DATA IN PAST PERFORMANCES

Past Performances include lifetime turf statistics for every horse who has raced on the grass in the U.S. and foreign countries; an indication of races for 3-year-olds and upward 3↑; a symbol Ⓕ denoting races for fillies or fillies and mares; a symbol Ⓢ pointing out races restricted to horses foaled in a specific state, and a "bullet" ● denoting superior workouts (the best workout of the day at the track and distance).

FOREIGN-BRED: An asterisk (*GOOD HOPES) preceding the horse's name indicates he was not bred in the United States or Canada. The country of origin (abbreviated) appears after the breeder's name, as does the state or place of origin of all horses foaled in the United States, Puerto Rico or Canada.

MUD MARKS: One of the following symbols after a horse's name reflects an expert's opinion of his ability on an off track:

✳ Fair Mud Runner ✕ Good Mud Runner ⊗ Superior Mud Runner

RECORD OF STARTS AND EARNINGS: Each horse's complete racing record is given for the current and prior year, or the last two years in which he competed. The letter M in the current year's record indicates the horse is a maiden. M in the previous year's record indicates the horse was a maiden at the end of that year. The Turf Record shows his lifetime number of starts, wins, seconds and thirds in races run on the grass.

Horse	Mud Mark	Claiming Price Color Sex Age	Pedigree	Today's Weight (With Apprentice Allowance Claimed)	Lifetime Turf Record				Complete Record For Two Years				
		Ch. f, 4,	by Ridan—Miss Hopes, by Jet Ribot		St.	1st	2nd	3rd		St.	1st	2nd	3rd	Amt.
Good Hopes	✳	→ $12,000	Br.—Jones H G (NY)	1175	6	2	1	0	1977	14	3	2	0	$9,825
Own.—Good Hope Farm			Tr.—Jones H G						1976	18	M	3	0	$1,750
LATEST WORKOUTS	May 31 Bel 3f fst :37 bg		●May 27 Bel 4f fst :46 h	May 23 Bel 3f fst :36⅗ b					May 14 Bel 4f gd :49 b				

NOTE: Latest workouts are printed under each horse's past performances when they are available. The "bullet" ● indicates it was the best workout of the day at the track and distance. Abbreviations used in workouts: b—breezing; d—driving; e—easily; h—handily; bo—bore out; g—worked from gate; (d)—worked around "dogs"; Ⓣ—turf course; trt—training track; ▣—inner dirt track.

EVERYTHING YOU WANT TO KNOW IS IN THE PAST PERFORMANCES!

30Jun77—6Bel fst 6f :22⅖ :46 1:11⅜ 3↑ⓑⓈ Clm c-12000 3 5 23 3hd 31 1no Smith T⁵ b 117 *.70e 88-14 Good Hopes 117no Bad Baya 112² Lacily 1071½ Blocked, just up 12

DATE RACE WAS RUN — The day, month and year. This race was run on June 30, 1977.

30Jun77—6Bel fst 6f :22⅖ :46 1:11⅜ 3↑ⓑⓈ Clm c-12000 3 5 23 3hd 31 1no Smith T⁵ b 117 *.70e 88-14 Good Hopes 117no Bad Baya 112² Lacily 1071½ Blocked, just up 12

NUMBER OF RACE AND TRACK RACED ON — This was the sixth race at Belmont Park. A complete list of track abbreviations is published in the past performance section of each issue of Daily Racing Form. A ◆ symbol preceding race number denotes track located in foreign country.

30Jun77—6Bel fst 6f :22⅖ :46 1:11⅜ 3↑ⓑⓈ Clm c-12000 3 5 23 3hd 31 1no Smith T⁵ b 117 *.70e 88-14 Good Hopes 117no Bad Baya 112² Lacily 1071½ Blocked, just up 12

TRACK CONDITION — The track was fast. Track condition abbreviations are, for dirt tracks: fst-fast; fr-frozen; gd-good; sl-slow; sly-sloppy; my-muddy; hy-heavy; for turf, steeplechase and hurdle races: hd-hard; fm-firm; gd-good; yl-yielding; sf-soft.

30Jun77—6Bel fst 6f :22⅖ :46 1:11⅜ 3↑ⓑⓈ Clm c-12000 3 5 23 3hd 31 1no Smith T⁵ b 117 *.70e 88-14 Good Hopes 117no Bad Baya 112² Lacily 1071½ Blocked, just up 12

DISTANCE OF RACE — The race was at 6 furlongs (or 3/4 of a mile — there are 8 furlongs to a mile). An asterisk * before distance means it was not exact ('6f—"about" 6 furlongs). Turf course symbols (following distance): Ⓣ—main turf course; Ⓣ—inner turf course; ⊡—inner dirt track (at racecourses that have two dirt strips).

30Jun77—6Bel fst 6f :22⅖ :46 1:11⅜ 3↑ⓑⓈ Clm c-12000 3 5 23 3hd 31 1no Smith T⁵ b 117 *.70e 88-14 Good Hopes 117no Bad Baya 112² Lacily 1071½ Blocked, just up 12

FRACTIONAL TIMES — The first fraction (.22 4/5) is the time of the horse in front at the quarter; the second fraction (.46) is the time of the horse in the lead after a half-mile. Fractional times used vary according to the distance of the race. For the fractional times printed at various distances, see table below.

30Jun77—6Bel fst 6f :22⅖ :46 1:11⅜ 3↑ⓑⓈ Clm c-12000 3 5 23 3hd 31 1no Smith T⁵ b 117 *.70e 88-14 Good Hopes 117no Bad Baya 112² Lacily 1071½ Blocked, just up 12

FINAL TIME — This is the time of the first horse to finish (when the winner is disqualified, this is HIS time, not the time of the horse awarded first money).

30Jun77—6Bel fst 6f :22⅖ :46 1:11⅜ 3↑ⓑⓈ Clm c-12000 3 5 23 3hd 31 1no Smith T⁵ b 117 *.70e 88-14 Good Hopes 117no Bad Baya 112² Lacily 1071½ Blocked, just up 12

RACE FOR 3-YEAR-OLDS AND UPWARD — This is used ONLY when 3-year-olds and upward were eligible to start in the race.

30Jun77—6Bel fst 6f :22⅖ :46 1:11⅜ 3↑ⓑⓈ Clm c-12000 3 5 23 3hd 31 1no Smith T⁵ b 117 *.70e 88-14 Good Hopes 117no Bad Baya 112² Lacily 1071½ Blocked, just up 12

RACE FOR FILLIES AND MARES — The symbol ⓕ means the race was restricted to fillies or fillies and mares.

30Jun77—6Bel fst 6f :22⅖ :46 1:11⅜ 3↑ⓑⓈ Clm c-12000 3 5 23 3hd 31 1no Smith T⁵ b 117 *.70e 88-14 Good Hopes 117no Bad Baya 112² Lacily 1071½ Blocked, just up 12

RACE FOR STATE-BREDS — The symbol Ⓢ means the race was restricted to horses foaled in a specific state (a closed race). The state where the horse was foaled follows the name of his breeder, directly below the horse's pedigree.

30Jun77—6Bel fst 6f :22⅖ :46 1:11⅜ 3↑ⓑⓈ Clm c-12000 3 5 23 3hd 31 1no Smith T⁵ b 117 *.70e 88-14 Good Hopes 117no Bad Baya 112² Lacily 1071½ Blocked, just up 12

CLAIMING PRICE OR TYPE OF RACE — The horse was entered to be claimed for $12,000. The letter c preceding the claiming price indicates the horse was claimed. For a complete list of the various race classifications, see table below.

30Jun77—6Bel fst 6f :22⅖ :46 1:11⅜ 3↑ⓑⓈ Clm c-12000 3 5 23 3hd 31 1no Smith T⁵ b 117 *.70e 88-14 Good Hopes 117no Bad Baya 112² Lacily 1071½ Blocked, just up 12

POST POSITION — The horse left the starting gate from post position number 3. This figure can differ from the official program number because of late scratches, horses coupled in the wagering (an "entry") or horses grouped in the mutuel field.

30Jun77—6Bel fst 6f :22⅘ :46 1:11⅜ 3 ↑ ⓔⓈ Clm c-12000 3 5 2^3 3^{hd} 31 1no Smith T^5 b 117 * .70e 88-14 Good Hopes 117no Bad Baya 112^2 Lacily $107^{1\frac{1}{2}}$ **Blocked, just up 12**

FIRST CALL — The horse's position immediately after leaving the starting gate. He was fifth at this point. Points of call vary according to the distance of the race. In races of 1 mile and longer, the start call is omitted and the horse's position at the 1/4-mile or 1/2-mile is given instead. A table listing the points of call for races at the most frequently run distances is printed below.

30Jun77—6Bel fst 6f :22⅘ :46 1:11⅜ 3 ↑ ⓔⓈ Clm c-12000 3 5 2^3 3^{hd} 31 1no Smith T^5 b 117 * .70e 88-14 Good Hopes 117no Bad Baya 112^2 Lacily $107^{1\frac{1}{2}}$ **Blocked, just up 12**

SECOND CALL — The horse was second, three lengths behind the leader (2^3) at the 1/4-mile point. The large figure indicates the horse's running position; the small one his margin behind the leader. If the horse had been in front at this point (1^3), the small figure would indicate the margin by which he was leading the second horse.

30Jun77—6Bel fst 6f :22⅘ :46 1:11⅜ 3 ↑ ⓔⓈ Clm c-12000 3 5 2^3 3^{hd} 31 1no Smith T^5 b 117 * .70e 88-14 Good Hopes 117no Bad Baya 112^2 Lacily $107^{1\frac{1}{2}}$ **Blocked, just up 12**

THIRD CALL — The horse was third at this call at the 1/2-mile point, a head behind the leader (3^{hd}).

30Jun77—6Bel fst 6f :22⅘ :46 1:11⅜ 3 ↑ ⓔⓈ Clm c-12000 3 5 2^3 3^{hd} 31 1no Smith T^5 b 117 * .70e 88-14 Good Hopes 117no Bad Baya 112^2 Lacily $107^{1\frac{1}{2}}$ **Blocked, just up 12**

STRETCH CALL — The horse was third, one length behind the leader (3^1), at this point. The stretch call is made 1/8 mile from the finish.

30Jun77—6Bel fst 6f :22⅘ :46 1:11⅜ 3 ↑ ⓔⓈ Clm c-12000 3 5 2^3 3^{hd} 31 1no Smith T^5 b 117 * .70e 88-14 Good Hopes 117no Bad Baya 112^2 Lacily $107^{1\frac{1}{2}}$ **Blocked, just up 12**

FINISH — The horse finished first, a nose before the second horse (1no). If the horse is second, third or unplaced, the small figure indicates the total distance he finished behind the winner.

30Jun77—6Bel fst 6f :22⅘ :46 1:11⅜ 3 ↑ ⓔⓈ Clm c-12000 3 5 2^3 3^{hd} 31 1no Smith T^5 b 117 * .70e 88-14 Good Hopes 117no Bad Baya 112^2 Lacily $107^{1\frac{1}{2}}$ **Blocked, just up 12**

JOCKEY — The horse was ridden by T. Smith. The small figure following the jockey's name (Smith T^5) indicates the amount of the apprentice allowance claimed. When an apprentice allowance is claimed the exact number of pounds of the claim is listed.

30Jun77—6Bel fst 6f :22⅘ :46 1:11⅜ 3 ↑ ⓔⓈ Clm c-12000 3 5 2^3 3^{hd} 31 1no Smith T^5 b 117 * .70e 88-14 Good Hopes 117no Bad Baya 112^2 Lacily $107^{1\frac{1}{2}}$ **Blocked, just up 12**

EQUIPMENT CARRIED — The letter b indicates the horse was equipped with blinkers. Other abbreviations which may appear here: s-spurs; sb-spurs and blinkers.

30Jun77—6Bel fst 6f :22⅘ :46 1:11⅜ 3 ↑ ⓔⓈ Clm c-12000 3 5 2^3 3^{hd} 31 1no Smith T^5 b 117 * .70e 88-14 Good Hopes 117no Bad Baya 112^2 Lacily $107^{1\frac{1}{2}}$ **Blocked, just up 12**

WEIGHT CARRIED IN THIS RACE — The horse carried 117 pounds. This is the weight of the rider and equipment (saddle, lead pads, etc.) and includes the apprentice allowance when an allowance is claimed.

30Jun77—6Bel fst 6f :22⅘ :46 1:11⅜ 3 ↑ ⓔⓈ Clm c-12000 3 5 2^3 3^{hd} 31 1no Smith T^5 b 117 * .70e 88-14 Good Hopes 117no Bad Baya 112^2 Lacily $107^{1\frac{1}{2}}$ **Blocked, just up 12**

CLOSING ODDS — The odds were 70 cents to the dollar (he was 7-10 in the wagering). The star preceding the odds indicates he was the favorite. The symbol ♦ between the weight and the odds would mean he finished in a dead-heat with one or more horses. The letter e following the odds means the horse was coupled in the betting (an entry) with one or more horses. The letter f in this position would indicate he was in the mutuel field; the symbol Ⓓ means that the horse was disqualified.

30Jun77—6Bel fst 6f :22⅘ :46 1:11⅜ 3 ↑ ⓔⓈ Clm c-12000 3 5 2^3 3^{hd} 31 1no Smith T^5 b 117 * .70e 88-14 Good Hopes 117no Bad Baya 112^2 Lacily $107^{1\frac{1}{2}}$ **Blocked, just up 12**

SPEED RATING AND TRACK VARIANT — The first figure is the speed rating, a comparison of this horse's time with the 100-par track record; the second figure is the track variant, showing how much below par the times for all races were that day.

30Jun77—6Bel fst 6f :22⅖ :46 1:11⅜ 3↑ⒸⓈ Clm c-12000 3 5 23 3hd 31 1no Smith T⁵ b 117 *.70e 88-14 Good Hope 117no Bad Baya 1122 Lacily 1071½ Blocked, just up 12

FIRST, SECOND AND THIRD HORSES AT THE FINISH — The horses who finished 1-2-3 in the race, the weight each carried and the margins separating each one from the next horse If any of these horses was disqualified or finished in a dead-heat, the symbol Ⓓ for disqualified or ⒹⒽ for dead-heat precedes the horse's name.

30Jun77—6Bel fst 6f :22⅖ :46 1:11⅜ 3↑ⒸⓈ Clm c-12000 3 5 23 3hd 31 1no Smith T⁵ b 117 *.70e 88-14 Good Hopes 117no Bad Baya 1122 Lacily 1071½ Blocked, just up 12

COMMENT LINE — A capsule description of the horse's performance, with special emphasis on pointing out any trouble he may have encountered.

30Jun77—6Bel fst 6f :22⅖ :46 1:11⅜ 3↑ⒸⓈ Clm c-12000 3 5 23 3hd 31 1no Smith T⁵ b 117 *.70e 88-14 Good Hopes 117no Bad Baya 1122 Lacily 1071½ Blocked, just up 12

NUMBER OF STARTERS — Twelve horses started in this race.

ABBREVIATIONS USED FOR RACE CLASSIFICATIONS

"Allowance"—Allowance race.
"Clm 10000"—Claiming race. (Entered for $10,000.)
"Stk 50000"—Claiming stakes. (Entered for $50,000.)
"Ⓕ-M 10000"—Fillies or fillies & mares, maidens, claiming. (Entered for $10,000.)
"Handicap"—Handicap.
"Hcp 10000"—Handicap, claiming. (Entered for $10,000.)
"Inv. H'cap"—Invitational handicap.
"Md Allow"—Maidens, allowances.
"Md 10000"—Maidens, claiming. (Entered for $10,000.)
"Md Sp Wt"—Maidens, special weight.

"Match R"—Match race.
"Clm º10000"—Optional claiming race—NOT entered to be claimed.
"Clm 10000º"—Optional claiming race—WAS entered to be claimed.
"Hcp º10000"—Optional claiming handicap—NOT entered to be claimed.
"Hcp 10000º"—Optional claiming handicap—WAS entered to be claimed.
"Spec'l Wt"—Special Weight.
"Alw 10000s"—Starter allowance race.
"Hcp 10000s"—Starter handicap.
"Md 10000s"—Starter maiden race.
"Spw 10000s"—Starter special weight race.

In stakes races, with the exception of claiming stakes, the name or abbreviation of name is shown in the class of race column. The letter "H" after name indicates the race was a handicap stakes. The same procedure is used for the rich invitational races for which there are no nomination or starting fees. The letters "Inv" following the abbreviation indicate the race was by invitation only.

POINTS OF CALL AND FRACTIONAL TIMES IN PAST PERFORMANCES

The points of call and the fractional times in the past performances vary according to the distance of the race. The points for which the fractional times are given correspond to the points of call of the running positions (except in some races at odd distances). In all races, the stretch call is made 1/8 mile from the finish. The points of call and fractional times for the most frequently raced distances are:

Distance of Race	1st Call	2nd Call	Points of Call 3rd Call	4th Call	5th Call	Fractional Times Given At These Points of Call	
2 Furlongs	Start	—	—	Stretch	Finish	—	Finish
2 1/2 Furlongs	Start	—	—	Stretch	Finish	—	Finish
3 Furlongs	Start	—	—	Stretch	Finish	1/4	Finish
3 1/2 Furlongs	Start	1/4	—	Stretch	Finish	1/4	3/8 Finish
4 Furlongs	Start	1/4	—	Stretch	Finish	1/4	Finish
4 1/2 Furlongs	Start	1/4	—	Stretch	Finish	1/4	1/2 Finish
5 Furlongs	Start	3/16	3/8	Stretch	Finish	1/4	1/2 Finish
5 1/2 Furlongs	Start	1/4	3/8	Stretch	Finish	1/4	1/2 Finish
6 Furlongs	Start	1/4	1/2	Stretch	Finish	1/4	1/2 Finish
6 1/2 Furlongs	Start	1/4	1/2	Stretch	Finish	1/4	1/2 Finish
7 Furlongs	Start	1/4	1/2	Stretch	Finish	1/4	1/2 Finish
1 Mile	1/4	1/2	3/4	Stretch	Finish	1/2	3/4 Finish
1 Mile 70 Yards	1/4	1/2	3/4	Stretch	Finish	1/2	3/4 Finish
1 1/16 Miles	1/4	1/2	3/4	Stretch	Finish	1/2	3/4 Finish
1 1/8 Miles	1/4	1/2	3/4	Stretch	Finish	1/2	3/4 Finish
1 3/16 Miles	1/4	1/2	3/4	Stretch	Finish	1/2	3/4 Finish
1 1/4 Miles	1/4	1/2	1 mile	Stretch	Finish	1/2	1 mile Finish
1 5/16 Miles	1/4	1/2	1 mile	Stretch	Finish	1/2	1 mile Finish
1 3/8 Miles	1/4	1/2	1 mile	Stretch	Finish	1/2	1 mile Finish
1 1/2 Miles	1/4	1/2	1 1/4	Stretch	Finish	1/2	1 1/4 Finish
1 5/8 Miles	1/4	1/2	1 3/8	Stretch	Finish	1/2	1 1/4 Finish
1 3/4 Miles	1/2	1 mile	1 1/2	Stretch	Finish	1/2	1 1/2 Finish
1 7/8 Miles	1/2	1 mile	1 5/8	Stretch	Finish	1/2	1 3/4 Finish
2 Miles	1/2	1 mile	1 3/4	Stretch	Finish	1/2	1 3/4 Finish
2 1/16 Miles	1/2	1 mile	1 3/4	Stretch	Finish	1/2	1 3/4 Finish
2 1/8 Miles	1/2	1 mile	1 3/4	Stretch	Finish	1/2	1 3/4 Finish
2 1/4 Miles & Longer	1/2	1 mile	2 miles	Stretch	Finish	1/2	2 miles Finish

NOTE: When the 1/4 mile or 1/2 mile call is substituted for the start call, only the horse's position at that point is indicated. The margin separating the horse from the leader is not given.

Day
Month
Year
Number of Race
Track Raced On
Distance
Fractional Times of Horse in Lead at Each of These Points
Time of Winner
Track Condition
Closing Odds
Denotes Favorite
Weight Carried
Apprentice Allowance
First Call
Second Call
In Stretch
At Finish
Winning Margin
Jockey
Post Position
Denotes Claim
Type of Race or Claiming Price
Speed Rating
Race Exclusively for Fillies & Mares
First Two Horses in Order of Finish
(With Weight Carried by First Horse)
Number of Starters

27Jun 74² AP   6f   :22⁴ :46 1:11³   ft   9-5   ▲117⁵   5³   4²   2ʰ   1¹½   JonesJ⁵   c5000 87   Ⓟ Donnie 117 Lovely Day   8

EVERYTHING YOU WANT TO KNOW IS IN THE P.P.'s!

27Jun 74² AP   6f   :22⁴ :46 1:11³ ft 9-5 ▲117⁵ 5³ 4² 2ʰ 1¹½ JonesJ⁵   c5000 87   Ⓟ Donnie 117 Lovely Day 8
DATE RACE WAS RUN—The day, month and year. This race was run June 27, 1974.

27Jun 74² AP   6f   :22⁴ :46 1:11³ ft 9-5 ▲117⁵ 5³ 4² 2ʰ 1¹½ JonesJ⁵   c5000 87   Ⓟ Donnie 117 Lovely Day 8
NUMBER OF RACE AND TRACK RACED ON—This was the second race at Arlington Park (AP). See the past performances section of Daily Racing Form for a complete list of track abbreviations.

27Jun 74² AP   6f   :22⁴ :46 1:11³ ft 9-5 ▲117⁵ 5³ 4² 2ʰ 1¹½ JonesJ⁵   c5000 87   Ⓟ Donnie 117 Lovely Day 8
DISTANCE OF RACE—The race was six furlongs or ¾ of a mile (there are 8 furlongs to a mile). An "a" before the distance (a6f) denotes an "about" or inexact distance ("about six furlongs"). A circled Ⓣ before the distance denotes the race was run on the main turf course; a squared Ⓣ a race run on track's inner turf course.

27Jun 74² AP   6f   :22⁴ :46 1:11³ ft 9-5 ▲117⁵ 5³ 4² 2ʰ 1¹½ JonesJ⁵   c5000 87   Ⓟ Donnie 117 Lovely Day 8
FRACTIONAL TIMES—The first fraction (:22 4/5) is the time of the horse in front at the ¼; the second fraction (:46) is the time of the horse in front at the ½. For a listing of the fractions at other distances, see Fractional Times explanation below.

27Jun 74² AP   6f   :22⁴ :46 1:11³ ft 9-5 ▲117⁵ 5³ 4² 2ʰ 1¹½ JonesJ⁵   c5000 87   Ⓟ Donnie 117 Lovely Day 8
FINAL TIME OF FIRST HORSE TO FINISH—This is the winner's final time (the six furlongs were run in 1:11 3/5). In all cases, this is the time of the first horse to finish (when the winner is disqualified, this is HIS time, not the time of the horse awarded first money).

27Jun 74² AP   6f   :22⁴ :46 1:11³ ft 9-5 ▲117⁵ 5³ 4² 2ʰ 1¹½ JonesJ⁵   c5000 87   Ⓟ Donnie 117 Lovely Day 8
TRACK CONDITION—The track was fast (ft). See reverse side for all other track condition abbreviations.

27Jun 74² AP   6f   :22⁴ :46 1:11³ ft 9-5 ▲117⁵ 5³ 4² 2ʰ 1¹½ JonesJ⁵   c5000 87   Ⓟ Donnie 117 Lovely Day 8
APPROXIMATE CLOSING ODDS—The odds were approximately 9-5 in the wagering. A triangle ▲ following the odds indicates the horse was the favorite; an "e" that he was part of an entry (two or more horses coupled in the wagering); an "f" that he was in the mutuel field.

27Jun 74² AP   6f   :22⁴ :46 1:11³ ft 9-5 ▲117⁵ 5³ 4² 2ʰ 1¹½ JonesJ⁵   c5000 87   Ⓟ Donnie 117 Lovely Day 8
WEIGHT CARRIED IN THIS RACE—The horse carried 117 pounds. The small figure following the weight indicates the amount of the apprentice allowance claimed. When an apprentice allowance is claimed the exact amount of the claim is listed.

27Jun 74² AP   6f   :22⁴ :46 1:11³ ft 9-5 ▲117⁵ 5³ 4² 2ʰ 1¹½ JonesJ⁵   c5000 87   Ⓟ Donnie 117 Lovely Day 8
FIRST CALL—The horse was running fifth, three lengths behind the leader, at this stage of the race (at the ¼ mile in this instance). The larger figure indicates the horse's running position; the small one his total margin behind the first horse. If he was in front at this point (1²) the superior figure would indicate the margin by which he was leading the second horse.

27Jun 74² AP   6f   :22⁴ :46 1:11³ ft 9-5 ▲117⁵ 5³ 4² 2ʰ 1¹½ JonesJ⁵   c5000 87   Ⓟ Donnie 117 Lovely Day 8
SECOND CALL—The horse was fourth at this stage of the race (at the ½ mile in this case) a total of two lengths behind the leader.

27Jun 74² AP   6f   :22⁴ :46 1:11³ ft 9-5 ▲117⁵ 5³ 4² 2ʰ 1¹½ JonesJ⁵   c5000 87   Ⓟ Donnie 117 Lovely Day 8
STRETCH CALL—The horse was second at this stage of the race, a head behind the leader.

27Jun 74² AP   6f   :22⁴ :46 1:11³ ft 9-5 ▲117⁵ 5³ 4² 2ʰ 1¹½ JonesJ⁵   c5000 87   Ⓟ Donnie 117 Lovely Day 8
FINISH—The horse finished first, 1½ lengths in front of the second horse. If second, third or unplaced, the superior figure indicates his margin behind the winner.

27Jun 74² AP   6f   :22⁴ :46 1:11³ ft 9-5 ▲117⁵ 5³ 4² 2ʰ 1¹½ JonesJ⁵   c5000 87   Ⓟ Donnie 117 Lovely Day 8
JOCKEY AND POST POSITION—J. Jones rode the horse, who started from post position number 5.

27Jun 74² AP   6f   :22⁴ :46 1:11³ ft 9-5 ▲117⁵ 5³ 4² 2ʰ 1¹½ JonesJ⁵   c5000 87   Ⓟ Donnie 117 Lovely Day 8
CLAIMING PRICE OR TYPE OF RACE—The horse was entered to be claimed for $5,000 and the "c" indicates he was claimed. See reverse side for a complete list of the race classification abbreviations used in this portion of the past performance line.

27Jun 74² AP   6f   :22⁴ :46 1:11³ ft 9-5 ▲117⁵ 5³ 4² 2ʰ 1¹½ JonesJ⁵   c5000 87   Ⓟ Donnie 117 Lovely Day 8
SPEED RATING—The horse's speed rating was 87. See reverse side for an explanation of speed ratings.

27Jun 74² AP   6f   :22⁴ :46 1:11³ ft 9-5 ▲117⁵ 5³ 4² 2ʰ 1¹½ JonesJ⁵   c5000 87   Ⓟ Donnie 117 Lovely Day 8
FIRST TWO FINISHERS—These are the first two finishers in the race, with the weight carried by the first horse. The Ⓟ preceding the first horse's name indicates the race was exclusively for fillies or fillies and mares.

27Jun 74² AP   6f   :22⁴ :46 1:11³ ft 9-5 ▲117⁵ 5³ 4² 2ʰ 1¹½ JonesJ⁵   c5000 87   Ⓟ Donnie 117 Lovely Day 8
NUMBER OF STARTERS—Eight horses started in this race.

POINTS OF CALL IN PAST PERFORMANCES

The points of call in the past performances vary according to the distance of the race. The points of call of the running positions for the most frequently raced distances are:

Distance		1st Call	2nd Call	3rd Call	4th Call		Distance	1st Call	2nd Call	3rd Call	4th Call
2	Furlongs	Start	—	Stretch	Finish		1 Mile	½ mile	¾ mile	Stretch	Finish
5/16	Mile	Start	—	Stretch	Finish		1 Mile, 70 Yds	½ mile	¾ mile	Stretch	Finish
3	Furlongs	Start	—	Stretch	Finish		1¹⁄₁₆ Miles	½ mile	¾ mile	Stretch	Finish
3½	Furlongs	Start	—	Stretch	Finish		1⅛ Miles	½ mile	¾ mile	Stretch	Finish
4	Furlongs	Start	¼ mile	Stretch	Finish		1³⁄₁₆ Miles	½ mile	¾ mile	Stretch	Finish
4½	Furlongs	Start	¼ mile	Stretch	Finish		1¼ Miles	½ mile	1 mile	Stretch	Finish
5	Furlongs	¼ mile	⅜ mile	Stretch	Finish		1⅜ Miles	½ mile	1 mile	Stretch	Finish
5½	Furlongs	¼ mile	⅜ mile	Stretch	Finish		1½ Miles	½ mile	1¼ miles	Stretch	Finish
6	Furlongs	¼ mile	½ mile	Stretch	Finish		1⅝ Miles	½ mile	1⅜ miles	Stretch	Finish
6½	Furlongs	¼ mile	½ mile	Stretch	Finish		1¾ Miles	½ mile	1½ miles	Stretch	Finish
7	Furlongs	¼ mile	½ mile	Stretch	Finish						

NOTE: The second call in most races is made ¼ mile from the finish; the stretch call ⅛ mile from the finish.

FRACTIONAL TIMES

In races at less than one mile, fractional times are given for the horse in the lead at the quarter-mile and half-mile. In races at one mile or more, fractional times are given for the half-mile and three-quarter mile.

NOTE: In races at the shorter distances, only the fraction for the quarter-mile is used, except for races at three and one-half furlongs, in which the fractions are given for the quarter-mile and three-eighths mile.

KEY TO SYMBOLS, ABBREVIATIONS IN PAST PERFORMANCES

FOREIGN-BRED HORSES
An asterisk(*) preceding the name of the horse indicates foreign-bred. (No notation is made for horses bred in Canada and Cuba.

MUD MARKS
* —Fair mud runner   X—Good mud runner
⊗—Superior mud runner

COLOR
B.—Bay	Blk.—Black	Br.—Brown	Ch.—Chestnut
	Gr.—Gray Ro.—Roan Wh.—White		
	Dk. b. or br.—Dark bay or brown		
	(Lt. before color denotes Light)		

SEX
c—colt   h—horse   g—gelding   rig—ridgling
f—filly   m—mare

PEDIGREE
Each horse's pedigree lists, in the order named, color, sex, year foaled, sire, dam and grandsire (sire of dam).

BREEDER
Abbreviation following breeder's name indicates the state, place of origin or foreign country in which the horse was foaled.

TODAY'S CLAIMING PRICE
Claiming prices for horses entered today appear in bold face type to right of trainer's name.

RECORD OF STARTS AND EARNINGS
The horse's racing record for his most recent two years of competition appears to the extreme right of the name of the breeder. This lists the year, number of starts, wins, seconds, thirds and earnings. The letter "M" in the win column of the upper line indicates the horse is a maiden. If the letter "M" is in the lower line only, it indicates the horse was a maiden at the end of that year.

DISTANCE
a— preceding distance (a6f) denotes "about" distance (about 6 furlongs in this instance.)

TURF COURSES
Ⓣ— before distance indicates turf (grass) course race.

Ⓣ— before distance indicates inner turf course.

TRACK CONDITIONS
ft—fast	fr—frozen	gd—good	sl—slow
sy—sloppy	m—muddy	hy—heavy	

Turf course races, including steeplechase and hurdles:
hd—hard	fm—firm	gd—good yl—yielding	sf—soft

Note: SC in place of track condition indicates Synthetic Course in use at various tracks. The condition of this synthetic course is fast at all times.

CLOSING ODDS
2▲—favorite   2e—entry   15f—mutuel field

APPRENTICE OR RIDER WEIGHT ALLOWANCES
Allowance (in pounds) indicated by superior figure following weight—1175

ABBREVIATIONS USED IN POINTS OF CALL
no—nose   h—head   nk—neck

POST POSITION
Horse's post position appears after jockey's name—Wilson R⁴.

RACE CLASSIFICATIONS
10000— Claiming race (eligible to be claimed for $10,000). Note: The letter c preceding claiming price (c10000) indicates horse was claimed.

M10000—Maiden claiming race (non-winners—eligible to be claimed).

10000H—Claiming handicap (eligible to be claimed).

o10000—Optional claiming race (entered NOT to be claimed).

10000o—Optional claiming race (eligible to be claimed).

Mdn—Maiden race (non-winners).

AlwM—Maiden allowance race (for non-winners with special weight allowance for those having started in a claiming race).

Alw—Allowance race.

HcpO—Overnight handicap race.

SplW—Special weight race.

Wfa—Weight-for-age race.

Mtch—Match race.

A10000—Starter allowance race (horses who have started for claiming price shown, or less, as stipulated in the conditions).

H10000—Starter handicap (same restriction as above).

S10000— Starter special weight (restricted as above). Note: Where no amount is specified in the conditions of the "starters" race dashes are substituted, as shown below:

A————   H————   S————

STEEPLECHASE AND HURDLE RACES
[S—Steeplechase   [H—Hurdle race

STAKES RACES
AlwS—Allowance stakes.

HcpS—Handicap stakes.

ScwS—Scale weight stakes.

SpwS—Special weight stakes.

WfaS—Weight-for-age stakes.

50000S—Claiming stakes (eligible to be claimed).

INVITATIONAL RACES
InvH—Invitational handicap.

InvSc—Invitational scale weight

InvSp—Invitational special weights.

InvW—Invitational weight-for-age.

RACES EXCLUSIVELY FOR FILLIES, MARES
Ⓕ— Immediately following the speed rating indicates races exclusively for fillies or fillies and mares.

SPEED RATINGS
This is a comparison of the horse's time with the track record established prior to the opening of the meeting. The track record is given a rating of 100 and one point is deducted for each one-fifth second slower than the record. When a horse breaks the track record one point is added to the par 100 for each one-fifth second faster than the record. One-fifth of a second is considered the equivalent of one length.

No ratings are given for hurdle or steeplechase events, for races of less than three furlongs, for races where the horse's speed rating is less than 25.

NOTE: Speed ratings for new distances are computed and assigned when adequate time standards are established. At Caliente, Mexico, which operates throughout the year, rating changes are made whenever a track record is broken.

EACH HORSE'S MOST RECENT WORKOUTS APPEAR DIRECTLY UNDER THE PAST PERFORMANCES
For example, July 30 Bel 3f ft :38b indicates the horse worked on July 30 at Belmont Park. The distance of the trial was 3 furlongs over a fast track and the horse was timed in 38 seconds, breezing. The following abbreviations are used to describe how each horse worked:

b—breezing	d—driving	e—easily	g—worked from stall gate	h—handily	bo—bore out

trt following track abbreviation indicates horse worked on training track.   tc—turf course   TR-Trial race
HC—Hillside Course

Abbreviations for North American Tracks

Abbreviations below designate tracks in DAILY RACING FORM charts and past performances.

AC	Agua Caliente, Mex.	Det	Detroit Race Course, Mich.
Aks	Ak-Sar-Ben, Neb.	Dmr	Del Mar, Calif.
Alb	Albuquerque, N. Mex.	EIP	James C. Ellis Park, Ky.
AP	Arlington Park, Ill.	EP	Exhibition Park, Can.*
Aqu	Aqueduct, N.Y.	EvD	Evangeline Downs, La.*
AsD	Assiniboia Downs, Can.*	FD	Florida Downs, Fla.[2]
Atl	Atlantic City, N.J.	FE	Fort Erie, Can.
Ato	Atokad Park, Neb.*	Fer	Ferndale, Calif.*
BB	Blue Bonnets, Can.*	FG	Fair Grounds, La.
BD	Berkshire Downs, Mass.*	FL	Finger Lakes, N.Y.
Bel	Belmont Park, N.Y.	Fno	Fresno, Calif.
Beu	Beulah Park, Ohio	Fon	Fonner Park, Neb.*
BF	Brockton Fair, Mass.*	FP	Fairmount Park, Ill.
Bil	Billings, Mont.*	GBF	Great Barrington, Mass.*
BM	Bay Meadows, Calif.	GF	Great Falls, Mont.*
Bmf	Bay Meadows Fair, Calif.	GG	Golden Gate Fields, Calif.
Boi	Les Bois Park, Boise, Idaho*	GM	Green Mountain, Vt.*
Bow	Bowie, Md.	GP	Gulfstream Park, Fla.
CD	Churchill Downs, Ky.	Grd	Greenwood, Can.*
CdA	Coeur d'Alene, Idaho*	GS	Garden State Park, N.J.
Cen	Centennial Race Track, Colo.	Haw	Hawthorne, Ill.
Cka	Cahokia Downs, Ill.*	Hia	Hialeah Park, Fla.
Cls	Columbus, Neb.*	Hol	Hollywood Park, Calif.
Com	Commodore Downs, Pa.*	HP	Hazel Park, Mich.*
Crc	Calder Race Course, Fla.	JnD	Jefferson Downs, La.*
CT	Charles Town, W.Va.*	Jua	Juarez, Mex.
Cwl	Commonwealth Race Course, Ky.[1]*	Kee	Keeneland, Ky.
		Key	Keystone Race Track, Pa.
DeD	Delta Downs, La.*	LaD	Louisiana Downs, La.
Del	Delaware Park, Del.	LaM	La Mesa Park, N.M.*

Lat	Latonia, Ky.		Suf	Suffolk Downs, Mass.
Lbg	Lethbridge, Can.*		Sun	Sunland Park, N.M.
LD	Lincoln Downs, R.I.*		Tdn	Thistledown, Ohio
Lga	Longacres, Wash.		Tim	Timonium, Md.*
LnN	Lincoln State Fair, Neb.*		TuP	Turf Paradise, Ariz.
Lrl	Laurel Race Course, Md.		Was	Washington Park, Ill.
MD	Marquis Downs, Can.*		Wat	Waterford Park, W.Va.
Med	Meadowlands, N.J.		Wey	Weymouth Fair, Mass.*
Mex	Mexico City, Mex.*		WO	Woodbine, Can.
MF	Marshfield Fair, Mass.*		YM	Yakima Meadows, Wash.
Mth	Monmouth Park, N.J.			
Nar	Narragansett Park, R.I.			**HUNT MEETINGS**
Nmp	Northampton, Mass.*			
NP	Northlands Park, Can.*		Aik	Aiken, S.C.
OP	Oaklawn Park, Ark.		AtH	Atlanta, Ga.
Pen	Penn National, Pa.		Cam	Camden, S.C.
Pim	Pimlico, Md.		Clm	Clemmons, N.C.
PJ	Park Jefferson, S.D.*		Fai	Fair Hill, Md.
Pla	Playfair, Wash.*		Fax	Fairfax, Va.
Pln	Pleasanton, Calif.		FH	Far Hills, N.J.
PM	Portland Meadows, Ore.		Gln	Glyndon, Md.
Pmf	Portland Meadows Fair, Ore.		GN	Grand National, Md.*
Poc	Pocono Downs, Pa.*		Lex	Lexington, Ky.
Pom	Pomona, Calif.*		Lig	Ligonier, Pa.
PR	Puerto Rico		Mal	Malvern, Pa.
Pre	Prescott Downs, Ariz.*		Mid	Middleburg, Va.
RD	River Downs, Ohio		Mon	Monkton, Md.
Reg	Regina, Can.*		Mtp	Montpelier, Va.
Ril	Rillito, Ariz.*		Oxm	Oxmoor, Ky.
Rkm	Rockingham Park, N.H.		Pro	Prospect, Ky.
Rui	Ruidoso Downs, N.M.*		PW	Percy Warner, Tenn.
SA	Santa Anita Park, Calif.		RB	Red Bank, N.J.
Sac	Sacramento, Calif.		SH	Strawberry Hill, Va.
Sal	Salem, Ore.*		SoP	Southern Pines, N.C.
San	Sandown Park, Can.*		Try	Tryon, N.C.
Sar	Saratoga, N.Y.		Uni	Unionville, Pa.
SFe	Santa Fe Downs, N.M.*		War	Warrenton, Va.
ShD	Shenandoah Downs, W.Va.*		Wel	Wellsville, Pa.
Sol	Solano, Calif.*			
Spt	Sportsman's Park, Ill.*			
SR	Santa Rosa, Calif.*			
Stk	Stockton, Calif.			
StP	Stampede Park, Can.[3]*			

* Indicates tracks less than one mile in circumference.
[1] Formerly named Miles Park.
[2] Formerly named Sunshine Park.
[3] Formerly named Victoria Park.

Abbreviations for Foreign Tracks

AbA	Aberdeen, Aus.		**Bda**	Budapest, Hungary
Af	Africa		**Cgs**	Cagnes, Fra.
Ain	Aintree, Eng.		**Can**	Canterbury, Aus.
AEP	Aix-En-Provence, Fra.		**Cara**	Caracas, Venez.
Alx	Alexandra Park, Eng.		**Car**	Carlisle, Eng.
Amie	Amiens, Fra.		**Ctk**	Catterick, Eng.
And	Andelys, Fra.		**Cau**	Caulfield, Aus.
Ang	Angers, Fra.		**Cav**	Cavaillon, Fra.
Ast	Ascot, Eng.		**CeA**	Cessnock, Aus.
Auc	Auckland, N.Z.		**Cha**	Chantilly, Fra.
Aus	Australia		**Che**	Cheltenham, Eng.
Aut	Auteuil, Fra.		**ChA**	Cheltenham, Aus.
Ayr	Ayr, Scot.		**Chep**	Chepstow, Eng.
BaB	Baden Baden, Ger.		**Chs**	Chester, Eng.
Bal	Baldoyle, Ire.		**CiJ**	Cidare Jardim, Brazil
Bo-D	Bangor-on-Dee, Eng.		**Cla**	Clairfontaine, Fra.
Bat	Bath, Eng.		**Cln**	Clarendon, Aus.
BtA	Beaudesert, Aus.		**HdS**	Club Hipico de Santiago, Chile
Belg	Belgium		**Clge**	Cologne, Ger.
Bell	Bellestown, Ire.		**CSA**	Columbia, S.A.
BlnE	Berlin, East Germany		**Com**	Compiegne, Fra.
Bern	Bernay, Fra.		**Cor**	Cordoba, Arg.
Bev	Beverley, Eng.		**Cd'A**	Cote d'Azur, Fra.
Brtz	Biarritz-Bayonne, Fra.		**Cra**	Craon, Fra.
Bir	Birmingham, Eng.		**C-L**	Croise-Laroche, Fra.
Bgta	Bogota, Col.		**Cur**	Curragh, Ire.
Bog	Bogside, Scot.		**Dea**	Deauville, Fra.
Boik	Boiktort, Belgium		**Dev**	Devon-Exeter, Eng.
Bor	Bordeaux, Fra.		**Diep**	Dieppe, Fra.
Braz	Brazil		**Don**	Doncaster, Eng.
Bri	Brighton, Eng.		**Dor**	Dortmund, Ger.
Bris	Brisbane, Aus.		**DRoy**	Down Royal, Ire.
Bru	Brussels, Belgium		**Ddt**	Duindigt, Holland
Bgh	Buckfastleigh, Eng.		**Dun**	Dundalk, Ire.

Dus	Dusseldorf, Ger.	Lud	Ludlow, Eng.
Edn	Edinburgh, Scot.	Lvov	Lvov, Ukrania
Elb	Elbeut, Fra.	Lyon	Lyons, Fra.
Eng	Enghien, Fra.	Mai	Maissons-Laffitte, Fra.
Epm	Epsom, Eng.	Mall	Mallow, Ire.
Esk	Esk, Australia	Man	Manchester, Eng.
Fy	Fairyhouse, Ire.	Msl	Marseille, Fra.
FlA	Flemington, Aus.	Mas	Masterton, N.Z.
Fol	Folkestone, Eng.	Mtu	Manawatu, N.Z.
Font	Fontainebleau, Fra.	Mda	Mendoza, Arg.
Fwl	Fontwell, Eng.	Mer	Merano, Italy
Fra	Frankfort, Ger.	Mil	Milan, Italy
Gal	Galway, Ire.	Mto	Monterrico, Peru
Gwd	Goodwood, Eng.	MVA	Moonee Vly, Aus.
GoA	Gosford, Aus.	Mor	Mornington, Aus.
GoP	Gowran Park, Ire.	Mrpt	Morphetville, Aus.
Ham	Hamburg, Ger.	Mos	Moscow, Russia
Hml	Hamilton, Scot.	Muh	Mulheim, Ger.
Han	Hanshin, Japan	Mul	Mullinger, Ire.
H.B	Hawkes Bay, N.Z.	Naas	Naas, Ire.
Hay	Haydock Park, Eng.	Nak	Nakayama, Japan
HnA	Hazeldean, Aus.	Nan	Nantes, Fra.
Hfd	Hereford, Eng.	Nap	Naples, Italy
HAr	Hipodromo Argentino, S.A.	Nav	Navan, Ire.
HCh	Hipodromo Chile, Chile	Nus	Neuss, Ger.
Hor	Horst-Emscher, Ger.	Nby	Newbury, Eng.
HuP	Hurst Park, Eng.	NeA	Newcastle, Aus.
If-Ba	Iffezheim-Baden, Ger.	Nec	Newcastle, Eng.
I.S	Isle Sorgue, Fra.	New	Newmarket, Eng.
BWl	Jamaica, B.W.I.	Ntn	Newton Abbott, Eng.
Kel	Kelso, Scot.	N.Z	New Zealand
KG	Kembia Grange, Aus.	NoE	Nort Erdre, Fra.
Kem	Kempton Park, Eng.	Not	Nottingham, Eng.
Kilb	Kilbeggan, Ire.	Orl	Orleans, Fra.
Kill	Killarney, Ire.	Oslo	Oslo, Norway
Kfd	Knutsford Park, B.W.I.	Ost	Ostend, Belgium
Koi	Koin, Ger.	OtM	Otaki Maori, N.Z.
Kre	Krefeld, Ger.	Pal	Palermo, Arg.
Kret	Kretein, Ger.	Pan	Panama
Kyo	Kyoto, Japan	Per	Perth, Scot.
LaC	La Capelle, Fra.	PhP	Phoenix Park, Ire.
Lan	Lanark, Scot.	Plu	Plumpton, Eng.
LaP	La Plata, S.A.	Pomp	Pompadour, Fra.
Layt	Layton, Ire.	Pon	Pontefract, Eng.
Lgn	Leghorn, Italy	Pow	Powerstown Park, Ire.
Lei	Leicester, Eng.	Pun	Punchestown, Ire.
Leo	Leopardstown, Ire.	QdA	Queensland, Aus.
Tre	Le Tremblay, Fra.	Raf	Rafaela, Arg.
Lew	Lewes, Eng.	Rand	Randwick, Aus.
Peru	Lima, Peru	Red	Redcar, Eng.
LimJ	Limerick Junction, Ire.	Rei	Reims, Fra.
Lin	Lincoln, Eng.	Rei	Rennes, Fra.
Lfd	Lingfield, Eng.	Rin	Rinconada, Venez.
List	Listowel, Ire.	R.J	Rio de Janiero, Brazil
Liv	Liverpool, Eng.	Rip	Ripon, Eng.
Lon	Longchamp, Fra.	Rom	Rome, Italy
Lou	Loudeac, Fra.	Rio	Rosario, Arg.

Rmn	Roscommon, Ire.	**Tur**	Turin, Italy
Ros	Rosehill, Aus.	**Uru**	Uruguay
Rou	Rouen, Fra.	**Utx**	Uttoxetter, Eng.
StC	Saint-Cloud, Fra.	**Val**	Valparaiso, Chile
Sby	Salisbury, Eng.	**Van**	Vannes, Fra.
Sdn	Sandown, Eng.	**Var**	Varese, Italy
SF	San Felipe, Peru	**Ver**	Vernon, Fra.
SI	San Isidro, Arg.	**Vich**	Vichy, Fra.
Sant	Santiago, Chile	**Vic**	Victoria, Aus.
Sed	Sedgefield, Eng.	**Vna**	Vienna, Austria
Sli	Sligo, Ire.	**Wto**	Waikato, N.Z.
SthA	South Africa	**Wan**	Wanganui, N.Z.
Sll	Southwell, Eng.	**Wsw**	Warsaw, Poland
StM	St. Malo, Fra.	**Wak**	Warwick, Eng.
Stkl	Stockel, Belgium	**WarF**	Warwick Farm, Aus.
Stock	Stockholm, Sweden	**Wa-T**	Waterford-Tramore, Ire.
Stn	Stockton, Eng.	**Wel**	Wellington, N.Z.
SoA	Stratford-on-Avon, Eng.	**Wer**	Werribee, Aus.
Syd	Sydney, Aus.	**Wet**	Wetherby, Eng.
Tau	Taunton, Eng.	**Win**	Windsor, Eng.
Tsk	Thirsk, Eng.	**Wolv**	Wolverhampton, Eng.
Thur	Thurles, Ire.	**Wdn**	Woodend, Aus.
Tok	Tokyo, Japan	**Wor**	Worcester, Eng.
ToA	Toowoomba, Aus.	**Wye**	Wye, Eng.
Toul	Toulouse, Fra.	**Wvo**	Wyong, Aus.
Tou	Touquest, Fra.	**Yar**	Yarmouth, Eng.
Tow	Towcester, Eng.	**Yor**	York, Eng.
Tra	Tralee, Ire.	**Yugo**	Yugoslavia
Trm	Tramore, Ire.		

21

The Racegoer's Dictionary

Acey deucy—Riding style in which right stirrup is shorter than left, enabling jockey to balance more easily on turns.

Across the board—Three bets—win, place and show—on one horse.

Added money—Purse money with which track management supplements stakes posted by owners and breeders.

Aged—Of a horse, aged seven or older.

Airing—A workout; a racing performance in which horse runs as if it were only out for exercise.

All-out—Maximum exertion.

Allowance race—A non-claiming affair in which published conditions stipulate weight allowances according to previous purse earnings and/or number or type of victories.

Also eligible—Official entrants that will not run unless other horses are scratched and vacancies occur in field.

Also-ran—Horse that finished out of the money.

Alter—To castrate, geld.

Ankle boot—Protective covering for fetlock, usually leather or rubber.

Ankle cutter—Horse that cuts a fetlock with opposite foot while running.

Apprentice—Student jockey.

Apprentice allowance—Weight concession granted animal ridden by apprentice.

Arm—Foreleg, between elbow and knee; forearm.

Armchair ride—Easy victory without urging by rider.

Baby—Two-year-olds, especially during first months of year.

Baby race—Two-, three- or four-furlong race for two-year-olds, early in year.

Back at the knee—Defective conformation in which foreleg bends slightly backward at knee.

Backstretch—Straight part of track on far side; stable area.

Back up—Slow down noticeably.

Bad actor—Fractious horse.

Bad doer—Horse that lacks appetite, usually because of illness, pain, fatigue, nervousness or loneliness.

Badger—Cheap horse that qualifies owner for track privileges; "badge horse."

Bald—Of a horse, with a white face.

Ball—Pill; physic.

Bandage—Leg wrapping.

Bangtail—Tail bobbed or tied short; journalese for horse.

Bar plates—Horseshoes with bars across rear.

Barrel—Horse's torso.

Barrier—Starting gate.

Baseball—Daily-double play in which bettor couples a horse in one race with all horses in the other; "wheeling."

Bat—Whip (a term used by writers, not jockeys).

Bay—Brown or tan horse with black mane and tail.

Bear in—Running toward inside rail instead of straight.

Bear out—Running toward outside, especially on turns.

Beef—Protest, usually by jockey about another's riding tactics.

Bell—Signals start of race and termination of betting.

Bend—A turn of the track.

Big Apple—A major racing circuit.

Bill Daly—Rider who takes lead as soon as possible is "on the Bill Daly." Famous trainer, "Father Bill" Daly, used to tell jockeys, "Get on top right away and improve your position."

Bit—Metal mouth bar to which reins are attached.

Blanket finish—Extremely close finish.

Blaze—Large white marking on horse's face.

Bleeder—Horse that bleeds during heavy exertion, usually from ruptured blood vessels of nose.

Blind switch—In which rider finds his mount pocketed behind horses and must decide whether to hope for an opening or take back and go around.

Blinkers—Eye pieces that limit a horse's vision and sometimes help him to concentrate on running.

Blister—Treatment of damaged tissue with chemical irritant or heat, causes blistering and encourages development of scar tissue.

Block heel—Horseshoe with raised heel, to prevent running down.

Bloodline—Pedigree.

Blow out—Short exercise to limber a horse before its race.

Blue roan—Horse with coat of black, white and yellow hairs, producing blue-gray effect.

Boat race—A fixed race.

Bobble—Stumble; break stride clumsily.

Bog Spavin—Puffy swelling on inside of hock. Caused by strain.

Bold eye—Prominent eye, supposedly sign of courage.

Bold front—Long, well-muscled neck, another sign of courage.

Bolt—To run off in wrong direction, as when horse tries to return to barn instead of going to starting gate.

Bone spavin—Bony swelling, usually below the hock joint.

Book—Jockey's schedule of riding assignments; bookmaker; bookmaker's tally of amounts bet on each horse and odds necessary to assure him of profit.

Boot—To kick horse, as when booting it home in race; rubber or leather anklet.

Boots and Saddles—Bugle call sounded when riders mount and when horses enter track for post parade.

Bottom—Equine stamina; horse assigned outside post position and listed last in program of race; sub-surface of racing strip.

Bottom line—Bottom, or female side of pedigree.

Bow—When strained sheath of flexor tendon ruptures, allowing tendon to stand out behind cannon bone like string of a bow.

Boy—Jockey.

Brace—Horse liniment.

Brackets—Victory, because index numbers with which official result charts identify previous race of each horse are enclosed in brackets if horse won that race.

Break—Start of race; accustoming young horse to saddle, bridle and rider.

Breakage—Difference between true mutuel odds and lesser, rounded amounts given to winning players. The resultant millions usually are divided between track and state.

Break down—Become unable to race because of lameness or injury.

Break in the air—Leap upward at the start, instead of hustling forward.

Break maiden—When horse or rider wins first race of career.

Breastplate—Leather passed across chest of horse and fastened to each side of saddle, keeping it in place. Used on thin horses.

Breather—Restraining horse to rest and relax it before stretch drive.

Breed—To mate horses.

Breeder—Owner of mare at time she drops foal.

Breeze—Running under a stout hold, easily, without encouragement.

Bridge-jumper—Bettor who specializes in large show bets on odds-on favorites.

Brisket—Area of horse's body between forelegs.

Brittle feet—Hooves that chip easily and are difficult to shoe.

Broken knees—Skin lesions at knee.

Broken wind—When overstrained lung tissue breaks down, causing breathing problems; "heaves."

Broodmare—Female Thoroughbred used for breeding.

Broodmare dam—Mare whose female offspring become good broodmares.

Broodmare sire—Male horse whose female offspring become good broodmares.

Bruce Lowe system—A method of identifying Thoroughbred families by number, according to the female ancestor from which each family descends.

Brushing—Horse scrapes fetlock with opposite shoe. Caused by improper balance, poor shoes or fatigue.

Bucked shins—Shins painfully inflamed by overstrain.

Bug boy—Apprentice jockey, because of asterisk with which newspapers identify apprentice in entry lists.

Bull ring—Small track, because of sharp turns.

Bushes—Small-time, bush-league racing.

Buy the rack—Purchase every possible daily-double ticket.

Buzzer—Battery-powered oscillator or vibrator used illegally to frighten horse into running.

Calculator—Clerk who computes parimutuel odds.

Calk—Horseshoe cleat for greater purchase in mud or on grass.

Call—To announce progress of race for purposes of official result charts (chart-caller); to describe race to audience; stage of race at which running positions are recorded, like "half-mile call."

Canker—Foot infection that softens the hoof.

Cannon—Foreleg between knee and ankle. Rear leg between hock and ankle.

Canter—Slow gallop; lope.

Capped—Swollen, as of elbow or hock rubbed or bumped in stall.

Card—Program of racing.

Car fit—Severe fright while being shipped in van, train or plane.

Carry the target—Run last all the way.

Cast—Fallen and unable to rise, as of a horse; lost or "thrown," as of a horseshoe.

Chalk horse—Betting favorite.

Chalk player—Bettor on favorites.

Challenge—To vie for lead.

Chart—Result chart.

Chase—Steeplechase.

Chestnut—Brown or tan horse with brown tail and mane; horny growth (called "night eyes") on inside of horse's legs.

Choppy—Of stride, shortness, often reveals soreness.

Chute—Extension of stretch to permit long, straight run from starting gate to first turn.

Circuit—Geographical grouping of tracks whose meetings are coordinated to run in sequence.

Claim—To buy horse in claiming race.

Claimer—Claiming race; horse that runs in such races.

Claiming box—Where claims are deposited before race.

Clerk of the scales—Weighs riders and tack before and after race.

Clever—Of a horse, kindly, easily managed, able.

Client—Purchaser of betting information from horseman or other tipster.

Climb—To run with unusually high motion of forelegs, usually when flustered or tired.

Clocker—Person who times workouts, usually for betting information.

Close—Of final odds on horse ("closed at 2 to 1"); to gain ground on leader.

Close-coupled—Of a horse, short-backed.

Close fast—Finish fast, gaining on leader.

Clothes—Horse blanket.

Clubhouse turn—Turn of track nearest clubhouse; first turn of races that begin on homestretch.

Coffin bone—Main bone in equine foot.

Cold—Of a horse, unreadiness to win because of physical condition or stable's intentions.

Cold-blooded—Of a non-Thoroughbred horse.

Colors—Distinctively patterned rider's costumes identifying owner.

Colt—Unaltered male horse aged four or less.

Combination—Across-the-board bet for which a single mutuel ticket is issued.

Come back to—Of a horse, to tire and slow down, allowing other horse to close gap.

Condition—Equine form or fitness; to train a horse.

Condition book—Publication in which track announces purses, terms of eligibility and weight formulas of races.

Conditions—Terms of race, including purse size, eligibility for entry, and weight concessions.

Connections—Owner, trainer and other custodians of horse.

Consolation double—When horse is scratched from second race after daily-double betting begins, money is set aside to pay those who have bought tickets pairing horse with winner of first race.

Contract rider—Jockey on whose services an owner, by contract, has first call.

Cooler—Covering draped on horse while it cools out after race or workout; horse that is restrained to prevent it from running well.

Corn—Horny callus caused by irritation from horseshoes.

Coronet—Area just above hoof; "crown of hoof."

Cover—Of a stallion, act of coupling with a mare.

Cow hocks—Hocks that turn toward each other, like cow's.

Cresty—Of horse, thick-necked and probably not nimble.

Cribber—Horse that bites parts of its stall, sucking air into lungs; "windsucker"; "crib-biter."

Cropper—Spill, usually in jump race.

Croup—Top hindquarters of horse.

Crowd—To race too close to another horse, forcing its rider to take up or change course.

Cryptorchid—Male horse with undescended testicle.

Cuff—Horse anklet; credit ("on the cuff").

Cull—Unwanted horse disposed of by owner.

Cup—Type of blinker.

Cup horse—Good router.

Cuppy—Of a track, when surface breaks into clods and shows hoofprints.

Curb—Sprain at back of hock; a powerful bit equipped with extra strap or chain beneath horse's chin.

Cushion—Subsurface of track.

Cut down—Of a horse, injured during race by shoe of another horse or by striking itself with own shoe.

Daily double—Form of mutuel betting in which player attempts to pick winners of two races, buying a single ticket on the double choice.

Dam—Horse's mother.

Dark—Of a track at which or a day on which there is no racing.

Dark horse—Underrated animal that wins or has good prospects of winning.

Dash—Sprint race.

Dead heat—When two or more horses reach finish wire simultaneously.

Dead weight—Lead slabs carried in saddle to increase weight of jockey and tack.

Declaration to win—Public announcement by owner of more than one entrant in a race that he will try to win with one but not with the others.

Declare—To withdraw horse from race.

Deep—Of racing surface recently harrowed or to which extra top soil has been added, increasing holding qualities.

Derby—Stakes race for three-year-olds.

Destroy—To kill a horse.

Disqualify—To lower horse's actual finishing position by official act after deciding it interfered with others during race, or carried improper weight or was drugged.

Distaff side—Female ancestry, shown in lower half of pedigree.

Distance of ground—A route race.

Division—When too many entries are made in an important race, track may divide it into two races.

Doer—Of a horse, eater.

Dog—Obstructions placed near rail when track is muddy, to prevent horses from running there and kicking up the surface during workouts; cheap horse; quitter.

Dope—Information about races or horses; drugs.

Draw Away—To win going away; "draw clear"; "draw out."

Drench—To give horse liquid medicine.

Drive—All-out exertion, under heavy punishment, especially in home-stretch.

Drop—Give birth to foal.

Dun—Mousy, grayish color in brown to gold range, usually with black mane and tail.

Dutch—To take advantage of booking percentages by eliminating heavily bet non-contenders, betting on others in exact proportions necessary to yield profit no matter which wins.

Dwell—Of a horse that breaks slowly from the gate.

Early foot—Good speed at beginning of race.

Ease up—To slow horse's stride, sparing it exertion.

Easy ride—Performance in which jockey fails to try.

Eggs (walking on)—Of a sore horse.

Eighth—Furlong; 220 yards; 660 feet.

Eighth pole—Colored post at the inside rail exactly one furlong from finish wire.

Empty—Of a horse that lacks energy for finishing drive.

English Stud Book—Official repository of English Thoroughbred records.

Entire—Of an unaltered male horse.

Entry—Two or more horses owned by same interests, or trained by same person, entered in same race and coupled in the betting.

Ewe-necked—Of a horse with concave neck, a sign of clumsiness.

Exacta—Form of betting in which player attempts to pick winner and second horse, buying one mutuel ticket on the double choice.

Excused—Permitted to withdraw horse after official scratch time.

Exercise boy—Rider in training workouts.

Extend—To force horse to go all out.

Fade—To tire and drop out of contention.

False quarter—Horizontal crack in hoof, caused by coronet injury.

Falter—To tire badly.

Farrier—Horseshoer.

Fast track—Dry, hard strip on which horses run fastest; a track at which typical running times are relatively fast by comparison with most other tracks.

Feather—Extremely light weight.

Fetlock—Horse's ankle.

Field—All entrants in race; in pari-mutuel betting, two or more lightly regarded horses grouped as a single betting entry.

Filly—Female horse, aged four or less.

Film patrol—Crew that records running of each race on movie film or television tape, for possible review by stewards when questions arise about behavior of horse or rider.

Fire—Cauterization of ailing tissue with red-hot needle or firing iron.

Fit—Of a horse, physical readiness.

Five-eighths pole—Post at inside rail, exactly five furlongs from finish wire.

Flag—Signal held by official flag man a few yards in front of the gate, where race actually starts. Timing begins when horses reach that point and he drops flag.

Flag down—To wave at an exercise rider to indicate horse is working too hard.

Flash—Change of odds information on tote board.

Flat—Conventional racing surface, contrasted with grass or jump course.

Flatten out—Of an exhausted horse that stops, often dropping its head flat-level with body.

Foal—Newborn horse; of a mare, to give birth.

Foot—Speed; soft tissue beneath hoof.

Footing—Condition of track surface.

Forearm—Horse's foreleg between elbow and knee.

Forked—Of horse's conformation where forelegs join body.

Form—Of a horse, current condition; *Daily Racing Form*.

Form player—Bettor who makes selections from past-performance records.

Fractions—Clockings at quarter-mile intervals in races and workouts.

Free lance—Jockey not under contract to one stable.

Freemartin—Filly twin of a colt.

Freshener—Layoff designed to restore energies of overworked horse.

Frog—Triangular fleshy cushion on sole of horse's foot.

Front runner—Horse that prefers to run in front.

Furlong—One eighth of a mile.

Futurity—Race in which horses are entered before birth.

Gad—Jockey's whip.

Gait—Equine walk, trot or gallop; horse's action or "way of going."

Gallop—Fastest gait; workout; an easy race or workout, compared with one in which horse is urged.

Garrison finish—Victory by a come-from-behind horse, such as those ridden by the famous Snapper Garrison.

Gaskin—Hind leg between thigh and hock.

Gate—Starting gate; entrance to track.

Gelding—Castrated male horse.

Gentleman jockey—Amateur rider.

Get—Offspring of stallion.

Getaway day—Last day of race meeting.

Get into—Of a rider, to whip horse.

Gimpy—Of a lame, sore, "ouchy" horse.

Girth—Saddle band.

Go—Of a stable or horse, to start in a race; an effort to win.

Going—Condition of racing surface; of a horse, its stride ("way of going").

Going away—Winning while increasing the lead.

Good bone—Impressive bone structure indicative of weight-bearing ability and ruggedness.

Good doer—Of a horse, a hearty eater.

Go on—Of a horse, to win at a new, longer distance. "I think he'll go on."

Goose-rumped—Of a horse, high hindquarters with a sharp slope at base of tail.

Grab—To catch foreleg with a hind foot, because of faulty conformation. Causes stumbling, loss of stride.

Graded race—One in which eligibility is limited to horses in one or another classification, as determined by racing secretary. Graded allowances and grade handicaps are common.

Graduate—To break maiden.

Grandam—Equine grandma.

Grandsire—Equine grandpa.

Gray—Equine color composed of black and white hairs.

Groom—Stable employee who tends horse, brings it to paddock for race.

Grounded—Of a jockey, suspended from competition for infractions of rules.

Grunter—Horse whose noisy breathing indicates unreadiness for hard exertion.

Guinea—Stablehand, because winning British owners used to tip the groom a guinea.

Gumbo—Heavy mud.

Gun—All-out effort by jockey.

Gypsy—Itinerant owner-trainer; "gyp."

Half—Half-mile; time "to the half" is fractional time after half a mile of running.

Half brother—Male horse out of same dam as, but by different sire than another horse.

Half-mile pole—Vertical pole at infield rail exactly four furlongs from finish line.

Half-miler—A track of that distance; horse that prefers such a track.

Half sister—Female horse out of same dam as, but by different sire than another horse.

Halter—Hand-held rope or strap by which horses are led; to claim a horse.

Halter man—Owner or trainer who specializes in buying horses from claiming races.

Hand—Four inches of equine height.

Handicap—Race in which racing secretary or track handicapper assigns weights designed to equalize winning chances of entrants; to study horses' records in effort to determine winner of race.

Handicap Triple Crown—Mythical award to horse that wins the three classic handicaps—the Brooklyn, Suburban and Metropolitan—in one season.

Handily—Of a comparatively easy victory achieved without hard urging; of a fairly strenuous workout under a hand ride without whipping.

Handle—Total sum bet on a race or in a day or some other period.

Hand ride—Urging horse toward longer, faster, more rhythmic stride by rolling hands on its neck, lifting its head at beginning of stride.

Handy—Of a nimble, trappy, lightfooted, easily guided horse.

Hang—Of a horse unable to produce the expected finishing kick and therefore unable to improve its position in the stretch.

Hardboot—A Kentucky horseman of the old school, because of the legendary mud caked on his boots.

Hat trick—The winning, usually by a jockey, of three races on a single program.

Have one in the boot—To ride a horse whose owner or trainer has made bets, including one for the rider.

Hayburner—Horse that fails to pay its own feed bill; "oatburner."

Headed—Beaten by a head to the wire.

Head of the stretch—End of the final turn; top of the stretch.

Heat—A race.

Heavy-fronted—Of a horse with extremely wide, muscular chest. Supposedly a sign of poor quality.

Heavy-headed—Of a horse that fights the reins, responds slowly to guidance, or prefers to run with its head low.

Heavy-topped—Of a horse with an unusually large, muscular body by comparison with its legs. A sign of susceptibility to soreness and lameness.

Heavy track—A running surface drier than muddy, and often slower.

Height—Of a horse, distance from ground to withers.

Herd—To alter horse's course so as to prevent another from improving its position.

Herring-gutted—A poor doer with practically no depth of abdomen.

Hind sticker—Horseshoe similar to mud calk, except cleat is on outside edge.

Hip number—Identification number attached to horse's hip at Thoroughbred sales.

Hock—Hind elbow joint between gaskin and cannon.

Homebred—Horse foaled in state where it races.

Homestretch—Straight part of track from final turn to finish wire.

Honest—Of a kind, reliable horse.

Hood—Head covering containing blinkers.

Hop—To drug a horse illegally.

Horse—Technically, any entire male aged five or more.

Horseman—An owner or trainer.

Horseman's Benevolent and Protective Association—Trade association of owners and trainers.

Horsing—Of a mare in heat.

Hot—Of a horse expected to win; of a jockey or stable on a winning streak; of a horse overheated from exertion.

Hot-walker—Stablehand who walks horse while it cools out after a race or workout.

Hunt—Amateur racing, mainly on grass and over jumps.

Hurdle race—A race over low obstacles.

Ice—To anesthetize a horse's painful feet or legs by standing it in ice.

Impost—Weight carried by horse.

In-and-outer—Inconsistent horse that "runs hot and cold."

Index—Number that identifies a specific result chart. When printed in racing papers, directs player to chart of horse's most recent race.

Infield—The area on the inner circumference of the track, where grass and jump races are run and the tote board is found.

In hand—Of a horse running under restraint.

In light—Carrying relatively little weight.

Inquiry—Official investigation of the running of a race to see whether it was fairly won.

In shape—Of a horse ready to win.

Inside—Anything to the left of a horse during the race; position closest to the rail.

Inside rail—Fence separating racing strip from infield.

Interfere—Of a horse, to strike a leg with opposite hoof; to impede another horse in the race.

In the can—An out-of-the-money finish; "in the crapper," etc.

In the money—Technically, a finish in the first four, entitling the owner to a share of the purse; among bettors, a finish in the first three, resulting in a mutuel payoff.

In tough—Of a horse entered with animals it is unlikely to beat.

Irons—Stirrups.

Jail—Of the first month that a claimed horse is in the new barn, when racing law requires it to run at a 25 percent higher claiming price or remain idle.

Jam—Traffic jam during a race.

Jockey—Race rider; to maneuver for position during a race.

Jockey agent—Person who helps rider obtain mounts in return for 20 percent or more of the rider's earnings.

Jockey Club—Name taken by organizations that operate tracks; New York organization that maintains the American Stud Book and approves Thoroughbred names and registry; the governing body of British racing.

Jockeys' Guild—National association of race riders.

Jog—Slow, easy gait, similar to a trot.

Jostle—To bump another horse during a race.

Journeyman—A full-fledged professional jockey.

Jumper—Horse that runs in steeplechase or hurdle races.

Jump up—Of a horse that wins in a surprising reversal of form.

Juvenile—Two-year-old.

Kiss the eighth pole—Of a horse, to finish far behind.

Kitchen—Horsemen's restaurant in backstretch area.

Knee spavin—Bony growth behind knee, caused by blow or overstrain. More serious than hock spavin.

Laminitis—Serious inflammation of equine foot.

Lay—To occupy a certain running position deliberately, while waiting to make strategic move. "Lay fourth, off the pace."

Lead pad—Saddle pocket in which lead weights can be placed.

Lead pony—Horse on which outrider escorts Thoroughbreds to the post.

Leaky roof circuit—Minor tracks.

Leather—A whip.

Leathers—Stirrup straps.

Leg lock—When jockey illegally hooks legs with another rider, impeding the other horse.

Leg up—To build horse's speed and stamina with work; a jockey's riding assignment.

Length—Eight or nine feet.

Light over the kidney—Of a horse, slender-loined; wasp-waisted.

Line—Pedigree; male side of the pedigree as contrasted with family, or female side.

Live weight—The weight of the jockey, as contrasted with dead weight.

Loaded shoulder—Unusually thick shoulder and unimpressive withers, making for an awkward gait.

Loafer—Horse unwilling to run well without hard urging.

Lob—A cooler or stiff.

Lock—A sure thing.

Look for hole in fence—Of a quitter that acts as if it would rather run back to the barn than continue in the race.

Look of eagles—The proud look in the eyes of many good horses, as if they knew they were good.

Loose-coupled—Opposite of close-coupled; slack-coupled.

Loose mount—Horse that continues running after losing rider.

Lug in—Bear in.

Machine—Battery.

Machines—The mutuels.

Maiden—Of a horse or jockey, a non-winner; of a race, one for non-winners.

Make a run—Of a horse that turns on the speed, makes a move, makes a bid.

Marathon—A race longer than 1¼ miles.

Mare—A female horse of five or older.

Martingale—Straps attached to bit or noseband and girth, preventing horse from rearing.

Match race—A race between two horses, winner-take-all.

Maturity—A race for four-year-olds in which entries are made before their birth.

Meant—Of a horse whose stable intends to win; "well-meant."

Meat ball—Cathartic pill.

Meet—Race meeting.

Middle distance—Of a race longer than seven furlongs but less than 1⅛ miles.

Mile pole—Colored post at infield rail exactly a mile from finish wire.

Minus pool—In pari-mutuel betting, a situation in which so much money is bet on a horse (usually to show) that the pool is insufficient, after take and breakage, to pay holders of winning tickets the legal minimum odds of 1 to 10 or 20. The track is required to make up the difference from its own funds.

Monkey crouch—Riding style popularized by Tod Sloan in which jockey bends forward over horse's withers; "monkey-on-a-stick."

Morning glory—Horse that runs well in workouts but not in races.

Morning line—Forecast of probable odds.

Move up—Gain ground; run in a higher-class race.

Muck out—Clean a horse's stall.

Mudder—Horse that prefers muddy going; "mudlark."

Muddy track—Soft, wet and holding.

Mutuel pool—Total amount bet to win, place or show in a race; total amount bet on daily double, exacta, quinella, etc.

Muzzle—Straps that keep horse's mouth closed, prevent it from biting.

Name—To enter a horse in a race.

Nape—Top of horse's neck; poll.

Navicular disease—A crippling, sometimes fatal ulcer which corrodes the navicular bone of the foot. Usually found in forefoot.

Near side—Horse's left side.

Neck—About ¼ length.

Nerve—To remove a nerve, eliminating pain but not the infirmity that causes it. Illegal in major racing.

Nick—To nerve a horse; a supposedly strategic feature of a pedigree, representing a particular mating or crossbreeding worthy of repetition.

Nightcap—Last race on the program.

Nod—Lowering of head; permission to a jockey to dismount after race.

Nom de course—Stable name.

Nose—The narrowest possible winning margin.

Number ball—Numbered ball drawn from number box to assign post positions.

Nursery race—Baby race.

Oaks—Stakes race for three-year-old fillies.

Oatburner—Hayburner.

Objection—Complaint by jockey that a foul has been committed.

Odds board—Tote board.

Odds man—At tracks where electronic computers are not in use, an employee who calculates changing odds as betting progresses.

Odds on—Odds of less than even money.

Off—The start, or the time of the start; difference between track record and final clocking of a horse; slowness of a horse, expressed in a time comparison or a lengths comparison between its current performance and what it should do, or what other horses have done or are likely to do. "He's off at least three lengths."

Off side—Right side of a horse.

Off the board—Of a horse so lightly bet that its odds exceed 99 to 1; failure to finish in the money.

Off the pace—To run behind the early leaders.

Off the top—Of the practice of deducting a fixed "take" percentage from the mutuel pool before paying holders of winning tickets.

Off track—A racing surface other than fast; of betting conducted away from the track.

On edge—Nervous; sharply conditioned.

On the bit—Of a horse eagerly straining against the bit.

On the chin strap—Winning by a wide margin.

On the ground—Of a suspended jockey.

On the nose—A bet that horse will win.

On the rail—Running close to the infield rail.

On top—In the lead.

One-run—Of a horse that expends all its energy in a single burst of speed, usually in stretch.

Open race—A race with lenient eligibility conditions, permitting entry of a wide variety of horses.

Optional claimer—A race for horses entered to be claimed at a fixed price or a price within a limited range, and open also to horses that have run at such a price in the past but are not entered to be claimed today.

Osselets—Bony growths on injured membrane of ankle joint.

Ouchy—Sore.

Out of—In discussing a horse's parentage, one says that it is "by" a sire "out of" a dam.

Outrider—Mounted employee who escorts horses to post.

Over at the knee—The foreleg curves forward at the knee.

Overland—Of the course followed by a horse that runs wide on the turns, losing ground.

Overlay—Horse whose odds are high by comparison with its good winning chances.

Overnight race—One for which entries close less than three days before the start of the program.

Overnights—Tomorrow's entries, as released by the racing secretary's office.

Overreach—To strike a forefoot with a hind shoe while running.

Overweight—Pounds that a horse carries in excess of officially assigned weight, because jockey is too heavy.

Pace—The speed of the leaders at each stage of the race.

Paddock—Saddling enclosure.

Pari-mutuels—From Paris ("Paree") Mutuels, system invented by Frenchman, whereby winning bettors get all money wagered by losers, after deduction of house percentage.

Pasteboard track—Fast racing strip, so-called because thin and hard.

Pastern—Area between fetlock and coronet.

Peacocky—High-headed, flighty horse.

Periodic ophthalmia—Periodic loss of vision by horse; "moonblindness."

Pigeye—Small equine eye, supposed sign of meanness.

Pinched back—Caught in a jam and forced back during race.

Pink—Uniformed Pinkerton guard at track.

Pipe opener—Short workout; blow out.

Plater—Horseshoer, farrier; claiming horse, because of silver plates formerly awarded to winners of such races.

Pocket—Racing predicament in which horse is surrounded by others and unable to increase speed until opening occurs.

Points—In Thoroughbred conformation, a physical feature; the lower legs of a horse, especially in describing color ("Dark brown or bay horses always have black points").

Poll—Top of horse's head.

Pony—Any workhorse at a track, such as lead pony.

Pool—Total amount bet for win, place or show, or in daily double, etc.

Post—Starting gate.

Powder—Minor physical contact between horses during race.

Preferred—Of horses given preference in entry for particular race, usually previous winners or horses bred or foaled in the local jurisdiction.

Prepotent—Of horse whose offspring breed comparatively true to type, inheriting the desired characteristics.

Prod—Illegal battery, as in cattleprod.

Produce—Offspring of mare.

Prop—Refusing to break at start; standing flat-footed.

Public stable—Enterprise of "public trainer" who handles horses on free-lance basis, as contrasted with one who trains stock of only one owner.

Puett gate—Widely used brand of starting gate.

Pull—To restrain horse deliberately, preventing it from winning; to "stiff."

Pull in the weights—A weight advantage.

Pull up—To stop or slow a horse during or after race or workout.

Punter—Horseplayer.

Quarter—Quarter-mile; two furlongs; side of hoof.

Quarter crack—Separation of inner and outer walls of hoof in quarter area.

Quarter horse—Extremely speedy breed used for ranch work and racing up to a quarter-mile.

Quarter pole—Colored post at infield rail exactly two furlongs from finish wire.

Quinella (quiniela; quinela)—Form of mutuel betting in which player tries to pick first two finishers, regardless of order.

Racing plate—Shoe worn for racing purposes.

Racing secretary—Official who prescribes conditions of races at his track and usually serves as track handicapper, assigning weights to entrants in handicap races.

Racing sound—Of a horse able to race, although not necessarily in prime health.

Rack up—To interfere with several other horses so severely that they all slow down.

Rail runner—Horse that prefers to run along inside rail.

Raised bar—Bar plate which helps prevent running down.

Rank—Of a fractious horse, especially when, "running rank," it refuses to be rated early in race.

Rate—To restrain a horse early in race, conserving its energies for later challenges.

Receiving barn—Where horses stabled at other tracks are kept before they go to the paddock for their races.

Red roan—Of a horse whose coat consists of red, yellow and white hairs.

Refuse—Of a horse that fails to break at the start or, in jump races, fails to attempt one of the fences.

Ridden out—Of a horse that wins under an active but not a driving ride, and probably has racing energy left; sometimes, contradictorily, a winner whose jockey parcels out its energy so that none is left after it passes finish line.

Ride short—To ride with short stirrup leathers.

Ridgling—Partly castrated horse; "rigling."

Right price—Among players, mutuel odds high enough to warrant risking a bet on a particular animal; among horsemen, odds high enough to warrant an all-out try with horse.

Rim—Horseshoe with long cleat or grab on outer rim, sometimes helps horses with bad tendons.

Ringbone—Bony overgrowth at top of hoof or near pastern bones, found often in horses with straight pasterns. Formerly treated by nerving.

Ringer—Of a horse entered under another's name.

Roan—Striking reddish or grayish color.

Roar—Of a horse, noisy breathing like coughing.

Rogue—Chronically fractious horse.

Rogue's badge—Blinkers.

Romp—An easy race.

Roping—Training or exercising a horse by having it move in circles at end of a tether.

Route—A relatively long race.

Router—Horse that does its best in races of 1⅛ miles or longer.

Rug—Heavy horse blanket.

Rule off—To bar from racing.

Run down—Of a horse, to scrape the flesh of the heels on the track surface while racing. Associated with weak pasterns; "run down behind."

Run in—To win unexpectedly.

Runner—Messenger to and from mutuel windows for occupants of clubhouse boxes.

Run out—To finish out of the money; to run toward outside rail.

Run-out bit—Bit that gives rider extra leverage on one side, helping prevent animal from lugging in or bearing out.

Run wide—To race far from inside rail, covering extra ground.

Saddlecloth—Piece of fabric between saddle and horse.

Saliva test—Chemical analysis of horse's saliva, routinely performed on in-money finishers, in attempt to see whether animal was dosed with illegal drugs.

Salute—Of jockey who raises whip in greeting to stewards after race, in customary request to dismount.

Sand crack—Vertical crack on hoof from coronet downward.

Sanitary ride—Of a horse that did not try its best in a race, or of a jockey that took the animal wide to avoid tight spots or flying mud, harming its chances.

Savage—Of a horse, to bite.

Save ground—To cover the shortest possible distance in a race, hugging the rail on turns, running in direct, straight line on stretches.

Scale of weights—Official tabulation of correct weights for various age groups at all distances and all times of year; "the scale."

Scale weights—Weights carried in an official weight-for-age race.

Scenic route—When a horse loses ground by running far from rail; overland.

School—To train a horse, especially at the gate, in the paddock or over jumps.

Score—To win a race or a bet; a victory.

Scratch—To withdraw an entrant from its race.

Scratch sheet—Daily publication that includes graded handicaps, tips, and scratches.

Season—The period in which racing is conducted on a particular circuit or at a particular track; of a filly or mare, the period of estrus or "heat."

Seat—The posture of a rider on a horse.

Second dam—Horse's maternal grandmother.

Second sire—Horse's paternal grandfather.

Selling plater—Claiming horse; plater.

Selling race—Claiming race; type of race that antedated claimers and no longer is run, in which rules required that winner be auctioned off afterward.

Send—To enter a horse in a race; of a horseman, to try to win with the horse.

Send away—Of an official starter, opening the gate and beginning the race.

Sesamoiditis—Bone inflammation above and behind fetlock.

Set down—To suspend horseman, rider, stablehand from racing for a period; to shake up a horse and ask it for speed in a race or workout.

Sex allowance—Weight concession that is given to female horses in races against males.

Shadow roll—Sheepskin or cloth cylinder strapped across horse's nose to bar its vision of ground, prevent it from shying at shadows.

Shake up—To hit a horse in effort to make it run.

Shank—Rope or strap attached to halter or bridle, for leading a horse by hand.

Sheath—Fleshy pocket containing genital organs of male horse.

Shed row—Racetrack barns; the backstretch community.

Ship—To transport a horse.

Shipping fever—Respiratory ailment of horses, associated with move from one climate to another.

Shoe board—Sign that tells what kind of shoes each entrant wears.

Shoo in—A supposed cinch bet or guaranteed victor; a fixed race.

Short—Of a horse that tires in stretch after long layoff, demonstrating need for more work.

Short price—Small mutuel payoff.

Show wear—Fetlocks swollen by overwork.

Shuffle—Of jockey who hand rides, pumping his hands and moving his feet.

Shuffled back—Of a horse that loses ground or racing position because of jams.

Shut off—To cross in front of another horse during race, forcing it to take up or go around.

Shut out—What happens to the player who gets on the betting line too late and is still waiting in line when the window closes.

Silks—Nylon or other costume worn by rider in race.

Sire—Horse's father.

Sit-still—A type of riding dependent more on patience, knowledge of pace than active, "whoop-de-doo" whipping; of a jockey who loses the race through inactivity with the whip.

Sixteenth pole—Vertical post on infield rail exactly half a furlong from finish wire.

Skin—To make a track faster by rolling and hardening the surface.

Skittish—Of a nervous horse.

Slab-sided—Of a horse with flat, narrow rib cage, indicative of poor lung capacity.

Slack of rib—Of a horse whose last rib is not close to its hip, indicating a long, weak back.

Sleeper—An underrated horse that could, or does, surprise.

Sloppy track—When racing strip is covered with puddles, but is not yet muddy, the surface remaining hard.

Slot—Post position.

Slow pill—Drug that dulls horse's nervous system, preventing it from performing alertly.

Slow track—A track wetter than good, not as thick as muddy.

Smart money—Insiders' bets, insiders themselves.

Snatch—Any violent, sudden action with reins or halter; "snatch up," "snatch around."

Snip—White or flesh-colored marking on horse's nose.

Snug—To keep a tight hold on horse while rating it during race; "snug back," "snug hold."

Socks—White ankles, allegedly a sign of weakness.

Solid—Of a ready horse, suitably placed.

Sophomore—Three-year-old.

Spanish bit—Type of bit that causes pain under pressure of reins. Used as last resort in schooling rebellious horses.

Spark—To use a battery in a race.

Spavin—Bony outcropping caused by inflammation of equine joints.

Special weights—Even weights, except for sex and apprentice allowances, assigned by racing secretary without recourse to official weight scale. Used mainly in races for better maidens.

Speedy cut—Leg injury caused by blow from opposite foot while running.

Spit out the bit—When an exhausted horse "backs up" and stops pressing against the bit.

Splint—Bony growth on horse's shin.

Split race—When an oversubscribed race is divided into two.

Sponge—To insert a piece of sponge or other foreign substance in a horse's nostrils, impeding its breathing and preventing it from performing well.

Spot—To concede weight to another horse.

Spot play—Type of play in which bettor risks money only on types of races and horses which seem relatively worthwhile risks.

Spring halt—Nerve-muscle ailment causing spasmodic elevation of rear legs.

Sprint—Short race, seven furlongs or less.

Stake—Commission paid winning jockey, trainer or groom.

Stakes—A race in which purse consists of nomination, entrance and starting fees plus money added by track itself. Improperly called "stake" race.

Stale—Of a jaded, overworked horse; of a horse, to urinate.

Stall gate—Starting gate in which each horse has its own compartment.

Stallion—Entire male horse.

Stall walker—Horse that paces its stall, consuming energy.

Stand—Of a stallion, to be at stud.

Star—White marking on horse's forehead.

Starter's list—List of horses ruled out of action by official starter because of chronic misbehavior at gate and, therefore, ineligible for racing until bad habits are corrected.

Stayer—A reliable, determined router.

Steeplechase—A race over jumps higher and broader than hurdles.

Stewards—The three duly-appointed arbiters of racing law who judge human and equine conduct at a race meeting.

Stick—Whip; to whip.

Sticker—Cleat on a horseshoe.

Stick horse—Horse that runs better when whipped.

Stiff—To prevent a horse from winning by deliberately riding poorly or by drugging it or training it inappropriately; an unfit or outclassed horse; a horse that has been stiffed.

Stifle—Forward area of horse's thigh.

Sting—To use a battery in a race.

Stirrup—Where jockey's feet go when he is mounted; irons.

Stockings—White leg markings, longer than socks.

Stooper—One of several dozen Americans who make a precarious living picking up discarded mutuel tickets at tracks and cashing those that have been thrown away by mistake.

Straight—Another term for a bet to win; "straight, place and show."

Straight as a string—Of a horse going all-out; "strung out."

Straightaway—Straight part of a race course; stretch.

Stretch call—Position in stretch where call is made for charting purposes. Usually a furlong from the wire.

Stretch turn—The turn into the homestretch.

Stride—Of a horse, its way of running or the ground it covers after each foot has been in contact with the track once.

String—The horses owned by one stable or handled by one trainer.

Strip—Racing strip; narrow white marking on horse's face.

Stripe—Marking similar to strip, but longer.

Stud—Stallion; breeding farm; horses at a breeding farm.

Studbook—Official registry of Thoroughbreds; a stallion's date book.

Stud fee—What the stallion's owner gets for its breeding services.

Subscription—Fees required of owner who enters horse in stakes race.

Sulk—Of a horse that refuses to run or respond to jockey's guidance.

Surcingle—Buckled strap that holds blanket on horse.

Suspension—Punishment, usually temporary, that declares jockey, horseman or stablehand ineligible for participation in sport.

Swamp fever—Infectious equine anemia.

Sweat the brass—To overwork a horse.

Sweepstakes—Stakes race.

Tack—What goes on the horse in addition to the rider.

Tag—Claiming price.

Tail female—Horse's female ancestry on dam's side.

Tail male—Horse's male ancestry on sire's side.

Take—Money deducted from each mutuel pool for track revenue and taxes.

Take back—To restrain a horse, either to rate it or prevent running into trouble.

Take care of—Of a jockey, to give the works to another in a race.

Take down—To disqualify a horse after it has finished in the money. Its number literally is removed from the list of early finishers.

Take out—Track take.

Take up—To slow sharply in effort to avoid collision or other racing trouble.

Tea—Any illegal chemical used to drug a horse and worsen or improve its performance.

Teaser—Stallion that tests mare's readiness for mating.

Teletimer—Electronic timer that flashes the fractional and final times of races on the tote board.

Tenderfoot—Sore-footed horse.

Thief—Unreliable horse that runs worst when its chances seem best.

Third sire—Horse's paternal great-grandfather.

Thoroughbred Racing Association—Trade association of track owners and managers.

Thoroughbred Racing Protective Bureau—The TRA's FBI, an intelligence network which combats corruption by investigating suspected evildoers and exposing those it catches.

Thoroughpins—A larger version of bog spavin that often goes right through the upper hock.

Three-eighths pole—Colored pole at inside rail, exactly three furlongs from finish wire.

Three-quarters pole—Colored pole at inside rail, exactly six furlongs from finish wire.

Throat latch—Upper part of horse's throat.

Thrush—Inflammation of the frog.

Tied on—Reins knotted and crossed, for stouter hold.

Tight—Fit and ready.

Tightener—A race intended to bring a horse to its peak.

Timber—Hurdle or other obstacle in jump race.

Timber rider—Steeplechase jockey.

Timber topper—A horse that runs in jump races.

Toe plate—Horseshoe with cleat in front, prevents sliding.

Tongue strap—Leather or cloth band that holds horse's tongue down to prevent horse from swallowing it during race or workout.

Top horse—Horse listed first in program of the race.

Top line—Male side of Thoroughbred pedigree.

Top weight—Heaviest impost in race.

Totalisator—Automated pari-mutuel machine which records bets as soon as tickets are dispensed at betting windows.

Tout—To give or sell betting advice; one who does so.

Trackmaster—Employee in charge of maintaining racing strip.

Training track—Separate track where workouts are held.

Trappy—Of a nimble, kind Thoroughbred.

Travel in straw—To travel with the horses in shipping vans, as stablehands do.

Trial—A preparatory race; a workout in which horse is asked for speed.

Triple Crown—Mythical award to any three-year-old that wins Kentucky Derby, Preakness Stakes and Belmont Stakes.

Trouble line—Words at end of each past-performance line in the Eastern edition of the Daily Racing Form, appraising horse's effort or stating any legitimate excuse it might have had for losing.

Turf course—A grass-covered track.

Turn out—To send a horse to the farm for pasturage and rest.

Twitch—Noose that can be tightened painfully around horse's nose and upper lip, keeping it quiet in starting gate, elsewhere "tongs."

Under wraps—Of a horse showing less than its best, probably because trainer does not want to extend it.

Untrack—What a horse is said to do to itself when it finally generates momentum and shows its talent.

Unwind—To taper off a horse's training preparatory to resting it.

Up—Of a jockey's assignment ("Buckpasser, Baeza up"), or an order to jockeys ("Riders, up!").

Urine test—Chemical analysis of horse's urine in effort to tell whether animal was drugged.

Used up—Of an exhausted horse.

Valet—Employee who takes care of jockey's clothing, carries his tack.

Van—A motor truck in which horses are shipped.

Veer—Of a horse, to swerve.

Vet's list—List of ill or injured horses declared ineligible for racing by the track veterinarian.

Vice—Any undesirable habit of a horse.

Walking ring—Oval near paddock enclosure, where horses walk and riders mount before start of post parade.

Walkover—A race from which all but one horse are scratched, permitting the horse to win by walking the distance.

Walk-up start—In contrast with the standing start at the stall gate, a start in which riders walk horses toward the starting point, and begin to run at the starter's command.

Warm up—Pre-race gallop.

Washy—Of a nervously sweating horse.

Water out—To water horse while it cools out after exertion.

Weanling—A newly weaned horse.

Weave—Of a horse, to move with a swaying, rocking motion in stall, or to pursue erratic course during a race.

Webfoot—A mudder.

Weigh in—Of jockeys, to be weighed with tack after race.

Weigh out—Of jockeys, to be weighed with tack before race.

Weight-for-age race—In which horses carry weights as prescribed by the official scale of weights.

Well let down—Of a horse with long, arched ribs, long forearms and short cannon bones, signifying good lung capacity and an easy, long stride.

Well ribbed up—Of a horse whose last rib is close to its hip, signifying a short, strong back.

Well-sprung ribs—Full, arched ribs for maximum lung capacity.

Welterweights—Weights 28 pounds over the official scale of weights, to test weight-bearing ability of entrants.

Wheel—Of a horse, to turn sharply, almost pinwheeling; a form of betting in which daily-double, perfecta or quinella player makes every possible combination bet on his favored horse or horses.

Whistle—Noisy equine breathing, like a whistle, caused by overstrained respiratory system.

Whoop-de-doo—A riding style that stresses an effort to get the lead immediately and run as fast as possible, with much whip action and little effort at rating; "whoop-de-hoo."

Wind sucker—Of a horse that swallows air, often with spasmodic motions of chin.

Winter—To spend the winter away from competition.

Wound up—Of a fit, ready horse.

Index

fundamentals, 109
  distance priority and, 149
  in systems, 359–60

gadgets, 26
Gallant Fox, 102
gambling:
  handicapping vs., 7–8, 48
  multiple betting as, 71
Gaver, John M., Jr., 295–96
geldings, 97, 215
Gentry, Loyd (Boo), 343
Gentry, Olin, 343
Globemaster, 83
Godolphin Barb, 79, 80
Golden Gate Fields, Calif., 39, 253
"Golden Notebook, The," 204–8
Gomez, Avelino, 307
Graell, Antonio, 308, 320
Graustark, 343
Greentree Stable, 278, 279, 280
Gulfstream Park, Fla., 39, 176, 253
Gun Bow, 98

Hail to Reason, 98
handicappers:
  information available to, 12–13
  as public selectors, 51–53
  as racing officials, 222–23
  weight formulas of, 227
handicapping:
  education needed in, 6, 7, 8
  fundamentals in, 109, 149, 359–60
  gambling vs., 7–8, 48
  as game in itself, 5–6
  individual differences in, 40–41,
    106–8
  mishaps and errors as factors in,
    19–20
  odds wagering vs., 48
  predictability in, 9–12
  prescription for success in, 109–11
  reasons for defeats in, 113
  reasons for victories in, 112–13
  recovery of costs in, 77–78
  skills in, 8
  theories of, 106–11
  tools of, 19–30
handicapping literature, 9
  growth of, 13–14
  unreadable or fraudulent, 14–15

handicap races, 49, 138
  class in, 215, 216, 221, 259
  recent action and, 168, 171
  starter, 138–39
  weight in, 226, 228–29
Handy, George, 210
Hanford, Carl, 98
harness racing, 7, 72
Hatton, Charles, 95
Hawley, Sandy, 307, 311, 312, 315,
    316, 320–21
Hazelton, Richard, 296
head, conformation of, 102
hedging, 66–67
  in betting on more than one horse
    to win, 67
Hernandez, Ruben, 308, 321
Hialeah Park, Fla., 39, 176
hips, conformation of, 102
Hirsch, Max, 85, 285
hocks, conformation of, 101
Hollingsworth, Kent, 83
Hollywood Park, Calif., 234, 248,
    361, 387
hoofprints, 99
hooves, conformation of, 98–99
"horseplayers" vs. "racing fans," 7
Horse Sense (Fabricand), 46
"horses for courses," meaning of,
    175–76
Hough, Stanley M., 296
house percentage, *see* breakage; take
Howard, C. S., 84
How To Select Winning Horses, 248
hurdle races, 140
Hyperion, 84

Illinois, 114, 115
information:
  availability and use of, 12–13
  main sources of, 24–25
  tips as, 21
insiders, as losers, 21
Iselin, Jimmy, 210

Jacobs, Hirsch, 85, 87–88, 201, 281
Jennings, Larry, 210, 296
Jerkens, H. Allen, 88, 137, 168, 292
Jockey Club of New York Rules of
    Racing, 407–29

excuses for, 179–82
knowledge of form vs., 160, 165–166
"last-out-in-the-money," 176–77
signs of improvement in, 182–84, 192
in speed handicapping, 235, 241–42
track significant in, 175–76
see also layoffs; workouts
Reine Enchanteur, 85
result charts, 12–13, 24, 259, 265
allowance races and, 130, 204–5
condition factor and, 76–77, 177
purse and eligibility conditions in, 204–5, 210
Rivera, Miguel A., 324
Rokeby Stables, 279
Roman Brother, 65, 97, 98, 102
Rondinello, Thomas L. (Lou), 301
Rotz, John L., 193–99
roulette, racing bets compared with, 44
Round Table, 102
Rous, John Francis, 223–24
route races, sprinters in, 143, 157–59
Rowe, Howard, 147, 234
Rowe, Robert V., 46, 48, 398–99
Rules of Racing (Jockey Club), 407–429
running styles, pace and, 250, 251, 252, 255, 267, 271
running times, 192, 240, 260, 261–62
see also final times; fractional times
Runyon, Damon, 255
Russell, John, 301

Saggy, 83–84
Samyn, Jean-Luc, 308, 313, 324
Santa Anita Park, Calif., 39, 234
Santiago, Angel, 324
Saratoga, N.Y., 115, 210, 234, 261
Saumell, Larry, 324
Science in Betting (DaSilva and Dorcus), 361
Sea-Bird, 85
Seabiscuit, 84
seasons, racing, 114–15
Seattle Slew, 74, 84, 85–86
Sechrest, Sam, 285
Second Venture, 193–99

Secretariat, 85
selection systems, *see* systems
Sermon, 198–99
sex of horse, class and, 206–7, 216–217, 219
Shenandoah Downs, W.Va., 39, 208
shippers:
condition factor and, 175–76
track class and, 208–11
shoe board, 34–35
Shoemaker, Willie, 54, 254, 307, 311, 312, 324–25, 344
shoes, 20, 350
shoulders, conformation of, 101
Silberman, Saul, 185
sires:
dams vs., 81–82
leading, 90–91
leading broodmare, 91–92
leading juvenile, 91
Sires and Dams, 136
Smith, Robyn C., 325
Snyder, Larry, 325–26
social order of horses, 200
Solomone, Mickey, 326
speed, 232–49
class and, 193–99, 200–201, 236–238, 242, 245–46
form and, 235, 241–42, 250, 251
as handicapping basis, 157, 202, 235–36, 385
lengths per second and, 238–39
pace vs., 254–55, 256, 265
sophisticated approaches to, 248–249
in systems, 385–89
theory of, 233–35
U.S. records for, 237
U.S. turf-course records for, 238
see also early speed; pace; stretch speed
speed charts, 239–40, 243–44, 255, 265
distance and, 157, 239–40
guidelines for use of, 240
for races with one turn, 243
for races with two turns, 244
speed ratings:
distance and, 151–53, 154–55, 245–248
"respectable time" in, 154–55